MW00681593

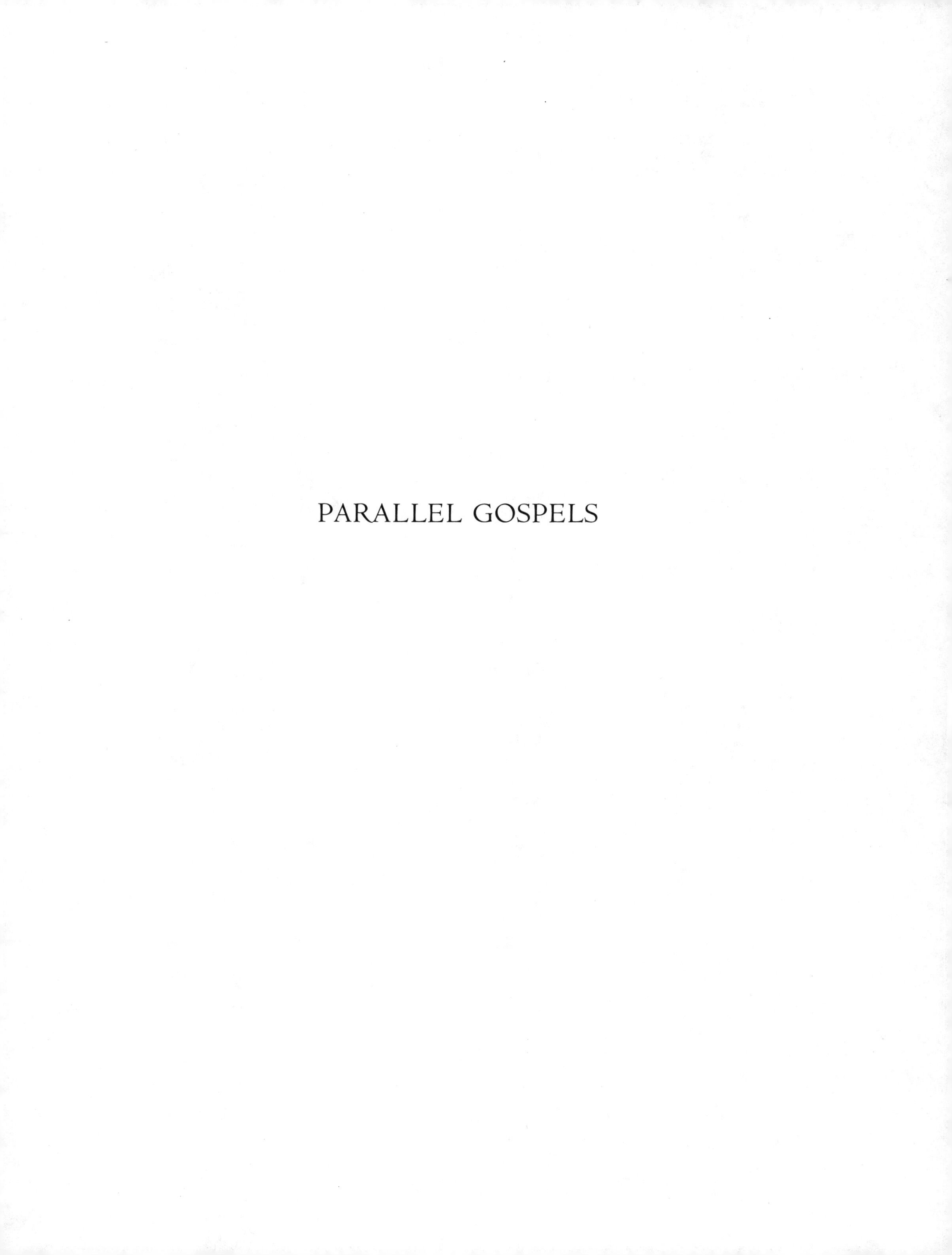

PARALLEL GOSPELS

PARALLEL GOSPELS

A Synopsis of Early Christian Writing

Zeba A. Crook

Carleton University

New York Oxford

OXFORD UNIVERSITY PRESS

Oxford University Press, Inc., publishes works that further Oxford University's objective of excellence in research, scholarship, and education.

Oxford New York
Auckland Cape Town Dar es Salaam Hong Kong Karachi
Kuala Lumpur Madrid Melbourne Mexico City Nairobi
New Delhi Shanghai Taipei Toronto

With offices in
Argentina Austria Brazil Chile Czech Republic France Greece
Guatemala Hungary Italy Japan Poland Portugal Singapore
South Korea Switzerland Thailand Turkey Ukraine Vietnam

For titles covered by Section 112 of the US Higher Education Opportunity Act, please visit www.oup.com/us/he for the latest information about pricing and alternate formats.

Published by Oxford University Press, Inc.
198 Madison Avenue, New York, New York 10016
http://www.oup.com

Library of Congress Cataloging-in-Publication Data

Bible. N.T. Gospels. English. Crook. 2011.
Parallel Gospels : a synopsis of early Christian writing / [translated by] Zeba A. Crook.
p. cm.
Includes index.
ISBN 978-0-19-973941-7 (main edition)
1. Bible. N.T. Gospels—Harmonies, English. I. Crook, Zeba A. II. Title.
BS2560.C76 2012
226′.065—dc22
2011014045

9 8 7 6 5 4 3 2 1

Printed in the United States of America
on acid-free paper

Contents

Acknowledgments

When a project takes over ten years to complete, the number of people who participate—wittingly or unwittingly—in the process becomes rather large. If I have forgotten you, please don't hold it against me.

First of all, I wish to thank two deans of the Faculty of Arts and Social Sciences at Carleton University, Drs. Michael Smith and John Osbourne, for unprecedented financial support of this project.

The number of people who have believed in this project has been heartening. Some were supportive from the start, others came along near the end: to them I am extremely grateful. First and foremost among them must be John S. Kloppenborg, University of Toronto, whose expertise and ideas were required practically every second day, and whose support was unstinting. The only person who solved more problems than John Kloppenborg is my wife, Dr. Kelly Quinn. Robert Miller accepted this work and showed great enthusiasm, as well as a guiding hand, and those who work with him were indispensable: Lisa Grzan, Christina Mancuso, Kristin Maffei, Brenda Griffing, and Lauren Roth. Mark Goodacre, Duke University, supported the project on- and offline, was instrumental in guiding Oxford University Press to me, and read the cameo essays, as did Robert Derrenbacker. David Bivin and the Jerusalem Perspective were among the earliest enthusiastic supporters of this project. Eric Tindale, an undergraduate student at the time and now a doctoral candidate in classics at the University of Toronto, did what no else would have had the patience to: he proofread the entire work with my vocabulary key. Terence L. Donaldson, Wycliffe College, was a reader for OUP and used pages from the synopsis in some of his courses. Daniel A. Smith, Huron University College, was a careful reader and a good friend. David L. Barr, Wright State University; Nicola Denzey Lewis, Brown University; Brad Kirkegaard, San Diego State University; Sheila McGinn, John Carroll University; Anne McGuire, Haverford College; Colleen Shantz, University of St. Michael's College; and the anonymous OUP reviewers also provided considerable direction and correction. If only I could hold them responsible for any of the shortcomings!

And finally, I acknowledge Humayra Kabir, who came out of nowhere with a fastidious eye and unquenchable work ethic to help me complete this work in a timely fashion.

To Humarya, and to all of you: Thank you.

Introduction

The New Testament gospels tell the story of the life and death of Jesus Christ. It is not surprising to anyone therefore that they share many episodes. What has been surprising to many readers throughout history is that almost always the gospels tell these shared episodes with different details. Either the stories are set at different points in Jesus' career, or the question posed by Jesus' opponents is different in each gospel, or Jesus' response is different, or the names of those present are different. Placing two, three, or more stories side by side allows the reader to compare the precise wordings. Do any of the gospels use the same words? Do they use any of the same words in the same order? Do all agree, or do some agree against others? What is the pattern of agreements and disagreements? The synopsis is the best tool to help you compare at any level—from the order of the stories to the words used—where the gospels agree and disagree.

The synopsis has been a tremendously important and useful tool for New Testament scholarship, and this is because of what it allows one to see. A synopsis is useful for analyzing the literary relationship among the gospels (see Synoptic Study Guide 1), also known as source criticism: Which gospel was written first? Which gospel was written third? Did John rely on any of the synoptic gospels (Matthew, Mark, and Luke)? In this synopsis, I include a column for Q, not to give Q an official or material status it currently lacks, but to give students access to this "text." It is not the case that simply including Q here in a column prejudices the source-critical debate; it is just as likely that its presence here will highlight the problems with Q's putative existence and textual reconstruction. Neither proving nor disproving Q has been my concern here.

The synopsis also allows one to see more clearly how each gospel is unique. With a synopsis, one can notice that Matthew and Luke frequently have the same story as Mark but with fewer superfluous details. One can notice that Matthew and Luke both use the word "immediately" far less often than Mark. When a pattern emerges, and there are many others beyond these two, one understands a little bit more about the author in question (see Synoptic Study Guide 12), their stylistic preferences, their theology, perhaps even their ideology.

Because the Gospels were originally written in Greek, the best synopses are in Greek. Something is always lost in translation, in this case details of the Greek language that do not carry over into English but do reveal a great deal about how the Gospels interrelate. English translations of synopses are also exceedingly common. English synopses are intended to serve readers without formal training in Greek, allowing them to study the way the Gospels are similar or different. But how well do they really serve these readers?

The standard practice of synopsis creators has been to use whichever English translation of the New Testament is current at the time and plug it into the parallel columns that make up the structure of the synopsis. There are synopses that use the Revised Standard Version (RSV), the New Revised Standard Version (NRSV), and the New International Version (NIV). There is nothing particularly wrong with these translations, but they were not intended to be placed side by side in parallel columns. I shall illustrate why in the coming paragraphs.

There are two extremes between which every translator must, in some way, navigate: the need to *follow the original text*, not departing too much from its contents, and the need to *create a translation that feels natural, that is attractive and pleasing in the target language.* Concern for the target language product is paramount in the mind of almost all translators, because the point of a translation is to encourage people to read it, whether a novel in the original French or Russian, or Homer's Iliad. But concern with the target language is even more paramount with English Bible translators because they must create a translation that can serve a living faith community. Likewise, the goal of any target-language translation is to take a foreign text and make it appear indigenous, local, and familiar. The gospel writers were not tremendously erudite writers, especially in comparison with other Greek writers (e.g., Homer, Aristotle, or Plutarch). New Testament vocabulary can be repetitive, and sentence construction simplistic. English translators often add variety to a Gospel's vocabulary, or make its syntax more complex than it actually is. All this is perfectly fair when producing a target-language translation, but inevitably something is lost: one might come away with the impression that, for example, Mark had a larger vocabulary and better writing style than he actually did, and from there one might conclude that he was much better educated than he probably was.

When a target-language translation is placed in the parallel columns of a synopsis, what is lost is both subtle and profound. To account for what is lost, this synopsis features not an English target-language translation, but *a Greek source-language translation*. The result is not an idiomatic, readable, English translation of the gospels, such as you necessarily find in NRSV Bibles. Rather, the result is a translation that is difficult to read sometimes. But there is much to be gained with this approach.

In what follows, I have taken the pericope of the Baptism of Jesus from my synopsis and from Throckmorton's and drawn attention to the various patterns of agreement among Matthew, Mark and Luke.

- *Italic* represents words shared between Matthew and Mark, but different or missing in Luke.
- Wavy underlined words are those shared by Mark and Luke, but different or missing in Matthew.
- **Bolded** words are those shared by Matthew and Luke, but different or missing in Mark.

I limit our focus to these agreements because it is these agreements (two against a third) that provide our most meaningful data concerning literary interdependence. If Matthew and Mark used each other directly, we would expect to see instances of their agreeing together against Luke. Likewise for the other two patterns of agreement. Conversely, triple agreements (words shared exactly by all three) show us that they all tell the same story.

21. The Baptism of Jesus (*Parallel Gospels,* Crook)

Matt 3:13-17	Mark 1:9-11	Luke 3:21-22
[13]Then *Jesus* arrives *from* *the Galilee* upon [=at] *the* *Jordan* to John **to-be-** **baptized** *under* [=by] him. [14]So [=But] John was- preventing him saying "I have need to-be-baptized under [=by] you, and you come to me?" [15]So having- answered Jesus said to him, "Excuse [=Allow it] right-now, for it-is suitable thus for-us to-fulfill all righteousness." Then he- excused [=he allowed] him [to	[9]And it-happened in those days, *Jesus* came *from* Nazareth *of-the Galilee*	[21]So it-happened in the [=while] every-one [of] the whole-people **to-be-** **baptized** [=was being baptized]

be baptized]. 16So **Jesus**, **having-been-baptized**, *immediately ascended* from *the water*;	and was-baptized into [=in] *the Jordan under* [=by] John. 10And *immediately ascending* out *of-the water*	and **Jesus** having-been-**baptized** and praying,
and look! the *heavens* **were-opened**, and *he-saw* [the] spirit of-god *descending* as [a] dove, coming **upon** him; 17and look! [a] voice out of-the heavens saying, "This is my son the beloved, in whom I-was-content."	*he-saw* the *heavens* being-torn and the spirit *descending* like [a] dove into him; 11and [a] voice happened [=came] out of-the heavens, "You [yourself] are my son the beloved, in you I-was-content."	the heaven **to-be-opened** [=was opened] 22and the holy spirit to-descend [=was descending] in-bodily form like [a] dove **upon** him, and [a] voice out of-heaven to-happen [=came], "You [yourself] are my son the beloved, in you I-was-content."

6. The Baptism of Jesus (*Gospel Parallels,* Throckmorton, fifth ed.)

Matt 3:13-17	**Mark 1:9-11**	**Luke 3:21-22**
13Then *Jesus came from Galilee* to *John* at *the Jordan*, **to be baptized** by him. 14John would have prevented him, saying, "I need to be baptized by you, and do you come to me?" 15But Jesus answered him, "Let it be so now; for it is proper for us in this way to fulfill all righteousness." Then he consented.	9In those days *Jesus came from* Nazareth of *Galilee*	
16And when **Jesus had been baptized**, *just as he came up* from *the water*, suddenly	and was baptized by *John* in *the Jordan*. 10And *just as he* was *coming up* out of *the water*,	21Now when all the people **were baptized**, and when **Jesus** also **had been baptized** and was praying,
the *heavens* **were opened** to him and *he saw* the Spirit of God *descending* like a dove and alighting *on* him. 17And a voice from heaven said, "This is my Son, the Beloved, with whom I am well pleased."	*he saw* the *heavens* torn apart and the Spirit *descending* like a dove *on* him. 11And a voice came from heaven, "You are my Son, the Beloved; with you I am well pleased."	the heaven **was opened**, 22and the Holy Spirit descended upon him in bodily form like a dove. And a voice came from heaven, "You are my Son, the Beloved; with you I am well pleased."

A summary of agreements:

	Crook	**The Greek Text**	**Throckmorton**
Mt/Mk≠Lk Verbatim	Jesus, from, the Galilee, the Jordan, under, immediately, the water, he-saw, heavens, descending **(12)**	Jesus, from, the Galilee, the Jordan, under, immediately, the water, saw, descending **(12)**	Jesus, came, from, Galilee, John, the Jordan, just as he, up, the water, heavens, he saw, descending, on **(18)**

Mt/Mk≠Lk Near-Verbatim	the/of-the, the/of-the, ascended/ ascending **(3)**	John, ascended/ ascending, the heavens **(4)**	came/coming **(1)**
Mk/Lk≠Mt Verbatim	it-happened, in, and, the, like, you, are, you **(8)**	happened, in, and, the, like, you, are, you **(8)**	came, you, are, you **(4)**
Mk/Lk≠Mt Near-Verbatim	happened/to-happen **(1)**	happened/to happen **(1)**	**(0)**
Mt/Lk≠Mk Verbatim	to-be-baptized, Jesus, having-been-baptized, upon **(4)**	to be baptized, Jesus, upon **(3)**	when, Jesus, had been baptized **(3)**
Mt/Lk≠Mk Near-Verbatim	were-opened/to-be-opened **(1)**	having been baptized, were opened/to be opened **(2)**	were baptized /to be baptized, was opened/were opened **(2)**

As the preceding tables illustrate, the pattern of agreements between my synopsis and the Greek is nearly identical. There are two places where I have made a near-verbatim agreement look like a verbatim agreement, and this is because I was not able to reflect *in English* the different case ending for the same Greek word. Conversely, Throckmorton's pattern of agreements is considerably different in almost every respect. In Throckmorton, Matthew and Mark look much more like each other than they should, Luke and Mark look less like each other than they should, and although the Matthew-Luke agreements against Mark (the 'minor agreements': see Synoptic Study Guides 9 and 15) are the same in number, the number of minor agreements is an illusion.

There is another critical difference between Throckmorton's synopsis and mine: while the limitations of my translation have forced me to make two near-verbatim agreements into verbatim agreements, I have not *created* any agreements in English where they do not exist in the Greek. In contrast, Throckmorton has done so three times in this short pericope: he has created a minor agreement ('when') and a Matt/Mark agreement against Luke ('came'), and, in the third case, has taken away a minor agreement and turned it into a Matt/Mark agreement against Luke (the dove's landing "on" Jesus)! But these are exactly the sorts of things one *needs* to be able to see when using a synopsis, and Throckmorton does not allow you to see them.

I was inspired in 1999 to start the long process of creating this synopsis by the repeated frustration of explaining to students, while using Throckmorton, that what appear to be agreements and disagreements in English are not actually so in the Greek. This synopsis makes it possible for students actually to see how Matthew, Mark, Luke, and Q interrelate directly, and how John and Thomas are related in some way.

John, Q, and Thomas

You will note that there is always a double line on the left border of the Gospel of John and Gospel of Thomas columns, whereas Matthew, Mark, and Luke always have a single line (either solid or broken) on their left. This is to remind the reader that the Gospels of John and Thomas are not given in their entirety in this synopsis. Both are given space in a column only when they have a directly parallel passage. Some synopses contain only the synoptic gospels, some also contain all of John. The problem with the latter approach is that it is a waste of paper: nine times out of ten, when the synoptic columns are full, John is empty, and when the John column is full, the others are empty. I have provided only those John passages that are directly parallel in one or another synoptic gospel. This is the first time in a synopsis that the Gospel of Thomas has appeared in a column alongside the canonical gospels. It is presented here only for ease of access, not as a claim to the relative authority or historical reliability of the Gospel of Thomas (see Synoptic Study Guide 13).

The Gospel of John has been translated with precisely the same principle as Matthew, Mark, Luke, and Q. I have not translated the Gospel of Thomas in this way for two reasons. First of all, I cannot read Coptic, the language in which Thomas survives. But even if I could, it would be misleading to have translated Thomas according to the same principle because it would have implied that Thomas and the canonical gospels share (or do not share any) words. Yet, how can they, if they are in different languages?

The translation of Thomas used here, an open-source free translation done by Stephen Patterson and Marvin Meyer, is available widely on the Internet. You will notice that Thomas has its own brackets (< >). These come from the translators and typically imply words the translators had to supply to generate a meaningful translation or to indicate that there was a gap in the manuscript; the words in the angle brackets are the translators' reconstruction of the missing words. The angle brackets thus function differently from the square brackets used in my rendering of the canonical gospels.

Q has also been translated with the same principles as the canonical Gospels, and for its text I have relied upon the reconstruction of the International Q Project (James M. Robinson, Paul Hoffman, and John S. Kloppenborg, *The Critical Edition of Q: Synopsis including the Gospels of Matthew and Luke, Mark and Thomas with English, German, and French Translations of Q and Thomas*, Minneapolis: Fortress; Leuven: Peeters, 2000). Where I have deviated from their work, which is not often, it is because I disagree on whether a passage really was in Q; I do not disagree on the reconstruction of individual passages. This is key because while, by convention, Q's verse numbers are the same as Luke's, it is not the case that the text of Q is a reproduction of Luke. The IQP has attempted, through the principles of redaction criticism (see Synoptic Study Guide 12), to discern when it is Matthew and when it is Luke that is most likely to have altered the wording of Q.

The Challenges of Translation

Recall that the problem with target-language synopses is that they obscure too much of what is happening in the Greek because they are too focused on the English end result. I felt that the solution to this was to translate every Greek word the same way in English every time it occurs. This way, a student without training in Greek would know with certainty that if something looks like an agreement in English, it is in fact an agreement in Greek. The same concern for consistency applies not only to vocabulary but to verb tenses, moods, and voices, as well. If one notices that Matthew 3:16 and Mark 1:10 agree on the participle "going-down" and Luke 3:22 has the infinitive "to-go-down," then one can be certain that is what is happening in the Greek too. Likewise if the verb appears in the subjunctive ("might-marry") in Matthew 5:32, but the participle ("marrying") in Q and Luke 16:18. Every Greek word is translated with only one English option, and that English option is used only for that Greek word and never for another Greek word in addition.

"One English word for one Greek word" is the sole translation principle that governs this synopsis. This was far from easy to execute, however. In what follows, I shall explain some of the challenges generated by this translation principle, and also some of the places where I felt I had to let go of the principle.

To start, "One English word for one Greek word" is just not how language works. Practically every word in Greek (or any language for that matter) has multiple senses, meanings, uses, or applications. So for example, the Greek verb *ginomai* has two very common uses: "to happen" and "to become." When an event "happens" and when someone "becomes" 12 years old, the same Greek verb is used. But my translation principle required me to choose one or the other, and to be consistent throughout the synopsis. This synopsis goes with "to-happen" for *ginomai*. As will be the case with every single choice I have made, sometimes this will work fine, and sometimes it will not. It works in Luke 1:59: "And it-happened in [=on] the eighth day, they-went to-circumcise the young-child." But it does not work as easily in Luke 2:42, when we read that Jesus "happened twelve years." In cases like these, I supply the *meaning* in reduced-font brackets right after: he-happened [=he became] twelve years [old]." Because of the nature of language, there are many instances of this. It makes for challenging reading, but it also allows you to know with certainty that the same Greek word stands behind both English translations.

This translation principle can result in many strange-looking words. This is because the Greek language is so different from English. For instance, Greek is a highly inflected language, meaning that a single Greek word carries much more grammatical information than an English word does: number (singular or plural), person (first, second, third), case (nominative, genitive, dative, accusative), tense (past, present, future), mood (participle, infinitive, indicative, subjunctive, imperative), voice (active, passive, middle), aspect (completed or continuous). What English does with extra words (to, have, had, he, she, in, of, was, used to, would, etc.) Greek can often do by changing the form of the single verb. As a result, I have rendered single words in Greek as single words in English: not "to have been restrained" but "to-have-been-restrained" (Mark 5:4) because the perfect passive infinitive of "restrain" is one word; not "in the Temple" but "in-the Temple" because the definite article "the" is in the dative (which in this case expresses location, or 'in').

Or consider this example: the Greek word *thaumazō* means "to-be-astonished." Attach *ek* to the front of it (*ekthaumazō*), and it intensifies the original ("completely astonished"): put this in the third person plural imperfect and you get "they-were-completely-astonished." Or take the verb *methistēmi*, which I render "to-banish." Luke 16:4 is the only place this word occurs, and it is in the first person singular ('I'), subjunctive ('might'), and passive ('have been'). What English would express with five words, Greek can do with one: "I-might-have-been-banished."

The greatest challenge posed by my translation principle was to find English alternatives to words I had already used. Greek, for example, has three verbs for talking: *laleō*, *phēmi*, *legō*. They are used pretty much interchangeably in the Greek, meaning at various times "to talk," "to speak," and "to say." But I had to choose a unique English word for each one. Sometimes it works, but sometimes it requires square brackets to provide some English idiom. The challenge of avoiding English words already used hits its peak in the impossible-looking "y'all's-own" (Luke and Q 6:20 and Luke 16:12). The problem is that *su* in Greek means "you." In the genitive is means "your," and that is how I translate it the 481 times it occurs in the gospels. But Greek also has *sos*, which occurs only 27 times in the whole New Testament and also means "your." So I rendered this as the stronger "your-own." This is all fine until we encounter the rare word *humeteros*, which occurs only twice in the whole New Testament (Luke 6:20 and 16:12), and which also means "your." I render *humeteros* as "y'all's-own." I made this choice only because I needed another way to express "your." I did not choose it in order to make Luke appear folksy or Texan. We can be thankful the word occurs so rarely!

This single issue (how to translate *humeteros*) nicely illustrates the challenge of a one-to-one translation. It also raises a related issue: as often as I could and with as much attention to detail as I could muster, I reserved common English words to render common Greek words. Thus when you come across an English word that is rare, or sounds archaic, ideally it is because the Greek word is also rare or archaic. Hence, I render *enantion* (which occurs three times in Luke) as "ere" because "before" was reserved for the more common *pro*, which occurs twenty times in the gospels. Having said that, there were times when synonyms were in short supply and I had to take what I could get.

Another unfortunate side effect of my translation principle is that the gospel writers, who use the wrong word here or there, are sometimes made to look stupid. This poses another challenge because sometimes the writers are actually using the wrong word and sometimes this does appear to be the result of their low level of education. For instance, Q 17:37 (§284) refers to *aetoi* gathered at a corpse. Now we know that these are in all likelihood vultures, but Q uses the Greek word for "eagle," not the Greek word for "vulture." But there are other instances in which it is the fault of my translation principle that makes it appear that one of the writers has used the wrong word. Likewise, at times my translation might raise interpretive options you had not considered. For instance, I translate *pistis* as "loyalty" rather than "faith" because of research I have done on this particular issue. I do it deliberately and provocatively. But at other times, I have chosen an English term only because it was available or because it was a satisfactory choice. On the whole, one should avoid reading too much into my vocabulary choices: they were for the most part governed by *the need to use English words only once.*

Sometimes, the strangeness of the translation is entirely the fault of the strangeness of the Greek. The ancient understanding of physiology in general and gynecology in particular would be comical if it were not so often tragic. For instance, the ancients believed that the womb wandered around in a woman's body, and this caused her uniquely female ailments. One of these was hysteria, derived from the Greek for womb, *hystera*. A relatively common way of expressing conception in Greek was with the verb *sullambanō* (to collect, gather, seize, etc.) plus *en gastri*. In this synopsis I have had to translate this literally ("to-grip in stomach"). Why not translate it in the more obvious way, "to-conceive"? For three reasons: (1) Because "to-conceive" is one word, while the Greek uses a three-word phrase. (2) Because *sullambanō* (to-grip) occurs in other places in the gospels where it has nothing to do with conception. This allows the reader to see exactly how odd the Greek way of expressing conception is. To use "to-conceive" might be perfectly accurate, but it obscures the strangeness of the Greek. (3) Because *gastēr* (the dictionary form of *gastri*) does not mean womb; it clearly means "stomach" (think: gastronomical, gastroenterologist, gastric, etc.). There is a word for womb, and the gospel writers did not use it. Either they thought the baby was in the "stomach" or this was simply a manner of expression; but either way, it is interesting enough not to hide it behind an English gloss like "to-conceive."

My translation principle results in another issue that will pain those who know Greek. In Greek, many prepositions (in, upon, to, from, under, above, through, etc.) have multiple meanings. *Dia* for instance usually means "through" but it can also mean "because of," depending on the "case" of the following word. But English does not use "case," and I had to designate one English word to render *dia*; otherwise it becomes unclear to the reader what Greek word is actually being used. It will strike many readers, therefore, that when it comes to the Greek prepositions especially, I have simply translated them incorrectly. All I have done is impose upon them the same translation principle as I used in the rest of the text: *one English word for one Greek word.*

I have strived for consistency, but there had to be a limit on this. For instance, case endings on nouns express many things. For the most common uses of the dative, I retain the dative in the noun itself by using hyphenation. When the dative expresses "to" (something is given "to" someone), "for" (something is done "for" you), or "in" (someone is "in" the Temple), I have attached it to the appropriate word (e.g., "to-him," "for-you," and "in-the" are all like that because they are in the dative). In other instances, however, it seemed that retaining the dative in the noun would be overly confusing. So with less common uses of the dative, I detached the dative sense from the noun. When the dative is used to express "with" (praising God "with" a great voice), "on" (riding "on" a donkey), or "by" (gripped "by" fear), I have done so in square brackets (e.g., [with] them, [on a] donkey, [by] fear). The cost is that the reader does not realize that "them" here is in the dative. The benefit is that it is ever so slightly more readable. The same applies for those times when Greek verbs take their direct object in the dative or genitive, which English never does: in Greek, if a disciple "hears" Jesus, "Jesus" will be in the genitive. This is how that verb works in Greek. But it would make the translation even less readable to have "of-Jesus" every time someone hears him.

Likewise, some verbal forms in Greek cannot be differentiated from each other in English. English has one form of the infinitive: to run. But Greek has an aorist infinitive as well, the precise sense of which is impossible to reproduce in English. I have not in my translation distinguished between present and aorist infinitives. Likewise, Greek has an aorist participle, which I typically render "having-" as in "having-attended (Luke 1:3). But Greek also has a perfect participle, which English would want to express with "have" because that is our marker of the perfect tense. So perfect participles are also rendered "having-". In the end, the reader of this synopsis will not be able to tell the difference between the present and aorist infinitive, and between the aorist and perfect participle, but everything else will be visible and consistent.

These are some of the ways then in which my translation principle hit its limit either in practicality or usability, and that is because proper translation does not work as I have tried to make it work here. One might even claim that this work is not a translation at all. All too often I have not translated the text; I have simply "rendered" it in English. It might be useful to keep the distinction between translating and rendering in mind when reading this work becomes particularly frustrating.

One final comment on the translation. The noncapitalization of some terms might surprise you. I decided to capitalize in English only those words that are capitalized in the Greek New Testament (Nestle-Aland^{27}). It might surprise you to learn that words and phrases like God, Holy Spirit, Lord, Son of God, Sabbath, Law, and Prophets are never capitalized in the Greek the way they are in English. Now the first words of sentences in Greek are not capitalized either, but I decided to do it here because the convention of capitalizing the first words in sentences is so deeply embedded in English usage. But in Greek, the only words that are capitalized are the names of people, cities, and countries.

Textual Criticism

At the bottom of most pericopae in this synopsis, you will find a jumble of letters and numbers. This is called a critical apparatus, and its job is to list variant readings and the manuscripts, in shorthand markings called sigla, that support those readings. Look at the bottom of §1 and you'll find this:

> [a] *son of-god* $\aleph^1$ A B D L W f^1 f^{13} 33 892 1006 1342 1506 2427 𝔐; *omit* $\aleph^*$ Θ 28 2211 *pc* cop^{sa};
> *son of-the lord* 1241.

The superscript 'a' here corresponds to the superscript 'a' at the end of Mark 1:1 "son of-god[a]". The critical apparatus tells you that our surviving manuscripts of Mark have three different variants, or wordings, at this spot. All the manuscripts agree that the Gospel of Mark opened with "[The] beginning of-the proclamation of-Jesus Anointed-one," so the first part is easy to reconstruct. From there, some manuscripts have "son of-god"; some just end with "Anointed-one"; one other ends with "son of-the lord." In this section, I will briefly explain what these sigla represent, and the principles of textual criticism. By the end, you should understand why the critical apparatus looks like it does, and why I have chosen the variant I have.

Why do we need a critical apparatus at all? Because we do not have any original manuscripts of any book of the Bible. All we have are copies of copies of copies. And while we do have an unprecedented number of these copies, nearing 6000 in number, in different writing styles, on different types of material, and in different languages, one cannot help but be struck, and a little terrified, by the fact that no two of these manuscripts are exactly the same in every way. It is hard to count the differences among them; it could be as staggeringly high as 250,000.

Let me put this into perspective. Imagine that I have an ancient manuscript containing the whole New Testament, and that I am standing before you reading out loud from it. Now imagine that there are about 6000 of you listening to me, and each of you is holding *something* with a part or all of the New Testament written on. (It might be a tiny fragment or a whole New Testament; it might be written in Greek or another language; it might be a copy of the New Testament itself or a sermon written by a church father that quotes from the New Testament.) Now, if every time I read out something that is different from what is written on the manuscript you all are holding, one of you raises a hand, one hand or another would be raised as many as 250,000 times by the time I finish reading from my manuscript. There are, by some counts, only 138,020 words in the Greek New Testament, which means there are more variants than there are words in the New Testament. Almost twice as many.

Every time a hand is raised, we have a variant. We call these variants, and not errors or mistakes. Only when you have an original can you know which variant is a mistake; but we do not have any originals of any New Testament work. *The task of textual criticism then is to reconstruct the best text we can from the surviving manuscripts.*

It is worth explaining how there came to be so many variants. The followers of Jesus—Paul, the gospel writers, and others—wrote their letters and gospels and so on, and at some point afterward, these works were copied and shared. Copies were made of those copies, and this was repeated many times over. Initially, everything was done (written *and* copied) on papyrus, an ancient form of paper. But as Christianity gained in status and wealth in the fourth century, thanks to the Roman emperor Constantine, Christians began copying their texts onto parchment, which is made from animal skins and lasts much longer. But Christians moved around a good deal, and everywhere they went they were commanded to convert people, so their writings also had to be translated as well as copied: Latin for Roman areas, Coptic in Egypt, Syriac in Syria, and so on. We call these translations *versions*.

For more than a thousand years, then, Christian texts were being copied, transported, translated, and copied again, in a cycle that ended only with the invention of the printing press in the fifteenth century. Initially, all texts in the ancient Mediterranean were written with majuscule or capital letters (ALL-CAPS). It was not until the ninth century that someone realized it was faster to write with cursive letters (*lowercase handwriting*). Our papyrus manuscripts are all written with majuscule letters. Our oldest parchment manuscripts are also written with majuscule letters; we call these manuscripts uncials. When minuscule letters took over in popularity, parchment manuscripts of the New Testament used them too; we call these manuscripts minuscules because of their cursive handwriting.

Whether written on papyrus or parchment, in majuscule or minuscule lettering, in Greek or Latin or Coptic, we call these documents *witnesses* because they witness some or all of the text of the New Testament. There are two more witnesses for us to consider: lectionaries and church fathers. Lectionaries were used in worship settings, offering just that portion of a New Testament text necessary for that day's worship. Church fathers, or patristic writers, are those traditionally honored for defending and defining this new religion, especially in its contest with, and eventual transformation into, an empire. These men wrote letters and delivered fiery sermons in which the New Testament might be quoted or paraphrased—often, it appears, from memory. These passages also comprise witnesses to the text of the New Testament, though generally not very good ones.

Christians traveled and settled around the Mediterranean and began copying their manuscripts. It is generally possible to tell what region of the Mediterranean a manuscript was copied in because it seems that certain practices became standard in certain areas. For instance, in some areas the rule was that the scribe should alter the text he is copying—by accident or on purpose—as little as possible. In other areas it was quite acceptable for a scribe to alter the text, especially if the point was to make it clear. But then there is always the issue of ability, and some areas appear to have had access to better-trained scribes, who would be less prone to making errors while copying. Well-trained scribes were by no means infallible; but they were less likely to misspell words, repeat the same line, skip lines, repeat groups of letters or skip them too. But even a talented scribe could be confused by a note in the margin of a manuscript. Had the previous scribe jotted down there a thought that occurred to him while copying, or had he missed a verse and put it there? A well-trained scribe would be as likely to insert that marginal gloss into the text as an untrained copier. The point is important: not all scribes who copied the New Testament were equally well trained, equally careful, or equally interested in maintaining the text unchanged.

All this is to explain how the New Testament came to have so many copies and yet no originals, and how those copies came to be spread so far and wide and to have so many varieties in terms of language, writing style, material, and reliability. At any rate, textual critics divide our surviving manuscripts up into *family types*, which correspond to geographical areas, and to the ethos of the copying environment. The family types (sometimes also called text types) are as follows.

Alexandrian: Texts that come from Egypt are normally of this family. It is thought to be the most consistently reliable family type, and is found in manuscripts from as early as the second to third centuries CE. The Alexandrian type of text is found in the papyri, since they almost all come from Egypt, in the most important uncials, and in the Alexandrian church fathers. The Alexandrian family type of text is characterised by austerity and brevity; it does not exhibit the degree of grammatical or stylistic polishing evidenced by other family types.

Western: Comes from Greece and Italy. This family type is also attested since the second century CE, in some of the early church fathers like Tatian, Marcion, Irenaeus, and Tertullian. It even appears in some early papyri, as well as the Old Latin (it) and Syriac translations (sy). Its main representative among the uncials is Codex Beza (D). The text in Western manuscripts is characterized by omissions and insertions for clarification, readings found only in Codex Beza, paraphrasing, and harmonization.

Caesarean: Geographically, this area refers to what lies between modern-day Turkey and Egypt. In terms of reliability and characteristics of the text, the Caesarean family type falls between the Western and the Alexandrian text types. No serious scholars question whether the other family types are legitimate types, but there is considerable debate over the legitimacy of the Caesarean family type.

Byzantine: The term "Byzantine" refers to the old empire of Byzantium, more or less modern Turkey, which was the seat of power in Christianity until Rome took over in the tenth century. This is the latest and least reliable of the family types, but it is also the most widely attested because of the vast majority of minuscules produced in Byzantine scriptoria (copying auditoriums). This family type is also found in some uncials. Because there can be as many as 3000 manuscripts with the same Byzantine variant, they can all be represented by a single letter: in this synopsis 𝔐 (for majority). While this type of text does preserve *some* good readings, for the most part it is inferior to the other text types. The Byzantine type of text is characterized by conflations and revisions carried out in the interest of smoothness and intelligibility, and theological "correction." The text in Byzantine manuscripts is highly polished and readable.

One final comment on family types should be made: some manuscripts can contain more than one type of text. This might start when a scribe has two partial manuscripts before him. If a scribe is producing a full New Testament from two incomplete manuscripts, and the manuscript with Paul's letters comes from Alexandria while the manuscript with the Gospels in it comes from Byzantium, then the manuscript that scribe produces will have two types of text in it (Alexandrian and Byzantine), and so, of course, will the copies made of it.

The Manuscripts of This Synopsis

In the following table, I present and describe the various witnesses, their sigla and annotations that appear in the critical apparatuses, but I do so with three caveats:

- I discuss only those manuscripts that appear in this synopsis. Lectionaries do not appear in this table, since, in the interest of simplicity, I have not listed them in the critical apparatuses. This does mean that some of the more famous or important manuscripts, say $\mathfrak{P}^{52}$ (a mid-second-century fragment from the Gospel of John) or $\mathfrak{P}^{66}$, a full copy of John from c. 200) are not mentioned in this table because they do not play any role in the reconstruction of any of the text that appears in *this* synopsis. Beware then that the following table is anything but thorough.
- I note only the *gospel* material that appears in each manuscript witness, not other New Testament material (Pauline and other letters, Acts, Revelation), since only gospel material is relevant to our immediate needs.
- Since the minuscules are so numerous, I list here only those with an Alexandrian text or those that are otherwise well known and important. If a minuscule is given in a critical apparatus in the synopsis but is not in this table, one can assume it is has a Byzantine-family-type text.

Siglum	Name/Location	Date	Family Type	Brief Description and Comments
			PAPYRI	
$\mathfrak{P}^{1}$	Philadelphia	3rd c.	Alexandrian	Parts of Matt 1 and 13
$\mathfrak{P}^{4}$	Paris	3rd c.	Alexandrian	Parts of Luke 1-6
$\mathfrak{P}^{19}$	Oxford	4th-5th c.	Mixed	Parts of Matt 10-11
$\mathfrak{P}^{21}$	Allentown	4th-5th c.	Agrees with ℵ and D	Part of Matt 12
$\mathfrak{P}^{25}$	Berlin	late 4th	Western	Parts of Matt 18-19
$\mathfrak{P}^{37}$	Ann Arbor	3rd-4th c.	Caesarean	Part of Matt 26
$\mathfrak{P}^{44}$	New York	6th-7th c.	Mixed	Parts of Matt 17-18, 25 and John 9, 10, 12
$\mathfrak{P}^{45}$	Dublin	3rd	Alexandrian	Parts of Matt 20-21, 25-26; Mark 4-9, 11-12; Luke 6-7, 9-14; John 4-5, 10-11
$\mathfrak{P}^{53}$	Ann Arbor	3rd	Mixed	Part of Matt 26
$\mathfrak{P}^{64}$	Oxford	200 CE	Alexandrian	Parts of Matt 3, 5, 26
$\mathfrak{P}^{69}$	Oxford	3rd	Mixed	Parts of Luke 22
$\mathfrak{P}^{70}$	Oxford	3rd	Unclassified	Parts of Matt 2-3, 11-12, 24
$\mathfrak{P}^{75}$	Geneva	early 3rd c.	Alexandrian	Parts of Luke 3-18, 22-24 and John 1-15
$\mathfrak{P}^{86}$	Cologne	4th	Unclassified	Parts of Matt 5
$\mathfrak{P}^{88}$	Milan	4th	Unclassified	Most of Mark 2
$\mathfrak{P}^{97}$	Dublin	6th-7th c.	Unclassified	Part of Luke 14
			UNCIALS	
ℵ	Sinaiticus	4th c.	Alexandrian	Matthew, Mark, Luke, John (see below for $\aleph^{*}$ $\aleph^{1}$ $\aleph^{2}$)
A	Alexandrinus	5th c.	Byzantine in the Gospels	Matthew (except 25:6-end), Mark, Luke, John (except 6:50-8:52)
B	Vaticanus	4th c.	Alexandrian	Matthew, Mark, Luke, John
C	Ephraemi Rescriptus	5th c.	Alexandrian	Most of Matthew, Mark, Luke, John (see below for C^{*} C^{2} C^{3})
D	Beza	5th	Western	Matthew (except 1:1-20; 6:20- 9:2; 27:2-12), Mark, Luke, John (except 1:16- 3:26) (see below for D^{*} D^{1})
E	Basilensis	8th	Byzantine	Matthew, Mark, Luke, John
F	Boreelianus	9th	Byzantine	Most of Matthew, Mark, Luke, John
G	Seidelianus I	9th	Byzantine	Most of Matthew, Mark, Luke, John
H	Seidelianus II	9th	Byzantine	Part of Matthew; most of Mark, Luke, and John
K	Cyprius	9th	Byzantine	Matthew, Mark, Luke, John
L	Regius	8th	Alexandrian	Matthew, Mark, Luke, John
N	Petropolitanus Purpureus	6th	Byzantine	Most of Matthew, Mark, Luke, John
P	Guelferbytanus	6th	Byzantine	Parts of Matthew, Luke, John
T	Borgianus	5th	Alexandrian	Luke, John
W	Washingtoniensis	5th	Mixed	Most of Matthew, Mark, Luke, John
X	Monacensis	10th	Byzantine	Very little of Matthew, Luke, and John; part of Mark
Y	Macedoniensis	9th	Byzantine	Most of Matthew, Luke, John; all of Mark
Z	Dublinensis	6th	Caesarean	Matthew
Γ	Tischendorfianus	10th	Byzantine	Most of Matthew and Mark; all of Luke and John
Δ	Sangallensis	9th	Alexandrian in Mark; Byzantine in the rest	Matthew, Mark, Luke, John
θ	Koridethi	9th	Mixed	Matthew, Mark, Luke, John
Ξ	Zacynthius	6th	Alexandrian	Part of Luke
Π	Petropolitanus	9th	Byzantine	Matthew, Mark, Luke, John
Σ	Rossanensis	6th	Byzantine	Matthew, Mark
Φ	Beratinus	6th	Byzantine	Matthew and Mark

UNCIALS *(Continued)*				
Ψ	Athous Lavrensis	8th-9th	Alexandrian	Matthew, Mark, Luke, John
058		4th	Alexandrian	Part of Matt 18
070		6th	Alexandrian	Luke and John
083		6th-7th	Alexandrian	Parts of John 1, 2-4
085		6th	Alexandrian	Part of Matt 20, 22
087		6th	Alexandrian	Parts of Matt 1, 2, 19, 21 and John 18
0106		7th	Alexandrian	Matt 12-15
0130		9th	Alexandrian	Parts of Mark and Luke
0181		4th-5th	Alexandrian	Part of Luke 9-10
0233		8th	Alexandrian	Matthew, Mark, Luke, John
0250	Climaci rescriptus	8th	Alexandrian	Matthew, Mark, Luke, John
0274		5th	Alexandrian	Mark 6-10
MINUSCULES				
1		12th	Caesarean	Most of the NT
13		13th	Alexandrian	Most of Matthew, Mark, and John; all of Luke
28		11th	Caesarean in Mark, Byzantine for the rest	Most of Matthew, Luke; all of Mark; part of John
33		9th	Alexandrian	All of Matt and John; most of Mark and Luke
205		15th	Caesarean	Matthew, Mark, Luke, John
209		14th	Caesarean	Matthew, Mark, Luke, John
237		11th	Byzantine	Matthew, Mark, Luke, John
565		9th	Caesarean/Mixed	Matthew, Mark, Luke, John, but with many holes. This manuscript, like N above, is purple.
579		13th	Alexandrian in Mk/Lk	All of Matt and Luke; most of Mark and John
700		11th	Caesarean	Matthew, Mark, Luke, John
788		11th	Caesarean	Matthew, Mark, Luke, John
892		9th	Alexandrian	Matthew, Mark, Luke, John
983		12th	Mixed	Matthew, Mark, Luke, John
1006		11th	Byzantine	Matthew, Mark, Luke, John
1241		12th	Caesarean	Matthew, Mark, Luke, John
1342		13th-14th	Alexandrian in Mark	Matthew, Mark, Luke, John
1424		9th-10th	Mixed	Matthew, Mark, Luke, John
1506		1320 CE	Byzantine	Matthew, Mark, Luke, John
1582		949 CE	Mixed	Matthew, Mark, Luke, John
2427		14th	Alexandrian	Mark
2542		13th	Mixed	Matt, Mark, Luke
f^{1}	Lake Group	12th-13th	Caesarean	1, 118, 131, 209, 1582 and others
f^{13}	Ferrar Group	11th-12th	Caesarean	13, 69, 124, 174, 230, 346, 543, 788, 826, 828, 983, 1689, 1709, and others
𝔐	Majority	9th-15th	Byzantine	Refers to the majority of all manuscripts, which will naturally be mostly Byzantine minuscules
pc		9th-15th	Byzantine	A **few** minuscules normally counted in 𝔐 but which differ from 𝔐
al		9th-15th	Byzantine	**Some** minuscules normally counted in 𝔐 but which differ from 𝔐
pm		9th-15th	Byzantine	A **large number** of minuscules normally counted in 𝔐 but which differ from 𝔐

VERSIONS			
Language	**Dialect**	**Date**	**Family Type**
Coptic	cop alone refers to all or most Coptic versions		
	copsa = Sahidic	3rd c.	Alexandrian
	copbo = Bohairic	3rd c.	Alexandrian
Old Latin	it	4th-13th c.	Western
Syriac	sy alone refers to all or most Syriac versions		
	sy^{c} = Curetonian	3rd-4th c.	Western
	sy^{h} = Harclensis	2nd-3rd c.	Western
	sy^{p} = Peshitta	5th c.	Byzantine
	sy^{s} = Sinaitic	3rd-4th c.	Western
Latin	vg	383 CE	Mixed
CHURCH FATHERS			
Augustine		5th	Alexandrian
Origen		3rd	Alexandrian
Jerome		4th	Western
Justin		2nd	Western

A note about the following superscript add-ons that appear at times with the manuscript sigla:

- * (e.g., א*) refers to the original reading on a manuscript if correctors' hands are present.
- ^{1}, ^{2}, ^{3}, ^{C} (e.g., $א^{C}$, C^{2}, D^{3}), all refer either to the corrector's hand (^{C}) or to successive correctors (^{1}, ^{2}, ^{3}).
- ^{mss} (e.g., it^{mss}) tells you that several manuscripts in that group (in this case the Old Latin texts) have that reading.

The Principles of Textual Criticism

The goal of Textual Criticism is to reconstruct the text of the New Testament word by word. The challenge is to do so from the thousands of manuscripts and their astonishing number of variants. Modern textual criticism has a number of principles that help in attaining this goal. They are not perfect, and like all things scholarly they are open to constant revision, but they do result in a text that most scholars agree upon.

The single most important principle of Textual Criticism is that manuscripts are not counted; they are weighed. For example, let us imagine, hypothetically, that there are 1500 manuscripts that all have the longer ending of Mark (Mark 16:9-22), and only 100 manuscripts that end at Mark 16:8. Instinct might lead one to think democratically: the longer ending has fifteen times more manuscript support, so it must be better. This was the thinking of the creators of the King James Bible.

But modern text critics think differently. First of all, if those 1500 witnesses to the longer ending of Mark can be traced back to 75 originally different copies, then we do not actually have 1500 witnesses, but only 75. Numbers can be deceiving if one does not consider them in the context of genealogy—which manuscripts derive from which? Alternatively, if those 1500 manuscripts, again hypothetically, all date to after the ninth century, and the 100 witnesses to the shorter ending all date from before the sixth century, then again, we are not best served by thinking democratically. And finally, if those 1500 witnesses come from scribes with a noted history of altering the texts they are copying, but the 100 witnesses of the shorter ending were produced by scribes we know did not meddle with the text, then surely the quality of manuscript is more important than their number. The bottom line is that modern text critics consider the number of manuscripts that attest a certain reading to be irrelevant.

In the event that a text critic needs to decide which reading among variants is better, she considers two factors: the manuscripts that the variants are found in (external criteria) and the logic of the variants themselves (internal criteria).

External criteria focus on the three features of the texts: date of manuscripts, the assumption being that earlier is usually better; whether the reading is found in other types of manuscripts and locales, since a widely distributed variant has a stronger claim to being original than a variant found in only one location; and the tendencies of the scribes responsible for the copying of *that* manuscript: were the scribes respectful of the text, or did they alter it deliberately in any way?

Internal criteria focus on the variants themselves. Above all, the text critic wants to be able to understand how variants come about. If one can explain how one variant derived from another, then it is possible to ascertain which of the surviving variants is earliest. Three considerations aid scholars in this. (1) *Lectio difficilior* is the principle that scribes are more likely to clarify things than to introduce lack of clarity. (2) *Lectio brevior* is the principle that a longer variant is longer because a scribe elaborated upon it, most likely in the interest of clarification. These two criteria are clearly related. Both work especially well for theological issues that require clarification. If one variant reflects badly on Jesus, and another well, then it is unreasonable to imagine that a scribe deliberately put Jesus in a bad light. It is more reasonable to imagine that the reading that reflects well on Jesus is later, or secondary. And finally (3) there is the issue of harmonization. Particularly when copying gospels, scribes were prone to bring sayings of Jesus into line with one another, rather than have him respond differently in different gospels to the same question. This might be done accidentally, whereby a scribe who is copying Matthew thinks he knows the text so well that he does not need to look up at his exemplar, but in fact the words he has in his head are Mark's. But it can also happen deliberately, whereby a scribe thinks it is a theological problem that the gospels have Jesus saying different things at the same event; harmonization is that scribe's solution to that problem.

There is one final criterion that can help scholars distinguish later additions to a text from its original wording. People have writing styles nearly as unique as fingerprints. If a variant is long enough, as is the case with the longer ending of Mark, there might be vocabulary or grammatical constructions in it that cannot be found in the rest of Mark. This suggests very strongly that the longer ending was not written by the same person who wrote the rest of Mark. The same logic applies in cases where there are theological ideas found in a variant that cannot be found in the rest of a piece of writing, or an author's corpus, or theological ideas that come from later periods, not from the period of the original writing.

Keep in mind that we are dealing here with tendencies, likelihoods, and probabilities, not hard and fast rules. Scribes were people, not machines! A missing word that results in unintelligibility is clearly a difficult reading, but it is not immediately obvious that the unintelligibility goes back to the original. It might; but it might also be the fault of a scribe working in haste. This and other challenges make Text Criticism more art than science, and it means that all criteria must be applied together and a judgment made based on all of them, not just one (e.g., the date of the manuscript).

The most interesting thing about the finished product at the end of this process is that the text produced does not have a twin in any ancient manuscript. In other words, even though text critics can deem Vaticanus (B) the very best of our surviving manuscripts, modern Bibles are not just translations of Vaticanus. This is because even Vaticanus has readings that are secondary, or scribal. It means that the Greek New Testament produced by modern text critics is an "eclectic" text, because the words that make it up are "chosen" from all the surviving manuscripts, not just from one.

How to Read a Synopsis Page

The broken lines here tell you that this story is found in a different place in Matthew and Mark than it is in Luke. At this point in the synopsis, we are in Luke's order, so Luke's heading appears in bold and the Luke column has a solid line to its left. The information in parentheses (→ §164) tells you that you will find the same story (or pericope) at pericope number 164. At that point, the story is in Matthew's and Mark's order, so the table there appears with solid lines to the left of the Matthew and Mark columns and a broken line beside Luke, and the headings "Matt 14:3-4" and "Mark 6:17-18" in bold and "Luke 3:18-20" unbolded.

Each table, which generally corresponds to a whole story, is called a pericope, in this case pericope 20.

The roman font material tells you what the words say: "exhorting many others"; but this is not really what the words mean. In places where my translation principles have resulted in unclear meanings, I have provided that meaning in the square brackets immediately following: [=other things]. That means you should read the whole phrase: "exhorting many other things." It is important always to remember that the text outside the square brackets tells you what the words literally *say*; the material inside the brackets tells you what the words *mean*.

20. The Imprisonment of John (→ §164)

Matt 14:3-4	Mark 6:17-18	**Luke 3:18-20**
		[18]And therefore for-one, [while] exhorting many others [=other things], he-was-proclaiming [=preaching to] the whole-people.
[3]For Herod, having-seized John, restrained and deposited [him] in prison through [=because of] Herodias, the woman [=wife] of-Philip his brother[a];	[17]For Herod, having-sent-off [soldiers], he [himself] seized John and restrained him in prison through [=because of] Herodias, the woman [=wife] of-Philip his brother, that [=because] he-married her;	[19]So [=on the other hand] Herod the tetrarch, being-exposed under [=by] him around [=concerning] <u>Herodias</u>, the woman [=wife of] his brother and around [=concerning] all [the] evils which Herod did,
[4]for John was-saying to-him, "It-is-permitted not for-you to-have her."	[18]for John was-saying to-Herod that "It-is-permitted not for-you to-have the woman [=wife of] your brother."	
		[20]and added this upon [=to it] all: he-shut-up John in prison[b].

[a] *of-Philip his brother* ℵ B C L W Δ Θ 0106 f^1 f^{13} 28 33 𝔐 sy cop Origen; *his brother* D it vg Jer Aug.
[b] *in prison* $\mathfrak{p}^4$ ℵ B D L Ξ 070 f^1 565; *in the prison* A W Θ Ψ f^{13} 33 892 1006 1342 𝔐.

With practice, you will learn to read from roman font to square brackets fluidly, like this: "For Herod, having seized John, restrained and deposited him in prison because of Herodias, the wife of Philip his brother."

In most pericopae, small superscript letters will appear, alerting the reader to a textual variant that can be found below the pericope in a critical apparatus. The critical apparatus shows the variants and the manuscripts that support each variant. For an explanation of the critical apparatus and the principles of textual criticism, see the preceding section. When the raised letter is attached to a word or phrase, as both are here, the variants replace it; when it sits in an open space, the variants represent inserted material.

Some words are underlined because they are spelled slightly differently from the same word in another gospel. In this case, Matthew and Mark both have the word "Herodias" spelled the same way, but Luke's is spelled differently. Sometimes the same word is spelled differently in all three gospels, in which case you will find double-underlining used.

Sometimes, the material inside the square brackets tells you what the words mean, using the = sign. At other times, as here with [the], the brackets give you a missing but often implied word. It is important to recognize that the word is implied in the Greek but is not actually there in the text.

There are a few items you will see with some pericopae that do not appear with this one. Below the critical apparatus, one might find:

📖 Lk 1:10 – Lev 16:17; 📖 Lk 1:17 – Mal 4:5, 6

This indicates citations and allusions to the Hebrew Bible (NRSV). If there is a direct quote of the Hebrew Bible, it will appear in ALL-CAPS in the gospel itself.

Notes on the Synoptic Study Guides

There are 17 Synoptic Study Guides distributed throughout the synopsis. There are myriad topics relevant to the study of the gospels, so there could have been many more of these. I elected to limit the Study Guides to topics directly relevant to the study of the Synoptic Problem, the main target of a synopsis. Each Study Guide is placed at the point at which the information becomes relevant; the units are not in a logical order as a whole, so it is possible that information contained in one assumes knowledge gained in a later guide. When that happens, you will be directed to the relevant Study Guide.

List of Pericopae

Prologues and Infancy Narratives

§	Matt	Mark	Q	Luke	John	Thomas	Parallel §
1.	**1:1**	**1:1**	———	**1:1-4**	———	———	———
2.	———	———	———	**1:5-25**	———	———	———
3.	———	———	———	**1:26-38**	———	———	———
4.	———	———	———	**1:39-56**	———	———	———
5.	———	———	———	**1:57-80**	———	———	———
6.	**1:2-17**	———	———	3:23-38	———	———	§22
7.	**1:18-25**	———	———	———	———	———	———
8.	———	———	———	**2:1-7**	———	———	———
9.	**2:1-12**	———	———	———	———	———	———
10.	———	———	———	**2:8-20**	———	———	———
11.	———	———	———	**2:21-38**	———	———	———
12.	**2:13-21**	———	———	———	———	———	———
13.	**2:22-23**	———	———	———	———	———	———
14.	———	———	———	**2:39-40**	———	———	———
15.	———	———	———	**2:41-52**	———	———	———

The Start of the Galilean Ministry

§	Matt	Mark	Q	Luke	John	Thomas	Parallel §
16.	**3:1-6**	**1:2-6**	**3:3a**	**3:1-7a**	1:19-23	———	———
17.	**3:7-10**	———	**3:7b-9**	**3:7b-9**	———	———	———
18.	———	———	———	**3:10-14**	———	———	———
19.	**3:11-12**	**1:7-8**	**3:16-17**	**3:15-17**	1:25-28, 33	———	———
20.	14:3-4	6:17-18	———	**3:18-20**	———	———	§164
21.	**3:13-17**	**1:9-11**	———	**3:21-22**	1:29-34	———	———
22.	1:1-16	———	———	**3:23-38**	———	———	§6
23.	**4:1-11**	**1:12-13**	**4:1-4, 9-12 5-8, 13**	**4:1-13**	———	———	———
24.	**4:12**	**1:14a**	———	**4:14-15**	4:1-3, 43, 45	———	———
25.	**4:13a**	———	**4:16**	**4:16a**	———	———	———
26.	**4:13b-16**	———	———	———	———	———	———
27.	**4:17**	**1:14b-15**	———	———	———	———	———
28.	13:53-58	6:1-6	———	**4:16b-30**	7:15; 6:42; 4:44; 10:39	31	§161
29.	**4:18-22**	**1:16-20**	———	———	1:35-51	———	———

Matthew's Sermon on the Mount

§	Matt	Mark	Q	Luke	John	Thomas	Parallel §
30.	**4:23-5:1**	———	———	———	———	———	———
31.	**5:2-12**	———	6:20-23	6:20-23	———	54; 68; 69	§74, §75
32.	**5:13**	9:50	14:34-35	14:34-35	———	———	§187, §263
33.	**5:14-16**	———	11:33	11:33	———	33	§220
34.	**5:17-20**	———	16:17	16:17	———	———	§273
35.	**5:21-26**	———	12:58-59	12:58-59	———	———	§243
36.	**5:27-30**	———	———	———	———	———	———

37. **5:31-32**	———	16:18	16:18	———	———	§274
38. **5:33-37**	———	———	———	———	———	———
39. **5:38-42**	———	6:29-30	6:29-30	———	95	§78
40. **5:43-48**	———	6:27-28, 32, 34-36	6:27-28, 32-36	———	———	§77, §80, §81
41. **6:1-4**	———	———	———	———	62	———
42. **6:5-6**	———	———	———	———	14	———
43. **6:7-13**	———	11:2-4	11:1-4	———	———	§210
44. **6:14-15**	11:25-26	———	———	———	———	§311
45. **6:16-18**	———	———	———	———	———	———
46. **6:19-21**	———	12:33-34	12:33-34	———	76	§233, §237
47. **6:22-23**	———	11:34-35	11:34-36	———	24	§221
48. **6:24**	———	16:13	16:13	———	47	§264, §270
49. **6:25-34**	———	12:22-31	12:22-32	———	36	§236
50. **7:1-2**	4:24	6:37-38	6:37-38	8:7	———	§82, §147
51. **7:3-5**	———	6:41-42	6:41-42	———	26	§85
52. **7:6**	———	———	———	———	93	———
53. **7:7-11**	———	11:9-13	11:9-13	16:24; 14:13-14; 15:7	92; 94; 2	§212
54. **7:12**	———	6:31	6:31	———	6	§79
55. **7:13-14**	———	13:24	13:24	———	———	§248
56. **7:15-20**	———	6:43; 44	6:43; 44	———	———	§86
57. **7:21-23**	———	6:46; 13:26-27	6:46; 13:26-27	———	———	§87, §248
58. **7:24-27**	———	6:47-49	6:47-49	———	———	§88
59. **7:28-29**	**1:21-22**	———	**4:31-32**	2:12; 7:46	———	———

The Galilean Ministry Continues

60. ———	**1:23-28**	———	**4:33-37**	———	———	———
61. 8:14-15	**1:29-31**	———	**4:38-39**	———	———	§91
62. 8:16-17	**1:32-34**	———	**4:40-41**	———	———	§92
63. ———	**1:35-39**	———	**4:42-44**	———	———	———
64. ———	———	———	**5:1-11**	21:1-11	———	———
65. **8:1-4**	**1:40-45**	———	**5:12-16**	———	———	———
66. 9:1-8	**2:1-12**	———	**5:17-26**	5:1-9a	———	§89, §96
67. 9:9-13	**2:13-17**	———	**5:27-32**	———	———	§97
68. 9:14-17	**2:18-22**	———	**5:33-39**	3:29-30	104; 47	§98
69. 12:1-8	**2:23-28**	———	**6:1-5**	———	———	§130
70. 12:9-14	**3:1-6**	———	**6:6-11**	———	———	§131
71. ———	3:7-12	———	6:17-19	———	———	§73
72. 10:1-4	**3:13-19**	———	**6:12-16**	1:42	———	§103

Luke's Sermon on the Plain

73. ———	3:7-12	———	**6:17-19**	———	———	§71
74. 5:3-6	———	**6:20-21**	**6:20-21**	———	54; 69	§31
75. 5:11	———	**6:22-23**	**6:22-23**	———	68; 69	§31
76. ———	———	———	**6:24-26**	———	———	———
77. 5:43-45	———	**6:27-28, 35**	**6:27-28**	———	———	§40
78. 5:38-42	———	**6:29-30**	**6:29-30**	———	95	§39
79. 7:12	———	**6:31**	**6:31**	———	6	§54
80. 5:46-47	———	**6:32, 34**	**6:32-35**	———	———	§40
81. 5:48	———	**6:36**	**6:36**	———	———	§40
82. 7:1-2	4:24	**6:37-38**	**6:37-38**	8:7	———	§50, §147
83. 15:14	———	**6:39**	**6:39**	———	34	§169

84. 10:24-25a	———	**6:40**	**6:40**	13:16	———	§112
85. 7:3-5	———	**6:41-42**	**6:41-42**	———	26	§51
86. 7:18; 12:33b; 7:16b; 12:35; 12:34b	———	**6:43-45**	**6:43-45**	———	45	§56, §140
87. 7:21	———	**6:46**	**6:46**	———	———	§57
88. 7:24-27	———	**6:47-49**	**6:47-49**	———	———	§58

The Galilean Ministry Continues Again

89. **8:5-13**	2:1	**7:1, 3, 6-9**	**7:1-10**	4:46b-54	———	§66, §96, §249-51
90. ———	———	———	**7:11-17**	———	———	———
91. **8:14-15**	1:29-31	———	4:38-39	———	———	§61
92. **8:16-17**	1:32-34	———	4:40-41	———	———	§62
93. **8:18-22**	———	9:57-60	9:57-62	———	86	§195
94. **8:23-27**	4:35-41	———	8:22-25	———	———	§158
95. **8:28-34**	5:1-20	———	8:26-39	———	———	§159
96. **9:1-8**	2:1-12	———	5:17-26	5:1-9a	———	§66, 89
97. **9:9-13**	2:13-17	———	5:27-32	———	———	§67
98. **9:14-17**	2:18-22	———	5:33-39	3:29-30	104; 47	§68
99. **9:18-26**	5:21-43	———	8:40-56	———	———	§160
100. **9:27-31**	———	———	———	———	———	§301
101. **9:32-34**	3:22	11:14-15	11:14-15	10:20; 8:48	———	§136, §137, §213
102. **9:35-38**	6:34	10:2	10:2	4:35	73	§161, §197
103. **10:1-4**	3:13-19	———	6:12-16	1:42	———	§72
104. **10:5-6**	6:7-8a	———	9:1-2	———	———	§162
105. **10:7-8**	———	10:9	10:9	———	———	§200
106. **10:9-10**	6:8b-9	10:4, 7	10:4, 7	———	14	§199, §200
107. **10:11-13**	6:10	10:8, 5-6	10:8, 5-6	———	———	§200
108. **10:14**	6:11	10:10-11	10:10-11	———	———	§201
109. **10:15**	———	10:12	10:12	———	———	§201
110. **10:16**	———	10:3	10:3	———	39	§198
111. **10:17-23**	13:9-13	12:11-12	21:12-13; 12:11-12; 21:16-17	———	———	§232, §326, §327
112. **10:24-25**	———	6:40	6:40	13:16	———	§84
113. **10:26-27**	———	12:2-3	12:2-3	———	5; 33	§227
114. **10:28**	———	12:4-5	12:4-5	———	———	§228
115. **10:29-31**	———	12:6-7	12:6-7	———	———	§229
116. **10:32-33**	———	12:8-9	12:8-9	———	———	§230
117. **10:34-36**	———	12:51, 53	12:51-53	———	16	§241
118. **10:37-39**	———	14:26-27; 17:33	14:25-27; 17:33	12:25	55; 101	§260, §262, §287
119. **10:40-41**	———	10:16	10:16	13:20	———	§203
120. **10:42**	9:41	———	———	———	———	§185
121. **11:1**	———	———	———	———	———	———
122. **11:2-6**	———	**7:18-19, 22-23**	**7:18-23**	———	———	———
123. **11:7-11**	———	**7:24-28**	**7:24-28**	———	78; 46	———
124. ———	———	———	**7:29-30**	———	———	———
125. **11:12-15**	———	16:16	16:16	———	———	§272
126. **11:16-19**	———	**7:31-35**	**7:31-35**	———	———	———
127. **11:20-24**	———	10:13-15	10:13-15	———	———	§202

128.	**11:25-27**	———	10:21-22	10:21-22	3:35; 7:29; 10:15a; 13:3a; 17:2a	61	§205
129.	**11:28-30**	———	———	———	———	90	———
130.	**12:1-8**	2:23-28	———	6:1-5	———	———	§69
131.	**12:9-14**	3:1-6	———	6:6-11	———	———	§70
132.	**12:15-21**	———	———	———	———	———	———
133.	———	———	———	**7:36-50**	———	———	§209, §345
134.	———	———	———	**8:1-3**	———	———	———
135.	———	**3:20-21**	———	———	———	———	———
136.	9:34	**3:22**	11:15	11:15	10:20; 8:48	———	§101, §213
137.	**12:22-24**	———	———	———	———	———	§101
138.	**12:25-29**	**3:23-27**	11:17-20	11:17-21	———	35	§213, § 214
139.	**12:30**	———	11:23	11:23	———	———	§215
140.	**12:31-37**	**3:28-30**	12:10; 6:44-45	12:10; 6:44-45	———	44; 45	§86, §231
141.	**12:38-42**	———	11:16, 29-30, 32, 31	11:16, 29-30 32, 31	———	———	§173, §213, §218, §219
142.	**12:43-45**	———	11:24-26	11:24-26	———	———	§216
143.	**12:46-50**	**3:31-35**	———	8:19-21	15:14	99	§157
144.	**13:1-9**	**4:1-9**	———	**8:4-8**	———	9	———
145.	**13:10-17**	**4:10-12**	10:23-24	**8:9-10**; 10:23-24	9:39b; 12:37-40	62; 41; 17	§206
146.	**13:18-23**	**4:13-20**	———	**8:11-15**	———	———	———
147.	13:12	**4:21-25**	———	**8:16-18**	———	33; 5; 6 ; 41	§50, §82, §145
148.	———	**4:26-29**	———	———	———	———	———
149.	**13:24-30**	———	———	———	———	57	———
150.	**13:31-32**	**4:30-32**	13:18-19	13:18-19	———	20	§246
151.	**13:33**	———	13:20-21	13:20-21	———	96	§247
152.	**13:34-35**	**4:33-34**	———	———	———	———	———
153.	**13:36-43**	———	———	———	———	———	———
154.	**13:44-46**	———	———	———	———	109; 76	———
155.	**13:47-50**	———	———	———	———	8	———
156.	**13:51-52**	———	———	———	———	———	———
157.	12:46-50	3:31-35	———	**8:19-21**	15:14	99	§143
158.	8:23-27	**4:35-41**	———	**8:22-25**	———	———	§94
159.	8:28-34	**5:1-20**	———	**8:26-39**	———	———	§95
160.	9:18-26	**5:21-43**	———	**8:40-56**	———	———	§99
161.	**13:53-58;** 9:35	**6:1-6**	4:16	4:16-24	7:15; 6:42; 4:44	31	§25, §28
162.	10:5-6; 9-11, 14	**6:7-13**	———	**9:1-6**	———	———	§104, §106-08, 201
163.	**14:1-2**	**6:14-16**	———	**9:7-9**	———	———	———
164.	**14:3-12**	**6:17-29**	———	3:19-20	———	———	§20
165.	———	**6:30-31**	———	**9:10a**	———	———	———
166.	**14:13-21**	**6:32-44**	———	**9:10b-17**	6:1-13	———	———
167.	**14:22-33**	**6:45-52**	———	———	6:16-21	———	———
168.	**14:34-36**	**6:53-56**	———	———	6:22-25	———	———
169.	**15:1-20**	**7:1-23**	6:39	6:39	———	14; 40; 34	§83
170.	**15:21-28**	**7:24-30**	———	———	———	———	———
171.	**15:29-31**	**7:31-37**	———	———	———	———	———
172.	**15:32-39**	**8:1-10**	———	———	———	———	———
173.	**16:1-4**	**8:11-13**	———	———	6:30	———	§141
174.	**16:5-12**	**8:14-21**	———	12:1	———	———	§226

175.	———	**8:22-26**	———	———	———	———	———
176.	**16:13-20**	**8:27-30**	———	**9:18-21**	6:67-69	13	———
177.	**16:21-23**	**8:31-33**	———	**9:22**	———	———	———
178.	**16:24-28**	**8:34-9:1**	———	**9:23-27**	12:25	55	———
179.	**17:1-9**	**9:2-10**	———	**9:28-36**	12:28-30	———	———
180.	**17:10-13**	**9:11-13**	———	———	———	———	———
181.	**17:14-21**	**9:14-29**	———	**9:37-43a**	———	48; 106	———
182.	**17:22-23**	**9:30-32**	———	**9:43b-45**	7:1	———	———
183.	**17:24-27**	———	———	———	———	———	———
184.	**18:1-5**	**9:33-37**	———	**9:46-48**	3:3, 5; 13:20	22	———
185.	10:42	**9:38-41**	———	**9:49-50**	———	———	§120
186.	**18:6-9**	**9:42-48**	17:2, 1	17:2, 1	———	———	§276
187.	5:13	**9:49-50**	14:34-35	14:34-35	———	———	§32, §263
188.	**18:10-14**	———	15:4-5a, 7	15:3-7	———	107	§265, §277
189.	**18:15-18**	———	17:3	17:3	20:23	———	§276, §278
190.	**18:19-20**	———	———	———	———	30; 77	———
191.	**18:21-22**	———	17:4	17:4	———	———	§278
192.	**18:23-35**	———	———	———	———	———	———
193.	**19:1-2**	**10:1**	———	**9:51**	———	———	———

Luke's Journey toward Jerusalem

194.	———	———	———	**9:52-56**	———	———	———
195.	8:19-22	———	**9:57-60**	**9:57-62**	———	86	§93
196.	———	———	———	**10:1**	———	———	———
197.	9:37-38	———	**10:2**	**10:2**	4:35	73	§102
198.	10:16	———	**10:3**	**10:3**	———	39	§110
199.	10:9-10a	———	**10:4**	**10:4**	———	———	§106
200.	10:12-13, 10b-11, 7	6:10	**10:5-9**	**10:5-9**	———	14	§105, §107
201.	10:14-15	6:11	**10:10-12**	**10:10-12**	———	———	§108, §109, §162
202.	11:21-23a	———	**10:13-15**	**10:13-15**	———	———	§127
203.	10:40	———	**10:16**	**10:16**	13:20	———	§119
204.	———	———	———	**10:17-20**	———	———	———
205.	11:25-27	———	**10:21-22**	**10:21-22**	3:35; 7:29; 10:15a; 13:3a; 17:2a	61	§128
206.	13:16-17	———	**10:23-24**	**10:23-24**	———	17	§145
207.	22:34-40	12:28-34	———	**10:25-28**	———	———	§318
208.	———	———	———	**10:29-37**	———	———	———
209.	———	———	———	**10:38-42**	11:1; 12:1-3	———	§133, §345
210.	6:7-13	———	**11:2-4**	**11:1-4**	———	———	§43
211.	———	———	———	**11:5-8**	———	———	———
212.	7:7-11	———	**11:9-13**	**11:9-13**	16:24; 14:13-14; 15:7	92; 94; 2	§53
213.	9:32-34; 12:25-29	3:22-26	**11:14-15**, 11:16 **11:17-20**	**11:14-20**	7:20; 10:20; 8:48, 52a	———	§101, §136, §138, §218
214.	12:29	3:27	———	**11:21-22**	———	35	§138
215.	12:30	———	**11:23**	**11:23**	———	———	§139
216.	12:43-45	———	**11:24-26**	**11:24-26**	———	———	§142
217.	———	———	———	**11:27-28**	———	79	———
218.	12:38-40	———	**11:16, 29-30**	11:16, **29-30**	———	———	§141, §213
219.	12:41-42	———	**11:31-32**	**11:31-32**	———	———	§141
220.	5:15	———	**11:33**	**11:33**	———	33	§33

221.	6:22-23	———	**11:34-35**	**11:34-36**	———	———	§47
222.	23:23, 25-26, 6-7, 27	———	**11:42, 39b, 41, 43-44**	**11:37-44**	———	89	§321
223.	23:4, 13, 29-32	———	**11:46b, 52, 47-48**	**11:45-46**, 52, **47-48**	———	———	§225, §321
224.	23:34-36	———	**11:49-51**	**11:49-51**	———	———	§321
225.	23:13	———	11:52	**11:52-54**	———	39, 102	§223, §321
226.	16:5-6	8:14-15	———	**12:1**	———	———	§174
227.	10:26-27	———	**12:2-3**	**12:2-3**	———	5; 33	§113
228.	10:28	———	**12:4-5**	**12:4-5**	———	———	§114
229.	10:29-31	———	**12:6-7**	**12:6-7**	———	———	§115
230.	10:32-33	———	**12:8-9**	**12:8-9**	———	———	§116
231.	12:32	———	**12:10**	**12:10**	———	44	§140
232.	10:19-20	13:11	**12:11-12**	**12:11-12**	———	———	§111, §326
233.	6:19-21	———	**12:33-34**	12:33-34	———	76	§46, §237
234.	———	———	———	**12:13-15**	———	72	———
235.	———	———	———	**12:16-21**	———	63	———
236.	6:25-34	———	**12:22-31**	**12:22-32**	———	36	§49
237.	6:19-21	———	12:33-34	**12:33-34**	———	76	§46, §233
238.	———	———	———	**12:35-38**	———	———	§173
239.	24:43-44	———	**12:39-40**	**12:39-41**	———	21	§338
240.	24:45-51	———	**12:42-46**	**12:42-48**	———	———	§339
241.	10:34-36	———	**12:51, 53**	**12:49-53**	———	10; 16	§117
242.	———	———	———	**12:54-56**	———	91	———
243.	5:25-26	———	**12:58-59**	**12:57-59**	———	———	§35
244.	———	———	———	**13:1-9**	———	———	———
245.	———	———	———	**13:10-17**	———	———	———
246.	13:31-32	4:30-32	**13:18-19**	**13:18-19**	———	20	§150
247.	13:33	———	**13:20-21**	**13:20-21**	———	96	§151
248.	7:13-14; 25:10-12; 7:22-23	———	**13:24-27**	**13:22-27**	———	———	§55, §57, §340
249.	8:11a	———	**13:29**	13:29	———	———	§89, §251
250.	8:11b-12	———	**13:28**	**13:28**	———	———	§89
251.	8:11a	———	13:29	**13:29**	———	———	§89, §249
252.	20:16	———	**13:30**	**13:30**	———	4	§297
253.	———	———	———	**13:31-33**	———	———	———
254.	23:37-39	———	**13:34-35**	**13:34-35**	———	———	§322
255.	———	———	———	**14:1-6**	———	———	———
256.	———	———	———	**14:7-10**	———	———	———
257.	23:12	———	**14:11**	**14:11**	———	———	§321
258.	———	———	———	**14:12-14**	———	———	———
259.	22:1-14	———	**14:16-18, 21, 23**	**14:15-24**	———	64	§315
260.	10:37-38	———	**14:26-27**	**14:25-27**	———	55; 101	§118
261.	———	———	———	**14:28-33**	———	———	———
262.	10:39	———	**17:33**	17:33	12:25	———	§118, §287
263.	5:13	9:50	**14:34-35**	**14:34-35**	———	———	§32, §187
264.	6:24	———	**16:13**	16:13	———	47	§48, §270
265.	18:12-14	———	15:4-5, 7	**15:1-7**	———	107	§188, §277
266.	———	———	———	**15:8-10**	———	———	———
267.	———	———	———	**15:11-32**	———	———	———
268.	———	———	———	**16:1-9**	———	———	———
269.	———	———	———	**16:10-12**	———	———	———

270. 6:24	———	16:13	**16:13**	———	47	§48, §264
271. ———	———	———	**16:14-15**	———	———	———
272. 11:12-13	———	**16:16**	**16:16**	———	———	§125
273. 5:18	———	**16:17**	**16:17**	———	———	§34
274. 5:32	———	**16:18**	**16:18**	———	———	§37
275. ———	———	———	**16:19-31**	———	———	———
276. 18:7, 6	9:42	**17:1-2**	**17:1-3a**		———	§186
277. 18:12-13	———	**15:4-5a, 7**	15:4-5a, 7	———	107	§188, §266
278. 18:15a; 21b-22	———	**17:3b-4**	**17:3b-4**	———	———	§186, §189, §191
279. 17:20	———	**17:6**	**17:5-6**	———	48; 106	§181
280. ———	———	———	**17:7-10**	———	———	———
281. ———	———	———	**17:11-19**	———	———	———
282. 24:23	13:21	———	**17:20-21**	———	3	§329
283. 24:26-27	———	**17:23-24**	**17:22-25**	———	———	§330
284. 24:28	———	**17:37**	17:37	———	———	§288, §331
285. 24:37-39	———	**17:26-27**, 30	**17:26-30**	———	———	§335
286. 24:17-18	13:15-16	———	**17:31-32**	———	———	§328
287. 10:39	———	17:33	**17:33**	12:25	———	§118, §262
288. 24:40-41, 28	———	**17:34-35**, 37	**17:34-37**	———	———	§284, §331, §336
289. ———	———	———	**18:1-8**	———	———	———
290. ———	———	———	**18:9-14**	———	———	———

Jesus' Ministry in Judea

291. **19:3-9**	**10:2-12**	———	———	———	———	———
292. **19:10-12**	———	———	———	———	———	———
293. **19:13-15**	**10:13-16**	———	**18:15-17**	———	22	———
294. **19:16-22**	**10:17-22**	———	**18:18-23**	———	———	———
295. **19:23-30**	**10:23-31**	———	**18:24-30**	———	———	§352
296. **20:1-15**	———	———	———	———	———	———
297. **20:16**	———	13:30	13:30	———	4	§252
298. **20:17-19**	**10:32-34**	———	**18:31-34**	———	———	———
299. **20:20-23**	**10:35-40**	———	———	———	———	———
300. **20:24-28**	**10:41-45**	———	22:24-27	13:4-5, 12-17	———	§351
301. **20:29-34**	**10:46-52**	———	**18:35-43**	———	———	§100
302. ———	———	———	**19:1-10**	———	———	———
303. 25:14-30	———	**19:12-13, 15-24, 26**	**19:11-27**	———	———	§341
304. **21:1-9**	**11:1-10**	———	**19:28-40**	12:12-15	———	———
305. ———	———	———	**19:41-44**	———	———	———

Jesus in Jerusalem

306. ———	**11:11**	———	———	———	———	———
307. **21:10-17**	11:15-19	———	19:45-48	2:13-17	———	§309
308. **21:18-19**	**11:12-14**	———	———	———	———	———
309. 21:10-17	**11:15:19**	———	**19:45-48**	2:13-17	———	§307
310. **21:20-22**	**11:20-24**	———	———	———	48; 106	———
311. 6:14-15	**11:25-26**	———	———	———	———	§44
312. **21:23-27**	**11:27-33**	———	**20:1-8**	———	———	———
313. **21:28-32**	———	———	———	———	———	———
314. **21:33-46**	**12:1-12**	———	**20:9-19**	———	65; 66	———
315. **22:1-14**	———	14:16-18, 21, 23	14:15-24	———	64	§259

316.	**22:15-22**	**12:13-17**	———	**20:20-26**	———	100	———
317.	**22:23-33**	**12:18-27**	———	**20:27-40**	———	———	———
318.	**22:34-40**	**12:28-34**	———	10:25-28	———	———	§207
319.	**22:41-46**	**12:35-37a**	———	**20:41-44**	———	———	———
320.	———	**12:37b-40**	———	20:45-47	———	———	———
321.	**23:1-36**	———	11:46b, 43; 14:11; 11:52, 43, 39b, 41, 44, 47-51	11:46b, 43; 14:11; 11:52, 43, 39b, 41, 44, 47-51	———	89; 39	§222-225, §257
322.	**23:37-39**	———	13:34-35	13:34-35	———	———	§254
323.	———	**12:41-44**	———	**21:1-4**	———	———	———
324.	**24:1-2**	**13:1-2**	———	**21:5-6**	———	———	———
325.	**24:3-8**	**13:3-8**	———	**21:7-11**	———	———	———
326.	10:17-23	**13:9-13**	12:11-12	**21:12-19**; 12:11-12	———	———	§111, §232
327.	**24:9-14**	———	———	———	———	———	§111
328.	**24:15-22**	**13:14-20**	———	**21:20-22**; 17:31-32; **21:23-24**	———	———	§286
329.	**24:23-25**	**13:21-23**	———	17:21	———	3	§282
330.	**24:26-27**	———	17:23-24	17:22-25	———	———	§283
331.	**24:28**	———	17:37	17:37	———	———	§284, §288
332.	**24:29-31**	**13:24-27**	———	**21:25-28**	———	———	———
333.	**24:32-36**	**13:28-32**	———	**21:29-33**	———	11	———
334.	———	———	———	**21:34-36**	———	———	———
335.	**24:37-39**	———	17:26-27, 30	17:26-30	———	———	§285
336.	**24:40-41**	———	17:34-35	17:34-36	———	———	§288
337.	**24:42**	**13:33-37**	———	———	———	———	———
338.	**24:43-44**	———	12:39-40	12:39-40	———	21	§239
339.	**24:45-51**	———	12:42-46	12:42-46	———	———	§240
340.	**25:1-13**	———	13:25	13:25	———	———	§248
341.	**25:14-30**	———	19:12-13, 15-24, 26	19:11-27	———	———	§303
342.	**25:31-46**	———	———	———	———	———	———
343.	———	———	———	**21:37-38**	8:1-2	———	———

The Passion Narratives

344.	**26:1-5**	**14:1-2**	———	**22:1-2**	11:47-53	———	———
345.	**26:6-13**	**14:3-9**	———	———	12:1-8	———	§133, §209
346.	**26:14-16**	**14:10-11**	———	**22:3-6**	13:2, 27; 6:70-71	———	———
347.	**26:17-20**	**14:12-17**	———	**22:7-14**	———	———	———
348.	**26:21-25**	**14:18-21**	———	22:21-23	13:21-30	———	§350
349.	**26:26-29**	**14:22-25**	———	**22:15-20**	6:51-56	———	———
350.	26:21-25	14:18-21	———	**22:21-23**	13:21-30	———	§348
351.	20:24-28	10:41-45	———	**22:24-27**	13:4-5, 12-17	———	§300
352.	19:28	———	**22:28, 30**	**22:28-30**	———	———	§295
353.	**26:30-35**	**14:26-31**	———	**22:31-34**	13:36-38	———	———
354.	———	———	———	**22:35-38**	———	———	———
355.	**26:36-46**	**14:32-42**	———	**22:39-46**	18:1; 12:27	———	———
356.	**26:47-56**	**14:43-52**	———	**22:47-53**	18:2-11	———	———
357.	**26:57-58**	**14:53-54**	———	**22:54-55**	18:12-16	———	———
358.	26:69-75	14:66-72	———	**22:56-62**	18:17, 25-27	———	§364
359.	26:67-68	14:65	———	**22:63-65**	———	———	§363
360.	27:1	15:1a	———	**22:66**	———	———	§365

361.	**26:59-61**	**14:55-59**	———	———	———	71	———
362.	**26:62-66**	**14:60-64**	———	**22:67-71**	———	———	———
363.	**26:67-68**	**14:65**	———	22:63-65	———	———	§359
364.	**26:69-75**	**14:66-72**	———	22:56-62	18:17, 25-27	———	§358
365.	**27:1-2**	**15:1**	———	22:66; **23:1**	18:28	———	§360
366.	**27:3-10**	———	———	———	———	———	———
367.	**27:11-14**	15:2-5	———	**23:2-5**	18:29-38	———	———
368.	———	———	———	**23:6-12**	———	———	———
369.	———	———	———	**23:13-16**	———	———	———
370.	**27:15-23**	**15:6-14**	———	**23:17-23**	18:39-40	———	———
371.	**27:24-26**	**15:15**	———	**23:24-25**	———	———	———
372.	**27:27-31a**	**15:16-20a**	———	———	19:2-3	———	———
373.	**27:31b-32**	**15:20b-21**	———	**23:26**	19:16-17a	———	———
374.	———	———	———	**23:27-31**	———	79	———
375.	**27:33-38**	**15:22-28**	———	**23:32-34**	19:17b-24	———	———
376.	**27:39-43**	**15:29-32a**	———	**23:35-38**	———	———	———
377.	**27:44**	**15:32b**	———	**23:39-43**	———	———	———
378.	**27:45-54**	**15:33-39**	———	**23:44-48**	19:28-30	———	———
379.	**27:55-56**	**15:40-41**	———	**23:49**	19:25-27	———	———
380.	**27:57-61**	**15:42-47**	———	**23:50-56**	19:38-42	———	———
381.	**27:62-66**	———	———	———	———	———	———

Resurrection Narratives

382.	**28:1-8**	**16:1-8**	———	**24:1-12**	20:1-13	———	———
383.	**28:9-10**	———	———	———	20:14-18	———	———
384.	**28:11-15**	———	———	———	———	———	———
385.	———	———	———	**24:13-35**	———	———	———
386.	———	———	———	**24:36-43**	20:19-23	———	———
387.	**28:16-20**	———	———	———	———	———	———
388.	———	———	———	**24:44-53**	———	———	———

Index of Pericope Headings

The Galilean Ministry Continues Again *(Continued)*

Prologues and Infancy Narratives

I. Prologues

Matt 1:1	Mark 1:1	Luke 1:1-4
[1][The] book [of the] genesis of-Jesus [the] Anointed-one, son of-David son of-Abraham.	[1][The] beginning of-the proclamation of-Jesus Anointed-one, son of-god[a].	[1]In-as-much-as many attempted to-compile [a] narrative around [=concerning] the events having- been-realized in [=among] us, [2]just- as the having-happeneds [=ones who were] from [the] beginning eyewitnesses and attendants of-the word delivered to-us, [3]it-supposed [=it seemed] to-me-too [worthwhile], having-attended [=that having paid careful attention], to-write for-you all [=everything] accurately, from-the- start, successively, most-excellent Theophilus, [4]in-order-that you- might-understand the certainty [of the] words around [=concerning] which you-were-educated.

[a] *son of-god* ℵ[1] A B D L W *f*[1] *f*[13] 33 892 1006 1342 1506 2427 𝔐; *omit* ℵ* Θ 28 2211 *pc* cop[sa]; *son of-the lord* 1241.

SYNOPTIC STUDY GUIDE I

Source Criticism/Synoptic Problem

Matthew, Mark, and Luke are called the Synoptic Gospels because their deep similarities allow them to be "seen together," as they are in this book in parallel columns. Readers of the gospels have long noticed the shared stories and the sometimes very close verbal parallels within those stories. In a precritical era of New Testament scholarship, people explained these close verbal parallels in a number of ways. One explanation was that the gospels were written by eyewitnesses (or their close associates) who simply recorded the facts of Jesus' life. Where the details were different, this could be attributed to differences in the writers' audiences or perspectives. Another precritical explanation was that the Holy Spirit "inspired" all three writers. Other readers have sought more rational explanations than these. They might find troubling the assumed portrait of the Holy Spirit in the second explanation (Was the Holy Spirit not able to ensure that the gospels agree completely, instead of just sometimes?) and decide it was best to leave the Holy Spirit out of the process of Gospel composition.

Both of these are positions of faith grounded in an inerrantist view of the text, and thus are incompatible with how historians approach the past. They are also inconsistent with the data provided by the stories themselves. The stories do not have the qualities of eyewitness testimony. They have the qualities of stories that have been orally transmitted for some time, and then written down, and only at that point were they used by the gospel writers. The process of oral transmission tends to round off the rough edges from stories (much like a rolling stone eventually becomes rounded): rare words are replaced with common words, tongue twisters are replaced with easy alliteration, and so on. And the verbatim agreements suggest shared written sources for this reason: while word order in English is quite fixed, Greek word order is extremely variable. A sentence of five words can often be written in fifteen or more different ways without altering the meaning. Therefore, when two sources share lengthy verbatim agreements in the same word order, then the more rational explanation is not reliance on *oral* transmission or eyewitnesses alone but shared access to *written* sources.

And evidence of this abounds in the synoptic gospels. When two gospels have the same words in the same forms, they will often have the same order. When an author starts to put things in his own words, or in different grammatical forms, often other things change too. In other words, when everything is the same, it is because someone was copying from someone else.

SYNOPTIC STUDY GUIDE I

What is certain is that there is a very close *literary* relationship between the gospels of Matthew, Mark, and Luke: either their authors used each other's writings or they had written sources in common. On this all New Testament scholars agree. What they disagree on is the solution to this problem: Was Matthew the first Gospel written, or was it Mark or Luke? Was Mark first or third? Was there a sayings-source (known as Q) to which the authors of Matthew and Luke each had access? *This* is the Synoptic Problem, and in the Synoptic Study Guides that follow, I shall take you through the most probable solutions and the weaknesses of each, as well as other topics pertaining to the study of the Synoptic Problem.

2. Luke's Promise of the Birth of John the Baptist

Luke 1:5-25

5 It-happened in the days of-Herod, king[a] of-Judea, some priest, Zachariah [by] name, out [=from
the] priestly-division of-Abija, and woman to-him out [=he had a wife from] the daughters of-Aaron,
and her name [was] Elizabeth. 6 So [=Now] both were righteous ere[b] [=before] god, faultless traveling
in all the commandments and requirements of-the lord. 7 And there-was not [any] descendant for-
them on-account-that Elizabeth was sterile, and both were having-been-advanced [=advanced] in
their days. 8 So it-happened in the him to-be-priest [=while he was serving as priest], in the turn [of]
his priestly-division out-front-of [=before] god, 9 according-to the custom of-the priestly-office he-
had-as-his-lot having-entered [=to enter] into the sanctuary of-the lord to-burn-incense, 10 and all
the multitude of-the whole-people was praying outside [at] the hour of-the incense. 11 So [=And an]
announcer [=angel of the] lord was-seen [by] him having-stood out [=to the] right of-the sacrificial-
altar of-the incense. 12 And Zachariah, having-seen, was-disturbed and fear assailed upon him.
13 So [=But] the announcer said to him, "Fear no [=not], Zachariah, through-that [=because] your
petition has-been-paid-attention-to and your woman [=wife] Elizabeth will-beget [a] son to-you
and you-will-call his name John. 14 And there-will-be joy for-you and jubilation and many will-
rejoice upon [=at] his genesis [=birth]. 15 For he-will-be great in-the-sight of-the lord, and wine and
strong-drink will-he-drink not no [=ever], and he-will-be-filled [by the] holy spirit still [=before he
is] out [=of the] abdomen [of] his mother, 16 and many of-the sons of-Israel will-turn-back [=will
return] upon [=to the] lord their god. 17 And he [himself] will-precede in-the-sight of-him in [the]
spirit and power of-Elijah, to-turn-back [the] hearts of-fathers upon [=toward their] descendants,
and disobedients [=those who are disobedient] in [the] sensibility [of the] righteous, to-make-ready
[for the] lord [a] whole-people having-been-prepared." 18 And Zachariah said to the announcer,
"According-to what [=How] will-I-know this? For I [myself] am elderly and my woman [=wife]
having-been-advanced [=is advanced] in her days." 19 And having-answered, the announcer said
to-him, "I am Gabriel, the [one] being-present in-the-sight of-god, and I-was-sent-off to-talk to
you and to-proclaim these [things] to-you. 20 And look! you-will-be being-silent and being-able no
[=not] to-talk till which day these [things] might-happen, in-place of-which [=because] you-believed
not my words, whichever will-be-fulfilled into [=in] their proper-time." 21 And the whole-people
was expecting Zachariah and were-astonished [at] him in to-delay [=for delaying] in the sanctuary.
22 So having-gone-out, he-was-able not to-talk to-them, and they-understood that he-has-seen
[a] vision in the sanctuary, and he [himself] was making-signs to-them and was-remaining mute.
23 And it-happened like [=when] the days [of] his ministry were-filled [=were finished], he [himself]
went-away into his house. 24 So with [=after] these days, Elizabeth, his woman [=wife], gripped
[=conceived] and kept-in-seclusion herself [for] five months, saying 25 that "Thus[c] [the] lord has-done
to-me in days in-which he-took-notice-of [me] to-take-away my disgrace in [=among] people."

[a] *king* ℵ B L W Ξ Ψ *pc*; *the king* A C D Θ f^1 f^{13} 33 892 1006 1342 1506 𝔐 cop^{sa} cop^{bo}.
[b] *ere* ℵ B C* Ψ 579 892 *pc*; *in-the-sight* A C^3 D L W Θ Ξ f^1 f^{13} 33 1006 1342 1506 𝔐.
[c] *lord* ℵ C D L W 33 *pc*; *the lord* A B Θ Ψ f^1 f^{13} 892 1006 1342 1506 𝔐.
📖 Lk 1:10 – Lev 16:17; 📖 Lk 1:17 – Mal 4:5, 6

3. Luke's Annunciation

Luke 1:26-38

26So in the sixth month the announcer [=angel] Gabriel was-sent-off from[a] god into [a] city of-the
Galilee, [the] name [of] which [was] Nazareth, 27to [an] unmarried-girl having-been-promised-in-
marriage [to a] man, [the] name [of] which [was] Joseph, out [of the] house of-David, and the name
of-the unmarried-girl [was] Mary. 28And having-entered to her, he-said[b], "Rejoice, having-received-a-
benefaction [=favored one], the lord [is] with you[c]." 29So [=But] she-was-disturbed-deeply upon [=by]
the word and was-pondering what-sort-of greeting this might-be. 30And the announcer said to-her,
"Fear no [=not] Mary, for you-found [a] benefaction along [=from] god. 31And look! you-will-grip in
stomach [=you will conceive] and you-will-give-birth-to [a] son and you-will-call his name Jesus. 32This
[one] will-be great and will-be-called son [of the] most-high, and [the] lord god will-give to-him the
throne of-David his father, 33and he-will-be-king upon [=over] the house of-Jacob into the eons and
there-will-be [an] end not [of] his kingdom." 34So Mary said to the announcer, "How will-be this, as-
a-result-of [=because] I-know not [a] man?" 35And having-answered, the announcer said to-her, "[The]
holy spirit will-come-upon upon you and [the] power [of the] most-high will-overshadow you; and
for-this-reason the [one] having-been-begotten [will be] holy, he-will-be-called son of-god. 36And look!
Elizabeth your kinswoman she [herself] and [=also] has-gripped [=has conceived a] son in her agedness,
and this is [the] sixth month for-her the [=who was] being-called sterile; 37that [=because] not all speech
[=nothing] will-be-impossible along [=for] god." 38So Mary said, "Look! the female-slave [of the] lord;
might-it-happen for-me according-to your speech." And the announcer went-away from her.

[a] *from* ℵ B L W Ψ 0130 f^1 f^{13} 565 579 700 892 *pc*; *under* A C D Θ 33 1006 1342 𝔐.
[b] *he-said* B L W Θ Ξ Ψ f^1 565 *pc* cop; *the announcer said* ℵ A C D f^{13} 33 892 1006 1342 1506 𝔐 it vg sy.
[c] *omit* ℵ B L W Ψ f^1 565 579 700 *pc* cop; *blessed you in women* A C D Θ f^{13} 33 892 1006 1342 1506 𝔐 it vg sy.
🕮 Lk 1:32 – Ps 132:11; 🕮 Lk 1:33 – Mic 4:7; Dan 4:3

4. Luke's Mary and Elizabeth

Luke 1:39-56

39So Mary, having-gotten-up in these days, traveled into the mountainous [area] with haste, into [a] city
of-Judah, 40and she-entered into the house of-Zachariah and greeted Elizabeth. 41And it-happened,
like [=when] Elizabeth heard the greeting of-Mary, the baby leapt in her abdomen [=womb], and
Elizabeth was-filled [by the] holy spirit, 42and she-exclaimed [with a] great scream[a] and said, "Having-
been-blessed [are] you in [=among] women and having-been-blessed [is] the fruit [of] your abdomen
[=womb]. 43And from-where [=why is] this [happening] to-me in-order-that the mother [of] my lord
might-come to me? 44For look! like [=when] the voice [of] your greeting happened [=went] into my
ears, the baby in my abdomen leapt in jubilation." 45And fortunate [is] the [one] having-believed that
there-will-be fulfilment of-the having-been-talkeds [=of the things that were told] to-her along [=by
the] lord. 46And Mary said, "My soul magnifies the lord, 47and my spirit was-glad upon [=in] god my
savior, 48that [=because] he-looked-upon the humiliation [of] his female-slave. For look! from the now
[=from now on] all the generations will-congratulate me, 49that [=because] the possible [=God] did great
[things] to-me. And holy [is] his name. 50And his mercy [is] into generations and generations to-the
fearings [=to those who fear] him. 51He-did [=He showed] strength in his arm, he-scattered arrogants
[those who are proud of the] mind [=thoughts of] their heart. 52He-brought-down princes from thrones
and exalted humbles [=the humble], 53hungerings [=those who hunger] he-satisfied [with] goods [=good
things] and being-wealthies [=those who were wealthy] he-sent-forth empty. 54He-aided Israel his child
[=servant] to-remember mercies, 55just-as he-talked to our fathers, to-Abraham and his seed into the
eon." 56So Mary stayed together-with her like[b] [=about] three months, and she-returned into her house.

[a] *exclaimed great scream* B L W Ξ 565 579; *exclaimed great voice* A D Ψ f^1 1006 1342* 𝔐; *wailed great voice* ℵ C F Θ f^{13} 33 892 1342[c] 1424 1506 *pc*.
[b] *like* ℵ B L W Ξ Ψ f^1 565 *pc*; *as* A C Θ f^{13} 33 892 1006 1342 1506 𝔐; *omit* D 69 *pc* it cop.
🕮 Lk 1:55 – Gen 17:19; 22:18

5. Luke's Birth of John the Baptist

Luke 1:57-80

57 So for-Elizabeth the time [for] her to-give-birth-to [her child] was-filled, and she-begat [a] son.
58 And the nearby-dwellers and her kin heard that [the] lord magnified his mercy with her and
they-were-rejoicing-with her. 59 And it-happened in [=on] the eighth day, they-went to-circumcise
the young-child and they-were-calling it upon [=after] the name [of] his father, Zachariah. 60 And
having-answered, his mother said, "Indeed-not, but he-will-be-called John." 61 And they-said to
her that "There-is no-one out [=from] your kindred who is-called [by] this name." 62 So they-were-
gesturing [to] his father [to find out] what ever he-might-wish it to-be-called. 63 And having-asked
[for a] writing-tablet, he-wrote saying, "His name is John." And all were-astonished. 64 So [=And
suddenly] his mouth was-opened and his tongue at-once, and he-talked, blessing god. 65 And fear
happened [=came] upon all the dwelling-nearbys [=those who dwelled nearby] them, and in the
whole mountainous [area] of-Judea all these speeches [=things] were-talked-about, 66 and all the
having-heards [=those who heard] put [them] in their heart saying, "What consequently will-be this
young-child?" For and [=even the] hand [of the] lord was with him. 67 And Zachariah his father was-
filled [with the] holy spirit and he-prophesied saying, 68 "Blessed [is the] lord, the god of-Israel, that
[=because] he-cared-for and did redemption [=redeemed] his whole-people, 69 and he-raised [a] horn
of-salvation to-us in [the] house of-David his child [=servant], 70 just-as he-talked [=he said] through
[the] mouth [of] his holy prophets from [=for] eons, 71 salvation out [=from] our enemies and out
[=from the] hand of-all the hatings [=those who hate] us 72 to-do [=to show] mercy with our fathers
and to-remember his holy covenant, 73 [a] sworn-oath which he-vowed to Abraham our father,
to-give us [that] 74 having-rescued [us] out [=from the] hand of-enemies[a] to-venerate him fearlessly
75 in holiness and righteousness in-the-sight of-him all [of] our days. 76 And so you, young-child,
will-be-called prophet [of the] most-high; for you-will-forerun in-the-sight[b] [of the] lord to-make-
ready his ways, 77 to-give knowledge of-salvation [to] his whole-people in [the] remission [of]
their sins 78 pity through [the] mercy [of] our god, in which east [=the dawn] out of-heights will-
care-for[c] us, 79 to-give-light to-the sittings [=those who sit] in darkness and [the] shade of-death,
to-guide our feet into [the] way of-peace." 80 So the young-child grew and was-being-made-strong
in-spirit, and was in the deserted [places] until [the] day [of] his public-appearance to Israel.

[a] *of-enemies* ℵ B L W f^1 f^{13} 565 892 *pc*; *our enemies* A C D Θ Ψ 33 1006 1342 1506 𝔐.
[b] *in-the-sight* 𝔓4 ℵ B W; *before face* A C D L Θ Ψ f^1 f^{13} 33 1006 1342 1506 𝔐 sy.
[c] *will-care-for* ℵ* B L W Θ sy; *cared-for* ℵ2 A D Ξ Ψ f^1 f^{13} 33 892 1006 1342 1506 𝔐 it vg.
📖 Lk 1:73 – Gen 12:3; 22:16; 📖 Lk 1:78 – Num 24:17; Mal 4:2; 📖 Lk 1:79 – Isa 9:2

6. Matthew's Genealogy of Jesus (→ §22)

Matt 1:2-17

2 Abraham begat Isaac, so Isaac begat Jacob, so Jacob
begat Judah and his brothers, 3 so Judah begat Perez
and Zerah out of-Tamar, so Perez begat Hezron, so
Hezron begat Aram, 4 so Aram begat Aminadab, so
Aminadab begat Nahshon, so Nahshon begat Salmon,
5 so Salmon begat Boaz out of-Rahab, so Boaz begat

Luke 3:23-38 (names only)

38 of-god, of-Adam, of-Seth, of-Enos,
37 of-Cainan, of-Malaleel, of-Jared,
of-Enoch, of-Methuselah, 36 of-Lamech,
of-Noah, of-Shem, of-Arphaxad, of-Cainan,
35 of-Shelah, of-Ever, of-Peleg, of-Reu,
of-Serug, 34 of-Nahor, of-Terah,
of-Abraham, of-Isaac, of-Jacob,
33 of-Judah,
of-Perez, of-Hezron,
of-Arni, of-Admin,
of-Aminadab, 32 of-Nahshon,
of-Sala[c],

Obed out of-Ruth, so Obed begat Jesse, 6so Jesse begat
King David. So David begat Solomon out of-the [wife]
of-Uriah, 7so Solomon begat Rehoboam, so Rehoboam
begat Abijah, so Abijah begat Asaph[a], 8so Asaph[a] begat
Jehosephat, so Jehosephat begat Joram, so Joram begat
Uzziah, 9so Uzziah begat Jotham, so Jotham begat
Ahaz, so Ahaz begat Hezekiah, 10so Hezekiah begat
Manasseh, so Manasseh begat Amos[b], so Amos[b] begat
Josiah, 11so Josiah begat Jechoniah and his brothers
upon [=at] the deportation to-Babylon. 12So with [=after]
the deportation to-Babylon, Jechoniah begat Salathiel,
so Salathiel begat Zerubbabel, 13so Zerubbabel begat
Abiud, so Abiud begat Eliakim, so Eliakim begat Azor,
14so Azor begat Zadok, so Zadok begat Achim, so
Achim begat Eliud, 15so Eliud begat Eleazar, so Eleazar
begat Matthan, so Matthan begat Jacob, 16so Jacob begat
Joseph the man [=husband] of-Mary, out of-whom Jesus,
the being-said [=who is called the] anointed-one, was-
begotten. 17Therefore all the generations from Abraham
until David [are] fourteen generations, and from
David until the deportation of-Babylon [are] fourteen
generations, and from the deportation of-Babylon
until the Anointed-one [are] fourteen generations.

of-Boaz,
of-Obed,
of-Jesse,
31of-David,
of-Natham[d], of-Mattatha, of-Menna,
of-Melea, 30of-Eliakim, of-Jonam, of-Joseph,
of-Judah, of-Simeon, 29of-Levi, of-Matthat,
of-Jorim, of-Eliezer, of-Joshua, 28of-Er,
of-Elmadam, of-Cosam, of-Addi, of-Melchi,
27of-Neri,
of-Salathiel, of-Zerubbabel,
of-Rhesa, of-Joanan, 26of-Joda, of-Josech,
of-Semein, of-Mattathias, of-Maath,
25of-Naggai, of-Esli, of-Nahum, of-Amos,
of-Mattathias, 24of-Joseph, of-Jannai, of-
Melchi, of-Levi, of-Matthat, 23[son] of-Heli
of-Joseph.

[a] *Asaph* $\mathfrak{p}^{1}$ ℵ B C f^{1} f^{13} 205 700 1506 *pc* it cop; *Asa* L W 33 892 1006 1342 𝔐 vg sy.
[b] *Amos* ℵ B C Δ Θ f^{1} 33 205 *pc* it vg^{mss} cop; *Amon* L W f^{13} 892 1006 1342 1506 𝔐 it^{mss} vg sy.
[c] *Sala* $\mathfrak{p}^{4}$ ℵ* B sy^{s} cop^{sa} cop^{bomss}; *Salmon* ℵ^{2} A D L Θ Ψ f^{1} f^{13} 33 892 1006 1506 𝔐 it vg sy^{p} cop^{bo}.
[d] *Natham* $\mathfrak{p}^{4}$ ℵ* B 1582 *pc* it; *Nathan* ℵ^{2} A L Θ Ψ f^{1} f^{13} 33 892 1006 1506 𝔐 sy cop^{bo}.

7. Matthew's Birth of Jesus

Matt 1:18-25

18So, thus was the genesis[a] [=birth] of-Jesus [the] Anointed-one. His mother Mary, having-been-
promised-in-marriage to-Joseph, prior-to or to-come-together them [=before they had lived
together], was-found having in stomach [=to be pregnant] out [=by the] holy spirit. 19So [=But]
Joseph, her man, being righteous and no [=not] wishing to-besmirch her, was-wanted [=wanted]
secretly to-release her. 20So his having-deliberated-on [=while he was contemplating] these [things],
look! [an] announcer [=angel of the] lord was-appeared [=was made apparent] to-him according-to
[a] dream saying, "Joseph, son of-David, might-you-be-feared no [=do not be made afraid] to-take-
along Mary [as] your woman [=wife]. For the [one] having-been-begotten in her is out [=from the]
holy spirit. 21So she-will-give-birth-to [a] son, and you-will-call his name Jesus. For he [himself]
will-save his whole-people from their sins." 22So this whole [thing] has-happened in-order-that the
having-been-said [=what had been said] under [=by the] lord through the prophet might-be-fulfilled,
saying, 23"LOOK! THE UNMARRIED-GIRL WILL-HAVE IN STOMACH [=will conceive] AND
SHE-WILL-GIVE-BIRTH-TO [a] SON AND THEY-WILL-CALL HIS NAME EMMANUEL,"
which is having-been-translated, "God [is] with us." 24So Joseph, having-risen[b] from sleep, did
like the announcer [of the] lord designated to-him, and took-along his woman 25and he-was-
knowing her not until which [time] she-gave-birth-to [a] son and he-called his name Jesus.

[a] *genesis* $\mathfrak{p}^{1}$ ℵ B C W Z Δ Θ f^{1} *pc*; *birth* L f^{13} 33 892 1006 1506 𝔐.
[b] *having-risen* ℵ B C* Z f^{1} 205 *pc*; *having-awoken* C^{3} D L W 087 f^{13} 33 892 1006 1506 𝔐.
📖 Mt 1:23 – Isa 7:14

8. Luke's Birth of Jesus

Luke 2:1-7

1So it-happened in those days [a] decree went-out along [=from] Caesar Augustus [for] all the
inhabited-earth to-be-registered. 2This first registration happened [with] Quirinius being-ruler
of-Syria. 3And all were-traveling to-register, each into the city of-himself[a]. 4So Joseph and [=also]
ascended from the Galilee out [=from the] city of-Nazareth into Judea into [the] city of-David
whoever [=which] is-called Bethlehem, through the to-be him [=because he was descended] out of-
the house and parentage of-David, 5to-be-registered together-with Mary the [one] having-been-
promised-in-marriage to-him, being pregnant. 6So it-happened in the to-be them [=while they were]
there, the days her to-give-birth-to were-filled [=the time came for her to give birth], 7and she-gave-
birth-to her first-born son, and she-wrapped-in-baby-clothes him and stretched-out him in [a]
feeding-trough[b], through-that [=since] there-was not [a] place for-them in the guest-room.

[a] *city of-himself* ℵ* B L W Ξ Ψ 565 579 *pc*; *own city* A C^3 Θ f^1 f^{13} 33 𝔐; *own region* C*; *homeland of-himself* D *pc* sy^s.
[b] *feeding-trough* ℵ* A B D L W Θ Ξ 700 *pc* cop; *the feeding-trough* Ψ f^1 f^{13} 33 892 1006 1342 1506 𝔐.

9. Matthew's Herod, the Magi, and the Infant Jesus

Matt 2:1-12

1So Jesus, having-been-begotten in Bethlehem of-Judea in [the] days of-Herod the king, look! Magi
from easts [=the east] arrived into Jerusalems 2saying, "Wheresoever is the [one] having-been-given-
birth-to [as] king of-the Judeans? For we-saw his star in the east and we-came to-worship him." 3So the
king Herod, having-heard [this] was-disturbed and all Jerusalem with him; 4and having-gathered all
the high-priests and scribes of-the whole-people, he-was-inquiring along [=from] them wheresoever
the anointed-one is-begotten [=was to be born]. 5So they-said to-him, "In Bethlehem of-Judea, for
thus it-has-been-written through the prophet, 6'AND YOU BETHLEHEM, LAND OF-JUDAH,
BY-NO-MEANS ARE-YOU LEAST IN [=among] THE RULERS OF-JUDAH. FOR OUT OF-YOU
WILL-GO-OUT RULING [=a ruler] WHOEVER [=who] WILL-SHEPHERD MY WHOLE-PEOPLE
ISRAEL.'" 7Then Herod secretly having-called the Magi, ascertained along [=from] them the time
of-the appearing star, 8and having-sent them into Bethlehem, said "Having-traveled, make-a-careful-
search accurately around [=concerning] the young-child; so [=and] as-soon-as you-might-find [him]
inform me, so-that I-too, having-come, might-worship him." 9So, having-heard the king, they-traveled
and look! the star which they-saw in the east was-leading-ahead [of] them, until having-come, it-
was-stood[a] [=it stood still] above which [=where] the young-child was. 10So, having-seen the star they-
rejoiced [a] very great joy. 11And having-come into the home they-saw the young-child with Mary his
mother and having-fallen [to their knees] they-worshiped him and having-opened their treasure-boxes
they-offered him gifts: gold and frankincense and myrrh. 12And having-been-warned according-to [a]
dream no [=not] to-head-back to Herod, they-retreated into their region through another way.

[a] *it-was-stood* ℵ B C D f^1 33 *pc*; *it-stood* L W 0233 f^{13} 𝔐.
📖 Mt 2:6 – Mic 5:2

10. Luke's Shepherds and the Infant Jesus

Luke 2:8-20

8And shepherds were in the it [=same] region living-outdoors and guarding prisons [=keeping watch
in] the night upon [=over] their flock. 9And [an] announcer [=angel of the] lord stood-by them and
[the] glory [=of the] lord shone-around them, and they-were-feared great fear [=they were made very
afraid]. 10And the announcer said to-them, "Fear no [=not]. For look! I-proclaim to-you [a] great joy
whichever [=which] will-be for-all the whole-people, 11that [=because] today [a] savior, who is [the]

anointed-one, [and] lord, was-given-birth-to for-you in [the] city of-David. [12]And this [is] the sign for-you: you-will-find [a] baby having-been-wrapped-in-baby-clothes and laying in [a] feeding-trough." [13]And suddenly [a] multitude [of the] army of-heaven happened [=appeared] together-with the announcer praising god and saying, [14]"Glory in [the] most-high to-god and peace [be] upon land [=the earth], [and] contentment in [=among] people." [15]And it-happened, like [=when] the announcers went-away from them into heaven, the shepherds were-talking[a] to one-another, "We-might-go-through indeed until [=even as far as] Bethlehem and we-might-see this speech [=thing] having-happened which the lord made-known to-us." [16]And having-hurried they-went and located even Mary and Joseph and the baby laying in the feeding-trough. [17]So having-seen, they-made-known[b] around [=concerning] the speech [=thing] having-been-talked to-them around [=concerning] this young-child. [18]And all the having-heards [=those who heard] were-astonished around [=concerning] the having-been-talkeds [=what had been said] to them under [=by] the shepherds. [19]So Mary was-protecting all these speeches [=things], mulling-over [them] in her heart. [20]And the shepherds returned glorifying and praising god upon [=for] all which they [themselves] heard and saw, just-as was-talked [=had been told] to them.

[a] *were-talking* ℵ B W 0233 565; *said* A D L Θ Ξ Ψ f^1 f^{13} 892 1006 1342 1506 𝔐.
[b] *made-known* ℵ B D L W Ξ 0233 205 209 565 579 *pc*; *reported-exactly* A Θ Ψ f^1 f^{13} 33 892 1006 1342 1506 𝔐.

11. Luke's Jesus Circumcised and Presented at the Temple

Luke 2:21-38

[21]And when [the] eight days were-filled [=had passed it was time] to-circumcise him, and his name was-called Jesus, having-been-called [so] under [=by] the announcer [=angel] before him to-be-gripped in the abdomen [=he was conceived]. [22]And when the days [of] their purification according-to the law of-Moses were-filled, they-led-up him into Jerusalems to-be-presented to-the lord, [23]just-as has-been-written in [the] law [of the] lord that "ALL [=every] MALE OPENING-UP [a] CERVIX WILL-BE-CALLED HOLY TO-THE LORD," [24]and to-give [a] sacrifice according-to the having-been-said [=what is written] in the law [of the] lord, "[A] PAIR OF-TURTLE-DOVES OR TWO YOUNG DOVES." [25]And look! [a] person was in Jerusalem [the] name of-which [was] Symeon and this person [was] righteous and god-fearing, waiting-for [the] consolation of-Israel, and [the] holy spirit was upon [=in] him. [26]And he-was having-been-warned to-him [=he himself had been warned] under [=by] the holy spirit no ever to-see [=that he would not see] death prior-to [=before] he-might-see the anointed-one [of the] lord. [27]And he-came in the spirit into the Temple. And the parents, in the to-lead-in [=when they were leading in] the young-child Jesus of-the to-do them [=so they could do] according-to the having-been-customary of-the law around him [=for him what was customary according to the Law], [28]and he [=Symeon himself] received it [=the child] into the [=his] forelimbs [=arms] and blessed god and said, [29]"Now release your slave, master, according-to your speech [=words], in peace; [30]that [=because] my eyes saw your saving-power [31]which you-made-ready according-to face [=in the presence] of-all the whole-people, [32][a] light into [=for the] revelation [to the] nations and [the] glory [of] your whole-people Israel." [33]And his father[a] and mother was [=were] being-astonished upon [=at] the being-talkeds [=what was being said] around [=concerning] him. [34]And Symeon blessed them and said to Mary his mother, "Look! this [child] lay into [=is destined for the] decline and rise of-many in Israel and into [=destined to be a] refuting [=controversial] sign, [35]and intense-sorrow will-go-through [=will pierce] your it [=own] soul—so-that [the] thoughts out [=from] many hearts might-be-revealed ever." [36]And there-was [a] prophetess, Anna, daughter of-Phanouel, out [=from the] tribe of-Asher—she [herself] having-advanced in many days [and] having-lived with [a] man seven years from [=after] her time-of-marriage [37]and she [herself had been a] widow until [=for] eighty four years who was-abandoning the temple not, venerating [with] fastings and petitions night and day. [38]And having-stood-by [at] the it [=same] hour she-was-confessing-freely to-god[b] and was-talking around [=about] him to-all the waiting-fors [=those waiting for the] redemption of-Jerusalem.

[a] *his father* ℵ B D L W f^1 700 *pc* sy^s cop^{sa}; *Joseph* A Θ Ψ f^{13} 33 892 1006 1342 1506 𝔐 it vg^{mss} sy^p.
[b] *to-god* ℵ B D L W Ξ 579 892 *pc* sy^{mss}; *lord god* A Θ f^1 f^{13} 33 1006 1342 1506 𝔐 it^{mss} vg sy cop.
📖 Lk 2:21 – Lev 12:3, 4; 📖 Lk 2:23 – Exod 13:2; 📖 Lk 2:24 – Lev 12:8; 📖 Lk 2:34 – Isa 8:14, 15

12. Matthew's Flight to and Return from Egypt

Matt 2:13-21

[13]So their having-retreated [=when the Magi were leaving], look! [an] announcer [=angel of the] lord appears according-to [a] dream to-Joseph saying, "Be-raised, take-along the young-child and his mother and flee into Egypt and be there until [when] ever I-might-say to-you, for Herod intends to-search [for] the child to-destroy it." [14]So having-been-raised, he-took-along the young-child and his mother [at] night and retreated into Egypt, [15]and he-was there until the expiration of-Herod, in-order-that the having-been-said [=what had been said] under [=by the] lord through the prophet might-be-fulfilled, saying, "OUT OF-EGYPT I-CALLED MY SON." [16]Then Herod, having-seen that he-was-mocked under [=by] the Magi, became-wrathful extremely and having-sent-off [soldiers] he-abolished all the children [=boys] from two-years-old and less in Bethlehem and in all the territories of-it, according-to the time which he-ascertained along [=from] the Magi. [17]Then the having-been-said [=what had been said] through Jeremiah the prophet was-fulfilled, saying, [18]"[A] VOICE IN RAMA WAS-HEARD, WAILING[a] AND MANY [=much] GRIEVING; RACHEL WEEPING [for] HER DESCENDANTS AND SHE-WISHED NOT TO-BE-EXHORTED [=to be comforted], THAT [=because] THEY-ARE NOT." [19]So Herod having-expired, look! [an] announcer [of the] lord appears according-to [a] dream to-Joseph in Egypt [20]saying, "Be-raised, take-along the young-child and his mother and travel into [the] land of-Israel, for the searchings [=those who search for] the soul [=life] of-the child have-died." [21]So having-been-raised, he-took-along the young-child and his mother and entered into [the] land of-Israel.

[a] *wailing* ℵ B 0250 f^1 it vg sy^p cop; *dirge and wailing* C D L W Δ 0233 f^{13} 33 892 1006 1506 𝔐 sy^c sy^s.
📖 Mt 2:15 – Hos 11:1; 📖 Mt 2:18 – Jer 31:15

13. Matthew's Childhood of Jesus at Nazareth

Matt 2:22-23

[22]So having-heard that Archelaus is-king of-Judea in-place [of] his father Herod, [Joseph] was-feared [=was made afraid] to-go-away there; so [=but] having-been-warned according-to [a] dream he-retreated into the parts [=regions] of-the Galilee, [23]and having-come, he-settled into [a] city being-called Nazaret[a], so-that the having-been-said [=what had been said] through the prophets might-be-fulfilled, that "He-will-be-called [a] Nazarite."

[a] *Nazaret* ℵ B D L 33 700 892 1241 1424; *Nazareth* C E K N W Γ 0233 f^1 f^{13} 565 it^{mss} vg cop; *Nazara* 𝔓^{70}.

14. Luke's Childhood of Jesus at Nazareth

Luke 2:39-40

[39]And like [=when] they-completed all [things] according-to the law [of the] lord, they-turned-back into the Galilee, into city of-themselves, Nazareth. [40]So the young-child was-growing and was-being-made-strong[a], being-filled [with] wisdom, and [the] benefaction of-god was upon him.

[a] *omit* ℵ B D L W *pc* it^{mss} vg sy^s cop; *in-spirit* A Θ Ψ f^1 f^{13} 33 892 1006 1342 1506 𝔐 it^{mss}.

15. Luke's Jesus as a Boy in the Temple

Luke 2:41-52

41 And his parents were-traveling according-to year [=every year] into Jerusalem for-the feast of-the passover. 42 And when he-happened [=he became] twelve years [old], their ascending[a] [=they went] according-to the custom of-the feast; 43 and having-finished the days [of the feast], in the to-return them [=when they were returning], Jesus the child stayed-behind in Jerusalem, and his parents[b] knew not. 44 So having-thought him to-be in the company, they-went way of-day [=a day's journey] and tracked-down [=they looked for] him in [=among] their kins and acquaintances, 45 and no [=not] having-found[c] they-returned into Jerusalem tracking-down him. 46 And it-happened, with [=after] three days, they-found him in the temple seating-himself in [the] middle of-the teachers and hearing them and questioning them. 47 So all his hearings [=those who heard him] were-surprised upon [=at] his comprehension and answers. 48 And having-seen him they-were-amazed, and his mother said to him, "Descendant, what [=why] did-you-do to-us thus? Look! your father, I-too, fretting, were-searching [for] you." 49 And he-said to them, "What [=Why is it] that you-were-searching [for] me? Do-you-recognize not that it-is-necessary [for] me to-be in the [=house of] my father?" 50 And they [themselves] comprehended not the speech [=words] which he-talked [=he said] to-them. 51 And he-descended with them and went into Nazareth and was submitting to-them. And his mother was-preserving all the speeches [=these things] in her heart. 52 And Jesus was-progressing in-wisdom and in-age and in-benefaction [=in grace] along god and people.

[a] *omit* ℵ B D L W 579 *pc* sy[s] sy[p] cop; *into Jerusalem* A Θ Ψ *f*[1] *f*[13] 33 892 1006 1342 1506 𝔐 it[mss] vg.
[b] *his parents* ℵ B D L W Θ *f*[1] 33 205 579 vg sy[s] cop[sa]; *Joseph and his mother* A C Ψ *f*[13] 1006 1342 1506 𝔐 it sy[p].
[c] *omit* ℵ B C* D L W *f*[1] 33 205 579 892 *pc*; *him* A Θ Ψ *f*[13] 1006 1342 1506 𝔐 it sy cop.

The Start of the Galilean Ministry

16. John the Baptizer

Matt 3:1-6	Mark 1:2-6	Q 3:3a	Luke 3:1-7a	John 1:19-23
1 So in those days, John the baptist arrives preaching in the deserted [=desert] of-Judea, 2 saying, "Repent, for the kingdom of-the heavens has-neared."			1 So in [the] fifteenth year of-the rule of-Tiberius Caesar, [with] Pontius Pilate being-ruler of-Judea and Herod being-tetrarch of-the Galilee, so [=and] Philip his brother being-tetrarch of-Ituraea and [the] region of-Trachonitis, and [with] Lysanius being-tetrarch of-Abilene, 2 upon [=when] Annas and Caiaphas [were] high-priest, [the] speech [=word] of-god happened upon John, son of-Zachariah	19 And this is the witness-testimony of-John when the Judeans sent-off priests and Levites out of-Jerusalems to him in-order-that they-might-beg [=they might ask] him, "What [=Who] are you?" 20 And he-confessed and denied not, and confessed that, "I am not the anointed-one." 21 And they-begged him, "What [=Who] therefore? Are you Elijah?" And he-says, "I-am not." "Are you the prophet?" And he-answered, "Not."

Matt 3:3-6

3For this is the [one] having-been-spoken [of] through Isaiah the prophet, saying,

“[A] VOICE [of one] SHOUTING IN THE DESERTED [=desert]: ‘MAKE-READY THE WAY [of the] LORD, DO [=make] STRAIGHT HIS PATHS.’” 4So John he [himself] was-having his clothes [made] from camel hairs and [a] leather belt around his waist, so [=and] his nourishment was locusts and wild honey. 5Then Jerusalems was-traveling-out to him and all Judea and all the surrounding-region of-the Jordan, 6and they-were-being-baptized in the Jordan river under [=by] him, acknowledging their sins.

Mark 1:2-6

2Just-as it-has-been-written in Isaiah the prophet[a]: “LOOK! I-SEND-OFF MY ANNOUNCER BEFORE YOUR FACE, WHO WILL-PREPARE YOUR WAY; 3[a] VOICE [of one] SHOUTING IN THE DESERTED [=desert]: ‘MAKE-READY THE WAY [of the] LORD, DO [=make] STRAIGHT HIS PATHS.’” 4John happened [=came] baptizing in the deserted [=desert] and preaching [a] baptism of-repentance into [=for the] forgiveness of-sins. 5And all the region of-the Judeans was-traveling-out to him and all the Jerusalemites, and they-were-being-baptized under [=by] him in the Jordan river, acknowledging their sins. 6And John was having-been-clothed [in] camel hairs and [a] leather belt around his waist, and [was] eating locusts and wild honey.

Q 3:3a

3aall [the] surrounding-region of-the Jordan

Luke 3:3-7a

in the deserted [=desert]. 3And he-went into all [the] surrounding-region of-the Jordan preaching [a] baptism of-repentance into [=for the] remission of-sins, 4like it-has-been-written in [the] book of-words of-Isaiah the prophet[b]:

“[A] VOICE [of one] SHOUTING IN THE DESERTED [=desert]: ‘MAKE-READY THE WAY [of the] LORD, DO [=make] STRAIGHT HIS PATHS. 5ALL [=Every] VALLEY WILL-BE-FULFILLED [=will be filled up], AND ALL [=every] MOUNTAIN AND HILL WILL-BE-HUMBLED [=flattened], AND THE CROOKED WILL-BE [made] INTO STRAIGHT, AND THE ROUGH INTO SMOOTH WAYS; 6AND ALL FLESH WILL-SEE THE SAVING-POWER OF-GOD.’” 7aTherefore he-was-saying to-the crowds traveling-out to-be-baptized under [=by] him . . .

John

22Therefore they-said to-him, “What [=Who] are-you?” In-order-that we-might-give [an] answer to-the having-sents [=to those who sent] us, what do-you-say around [=about] yourself?”

23He-spoke “I [am the] VOICE [of one] SHOUTING IN THE DESERTED [=desert]. ‘MAKE-STRAIGHT THE WAY [of the] LORD’, just-as Isaiah the prophet said.”

[a] *in Isaiah the prophet* ℵ B D L Δ Θ f^1 33 565 892 2427; *in the prophets* A W f^{13} 1006 1342 𝕸.
[b] *Isaiah the prophet* ℵ B D L W Δ f^1 205 579 700 892 1424 2542 *pc*; *Isaiah the prophet, saying* A C Θ Ψ f^{13} 33 1006 1342 1506 𝕸 it.
🕮 Mt 3:3 – Isa 40:3; 🕮 Mk 1:2 – Mal 3:1; Isa 40:3; 🕮 Lk 3:4-6 – Isa 40:3-5; 🕮 Jn 1:23 – Isa 40:3

SYNOPTIC STUDY GUIDE 2

Two-Document Hypothesis

The Two-Document Hypothesis (2DH) is also known as the Two-Source Hypothesis and the Four-Source Hypothesis. The latter term is somewhat problematic, for it implies that M (Synoptic Study Guide 10) and L (Synoptic Study Guide 11) are sources in the same way that Mark and Q (Synoptic Study Guide 3) are sources, which is unlikely. The 2DH has been the most widely held solution to the Synoptic Problem among New Testament scholars for a hundred years, and its dominance continues today. Nonetheless, as we shall see (Synoptic Study Guides 9 and 15), this solution is not without its problems, and thus there are also legitimate alternative solutions (though they too have their limitations).

It is impossible to ascribe the development of the 2DH to a single scholar because there are three distinct stages in the formulation of this hypothesis: (1) that Mark is the earliest gospel written (what scholars call 'Markan Priority'); (2) that the writers of the Gospels of Matthew and Luke used Mark but wrote independently of each other; and (3) that the writers of Matthew and Luke had access also to a second now lost written source comprised mostly of sayings of Jesus (known as Q). The first two conclusions came about late in the nineteenth century as scholars reacted against the dominant Griesbach Hypothesis, with its claims of Matthean Priority, Lukan dependence upon Matthew, and the posteriority of Mark (see Synoptic Study Guide 5). It is important to note therefore that scholars did not posit the existence of Q for the sake of novelty, but hypothesized it to explain the existence of stories shared by Matthew and Luke (often with very high verbal agreement) that cannot have derived from the Gospel of Mark (this material is known as the Double Tradition—see Synoptic Study Guide 3).

It has been very difficult for some scholars to accept the idea of a hypothetical "gospel": no document like it is ever explicitly referred to in other early Christian writings, and there are no surviving manuscripts of it. The theory requires one to accept that Q was so important to Matthew and Luke, but that it was not important enough to anyone else to warrant referring to or keeping. Of course, we know of letters of Paul that did not survive, so perhaps we should not be too troubled by Q's disappearance. Another long-standing objection to Q is that a "gospel" that lacks narrative in general, and especially any stories of Jesus' birth, death, or resurrection, can never have existed among Christians. This objection is no longer tenable, as the discovery of the Gospel of Thomas shows that early Christian gospels could take more forms than the predominantly narrative canonical gospels. It is important to realize, however, that the Gospel of Thomas is *not* Q; they do not share enough material in common for this to be so.

17. John the Baptist's Preaching of Repentance

Matt 3:7-10

7 So having-seen many of-the
Pharisees and Sadducees coming
upon [=to] his[a] baptism, he-said
to-them, "Offspring of-vipers, what
[=who] displayed [to] you [how]
to-flee from the intending anger?
8 Therefore, do [=make] fruit worthy
of-repentance, 9 and suppose no
[=not] to-say in themselves [=to
yourselves], 'We-have Abraham [as]
father.' For I-say to-you that god
is-able to-raise descendants to-
Abraham out of-these stones. 10 So[b]
already the axe lies to [=at] the root
of-the trees; therefore all [=every]
tree doing [=making] no fine fruit is-
cut-off and is-thrown into [the] fire."

Q 3:7b-9

7b "Offspring of-vipers, what [=who]
displayed [to] you [how] to-flee from
the intending anger? 8 Therefore, do
[=make] fruit worthy of-repentance,
and suppose no [=not] to-say in
themselves [=to yourselves], 'We-
have Abraham [as] father.' For I-say
to-you that god is-able to-raise
descendants to-Abraham out of-
these stones. 9 So already the axe
lies to [=at] the root of-the trees;
therefore all [=every] tree doing
[=making] no fine fruit is-cut-off
and is-thrown into [the] fire."

Luke 3:7b-9

7b "Offspring of-vipers, what [=who]
displayed [to] you [how] to-flee from
the intending anger? 8 Therefore,
do [=make] fruits worthy of-
repentance, and begin no [=not]
to-say in themselves [=to yourselves],
'We-have Abraham [as] father.' For
I-say to-you that god is-able to-
raise descendants to-Abraham out
of-these stones. 9 And so already the
axe lies to [=at] the root of-the trees;
therefore all [=every] tree doing
[=making] no fine fruit is-cut-off
and is-thrown into [the] fire."

[a] *his* ℵ* B *pc* cop^{sa}; *omit* ℵ^{1} C D L W f^{1} f^{13} 33 892 1006 1506 𝔐 sy^{c} sy^{s} cop^{bo}.
[b] *So* ℵ B C D W Δ 0233 f^{1} 700 *pc* cop; *And so* L f^{13} 33 892 1006 1506 𝔐.

SYNOPTIC STUDY GUIDE 3

Double Tradition/Reconstruction of Q

As a rule of thumb, gospel material can be divided up into four categories: Double Tradition, Triple Tradition (see Synoptic Study Guide 4), Special Matthew (see Synoptic Study Guide 10), and Special Luke (see Synoptic Study Guide 11). Importantly, the designation of these categories is common to all synoptic theories.

Double Tradition refers to blocks of material—interestingly almost always sayings, not stories—that are common to the Gospels of Matthew and Luke but are absent from Mark. The Two-Document Hypothesis (2DH) argues that the Double Tradition came from Q and that the authors of Matthew and Luke fit this material into the narrative framework provided by the Gospel of Mark. What is more, Matthew and Luke appear to have had deep regard for Q, since the degree of verbatim agreement in this material is generally extremely high. For the Griesbach Hypothesis (see Synoptic Study Guide 5), the Double Tradition is any material that the writer of Luke took over from the Gospel of Matthew but that the author of Mark ignored. The Farrer Hypothesis argues that the author of Matthew added about 300 verses of unique material to his rewriting of Mark, and what is adopted by Luke (about 230 verses) is the Double Tradition material. In other words, the Farrer Hypothesis does not rely on the existence of a hypothetical source to explain the Double Tradition; it is simply the material that the writer of Matthew added to Mark that the writer of Luke took over.

You will notice that the verse numbers of Q are the same as the verse numbers in Luke. This is because originally Q scholars believed that the author of Luke tended to leave Q in its original order (there are exceptions, however: see §213 + §218, and §233 + §237), while the author of Matthew tended to collect Q material into longer sections (see Matthew's Sermon on the Mount). Scholars acknowledge, on the other hand, that these two gospel writers had an equal propensity to alter the *wording* of Q; therefore, the reconstruction of the text of Q proceeds on a word-by-word basis, pausing to consider whether there are signs that the author of Matthew or Luke (or both) could have reworded Q. It is the hypothetical (textual reconstruction) stacked on top of the hypothetical (mere existence); but this is not greatly different in principle from modern textual criticism, which proceeds in similar fashion in the reconstruction of the entire New Testament, for which there are no original documents (though the texts of the New Testament reflect certainly *extant* literary works).

18. Luke's John Replies to Questions

Luke 3:10-14

10 And the crowds were-questioning him saying, "What therefore might-we-do?" 11 So having-
answered, he-was-saying to-them, "The [one] having two tunics, let-him-share-with the [one]
having no [=not], and the [one] having sustenances [=food], let-him-do likewise." 12 So and [=even]
tax-collectors came to-be-baptized, and they-said to him, "Teacher, what might-we-do?" 13 So
he-said to them, "Practice [=Collect] not-one [=nothing] more along [=than] the having-been-
appointed [=what has been allotted] to-you." 14 So and [=even] being-soldiers [=some soldiers] were-
questioning him saying, "And we, what will-we-do?[a]" And he-said to-them, "Might-you-bribe
not-one [=no one] nor might-you-blackmail and be-enough [=be satisfied with] your pay."

[a] *And we, what will-we-do?* 𝔓4 ℵ A B C L W Θ Ξ Ψ f^1 f^{13} 33 892 1006 1342 1506 𝔐 sy; *What we will-do in-order to-be-saved?* D

19. John's Preaching

Matt 3:11-12	Mark 1:7-8	Q 3:16-17	Luke 3:15-17	John 1:25-28, 33
			[15]So the whole-people [were] expecting and all [were] pondering in their hearts around [=concerning] John, lest he [himself] might-be the anointed-one,	[25]And they-begged him and said to-him, "What [=Why] therefore do-you-baptize if you are not the anointed-one nor Elijah, nor the prophet?" [26]John answered them
[11]"I, for-one, baptize you in water into [=for] repentance,	[7]And he-was-preaching saying,	[16]"I, for-one, baptize	[16]John answered all, saying[b], "I, for-one, in-water baptize	saying, "I baptize in water. [In the] middle of-you has-stood [one] who you recognize not,
so [=but] the [one] coming behind me is stronger [than] me, of-whom I-am not fit to-bear the	"The [one who is] stronger [than] me comes behind me, of-whom I-am not fit, having-bent [down], to-loose the strap [of] his sandals. [8]I baptized you in-water, so	you in water, so [=but] the [one] coming behind me is stronger [than] me, of-whom I-am not fit to-bear the	you, so [=but] the [one who is] stronger [than] me comes, of-whom I-am not fit to-loose the strap [of] his sandals.	[27]the [one who is] coming behind me of-who I-am not worthy in-order-that I-might-loose the strap [of] his sandal." [28]These [things] happened in Bethany beyond
sandals. He [himself] will-baptize you in [the] holy spirit and fire; [12]who, [with] the winnowing-shovel in his hand, and [=both] will-purge his threshing-floor and will-gather his wheat[a] into the storehouse, so [=but] the chaff he-will-incinerate [with] unquenchable fire."	[=but] he [himself] will-baptize you in [the] holy spirit."	sandals. He [himself] will-baptize you in-[the]-holy spirit and fire; [17]who, [with] the winnowing-shovel in his hand, and [=both] will-purge his threshing-floor and will-gather the wheat into his storehouse, so [=but] the chaff he-will-incinerate [with] unquenchable fire."	He [himself] will-baptize you in [the] holy spirit and fire; [17]who, [with] the winnowing-shovel in his hand to-cleanse [=will cleanse] his threshing-floor and to-gather[c] [=will gather] the wheat into his storehouse, so [=but] the chaff he-will-incinerate [with] unquenchable fire."	the Jordan where John was baptizing. [33] . . . this is the [one] baptizing in [the] holy spirit.

[a] *his wheat* ℵ C D 0233 f^{1} 33 1006 $\mathfrak{M}$ it^{mss} vg cop; *the wheat* f^{13} *pc*.
[b] *John answered all, saying* A B C 892 1006 1342 $\mathfrak{M}$; *knowing their thoughts, he-said* D.
[c] *to-cleanse . . . to-gather* $\mathfrak{P}^{4}$ ℵ B *pc* it vg; *will-purge . . . will-gather* A C L W Θ Ξ Ψ f^{1} f^{13} 33 892 1006 1342 $\mathfrak{M}$.

20. The Imprisonment of John (→ §164)

Matt 14:3-4	Mark 6:17-18	**Luke 3:18-20**
		18And therefore for-one, [while] exhorting many others [=other things], he-was-proclaiming [=preaching to] the whole-people.
3For Herod, having-seized John, restrained and deposited [him] in prison through [=because of] Herodias, the woman [=wife] of-Philip his brother[a];	17For Herod, having-sent-off [soldiers], he [himself] seized John and restrained him in prison through [=because of] Herodias, the woman [=wife] of-Philip his brother, that [=because] he-married her;	19So [on the other hand] Herod the tetrarch, being-exposed under [=by] him around [=concerning] Herodias, the woman [=wife of] his brother and around [=concerning] all [the] evils which Herod did,
4for John was-saying to-him, "It-is-permitted not for-you to-have her."	18for John was-saying to-Herod that "It-is-permitted not for-you to-have the woman [=wife of] your brother."	
		20and added this upon [=to it] all: he-shut-up John in prison[b].

[a] *of-Philip his brother* ℵ B C L W Δ Θ 0106 f^1 f^{13} 28 33 𝔐 sy cop Origen; *his brother* D it vg Jer Aug.
[b] *in prison* 𝔓[4] ℵ B D L Ξ 070 f^1 565; *in the prison* A W Θ Ψ f^{13} 33 892 1006 1342 𝔐.

SYNOPTIC STUDY GUIDE 4

Triple Tradition

Triple Tradition refers to stories or blocks of material—regardless of placement—shared by the Gospels of Matthew, Mark, and Luke. It is the most common form of material in the Gospels (§20). Triple Tradition material is not very controversial, since all three synoptic hypotheses we will look at agree that the authors of Matthew, Mark, and Luke each used the other's works in some way at some point: Triple Tradition material is simply that material which two later writers took from an earlier gospel, whether that earlier gospel is Mark (Two-Document Hypothesis; Farrer Hypothesis) or Matthew (Griesbach Hypothesis). Nonetheless, there are some interesting features of Triple Tradition material.

The most interesting feature is what this material illustrates about Mark's relationship to Matthew and Luke. Notice that before Mark's Gospel begins (see §1-15) the Gospels of Matthew and Luke look very different from each other. Yes, they both open with infancy narratives (which is interesting!), but their narratives about the circumstances of Jesus' birth are almost completely different. Notice the preponderance of Single Tradition material in the first two chapters of Matthew and Luke (see Synoptic Study Guides 10 and 11). And yet, as soon as Mark's story starts (§16), the Gospels of Luke and Matthew simultaneously start agreeing much more closely with each other and with Mark! The very same phenomenon occurs at the end of Mark: as soon as Mark's narrative ends, the extent of verbal agreement between Matthew and Luke plummets.

Another, and related, piece of evidence concerns the order of gospel stories: sometimes Matthew and Mark have a story in the same place, and Luke has it differently. Sometimes Mark and Luke have a story in the same place, and Matthew differs. But in the Triple Tradition Matthew and Luke never have a story in the same place unless Mark also has it there. In other words, they never agree together against Mark in the placement of a Triple Tradition story.

Neither of these two pieces of evidence tells us what order the Synoptic Gospels were composed in, nor whether Mark was composed first or third. They do, however, tell us that Mark plays some sort of mediating role between the Gospels of Matthew and Luke: either Mark is the source for Matthew and Luke, or its author used Matthew and Luke. Any solution that does not have "Mark in the middle" has not survived scholarly scrutiny (which is why Mark cannot be second in order). Each of the three solutions considered here has "Mark in the middle."

21. The Baptism of Jesus

Matt 3:13-17

13Then Jesus arrives from
the Galilee upon [=at]
the Jordan to John to-be-
baptized under [=by] him.
14So [=But] John was-
preventing him saying "I
have need to-be-baptized
under [=by] you, and you
come to me?" 15So having-
answered Jesus said to
him, "Excuse [=Allow it]
right-now, for it-is suitable
thus for-us to-fulfill all
righteousness." Then he-
excused [=he allowed] him
[to be baptized]. 16So Jesus,
having-been-baptized,
immediately ascended
from the water; and
look! the heavens were-
opened[a], and he-saw
[the] spirit of-god
descending as [a] dove,
coming upon him; 17and
look! [a] voice out of-the
heavens saying, "This is
my son the beloved, in
whom I-was-content."

Mark 1:9-11

9And it-happened in
those days, Jesus came
from Nazareth [of] the
Galilee and was-baptized
into [=in] the Jordan
under [=by] John.
10And immediately
ascending out of-the
water he-saw the heavens
being-ripped and the
spirit descending like
[a] dove into[b] him;
11and [a] voice happened
[=came] out of-the
heavens, "You [yourself]
are my son the beloved,
in you I-was-content."

Luke 3:21-22

21So it-happened in
the [=while] everyone
[of] the whole-people
to-be-baptized [=was
being baptized] and
Jesus having-been-
baptized and praying,
the heaven to-be-opened
[=was opened] 22and the
holy spirit to-descend
[=was descending] in-
bodily form like [a] dove
upon him, and [a] voice
out of-heaven to-happen
[=came], "You [yourself]
are my son the beloved,
in you I-was-content[c]."

John 1:29-34

29[On] the next-day, he-
looks [at] Jesus coming to
him and he-says, "Look,
the lamb of-god, the [one]
removing the sin of-the
world. 30This is [the one]
on-behalf of-whom I-said,
'Behind me comes [a]
man who has-happened
in-front of-me [=is better
than me] that [=because]
he-was first of-me [=before
me].' 31I-too recognized
him not, but in-order-
that he-might-be-made-
visible to-Israel, through
[=because of] this I [myself]
came baptizing in water."
32And John testified saying
that "I-had-noticed the
spirit descending like [a]
dove out of-heaven, and
it-stayed upon him. 33I-too
recognized him not, but
the [one] having-sent me
to-baptize in water, that
[one] said to-me, 'Upon
who ever you-might-see
the spirit descending and
staying upon him, this
is the [one] baptizing in
[=with the] holy spirit.
34I-too have-seen and
have-testified that this
is the son of-god."

[a] *opened* ℵ B sy^{c} sy^{s} cop^{sa}; *opened to-him* C D L W Δ f^{1} f^{13} 𝔐 it vg sy^{p} cop^{bo}.
[b] *into* B D f^{13} 2427; *upon* ℵ A L W Θ f^{1} 33 𝔐 sy.
[c] *You are my son the beloved, in you I-was-content* 𝔭^{4} ℵ 070 A B L W Δ Θ f^{1} f^{13} 28 33 𝔐 vg sy^{s} sy^{p} cop Aug; *You-are my son, today I-have begotten you* (📖 Ps 2:7) D it Justin.

22. Luke's Genealogy of Jesus (→ §6)

Matt 1:2-16 (names only)

16Jacob, Joseph,
15Matthan, Eleazar,
Eliud, 14Achim, Zadok, Azor, 13Eliakim, Abiud,

Luke 3:23-38

23And Jesus he [himself] was beginning [to teach]
as [=at] thirty years, being [the] son, like [=so]
it-was-thought, of-Joseph, [son] of-Heli, 24of-
Matthat, of-Levi, of-Melchi, of-Jannai, of-Joseph,
25of-Mattathias, of-Amos, of-Nahum, of-Esli,
of-Naggai, 26of-Maath, of-Mattathias, of-Semein,

Zerubbabel, 12 Salathiel, Jechoniah, 11 Josiah 10 Amos[a], Manasseh, Hezekiah, 9 Ahaz, Jotham, Uzziah, 8 Joram, Jehosephat, Asaph[b], 7 Abijah, Rehoboam, Solomon, 6 David, so Jesse begat King David, 5 Obed, Boaz, Salmon, 4 Nahshon, Aminadab, Aram, 3 Hezron, Perez, Judah, 2 Jacob, Isaac, Abraham	of-Josech, of-Joda, 27 of-Joanan, of-Rhesa, of-Zerubbabel, of-Salathiel, of-Neri, 28 of-Melchi, of-Addi, of-Cosam, of-Elmadam, of-Er, 29 of-Joshua, of-Eliezer, of-Jorim, of- Matthat, of-Levi, 30 of-Symeon, of-Judah, of-Joseph, of-Jonam, of-Eliakim, 31 of-Melea, of-Menna, of- Mattatha, of-Natham[c], of-David, 32 of-Jesse, of-Obed, of-Boas, of-Sala[d], of-Nahshon, 33 of-Aminadab, of-Admin, of-Arni, of-Hezron, of-Perez, of-Judah, 34 of-Jacob, of-Isaac, of-Abraham, of-Terah, of-Nahor, 35 of-Serug, of-Reu, of-Peleg, of-Eber, of-Sala, 36 of- Cainan, of-Arphaxad, of-Shem, of-Noah, of-Lamech, 37 of-Methuselah, of-Enoch, of-Jared, of-Mahalaleel, of-Cainan, 38 of-Enos, of-Seth, of-Adam, of-god.

[a] *Amos* ℵ B C Δ Θ *f*^{1} 33 205 *pc* it vg^{mss} cop^{sa} cop^{bo}; *Amon* L W *f*^{13} 892 1006 1342 1506 𝔐 it^{mss} vg sy.
[b] *Asaph* 𝔭^{1} ℵ B C *f*^{1} *f*^{13} 205 700 1506 *pc* it cop; *Asa* L W 33 892 1006 1342 𝔐 vg sy.
[c] *Natham* 𝔭^{4} ℵ* B 1582 *pc* it; *Nathan* ℵ^{2} A L Θ Ψ *f*^{1} *f*^{13} 33 892 1006 1506 𝔐 sy cop^{bo}.
[d] *Sala* 𝔭^{4} ℵ* B sy^{s} cop^{sa} cop^{bomss}; *Salmon* ℵ^{2} A D L Θ Ψ *f*^{1} *f*^{13} 33 892 1006 1506 𝔐 it vg sy^{p} cop^{bo}.

23. The Temptation

Matt 4:1-11	Mark 1:12-13	Q 4:1-4, 9-12, 5-8, 13	Luke 4:1-13
1 Then Jesus was-led-up into the deserted [places] under [=by] the spirit to- be-tested under [=by] the devil. 2 And having-fasted days forty and nights forty,	12 And immediately the spirit casts-out him into the deserted [places]. 13 And he-was in the deserted[b] [places] forty days being-tested under [=by] the adversary.	1 So Jesus, was-led-up into the deserted [places] under [=by] the spirit 2 to-be- tested under [=by] the devil. And [for] days forty	1 So Jesus, full [of the] holy spirit, returned from the Jordan and was-being-led in [=by] the spirit in [=into] the deserted [places], 2 days forty being-tested under [=by] the devil. And he-ate not no-one [=nothing at all] in those days and their [=when they were] having-been- concluded, he-hungered.
afterward he-hungered. 3 And the testing [one], having-approached, said to-him, "If you-are [the] son of-god, say [=speak] in-order-that these stones bread might-happen [=might become]." 4 So [=But] having-answered, he-said, "It-has-been- written, 'THE PERSON WILL-LIVE NOT UPON BREAD ALONE, BUT UPON ALL [=every] SPEECH TRAVELING- OUT THROUGH [the] MOUTH OF-GOD.'" 5 Then the devil takes- along him into the holy		he-hungered. 3 And the devil said to- him, "If you-are [the] son of-god, say [=speak] in-order-that these stones bread might-happen [=might become]." 4 And Jesus answered to- him, "It-has-been-written that 'THE PERSON WILL-LIVE NOT UPON BREAD ALONE[c].'" 9 The devil takes-along him into Jerusalem and stood him upon the pinnacle of-the temple and said to-him, "If you-are [the] son of-god, throw yourself below,	3 So the devil said to- him, "If you-are [the] son of-god, say [=speak] to-this stone in-order- that it-might-happen [=it might become] bread." 4 And Jesus answered to him, "It-has-been-written that 'THE PERSON WILL-LIVE NOT UPON BREAD ALONE[c].'" 5 And having-led-up him, he-showed to-him all the kingdoms of- the inhabited-earth in [a] moment of-time, 6 and the devil said to- him, "I-will-give to-you

city and stood[a] him upon
the pinnacle of-the temple
6and says to-him, "If
you-are [the] son of-god,
throw yourself below, for
it-has-been-written that,
'HE-WILL-CHARGE
HIS ANNOUNCERS
AROUND [=concerning]
YOU,' and 'UPON
HANDS THEY-WILL-
REMOVE YOU, LEST
YOU-MIGHT-BATTER
YOUR FOOT TO
[=against a] STONE.'"
7Jesus spoke to-him,
"Again it-has-been-
written, 'TRY NOT [the]
LORD YOUR GOD.'"
8Again the devil takes-
along him into [=to an]
extremely high mountain
and shows to-him all the
kingdoms of-the world
and their glory 9and
said to-him, "I-will-give
all these [things] to-you
if-ever having-fallen
you-might-worship me."
10Then Jesus says to-him,
"Leave, adversary; for it-
has-been-written, 'YOU-
WILL-WORSHIP [the]
LORD YOUR GOD AND
YOU-WILL-VENERATE
HIM ALONE.'" 11Then
the devil excuses [=leaves]
him and look! announcers
[=angels] approached
and were-serving him.

and he-was with
the beasts and the
announcers [=angels]
were-serving him.

10for it-has-been-written
that 'HE-WILL-CHARGE
HIS ANNOUNCERS
[=angels] AROUND
[=concerning] YOU,' 11and
'UPON HANDS THEY-
WILL-REMOVE YOU,
LEST YOU-MIGHT-
BATTER YOUR FOOT
TO [=against a] STONE.'"
12And having-answered
Jesus said to-him, "It-
has-been-written 'TRY
NOT [the] LORD YOUR
GOD.'" 5And the devil
takes-along him into
[=to an] extremely high
mountain and shows
to-him all the kingdoms
of-the world and their
glory 6and said to-him,
"I-will-give all these
[things] to-you 7if-ever
you-might-worship me."
8And having-answered,
Jesus said to-him, "It-
has-been-written, 'YOU-
WILL-WORSHIP [the]
LORD YOUR GOD AND
YOU-WILL-VENERATE
HIM ALONE."

13And the devil excuses
[=leaves] him.

everyone [=every bit of]
this authority and their
glory that [=because] it-
has-been-delivered to-me
and I-give it to-whom
if-ever I-might-wish.
7Therefore, if-ever
you-might-worship
in-the-sight of-me, all
[things] will-be yours."
8And having-answered,
Jesus said to-him, "It-
has-been-written, 'YOU-
WILL-WORSHIP [the]
LORD YOUR GOD AND
YOU-WILL-VENERATE
HIM ALONE."
9So he-led him into
Jerusalem and stood
[him][d] upon the pinnacle
of-the temple and said
to-him, "If you-are [the]
son of-god, throw yourself
below from-here, 10for
it-has-been-written that
"HE-WILL-CHARGE HIS
ANNOUNCERS [=angels]
AROUND [=concerning]
YOU, TO-SAFEGUARD
YOU,' 11and that 'UPON
HANDS THEY-WILL-
REMOVE YOU, LEST
YOU-MIGHT-BATTER
YOUR FOOT TO
[=against a] STONE."
12And having-answered
Jesus said to-him that
"It-has-been-said 'YOU-
WILL-TRY NOT [the]
LORD YOUR GOD."
13And having-concluded
all [=each] test, the devil
abandoned from him
till [a] proper-time.

[a] *stood* ℵ B C D f^1 33 205 *pc*; *stands* L W Θ f^{13} 892 1006 1506 𝔐.
[b] *in the deserted* ℵ A B D L Θ f^{13} 33 892 1006 1342 2427 *pc* it[mss] vg cop; *there* f^1 69 205 565 700 1424 2542 *al* sy[s]; *there in the deserted* W 1506 𝔐 sy[p].
[c] *omit* ℵ B L W *pc* sy[s] cop[sa] cop[bomss]; *but upon all speech of-god* A D Θ Ψ f^1 f^{13} 33 892 1006 1342 𝔐 it vg sy[p] cop[bomss].
[d] *omit* ℵ B L Ξ 579 700 892 *pc*; *him* A D W Θ Ψ f^1 f^{13} 1006 1342 𝔐 it[mss] vg sy cop.
🕮 Mt 4:4 – Deut 8:3l; 🕮 Mt 4:6 – Ps 91:11,12 ; 🕮 Mt 4:7 – Deut 6:16; 🕮 Mt 4:10 – Deut 6:13, Deut 10:20; 🕮 Lk 4:4 – Deut 8:3; 🕮 Lk 4:8 – Deut 6:13; 10:20, 🕮 Lk 4:10 – Ps 91:11,12; 🕮 Lk 4:12 – Deut 6:16

24. Jesus Returns to the Galilee

Matt 4:12	**Mark 1:14a**	**Luke 4:14-15**	John 4:1-3, 43, 45
[12]So having-heard that John was-delivered [=had been arrested], he-retreated into the Galilee.	[14a]So with the to-be-delivered [=arrest of] John, Jesus[a] went into the Galilee . . .	[14]And Jesus returned in the power of-the spirit into the Galilee. And gossip went-out according-to [=through the] whole of-the surrounding-regions around [=concerning] him. [15]And he [himself] was-teaching in their synagogues, being-glorified under [=by] all.	[1]Therefore like [=when] Jesus knew that the Pharisees heard that "Jesus does [=makes] and baptizes more disciples or [=than] John"—[2]and-yet Jesus he [himself] was-baptizing not but [it was] his disciples—[3]he-excused [=he left] Judea and went-away again into the Galilee. [43]So with [=after] the two days he-went-out from-there into the Galilee. [45]Therefore when he-came into the Galilee, the Galileans received him, having-seen all whatsoever he-did in Jerusalems in [=during] the feast, for they [themselves] and [=also] went into [=to] the feast.

[a] *Jesus* ℵ A B D L Δ f^1 f^{13} 33 205 565 892 1006 1424 1506 2427 2542 *al.*; *omit* A Θ W 1342 𝔐.

25. Jesus in "Nazara"

Matt 4:13a	**Q 4:16**	**Luke 4:16a**
[13a]And having-quit Nazara[a] . . .	. . . Nazara . . .	[16]And he-came into Nazara[b], which [is where] he-was nourished [=he was brought up]...

[a] *Nazara* ℵ[1] B* 33; *Nazareth* ℵ* D E W Θ 0233 f^1 f^{13} 579 1006 *pc* it^{mss} vg cop; *Nazarath* C Δ *pc.*

[b] *Nazara* ℵ B* Δ Ξ 33 *pc* it^{mss}; *Nazaret* B[2] F L 0233 205 209 565 579 892 1342 1424 1506 1582 2542; *Nazareth* D E G H W Ψ f^1 f^{13} 788 1006 *pc*; *Nazarat* A Θ *pc.*

26. Matthew's Explanation of Nazareth

Matt 4:13b-16

[13b][and] having-come he-settled into sea-side Capharnaum[a] in [the] territories of-Zebulon and Nephthali, [14]in-order-that the having-been-said [=what was said] through Isaiah the prophet might-be-fulfilled, saying: [15]"LAND OF-ZEBULON AND LAND OF-NEPHTHALI, [the] WAY [by the] SEA, BEYOND THE JORDAN, GALILEE OF-THE NATIONS, [16]THE WHOLE-PEOPLE SITTING IN DARKNESS SAW [a] GREAT LIGHT, AND TO-THE SITTINGS [=those who sat] IN [a] REGION AND SHADE OF-DEATH, [a] LIGHT AROSE TO-THEM."

[a] *Capharnaum* ℵ B D W Z 0233 33 *pc* vg it^{mss} cop; *Capernaum* C L Θ f^1 f^{13} 892 1006 1506 𝔐.

📖 Mt 4:15-16 – Isa 9:1-2

27. Jesus Preaches Concerning the Kingdom

Matt 4:17	**Mark 1:14b-15**
17 From then Jesus began to-preach and to-say, "Repent, for the kingdom of-the heavens has-neared."	14b preaching the proclamation of-god 15 and saying that "The proper-time has-been-fulfilled, and the kingdom of-god has-neared; repent and believe in the proclamation."

There are no variants in this pericope that appear in English.

28. Jesus' Preaching at Nazareth (→ §161)

Matt 13:53-58	Mark 6:1-6	**Luke 4:16b-30**	John 7:15; 6:42; 4:44; 10:39	Thomas 31
53 And it-happened when Jesus completed these parables,	1 And	16b and		
he-took-leave from-there. 54 And having-come into his homeland	he-went-out from-there and comes into his homeland and his disciples follow him.			
	2 And [when] sabbath having-happened [=started],	according-to the having-been-accustomed for-him [=as was his custom]		
he-was-teaching them in their synagogue	he-began to-teach in the synagogue	he-entered into the synagogue in [=on] the day of-the sabbaths, and he-got-up to-read. 17 And [a] booklet of-the prophet Isaiah was-given-to him and having-unrolled[c] the booklet he-found the place which [=where] it-was having-been-written, 18 "[The] SPIRIT [of the] LORD [is] UPON ME BECAUSE OF-WHICH HE-ANOINTED ME TO-PROCLAIM TO-POORS [=to poor people], HE-HAS-SENT-OFF ME TO-PREACH REMISSION [=release] TO-CAPTIVES AND RESTORATION-OF-SIGHT TO-BLINDS [=to blind people], TO-SEND-OFF HAVING-BEEN-OPPRESSEDS [=the oppressed] IN REMISSION [=freedom], 19 TO-PREACH [the] ACCEPTABLE		

with-the-result-that they to-be-amazed [=were amazed] and to-say [=said], "From-where [did] this [man get] this wisdom and the [=these] powers? 55 Is this not the son of-the carpenter? [Is] not his mother said [=called] Mary and his brothers James and Joseph[a] and Simon and Judah? 56 And are indeed-not his sisters all to [=with] us? Therefore from-where [did] this [man get] all these [abilities]?" 57 And they-were-being-caused-to-stumble [=they were offended] in [=by] him. So Jesus said to-them,

"[A] prophet is not dishonorable if no [=except] in [his] homeland and in his home." 58 And he-did not many [works with his] powers there through [=because of] their disloyalty.

and many hearing were-being-amazed, saying, "From-where [did] this [man get] these [things] and what [is] the wisdom having-been-given to-this[b] [man], and [what are] the powers such-as-these happening through his hands? 3 Is this not the carpenter, the son of-Mary and brother of-James and of-Joses and of-Judah and of-Simon? And are not his sisters here to [=with] us?"

And they-were-being-caused-to-stumble [=they were offended] in [=by] him. 4 And Jesus was-saying to-them that,

"[A] prophet is not dishonorable if no [=except] in his homeland and in [=among] his kin and in his home." 5 And he-was-being-able not to-do no-one [=any deeds of] power

ANNUM [=year of the] LORD." 20 And having-ravelled the booklet, [and] having-given-over [it] to-the attendant, he-was-seated; and the eyes of-all in the synagogue were being-fixed on him. 21 So he-began to-say to them that "Today this writing has-been-fulfilled in your ears." 22 And all were-testifying him and were-being-astonished upon [=by] the words of-benefaction [=of grace] traveling-out out [of] his mouth and were-saying, "Is indeed-not this [a] son of-Joseph?"

23 And he-said to them, "By-all-means you-will-say this parable to-me, 'Physician, heal yourself,' [and] 'Whatsoever we-heard having-happened into [=at] Capharnaum do and [=also] here in your homeland.'" 24 So he-said, "Amen I-say to-you that 'No-one [=No prophet is acceptable in

his homeland.'

7:15 Therefore the Judeans were-being-astonished, saying, "How [does] this [man] recognize letters [=writing], no [=despite never] having-been-learned [=having been trained]." 6:42 And they-were-saying, "Is this not Jesus the son of-Joseph, the father and the mother of-whom we [ourselves] recognize? Now how [does] he-say that, 'I-have-descended out of-heaven'"?

Jesus said, "No prophet is welcome on his home turf; doctors don't cure those who know them."

there, if no [=except] having-placed the hands [on them] he-healed [a] few unwell. 6 And he-was-being-astonished through [=by] their disloyalty.

And he-was-leading-around among the villages teaching.

25 So I-say to-you upon [=in] truth, there-were many widows in the days of-Elijah in Israel, when the heaven was-locked upon [=for] three years and six months, like [=when a] great famine happened upon all the land, 26 and Elijah was-sent to no-one of-them if no [=except] into [=to] Zarepheth the Sidonite [city], to [a] woman [who was a] widow. 27 And there-were many leprouses [=lepers] in Israel upon [=in the time of] Elisha the prophet, and no-one of-them was-purified if no [=except] Naaman the Syrian." 28 And hearing these [things], all in the synagogue were-filled [with] wrath 29 and having-gotten-up, they-cast-out him outside of-the city and lead him until [=as far as the] brow of-the mountain [=cliff], upon which their city had-been-built, with-the-result-that [=intending] to-toss-over him. 30 So [=But] he, having-come-through through [the] middle of-them, was-traveling [on].

4:44 For Jesus he [himself] testified that [a] prophet has not honor in the [=his] own homeland.

10:39 Therefore they-were-; it-searching [for] him again [in order] to-apprehend [him], and he-went-out out [=escaped from] their hands.

[a] *Joseph* ℵ[2] B C Θ *f*[1] 33 892 it[mss] vg; *Joses* L W Δ 0106 *f*[13] 565 1006 1342 1506 𝔐 it[mss] cop[sa]; *John* ℵ* D E G 579 1424 vg[mss].
[b] *this* ℵ B C L Δ 892 1342 cop[samss] cop[bo]; *him* A D W Θ *f*[1] *f*[13] 1006 1506 2427 𝔐 sy cop[samss].
[c] *unrolled* ℵ D * K Δ Θ Ψ *f*[1] *f*[13] 28 565 700 𝔐 it vg; *opened* A B L W Ξ 33 579 892 1241 *pc* sy cop.
🕮 Lk 4:18-19 – Isa 61:1-2; 🕮 Lk 4:25 – 1 Kgs 17:1, 9; 18:1, 2; 🕮 Lk 4:27 – 2 Kgs 5:14

29. The Call of the Disciples

Matt 4:18-22

18So, walking-around along [=along] the sea of-the Galilee, he-saw two brothers, Simon the [one] being-said [=being called] Peter, and Andrew his brother, throwing [a] casting-net into the sea, for they-were fishers. 19And he-says to-them, "Come-on! behind me and I-will-do [=I will make] you fishers of-people." 20So instantly having-excused [=leaving] the nets, they-followed him. 21And having-advanced from-there, he-saw another two brothers, James the [son] of-Zebedee and John his brother in the boat with Zebedee their father mending their nets, and he-called them. 22So instantly having-excused [=having left] the boat and their father, they-followed him.

Mark 1:16-20

16And passing-by[a] along [=along] the sea of-the Galilee, he-saw Simon and Andrew the brother of-Simon[b], throwing-a-net in the sea, for they-were fishers. 17And Jesus said to-them, "Come-on! behind me and I-will-do [=I will make] you to-happen [=become] fishers of-people." 18And immediately[c] having-excused [=having left] the nets, they-followed him. 19And having-advanced [a] little[d] he-saw James the [son] of-Zebedee and John his brother, and they [were] in the boat mending the nets, 20and immediately he-called them. And having-excused [=having left] their father Zebedee in the boat with the hired-laborers, they-went-away behind him.

John 1:35-51

35On-the next-day again John and two out [of] his disciples had-stood [=were standing around] 36and having-beheld Jesus walking-around he-says, "Look, the lamb of-god." 37And the two disciples heard him talking and they-followed Jesus. 38So Jesus, having-been-turned and having-noticed them following says to-them, "What are-you-searching [for]?" So they-said to-him, "Rabbi," which being-translated says [=means] teacher, "wheresoever are-you-staying?" 39He-says to-them, "Come and you-will-see." Therefore they-came and saw wheresoever he-stays, and they-stayed along [=with] him that day. It-was like [=about the] tenth hour. 40Andrew the brother of-Simon Peter was one out of-the two having-heards along [=who had been listening to] John and having-followeds [=who was following] him. 41This [one] finds the [=his] own brother Simon first and says to-him, "We-have-found the messiah," which is being-translated anointed-one. 42He-led him to-Jesus. Having-beheld him, Jesus said, "You are Simon the son of-John; you [yourself] will-be-called Cephas" which is-meant [=means] Peter. 43On-the next-day he-wished to-go-out into the Galilee and he-finds Philip. And Jesus says to-him, "Follow me." 44So [=Now] Philip was from Bethsaida, out of-the city of-Andrew and Peter. 45Philip finds Nathanael and says to-him, "We-have-found [the one about] whom Moses in the law and [about whom] the prophets wrote, Jesus son of-Joseph from Nazaret." 46And Nathanael said to-him, "Is-able some [thing] good to-be out [=to come from] Nazaret?" Philip says to-him, "Come and see." 47Jesus saw Nathanael coming to him and says around [=concerning] him, "Look, truly [an] Israelite in whom there-is no cunning." 48Nathanael says to-him, "From-where do-you-know me?" And Jesus answered and said to-him, "Before Philip yelled [for] you, I-saw you being under the fig-tree." 49Nathanael answered him, "Rabbi, you [yourself] are the son of-god, you [yourself] are king of-Israel." 50Jesus answered and said to-him, "Do-you-believe that [=because] I-said to-you that 'I-saw you beneath the fig-tree'? You-will-see greater [things] of-these [=than these]." [51]And he-says to-him, "Amen amen I-say to-you, you-will-see heaven having-been-opened and the announcers [=angels] of-god ascending and descending upon the son of-the person."

[a] *And passing-by* ℵ B D f^{13} 33 892 1342 2427 it vg cop; *So walking-around* A W Θ f^{1} 1006 1506 𝔐; *So passing-by* 565 700 983 *pc*; *And walking-around* sy[s] sy[p].
[b] *the brother of-Simon* ℵ A B Δ L f^{1} f^{13} 205 565 700 892 2427; *his brother* D G W Θ 33 579 1342 2542 it[mss] vg sy[s] sy[p] cop[bo].
[c] *immediately* ℵ L Θ 33 892 *pc*; *instantly* A B C D W f^{1} f^{13} 1006 1342 1506 2427 𝔐.
[d] *little* B D L W Θ f^{1} f^{13} 33 205 565 579 892 1424 2427; *from-there* ℵ*; *little from-there* ℵ[2] C 1006 1342 1506 𝔐 it[mss] vg.
📖 Jn 1:51 – Gen 28:12

SYNOPTIC STUDY GUIDE 5

The Griesbach/Two-Gospel Hypothesis

J. J. Griesbach (1745-1812) was the pioneer of the modern synopsis, and of the critical study of the gospels. He was among the earliest in the modern period to take seriously that there was a literary relationship between and among the Synoptic Gospels (see Synoptic Study Guide 1). Griesbach argued that Matthew was the earliest gospel written (Matthean Priority). We can therefore know little about that gospel's sources. The writer of Luke came next, taking a good part of Matthew over and adding about 500 verses of his own material. The author of Mark then came third and conflated both longer gospels to create a shorter gospel. The author of Mark exercises very little creativity here (there are only about 12 verses unique to Mark). Q is not necessary in this hypothesis because it is simply material that Luke took directly from Matthew but that Mark did not take.

Two assumptions common at the time likely propelled Griesbach toward his solution: that Matthew appears first in the New Testament because it was the earliest and most authoritative gospel; and that Christianity as we know it emerged from a contest between Jewish Christianity (represented by the Gospel of Matthew) and Gentile Christianity (represented by the Gospel of Luke and the letters of Paul), which the author of Mark forged into a new universal movement by bringing those two branches together. Griesbach argued that the writer of Mark moved back and forth in blocks between Matthew and Luke in his synthesis of Jewish and Gentile Christianities. There is some merit to this.

Assuming that Mark used Matthew and Luke, if you look back from here, you'll see that Mark 1:1-20 is most closely parallel to Matthew 3:1-4:22 (the only exceptions being that the author of Mark has left out §17 and postponed §20 and §28; but otherwise the stories and their order come from Matthew). Then at Mark 1:21 (§59), the writer of Mark appears to put Matthew down and pick up Luke, following Luke's stories and order for the next 13 pericopae (as far as Mark 3:19, leaving out only one Lukan story (§64) in this section and rearranging none).

In a sense, then, Griesbach understood Mark as a lesser gospel: less original and less important. The more modern name for this hypothesis, Two-Gospel Hypothesis, makes sense as it implies that there are *two* gospels at the heart of the New Testament, Matthew and Luke; and Mark is a digested summary of the two, contributing little to the story.

Mark 1:20 (§29, p. 22) Q 4:16 (§25, p. 18)
Luke 4:30 (§38, p. 21)

Matthew's Sermon on the Mount

30. The Occasion of Matthew's Sermon

Matt 4:23-5:1

23And[a] he-was-leading-around in [the] whole [of] the Galilee teaching in their synagogues and
preaching the proclamation of-the kingdom and healing all [=every] disease and all [=every]
sickness in [=among] the whole-people. 24And the rumor of-him went-away into whole [=all]
Syria; and they-offered to-him all the havings [= those who were sick] badly, [those who were] being-
controlled [by] various diseases and torments,[b] being-demon-possesseds [=demoniacs] and being-
epileptics [=epileptics] and paralytics, and he-healed them. 25And many crowds followed him from
the Galilee and Decapolis and Jerusalems and Judea and beyond the Jordan. 5:1So having-seen the
crowds he-ascended into the mountain and his having-been-seated [=when he had sat down] his
disciples approached him.

[a] *omit* B it cop^{sa}; *Jesus* ℵ C D W f^1 f^{13} 33 892 1424 𝔐 it^{mss} vg sy cop^{bo}.
[b] *omit* B C* f^{13} 892 pc; *and* ℵ C^2 D W f^1 33 1006 1506 𝔐 it vg cop^{sa}.

31. The Beatitudes (→ §74, §75)

Matt 5:2-12	Q 6:20-23	Luke 6:20-23	Thomas 54; 68; 69
2And having-opened his mouth he-taught them saying, 3"Fortunate [are] the poors in-the spirit, that [=because] theirs is the kingdom of-the heavens.	20And having-lifted-up his eyes into [=to] his disciples, saying, "Fortunate [are] the poors that [=because] y'all's-own [reward] is the kingdom of-god.	20And he, having-lifted-up his eyes into [=to] his disciples, was-saying, "Fortunate [are] the poors that [=because] y'all's-own [reward] is the kingdom of-god.	54"Fortunate are the poor, for to you belongs Heaven's kingdom."
4Fortunate [are] the languishings [=those who languish], that [=because] they [themselves] will-be-exhorted [=will be comforted]. 5Fortunate [are] the gentles, that [=because] they [themselves] will-inherit the land.			
6Fortunate [are] the hungerings [=those who hunger] and the being-thirsties [=those who thirst for] righteousness, that [=because] they [themselves] will-be-fed.	21Fortunate [are] the hungerings [=those who hunger], that [=because] you-will-be-fed.	21Fortunate [are] the hungerings [=those who hunger] now, that [=because] you-will-be-fed.	

Mark 1:20 (§29, p. 22) **Q 4:16 (§25, p. 18)**
Luke 4:30 (§38, p. 21)

	Fortunate [are] the languishings [=those who languish], that [=because] you-will-be-comforted.	Fortunate [are] the weepings [=those who weep] now, that [=because] you-will-laugh.	
7Fortunate [are] the mercifuls, that [=because] they [themselves] will-be-mercifulled [=will be shown mercy]. 8Fortunate [are] the pures [=those who are pure] in-the heart, that [=because] they [themselves] will-see god. 9Fortunate [are] the peacemakers, that [=because] they [themselves] will-be-called sons [=children] of-god. 10Fortunate [are] the having-been-pursueds [=those who are pursued] because-of righteousness, that [=because] theirs is the kingdom of-the heavens.			
11Fortunate are-you whenever they-might-denounce you and they-might-pursue [you] and they-might-say all evil, lying[a], according-to [=against] you because-of me. 12Rejoice and be-glad, that [=because] your wages [will be] many [=great] in the heavens; for thus they-pursued the prophets before you."	22Fortunate are-you whenever they-might-denounce you and they-might-pursue [you] and they-might-say all evil according-to [=against] you because-of the son of-the person. 23Rejoice and be-glad, that [=because] your wages [will be] many [=great] in heaven; for thus they-pursued the prophets before you."	22Fortunate are-you whenever the people might-hate you, and whenever they-might-exclude you and they-might-denounce [you] and they-might-cast-out your name like [=as] evil because-of the son of-the person. 23Rejoice in that day and leap [for joy], for look! your wages [will be] many [=great] in heaven. For their fathers were-doing according-to the them[b] [=the same things] to-the prophets."	68Jesus said, "Fortunate are you when you are hated and persecuted; and no place will be found, wherever you have been persecuted." 69Jesus said, "Fortunate are those those who have been persecuted in their hearts: they are the ones who have truly come to know the Father."

[a] *lying* ℵ B C W Δ Θ f^1 f^{13} 28 33 892 1006 1424 𝔐 it^{mss} vg sy^c sy^p cop; *omit* D it^{mss} sy^s.
[b] *the them* 𝔭^{75} B D Q W Ξ Ψ 33^c 892 *pc*; *these* ℵ A L Θ f^1 f^{13} 33* 1006 1342 1506 𝔐 it vg.
📖 Mt 5:5 – Ps 37:11

32. The Parable of the Salt (→ §187, §263)

Matt 5:13	Mark 9:50	Q 14:34-35	Luke 14:34-35
13“You are the salt of-the land; so [=but] if-ever the salt might-become-tasteless, in what [=how] will-it-be-made-salty?	50“The salt [is] fine, so [=but] if-ever the salt might-happen [=becomes] unsalty, in what will-you-flavor it [=will you use it as flavoring]? Have salt in themselves [=yourselves] and be-at-peace in [=with] one-another.”	34“The salt [is] fine so if-ever the salt might-become-tasteless, in what will-it-be-flavored [=will it be used as flavoring]?	34“Therefore[b] the salt [is] fine, and so[c] if-ever the salt might-become-tasteless, in what will-it-be-flavored [=will it be used as flavoring]?
		35Neither into [=for the] land neither [=nor] into [=for the] dung-heap is-it usable;	35Neither into [=for the] land neither [=nor] into [=for the] dung-heap is-it usable;
It-has-the-strength into no-one [=It is good for nothing] yet if no [=except], having-been-thrown[a] outside, to-be-tread-upon under [=by] the people.”		they-throw it outside.”	they-throw it outside.
			The [one] having ears to-hear, let-him-hear.”

[a] *having-been-thrown* 𝔓^{86} ℵ B C f^1 33 205 892 *pc*; *to-be-thrown* D W Θ f^{13} 1006 1342 1506 𝔐.
[b] *Therefore* 𝔓^{75} ℵ B L Θ f^{13} 579 892 *pc*; *omit* A D W Ψ f^1 1006 1506 𝔐 it vg sy cop^{samss}.
[c] *so* ℵ B D L Θ Ψ 0233 579 *pc* it^{mss} sy^p cop^{samss}; *omit* 𝔓^{75} A W f^1 f^{13} 892 1006 1342 1506 𝔐 it^{mss} vg sy^s sy^c cop.

33. The Parable of the Light (→ §220)

Matt 5:14-16	Q 11:33	Luke 11:33	Thomas 33
14“You are the light of-the world. [A] city laying above [=atop a] mountain [is] not able to-be-hidden; 15nor do-they-kindle [a] lantern and put it under the bushel but upon the lamp-stand and it-shines for-all the [ones who are] in the home. 16Thus, let-shine your light in-front of-the people so-that they-might-see your fine works and they-might-glorify your father in the heavens.”	33“No-one kindles [a] lantern and puts it into [a] cellar but upon the lamp-stand it-shines for-all the [ones who are] in the home.”	33“No-one having-touched [=having lit a] lantern puts [it] into [a] cellar nor under the bushel[a] but upon the lamp-stand, in-order-that the traveling-ins [=those who enter] might-look [at] the light.”	Jesus said, “What you will hear in your ear, in the other ear proclaim from your rooftops. After all, no one lights a lamp and puts it under a basket, nor does one put it in a hidden place. Rather, one puts it on a lampstand so that all who come and go will see its light.”

[a] *nor under the bushel* ℵ A B C D W Θ Ψ f^{13} 𝔐 it vg sy^c sy^p; *omit* 𝔓^{45} 𝔓^{75} L Γ Ξ 070 f^1 700* 1241 2542 *pc* sy^s cop^{sa}.

34. The Law and the Prophets (→ §273)

Matt 5:17-20

[17]“Think no [=not] that I-came to-demolish the law or
the prophets; I-came not to-demolish but to-fulfill.
[18]For amen I-say to-you, until ever might-pass-away
the heaven and the land, no [=not] one iota or one
stroke [=hook of a letter] might-pass-away not from
the law, until ever all [this] might-happen. [19]Therefore,
who if-ever might-loose [=might abolish] one of-the
least of-these commandments and might-teach the
people thus will-be-called least in the kingdom of-the
heavens; so [=but] who ever might-do and might-teach
[the commandments], this [one] will-be-called great in
the kingdom of-the heavens. [20]For I-say to-you that
if-ever your righteousness might-exceed no more [than
that of] the scribes and Pharisees, you-might-enter
not no [=at all] into the kingdom of-the heavens.”

There are no variants in this pericope that appear in English.

Q 16:17

[17]“So, it is easier [for]
the heaven and the land
to-pass-away or [=than
for] one stroke [=hook of a
letter] of-the law to-fall.”

Luke 16:17

[17]“So, it-is easier [for]
the heaven and the land
to-pass-away or [=than
for] one stroke [=hook of a
letter] of-the law to-fall.”

35. Murder, Wrath, and Resolution (→ §243)

Matt 5:21-26

[21]“You-heard that it-was-said to-the ancients, ‘YOU-
WILL-MURDER NOT.’ So, who ever might-murder,
he-will-be answerable to-judgment. [22]So [=But] I
[myself] say to-you that all the [=anyone] being-angered
[with] his brother will-be answerable to-judgment.
So, who ever might-say [to] his brother, ‘Fool’, he-will
[be] answerable to-the Sanhedrin. So [=And] who ever
might-say ‘Moronic’, will-be answerable into [=to] the
Gehenna of-fire. [23]Therefore, if-ever you-might-offer
your gift upon the sacrificial-altar and-there might-
remember that your brother has some [grievance]
according-to [=against] you, [24]excuse [=leave] your gift
there in-front of-the sacrificial-altar and leave, make-
peace first [with] your brother, and then having-come
offer your gift. [25]Be making-friends quickly [with] your
opponent until whoever [=while] you-are with him in
[=on] the way [to court], lest the opponent might-deliver
you to-the judge and the judge [a] to-the attendant,
and you-will-be-thrown into prison. [26]Amen I-say
to-you, you-might-go-out not no [=at all] from-there
until ever you-might-give-over the last quadrans.”

Q 12:58-59

[58]“Until whoever [=While
you are] with your
opponent in [=on] the
way [to court], give [an]
effort to-be-resolved from
[=to settle the case with]
him, lest your opponent
might-deliver you to-
the judge, and the judge
to-the attendant, and the
attendant will-throw you
into prison. [59]I-say to-you,
you-might-go-out not
no [=at all] from-there
until the last quadrans
you-might-give-over.”

Luke 12:58-59

[58]“For like [=when] you-
leave with your opponent
upon [=to go to the]
magistrate, in [=on] the
way [to court] give [an]
effort to-be-resolved from
[=to settle the case with]
him, lest he-might-drag
you to the judge, and
the judge will-deliver[b]
you to-the bailiff and the
bailiff will-throw you into
prison. [59]I-say to-you,
you-might-go-out not no
[=at all] from-there until
and [=even] the last lepton
you-might-give-over.”

[a] *omit* 𝔓[64] ℵ B *f*[1] *f*[13] 205 892 *pc*; *might-deliver you* D L W Θ 33 1006 1342 1506 𝔐 it[mss] vg sy[c] sy[p].
[b] *will-deliver* 𝔓[45] ℵ A B D E *f*[13] 579 2427 *pc*; *might-deliver* L W Ψ *f*[1] 33 892 1006 1342 1506 𝔐.
📖 Mt 5:21 – Exod 20:13; Deut 5:17

36. Matthew's Jesus on Adultery

Matt 5:27-30

27“You-heard that it-was-said, ‘YOU-WILL-COMMIT-ADULTERY NOT,’ 28so [=but] I [myself] say to-you that all the lookings [=those who look at a] woman to [=in order] to-desire her already committed-adultery [with] her in his heart. 29So [=And] if your right eye causes-to-stumble you, pull-out it and throw [it] from you; for it-is-profitable for-you in-order-that one [of] your body-parts might-be-destroyed and [that] your whole body might-be-thrown no [=not] into Gehenna. 30And if your right hand causes-to-stumble you, cut-off it and throw [it] from you; for it-is-profitable for-you in-order-that one [of] your body-parts might-be-destroyed and [that] your whole body might-go-away[a] no [=not] into Gehenna.”

[a] *might-go-away* ℵ B f^1 33 205 892 *pc* sy^{c} cop^{bo}; *might-be-thrown* L W Θ f^{13} 1006 1342 2506 𝔐 it^{mss} vg^{mss} sy^{p} cop^{sa}.
🕮 Mt 5:27 – Exod 20:14; Deut 5:18

37. Jesus on Divorce (→ §274)

Matt 5:31-32	Q 16:18	Luke 16:18
31“So it-was-said, ‘WHO EVER MIGHT-RELEASE [=might divorce] HIS WOMAN [=wife] LET-HIM-GIVE HER [a] BILL-OF-DIVORCE.’ 32So [=But] I [myself] say to-you		
that all the [=every person] releasing his woman [=wife] except-for [the] word [=matter] of-fornication	18“All the [=every person] releasing his woman [=wife]	18“All the [=every person] releasing his woman [=wife]
does [=causes] her to-commit-adultery, and who if-ever might-marry [a] having-been-released [=divorcée] becomes-an-adulterer.”	and marrying another commits-adultery, and the [one] marrying [a] having-been-released [=divorcée] commits-adultery.”	and marrying [an] other commits-adultery, and the[a] [one] marrying [a] having-been-released [=divorcée] from [a] man commits-adultery.”

[a] *the* 𝔓^{75} B D L 69 788 983 2542 *pc* vg it^{mss} sy^{s} cop; *all the* ℵ A W Θ Ψ f^1 f^{13} 892 1006 1342 1506 𝔐 sy^{p} sy^{h}.
🕮 Mt 5:31 – Deut 24:1

38. Matthew's Jesus on Oaths

Matt 5:33-37

33“Again you-heard that it-was-said to-the ancients, ‘YOU-WILL-SWEAR-FALSELY NOT, SO [but] YOU-WILL-GIVE-OVER YOUR SWORN-OATHS TO-THE LORD.’ 34So [=But] I [myself] say to-you no [=not] to-vow at-all, not-even in [=on] the heaven, that [=because] it-is [the] throne of-god; 35not-even in [=on] the land [=earth], that [=because] it-is [a] footstool [of] his feet; not-even into [=on] Jerusalems, that [=because] it-is [a] city of-the great king; 36you-might-vow not-even in [=on] your head, that [=because] you-are-able not to-do [=to make even] one hair white or black; 37so let-be your word [=speech] yes yes [or] not not; so [=but] the excessive of-these [=anything more than this] is out of-the [=comes from the] evil [one].”

There are no variants in this pericope that appear in English.
🕮 Mt 5:33 – Exod 20:7; Lev 19:12

39. Retaliation (→ §78)

Matt 5:38-42	Q 6:29-30	Luke 6:29-30	Thomas 95
38“You-heard that it-was-said, ‘[An] EYE IN-PLACE [of an] EYE, AND [a] TOOTH IN-PLACE [of a] TOOTH.’ 39So [=But] I [myself] say to-you no [=not] to-resist the evil [one].			
But whoever slaps[a] you into[b] [=on] your right cheek, turn to-him and [=also] the another [=other]; 40and to-the [one] wishing to-judge you and to-take your tunic, excuse [=offer] him and the [=also your] coat; 41and whoever will-enlist you [for] one mile, leave [=go] with him [for] two.	29“Whoever slaps you into [=on] your cheek, turn to-him and [=also] the another [=other]; and to-the [one] wishing to-judge you and to-take your tunic, excuse [=offer] him and the [=also your] coat; and whoever will-enlist you [for] one mile, leave [=go] with him [for] two.	29“To-the [one] hitting you upon the cheek, present and [=also] the another [=other]; and from the [one] removing your coat may-you-hinder [=withhold] no and [=not even your] tunic.	
42Give to-the [one] asking [of] you, and may-you-turn-away no [=do not refuse] the [one] wishing to-loan [=to borrow] from you.”	30Give to-the [one] asking [of] you, and from the [one] lending [=borrowing] the [things of] yours demand-back no [=not].”	30Give to-all asking [of] you[c], and from the [one] removing your-own [things] demand-back no [=not].”	<Jesus said>, “If you have money, don’t lend it at interest. Rather, give <it> to someone from whom you won’t get it back.”

[a] *slaps* ℵ B W 33 700 1424 *pc*; *will-slap* D L Θ f^1 f^{13} 892 1006 1342 1506 𝔐 cop[bo].
[b] *into* ℵ* B W 983 1342; *upon* ℵ[2] D L Θ f^1 f^{13} 33 892 1006 1506 𝔐.
[c] *Give to-all asking you* ℵ B W 579 700 892* *pc*; *Give to-all the asking you* L f^1 205 565 1006 1424 1506 2542 *pc*; *So give to-all the asking you* A D Θ Ψ f^{13} 33 892[c] 1342 𝔐 it[mss] vg.
🕮 Mt 5:38 – Exod 21:24; Lev 24:20; Deut 19:21

40. Loving One’s Enemies and Having Mercy (→ §77, §80, §81)

Matt 5:43-48	Q 6:27-28, 32, 34-36	Luke 6:27-28, 32-36
43“You-heard that it-was-said, ‘YOU-WILL-LOVE YOUR NEIGHBOR AND YOU-WILL-HATE YOUR ENEMY.’ 44So [=But] I [myself] say to-you ‘Love your enemies and pray on-behalf of-the	27“Love your enemies 28and	27“But I-say to-you, to-the hearings [=to those willing to hear], ‘Love your enemies, do well to-the hatings [=to those who hate] you, 28bless the cursings [=those who curse] you, pray around[c]
pursuings [=of those who pursue] you[a], 45so-that you-might-happen [=you might become] sons [of] your father in [the] heavens, that [=because] he-arises his sun upon [the] evil and [the] good [alike] and it-rains upon [the] righteous and	pray on-behalf of-the pursuings [=of those who pursue] you.	[=concerning] the mistreatings [=those who mistreat] you.

[the] unrighteous. 46For if-ever you-
might-love the lovings [=those who
love] you, what wages do-you-have?
[Do] indeed-not and [=even] the
tax-collectors do the it [=same thing]?

47And if-ever you-might-greet your
brothers only, what do-you-do [that
is] excessive [=more than what others
do]? [Do] indeed-not and [=even] the
Gentiles[b] do the it [=same thing]?

48Therefore you [yourselves]
will-be perfect like your
heavenly father is perfect."

32If you-love the lovings [=those who
love] you, what wages do-you-have?

[Do] indeed-not and [=even] the
tax-collectors do the it [=same thing]?

34And if-ever you-might-lend
[to someone] along [=from]
whom you-hope to-take,
what wages do-you-have?

[Do] indeed-not and [=even] the
Gentiles do the it [=same thing]?

35so-that you-might-happen [=you
might become] sons [of] your father,
that [=because] he-arises his sun
upon [the] evil and [the] good [alike]
and it-rains upon [the] righteous
and [the] unrighteous. 36Happen
[=Become] compassionate like
your father is compassionate."

32And if you-love the lovings
[=those who love] you, what-kind-of
benefaction is [there] for-you? For
and [=even] the sinfuls [=those
who are sinful] love the lovings
[=those who love] them.
33And for if-ever you-might-do-
good to-the doing-goods [=those
who do good] to-you, what-kind-of
benefaction is [there] for-you? And[d]
[=Even] the sinfuls [=those who are
sinful] do the it [=same thing].
34And if-ever you-might-loan [to
someone] along [=from] whom
you-hope to-take, what-kind-of
benefaction is [there] for-you? And
[=Even] sinfuls [=those who are sinful]
loan to-sinfuls [=to those who are
sinful] in-order-that they-might-
receive-back the equal [amount].

35Nevertheless love your enemies
and do-good and loan hoping-for
not-one [=nothing], and your wages
will-be many [=great], and you-will-
be sons [of the] most-high, that
[=because] he [himself] is kind upon
[=to the] thankless and [the] evil.

36Happen [=Become]
compassionate just-as[e] your
father is compassionate."

[a] *pray on-behalf of-the pursuings you* ℵ B f^{1} 205 *pc* sy^{c} sy^{s} cop; *bless the cursings you, do well to-the hatings you, pray around the mistreatings you and the pursuings you* D L W f^{13} 33 892 1006 1342 1506 𝔐 it^{mss} vg sy^{p}.
[b] *Gentiles* ℵ B D Z f^{1} 33 205 892 1424 *pc* it^{mss} vg sy^{c} cop; *tax-collectors* L W Θ f^{13} 1006 1342 1506 𝔐 sy^{p}.
[c] *around* 𝔓^{75} ℵ B L W Ξ 579 700 *pc*; *on-behalf* A D Θ Ψ f^{1} f^{13} 33 892 1006 1342 1506 𝔐 it vg.
[d] *And* ℵ B W 700 892* *pc* sy^{s}; *For and* A D L Θ Ξ Ψ f^{13} 33 892^{c} 1006 1342 1506 𝔐 it^{mss} vg sy^{p}.
[e] *omit* ℵ B L W Ξ Ψ f^{1} 205 579 *pc* it^{mss} sy^{s} cop; *and* A D Θ f^{13} 33 892 1006 1342 𝔐 it^{mss} vg sy^{p}.
🕮 Mt 5:43 – Lev 19:18

41. Matthew's Jesus on Almsgiving

Matt 6:1-4

1"Pay-close-attention[a] no [=not] to-do your righteousness in-front
of-the people to [in order] to-be-noticed [by] them; so [=but] if no
in-effect [=if you do this], you-have no wages [=reward] in-front
[of] your father in the heavens. 2Therefore, whenever you-might-
do almsgiving, you-might-sound-a-trumpet no [=not] in-front
of-you, even-as the hypocrites do in the synagogues and in the
laneways, so-that they-might-be-glorified under [=by] the people.
Amen I-say to-you they-receive-in-full their wages. 3So [when]
doing your almsgiving, let-know no [=not] your left-hand what

Thomas 62

Jesus said, "I disclose my mysteries to those <who are worthy> of <my> mysteries. Do not let your left hand know what your right hand is doing."

your right [hand] does, 4so-that your almsgiving might-be in the hidden [=secret], and your father looking [=watching] in the hidden [=secret] will-give-over [a reward] to-you[b]."

[a] *Pay-close-attention* B D W f^{13} 1006 1342 1506 𝔐 it^{mss} vg sy^{c}; *So, pay-close-attention* ℵ L Z Θ f^{1} 33 205 892 1424 sy^{p} cop^{bo}.
[b] *will-give over to-you* ℵ B D Z f^{1} f^{13} 33 205 it^{mss} vg sy^{c} cop; *will-give-over to-you in the known* L W Θ 892 1006 1342 1506 𝔐 it sy^{s} sy^{p}.

42. Matthew's Jesus on Prayer

Matt 6:5-6

5"And whenever you-might-pray, you-will-be not like the hypocrites, that [=because] they-like to-pray in the synagogues and having-stood in [=on] the corners of-the wide-streets, so-that they-might-appear to-the [=they might be seen by] people. Amen I-say to-you they-receive-in-full their wages. 6So [=But] whenever you [yourself] might-pray, enter into your private-room and, having-locked your door, pray [to] your father in the hidden [=secret]; and your father looking [=watching] in the hidden [=secret] will-give-over [a reward] to-you[a]."

Thomas 14

Jesus said to them, "If you fast, you will bring sin upon yourselves, and if you pray, you will be condemned, and if you give to charity, you will harm your spirits. When you go into any region and walk about in the countryside, when people take you in, eat what they serve you and heal the sick among them. After all, what goes into your mouth will not defile you; rather, it's what comes out of your mouth that will defile you."

[a] *will-give-over to-you* ℵ B D Z f^{1} 205 *pc* it^{mss} vg sy^{c} sy^{s} cop; *will-give-over to-you in the known* L W Θ f^{13} 33 892 1006 1342 1506 𝔐 it sy^{p}.

43. The Lord's Prayer (→ §210)

Matt 6:7-13

7"So, praying you-might-babble no [=not] even-as the Gentiles, for they-suppose that in their wordiness they-will-be-paid-attention-to. 8Therefore, be-compared no [=not] to-them, for your father recognizes [that] of-which you-have need before you [yourselves] to-ask [=ask] him. 9Therefore you [yourselves must] pray thus: 'Our father in the heavens, let-be-made-holy your name, 10let-come your kingdom, let-happen your wish like in heaven and [=also] upon land [=earth]. 11Give to-us today our bread [for] the coming-day, 12and excuse us our debts, like and [=also] we [ourselves] excused our debtors. 13And might-you-bring us no [=not] into [a] test, but rescue us from the evil [one][a].'"

Q 11:2-4

2"Whenever you-might-pray say, 'Father, let-be-made-holy your name, let-come your kingdom,

3give to-us today our bread [for] the coming-day, 4and excuse us our debts, like and [=also] we [ourselves] excused our debtors; and might-you-bring us no [=not] into [a] test.'"

Luke 11:1-4

1And it-happened in the to-be him [=while he was] in some place praying, like [=when] he-stopped, some [=one of] his disciples said to him, "Lord, teach us to-pray, just-as and [=even] John taught his disciples." 2So he-said to-them,

"Whenever you-might-pray say, 'Father, let-be-made-holy your name, let-come your kingdom,[b]

3give to-us according-to [a] day [=every day] our bread [for] the coming-day, 4and excuse us our sins, for and [=even] we [ourselves] excuse all [those] being-in-debt to-us; and might-you-bring us no [=not] into [a] test[c].'"

[a] *omit* ℵ B D Z f^{1} 205 *pc* it^{mss} vg; *that the kingdom and the power and the power and the glory is yours into the ages. Amen.* L W Θ f^{13} 33 892 1006 1342 1506 𝔐 it^{mss} sy cop^{sa}; *that the kingdom of-the father and the son and the holy spirit is yours into the ages. Amen.* 1253 *pc*.
[b] *omit* 𝔭^{75} B L f^{1} f^{13}42 *pc* vg sy^{s} sy^{c}; *let-happen your wish like in heaven and upon land* ℵ A C D W Θ Ψ f^{13} 33 892 1006 1506 𝔐 it cop^{bomss}; *let-happen your wish* vg^{mss} cop^{sa} cop^{bomss}.
[c] *omit* 𝔭^{75} ℵ* B L f^{1} 700 vg sy^{s} cop^{sa}; *but rescue us from the evil* A C D W Θ Ψ f^{13} 33 892 1006 1506 𝔐 it vg^{mss} sy^{c} sy^{p}.

44. The Conditions for Prayer (→ §311)

Matt 6:14-15

14“For if-ever you-might-excuse [=you might forgive]
the people their wrongdoings, your heavenly father
will-excuse [=will forgive] and [=also] you; 15so [=but]
if-ever you-might-excuse no [=not] the people, nor
[=neither] your father will-excuse your wrongdoings.”

Mark 11:25-26

25“And whenever you-persevere praying,
excuse [=forgive] if you-have some [=anything]
according-to [=against] some [=anyone], in-order-
that and [=also] your father in the heavens,
might-excuse you your wrongdoings.”[a]

[a] *omit* ℵ B L W Δ Ψ 205 565 700 892 2427 *pc* it^{mss} sy^{c} cop^{sa}; 26*So if you excuse not, nor your father in the heavens, will-excuse your wrongdoings.* A C D Θ *f*^{1} *f*^{13} 33 1342 1506 𝔐 it^{mss} vg sy^{p}.

45. Matthew’s Jesus on Fasting

Matt 6:16-18

16“So, whenever you-might-fast, happen [=become] no [=not] like[a] the gloomy hypocrites, for
they-disfigure their faces, so-that they-might-appear to-the people [to be] fasting; amen I-say
to-you,[b] they-receive-in-full their wages. 17So [=But when] you [are] fasting, smear your head and
wash your face, 18so-that you-might-appear no [=not] to-the people [=to be] fasting but [to] your
father in hiding[c], and your father looking [=watching] in hiding[c] will-give-over [a reward] to-you.”

[a] *like* ℵ B D Δ *f*^{1} 205 892 *pc*; *even-as* L E Θ *f*^{13} 33 1006 1342 1506 𝔐.
[b] *omit* ℵ B D 0233 0250 *f*^{1} *f*^{13} 205 565 700 1506 it; *that* L W Θ 33 892 1006 1342 𝔐 it^{mss} vg.
[c] *in hiding* ℵ B *f*^{1} *pc*; *in hidden* L W Θ *f*^{13} 33 892 1006 1342 1506 𝔐.

46. Treasures (→ §233, §237)

Matt 6:19-21

19“Store-treasure no [=not]
to-you [in] treasure-
boxes upon the land
[=earth], where moth and
rust disfigures [it] and
where thieves break-in
and steal [it], 20so [=but]
store-treasure to-you
[in] treasure-boxes in
heaven where neither
moth neither [=nor]
rust disfigures and
where thieves break-
in not nor steal [it].
21For where [ever] your
treasure-box is, there will-
be and [=also] your heart.”

Q 12:33-34

33“Store-treasure no [=not]
to-you [in] treasure-
boxes upon the land
[=earth], where moth and
rust disfigures [it] and
where thieves break-in
and steal [it], so [=but]
store-treasure to-you
[in] treasure-boxes in
heaven where neither
moth neither [=nor] rust
disfigures and where
thieves break-in not
neither [=nor] steal [it].
34For where [ever] your
treasure-box is, there will-
be and [=also] your heart.”

Luke 12:33-34

33“Sell your being-at-one’s-
disposals [=belongings]
and give almsgiving;

do [=make] for-themselves
[=yourselves] moneybags
[that are] no [=not]
becoming-old, [a] never-
decreasing treasure-box
in the heavens where
thief nears not nor
moth corrupts;

34for where your
treasure-box is, there
and [=also] your
heart will-be.”

Thomas 76

Jesus said, “The Father’s
kingdom is like a
merchant who had a
supply of merchandise
and found a pearl. That
merchant was prudent;
he sold the merchandise
and bought the single
pearl for himself. So
also with you, seek his
treasure that is unfailing,
that is enduring, where
no moth comes to eat
and no worm destroys.”

There are no variants in this pericope that appear in English.

47. The Healthy Eye (→ §221)

Matt 6:22-23	Q 11:34-35	Luke 11:34-36	Thomas 24
22“The lantern of-the body is the eye. Therefore, if-ever your eye might-be unencumbered[a] [=functioning properly], your whole body will-be full-of-light. 23So [=But] if-ever your eye might-be evil, your whole body will-be darksome. Therefore, if the light [which is] in you is darkness, how-great [must be] the darkness?”	34“The lantern of-the body is the eye. If-ever your eye, unencumbered [=functioning properly] might-be your whole body is full-of-light. So [=But] ever your eye might-be evil, your whole body and [=also is] darksome. 35Therefore, if the light [which is] in you is darkness, how-great [must be] the darkness?”	34“The lantern of-the body is your eye. [b] Whenever your eye unencumbered [=functioning properly] might-be, and [=also] your whole body is full-of-light. So [=But] as-soon-as it-might-be evil, your body and [=also is] darksome. 35Therefore be-concerned no [=not lest] the light in you is [actually] darkness. 36Therefore, if your whole body [is] full-of-light, no [=not] having some part darksome, [then the] whole will-be full-of-light like whenever the lantern might-illumine you in-the flashing-light.”	His disciples said, “Show us the place where you are, for we must seek it.” He said to them, “Anyone here with two ears had better listen! There is light within a person of light, and it shines on the whole world. If it does not shine, it is dark.”

[a] *if-ever your eye might-be unencumbered* ℵ B W 1342 *pc* it^{mss} vg; *if-ever unencumbered might-be your eye* L Θ f^1 f^{13} 33 892 1005 1506 𝔐 it.
[b] *omit* $𝔭^{45}$ $𝔭^{75}$ ℵ B D L W 070 579 *pc*; *Therefore* A C Θ Ψ f^1 f^{13} 33 892 1006 1342 1506 𝔐 sy.

48. Loyalty to Two Masters (→ §264, §270)

Matt 6:24	Q 16:13	Luke 16:13	Thomas 47
24“No-one [a] is-able to-be-a-slave for-two lords; for or [=either] he-will-hate the one, and he-will-love the other, or he-will-hold-fast [to the] one and he-will-despise the other. You-are-able not to-be-a-slave to-god and to-money.”	13“No-one is-able to-be-a-slave for-two lords; for or [=either] he-will-hate the one, and he-will-love the other, or he-will-hold-fast [to the] one and he-will-despise the other. You-are-able not to-be-a-slave to-god and to-money.”	13“No-one [=No] house-slave is-able to-be-a-slave for-two lords; for or [=either] he-will-hate the one, and he-will-love the other, or he-will-hold-fast [to the] one and he-will-despise the other. You-are-able not to-be-a-slave to-god and to-money.”	Jesus said, “A person cannot mount two horses or bend two bows. And a slave cannot serve two masters, otherwise that slave will honor the one and offend the other. Nobody drinks aged wine and immediately wants to drink young wine. Young wine is not poured into old wineskins, or they might break, and aged wine is not poured into a new wineskin, or it might spoil. An old patch is not sewn onto a new garment, since it would create a tear.”

[a] *omit* ℵ B D f^1 f^{13} 33 892 1006 1342 1506 𝔐 vg; *house-servant* L Δ 1242 *pc*.

49. Anxiety (→ §236)

Matt 6:25-34	Q 12:22-31	Luke 12:22-32	Thomas 36
25 “Through [=Because of] this, I-say to-you, worry no [=not about] your soul [=life] what you-might-eat, or what you-might-drink[a], so-not [=nor for] your body, [in] what you-might-be-clothed.	22 “Through [=Because of] this I-say to-you, worry no [=not about] your soul[d] [=life], what you-might-eat, so-not [=nor for] your body, [in] what you-might-be-clothed.	22 So he-said to his disciples[e], “Through [=Because of] this I-say to-you, worry no [=not about] the soul[d] [=life], what you-might-eat, so-not [=nor for] the body, [in] what you-might-be-clothed.	Jesus said, “Do not fret, from morning to evening and from evening to morning, <about your food—what you’re going to eat, or about your clothing—> what you are going to wear.
Is indeed-not the soul [=life] more [than] nourishment and the body [more than] clothes?	23 Is indeed-not the soul [=life] more [than] nourishment and the body [more than] clothes?	23 For the soul [=life] is more [than] nourishment and the body [more than] clothes.	
26 Behold into [=Look at] the birds of-heaven, that they-sow not nor do-they-harvest nor do-they-gather into storehouses, and your heavenly father nourishes them.	24 Think-about the crows, that they-sow not nor do-they-harvest, nor do-they-gather into storehouses, and god nourishes them.	24 Think-about the crows, that they-sow not nor do-they-harvest, to-whom there-is not [a] private-room nor storehouse, and god nourishes them.	
Are-superior rather not you of-them [=Are you not more important than them]?	Are-superior rather not you of-the birds [=How much more superior must you be than the birds]?	How-great rather you are-superior of-the birds [=How much more superior must you be than the birds]?	
27 So what [=who] out of-you, worrying, is-able to-add one cubit [=day] upon his age?	25 So what [=who] out of-you, worrying, is-able to-add [a] cubit [=day] upon his age?	25 So what [=who] out of-you, worrying, is-able [a] cubit [=day] to-add upon his age?	
		26 Therefore, if you-are-able [to change] nor [=not even the] least, what [=why] do-you-worry around [=concerning] the remainders [=rest]?	
28 And what [=why] do-you-worry around [=concerning] clothes?	26 And what [=why] do-you-worry around [=concerning] clothes?		
Observe the lilies of-the field, how they-grow; they-labor not nor do-they-spin[b].	27 Observe the lilies, how it-grows, it-labors not nor spins.	27 Think-about the lilies, how it-grows, it-labors not nor spins.	<You’re much better than the lilies, which neither card nor spin. As for you, when you have no garment, what will you put on? Who might add to your stature?
29 So I-say to-you that, nor [=not even] Solomon, in all his glory, was-arrayed like one of-these. 30 So if god thus dresses the food [=plants] of-the field, today being [alive] and tomorrow being-thrown into [a] furnace, not rather by-many you [=will he not dress	So I-say to-you, nor [=not even] Solomon, in all his glory, was-arrayed like one of-these. 28 So if god thus dresses the food [=plants] in [the] field, being [alive] today and tomorrow being-thrown into [a] furnace, not rather by-many you [=will he not dress you all the more],	So I-say to-you, nor [=not even] Solomon, in all his glory, was-arrayed like one of-these. 28 So if god thus attires the food [=plants] in [the] field, being [alive] today and tomorrow being-thrown into [a] furnace, how-great rather you [=how much more will he dress you], little-loyalties	

you all the more], little-loyalties [you of little faith]? 31 Therefore, you-might-worry no [=not], saying 'What might-we-eat?' or 'What might-we-drink?' or 'What [=How] might-we-be-arrayed? 32 For the nations seek all these [things]; for your heavenly father recognizes that you-need everyone of-these [things].	little-loyalties [you of little faith]? 29 Therefore, you-might-worry no [=not], saying 'What might-we-eat?' or 'What might-we-drink?' or 'What [=How] might-we-be-arrayed? 30 For the nations seek all these [things]; for your father recognizes that you-need everyone of-these [things].	[you of little faith]? 29 And you, search no [=not for] what you-might-eat and what you-might-drink and be-of-doubtful-mind not. 30 For the nations of-the world seek all these [things]; so [=but] your father recognizes that you-need these [things].	
33 So, search [for] his kingdom and righteousness[c] first and all these [things] will-be-added to-you.	31 So, search [for] his kingdom and all these [things] will-be-added to-you."	31 Nevertheless, search [for] his kingdom[f] and these [things] will-be-added to-you.	
34 Therefore, you-might-worry no [=not] into tomorrow, for tomorrow will-worry [about] itself; the wickedness of-it [is] enough [for this] day."		32 Fear no [=not], small fold, that [=because] your father was-content to-give to-you the kingdom."	That very one will give you your garment.>"

[a] *or what you-might-drink* B W f^{13} 33 205 109 1342 it cop^{samss} cop^{bo}; *and what you-might-drink* L Θ 1006 1506 𝔐 sy^{p}; *omit* ℵ f^{1} 892 *pc* it^{mss} sy^{s} cop^{samss}.

[b] *they-grow; they-labor not nor do-they-spin* ℵ^{1} Θ f^{1} 205 sy^{s}; *it-grows; it-labors not nor spins* L f^{13} 892 1006 1342 𝔐.

[c] *his kingdom and righteousness* ℵ it^{mss} cop^{sa} cop^{bo}; *his righteousness and kingdom* B; *the kingdom of-god and his righteousness* L W Θ f^{1} f^{13} 33 892 1006 1342 1506 𝔐 it^{mss} vg sy.

[d] *your soul* 𝔭^{45} Ψ f^{13} 33 892 1006 1342 𝔐 it^{mss} sy^{s} sy^{p} cop; *the soul* 𝔭^{75} ℵ A B D L Q W Θ f^{1} 700 2542 it^{mss} vg sy^{s}.

[e] *his disciples* 𝔭^{75} B *pc* it^{mss}; *the disciples* ℵ A D L W Θ Ψ f^{1} f^{13} 892 1006 1342 1506 𝔐 it^{mss} vg sy cop.

[f] *his kingdom* ℵ B D* L Ψ 579 892 *pc* it^{mss} cop; *the kingdom* 𝔭^{75}; *the kingdom of-god* 𝔭^{45} A D^{1} W Θ f^{1} f^{13} 33 1006 1342 1506 𝔐 it sy.

50. Judging (→ §82, §147)

Matt 7:1-2	Mark 4:24	Q 6:37-38	Luke 6:37-38	John 8:7
1 "Judge no [=not] in-order-that you-might-be-judged no [=not]		37 "Judge no [=not], you-might-be-judged no [=not]	37 "And judge no [=not] and you-might-be-judged not no [=at all], and condemn no [=not] and you-might-be-condemned not no [=at all]. Release and you-will-be-released. 38 Give and it-will-be-given to-you: [a] fine [=good] measure, having-been-pressed-down, having-been-shaken-up, having-	7 So like [=when] they-were-persisting-in begging him, he-straightened-up and said to-them, "The sinless [one among] you, let-him-throw [a] stone upon her first."

			been-overflowed, they-will-give into your bosom; for	
[2]for in [=by] which verdict you-judge you-will-be-judged,	[24]And he-was-saying to-them, "Look [=Take heed of] what you-hear. In [=By]	for in [=by that] verdict which you-judge you-will-be-judged,		
and in [=by] which measure you-measure, it-will-be-measured to-you."	which measure you-measure, it-will-be-measured to-you	[38]and in [=by] which measure you-measure, it-will-be-measured to-you."	[by] which measure[a] you-measure, it-will-be-measured-in-return to-you."	
	and [more] will-be-added to-you."			

[a] *for which measure* ℵ B D L Θ Ξ f^{1} 33 205 892 1342 *pc* sy^{p}; *for the it measure which* A C Θ Ψ f^{13} 1006 1506 𝔐 it^{mss} vg.

51. The Splinter and the Log (→ §85)

Matt 7:3-5	Q 6:41-42	Luke 6:41-42	Thomas 26
[3]"So what [=why] do-you-look [at] the splinter in the eye [of] your brother, so [=but] you-think-about not the log in your-own eye? [4]Or how will-you-say [to] your brother, 'Excuse [=Allow that] I-might-cast-out the splinter out [of] your eye' and look! the log [is] in your eye? [5]Hypocrite, first cast-out out [of] your eye the log[a] and then you-will-see-clearly to-cast-out the splinter out of-the eye [of] your brother."	[41]"So what [=why] do-you-look [at] the splinter in the eye [of] your brother, so [=but] you-think-about not the log in your-own eye? [42]How [will you say to] your brother, 'Excuse [=Allow that] I-might-cast-out the splinter out [of] your eye' and look! the log [is] in your eye? Hypocrite, first cast-out out [of] your eye the log and then you-will-see-clearly to-cast-out the splinter [=out of] the eye [of] your brother."	[41]"So what [=why] do-you-look [at] the splinter in the eye [of] your brother, so [=but] the log in [your] own eye you-think-about not? [42]How are-you-able to-say [to] your brother, 'Brother, excuse [=allow that] I-might-cast-out the splinter in your eye' not looking [=seeing] the log it [=itself] in your eye? Hypocrite, first cast-out the log out [of] your eye and then you-will-see-clearly the splinter in the eye [of] your brother to-cast-out [it]."	Jesus said, "You see the sliver in your friend's eye, but you don't see the timber in your own eye. When you take the timber out of your own eye, then you will see well enough to remove the sliver from your friend's eye."

[a] *cast-out out your eye the log* ℵ B C; *cast-out the log out your eye* L W Θ f^{1} f^{13} 33 892 1342 1506 𝔐 it vg.

52. Matthew's Jesus on Profaning the Holy

Matt 7:6	Thomas 93
[6]"Might-you-give no [=not] the holy to-the dogs so-not [=nor] might-you-throw your pearls in-front of-the pigs, lest they-will-tread-upon[a] them in [=with] their feet and having-been-turned they-might-devastate you."	"Don't give what is holy to dogs, for they might throw them upon the manure pile. Don't throw pearls <to> pigs, or they might . . . it <. . .>."

[a] *they-will-tread-upon* B C L W Θ f^{13} 33 205 *pc*; *they-might-tread-upon* ℵ f^{1} 892 1006 1342 1506 𝔐.

53. God's Answering of Prayer (→ §212)

Matt 7:7-11	Q 11:9-13	Luke 11:9-13	John 16:24; 14:13-14; 15:7	Thomas 92; 94; 2
7“Ask and it-will-be-given to-you, search and you-will-find, knock and it-will-be-opened to-you; 8for all [=each one] asking takes [=receives], and the [one] searching finds, and to-the [one] knocking it-will-be-opened.	9“I-say to-you, ask and it-will-be-given to-you, search and you-will-find, knock and it-will-be-opened to-you; 10for all [=each one] asking takes [=receives], and the [one] searching finds, and to-the [one] knocking it-will-be-opened.	9“I-too say to-you, ask and it-will-be-given to-you, search and you-will-find, knock and it-will-be-opened to-you; 10for all [=each one] asking takes [=receives], and the [one] searching finds, and to-the [one] knocking it-is-opened[b].	16:24“Until right-now you-asked not no-one [=for anything] in my name; ask and you-will-take in-order-that your joy might-be having-been-fulfilled.” 14:13“And [if] ever you-might-ask some which [=for anything at all] in my name, I-will-do this, in-order-that the father might-be-glorified in the son. 14If-ever you-might-ask me [for] some [thing] in my name, I [myself] will-do [it].” 15:7“If-ever you-might-stay [=you might remain] in me and my speech [=words] might-stay [=might remain] in you, ask which if-ever [=for whatever] you-might-wish, and it-will-happen for-you.”	92Jesus said, “Seek and you will find. In the past, however, I did not tell you the things about which you asked me then. Now I am willing to tell them, but you are not seeking them.” 94Jesus <said>, “One who seeks will find, and for <one who knocks> it will be opened.” 2Jesus said, “Those who seek should not stop seeking until they find. When they find, they will be disturbed. When they are disturbed, they will marvel, and will reign over all. <And after they have reigned they will rest.>”
9Or what person is [there] out of-you, who [when] his son will-ask [for] bread will-give-to him [a] stone no [=instead]?	11What person is [there] out of-you, who [when] his son will-ask [for] bread will-give-to him [a] stone no [=instead]?	11So what father out of-you [when] the son will-ask		
10Or and [=And if] he-will-ask[a] [for a] fish will-he-give-to him [a] snake no [=instead]?	12Or and [=And if] he-will-ask[a] [for a] fish will-give-to him [a] snake no [=instead]?	[for a] fish, and in-place of-fish will-give-to him [a] snake?		
		12Or and [=And if] he-will-ask [for an] egg he-will-give-to him [a] scorpion?		
11Therefore, if you, being	13Therefore, if you, being	13Therefore, if you, being-at-one's-disposals [=being by nature]		
evil, recognize [how] to-give good presents [to] your descendants, how-great rather [=how much more] your father in the heavens will-give good [things] to-the askings [=to those who ask] him.”	evil, recognize [how] to-give good presents [to] your descendants, how-great rather [=how much more] the father out of-heaven will-give good [things] to-the askings [=to those who ask] him.”	evil, recognize [how] to-give good presents [to] your descendants, how-great rather [=how much more] the father out of-heaven will-give [the] holy spirit to-the askings [=to those who ask] him.”		

[a] *he-will-ask* ℵ* B C Θ it^{mss} sy^{c} sy^{p}; *if-ever he-might-ask* ℵ^{1} L W f^1 f^{13} 33 892 1006 1506 𝔐 it^{mss} vg it.
[b] *it-is-opened* 𝔓^{75} B D; *it-will-be-opened* 𝔓^{45} ℵ C L Θ Ψ f^1 f^{13} 3 579 700 892 1241 2542 *pm*; *it-will-be-opened* A K W G Δ 565 1424 *pm*.

54. The Golden Rule (→ §79)

Matt 7:12	Q 6:31	Luke 6:31	Thomas 6
[12]"Therefore all whatsoever if-ever [=what ever] you-might-wish in-order-that [=that] people might-do to-you, thus and [=also] you [yourselves] do to-them; for this is the law and the prophets."	[31]"And just-as [=what ever] you-wish in-order-that [=that] people might-do to-you, thus you [yourselves] do to-them."	[31]"And just-as [=what ever] you-wish in-order-that [=that] people might-do to-you, do[a] to-them likewise."	His disciples asked him and said to him, "Do you want us to fast? How should we pray? Should we give to charity? What diet should we observe?" Jesus said, "Don't lie, and don't do what you hate, because all things are disclosed before heaven. After all, there is nothing hidden that will not be revealed, and there is nothing covered up that will remain undisclosed."

[a] *do* 𝔓75 B 579 700 *pc* it syp; *and you do* ℵ A D L W Θ Ξ Ψ *f*1 *f*13 33 892 1006 1342 1506 𝔐 itmss vg; *do good* itmss vgmss sys.

55. The Two Ways (→ §248)

Matt 7:13-14	Q 13:24	Luke 13:24
[13]"Enter through the narrow gate; that [=because it is a] wide gate and roomy way [=road] leading-away into destruction	[24]"Enter through the narrow door; that [=because]	[24]"Struggle to-enter through the narrow door[b], that [=because]
and many are the enterings [=those who enter] through it.	many search to-enter	many, I-say to-you, will-search to-enter and [=but] they-will-have-the-strength not."
[14]What [=How][a] narrow [is] the gate and having-been-pressed-against [=really narrow is] the way leading-away into life and few are the findings [=those who find] it."	and few are the enterings [=those who enter] through it."	

[a] *What* ℵ2 C L W Θ *f*1 *f*13 892 1006 1506 𝔐 itmss vg sy; *and* 205 209; *that* ℵ* 700c *pc* copsamss copbo; *so that* B* copsamss.
[b] *door* 𝔓75 ℵ B D L Θ *f*1 205 892 2542 *pc* copbo; *gate* A W Ψ *f*13 1006 1342 1506 𝔐 copsa.

56. "By their fruits . . ." (→ §86)

Matt 7:15-20	Q 6:44; 43	Luke 6:44; 43
[15]"Pay-close-attention [=Stay away] from the false-prophets, whoever [=who] come to you in clothes of-sheep, so [=but] from-within they-are ravenous wolves.		

16 You-will-understand [=You will know] them from their fruits. Surely-not do-they-pick bunches-of-grapes[a] from thorny-plants or figs from thistles? 17 Thus all [=every] good tree does [=makes] fine fruits, so [=and] the rotten tree does [=makes] evil fruits.
18 [A] good tree is-able not to-do [=make][b] evil fruits nor [a] rotten tree to-do [=to make][c] fine fruits. 19 All [=every] tree no [=not] doing [=making] fine fruit is-cut-off and is-thrown into [a] fire.
20 Consequently in-effect you-will understand them from their fruits."

44 "For out [=by] the fruit the tree is-known. Surely-not figs are-picked out [of] thorny-plants, or out [of] thistles bunches-of-grapes?

43 There-is not [a] fine tree doing [=making] rotten fruit, nor again[d] [a] rotten tree doing [=making] fine fruit."

44 "For each tree out [=by its] own fruit is-known. For they-pick not figs out of-thorny-plants nor do-they-glean [a] bunch-of-grapes out [of a] bramble-bush.

43 For there-is not [a] fine tree doing [=making] rotten fruit, nor again[d] [a] rotten tree doing [=making] fine fruit."

[a] *bunches-of-grapes* C L W Θ f^{13} 1006 1342 1506 𝔐; *bunch-of-grapes* ℵ B 0250 f^{1} 205 892 it^{mss} vg sy cop.
[b] *to-do* ℵ C L W Z Θ f^{1} f^{13} 33 892 1006 1342 1506 𝔐 it vg sy; *to-carry* B.
[c] *to-do* ℵ^{1} B C L W Z Θ f^{1} f^{13} 33 1006 1506 𝔐 it^{mss} vg sy cop^{samss}; *to-carry* ℵ*.
[d] *again* 𝔓^{75} ℵ B L W Ξ f^{1} f^{13} 579 892 1342 2542 *pc* vg^{mss} cop^{bo}; *omit* A C D Θ Ψ 33 1006 1506 𝔐 it^{mss} vg sy cop^{sa}.

57. "Lord, lord" (→ §87, §248)

Matt 7:21-23

21 "Not all [=each one] saying to-me, 'Lord, lord' will-enter into the kingdom of-the heavens, but the [one] doing the wish [of] my father in the[a] heavens.

22 Many will-say to-me in [=on] that day, 'Lord, lord, we-prophesied not [=did we not prophesy] in your-own name, and we-casted-out [=did we not cast out] demons in your-own name and did-we [not do] many powers [=miracles] in your-own name?' 23 And then I-will-confess to-them that I-knew you never; withdraw-back from me the workings [=you who work] lawlessness."

Q 6:46; 13:26-27

6:46 "What [=Why] do-you-call me, 'Lord, lord' and [=but] you-do not [do the things] which I [myself] say?"

13:26 "Then you-will-begin to-say, 'We ate and drank in-the-sight of-you and you-taught in our wide-streets.'

27 And he-will-say, saying to-you, 'I-recognize you not. Abandon from [=Leave] me the workings [=you who work] lawlessness.'"

Luke 6:46; 13:26-27

6:46 "So what [=why] do-you-call me, 'Lord, lord' and [=but] you-do not [do the things] which I-say?"

13:26 "Then you-will-begin to-say, 'We-ate and we-drank in-the-sight of-you and you-taught in our wide-streets.'

27 And he-will-say, saying to-you, 'I-recognize you not [nor] from-where you-are. Abandon from [=Leave] me all [you] workers of-unrighteousness.'"

[a] *the* ℵ B C Z Θ f^{1} 33 205 892 1424 1596; *omit* L W f^{13} 1006 1342 𝔐.
📖 Mt 7:23 – Ps 6:8

58. The House Built on Rock (→ §88)

Matt 7:24-27	Q 6:47-49	Luke 6:47-49
24“Therefore all [=each one] whoever [=who] hears these my words and does them	47“All [=Each one] hearing my words and doing them	47“All [=Each one] coming to me and hearing my words and doing them I-will-display [to] you what he-is comparable-to;
will-be-compared[a] [to a] sensible man, whoever [=who] built his home upon the rock.	48is comparable-to [a] person who built his home upon the rock.	48he-is comparable-to [a] person building [a] home, who dug and went-deep and put [the] foundation upon the rock.
25And the rain descended and the rivers came and the winds heaved and fell-to [=bombarded] that home, and it-fell not for it-had-been-founded upon the rock.	And the rain descended and the rivers came and the winds heaved and fell-to [=bombarded] that home, and it-fell not for it-had-been-founded upon the rock.	So [a] flood-tide having-happened, the river burst-upon that home and it-had-the-strength not to-shake-up it through [=because] it to-have-been-built [=had been built] well[b].
26And all [=each one] hearing these my words and no [=not] doing them	49And all [=each one] hearing my words and no [=not] doing them	49So [=But] the [one] having-heard [my words] and no [=not] having-done [them]
will-be-compared [to a] moronic man, whoever [=who] built his home upon the sand. 27And the rain descended and the rivers came and the winds heaved and battered that home, and it-fell	is comparable-to [a] person who built his home upon the sand. And the rain descended and the rivers came and the winds heaved and battered that home, and immediately it-fell	is comparable-to [a] person having-built [a] home upon the land without [a] foundation, which the river burst-upon and immediately it-collapsed[c]
and its decline was great.”	and its decline was great.”	and the devastation of-that home happened [=was] <u>great</u>.”

[a] *will-be-compared* ℵ B Z Θ f^{1} f^{13} 33 205 700 892 vg sy^{p} cop^{sa}; *I-will-compare* C L W 1006 1342 1506 𝔐 it^{mss} sy^{c} cop^{bo}.
[b] *through it to-have-been-built well* 𝔓^{75} ℵ B L W Ξ 33 579 892 1342 2542 *pc* cop^{sa}; *for it-had-been-founded upon the rock* A C D Θ Ψ f^{1} f^{13} 1006 1506 𝔐 it^{mss} vg sy^{p}; *omit* 𝔓^{45} 700* sy^{s}.
[c] *it-collapsed* 𝔓^{45} 𝔓^{75} ℵ B D L Θ Ξ f^{1} f^{13} 33 205 579 700 892 1342 2542 *pc*; *it-fell* A C W Ψ 1006 1506 𝔐.

59. The Effect of the Sermon

Matt 7:28-29	**Mark 1:21-22**	**Luke 4:31-32**	John 2:12, 7:46
28And it-happened when Jesus completed these words,	21And they-travel-in into Capharnaum;	31And he-went-down into Capharnaum, [a] city of-the Galilee. And	2:12With [=After] this, he-descended into Capharnaum, he and his mother and his brothers and his disciples and they-stayed there not many days.
	and immediately[a] having-entered into the synagogue [on] the sabbaths he-was-teaching.	he-was teaching them in [=on] the sabbaths.	
the crowds were-being-amazed upon [=at] his instruction; 29for he-was teaching them like [one] having authority and not like their scribes.	22And they-were-being-amazed upon [=at] his instruction; for he-was teaching them like [one] having authority and not like the scribes.	32And they-were-being-amazed upon [=at] his instruction, that [=because] his word was in [=with] <u>authority</u>.	7:46The attendants answered, “Never [has a] person talked thus [=like this].”

[a] *immediately* ℵ L f^{1} 33 205 565 579 700 892 1342 2542 *pc*; *instantly* A B C D W Θ f^{13} 1006 1506 2427 𝔐.

SYNOPTIC STUDY GUIDE 6

Problems with the Two-Gospel/Griesbach Hypothesis

Griesbach's idea that Mark worked in blocks, moving back and forth between Matthew and Luke, is a reasonable description of what Mark appears to be have done (see Synoptic Study Guide 5). It is possible in theory but is not the best description of what Mark actually does. As suggested earlier, Mark 1:21 (§59) is the point at which the writer of Mark turns from Matthew to Luke, according to Griesbach. Yet, the pattern is not as clear when you focus on the details. Yes, at 1:21 the writer of Mark follows Luke's order, and yes Mark's words here agree with Luke far more than they do with Matthew. But the pattern dissolves at the second clause of Mark 1:22—"for he-was teaching them like [one] having authority and not like the scribes"—which has no parallel in Luke, and in which 11/12 words are in verbatim agreement between Matthew and Mark, and the first ten are consecutive.

But the author of Mark had access to Matthew, so what is the problem? The problem is that this is not what Griesbach argued the writer of Mark was doing. He claimed that the author of Mark had put down Matthew and was now following Luke, which works only to a point. In other words, Mark was following the sequence of Luke but the wording of Matthew. This was one of the chief reasons that Griesbach's hypothesis fell out of favor with New Testament scholars.

Another problem was that many have difficulty making sense of Griesbach's depiction of the author of Mark as a conflator of Matthew and Luke. A conflator's job is to bring two sources together into one. This will be difficult where they disagree, but it should be perfectly straightforward where they are the same. And by the Griesbach Hypothesis, the writer of Mark omits about 230 verses where Matthew and Luke agree to an extremely high degree (the Double Tradition), most troublingly, the sermons of Jesus (on the mount and on the plain), the Lord's Prayer, and so many of Jesus' parables. Many scholars have asked what could possibly have compelled the author of Mark to omit the Lord's Prayer if he had it in two of his sources? This was a depiction of Mark's author that scholars could not abide (B. H. Streeter called Griesbach's Mark "a crank"!). Despite these problems, the Griesbach Hypothesis remains a viable option, with some scholars striving to explain these problems and improve the value of the hypothesis.

The Galilean Ministry Continues

60. A Demoniac in the Synagogue

Mark 1:23-28

[23]And immediately[a] [a] person in [=with an] unclean
spirit was in their synagogue and he-cried-out [24]saying,
"What to-us and to-you [=do you have to do with us],
Jesus Nazarene? Did-you-come to-destroy us? I-
recognize you, what you-are, the holy [one] of-god."
[25]And Jesus rebuked him saying, "Be-muzzled and
go-out out of-him." [26]And the unclean spirit, having-
convulsed him and having-yelled[b] [with a] great voice,
went-out out of-him. [27]And everyone were-astounded
with-the-result-that to-discuss to [=they discussed among]
themselves saying, "What is this? [A] new instruction
according-to [=with] authority. And he-presides-over
the spirits unclean, and they-obey him." [28]And [a]
rumor of-him went-out immediately everywhere into
[the] whole [of] the surrounding-region of-the Galilee.

Luke 4:33-37

[33]And in the synagogue [there] was [a] person having
[a] spirit [of an] unclean demon and he-cried-out
[with a] great voice,[c] [34]"Ah. What to-us and to-you
[=do you have to do with us], Jesus Nazarene? Did-you-
come to-destroy us? I-recognize you, what you-are,
the holy [one] of-god." [35]And Jesus rebuked him
saying, "Be-muzzled and go-out from[d] him." And the
demon, having-tossed him into the middle, went-out
from him, having-harmed him not-one [bit]. [36]And
wonder happened [=came] upon all and they-were-
talking-with to one-another saying, "What [is] this
word, that in authority and power he-presides-over
the unclean spirits and they-go-out?" [37]And [a]
report around [=concerning] him was-traveling-out
into all [=every] place of-the surrounding-region.

[a] *immediately* ℵ B L f^{1} 33 205 579 1342 2427 *pc* cop; *omit* A C D W Θ f^{13} 892 1006 1506 𝔐 it vg.
[b] *having-yelled* ℵ B L 33 579 1342 2427 *pc*; *having-cried* A C Θ f^{1} f^{13} 1006 1506 𝔐.
[c] *omit* ℵ B L 579 700* 2542; *saying* A C D Θ Ψ f^{1} f^{13} 33 892 1006 1342 1506 𝔐 it^{mss} vg.
[d] *from* ℵ B D L W Ξ f^{1} f^{13} 579 700 892 1424 2542; *out* 𝔓^{75} A C Θ Ψ 33 𝔐.

61. Peter's Mother-in-Law Healed (→ §91)

Matt 8:14-15	**Mark 1:29-31**	**Luke 4:38-39**
14 And Jesus, having-come into the home of-Peter saw his	29 And immediately having-gone-out out of-the synagogue they-went[a] into the home of-Simon and Andrew with James and John.	38 So having-gotten-up [=having departed] from the synagogue he-entered into the home of-Simon.
mother-in-law having-been-thrown [=sprawled out] and being-feverish;	30 So [=Now] the mother-in-law of-Simon was-lying-down, being-feverish, and immediately they-say [=they spoke] to-him around [=concerning] her.	So [=Now the] mother-in-law of-Simon was being-controlled [by a] great fever and they-begged him around [=concerning] her.
15 and he-touched her hand,	31 And having-approached he-raised her, having-seized the [=her] hand;	39 And having-stood-by above her he-rebuked the fever
and the fever excused [=left] her and she-was-raised and she-was-serving him.	and the fever excused [=left] her and she-was-serving them.	and it-excused [=it left] her; so at-once having-gotten-up she-was-serving them.

[a] *they-went* ℵ A C 𝔐 vg sy[s] sy[p] cop[bo]; *he-went* B D W Θ *f*[1] *f*[13] 565 2427 it.

62. The Sick Healed at Evening (→ §92)

Matt 8:16-17	**Mark 1:32-34**	**Luke 4:40-41**
16 So evening having-happened they-offered to-him many being-demon-possesseds [=demoniacs];	32 So evening having-happened when the sun set they-were-carrying to him all the havings [=those who are sick] badly and the being-demon-possesseds [=demoniacs]; 33 and the whole city was having-been-collected [=gathered] to [=at] the door.	40 So [while] the sun [=is] setting, everyone whatsoever [=who] had [any who were] being-ill [with] various diseases led them to him.
and he-cast-out the spirits [with a] word and he-healed all the havings [=those who are sick] badly	34 And he-healed many havings badly [=who were sick] various diseases and he-cast-out many demons	So placing hands [on] each one of-them, he-was-healing them. 41 So demons and [=also] were-going-out from many, screaming and saying that "You are the son[b] of-god."
	and he-was-excusing [=he would allow] not the demons to-talk that [=because] they-recognized him[a].	And rebuking he-was-permitting them not to-talk that [=because] they-recognized the anointed-one to-be him.
17 so-that the having-been-said [=what was said] through Isaiah the prophet might-be-fulfilled, saying "HE TOOK OUR ILLNESSES AND BORE [our] DISEASES."		

[a] *they-recognized him* ℵ A 1006 𝔐 sy[s] sy[p] cop[sa]; *they-recognized him to-be anointed-one* B C L W Θ *f*[1] *f*[13] 565 342 1424 2427 cop[bo].
[b] *you-are the son* ℵ B C D F L W Ξ 33 2542 it sy[s] cop[sa]; *you-are the anointed-one the son* A Θ Ψ *f*[1] *f*[13] 1006 1342 𝔐.
🕮 Mt 8:17 – Isa 53:4

63. Jesus Leaves Capharnaum

Mark 1:35-39

35And extremely early at-night [=long along daylight],
having-gotten-up, he-went-out and went-away
into [a] deserted place and-there he-was-praying.
36And Simon and the [ones] with him pursued-
closely him 37and they-found him and they-say
to-him that "All are-searching [for] you."
38And he-says to-them, "We-might-lead [=Let us go]
elsewhere[a] into the havings [=places that have] small-
towns, in-order-that there and [=also] I-might-preach,
for I-went-out into [=came for] this." 39And he-went[b]
preaching into [=in] their synagogues, into [the]
whole [of] the Galilee, and casting-out the demons.

Luke 4:42-44

42So [with] day having-happened, having-gone-out,
he-traveled into [a] deserted place, and the crowds
were-seeking him and they-came until [=right up
to] him and were-detaining him no [=they would
not allow him] to-travel from them. 43So he-said to
them that "It-is-necessary [for] me to-proclaim the
kingdom of-god and [=also] to-the other cities, that
[=because] I-was-sent-off upon [=for] this." 44And he-
was preaching into [=in] the synagogues of-Judea[c].

[a] *elsewhere* ℵ B C L 33 2427 cop; *omit* A D W Θ f^{1} f^{13} 892 1006 𝔐.
[b] *he-went* ℵ B L Θ 892 2427 *pc*; *he-was* A C D E F G W f^{1} f^{13} 33 700 1006 1342 1506 𝔐 it vg sy.
[c] *into the synagogues of-Judea* 𝔓^{75} ℵ B C L Q f^{1} 579 982 *pc* cop; *in the synagogues of-the Galilee* A Θ 1006 1342 1506 𝔐 it vg sy; *into the synagogues of-the Galilee* D Ψ f^{13}.

64. Luke's Miraculous Catch of Fish

Luke 5:1-11

1So it-happened in the to-lay-upon him the crowd
[=when he was being pressed in by the crowd] and to-hear
[=as they were hearing] the word of-god, and [when]
he [himself] was having-stood [=standing] along the
harbor of-Gennesaret 2and he [himself] saw two boats[a]
having-stood [=standing] along the harbor; so the fishers
having-gotten-out from them were-rinsing the nets.
3So having-embarked into one of-the boats, which was
[a boat] of-Simon, he-begged him to-put-out [a] little
from the land; so having-been-seated he-was-teaching
the crowds out of-the boat. 4So like [=when] he-stopped
talking he-said to Simon, "Put-out into the depth [=deep
water] and lower your nets into [=for a] catch [of fishes]."
5And having-answered, Simon said, "Overseer, having-
labored through [the] whole night[b], we-took no-one
[=we caught nothing]. So [=But] upon your speech [=at
your command] I-will-lower the nets." 6And having-done
this they-enclosed many [=a great] multitude of-fishes,
so their nets were-being-rent. 7And they-motioned-
toward the [=their] partners in the other boat, having-
come, to-grip [=to help] them. And they-came and
they-filled both the boats with-the-result-that to-be-
dragged-down them [=they were sinking]. 8So, Simon
Peter, having-seen, fell-to the knees of-Jesus saying,
"Go-out [=Get away] from me, that [=because] I-am [a]
sinful man, lord." 9For wonder overcame him and all the
[ones] together-with him, upon [=because of] the catch
of-the fishes which they-gripped [=they had caught],
10and so likewise James and John, sons of-Zebedee,

John 21:1-11

1With [=After] these [things] Jesus made-visible himself
again to-the disciples upon [=near] the sea of-Tiberias;
so he-made-visible [himself] thus: 2Simon Peter and
Thomas, being-said [=who is called] Twin, and Nathanael
from Cana of-the Galilee, and the [sons] of-Zebedee,
and two anothers [=others] out [of] his disciples were
close-by. 3Simon Peter says to-them, "I-am-leaving
to-catch-fish." They-say to-him, "We and [=also]
are-coming together-with you." They-went-out and
embarked into the boat, and in [=on] that night they-
apprehended no-one [=they caught nothing]. 4So morning
having-happened already, Jesus stood into [=on] the
beach; however, the disciples recognized not that it-is
Jesus. 5Therefore Jesus says to-them, "Young-children,
have-you no [=not] some something-to-eat?" They-
answered him, "Not." 6So he-said to-them, "Throw the
net into the right parts [=off the right side] of-the boat,
and you-will-find [some fish]." Therefore they-threw [the
nets], and no-longer were-they-having-the-strength
to-haul it from [=because] of-the multitude of-fishes.
7Therefore that disciple whom Jesus was-loving says
to-Peter, "It-is the lord." Therefore, Simon Peter, having-
heard that it-is the lord, encloaked the outer-garment
[around himself], for he-was naked, and he-threw
himself into the sea. 8So [=But] the another [=other]
disciples came in-the small-boat, for they-were not far-
away from the land but like [=about] two-hundred cubits
from [it], tugging the net of-the fishes. 9Therefore like
[=when] they-got-out into [=onto] the land, they-look

who were companions [with] Simon. And Jesus said
to Simon, "Fear no [=not]. From the now [=now on]
you-will-be capturing people." 11 And having-led-down
the boats upon [=to] the land [and] having-excused
[=having left behind] all [=everything], they-followed him.

[=they see a] charcoal-fire lying [there] and cooked-
food laying-upon [it] and bread. 10 Jesus says to-them,
"Carry from the cooked-food [=some of the fish] which
you-apprehended [=you caught just] now." 11 Therefore
Simon Peter ascended [=went aboard] and hauled the
net overflowing [with] great [=many] fishes into [=onto]
the land, one-hundred [and] fifty three; and [although]
being [=there were] so-many, the net was-ripped not.

[a] *two boats* 𝔓[75] ℵ B D W Θ f^1 f^{13} 579 892 𝔐 it[mss] vg; *two small-boats* A C* L Q Ψ 33 1241 1424.
[b] *night* 𝔓[75] ℵ B L W Ψ 33 *pc*; *the night* C D Θ f^1 f^{13} 𝔐.

65. The Healing of a Leper

Matt 8:1-4

1 So, [when] his having-descended
[=he came down] from the mountain,
many crowds followed him.
2 And look! [a] leprous
[person] having-approached
was-worshiping him
saying, "Lord, if-ever you-
might-wish, you-are-able
to-purify me." 3 And
having-reached-out
the hand, he-touched him saying,
"I-wish, be-purified." And instantly
his leprosy was-purified.

4 And Jesus says to-him,
"See [that] you-might-say [=you
might speak] to-not-one [=to no
one] but leave, yourself show
to-the priest and offer the gift
which Moses designated,

into [=as] testimony to-them."

Mark 1:40-45

40 And [a] leprous [person]
comes to him exhorting
him and kneeling[a] and
saying to-him that "If-ever you-
might-wish, you-are-able to-purify
me." 41 And having-had-pity[b], [and]
having-reached-out the hand
him he-touched[c] and says to-
him, "I-wish, be-purified." 42 And
immediately went-away from him
the leprosy and he-was-purified.
43 And having-censured him
immediately he-cast-out him [=he
threw him out], 44 and he-says to-
him, "See [that] you-might-say
not-one [=nothing] to-not-one [=to
any one] but leave, yourself show
to-the priest and offer [the things]
which Moses designated around
[=concerning] your purification,
into [=as] testimony to-them."
45 So [=But] having-gone-out he-
began to-preach many [things] and
to-speak-out the word, with-the-
result-that to-be-able him [=he
was able] not-any-longer to-enter
into [a] city visibly, but he-was
outside upon [=near] deserted
places; and they-were-coming
to him from-everywhere.

Luke 5:12-16

12 And it-happened in the to-be him
[=that he was] in one of-the cities,

and look! [there was a] man full
of-leprosy; so [=and] having-seen
Jesus, [and] having-fallen upon
[his] face, he-implored him saying,
"Lord, if-ever you-might-wish,
you-are-able to-purify me." 13 And
having-reached-out the hand,
he-touched him saying, "I-wish,
be-purified." And instantly the
leprosy went-away from him.

14 And he [himself] enjoined
him to-say [=to speak] to-not-
one [=to no one] but "Having-
gone-away show yourself to-the
priest and offer [the things] just-
as Moses designated around
[=concerning] your purification,
into [=as] testimony to-them."
15 So [=But] rather the word
around [=concerning] him was-
going-through [=went from place
to place] and many crowds
were-coming-together to-hear
and to-be-healed[d] from their
illnesses, 16 so he [himself] was
withdrawing in [=into] the
deserted [places] and praying.

[a] *and kneeling* ℵ L Θ f^1 205 565 892 1241 1424 it[ms] vg; *and kneeling to-him* A C Δ 0233 f^{13} 28 33 1006 1342 1505; *omit* B D G W 2427 it vg[ms] cop[sa].
[b] *having-had-pity* ℵ A B C L W Δ Θ 0130 0233 f^1 f^{13} 28 33 1241 1424 it vg sy cop[sa] cop[bo]; *having-become-angered* D it[ms].
[c] *him touched* ℵ B L 892 2427 *pc*; *touched him* A C W Θ f^1 f^{13} 33 1006 1342 1506 𝔐.
[d] *to-be-healed* ℵ B D L W f^1 f^{13} 205 579 892 2542 *pc* cop[sa]; *to-be-healed by-him* Θ Ψ 33 1006 1342 1506 𝔐 sy[h].
🕮 Mt 8:4 – Lev 14:2, 3; 🕮 Mk 1:44 – Lev 14:2; 🕮 Lk 5:14 – Lev 14:2

66. The Healing of a Paralytic (→ §89, §96)

Matt 9:1-8

[1]And having-embarked into [a] boat he-crossed-over and went into the [=his] own city.

[2]And look! they-were-offering to-him [a] paralytic

having-been-thrown upon [a] stretcher.

And Jesus, having-seen their loyalty said to-the paralytic, “Cheer-up, descendant, your sins are-excused.” [3]And look! some of-the scribes said in [=to] themselves, “This [man]

blasphemes.”

[4]And Jesus having-seen[a] their deliberations

Mark 2:1-12

[1]And having-entered again into Capharnaum through [=after some] days, it-was-heard that he-is in house [=at home]. [2]And[c] many were-gathered with-the-result-that not-any-longer to-accept so-not to [=there was no longer room even at] the door and he-was-talking [=he was speaking] the word to-them.
[3]And they-come carrying to him [a] paralytic

being-removed under [=by] four.

[4]And no [=not] being-able to-offer him through the crowd, they-unroofed the roof where he-was, and having-scooped they-lower the mattress where the paralytic was-lying-down.

[5]And Jesus, having-seen their loyalty, says to-the paralytic, “Descendant, your sins are-excused.”
[6]So some of-the scribes were there sitting and pondering in their hearts:
[7]“What this talks [=Why does this man speak] thus? He-blasphemes; what [=who] is-able to-excuse sins if no [=except] the one god?”
[8]And Jesus, having-understood immediately [in] his spirit that they-ponder thus in

Luke 5:17-26

[17]And it-happened in [=on] one of-the days and [=that] he [himself] was teaching and Pharisees and legal-teachers, who were having-come [=who had come] out of-all [=of every] village of-the Galilee and Judea and Jerusalem, were sitting; and [the] power [of the] lord was into [=with] him to-cure.
[18]And look! men carrying [a] person who was having-been-paralyzed

upon [a] stretcher; and they-were-searching [=they were trying] to-bring him [in] and to-put him in-the-sight of-him. [19]And no [=not] having-found what-kind-of [=by what way] they-might-bring him [in] through the crowd, having-ascended upon the housetop, they-let-down him through the tiles together-with the cot into the middle in-front of-Jesus. [20]And having-seen their loyalty, he-said, “Person, your sins have-been-excused for-you.” [21]And the scribes and Pharisees began to-ponder, saying, “What [=Who] is this who talks [=speaks] blasphemies? What [=Who] is-able to-excuse sins if no [=except] god alone?”
[22]So Jesus, having-understood their thoughts, [and] having-answered,

John 5:1-9a

[1]With [=After] these [things] there-was [a] feast of-the Judeans and Jesus ascended into Jerusalem. [2]So [=Now] there-is in Jerusalems upon [=near] the sheep-gate [a] pool, the being-called-on [=which is called] in-Hebrew Bethzatha, having [=which has] five porticos. [3]In these was-lying-down [a] multitude [of those] being-ill, blind, lame, withered.* [5]So, some person was there having [been] in his illness [for] thirty and eight years. [6]Jesus, having-seen this [person] lying-down and having-known that he-has already [been there] many [=for much] time, says to-him, “Do-you-wish to-happen [=to become] healthy?” [7]The [one who was] being-ill answered to-him, “Lord, I-have no person in-order-that, whenever the water might-be-disturbed, he-might-throw me into the pool. So, in which [=whenever] I [myself] come [down], another descends before me.”

Matt 8:4 (§65, p. 44)
Q 4:16 (§25, p. 18)

said,
"For-what-reason do-
you-deliberate-on evil
[things] in your hearts?
[5]For, what is easier
to-say: 'Your sins are-
excused[b], or to-say
'Rise and walk-around'?
[6]So [=But] in-order-that
you-might-recognize that
authority the son of-the
person has upon the
land [=earth] to-excuse
sins"—then he-says to-the
paralytic—"Having-
been-raised, remove your
stretcher and leave [=go]
into your house." [7]And
having-been-raised, he-
went-away into his house.
[8]So, having-seen, the
crowds were-feared
[=became afraid] and
they-glorified god,
having-given [=who
gave] authority such-
as-this to-people.

themselves, says[d] to-them,
"What [=Why] do-you-
ponder these [things]
in your hearts? [9]What
is easier to-say to-the
paralytic, 'Your sins
are-excused' or to-say
'Rise, and remove your
mattress and walk-
around'? [10]So [=But]
in-order-that you-might-
recognize that authority
the son of-the person
has to-excuse sins
upon the land [=earth]"—
he-says to-the paralytic—
[11]"I-say to-you, rise,
remove your mattress
and leave [=go] into your
house." [12]And he-was-
raised and immediately
having-removed the
mattress, he-went-out
in-front of-all, with-
the-result-that all to-be-
surprised [=were surprised]
and to-glorify [=they
glorified] god, saying that
"We-saw never thus
[=we have never seen
anything like this]."

said to them "What
[=Why] do-you-
ponder in your
hearts?
[23]What is easier to-say:
'Your sins have-been-
excused for-you'
or to-say 'Rise,
and walk-around'? [24]So
[=But] in-order-that
you-might-recognize that
the son of-the person
has authority upon the
land [=earth] to-excuse
sins"—he-said to-the [one]
having-been-paralyzed,
"I-say to-you, rise, and
having-removed your
cot, to-travel into your
house." [25]And having-
gotten-up at-once in-
the-sight of-them, [and]
having-removed [that]
upon which he-was-lying-
down, he-went-away
into his house glorifying
god. [26]And ecstasy took
everyone and they-
were-glorifying god and
they-were-filled [with]
fear saying that "We-saw
incredible [things] today."

[8]Jesus says to-him,
"Rise, remove your
mattress and walk-
around."
[9]And instantly the
person happened
[=became] healthy and
he-removed his
mattress and
was-walking-around.

[a] *having-seen* ℵ C D L W 0233 f^{13} 𝔐 it vg sy^{s} cop^{bo}; *having-known* B Θ f^{1} 565 700 1424 sy^{p} sy^{h} cop^{sa}.
[b] *are-excused* ℵ B D it^{mss} vg *pc*; *have-been-excused* C L W Θ 0233 f^{1} f^{13} 33 𝔐 it.
[c] *omit* ℵ B L W Q 33 579 892 1342 2427 *pc* it^{mss} vg sy^{p} cop; *instantly* A C D f^{1} f^{13} 1006 1506 𝔐.
[d] *says* 𝔓^{88} ℵ B L W 33 892 1342 2427 *pc*; *said* A C D Θ f^{1} f^{13} 1006 1506 𝔐.
* John 5:4 is missing from the oldest and most authoritative manuscripts.

67. The Call of Levi (→ §97)

Matt 9:9-13

[9]And passing-by from-there,
Jesus saw [a] person, sitting
upon [=in] the tax-booth,
being-said [=called] Matthew,
and he-says to-him,
"Follow me." And having-gotten-up,
he-followed him.

Mark 2:13-17

[13]And he-went-out again along the
sea; and all the crowd was-going to
him, and he-was-teaching them.
[14]And passing-by, he-saw
Levi the [son] of-Alpheus sitting
upon [=in] the tax-booth, and
he-says to-him, "Follow me."
And having-gotten-up,
he-followed him.

Luke 5:27-32

[27]And with [=after] these
[things], he-went-out
and
noticed [a] tax-collector [by the]
name Levi sitting upon [=in] the
tax-booth, and he-said to-him,
"Follow me." [28]And having-quit all
[=everything and] having-gotten-
up, he-was-following[d] him.

Matt	Mark	Luke
10 And it-happened [when] he [himself was] dining in the [=at] home and look! many tax-collectors and sinfuls [=those who are sinful], having-come, were-sitting-at-table [with] Jesus and his disciples.	15 And it-happens him to-recline [=as he was reclining] in his home and [=also] many tax-collectors and sinfuls [=those who are sinful] were-sitting-at-table [with] Jesus and his disciples, for there-were many and they-were-following him.	29 And Levi did [=made a] great dinner for-him in his home and there-was many [=a great] crowd of-tax-collectors and anothers [=others] who were lying-down with them.
11 And the Pharisees,	16 And the scribes of-the <u>Pharisees</u>, having-seen that he-eats with the sinfuls [=those who are sinful] and tax-collectors	30 And the Pharisees and their scribes
having-seen, were-saying[a] [to] his disciples, "Through what [=Why] your teacher eats [=does your teacher eat] with the tax-collectors and sinfuls [=those who sinful]?"	were-saying [to] his disciples "[How is it] that he-eats with the tax-collectors and sinfuls [=those	were-grumbling to his disciples saying, "Through what [=Why] do-you-eat and do-you-drink with the tax-collectors and sinfuls [=those who are sinful]?"
12 So having-heard, he-said, "The having-the-strengths [=those who have the strength] have not need [of a] physician but the havings [=those who are sick] badly.	who are sinful]?" 17 And having-heard, Jesus says to-them[c] that "The having-the-strengths [=those who have the strength] have not need [of a] physician but the havings [=those who are sick]	31 And having-answered, Jesus said to them, "The being-healthies [=those who are healthy] have not need [of a] physician but the havings [=those who are sick] badly;
13 So having-traveled, learn what is [the meaning of], 'I-WISH MERCY AND NOT SACRIFICE.'		
For I-came not to-call [the] righteous but sinful [people] [b]."	badly. I-came not to-call [the] righteous but sinful [people]."	32 I-have-come not to-call [the] righteous but sinful [people] into repentance."

[a] *were-saying* ℵ B C L W f^1 33 205 892; *said* D Θ f^{13} 1006 1342 𝔐.
[b] *omit* ℵ B D W Δ 0233 f^1 33 205 565 it^{mss} vg sy^p cop^{bo}; *into repentance* C L Θ f^{13} 892 1006 1342 1506 𝔐. it^{mss} sy^s cop^{sa}.
[c] *to-them* 𝔭^{88} B Δ Θ 565 2427 *pc*; *omit* ℵ A C D L W f^1 f^{13} 33 892 1006 1342 1506 𝔐 it vg sy.
[d] *he-was-following* B D L W Ξ 69 700 892 1506 *pc* it^{mss}; *they-were-following* ℵ A C Θ f^1 f^{13} 33 1006 11342 𝔐.
🕮 Mt 9:13 – Hos 6:6

68. A Question about Fasting (→ §98)

Matt 9:14-17	**Mark 2:18-22**	**Luke 5:33-39**	John 3:29-30	Thomas 104; 47
14 Then the disciples of-John	18 And the disciples of-John and the Pharisees[b] were fasting. And they-come and say	33 So they-said to him,		104 They said to Jesus, "Come, let us pray today, and let us fast." Jesus said, "What sin have I committed, or how have I been undone? Rather, when the groom leaves the bridal suite, then let people fast and pray."
approach him saying, "Through what [=Why do] we [ourselves] and the Pharisees fast [a]	to-him, "Through what [=Why do] the disciples of-John and the disciples of-the Pharisees fast,	"The disciples of-John fast frequently and do [=make] petitions and likewise the [disciples] of-the Pharisees,		
so [=but] your disciples fast not?" 15 And Jesus said to-them,	so [=but] your-own disciples fast not?" 19 And Jesus said to-them,	so [=but] your-own eat and drink." 34 So Jesus said to them,		

Matt 8:4 (§65, p. 44)
Q 4:16 (§25, p. 18)

“The sons of-the wedding-hall [=groom’s attendants] are-able no [=not] to-languish upon whatsoever [=while] is with them the bridegroom [are they]?	“The sons of-the wedding-hall [=groom’s attendants] are-able no [=not] to-fast in which [=while] the bridegroom is with them [are they]? Whatsoever time they-have the bridegroom with them they-are-able to-fast not.	“You-are-able no [=not] to-do [=to make] the sons of-the wedding-hall [=groom’s attendants] to-fast in which [=while] the bridegroom is with them [are you]?		
So days will-come whenever the bridegroom might-be-taken-up from them, and then they-will-fast.	20 So days will-come whenever the bridegroom might-be-taken-up from them, and then they-will-fast in [=on] that day.	35 So days will-come, and whenever the bridegroom might-be-taken-up from them, then they-will-fast in those days.”		
		36 And so he-was-saying [a] parable to them, that	29 “The [one] having the bride is [the] bridegroom; so the friend of-the bridegroom, having-stood and hearing him, rejoices [a] joy through [=because of] the voice of-the bridegroom. Therefore [in] this my-own joy has-been-fulfilled. 30 It-is-necessary [for] that [one] to-grow, so [=but for] me to-become-less-important.”	
16 So no-one throws-on [a] patch of-unshrunken piece-of-cloth upon [an] old coat; for the fullness of-it removes [it] from the coat and [a] worse rip happens.	21 No-one sews-on [a] patch [of] of-unshrunken piece-of-cloth upon [an] old coat; so if no [=if they do], the fullness removes [it] from it, the new [from] the old, and [a] worse rip happens.	“No-one, having-ripped [a] patch from [a] new coat, throws-on [it] upon [an] old coat. So if no in-effect [=indeed, if they do], and [=then] the new [one] will-rip and the patch from the new will-agree [=will fit] not [with] the old.		47 Jesus said, “A person cannot mount two horses or bend two bows. And a slave cannot serve two masters, otherwise that slave will honor the one and offend the other.
17 Nor do-they-throw [=do they put] fresh wine into old wine-skins; so if no in-effect [=indeed, if they do] the wine-skins are-devastated and the wine is-poured-out and the wine-skins are-destroyed; but they-throw [=they put]	22 And no-one throws [=puts] fresh wine into old wine-skins; so if no [=if they do] the wine will-devastate the wine-skins and the wine is-destroyed and the wine-skins[c]; but [they put]	37 And no-one throws [=puts] fresh wine into old wine-skins; so if no in-effect [=indeed, if they do] the fresh wine will-devastate the wine-skins and it will-be-poured-out and the wine-skins will-be-destroyed; 38 but one-must-throw [=one must		47 Nobody drinks aged wine and immediately wants to drink young wine. Young wine is not poured into old wineskins, or they might break, and aged wine is not poured into a new wineskin, or it might spoil. An

fresh wine into new wine-skins, and both are-protected."	fresh wine into new wine-skins."	pour] fresh wine into new wine-skins. [39]And no-one having-drunk old [wine] wishes fresh [wine], for he-says, 'The old is kind[d] [=better].'"		old patch is not sewn onto a new garment, since it would create a tear."

[a] *omit* ℵ* B *pc* cop^{sa}; *much* ℵ^{2} C D L W Θ f^{1} f^{13} 33 892 1006 1506 𝔐 it^{mss} cop^{bo}; *frequently* ℵ^{1} it^{mss} vg sy^{s}.
[b] *the Pharisees* 𝔓^{88} ℵ A B C D Θ f^{13} 565 1342 1424 2427 it^{mss} vg sy^{p}; *those of-the Pharisees* L f^{1} 33 892 1006 1506 𝔐 it^{mss} vg^{mss} cop^{samss} cop^{bomss}; *the disciples of-the Pharisees* W.
[c] *is-destroyed and the wine-skins* 𝔓^{88} B 892 2427 cop^{bo}; *is-poured-out and the wine-skins are destroyed* ℵ A C D L W Θ f^{1} f^{13} 33 1006 1342 𝔐 it^{mss} vg sy^{p} cop^{sa}.
[d] *kind* 𝔓^{4} ℵ B L W 1342 *pc* sy^{p}; *kinder* A C Θ Ψ f^{1} f^{13} 33 892 1006 1506 𝔐 it^{mss} vg.

69. Plucking Grain on the Sabbath (→ §130)

Matt 12:1-8	**Mark 2:23-28**	**Luke 6:1-5**
[1]In that proper-time [=season] Jesus traveled [on] the sabbaths through the grainfields; so [=and] his disciples hungered and they-began to-pluck ears-of-grain and to-eat [them]. [2]So the Pharisees, having-seen, said to-him, "Look! your disciples do [that] which is-permitted not to-do in [=on a] sabbath." [3]So [=But] he-said to-them, "Did-you-read not what David did when he-hungered and the [ones] with him, [4]how he-entered into	[23]And it-happened him [=he happened once] in [=on] the sabbaths to-travel-by through the grainfields, and his disciples began plucking ears-of-grain to-do way [=as they were made their way along]. [24]And the Pharisees were-saying to-him, "Look, what [=why] do-they-do [on] the sabbaths [that] which is-permitted not?" [25]And he-says[b] to-them, "Never did-you-read what David did when he-had need and he [himself] hungered and the [ones] with him, [26]how he-entered into the house of-god upon [=when] Abiathar [was] high-priest,	[1]So it-happened in [=on a] sabbath[d] him to-travel-through through grainfields and his disciples were-plucking and were-eating the ears-of-grain, rubbing [them] in-the [=in their] hands. [2]So [=But] some of-the Pharisees said, "What [=Why] do-you-do [that] which is-permitted not [on] the sabbaths?" [3]And having-answered, Jesus said to them, "Nor did-you-read this, [that] which David did when he [himself] hungered and the beings [=those who are] with him, [4]like [=when] he-entered into the house of-god, and having-taken the breads of-the presentation
the house of-god and they-ate[a] the breads of-the presentation [=the show bread], which was being-permitted not to-him to-eat nor to-the [ones] with him, if no [=only] to-the priests alone?	and he-ate the breads of-the presentation [=the show bread], which it-is-permitted not [to anyone] to-eat if no [=except]	[=the show bread] he-ate and gave to-the [ones] with him [that] which it-is-permitted not to-eat, if no
	the priests, and he-gave and [=also] to-the beings [=to those who are] together-with him?"	[=except] alone the priests?"
[5]Or did-you-read not in the law that [on] the sabbaths the priests in the temple profane the sabbath and they-are blameless? [6]So I-say to-you that [something] greater of-the [=than the] temple is here. [7]So if you-had-known what 'I-WISH MERCY AND NOT SACRIFICE' is [=means],		

you-condemned [=you would have condemned] not ever the blamelesses [=those who are blameless].		
	[27]And he-was-saying to-them, “The sabbath happened through [=because of] the person and not the person through [=because of] the sabbath,	[5]And he-was-saying to-them,
[8]For [the] lord of-the sabbath is the son of-the person.”	[28]with-the-result-that the son of-the person is lord and[c] [=even] of-the sabbath.”	“[The] lord of-the sabbath, is the son of-the person.”

[a] *they-ate* ℵ B *pc*; *he-ate* 𝔓[70] C D L W Θ *f* [1] *f* [13] 33 892[c] 1006 1506 𝔐 it vg sy cop; *he-took* 892*.
[b] *he-says* ℵ C L Θ *f* [13] 33 700 892 *pc*; *he was-saying* A *f* [1] 1006 1506 𝔐; *he says* 1424 *pc*; *having-answered he-said* D Θ 1342 it[mss]; *he-said* 𝔓[88] B 565 2427 cop[bo].
[c] *and* ℵ B C L Θ 13 2427; *omit* A *f* [1] *f* [13] 33 892 1006 1342 1506 𝔐 it[mss].
[d] *in sabbath* 𝔓[4] ℵ B L W *f* [1] 33 69* 205 579 2542 *pc* it sy[p] cop[sa] cop[bo]; *in next-to-last sabbath* A C D Θ Ψ *f* [13] 892 1006 1342 1506 𝔐 it[mss] vg.
📖 Mt 12:3 – 1 Sam 21:6; 📖 Mt 12:5 – Num 28:9, 10; 📖 Mt 12:7 – Hos 6:6; 📖 Mk 2:25 – 1 Sam 21:6; 📖 Lk 6:3 – 1 Sam 21:6

70. The Man with the Withered Hand (→ §131)

Matt 12:9-14	**Mark 3:1-6**	**Luke 6:6-11**
[9]And having-headed-out from-	[1]And he-entered again[b]	[6]So it-happened in [=on an] other sabbath to-enter him [=that he
there, he-went into their synagogue; [10]and look! [a] person having [=with a] withered hand[a].	into the synagogue. And [a] person was there having the having-been-withered [=with a withered] hand.	entered] into the synagogue and to-teach [=taught there]. And there-was [a] person there and his right hand was withered.
	[2]And they-were-watching-closely him [to see] if [on] the sabbaths he-will-heal him, in-order-that they-might-accuse him.	[7]So the scribes and the Pharisees were-watching-closely him [to see] if he-heals in [=on] the sabbath, in-order-that they-might-find [a way] to-accuse[c] him.
And	[3]And he-says to-the person the withered hand having, “Rise [=Get up and come] into the middle.”	[8]So [=But] he [himself] recognized their thoughts, so [=and] he-said to-the man having the withered hand, “Rise and stand into the middle.” And having-gotten-up, he-stood [there].
they-questioned him saying, if “Is-it-permitted to-heal [on] the sabbaths?”	[4]And he-says to-them, “Is-it-permitted [on] the sabbaths to-do good or to-do-ill, to-save [a] soul or to-kill [it]?”	[9]So Jesus said to them, “I-question you if it-is-permitted [on] the sabbath to-do-good or to-do-ill, to-save [a] soul or to-destroy [it]?”
in-order-that they-might-accuse him.		
[11]So [=But] he-said to-them, “What person will-there-be out of-you who will-have one sheep and if-ever [on] the sabbaths this [sheep] might-fall-in into [a] ditch will-seize it indeed-not and raise [=lift it out]? [12]Therefore, how-great is-superior	So [=But] they-were-being-silent.	

[=how much more superior is a] person
[than a] sheep? With-the-result-
that [=Therefore] it-is-permitted
[on] the sabbaths to-do well."

13 Then he-says to-the person,
"Reach-out your hand." And he-
stretched-out [it] and was-restored
[=it was made] healthy, like the
another [=other]. 14 So the Pharisees
having-gone-out took [=made a]
plot according-to [=against] him

so-that they-might-destroy him.

5 And having-looked-around
[at] them with anger, being-
grieved-deeply upon [=by] the
obstinacy [of] their heart,
he-says to-the person,
"Reach-out the [=your] hand."
And he-stretched-out [it] and
his hand was-restored.
6 And the Pharisees, having-gone-
out immediately gave [=made
a] plot with the Herodians
according-to [=against] him so-
that they-might-destroy him.

10 And having-looked-
around [at] all of-them,

he-said to-him,
"Your hand reach-out." So he-
did and his hand was-restored.

11 So they [themselves] were-filled
[with] madness and were-talking-
about to one-another what
ever they-might-do to-Jesus.

[a] *person having withered hand* ℵ B C W 892 *pc* vg; *there-was person having the withered hand* 𝔐 it^{mss} vg^{mss}; *person was there having the withered hand* D L Δ Q f^{1} f^{13} 33 1006 1342 1424 1506 sy^{p}.
[b] *he-entered again* A C D L W Θ f^{1} f^{13} 33 892 1006 1342 1506 2427 𝔐 cop^{sa}; *omit* ℵ B.
[c] *they-might-find to-accuse him* 𝔓^{4} ℵ* B Q 0233 f^{1} 205 *al* cop^{sa}; *they-might-find accusation him* ℵ^{2} A L W f^{13} 33 1006 1342 1506 𝔐 cop^{bo}; *they-might-find to-accuse* (NB. Contains an alternate spelling of accuse) *him* D; *they-might-accuse him* Ψ *pc.*

71. Jesus Heals Many by the Sea (→ §73)

Mark 3:7-12

7 And Jesus retreated with his disciples to the sea

and many [=a great] multitude from the Galilee
followed; and from Judea
8 and from Jerusalems
and from Idumea, and beyond the Jordan and
around Tyre and Sidon many [=a great] multitude,
hearing whatsoever he-was-doing[a], came to him.
9 And he-said [to] his disciples in-order-that [a] small-
boat might-be-ready for-him through [=because of]
the crowd, in-order-that they-might-press-against
him no [=not];
10 for he-healed many, with-the-
result-that whatsoever [=as many as] were-having
scourges to-assail [=came up to] him in-order-that
they-might-touch him.

11 And the unclean spirits whenever they-were-catching-
sight-of him, were-falling-to him and were-crying
saying that "You are the son of-god."
12 And he-was-
rebuking them many [=greatly] in-order-that they-
might-do [=they might make] him visible no [=not].

Luke 6:17-19

17 And having-descended with them, he-stood upon [a]
level place and many [=a great] crowd [of] his disciples
and many [=a great] multitude of-the whole-people
from all Judea and Jerusalem and the coastal-region
of-Tyre and of-Sidon,
18 who came to-hear him and
to-be-cured from their diseases; and the being-
aggravateds [=those who are bothered] from [=by] unclean

spirits were-being-healed,
19 and all the crowd were-
searching[b] to-touch him, that [=because] power was-
going-out along [=from] him and he-cured [them] all.

[a] *he-was-doing* ℵ A C D W Θ f^{1} f^{13} 33 1006 1342 1506 𝔐 it^{mss} vg; *he-does* B L 892 2427 cop^{sa}.
[b] *were-searching* 𝔓^{75} ℵ B L W Ψ 579 *pc* it^{mss} vg; *was-searching* A D Θ f^{1} f^{13} 33 892 1005 1342 1506 𝔐 it^{mss}.

Matt 8:4 (§65, p. 44)
Q 4:16 (§25, p. 18)

72. The Choosing of the Twelve (→ §103)

Matt 10:1-4	**Mark 3:13-19**	**Luke 6:12-16**	John 1:42
	13And he-ascends	12So it-happened in these days him to-go-out [=that he went out] into the	
1And	into the mountain and	mountain to-pray, and he-was spending-the-night in the prayer of-god. 13And when day	
having-summoned his	he-summons whom he was-wishing, and they-went-away to him. 14And he-did [=he made a group of] twelve, whom and	happened, he-addressed his disciples and having-chosen [=he chose] twelve from them, whom and	
twelve disciples he-gave	[=also] he-named apostles, in-order-that they-might-be with him[a] and in-order-that he-might-send-off them to-preach 15and to-have	[=also] he-named apostles:	
to-them authority [over] unclean spirits with-the-result-that [=for them] to-cast-out them and to-heal all disease and all sickness.	authority to-cast-out the demons.		
2So the names of-the twelve apostles is [=are]	16And he-did [=he appointed] twelve[b]: and he-placed [a] name on-		1:42He-led him to Jesus. Having-beheld him, Jesus said, "You are Simon the
these: first Simon the [one] being-said [=called] Peter, and Andrew his brother, and James the [son]	Simon, [namely] Peter, 17and James the [son]	14Simon whom and [=also] he-named Peter, and Andrew his brother,	son of-John; you [yourself] will-be-called Cephas, which is-meant [=means] Peter."
of-Zebedee, and John his brother, 3Philip and Bartholomew,	of-Zebedee, and John the brother of-James, he-placed [on] them [the] name Boanerges, which is 'sons of-thunder'; 18and Andrew, and Philip, and Bartholomew, and	and James and John, and Philip and Bartholomew[c], 15and	
Thomas and Matthew the tax-collector,	Matthew, and Thomas,	Matthew, and Thomas,	
James the [son] of-Alpheus, and Thadeus, 4Simon the Canaanean,	and James the [son] of-Alpheus, and Thadeus, and Simon the Canaanean,	and James [the son] of-Alpheus, and Simon the [one] being-called [=who was called a] zealot, 16and Judah [the son] of-James,	
and Judah the Iscariot, the [one] and [=also] having-delivered him.	19and Judah Iscariot, who and [=also] delivered him.	and Judah Iscariot who happened [=became a] traitor.	

[a] *twelve, whom and he-named apostles in-order-that they-might-be with him* ℵ B Θ f^{13} 28 cop[sa] cop[bo]; *twelve, in-order-that they-might-be with him* A K L P Π f^{1} 33 565 892 𝔐 it vg sy[s]; *twelve disciples in-order-that they-might-be with him whom and [=also] he-named apostles* W Δ.

Continued

Matt 8:4 (§65, p. 44)
Mark 3:19 (§72, p. 52)

[b] *And he-did twelve, and* ℵ B Δ 565; *and* A C[2] D K L P Θ Π *f*[1] 28 33 𝔐 it[mss] vg sy[s] sy[p] cop[bo]; *first Simon and* *f*[13] cop[sa]; *and leading-around to-preach the proclamation* W it[ms].

[c] *James and John, and Philip and Bartholomew* 𝔓[4] 𝔓[75] ℵ B D L W *f*[13] 33 565 2542 *al* it sy[s] sy[p]; *John and Bartholomew* A Θ Ψ *f*[1] 892 1006 1342 1506 𝔐 it[mss] vg cop[sa] cop[bo].

Luke's Sermon on the Plain

73. The Occasion of Luke's Sermon (→ §71)

Mark 3:7-12

[7]And Jesus retreated with his disciples to the sea

and many [=a great] multitude from the Galilee followed; and from Judea [8]and from Jerusalems and from Idumea, and beyond the Jordan and around Tyre and Sidon many [=a great] multitude, hearing whatsoever he-was-doing[a], came to him. [9]And he-said [to] his disciples in-order-that [a] small-boat might-be-ready for-him through [=because of] the crowd, in-order-that they-might-press-against him no [=not]; [10]for he-healed many, with-the-result-that whatsoever [=as many as] were-having scourges to-assail [=came up to] him in-order-that they-might-touch him.

[11]And the unclean spirits whenever they-were-catching-sight-of him, were-falling-to him and were-crying saying that "You are the son of-god." [12]And he-was-rebuking them many [=greatly] in-order-that they-might-do [=they might make] him visible no [=not].

Luke 6:17-19

[17]And having-descended with them, he-stood upon [a] level place and many [=a great] crowd [of] his disciples and many [=a great] multitude of-the whole-people from all Judea and Jerusalem and the coastal-region of-Tyre and of-Sidon, [18]who came to-hear him and to-be-cured from their diseases; and the being-aggravateds [=those who are bothered] from [=by] unclean spirits

were-being-healed, [19]and all the crowd were-searching[b] to-touch him, that [=because] power was-going-out along [=from] him and he-cured [them] all.

[a] *he-was-doing* ℵ A C D W Θ *f*[1] *f*[13] 33 1006 1342 1506 𝔐 it[mss] vg; *he-does* B L 892 2427 cop[sa].

[b] *were-searching* 𝔓[75] ℵ B L W Ψ 579 *pc* it[mss] vg; *was-searching* A D Θ *f*[1] *f*[13] 33 892 1005 1342 1506 𝔐 it[mss].

74. The Beatitudes (→ §31)

Matt 5:3-6

[3]"Fortunate [are] the poors in-the spirit, that [=because] theirs is the kingdom of-the heavens. [4]Fortunate [are] the languishings [=those who languish], that [=because] they [themselves] will-be-exhorted [=will be comforted]. [5]Fortunate [are] the gentles, that

Q 6:20-21

[20]And having-lifted-up his eyes into [=to] his disciples, <u>saying</u>, "Fortunate [are] the poors that [=because] y'all's-own [reward] is the kingdom of-god.

Luke 6:20-21

[20]And he, having-lifted-up his eyes into [=to] his disciples, was-saying, "Fortunate [are] the poors that [=because] y'all's-own [reward] is the kingdom of-god.

Thomas 54; 69

[54]Jesus said, "Fortunate are the poor, for to you belongs Heaven's kingdom."

[69]Jesus said, "Fortunate are those who have been persecuted in their hearts:

[=because] they [themselves] will-inherit the land. [6]Fortunate [are] the hungerings [=those who hunger] and the being-thirsties [=those who thirst for] righteousness, that [=because] they [themselves] will-be-fed."	[21]Fortunate [are] the hungerings [=those who hunger], that [=because] you-will-be-fed. Fortunate [are] the languishings [=those who languish], that [=because] you-will-be-comforted."	[21]Fortunate [are] the hungerings [=those who hunger] now, that [=because] you-will-be-fed. Fortunate [are] the weepings [=those who weep] now, that [=because] you-will-laugh."	they are the ones who have truly come to know the Father. Fortunate are those who go hungry, so the stomach of the one in want may be filled."

There are no variants in this pericope that appear in English.
🕮 Mt 5:5 – Ps 37:11

75. Beatitude for the Persecuted (→ §31)

Matt 5:11	**Q 6:22-23**	**Luke 6:22-23**	Thomas 68; 69
[11]"Fortunate are-you whenever	[22]"Fortunate are-you whenever	[22]"Fortunate are-you whenever the people might-hate you, and whenever they-might-exclude you and	[68]Jesus said, "Fortunate are you when you are hated and persecuted; and no place will be found, wherever you have been persecuted."
they-might-denounce you and they-might-pursue [you] and they-might-say all evil, lying[a], according-to [=against] you because-of me."	they-might-denounce you and they-might-pursue [you] and they-might-say all evil according-to [=against] you because-of the son of-the person. [23]Rejoice and be-glad, that [=because] your wages [will be] many [=great] in heaven; for thus they-pursued the prophets before you."	they-might-denounce [you] and they-might-cast-out your name like [=as] evil because-of the son of-the person. [23]Rejoice in that day and leap [for joy], for look! your wages [will be] many [=great] in heaven. For their fathers were-doing according-to the them[b] [=the same things] to-the prophets."	[69]Jesus said, "Fortunate are those who have been persecuted in their hearts: they are the ones who have truly come to know the Father. Fortunate are those who go hungry, so the stomach of the one in want may be filled."

[a] *lying* ℵ B C W Δ Θ f^1 f^{13} 28 33 892 1006 1424 𝔐 it^{mss} vg sy^{c} sy^{p} cop; *omit* D it^{mss} sy^{s}.
[b] *the them* 𝔭^{75} B D Q W Ξ Ψ 33^{c} 892 *pc*; *these* ℵ A L Θ f^1 f^{13} 33* 1006 1342 1506 𝔐 it vg.

76. The Woes of Luke's Jesus

Luke 6:24-26

[24]Nevertheless, woe to-you wealthies, that [=because] you-receive-in-full [already] your consolation. [25]Woe to-you, the having-been-satisfieds [=those who are satisfied] now, that [=because] you-will-hunger. Woe[a], the laughings [=those who laugh] now, that [=because] you-will-languish and you-will-weep. [26]Woe [to you], whenever all the people might-say [=might speak] well [of] you, for their fathers were-doing according-to the them [=the very same things] to-the false-prophets.

[a] *Woe* ℵ B L T W Θ Ξ f^1 f^{13} 205 579 700 892 2542 *al* sy^{s}; *Woe to-you* 𝔭^{75} A D Ψ 33 1006 1342 1506 𝔐 it^{mss} vg sy^{p} cop^{sa} cop^{bo}.
🕮 Lk 6:24 – Amos 6:1

77. Loving One’s Enemies (→ §40, §81)

Matt 5:43-45	**Q 6:27-28, 35**	**Luke 6:27-28**
43“You-heard that it-was-said, ‘YOU-WILL-LOVE YOUR NEIGHBOR AND YOU-WILL-HATE YOUR ENEMY.’ 44So [=But] I [myself] say		27“But I-say to-you, to-the hearings [=to those willing to hear],
to-you ‘Love your enemies and	27“Love your enemies	‘Love your enemies, do well to-the hatings [=of those who hate] you, 28bless the cursings [=of those who curse] you,
pray on-behalf of-the pursuings [=of those who pursue] you[a], 45so-that you-might-happen [=you might become] sons [of] your father in [the] heavens, that [=because] he-arises his sun upon [the] evil and [the] good [alike] and it-rains upon [the] righteous and [the] unrighteous.”	28and pray on-behalf of-the pursuings [=of those who pursue] you. 35so-that you-might-happen [=you might become] sons [of] your father, that [=because] he-arises his sun upon [the] evil and [the] good [alike] and it-rains upon [the] righteous and [the] unrighteous.”	pray around[b] [=concerning] the mistreatings [=of those who mistreat] you.”

[a] *pray on-behalf of-the pursuings you* ℵ B f^{1} 205 *pc* sy^{c} sy^{s} cop; *bless the cursings you, do well to-the hatings you, pray around the mistreatings you and the pursuings you* D L W f^{13} 33 892 1006 1342 1506 𝔐 it^{mss} vg sy^{p}.
[b] *around* 𝔓^{75} ℵ B L W Ξ 579 700 *pc*; *on-behalf* A D Θ Ψ f^{1} f^{13} 33 892 1006 1342 1506 𝔐 it vg.
📖 Mt 5:43 – Lev 19:18

78. Renouncing One’s Rights (→ §39)

Matt 5:38-42	**Q 6:29-30**	**Luke 6:29-30**	Thomas 95
38“You-heard that it-was-said, ‘[An] EYE IN-PLACE [of an] EYE, AND [a] TOOTH IN-PLACE [of a] TOOTH.’ 39So [=But] I [myself] say to-you no [=not] to-resist the evil [one]. But whoever slaps[a] you into[b] [=on] your right cheek, turn to-him and [=also] the another [=other]; 40and to-the [one] wishing to-judge you and to-take your tunic, excuse [=offer] him and the [=also your] coat; 41and whoever will-enlist you [for] one mile, leave [=go] with him [for] two.	29“Whoever slaps you into [=on] your cheek, turn to-him and [=also] the another [=other]; and to-the [one] wishing to-judge you and to-take your tunic, excuse [=offer] him and the [=also your] coat; and whoever will-enlist you [for] one mile, leave [=go] with him [for] two.	29“To-the [one] hitting you upon the cheek, present and [=also] the another [=other]; and from the [one] removing your coat may-you-hinder [=withhold] no and [=not even your] tunic.	

[42]Give to-the [one] asking [of] you, and may-you-turn-away no [=do not refuse] the [one] wishing to-loan [=to borrow] from you."	[30]Give to-the [one] asking [of] you, and from the [one] lending [=borrowing] the [things of] yours demand-back no [=not]."	[30]Give to-all asking [of] you[c], and from the [one] removing your-own [things] demand-back no [=not]."	<Jesus said?>, "If you have money, don't lend it at interest. Rather, give <it> to someone from whom you won't get it back."

[a] *slaps* ℵ B W 33 700 1424 *pc*; *will-slap* D L Θ f^{1} f^{13} 892 1006 1342 1506 𝔐 cop^{bo}.
[b] *into* ℵ* B W 983 1342; *upon* $ℵ^{2}$ D L Θ f^{1} f^{13} 33 892 1006 1506 𝔐.
[c] *Give to-all asking you* ℵ B W 579 700 892* *pc*; *Give to-all the asking you* L f^{1} 205 565 1006 1424 1506 2542 *pc*; *So give to-all the asking you* A D Θ Ψ f^{13} 33 892^{c} 1342 𝔐 it^{mss} vg.
📖 Mt 5:38 – Exod 21:24; Lev 24:20; Deut 19:21

79. The Golden Rule (→ §54)

Matt 7:12	**Q 6:31**	**Luke 6:31**	Thomas 6
[12]"Therefore all whatsoever if-ever [=what ever] you-might-wish in-order-that [=that] people might-do to-you, thus and [=also] you [yourselves] do to-them; for this is the law and the prophets."	[31]"And just-as [=what ever] you-wish in-order-that [=that] people might-do to-you, thus you [yourselves] do to-them."	[31]"And just-as [=what ever] you-wish in-order-that [=that] people might-do to-you, do[a] to-them likewise."	His disciples asked him and said to him, "Do you want us to fast? How should we pray? Should we give to charity? What diet should we observe?" Jesus said, "Don't lie, and don't do what you hate, because all things are disclosed before heaven. After all, there is nothing hidden that will not be revealed, and there is nothing covered up that will remain undisclosed."

[a] *do* $\mathfrak{p}^{75}$ B 579 700 *pc* it sy^{p}; *and you do* ℵ A D L W Θ Ξ Ψ f^{1} f^{13} 33 892 1006 1342 1506 𝔐 it^{mss} vg; *do good* it^{mss} vg^{mss} sy^{s}.

80. Impartial Love (→ §40)

Matt 5:46-47	**Q 6:32, 34**	**Luke 6:32-35**
[46]For if-ever you-might-love the lovings [=of those who love] you, what wages do-you-have? [Do] indeed-not and [=even] the tax-collectors do the it [=same thing]?	[32]If you-love the lovings [=of those who love] you, what wages do-you-have? [Do] indeed-not and [=even] the tax-collectors do the it [=same thing]?	[32]And if you-love the lovings [=those who love] you, what-kind-of benefaction is [there] for-you? For and [=even] the sinfuls [=of those who are sinful] love the lovings [=those who love] them.
		[33]And for if-ever you-might-do-good to-the doing-goods [=to those who do good] to-you, what-kind-of benefaction is [there] for-you? And [=Even] the sinfuls [=of those who are sinful] do the it [=same thing].
	[34]And if-ever you-might-lend [to someone] along [=to those from] whom you-hope to-take, what wages do-you-have?	

Matt	Q	Luke
47And if-ever you-might-greet your brothers only, what do-you-do [that is] excessive [=more than what others do]? [Do] indeed-not and [=even] the Gentiles[a] do the it [=same thing]?	[Do] indeed-not and [=even] the Gentiles do the it [=same thing]?	34And if-ever you-might-lend [to someone] along [=to those from] whom you-hope to-take, what-kind-of benefaction is [there] for-you? And [=Even] sinfuls [=those who are sinful] lend to-sinfuls [=to those who are sinful] in-order-that they-might-receive-back the equal [amount]. 35"Nevetheless love your enemies and do-good and lend hoping-for not-one [=nothing], and your wages will-be many [=great], and you-will-be sons [of the] most-high, that [=because] he [himself] is kind upon [=to the] thankless and [the] evil.

[a] *Gentiles* ℵ B D Z f^{1} 33 205 892 1424 *pc* it^{mss} vg sy^{c} cop; *tax-collectors* L W Θ f^{13} 1006 1342 1506 𝔐 sy^{p}.

81. Being Merciful (→ §40)

Matt 5:48	**Q 6:36**	**Luke 6:36**
48"Therefore you [yourselves] will-be perfect like your heavenly father is perfect."	36"Happen [=Become] compassionate like your father is compassionate."	36"Happen [=Become] compassionate just-as your father is compassionate."

There are no variants in this pericope that appear in English.

82. Judging (→ §50, §147)

Matt 7:1-2	Mark 4:24	**Q 6:37-38**	**Luke 6:37-38**	John 8:7
1"Judge no [=not] in-order-that you-might-be-judged no [=not]		37"Judge no [=not], you-might-be-judged no [=not]	37"And judge no [=not] and you-might-be-judged not no [=at all], and condemn no [=not] and you-might-be-condemned not no [=at all]. Release and you-will-be-released. 38Give and it-will-be-given to-you: [a] fine [=good] measure, having-been-pressed-down, having-been-shaken-up, having-been-over-flowed, they-will-give into	7So like [=when] they-were-persisting-in begging him, he-straightened-up and said to-them, "The sinless [one among] you, let-him-throw [a] stone upon her first."

[2]for in [=by] which verdict you-judge you-will-be-judged,		for in [=by that] verdict which you-judge you-will-be-judged,	your bosom; for	
and in [=by]	[24]And he-was-saying to-them, "Look [=Take heed of] what you-hear. In [=By]	[38]and		
which measure you-measure, it-will-be-measured to-you."	which measure you-measure, it-will-be-measured to-you and [more] will-be-added to-you."	in [=by] which measure you-measure, it-will-be-measured to-you."	[by] which measure[a] you-measure, it-will-be-measured-in-return to-you."	

[a] *for which measure* ℵ B D L Θ Ξ f^{1} 33 205 892 1342 *pc* sy^{p}; *for the it measure which* A C Θ Ψ f^{13} 1006 1506 𝔐 it^{mss} vg.

83. The Blind Leading the Blind (→ §169)

Matt 15:14	**Q 6:39**	**Luke 6:39**	Thomas 34
[14]"Excuse them [=Leave them alone], they-are blind escorts of-blind [people]; so if-ever [a] blind [person] might-escort [another] blind [person], they-will-fall both into [a] ditch."	[39]"Surely-not [is a] blind [person] able to-escort [another] blind [person]? Will-they-fall indeed-not both into [a] ditch?"	[39]And so he-said [a] parable to-them. "Surely-not [is a] blind [person] able to-escort [another] blind [person]? Will-they-fall-in[a] not both into [a] ditch?"	Jesus said, "If a blind person leads a blind person, both of them will fall into a hole."

[a] *Will-they-fall-in* B D L W Θ $f^{1\,(13)}$ 579 700 892 1006 1342 2542; *will-they-fall* ℵ A C Ξ Ψ 33 1506 𝔐.

84. Disciple and Teacher (→ §112)

Matt 10:24-25a	**Q 6:40**	**Luke 6:40**	John 13:16
[24]"[A] disciple is not on-behalf [=above] the teacher nor [a] slave on-behalf [=above] his lord.	[40]"[A] disciple is not on-behalf [=above] the teacher;	[40]"[A] disciple is not on-behalf [=above] the teacher[a],	[16]"Amen amen I-say to-you, [a] slave is not greater [than] his lord nor [an] apostle greater [than] the [one] having-sent him."
		so all [=each one] having-been-mended [=having been restored] will-be	
[25a][It is] enough for-the disciple in-order-that he-might-happen [=he might become] like his teacher and the slave like his lord."	[it is] enough for-the disciple in-order-that he-might-happen [=he might become] like his teacher."	like his teacher."	

[a] *the teacher* 𝔭^{75} ℵ B D L W Θ Ξ f^{1} f^{13} 33 205 700 892 1342 2542 *pc* it^{mss} vg; *his teacher* A C Ψ 1006 1506 𝔐 sy cop.

85. The Splinter and the Log (→ §51)

Matt 7:3-5	**Q 6:41-42**	**Luke 6:41-42**	Thomas 26
3 “So what [=why] do-you-look [at] the splinter in the eye [of] your brother, so [=but] you-think-about not the log in your-own eye? 4 Or how will-you-say [to] your brother, ‘Excuse [=Allow that] I-might-cast-out the splinter out [of] your eye’ and look! the log [is] in your eye? 5 Hypocrite, first cast-out out [of] your eye the log[a] and then you-will-see-clearly to-cast-out the splinter out of-the eye [of] your brother.”	41 “So what [=why] do-you-look [at] the splinter in the eye [of] your brother, so [=but] you-think-about not the log in your-own eye? 42 How [will you say to] your brother, ‘Excuse [=Allow that] I-might-cast-out the splinter out [of] your eye’ and look! the log [is] in your eye? Hypocrite, first cast-out out [of] your eye the log and then you-will-see-clearly to-cast-out the splinter [=out of] the eye [of] your brother.”	41 “So what [=why] do-you-look [at] the splinter in the eye [of] your brother, so [=but] the log in [your] own eye you-think-about not? 42 How are-you-able to-say [to] your brother, ‘Brother, excuse [=allow that] I-might-cast-out the splinter in your eye’ not looking [=seeing] the log it [=itself] in your eye? Hypocrite, first cast-out the log out [of] your eye and then you-will-see-clearly the splinter in the eye [of] your brother to-cast-out [it].”	Jesus said, “You see the sliver in your friend’s eye, but you don’t see the timber in your own eye. When you take the timber out of your own eye, then you will see well enough to remove the sliver from your friend’s eye.”

[a] *cast-out out your eye the log* ℵ B C; *cast-out the log out your eye* L W Θ *f*[1] *f*[13] 33 892 1342 1506 𝔐 it vg.

86. “By their fruits . . . ” (→ §56, §140)

Matt 7:18; 12:33b; 7:16b; 12:35; 12:34b	**Q 6:43-45**	**Luke 6:43-45**	Thomas 45
7:18 “[A] good tree is-able not to-do[a] [=make] evil fruits nor [a] rotten tree to-do[b] [=to make] fine fruits.” 12:33b For the tree is-known out of-the [=by its] fruit.	43 “There-is no fine tree doing [=making] rotten fruit, nor again[d] [a] rotten tree doing [=making] fine fruit. 44 For out [=by] the fruit the tree is-known.	43 “For there-is no fine tree doing [=making] rotten fruit, nor again[d] [a] rotten tree doing [=making] fine fruit. 44 For each tree out [=by its] own fruit is-known.	Jesus said, “Grapes are not harvested from thorn trees, nor are figs gathered from thistles, for they yield no fruit. Good persons produce good from what they’ve stored up; bad persons produce evil from the wickedness they’ve stored up in their hearts, and say evil things. For from the overflow of the heart they produce evil.”
7:16b “Surely-not do-they-pick bunches-of-grapes[c] from thorny-plants or figs from thistles?”	Surely-not figs are-picked out [of] thorny-plants, or out [of] thistles bunches-of-grapes?	For they-pick not figs out of-thorny-plants nor do-they-glean [a] bunch-of-grapes out [of a] bramble-bush.	
12:35 “The good person casts-out [=brings out] goods [=good things] out of-the good treasure-box, and the evil person casts-out [=brings out] evils [=evil things] out of-the evil treasure-box.”	45 The good person casts-out [=brings out] good [things] out of-the good treasure-box, and the evil person casts-out [=brings out] evil [things] out of-the evil treasure-box.	45 The good person produces the good out of-the good treasure-box of-the heart[e], and the evil [person] produces the evil out of-evil [treasure-box of the heart].	

12:34b“For the mouth talks out of-the excess of-the heart.”	For out of-excess of-heart [=from the excess of the heart] his mouth talks.”	For out of-excess of-heart [=from the excess of the heart] his mouth talks.”	

[a] *to-do* ℵ C L W Z Θ f^{1} f^{13} 33 892 1006 1342 1506 𝔐 it vg sy; *to-carry* B.
[b] *to-do* ℵ^{1} B C L W Z Θ f^{1} f^{13} 33 1006 1506 𝔐 it^{mss} vg sy cop^{samss}; *to-carry* ℵ*.
[c] *bunches-of-grapes* C L W Θ f^{13} 1006 1342 1506 𝔐; *bunch-of-grapes* ℵ B 0250 f^{1} 205 892 it^{mss} vg sy cop.
[d] *again* 𝔭^{75} ℵ B L W Ξ f^{1} f^{13} 579 892 1342 2542 *pc* vg^{mss} cop^{bo}; *omit* A C D Θ Ψ 33 1006 1506 𝔐 it^{mss} vg sy cop^{sa}.
[e] *of-the heart* 𝔭^{75}ℵ B *pc*; *his heart* A C L W Θ Ξ Ψ f^{1} f^{13} 33 893 1006 1342 1506 𝔐 cop.

87. “Lord, lord” (→ §57)

Matt 7:21	**Q 6:46**	**Luke 6:46**
21“Not all [=each one] saying to-me, ‘Lord, lord’ will-enter into the kingdom of-the heavens, but the [one] doing	46“What [=Why] do-you-call me,	46“So what [=why] do-you-call me,
	‘Lord, lord’ and [=but] you-do not [do the things] which I [myself] say?”	‘Lord, lord’ and [=but] you-do not [do the things] which I-say?”
The wish [of] my father in the[a] heavens.”		

[a] *the* ℵ B C Z Θ f^{1} 33 205 892 1424 1596; *omit* L W f^{13} 1006 1342 𝔐.

88. Houses Built on Rock or Sand (→ §58)

Matt 7:24-27	**Q 6:47-49**	**Luke 6:47-49**
24“Therefore all [=each one] whoever [=who] hears these my	47“All [=Each one] hearing my words and doing them	47“All [=Each one] coming to me and hearing my words and doing them I-will-display [to] you what he-is comparable-to;
words and does them will-be-compared[a] [to a] sensible man,	48is comparable-to [a] person	48he-is comparable-to [a] person
whoever [=who] built his home	who built his home	building [a] home, who dug and went-deep and put [the] foundation
upon the rock. 25And the rain descended and the rivers came and the winds heaved and fell-to [=bombarded] that home, and it-fell not for it-had-been-founded upon	upon the rock. And the rain descended and the rivers came and the winds heaved and fell-to [=bombarded] that home, and it-fell not for it-had-been-founded upon the rock.	upon the rock. So [a] flood-tide having-happened, the river burst-upon that home and it-had-the-strength not to-shake-up it through [=because] it to-have-been-built
the rock. 26And all [=each one] hearing these my words and no [=not] doing them will-be-compared [to a] moronic man, whoever [=who] built his home upon the sand. 27And the rain descended and the rivers	49And all [=each one] hearing my words and not doing them is comparable-to [a] person who built his home upon the sand. And the rain descended and the rivers came	[=had been built] well[b]. 49So [=But] the [one] having-heard [my words] and no [=not] having-done [them] is comparable-to [a] person having-built [a] home upon the land without [a] foundation, which

came and the winds heaved and battered that home, and it-fell	and the winds heaved and battered that home, and immediately it-	the river burst-upon and immediately it-collapsed[c] and the devastation of-that home
and its decline was great.”	fell and its decline was great.”	happened [=was] great.”

[a] *will-be-compared* ℵ B Z Θ *f*[1] *f*[13] 33 205 700 892 vg sy[p] cop[sa]; *I-will-compare* C L W 1006 1342 1506 𝔐 it[mss] sy[c] cop[bo].
[b] *through it to-have-been-built well* 𝔓[75] ℵ B L W Ξ 33 579 892 1342 2542 *pc* cop[sa]; *for it-had-been-founded upon the rock* A C D Θ Ψ *f*[1] *f*[13] 1006 1506 𝔐 it[mss] vg sy[p]; *omit* 𝔓[45] 700* sy[s].
[c] *it-collapsed* 𝔓[45] 𝔓[75] ℵ B D L Θ Ξ *f*[1] *f*[13] 33 205 579 700 892 1342 2542 *pc*; *it-fell* A C W Ψ 1006 1506 𝔐.

The Galilean Ministry Continues Again

89. The Centurion of Capharnaum (→ §66, §96, §249-251)

Matt 8:5-13	Mark 2:1	**Q 7:1, 3, 6-9**	**Luke 7:1-9;** 13:28-29; **7:10**	John 4:46b-54
[5]So, his	[1]And	[1]And it-happened when he-fulfilled [=he finished saying] these words,	[7.1]Since[c] [=When] he-fulfilled [=finished] all his speeches into the rumors [=hearing] of-the whole-people	[46b]And there-was some royal-official whose son was-ill
having-entered [=when he came]	having-entered again	he-entered	he-entered	
into Capharnaum,	into Capharnaum through [=after some] days, it-was-heard that he-is in house [=at home].	into Capharnaum.	into Capharnaum.	in Capharnaum. [47]This [man], having-heard that Jesus presses-forward out of-Judea, into the Galilee, went-away to him and begged [him] in-order-that he-might-descend and might-cure his son, for he-intended [=he was about] to-face-death [=to die].
[an] officer approached him exhorting him [6]and saying, “Lord, my child has-been-thrown [=is bedridden] in the [=at] home [a] paralytic, being-tormented terribly.”		[3][An] officer came to-him exhorting him and saying, “My child has [=is sick] badly.”	[2]So, [a] slave of-some officer, who was honored [=dear] to-him, having [=being sick] badly intended [=was about] to-expire [=to die].	[48]Therefore Jesus said to-him, “If-ever no [=Unless] you-might-see signs and omens, you-might-believe not no [=at all].”
[7]And he-says[a] to-him, “I, having-come, will-heal him.”		And he-says to-him, “I, having-come, will-heal him.”		
			[3]So having-heard around [=about] Jesus, he-sent-off elders of-the Judeans to him begging him so-that having-come he-might-bring-safely-	[49]The royal-official says to him, “Lord, descend [=go] prior-to to-face-death my young-child [=before my child dies].” [50]Jesus says to-him, “Travel [=Go], your son lives.” The person

Matt		Q	Luke	
			through his slave. 4So the having- arriveds [=those who came] to Jesus were-exhorting him hastily saying that "He-is worthy for- whom you-might- present this. 5For he- loves our nation and he [himself] built for- us the synagogue." 6So, Jesus traveled together-with them. So, already he [himself] receiving- in-full not far-away [=when he was not a great distance away] from the home,	believed in-the word which Jesus said to-him and traveled [=left].
8And the officer having-answered spoke, "Lord, I-am not fit in-order-that you-might-enter under my roof,		6And the officer having-answered spoke, "Lord, I-am not fit in-order-that you-might-enter under my roof,	the officer sent [d] friends saying to-him, "Lord, [do] no [=not] bother [coming], for I-am not fit in-order- that under my roof you-might-enter. 7Nor for-this- reason I-deemed- worthy myself to-come to you.	
but only say [it] in-word, and my child will-be-cured. 9And for [=For even] I [myself] am		7but say [it] in- word, and let-be- cured my child. 8And for [=For even] I [myself] am	But say [it] in- word, and let-be- cured[e] my child. 8And for [=For even] I [myself] am	
[a] person under authority, having under myself [=my very own] soldiers, and I-say to-this [one], 'Travel,' and he [himself] travels, and to-another, 'Come,' and he- comes, and to-my slave, 'Do this,' and he-does [it]."		[a] person under authority, having under myself [=my very own] soldiers. And I-say to-this [one], 'Travel,' and he [himself] travels, and to-another, 'Come,' and he- comes, and [to] my slave, 'Do this,' and he-does [it]."	[a] person being- consigned under authority, having under myself [=my very own] soldiers. And I-say to-this [one], 'Travel,' and he [himself] travels, and to-another, 'Come,' and he- comes, and [to] my slave, 'Do this,' and he-does [it]."	

10So, having-heard, Jesus was-astonished and said to-the followings [=to those who follow],

"Amen I-say to-you, along no-one [=in no one] so-many [=so much] loyalty in Israel have-I-found.
11So I-say to-you that many will-press-forward [=will come] from easts [=east] and wests [=west] and will-be-stretched-out [=will recline at table] with Abraham and Isaac and Jacob in the kingdom of-the heavens,
12so [=but] the sons of-the kingdom will-be-cast-out into the outermost darkness. There-will-be wailing and gnashing of-the teeth there."
13And Jesus said to-the officer, "Leave, let-it-happen for-you like you-believed [it would]." And the child[b] was-cured in that hour.

9So, having-heard, Jesus was-astonished and said to-the followings [=to those who follow],

"I-say to-you, nor in Israel so-many [=so much] loyalty have-I-found."

9So, having-heard these [things], Jesus was-astonished [at] him and having-turned to-the crowd [that was] following him said,

"I-say to-you, nor in Israel so-many [=so much] loyalty have-I-found."
13:28"There will-be wailing and grinding of-teeth whenever you-might-see Abraham and Isaac and Jacob and all the prophets in the kingdom of-god, so [=but] you being-cast outside.
29And they-will-press-forward from easts [=east] and wests [=west] and from north and south and they-will-be-stretched-out in the kingdom of-god."

7:10And the having-beens [=those who had been] sent, having-returned into the house, found the slave being-healthy.

51So already him [=as he was] descending, his slaves met him saying that his child lives.
52Therefore he-inquired along [=from] them [as to] the hour in which he-had more-nicely [=he started to recover]. Therefore they-said to-him that yesterday [in the] seventh hour the fever excused [=left] him.
53Therefore the father knew that [it was] in that hour in which Jesus said to-him, "Your son lives." And he believed and his whole home.
54So again this Jesus did this second sign having come out of-Judea into the Galilee.

a *he-says* ℵ B 892 *pc* it^mss cop^bo; *Jesus he-says* C L W Θ *f*^1 *f*^13 33 1006 1342 1506 𝔐 it^mss vg sy^s sy^p cop^sa.

b *the child* ℵ B 0250 *f*^1 33 205 *pc* it vg cop^bo; *his child* C L W Θ *f*^13 892 1006 1342 1506 𝔐 sy cop^sa.

c *Since* A B C* W 579; *So as* ℵ C^2 L X Y *f*^1 *f*^13 33 1006 1342 𝔐; *So when* Θ *pc*.

d *omit* 𝔓^75 ℵ* B 579 892 1342 *pc* cop^sa; *to him* ℵ^2 C D L Θ Ψ *f*^1 *f*^13 33 1006 1506 𝔐 it vg sy cop^bo.

e *let-be-cured* 𝔓^75 B L cop^sa; *will-be-cured* ℵ A C D W Θ Ψ *f*^1 *f*^13 33 892 1006 1342 1506 𝔐 it vg cop^bo.

90. Luke's Widow's Son at Nain

Luke 7:11-17

11 And it-happened in the following-day, he-traveled into [a] city being-called Nain and his
disciples and many crowds traveled-together-with him. 12 So like [=when] he-neared the gate of-
the city, and look! [someone] having-died, [an] only-born son [of] his mother—and she[a] was [a]
widow—was-being-conveyed-for-burial, and fit [=a large] crowd of-the city was together-with
her. 13 And having-seen her, the lord had-pity upon [=for] her and said to-her, "Weep no [=not]."
14 And having-approached, he-touched the bier, so the bearings [=those who bear it] stood [still], and
he-said, "Young-man, I-say to-you, be-raised." 15 And the dead [man] sat-up and began to-talk, and
he-gave him [to] his mother. 16 So fear took [=overtook] all [of them] and they-glorified god saying
that "[A] great prophet was-raised in [=among] us" and that "God cared-for his whole-people."
17 And this word [=story] around [=concerning] him went-out in the whole [of] Judea and all the
surrounding-regions.

[a] *she* 𝔓75 ℵ B* C D L W Θ Ψ Ξ f^{13} 33 1006; *this [woman]* B2 f^{1} 205 892 1342 1506 cop^{bo}.

91. Peter's Mother-in-Law Healed (→ §61)

Matt 8:14-15	Mark 1:29-31	Luke 4:38-39
14 And Jesus, having-come into the	29 And immediately having-gone-out out of-the synagogue they-went[a] into the home of-Simon and	38 So having-gotten-up [=having departed] from the synagogue he-entered into the home of-Simon.
home of-Peter saw his mother-in-law having-been-thrown	Andrew with James and John. 30 So [=Now] the mother-in-law of-Simon was-lying-down,	So [=Now the] mother-in-law of-Simon was being-controlled [by
[=sprawled out] and being-feverish;	being-feverish, and immediately they-say [=they spoke] to-him	a] great fever and they-begged him around [=concerning] her.
15 and he-touched her hand,	around [=concerning] her. 31 And having-approached he-raised her,	39 And having-stood-by above her he-rebuked the fever and it-excused
and the fever excused [=left] her and she-was-raised and she-was-serving him.	having-seized the [=her] hand; and the fever excused [=left] her and she-was-serving them.	[=it left] her; so at-once having-gotten-up she-was-serving them.

[a] *they-went* ℵ A C 𝔐 vg sy^{s} sy^{p} cop^{bo}; *he-went* B D W Θ f^{1} f^{13} 565 2427 it.

92. The Sick Healed at Evening (→ §62)

Matt 8:16-17	Mark 1:32-34	Luke 4:40-41
16 So evening having-happened they-offered to-him many being-demon-possesseds [=demoniacs];	32 So evening having-happened when the sun set they-were-carrying to him all the havings followings [=those who were] sick and the being-demon-possesseds [=demoniacs]; 33 and the whole city was having-been-collected [=gathered] to [=at] the door.	40 So [while] the sun [=is] setting, everyone whatsoever [=who] had [any who were] being-ill [with] various diseases led them to him.
and he-cast-out the spirits [with a] word and he-healed all the havings [=those who were sick] badly	34 And he-healed many havings badly [=who were sick] various diseases and he-cast-	So placing hands [on] each one of-them, he-was-healing them. 41 So demons and [=also] were-going-out from many, screaming

	out many demons and he-was-excusing [=he would allow] not the demons to-talk that [=because] they-recognized him[a].	and saying that "You are the son[b] of-god." And rebuking he-was-permitting them not to-talk that [=because] they-recognized the anointed-one to-be him.
17 so-that the having-been-said [=what was said] through Isaiah the prophet might-be-fulfilled, saying "HE TOOK OUR ILLNESSES AND BORE [our] DISEASES."		

[a] *they-recognized him* ℵ A 1006 𝔐 sy^s sy^p cop^{sa}; *they-recognized him to-be anointed-one* B C L W Θ f^1 f^{13} 565 1342 1424 2427 cop^{bo}.
[b] *you-are the son* ℵ B C D F L W Ξ 33 2542 it sy^s cop^{sa}; *you-are the anointed-one the son* A Θ Ψ f^1 f^{13} 1006 1342 𝔐.
🕮 Mt 8:17 – Isa 53:4

93. On Following Jesus (→ §195)

Matt 8:18-22	Q 9:57-60	Luke 9:57-62	Thomas 86
18 So Jesus having-seen [a] crowd[a] around him, ordered [for them] to-go-away into the beyond [=to the other side]. 19 And one scribe, having-approached, said to-him, "Teacher, I-will-follow you where if-ever you-might-go-away." 20 And Jesus says to-him, "The foxes have holes and the birds of-the heaven [have] nests, so [=but] the son of-the person has not [a place] wheresoever he-might-recline the [=his] head."	57 And some [one] said to-him, "I-will-follow you where if-ever you-might-go-away." 58 And Jesus said to-him, "The foxes have holes and the birds of-the heaven [have] nests, so [=but] the son of-the person has not [a place] wheresoever he-might-recline the [=his] head."	57 And their traveling [=while they were traveling] in [=on] the way [=road] some [one] said to him, "I-will-follow you where if-ever you-might-go-away[b]." 58 And Jesus said to-him, "The foxes have holes and the birds of-the heaven [have] nests, so [=but] the son of-the person has not [a place] wheresoever he-might-recline the [=his] head."	Jesus said, "<Foxes have> their dens and birds have their nests, but human beings have no place to lay down and rest."
21 So [=But an] other [of] his disciples said to-him, "Lord, first allow me to-go-away and to-bury my father." 22 So [=But] Jesus says to-him, "Follow me and excuse [=leave] the dead to-bury the dead themselves."	59 So [=but an] other said to-him, "Lord, first allow me to-go-away and to-bury my father." 60 So [=But] he-says to-him, "Follow me and excuse [=leave] the dead to-bury the dead themselves."	59 So he-said to-other [=to another disciple], "Follow me." So [=But] he-said, "Lord[c], allow me, having-gone-away, first to-bury my father." 60 So [=But] he-said to-him, "Excuse [=Leave] the dead to bury the dead themselves, so [=but] you, having-gone-away, give-notice [about] the kingdom of-god." 61 So [=But an] other said, "I-will-follow you,	

lord; so [=but] first allow me to-bid-goodbye to-the [ones] into [=in] my house [=family]." 62So Jesus said to him, "No-one having-thrown-on the [=putting his] hand upon [a] plow and looking into the behind [=back] is usable in-the kingdom of-god."

[a] *crowd* B cop^{samss}; *many crowds* ℵ^{2} C L Θ f^{13} 33 892 1006 1342 1506 𝔐 it^{mss} vg sy; *many crowd* W 1424 *pc* it^{mss} cop^{samss}; *crowds* ℵ* f^{1} *pc* cop^{bo}.
[b] *omit* 𝔓^{45} 𝔓^{75} ℵ B D L Ξ f^{1} 205 1342 pc it^{mss} vg sy^{s} sy^{c} cop^{sa}; *lord* A C W Θ Ψ f^{13} 33 892 1006 1506 𝔐 it^{mss} cop^{bo}.
[c] *Lord* 𝔓^{45} 𝔓^{75} ℵ A B^{2} C L W Θ Ξ Ψ 0181 f^{1} f^{13} 33 892 1006 1342 1506 𝔐 it sy^{c} sy^{p} cop; *omit* B* D pc sy^{s}.

94. Stilling the Storm (→ §158)

Matt 8:23-27

23And having-embarked him [=when he had gotten] into the boat his disciples followed him.

24And look! [a] great earthquake happened in the sea, with-the-result-that the boat to-be-covered [=was covered] under the waves, so [=but] he [himself] was-sleeping.

25And

having-approached,[a] they-raised [=they awoke] him saying, "Lord, save[b];

we-are-destroying [=we are perishing]." 26And he-says to-them, "What [=Why] are-you afraid, little-loyalties [=you of little faith]?" Then, having-been-raised [=having gotten up], he-rebuked the winds and the sea,

and [a] great calm happened.

27So the people were-astonished saying,

Mark 4:35-41

35And he-says to-them in [=on] that day, evening having-happened, "Let-us-go-through into the beyond [=to the other side]." 36And excusing [=leaving] the crowd they-take-along him in the boat like [=just as] he-was, and another [=other] boats were with him.
37And [a] great squall of-wind happens and the waves were-throwing-on [=were being thrown] into the boat, with-the-result-that the boat already to-be-stuffed [=was filled].
38And he [himself] was in the stern sleeping upon the cushion.

They-raise [=they wake] him and say to-him, "Teacher, is-it-of-concern not to-you that we-are-destroying [=we are perishing]?"

39And having-been-awoken, he-rebuked the wind and said to-the sea, "Be-silent, be-muzzled." And the wind ceased and [a] great calm happened.
40And he-said to-them, "What [=Why] are-you afraid? Have-you not-yet [any] loyalty[c]?"
41And they-were-feared great fear [=they were very afraid] and were-saying to one-another,

Luke 8:22-25

22So it-happened in [=on] one of-the days, and he [himself] embarked and his disciples into [a] boat and he-said to them, "Let-us-go-through into the beyond of-the harbor [=to the other side of the harbor], and they-were-led-up [=they launched the boat]."
23So their sailing [=while they were sailing] he-fell-asleep. And [a] squall of-wind descended into the harbor and they-were-being-swamped and they-were-being-endangered.

24So, having-approached they-awoke him saying, "Overseer, overseer,

we-are-destroying [=we are perishing]."

So having-been-awoken,[d] he-rebuked the wind and the rough-waves of-the water. And they-stopped and [a] calm happened. 25So he-said to-them,

"Wheresoever [is] your loyalty?"

So having-been-feared [=being afraid] they-were-astonished saying to one-another, "What

"What-sort-of [man] is this that and [=even] the winds and the sea obey him?"	"What [=Who] consequently is this that and [=even] the wind and the sea obeys him?"	[=Who] consequently is this that and [=even] he-presides-over the winds and the water and they-obey him?"

[a] *omit* ℵ B 33 892 it^{mss} vg cop^{sa} cop^{bo}; *the disciples* C^{2} L *f*^{13} 1005 1342 1506 𝔐; *his disciples* C* W Θ *f*^{1} 205 1424 it^{mss} sy.
[b] *omit* ℵ B C *f*^{1} *f*^{13} 33 205 892 pc cop^{bo}; *us* L W Θ 1006 1342 1506 𝔐 it vg sy.
[c] *What are-you afraid? Have-you not-yet loyalty?* ℵ B D L Δ Θ 565 579 700 892* 1342 1424 2427; *What are-you afraid thus? How have-you no loyalty?* A C 33 1006 1506 𝔐 sy^{p}; *What are-you afraid thus?* W; *What are-you thus afraid?* 𝔓^{45} *f*^{1} *f*^{13} 205 892^{C} 2542 *pc.*
[d] *having-been-awoken* 𝔓^{75} ℵ B L Q *f*^{13} 33 892; *having-been-raised* A D W Ψ *f*^{1} 1006 1342 1506 𝔐.

95. The Gadarene Demoniac (→ §159)

Matt 8:28-34	Mark 5:1-20	Luke 8:26-39
28 And his having-come [=when he went] into the beyond [=across] into the region of-the Gadarenes[a] two extremely fierce being-demon-possesseds [=demoniacs] going-out out of-the tombs met him,	1 And they-went into the beyond [=across] the sea into the region of-the Gerasenes[c]. 2 And his having-gone-out [=when he got] out of-the boat, immediately [a] person in [=with] [an] unclean spirit met[d] him out of-the tombs,	26 And they-sailed-along into the region of-the Gerasenes[e], whichever [=which] is opposite of-the Galilee. 27 So having-gone-out him [=when he got out] upon the land, some man out [=from] the city having[f] demons met [him], and in-time fit [=for a long time] he-was-clothed not [with a] coat and was-staying not in [a] home but in the graves.
with-the-result-that no some [=one] to-have-the-strength [=was strong enough] to-pass-away [=to pass] through that way.	3 who was-having [=had an] abode [=home] in the graves, and nor [=neither a] chain no-longer [=nor] no-one [=anyone] was-able to-restrain him, 4 through [=because] he [himself] to-have-been-restrained [=had been restrained] often [by] foot-shackles and chains and [=but] the chains to-have-been-broken-apart [=were broken apart] under [=by] him and the foot-shackles to-have-been-shattered [=were shattered], and no-one had-the-strength to-tame him. 5 And through all night and day in the graves and in the mountains he-was crying [out] and bruising himself [on] stones.	
29 And look! they-cried [out] saying, "What to-us and to-you [=What have you to do with us], son of-god? Did-you-come here before [the] proper-time to-torment us?"	6 And having-seen Jesus from far-off he-ran and worshiped him 7 and having-cried [with a] great voice he-says, "What to-me and to-you [=What have you to do with me], Jesus son of-god the most-high? I-swear [to] you [by] god, [that] you-might-torment me no [=not]." 8 For he-was-saying to-him, "Go-out, unclean spirit out [=from] the person."	28 So having-seen Jesus, having-cried-out he-fell-to him and said [with a] great voice, "What to-me and to-you [=What have you to do with me], Jesus son of-god the most-high? I-implore you, [that] you-might-torment me no [=not]." 29 For he-enjoin the unclean spirit to-go-out from the person. For many times it-had-grabbed him and he-was-being-bound in-chains and foot-shackles [while] being-guarded and [after] rending the bindings

30 So far-away from them [a] herd
of-many pigs was being-grazed.
31 So the evil-spirits were-exhorting
him saying, "If you-cast-out us,
send-off us[b] into the herd of-pigs."

32 And he-said to-them, "Leave."
So having-gone-out, they-went-
away into the pigs. And look! all
the herd rushed according-to
[=down] the steep-bank into the

sea and they-faced-death [=they
died] in the waters. 33 So the
grazings [=the herdsmen]
fled and having-gone-away into the
city informed all [=told everything]
and the [report] of-the being-
demon-possesseds [=demoniacs].

34 And look! all the city went-
out into [a] meeting [with]
Jesus and having-seen him

they-exhorted him so-
that he-might-head-out
from their territories.

9 And he-was-questioning him,
"What [is] your name?" And he-
says to-him, "My name [is] Legion,
that [=because] we-are many."
10 And he-was-exhorting him
many [times] in-order-that
he-might-send-off them no
[=not] outside of-the region.
11 So [=Now] to [=on] the mountain
great [a] herd of-pigs was there
being-grazed. 12 And they-
exhorted him saying, "Send
us into the pigs, in-order-that
we-might-enter into them."
13 And he-allowed them. And the
unclean spirits, having-gone-out
[of the man], entered into the pigs,
and the herd rushed according-to
[=down] the steep-bank into the
sea, like [=about] two-thousand,
and they-drowned in the sea.

14 And the grazings [=the herdsmen]
fled [from] them and informed
[=told of this] into [=in] the city and
into [=in] the fields [=countryside].
And they-went to-see what is the
having-happened [=had happened].

15 And they-come to Jesus and
they-catch-sight-of the being-
demon-possessed [=demoniac]
sitting, having-a-coat-on [=being
clothed] and being-sane, the [very
one] having-had the legion, and
they-were-feared [=they were afraid].
16 And the having-seens [=those
who saw it] narrated to-them how
[=what] happened to-the being-
demon-possessed [=demoniac] and
around [=concerning] the pigs.
17 And they-began

to-exhort him to-go-away
from their territories.

18 And his embarking into the boat,
the having-been-demon-possessed

[=his chains] he-was-being-driven
under [=by] the demon into the
deserteds [=deserted places].
30 So Jesus questioned him,
"What is your name?" So he-said,
"Legion" that [=because] many
demons entered into him. 31 And
they-were-exhorting him, in-order-
that he-might-preside-over them no
[=not] to-go-away into the abyss.

32 So [=Now a] fit [=large] herd of-pigs
was there being-grazed in [=on] the
mountain. And they-exhorted him
in-order-that he-might-allow them
to-enter into those [animals].

And he-allowed them. 33 So
the demons, having-gone-out
from the person, entered into
the pigs, and the herd rushed
according-to [=down] the
steep-bank into the harbor
and it-was-suffocated [=drowned].
34 So the grazings [=the herdsmen],
having-seen the having-happened
[=what had happened], fled and
informed [=told of this] into [=in]
the city and into [=in] the fields
[=countryside]. 35 So they-went-out
[=they went out] to-see the having-
happened [=what had happened]
and they-went to Jesus and found
sitting the person from whom the
demons went-out having-a-coat-
on and being-sane along [=at] the

feet of-Jesus, and they-were-feared
[=they were afraid]. 36 So the having-
seens [=those who saw it] informed
them how the having-been-demon-
possessed [=demoniac] was-saved.
37 And everyone [in] the multitude
[from] the surrounding-region
of-the Gerasenes begged
him to-go-away from them
that [=because] they-were-
controlled [by a] great fear.
So having-embarked into [a]
boat he [himself] returned.

[=demoniac] was-exhorting
him in-order-that he-might-
be [=he might go] with him.

19 And he-excused him not [=he
did not allow it], but says to-him,
"Leave into your house, to your-
own [people], and inform them
whatsoever [=of all the things] the
lord has-done for-you and [how]
he-was-merciful [to] you."
20 And he-went-away and began
to-preach in the Decapolis
whatsoever Jesus did to-him,

and all were-being-astonished.

38 So the man from whom the
demons had-gone-out implored
him to-be together-with him
[=allowed to go along with Jesus].
So [=But] he-released him saying,

39 "Return into your house and
narrate whatsoever [=all the
things] god did for-you."

And he-went-away according-
to [=throughout] the whole city
preaching whatsoever [=about
all the things] Jesus did to-him.

[a] *Gadarenes* B C Δ Θ *al* sy^{s} sy^{p}; *Gerasenes* 892^{C} it vg cop^{sa}; *Gergesenes* ℵ^{2} L W f^{1} f^{13} 892* 1006 1342 1506 𝔐 cop^{bo}; *Gazarenes* ℵ*.
[b] *send-off us* ℵ B Θ f^{1} 22 205 892 *pc* it^{mss} vg sy^{s} cop; *allow us to-go-away* C L W f^{13} 1006 1342 1506 𝔐 it^{mss}.
[c] *Gerasenes* ℵ* B D it vg sy; *Gadarenes* A C f^{13} 1006 1342 1506 𝔐 sy^{p}; *Gergustenes* W; *Gergesenes* ℵ^{2} L Δ Θ f^{1} 33 205 565 700 782 1424 2427 2542 *al* sy^{s} cop^{bo}.
[d] *met* ℵ B C D G L Δ Θ f^{1} f^{13} 205 565 579 700 1342 1424 2542 *al*; *encountered* A W 33 892 1006 1506 𝔐.
[e] *Gerasenes* 𝔭^{75} B D it vg; *Gergesenes* ℵ L Θ Ξ f^{1} 33 205 579 700* 1342 *pc*; *Gadarenes* A W Y f^{13} 892 1006 1506 𝔐 sy.
[f] *having* 𝔭^{75} ℵ* B 579 1342 *pc*; *who was-having* ℵ^{2} A D L Θ f^{1} f^{13} 33 892 1006 1506 𝔐.

96. The Healing of a Paralytic (→ §66, §89)

Matt 9:1-8

1 And having-embarked
into [a] boat he-crossed-
over and went into
the [=his] own city.

2 And look! they-
were-offering to-
him [a] paralytic

having-been-thrown
upon [a] stretcher.

Mark 2:1-12

1 And having-entered
again into Capharnaum
through [=after some] days,
it-was-heard that he-is
in house [=at home].
2 And[c] many were-
gathered with-the-result-
that not-any-longer
to-accept so-not to
[=there was no longer room
even at] the door and
he-was-talking [=he was
speaking] the word to-
them. 3 And they-come
carrying to him
[a] paralytic
being-removed
under [=by] four.

Luke 5:17-26

17 And it-happened in
[=on] one of-the days and
[=that] he [himself] was
teaching and Pharisees
and legal-teachers, who
were having-come [=who
had come] out of-all [=of
every] village of-the Galilee
and Judea and Jerusalem,
were sitting; and [the]
power [of the] lord was
into [=with] him to-cure.

18 And look! men
carrying [a] person
who was

having-been-paralyzed
upon [a] stretcher; and
they-were-searching
[=they were trying] to-bring
him [in] and to-put him
in-the-sight of-him.

John 5:1-9a

1 With [=After] these
[things] there-was [a]
feast of-the Judeans
and Jesus ascended into
Jerusalem. 2 So [=Now]
there-is in Jerusalems
upon [=near] the sheep-
gate [a] pool, the being-
called-on [=which is called]
in-Hebrew Bethzatha,
having [=which has] five
porticos. 3 In these was-
lying-down [a] multitude
[of those] being-ill, blind,
lame, withered.* 5 So, some
person was there having
[been] in his illness [for]
thirty and eight years.
6 Jesus, having-seen this
[person] lying-down and
having-known that he-has
already [been there] many
[=for much] time, says
to-him, "Do-you-wish

And Jesus, having-seen
their loyalty said to-
the paralytic, "Cheer-
up, descendant, your
sins are-excused."
3And look! some of-
the scribes said in
[=to] themselves,
"This [man]
blasphemes."
4And Jesus having-seen[a]
their deliberations
said, "For-what-reason
do-you-deliberate-on evil
[things] in your hearts?
5For, what is easier to-say:
'Your sins are-excused[b],
or to-say 'Rise
and walk-around'? 6So
[=But] in-order-that
you-might-recognize that
authority the son of-the
person has upon the
land [=earth] to-excuse
sins"—then he-says to-the
paralytic—"Having-
been-raised, remove your
stretcher and leave [=go]
into your house." 7And

4And no [=not] being-able
to-offer him through the
crowd, they-unroofed
the roof where he-was,
and having-scooped
they-lower the mattress
where the paralytic
was-lying-down.
5And Jesus, having-seen
their loyalty, says to-the
paralytic, "Descendant,
your sins are-excused."
6So some of-the scribes
were there sitting and
pondering in their
hearts: 7"What this
talks [=Why does this
man speak] thus? He-
blasphemes; what [=who]
is-able to-excuse sins if no
[=except] the one god?"
8And Jesus, having-
understood immediately
[in] his spirit that
they-ponder thus in
themselves, says[d] to-
them, "What [=Why]
do-you-ponder these
[things] in your hearts?
9What is easier to-
say to-the paralytic,
'Your sins are-excused' or
to-say 'Rise, and remove
your mattress and walk-
around'? 10So [=But]
in-order-that you-might-
recognize that authority
the son of-the person has
to-excuse sins upon the
land [=earth]"—he-says
to-the paralytic—11"I-
say to-you, rise, remove
your mattress and leave
[=go] into your house."
12And he-was-raised and
immediately having-
removed the mattress,

19And no [=not] having-
found what-kind-of [=by
what way] they-might-
bring him [in] through the
crowd, having-ascended
upon the housetop, they-
let-down him through
the tiles together-with
the cot into the middle
in-front of-Jesus.
20And having-seen
their loyalty, he-said,
"Person, your sins have-
been-excused for-you."
21And the scribes and
Pharisees began to-
ponder, saying, "What
[=Who] is this who talks
[=speaks] blasphemies?
What [=Who] is-able
to-excuse sins if no
[=except] god alone?"
22So Jesus, having-
understood their
thoughts, [and]
having-answered,
said to them "What
=Why] do-you-ponder
in your hearts?
23What is easier to-say:
'Your sins have-been-
excused for-you' or to-say
'Rise, and walk-around'?
24So [=But] in-order-that
you-might-recognize that
the son of-the person
has authority upon the
land [=earth] to-excuse
sins"—he-said to-the
[one] having-been-
paralyzed, "I-say to-you,
rise, and having-removed
your cot, travel into your
house." 25And having-
gotten-up at-once in-
the-sight of-them, [and]
having-removed [that]
upon which he-was-lying-

to-happen [=to become]
healthy?" 7The [one who
was] being-ill answered
to-him, "Lord, I-have
no person in-order-that,
whenever the water
might-be-disturbed,
he-might-throw me into
the pool. So, in which
[=whenever] I [myself]
come [down], another
descends before me."
8Jesus says to-him,
"Rise, remove your
mattress and walk-
around."
9aAnd instantly the
person happened
[=became] healthy and
he-removed his
mattress and
was-walking-around.

having-been-raised, he-went-away into his house. 8So, having-seen, the crowds were-feared [=became afraid] and they-glorified god, having-given [=who gave] authority such-as-this to-people.

he-went-out in-front of-all, with-the-result-that all to-be-surprised [=were surprised] and to-glorify [=they glorified] god, saying that "We-saw never thus [=we have never seen anything like this]."

down, he-went-away into his house glorifying god. 26And ecstasy took everyone and they-were-glorifying god and they-were-filled [with] fear saying that "We-saw incredible [things] today."

[a] *having-seen* ℵ C D L W 0233 f^{13} $\mathfrak{M}$ it vg sy^{s} cop^{bo}; *having-known* B Θ f^{1} 565 700 1424 sy^{p} sy^{h} cop^{sa}.
[b] *are-excused* ℵ B D it^{mss} vg *pc*; *have-been-excused* C L W Θ 0233 f^{1} f^{13} 33 $\mathfrak{M}$ it.
[c] *omit* ℵ B L W Q 33 579 892 1342 2427 *pc* it^{mss} vg sy^{p} cop; *instantly* A C D f^{1} f^{13} 1006 1506 $\mathfrak{M}$.
[d] *says* $\mathfrak{p}^{88}$ ℵ B L W 33 892 1342 2427 *pc*; *said* A C D Θ f^{1} f^{13} 1006 1506 $\mathfrak{M}$.
* John 5:4 is missing from the oldest and most authoritative manuscripts.

97. The Call of Levi (→ §67)

Matt 9:9-13

9And passing-by from-there, Jesus saw [a] person, sitting upon [=in] the tax-booth, being-said [=called] Matthew, and he-says to-him, "Follow me." And having-gotten-up, he-followed him. 10And it-happened [when] he [himself] [was] dining in the [=at] home and look! many tax-collectors and sinfuls [=those who are sinful], having-come, were-sitting-at-table [with] Jesus and his disciples. 11And the Pharisees, having-seen, were-saying[a] [to] his disciples, "Through what [=Why] your teacher eats [=does your teacher eat] with the tax-collectors and sinfuls [=those who are sinful]?" 12So having-heard, he-said, "The having-the-strengths [=those who have the strength] have not need [of a] physician but the havings [=those who are sick] badly.

Mark 2:13-17

13And he-went-out again along the sea; and all the crowd was-going to him, and he-was-teaching them. 14And passing-by, he-saw Levi the [son] of-Alpheus sitting upon [=in] the tax-booth, and he-says to-him, "Follow me." And having-gotten-up, he-followed him. 15And it-happens him to-recline [=as he was reclining] in his home and [=also] many tax-collectors and sinfuls [=those who are sinful] were-sitting-at-table [with] Jesus and his disciples, for there-were many and they-were-following him. 16And the scribes of-the Pharisees, having-seen that he-eats with the sinfuls [=those who are sinful] and tax-collectors were-saying [to] his disciples "[How is it] that he-eats with the tax-collectors and sinfuls [=those who are sinful]?" 17And having-heard, Jesus says to-them[c] that "The having-the-strengths [=those who have the strength] have not need [of a] physician but the havings [=those who are sick] badly.

Luke 5:27-32

27And with [=after] these [things], he-went-out and noticed [a] tax-collector [by the] name Levi sitting upon [=in] the tax-booth, and he-said to-him, "Follow me." 28And having-quit all [=everything and] having-gotten-up, he-was-following[d] him. 29And Levi did [=made a] great dinner for-him in his home and there-was many [=a great] crowd of-tax-collectors and anothers [=others] who were lying-down with them. 30And the Pharisees and their scribes were-grumbling to his disciples saying, "Through what [=Why] do-you-eat and do-you-drink with the tax-collectors and sinfuls [=those who are sinful]?" 31And having-answered, Jesus said to them, "The being-healthies [=those who are healthy] have not need [of a] physician but the havings [=those who are sick] badly;

[13]So having-traveled [forth], learn what is [the meaning of], 'I-WISH MERCY AND NOT SACRIFICE.' For I-came not to-call [the] righteous but sinful [people] [b]."	I-came not to-call [the] righteous but sinful [people]."	[32]I-have-come not to-call [the] righteous but sinful [people] into repentance."

[a] *were-saying* ℵ B C L W f[1] 33 205 892; *said* D Θ f[13] 1006 1342 𝔐.
[b] *omit* ℵ B D W Δ 0233 f[1] 33 205 565 it[mss] vg sy[p] cop[bo]; *into repentance* C L Θ f[13] 892 1006 1342 1506 𝔐. it[mss] sy[s] cop[sa].
[c] *to-them* 𝔓[88] B Δ Θ 565 2427 *pc*; *omit* ℵ A C D L W f[1] f[13] 33 892 1006 1342 1506 𝔐 it vg sy.
[d] *he-was-following* B D L W Ξ 69 700 892 1506 *pc* it[mss]; *they-were-following* ℵ A C Θ f[1] f[13] 33 1006 11342 𝔐.
🕮 Mt 9:13 – Hos 6:6

98. A Question about Fasting (→ §68)

Matt 9:14-17	Mark 2:18-22	Luke 5:33-39	John 3:29-30	Thomas 104; 47
[14]Then the disciples of-John	[18]And the disciples of-John and the Pharisees[b] were fasting. And they-	[33]So		
approach him saying, "Through what [=Why do] we [ourselves] and the Pharisees	come and say to-him, "Through what [=Why do] the disciples of-John and the disciples	they-said to him, "The disciples		
fast [a]	of-the Pharisees fast,	of-John fast frequently and do [=make] petitions and likewise the [disciples] of-the		
so [=but] your disciples fast not?" [15]And Jesus said	so [=but] your-own disciples fast not?" [19]And Jesus said	Pharisees, so [=but] your-own eat and drink." [34]So Jesus said to them, "You- are-able not to-do		
to-them, "The sons of-the wedding-hall [=groom's attendants] are-able no [=not] to-languish upon whatsoever [=while] is with them the bridegroom [are they]?	to-them, "The sons of-the wedding- hall [=groom's attendants] are-able no [=not] to-fast in which [=while] the bridegroom is with them [are they]? Whatsoever time they-have the bridegroom with them they-are-able to-fast no [=not].	[=to make] the sons of-the wedding-hall [=groom's attendants] to-fast in which [=while] the bridegroom is with them [are you]?		[104]They said to Jesus, "Come, let us pray today, and let us fast." Jesus said, "What sin have I committed, or how have I been undone? Rather, when the groom leaves the bridal suite, then let people fast and pray."

Mark 3:19 (§72, p. 52) Q 7:9 (§89, p. 63)
Luke 7:17 (§90, p. 64)

So days will-come whenever the bridegroom might-be-taken-up from them, and then they-will-fast.	20So days will-come whenever the bridegroom might-be-taken-up from them, and then they-will-fast in [=on] that day.	35So days will-come, and whenever the bridegroom might-be-taken-up from them, then they-will-fast in those days." 36And so he-was-saying [a] parable to them, that	29"The [one] having the bride is [the] bridegroom; so the friend of-the bridegroom, having-stood and hearing him, rejoices [a] joy through [=because of] the voice of-the bridegroom. Therefore [in] this my-own joy has-been-fulfilled. 30It-is-necessary [for] that [one] to-grow, so [=but for] me to-become-less-important."	
16So no-one throws-on [=sews on a] patch of-unshrunken piece-of-cloth upon [an] old coat; for the fullness of-it removes [it] from the coat and [a] worse rip happens.	21No-one sews-on [a] patch [of] of-unshrunken piece-of-cloth upon [an] old coat; so if no [=if they do], the fullness removes [it] from it, the new [from] the old, and [a] worse rip happens.	"No-one, having-ripped [a] patch from [a] new coat, throws-on [it] upon [an] old coat. So if no in-effect [=indeed, if they do], and [=then] the new [one] will-rip and the patch from the new will-agree [=will fit] not [with] the old.		47Jesus said, "A person cannot mount two horses or bend two bows. And a slave cannot serve two masters, otherwise that slave will honor the one and offend the other. Nobody drinks aged wine and immediately wants to drink young wine. Young wine is not poured into old wineskins, or they might break, and aged wine is not poured into a new wineskin, or it might spoil. An old patch is not sewn onto a new garment, since it would create a tear."
17Nor do-they-throw [=do they put] fresh wine into old wine-skins; so if no in-effect [=indeed, if they do] the wine-skins are-torn-devastated and the wine is-poured-out and the wine-skins are-destroyed; but they-throw [=they put] fresh wine into new wine-skins, and both are-protected."	22And no-one throws [=puts] fresh wine into old wine-skins; so if no [=if they do] the wine will-devastate the wine-skins and the wine is-destroyed and the wine-skins[c]; but [they put] fresh wine into new wine-skins."	37And no-one throws [=puts] fresh wine into old wine-skins; so if no in-effect [=indeed, if they do] the fresh wine will-devastate the wine-skins and it will-be-poured-out and the wine-skins will-be-destroyed; 38but one-must-throw [=one must pour] fresh wine into new wine-skins.		
		39And no-one having-drunk old [wine] wishes fresh [wine], for he-says, 'The old is kind[d] [=better].'"		

[a] *omit* ℵ* B *pc* cop^{sa}; *much* ℵ^{2} C D L W Θ f^{1} f^{13} 33 892 1006 1506 𝔐 it^{mss} cop^{bo}; *frequently* ℵ^{1} it^{mss} vg sy^{s}.

[b] *the Pharisees* 𝔭^{88} ℵ A B C D Θ f^{13} 565 1342 1424 2427 it^{mss} vg sy^{p}; *those of-the Pharisees* L f^{1} 33 892 1006 1506 𝔐 it^{mss} vg^{mss} cop^{samss} cop^{bomss}; *the disciples of-the Pharisees* W.

[c] *is-destroyed and the wine-skins* 𝔭^{88} B 892 2427 cop^{bo}; *is-poured-out and the wine-skins are destroyed* ℵ A C D L W Θ f^{1} f^{13} 33 1006 1342 𝔐 it^{mss} vg sy^{p} cop^{sa}.

[d] *kind* 𝔭^{4} ℵ B L W 1342 *pc* sy^{p}; *kinder* A C Θ Ψ f^{1} f^{13} 33 892 1006 1506 𝔐 it^{mss} vg.

99. A Magistrate's Daughter and the Hemorrhaging Woman (→ §160)

Matt 9:18-26	Mark 5:21-43	Luke 8:40-56
18 His talking [=After he had said] these [things] to-them	21 And the having-crossed-over of-Jesus again into the beyond [=when Jesus had gone back across the harbor a] many [=great] crowd was-gathered upon [=around] him, and he-was along [=by] the sea.	40 So[e] in the to-return Jesus [=when Jesus was returning] the crowd welcomed him, for all were expecting him.
look!	22 And[c]	41 And look! [a] man, whose name [was] Jairus, came and this [man] was-being-at-one's-disposal [=was a]
one magistrate having-come	one of-the synagogue-leaders comes, Jairus [by] name, and	magistrate of-the synagogue, and
was-worshiping him saying that	having-seen him he-falls to [=at] his feet 23 and exhorts him many [=much], saying that "My little-	having-fallen along the feet of-Jesus he-was-exhorting him to-enter into his house, 42 that [=because] there-was to-him [=he had an] only-born daughter like
"My daughter right-now expired [=just died]. But having-come, place your hand upon her,	daughter has lastly [=finally died], in-order-that having-come you-might-place the [=your] hands [on] her, in-order-that she-might-be-saved	[=about] twelve years [old] and she [herself] was-facing-death.
and she-will-live."	and she-might-live."	
19 And Jesus, having-risen, and his disciples, followed him.	24 And he-went-away with him. And many [=a great] crowd was-following him and was-pressing-upon him.	So in the to-leave him [=while he was leaving] the crowds were-choking him.
20 And look! [a] woman suffering-chronic-bleeding [for] twelve years,	25 And [a] woman being in [=with an] issue of-blood [=having been bleeding for] twelve years 26 and having-suffered many [things] under many physicians and having-spent all the along her [=her wealth] and having-been-achieved not-one [=having not improved] but rather having-come into worse [condition], 27 having-heard[d] around [=concerning]	43 And [a] woman being in [=with an] issue of-blood from [=for] twelve years, whoever [=who despite] having-expended the [=her] whole livelihood [on] physicians had-the-strength not from no-one to-be-healed [=had not been healed by anyone],
having-approached from-behind touched the tassel [of] his coat.	Jesus, having-come in the crowd from-behind [him], she-touched his coat.	44 having-approached [from] from-behind she-touched the tassel [of]
21 For she-was-saying in herself, "If-ever only I-might-touch his coat, I-will-be-saved."	28 For she-was-saying that "If-ever even-if [=If only] I-might-touch his coats, I-will-be-saved."	
	29 And immediately the flow [of] her blood was-withered [=was dried up] and she-knew in-the body that she-has-been-cured from the scourge.	his coat and at-once the issue [of] her blood stood [=stopped].
	30 And immediately Jesus having-understood in himself the power having-gone-out out of-him, having-turned in [=to]	45 And Jesus
	the crowd was-saying, "What [=Who] touched my coats?"	said, "What [=Who is] the [one] having-touched me?" So [=But] all denying [=when all denied it]

Mark 3:19 (§72, p. 52) Q 7:9 (§89, p. 63)
Luke 7:17 (§90, p. 64)

22 So Jesus having-been-turned[a] and having-seen her said, "Cheer-up, daughter. Your loyalty has-saved you." And the woman was-saved from that hour.

23 And Jesus having-come into the home of-the magistrate and having-seen the flute-players and the crowd being-stirred-up 24 was-saying, "Retreat,

for the girl faced-death not [=has not died] but sleeps." And they-were-laughing-heartily [at] him.

25 So when the crowd was-cast-out, having entered,

---

31 And his disciples were-saying to-him, "You-look [at] the crowd pressing-upon you, and you-say, 'What [=Who] touched me?'"
32 And he-was-looking-around to-see the [woman] having-done this.

33 So [=But] the woman having-been-feared [=being afraid] and trembling, having-recognized which [=what] happened to-her, came and fell-to him and said to-him all the truth [=told him everything].

34 So

he-said to-her, "Daughter, your loyalty has-saved you. Leave into [=Go in] peace and be-healthy [=be free] from your scourge."
35 Yet his talking [=while he was still talking] they-come from the synagogue-leader saying that, "Your daughter faced-death [=has died]. What [=Why] do-you-bother the teacher yet [=still]?" 36 So [=But] Jesus having-ignored the word being-talked [=what was said], says to-the synagogue-leader, "Fear no [=not], only believe."

37 And he-excused not no-one [=he would not let anyone] to-tag-along with him if no [=except] Peter and James and John the brother of-James.
38 And they-come into the house of-the synagogue-leader, and he-catches-sight-of [a] commotion and weeping and many [people] wailing-loudly, 39 and having-

entered, he-says to-them, "What [=Why] are-you-stirred-up and do-you-weep? The young-child faced-death [=has died] not but sleeps." 40 And they-were-laughing-heartily [at] him.

So having-cast-out all [=everyone], he [himself] takes-along the father

---

Peter[f] said, "Overseer, the crowds control and squeeze you."

46 So Jesus said, "Some [one] touched me, for I [myself] knew [=felt] power having-gone-out from me."
47 So the woman, having-seen that she-remained-hidden not, came trembling and having-fallen-to him she-informed [=she told] in-the-sight of-all the whole-people through which reason [=why] she-touched him and like [=how] she-was-cured at-once.
48 So

he-said to-her, "Daughter, your loyalty has-saved you. Travel into [=in] peace."

49 Yet his [=while he was still] talking some [person] comes along the synagogue-leader saying that "Your daughter has-died, bother the teacher not-any-longer."
50 So [=But] Jesus having-heard,

answered him[g], "Fear no [=not], only <u>believe</u>, and she-will-be-saved." 51 So having-come into the home he-excused [=he allowed] not some [=no one] to-enter together-with him if no [=except] Peter and John and James and the father of-the child and the

mother. 52 So all were-weeping and were-cutting [=mourning] her.

So he-said,

"Weep no [=not], for she-faced-death not [=she has not died] but sleeps."
53 And they-were-laughing-heartily [at] him recognizing that she-faced-death [=she had died]. 54 So

	of-the young-child and the mother and the [ones] with him and travels-in where the young-child was.	
he-seized her hand and	41 And having-seized the hand of-the young-child he-says to-her, "Talitha koum," which is being-translated,	he, having-seized her hand, yelled saying,
the girl was-raised.	"Girl, I-say to-you, rise."	"Child, rise."
	42 And immediately the girl got-up and was-walking-around; for she-was twelve years [old].	55 And her spirit turned-back [=returned to her] and she-got-up at-once
26 And this gossip[b] [=news] went-out into that whole land.		
		and he-appointed [=he asked for something] to-be-given to-her to-eat.
	And immediately they-were-surprised great ecstasy [=they are overcome with surprise].	56 And her parents were-surprised;
	43 And he-beseeched many [=emphatically of] them in-order-that not-one might-know [=they tell no one about] this and said [=asked for something] to-be-given to-her to-eat.	so he-enjoined them to-say to-not-one [=to no one] the having-happened [=what had happened].

[a] *having-been-turned* ℵ B f^{13} 33 205 892 *al*; *having-been-turned-to* C L W Θ f^{1} 1006 1442 1506 𝔐; *stood having-been-turned* D.
[b] *this gossip* B W Δ f^{13} 892 1006 1342 𝔐 it^{mss} vg sy; *her gossip* ℵ C Θ f^{1} 33 205 *pc* cop^{bo}; *his gossip* D 1424 1506 *pc* cop^{sa} cop^{bo}.
[c] *omit* ℵ B D L Δ 892 1342 2427 it^{mss} vg sy^{s} cop; *look!* $\mathfrak{P}^{45}$ A C W f^{1} f^{13} 33 1006 1506 𝔐 it^{mss}.
[d] *omit* ℵ^{C} A C^{2} D L W Θ f^{1} f^{13} 33 892 1006 1342 1506 𝔐 sy cop; *the* ℵ* B C* Δ 2427 *pc*.
[e] *omit* $\mathfrak{P}^{75}$ ℵ^{1} B L f^{1} 33 205 579 700* 1342 2542 pc sy^{s} sy^{p} cop^{sa}; *it-happened* ℵ* ℵ^{2} A C D W Θ Ψ f^{13} 892 1006 1506 𝔐 it vg.
[f] *omit* $\mathfrak{P}^{75}$ B 700* *al* sy^{s} cop^{sa}; *and the together-with him* ℵ A C D L W Θ Ξ Ψ f^{1} f^{13} 33 892 1342 𝔐 it vg sy^{p} cop^{bo}; *and the with him* Ψ 1006 1506 𝔐.
[g] *him* $\mathfrak{P}^{75}$ ℵ B L Ξ f^{1} 33 205 579 892 1342 1424 *pc* cop; *him saying* A C D W Θ Ψ f^{13} 1006 1506 𝔐 sy^{s}; *the father of-the child saying* 1229 it^{mss} vg sy^{p}.

100. Matthew's Two Blind Men (→ §301)

Matt 9:27-31

27 And [as] Jesus [was] passing-by from-there, two blinds [=blind people] followed[a] crying and saying, "Be-merciful [to] us son of-David." 28 So having-come into the home, the blinds [=blind people] approached him, and Jesus says to-them, "Do-you-believe that I-am-able to-do this?" They-say to-him, "Yes lord." 29 Then he-touched their eyes saying, "According-to your loyalty let-it-happen to-you." 30 And their eyes were-opened. And Jesus censured them saying, "See [that] not-one let-him-know [=no one knows about this]." 31 So [=And] having-gone-out they-spoke-out [about] it in that whole land.

[a] *omit* B D 892 *pc*; *him* ℵ C L W Θ f^{1} f^{13} 33 1006 1342 𝔐 it^{mss} vg sy.

101. The Mute Demoniac (→ §136, §137, §213)

Matt 9:32-34	Mark 3:22	Q 11:14-15	Luke 11:14-15	John 10:20; 8:48
[32]So their going-out [=when they were leaving], look! they-offered [=they brought] to-him [a] mute person[a] being-demon-possessed [=a mute demoniac].				[10:20]So many out of-them [=many of them] were-saying, "He-has [a] demon and is-insane. What [=Why do you] hear [=listen to] him?" [8:48]The Judeans answered and said to-him, "[Is it] not well [=right when] we [ourselves] say that 'You are [a] Samaritan and you-have [a] demon?'"
		[14]And he-cast-out [a] mute demon.	[14]And he-was casting-out [a] demon and it was mute. So	
[33]And the demon having-been-cast-		And the demon having-been-	it-happened the demon having-gone-out [=when the demon came	
out the mute [person] talked. And the crowds were-astonished saying, "Thus [=The likes of this] never appeared in Israel."		cast-out the mute [person] talked and the crowds were-astonished.	out that] the mute [person] talked and the crowds were-astonished.	
[34]So [=But] the Pharisees	[22]And the scribes having-descended from Jerusalems,	[15]So [=But] some	[15]So [=But] some out of-them [=some of them]	
were-saying,	were-saying that "He-has Beelzebul[b]"	said,	said,	
"In [=By] the magistrate of-the demons he-casts-out the demons."	and that "In [=By] the magistrate of-the demons he-casts-out the demons."	"In [=By] Beelzebul, the magistrate of-the demons, he-casts-out the demons."	"In [=By] Beelzebul, the magistrate of-the demons, he-casts-out the demons."	

[a] *person* C D L W Θ f^1 33 1006 1342 𝔐 it vg; *omit* ℵ B f^{13} 892 *pc* sy^s sy^p cop.
[b] *Beelzebul* ℵ A C D L W Θ Ψ f^1 f^{13} 33 892 1006 1342 1506 2427 𝔐 it vg^{mss} cop; *Beezebul* B; *Beelzebub* vg sy^s sy^p.

102. A Great Harvest (→ §161, §197)

Matt 9:35-38	Mark 6:34	Q 10:2	Luke 10:2	John 4:35	Thomas 73
[35]And Jesus was-leading-around all the cities and the villages teaching in their synagogues and preaching the proclamation of-the kingdom and healing all [=every] disease					

and all [=every] sickness.					
36 So having-seen the crowds he-had-pity around [=concerning] them, that [=because] they-were being-bothered and being-tossed as sheep no [=not] having [=without a] shepherd.	34 And having-gone-out he-saw many [=a great] crowd and he-had-pity upon [for] them that [=because] they-were like sheep no [=not] having [=without a] shepherd, and he-began to-teach them many [things].				
37 Then he-says [to] his disciples, "The harvest for-one [=on the one hand] many [=is great], so [=but] the workers little [=are few]. 38 Therefore implore the lord of-the harvest so-that he-might-cast-out [=he might send] workers [out] into his harvest."		2 He-says [to] his disciples, "The harvest for-one [=on the one hand] many [=is great], so [=but] the workers little [=are few]. Therefore implore the lord of-the harvest so-that he-might-cast-out [=he might send] workers [out] into his harvest."	2 So he-was-saying to them, "The harvest for-one [=on the one hand] many [=is great], so [=but] the workers little [=are few]. Therefore implore the lord of-the harvest so-that workers he-might-cast-out[a] [=he might send out] into his harvest."	35 "[Do] you not say that 'It-is four-month yet [four months to go] and [then] the harvest comes'? Look! I-say to-you, lift-up your eyes and notice the regions that are white to harvest [=that are ready for the harvest]."	Jesus said, "The crop is huge but the workers are few, so beg the harvest boss to dispatch workers to the fields."

[a] *workers he-might-cast-out* 𝔓75 B D 0181 700; *he-might-cast-out workers* ℵ A C L W Θ Ξ Ψ *f* 1 *f* 13 itmss vg.

103. The Choosing of the Twelve (→ §72)

Matt 10:1-4	Mark 3:13-19	Luke 6:12-16	John 1:42
	13 And he-ascends	12 So it-happened in these days him to-go-out [=that he went out] into the	
1 And	into the mountain and	mountain to-pray, and he-was spending-the-night in the prayer	

having-summoned his	he-summons whom he was-wishing, and they-went-away to him. 14 And he-did [=he made	of-god. 13 And when day happened, he-addressed his disciples and having-chosen [=he chose] twelve from them, whom and	
twelve disciples he-gave	a group of] twelve, whom and [=also] he-named apostles, in-order-that they-might-be with him[a] and in-order-that he-might-send-off them to-preach 15 and to-have	[=also] he-named apostles:	
to-them authority [over] unclean spirits with-the-result-that [=for them] to-cast-out them and to-heal all disease and all sickness.	authority to-cast-out the demons.		42 He-led him to Jesus. Having-beheld him, Jesus said, “You are Simon the son of-John; you [yourself] will-be-called Cephas, which is-meant [=means] Peter.”
2 So the names of-the twelve apostles is [=are]	16 And he-did [=he appointed] the twelve[b]: and he-placed [a] name		
these: first Simon the [one] being-said [=called] Peter, and Andrew his brother, and James the [son] of-Zebedee, and	on-Simon, [namely] Peter, 17 and James the [son]	14 Simon whom and [=also] he-named Peter, and Andrew his brother, and James and	
John his brother, 3 Philip and Bartholomew,	of-Zebedee, and John the brother of-James, he-placed [on] them [the] name Boanerges, which is ‘sons of-thunder’; 18 and Andrew, and Philip, and Bartholomew, and	John, and Philip and Bartholomew[c], 15 and	
Thomas and Matthew the tax-collector,	Matthew, and Thomas,	Matthew, and Thomas,	
James the [son] of-Alpheus, and Thadeus, 4 Simon the Canaanean,	and James the [son] of-Alpheus, and Thadeus, and Simon the Canaanean,	and James [the son] of-Alpheus, and Simon the [one] being-called [=who was called a] zealot,	
		16 and Judah [the son] of-James,	
and Judah the Iscariot, the [one] and [=also] having-delivered him.	19 and Judah Iscariot, who and [=also] delivered him.	and Judah Iscariot who happened [=became a] traitor.	

[a] *twelve, whom and he-named apostles, in-order-that they-might-be with him* ℵ B Θ f13 28 copsa copbo; *twelve, in-order-that they-might-be with him* A K L P Π f1 33 565 892 𝔐 it vg sys; *twelve disciples in-order-that they-might-be with him whom and he-named apostles* W Δ.

[b] *And he-did the twelve* ℵ B Δ 565; *omit* A C2 D K L P Θ Π f1 28 33 𝔐 itmss vg sys syp copbo; *first Simon* f13 copsa; *and leading-around to-preach the proclamation* W itms.

[c] *James and John, and Philip and Bartholomew* 𝔭4 𝔭75 ℵ B D L W f13 33 565 2542 *al* it sys syp; *John and Bartholomew* A Θ Ψ f1 892 1006 1342 1506 𝔐 itmss vg copsa copbo.

Mark 3:19 (§72, p. 52) Q 7:9 (§89, p. 63)
Luke 7:17 (§90, p. 64)

104. Sending Off the Twelve (→ §162)

Matt 10:5-6	Mark 6:7-8a	Luke 9:1-2
		1 So having-called-together the twelve,
5 These twelve Jesus sent-off	7 And he-summons the twelve and he-began to-send-off them two [by] two and he-was-giving authority to-them [over] the unclean spirits.	he-gave power to-them and authority upon [=over] all the demons and to-heal diseases.
	8a And he-enjoined them . . .	2 And he-sent-off them to-preach the kingdom of-god and to-cure the ills[a] [=those who are ill].
having-enjoined them saying, "Might-you-go-away no [=not] into way of-nations [=among the Gentiles], and into [any] city of-Samaritans might-you-enter no [=not]. 6 So [=But] travel rather to the destroyed [=lost] sheep [of the] house of-Israel."		

[a] *the ills* ℵ A D L Ξ Ψ 070 f^{1} 33 205 579 *pc* it^{mss}; *the being-ills* C W Θ f^{13} 892 1006 1342 1506 𝔐 vg it^{mss}; *omit* B sy^{s} sy^{c}

105. Preaching and Healing (→ §200)

Matt 10:7-8	Q 10:9	Luke 10:9
7 "So traveling, preach saying that	9 "And heal the being-ill in it [=those who are ill] and say to-them,	9 "And heal the ill in it [=those who have illness in themselves] and say to-them,
'The kingdom of-the heavens has-neared.'	'The kingdom of-god has-neared upon you.'"	'The kingdom of-god has-neared upon you.'"
8 Heal being-ills [=those who are ill], raise deads [=the dead], purify leprouses [=lepers], cast-out demons. You-took freely and [=so] give freely."		

There are no variants in this pericope that appear in English.

106. Missionary Provisions (→ §199, §200)

Matt 10:9-10	Mark 6:8b-9	Q 10:4, 7	Luke 10:4, 7	Thomas 14
9 "Might-you-acquire no	8b ". . . in-order-that they-might-remove not-one [=they might take nothing] into way [=for their journey] if no [=except a] staff only,	4 "Bear no [=not]	4 "Bear no [=not]	
	no bread, no pouch, [place],	[a] moneybag, no pouch, no	[a] moneybag, no pouch, no	
gold so-not [=nor] silver so-not [=nor] copper into your	no copper into the			

belts; [10]no pouch into way [=for the road] so-not [=nor] two tunics so-not [=nor] sandals so-not [=nor] staff[a],	belt, [9]but having- worn little-sandals	sandals, no staff and might-you-greet not-one [person] according-to [=along] the way.	sandals, and might-you-greet not-one [person] according-to [=along] the way.	Jesus said to them, "If you fast, you will bring sin upon yourselves, and if you pray, you will be condemned, and if you give to charity, you will harm your spirits. When you go into any region and walk about in the countryside, when people take you in, eat what they serve you and heal the sick among them. After all, what goes into your mouth will not defile you; rather, it's what comes out of your mouth that will defile you."
	and might-you-be-clothed no [not with] two tunics."			
for the worker [is] worthy [of] his nourishment."		[7]So stay in the it [=same] home eating and drinking the along of-them [=whatever they place along you]; for the worker [is] worthy [of] his wages. Head-out no [=not] out of-home into [another] home."	[7]So stay in it [=the same] home eating and drinking the along of-them [=whatever they place along you]; for the worker [is] worthy [of] his wages. Head-out no [=not] out of-home into [another] home."	

[a] *staff* ℵ B D Θ *f*[1] 33 205 892 1424 *al* vg it[mss] sy[p] cop[sa] cop[bo]; *staffs* C L W *f*[13] 1006 1342 1506 𝔐 it[mss].
📖 Lk 10:4 – 2 Kgs 4:29

107. Those Who Receive You (→ §200)

Matt 10:11-13	Mark 6:10	Q 10:8, 5-6	Luke 10:8, 5-6
	[10]And he-was-saying to-them, "Where if-ever you-might-enter into [a] home,	[8]"And into which ever city you-might-enter, and they-might-receive you, eat the being-placed-befores [=the things put before] you.	[8]"And into which ever city you-might-enter, and they-might-receive you, eat the [being-placed-befores [=the things put before] you.
[11]"So into which ever city or village you-might-enter, make-a-careful-search [for] what [=who] in it is worthy; and-there stay until ever you-might-go-out.	stay there until ever you-might-go-out from-there."		
[12]So entering into the home, greet it. [13]And if-ever for-one the home might-be worthy,		[5]So into which ever home you-might-enter, first say, 'Peace to-this house.' [6]And if-ever for-one [a] son of-peace might-be there, let-come your peace upon him; so [=but] if no,	[5]So into which ever home you-might-enter, first say, 'Peace to-this house.' [6]And if-ever [a] son of-peace might-be there, upon him your peace will-be-rested; so [=but] if no in-effect
let-come your peace upon it; so [=but] if-ever it-might-be no [=not] worthy, let-be-turned-back your peace to you."		let-turn-back your peace upon you."	[=on the other hand], it-will-head-back upon you."

There are no variants in this pericope that appear in English.

108. Shaking Off the Dust (→ §201)

Matt 10:14	Mark 6:11	Q 10:10-11	Luke 10:10-11
[14]"And who ever might-receive no [=not] you so-not [nor if] he-might-hear your words, going-out outside that home or city, shake- out the dust [from] your feet."	[11]"And which ever place might-receive you no [=not] so-not they- might-hear [=so they will not hear] you, traveling-out from-there shake-out the dirt beneath your feet into [=as] testimony to-them. [a]"	[10]"So into which ever city you-might-enter and they-might-receive you no [=not], going-out outside that city [11] shake- out the dust [from] your feet."	[10]"So [=But] into which ever city you-might-enter and they-might-receive you no [=not], having- gone-out into its wide- streets say, [11]'And [=Even] the dust out [of] your city having-been-clung to-us into the feet [=sticking to our feet], we-wipe-off [our feet] to- you; nevertheless, know this, that the kingdom of-god has-neared [b].'"

[a] *omit* ℵ B C D L W Δ Θ 565 892 1342 2427 2542 *pc* vg it^{mss} sy^{s} cop^{sa}; *Amen I-say to-you, more-tolerable will-it-be Sodoms or Gomorrahs in day of-judgment or that city* A f^{1} f^{13} 33 1006 1506 $\mathfrak{M}$ it^{mss} sy^{p} sy^{h}.
[b] *omit* $\mathfrak{p}^{45}$ $\mathfrak{p}^{75}$ ℵ B D L Ξ 0181 33 579 1342 1424 1582 2542 *pc* vg it^{mss} sy^{s} sy^{c} cop^{bo}; *upon you* A C W Θ Ψ f^{13} 1006 1506 $\mathfrak{M}$ sy^{p} sy^{h} cop^{sa}.

109. The Sin of Sodom (→ §201)

Matt 10:15	Q 10:12	Luke 10:12
[15]"Amen I-say to-you, more- tolerable will-it-be [in the] land of- Sodoms and of-Gomorrahs in [=on the] day of-judgment or [=than in] that city."	[12]"I-say to-you that it-will-be more-tolerable in-Sodoms in [=on] that day or [=than in] that city."	[12]"I-say to-you that in-Sodoms in [=on] that day it-will-be more-tolerable or [=than in] that city."

There are no variants in this pericope that appear in English.

110. Sheep and Wolves (→ §198)

Matt 10:16	Q 10:3	Luke 10:3	Thomas 39
[16]"Look! I send-off you like sheep in [the] middle of-wolves; therefore happen [=be] sensible like the snakes and guileless like the doves."	[3]"Leave. Look! I-send-off[a] you like sheep in [the] middle of-wolves."	[3]"Leave. Look! I-send-off[a] you like sacrificial-lambs in [the] middle of-wolves."	Jesus said, "The Pharisees and the scholars have taken the keys of knowledge and have hidden them. They have not entered nor have they allowed those who want to enter to do so. As for you, be as sly as snakes and as simple as doves.

[a] *I-send-off* $\mathfrak{p}^{75}$ ℵ A B 579 *pc* cop^{samss}; *I send-off* C D L W Θ Ξ 0181 f^{1} f^{13} 33 892 1006 1506 $\mathfrak{M}$ vg it^{mss} cop^{samss} cop^{bo}.

Mark 3:19 (§72, p. 52) Q 7:9 (§89, p. 63)
Luke 7:17 (§90, p. 64)

111. The Fate of the Disciples (→ §232, §326)

Matt 10:17-23	Mark 13:9-13	Q 12:11-12	Luke 21:12-13; 12:11-12; 21:16-17
17 "So pay-close-attention from the [=be aware of] people; for they-will-deliver you into Sanhedrins and in their synagogues they-will-scourge you. 18 And upon [=before] <u>rulers</u> so and [=and also] kings you-will-be-led because-of me into [=as] testimony to-them and to-the nations [=Gentiles].	9 "So you themselves [=yourselves] look [=beware]; [b] they-will-deliver you into Sanhedrins and into synagogues you-will-be-beaten and upon [=before] rulers and kings you-will-be-stood [=you will be put] because-of me into [=as] testimony to-them.		21:12 "So [=But] before all these [things] they-will-throw-on their hands upon [=they will beat] you and they-will-pursue [you], delivering [you] into the synagogues and prisons, being-led-away upon [=before] kings and rulers because-of my name. 13 It-will-get-out to-you into [=This will be your chance to offer] testimony."
	10 And it-is-necessary [for] the proclamation to-be-preached first into all the nations.		
19 So whenever they-might-deliver[a] you,	11 And whenever they-might-lead you, delivering [you],	11 "Whenever they-might-bring-into you [=When they bring you] into the synagogues,	12:11 "So whenever they-might-bring-into[c] you [=when they bring you] upon [=before] the synagogues, and the beginnings [=rulers], and the authorities,
you-might-worry no [=not] how or what you-might-talk [=you might say].	worry-ahead-of-time no [=not] what you-might-talk [=you might say], but talk [=say] this which if-ever [=whatever] might-be-given to-you in that hour,	you-might-worry no [=not] how or what you-might-say,	you-might-worry no [=not] how or [with] what you-might-defend [yourself] or what you-might-say.
For what you-might-talk will-be-given to-you in that hour.		12 for the holy spirit will-teach you what you-might-say in the [=that] hour."	12 For the holy spirit will-teach you in it [=in that very] hour [that] which it-is-necessary to-say."
20 For you-are not the talkings [=the ones doing the talking] but the spirit [of] your father [who is] talking in you.	for you-are not the talkings [=the ones doing the talking] but the holy spirit.		
21 So brother will-deliver brother into death and father descendant, and descendants will-turn-against upon parents, and they-will-put-to-death them.	12 And brother will-deliver brother into death and father descendant, and descendants will-turn-against upon parents, and they-will-put-to-death them.		21:16 "So you-will-be-delivered and [=even] under [=by] parents and brothers and kins and friends and they-will-put-to-death out [=some] of-you.

Matt	Mark	Q	Luke
[22]And you-will-be being-hated under [=by] all through [=because of] my name. So [=But] the having-stayed-behind [=the one who perseveres] into [the] end, this [one] will-be-saved. [23]So whenever they-might-pursue you in this city, flee into the other, for amen I-say to-you, you-might-complete not no [=at all] the cities of-Israel until ever the son of-the person might-come."	[13]And you-will-be being-hated under [=by] all through [=because of] my name. So [=But] the having-stayed-behind [=the one who perseveres] into [the] end, this [one] will-be-saved."		[17]And you-will-be being-hated under [=by] all through [=because of] my name."

[a] *they-might-deliver* ℵ B f^{1} 205 892 *pc*; *they-will-deliver* D G L W 33 579 1424 1596 *al* vg it^{mss}; *they-give* C Θ f^{13} 1006 1342 𝔐.
[b] *omit* B L Ψ 2427 *pc* cop^{samss} cop^{bo}; *for* ℵ A f^{13} 33 892 1006 1342 1506 𝔐 it^{mss} vg sy^{p} cop^{samss}; *and* W f^{1} *pc* sy^{s}; *moreover* D Θ 565 700 it.
[c] *they-might-bring-into* $\mathfrak{P}^{45}$ $\mathfrak{P}^{75}$ ℵ B L 070 f^{1} 33 579 700 892 2542 *pc* it^{mss} vg; *they-might-offer* A W Θ Ψ f^{13} 1006 1342 1506 𝔐 it^{mss}; *they-might-bring* D it^{mss}.
📖 Mk 13:12 – Mic 7:6

112. Disciple and Teacher (→ §84)

Matt 10:24-25	Q 6:40	Luke 6:40	John 13:16
[24]"[A] disciple is not on-behalf [=above] the teacher	[40]"[A] disciple is not on-behalf [=above] the teacher;	[40]"[A] disciple is not on-behalf [=above] the teacher[a],	[16]"Amen amen I-say to-you, [a] slave is not greater [than] his lord nor [an] apostle greater [than] the [one] having-sent him."
nor [a] slave on-behalf [=above] his lord.			
		so all [=each one] having-been-mended [=having been restored] will-be	
[25][It is] enough for-the disciple in-order-that he-might-happen [=he might become] like his teacher and the slave like his lord. If they-called-upon the master-of-the-house Beelzebul, how-great rather [=how much greater the insult to] his house-members."	[it is] enough for-the disciple in-order-that he-might-happen [=he might become] like his teacher."	like his teacher."	

[a] *the teacher* $\mathfrak{P}^{75}$ ℵ B D L W Θ Ξ f^{1} f^{13} 33 205 700 892 1342 2542 *pc* it^{mss} vg; *his teacher* A C Ψ 1006 1506 𝔐 sy cop.

Mark 3:19 (§72, p. 52) Q 7:9 (§89, p. 63)
Luke 7:17 (§90, p. 64)

113. Fearless Preaching (→ §227)

Matt 10:26-27	Q 12:2-3	Luke 12:2-3	Thomas 5; 33
[26]"Therefore might-you-be-feared no [=fear not] them, for		[2]"So	[5]Jesus said, "Know what is in front of your face, and what is hidden from you will be disclosed to you. For there is nothing hidden that will not be revealed. <And there is nothing buried that will not be raised.>" [33]Jesus said, "What you will hear in your ear, in the other ear proclaim from your rooftops. After all, no one lights a lamp and puts it under a basket, nor does one put it in a hidden place. Rather, one puts it on a lampstand so that all who come and go will see its light."
no-one is having-been-covered [=nothing is hidden] which will-be-revealed not and [nothing is] hidden which will-be-known not.	[2]"No-one having-been-covered is [=Nothing is hidden] which will-be-revealed not and [nothing is] hidden which will-be-known not.	no-one [=nothing] is having-been-concealed which will-be-revealed not and [nothing is] hidden which will-be-known not.	
[27]Which [=What] I-say to-you in the dark, say in the light and which [=what] you-hear [whispered] into the ear	[3]Which [=What] I-say to-you in the dark, say in the light and which [=what] you-hear into the ear [=whispered]	[3]In-place of-which [=Therefore] whatsoever you-said in the dark will-be-heard in the light, and [that] which you-talked [=you whispered] to the ear in the private-rooms	
preach upon [=from] the housetops."	preach upon [=from] the housetops."	will-be-preached upon [=from] the housetops."	

There are no variants in this pericope that appear in English.

114. Fear Not Death (→ §228)

Matt 10:28	Q 12:4-5	Luke 12:4-5
[28]"And fear[a] no [=not] from the killings [=those who kill] the body, so [=but] being-able no [=not] to-kill the soul.	[4]"And fear no [=not] from the killings [=those who kill] the body, so [=but] being-able no [=not] to-kill the soul.	[4]"So I-say to-you, [to] my friends, might-you-be-feared no from [=fear not] the killings [=those who kill] the body, and with these no having some to-do [=but cannot do] more-excessive [=more than this].
So [=But] rather fear[b] the [one] being-able to-destroy and [=both] soul and body in Gehenna."	[5]So [=But] fear the [one] being-able to-destroy and [=both] soul and body in the Gehenna."	[5]So I-will-display to-you what you-might-be-fear [=you should fear]. Might-you-be-feared [=You should fear] the [one] having [the] authority to-throw-in [people] into the Gehenna with to-kill [=after he has killed them]. Yes, I-say to-you fear this [one]."

[a] *fear* ℵ C K L Γ Δ f^{13} 565 579 700 *pm*; *might-you-be-feared* B D N W Θ f^{1} 33 892 1424 *pm*.
[b] *fear* ℵ B C W 892 *pc*; *might-you-be-feared* D L Θ f^{1} f^{13} 33 𝔐.

115. More Precious than Sparrows (→ §229)

Matt 10:29-31	Q 12:6-7	Luke 12:6-7
29“Two sparrows is-sold [for an] assarion, indeed-not [=are they not]? And not one out of-them will-fall upon the land apart [from the will of] your father. 30So and [=even] the hairs [on that] head [of] yours are all having-been-counted. 31Therefore fear no [=not], you [yourselves] are- superior [=are worth more than] many sparrows.”	6“Five sparrows are-sold [for] two assarions, indeed-not [=are they not]? And not one out of-them will-fall upon the land apart [from the will of] your father. 7So and [=even] the hairs [on that] head [of] yours are all having-been-counted. Fear no [=not], you [yourselves] are- superior [=are worth more than] many sparrows.”	6“Five sparrows are-sold[a] [for] two assarions, indeed-not [=are they not]? And not one out of-them is having- been-neglected in-the-sight of-god. 7But and [=even] all the hairs [of] your head have-been-counted. Fear no[b] [=not]; you-are-superior [=you are worth more than] many sparrows.”

[a] *are-sold* $\mathfrak{P}^{75}$ ℵ B Θ Ψ f^{13} 892 1241 2542 *pc*; *is-sold* $\mathfrak{P}^{45}$ D L W 070 f^{1} 33 𝔐.
[b] *Fear no* $\mathfrak{P}^{45}$ $\mathfrak{P}^{75}$ B L 070 579 *pc* it; *Therefore fear no* ℵ A D W Θ Ψ f^{1} f^{13} 33 892 1006 1342 1506 𝔐 vg it^{mss} sy.

116. Confessing and Denying (→ §230)

Matt 10:32-33	Q 12:8-9	Luke 12:8-9
32“Therefore all whoever will- confess in me in-front of-the people, I-too will-confess in him in-front [of] my father in the heavens[a]. 33So [=But] whoever ever might-deny me in-front of-the people, I-too will- deny him in-front [of] my father in the heavens[b].”	8“All who ever might-confess in me in-front of-the people, and [=even] the son of-the person will-confess in him in-front of-the announcers [=angels]. 9So [=But] who ever might- deny me in-front of-the people will-be-denied in-front of-the announcers [=angels].”	8“So I-say to-you, all who ever might-confess in me in-front of-the people, and [=even] the son of-the person will-confess in him in-front of-the announcers [=angels] of-god. 9So [=But] the [one] having-denied me in-the-sight of-the [=the] people will-be-disowned in-the-sight of- the announcers [=angels] of-god.”

[a] *in the heavens* B f^{13} 579 892 1424 *al*; *in heavens* $\mathfrak{P}^{19}$ ℵ C D L W Θ f^{1} 1006 1342 𝔐.
[b] *in the heavens* B C f^{13} 579 892 1506 *al*; *in heavens* $\mathfrak{P}^{19}$ ℵ D L W Θ f^{1} 1006 1342 𝔐.

117. Casting Disunity and Divisions (→ §241)

Matt 10:34-36	Q 12:51, 53	Luke 12:51-53	Thomas 16
34“You-might-think no [=Do not think] that I-came to-throw [=to bring] peace upon the land. I-came not to-throw [=to bring] peace but [the] sword. 35For I-came to-slice [=to separate a] person according-to [=from] his father and	51“Do-you-suppose that I-came to-throw [=to bring] peace upon the land. I-came not to-throw [=to bring] peace but [the] sword. 53For I-came to-slice [=to separate] son according-to [=from] father,	51“Do-you-suppose that I-arrived to-give peace in the land? Indeed-not, I- say to-you, but or [=rather] disunity. 52For from the now [=from now on] five in one house will- be having-been-divided- up, three upon [=against] two and two upon [=against] three, 53they-will-be-divided-up father upon [=from] son	Jesus said, “Perhaps people think that I have come to cast peace upon the world. They do not know that I have come to cast conflicts upon the earth: fire, sword, war. For there will be five in a house: there’ll be three against two and two against three, father against son and son against father, and they will stand alone.”

		and son upon [=from] father, mother upon [=from] the daughter and		
daughter according-to [=from] her mother, and	daughter according-to [=from] her mother, and	daughter upon [=from] the mother, mother-in-law upon [=from] her bride		
bride according-to [=from] her mother-in-law, 36 and enemies of-the person [will be] his house-members.”	bride according-to [=from] her mother-in-law.”	and bride upon [=from] the[a] mother-in-law.”		

[a] *the* 𝔓[45] 𝔓[75] א* B D L 579 892 *pc*; *her* א[2] A W Θ Ψ *f*[1] *f*[13] 33 1006 1342 1506 𝔐 it[mss] vg sy cop[sa] cop[bo].
📖 Mt 10:35 – Mic 7:6

118. Conditions of Discipleship (→ §260, §262, §287)

Matt 10:37-39	Q 14:26-27; 17:33	Luke 14:25-27; 17:33	John 12:25	Thomas 55; 101
		14:25 So many crowds were-traveling-together-with him, and having-been-turned he-said to them,		
37 “The [one]	14:26 “Who	26 “If some [one] comes to me and		55 Jesus said, “Whoever does not hate father and mother cannot be my disciple, and whoever does not hate brothers and sisters, and carry the cross as I do, will not be worthy of me.” 101 “Whoever does not hate <father> and mother as I do cannot be my <disciple>, and whoever does <not> love <father and> mother as I do cannot be my <disciple>. For my mother <. . .>, but my true <mother> gave me life.”
liking father or mother on-behalf [=more than] me is not worthy of-me,	hates not the father and the mother is-able not to-be my	hates not the father himself[a] [=his very own father] and the		
and the [one] liking son or daughter on-behalf [=more	disciple and who hates not the son and the daughter	mother and the woman [=wife] and the descendants and the brothers and the sisters and yet even [=also] the soul himself [=his		
than] me is not worthy of-me.	is-able not to-be my disciple.”	very own life], he-is-able not to-be my disciple.		
38 And who [ever] takes not his cross and follows	27 “Who takes not his cross and follows	27 Whoever bears not the cross himself [=his very own cross] and		
behind me is not worthy of-me.	behind me is-able not to-be my disciple.”	comes behind me is-able not to-be my disciple.”		
39 The [one] having-found his soul [=life] will-destroy [=will lose] it and the [one]	17:33 “The [one] having-found his soul [=life] will-destroy [=will lose]	17:33 “Who if-ever might-search to-make-secure his soul[b] will-destroy	25 “The [one] liking his soul [=life] destroys it and the [one] hating his	

having-destroyed his soul [=life] because-of me will-find it."	it and the [one] having-destroyed his soul [=life] because-of me will-find it."	it, so [=but] who ever might-destroy [his life] will-give-life [to] it."	soul [=life] in this world will-guard it into eternal life."

[a] *the father himself* $\mathfrak{P}^{75}$ B L Ψ *pc*; *his father* $\mathfrak{P}^{45}$ ℵ A D W Θ f^{1} f^{13} 892 1006 1342 𝔐; *the father* 579 1506 2542.
[b] *Who if-ever might-search to-make-secure his soul* $\mathfrak{P}^{75}$ B L 579; *Who if-ever might-search to-save his soul* ℵ A W Θ Ψ f^{1} f^{13} 892 1006 1342 1506 𝔐 it^{mss} vg; *Who ever might-wish to-give-life his soul* D sy^{s} sy^{p} cop^{sa}.
📖 Lk 14:26 – Mic 7:6

119. Receiving the One Who Sent Me (→ §203)

Matt 10:40-41	Q 10:16	Luke 10:16	John 13:20
40"The [one] receiving you receives me and the [one] receiving me receives the [one] having-sent-off me. 41The [one] receiving [a] prophet into [in the] name [of a] prophet will-take [the] wages [=reward of a] prophet, and the [one] receiving [a] righteous [person] into [in the] name [of a] righteous [person] will-take [the] wages [=reward of a] righteous [person]."	16"The [one] receiving you receives me and the [one] receiving me receives the [one] having-sent-off me."	16"The [one] hearing you hears me and the [one] refusing me refuses the [one] having-sent-off me."	20"Amen amen I-say to-you, the [one] taking [=who receives] ever some [=whoever] I-will-send takes [=receives] me, so [=and] the [one] taking [=receiving] me takes [=receives] the [one] having-sent me."

There are no variants in this pericope that appear in English.

120. Like Prophets and Children (→ §185)

Matt 10:42	Mark 9:41
42"And who ever might-give-a-drink [of] only [=even a] cup of-cold [=water to] one of-these smalls [=little ones] into [=in the] name [of a] disciple, amen I-say to-you might-he-destroy [=might he lose] not no [=at all] his wages."	41"For who ever might-give-a-drink [of a] cup of-water [to] you that [=because] you-are in [you bear the] name[a] [of the] Anointed-one, amen I-say to-you that might-he-destroy [=might he lose] not no [=at all] his wages."

[a] *name* ℵ^{2} B C* L Ψ f^{1} 205 579 892 1342 1424 2427 *al* sy; *my name* ℵ* D W Δ Θ f^{13} 1006 1506 𝔐 it vg cop.

121. Matthew's Completion of the Mission Instructions

Matt 11:1

1And it-happened [that] when Jesus completed appointing [=instructing] his twelve disciples, he-headed-out from-there to-teach and to-preach in their cities.

There are no variants in this pericope that appear in English.

122. John Questions Jesus

Matt 11:2-6	Q 7:18-19, 22-23	Luke 7:18-23
[2]So John having-heard in jail [about] the works of-the Anointed-one, [and] having-sent [a message] through his disciples[a], [3]said to-him, "Are you [yourself] the coming [one] or do-we-expect [an] other?"	[18]John having-heard around [=concerning] all of-these [things and] having-sent [a message] through his disciples, [19]said to-him, "Are you [yourself] the coming [one] or do-we-expect [an] other?"	[18]And his disciples informed John around [=concerning] all of-these [things]. And having-summoned what two [of] his disciples John [19]sent [them] to the lord saying, "Are you [yourself] the coming [one] or do-we-expect another?" [20]So having-arrived to him, the men said, "John the baptist sent-off[b] us to you saying, 'Are you [yourself] the coming [one] or do-we-expect another?'" [21]In that hour he-healed many from diseases and scourges and evil spirits and to-many blinds [=blind people] he-gave-as-a-benefaction to-look [=gave them sight].
[4]And Jesus having-answered said to-them, "Having-traveled inform John [the things] which you-hear and look [=see]: [5]blinds [=blind people] look-up and lames [=lame people] walk-around, leprouses [=lepers] are-purified and mutes [=deaf people] hear, and deads [=dead people] are-raised and poors [=poor people] are-proclaimed [to]. [6]And fortunate is who if-ever [=he who] might-be-caused-to-stumble no [=not] in [=by] me."	[22]And having-answered he-said to-them, "Having-traveled inform John [the things] which you-hear and look [=see]: blinds [=blind people] look-up and lames [=lame people] walk-around, leprouses [=lepers] are-purified and mutes [=deaf people] hear, and deads [=dead people] are-raised and poors [=poor people] are-proclaimed [to]. [23]And fortunate is who if-ever [=he who] might-be-caused-to-stumble no [=not] in [=by] me."	[22]And having-answered he-said to-them, "Having-traveled inform John [the things] which you-saw and you-heard: [c] blinds [=blind people] look-up, lames [=lame people] walk-around, leprouses [=lepers] are-purified and mutes [=deaf people] hear, deads [=dead people] are-raised, poors [=poor people] are-proclaimed [to]. [23]And fortunate is who if-ever [=he who] might-be-caused-to-stumble no [=not] in [=by] me."

[a] *through his disciples* ℵ B C* D W Z Δ Θ 0233 f^{13} 33 1006 *pc* sy[s] cop[sa]; *through two his disciples* C[3] L f^{1} 892 1342 1506 𝔐 it[mss] vg.
[b] *sent-off* 𝔓[75] ℵ B W 1006 1424 *pc*; *has-sent-off* A D L Θ Ξ Ψ f^{1} f^{13} 33 892 1342 𝔐.
[c] *omit* ℵ B L W Θ Ξ Ψ f^{1} f^{13} 205 579 700 892 1342 1424 2542 *pc* it cop[sa] cop[bo]; *that* A D 33 1006 1506 𝔐 it[mss] vg.
🕮 Mt 11:5 – Isa 35:5; 29:18

123. Jesus Praises John

Matt 11:7-11	Q 7:24-28	Luke 7:24-28	Thomas 78; 46
[7]So [=As] these travelings [=people were traveling]	[24]So [after] these having-gone-aways sinfuls	[24]So [after] the announcers [=messengers] of-John having-gone-away	
Jesus began to-say to-the crowds around [=concerning] John, "What did-you-go-out into the deserted [places] to-notice? [A] reed being-shaken-up under [=by] wind?	[=people left], he-began to-say to the crowds around [=concerning] John, "What did-you-go-out into the deserted [places] to-notice? [A] reed being-shaken-up under	[=left], he-began to-say to the crowds around [=concerning] John, "What did-you-go-out into the deserted [places] to-notice? [A] reed being-shaken-up under [=by] wind?	[78]Jesus said, "Why have you come out to the countryside? To see a reed shaken by the wind? And to see a person dressed in

8 But what did-you-go-
out to-see? [A] person
having-been-dressed in
soft [clothing]? Look! the
donnings softs [=ones
wearing soft clothes]
are in the houses of-kings.
9 But what did-you-go-out
to-see? [A] prophet?[a] Yes,
I-say to-you, and more-
excessive [=much more than
a] prophet.
10 This[b] is [the one] around
[=concerning] which
it-has-been-written,
'LOOK! I SEND-OFF
MY ANNOUNCER
BEFORE YOUR FACE,
WHO WILL-PREPARE
YOUR WAY IN-FRONT
OF-YOU.' 11 Amen I-say
to-you, in borns [=among
those born] of-women not
[=no one] has-been-raised
greater [than] John
the baptist. So [=But]
the smaller [one] in the
kingdom of-the heavens is
greater [than] him."

[=by] wind? 25 But what
did-you-go-out to-see? [A]
person having-been-
dressed in soft [clothing]?
Look! the donnings softs
[=ones wearing soft clothes]
are in the houses of-kings.
26 But what did-you-go-out
to-see? [A] prophet? Yes,
I-say to-you, and more-
excessive [=much more than
a] prophet.
27 This is [the one] around
[=concerning] which
it-has-been-written,
'LOOK! I SEND-OFF MY
ANNOUNCER BEFORE
YOUR FACE, WHO
WILL-PREPARE YOUR
WAY IN-FRONT OF-
YOU.' 28 I-say to-you
in borns [=among those
born] of-women no
[one] has-been-raised
greater [than] John the
baptist. So [=but] the
smaller [one] in the
kingdom of-god is greater
[than] him."

25 But what did-you-go-out
to-see? [A] person having-
been-dressed in soft coats?
Look! the being-at-one's-
disposals [=those who dress]
in glorious and luxurious
apparel are in the palaces.
26 But what did-you-go-out
to-see? [A] prophet? Yes,
I-say to-you, and more-
excessive [much more than
a] prophet.
27 This is [the one] around
[=concerning] which
it-has-been-written,
'LOOK! I-SEND-OFF MY
ANNOUNCER BEFORE
YOUR FACE, WHO
WILL-PREPARE YOUR
WAY IN-FRONT OF-
YOU.' 28 I-say to-you,
there-is no-one greater
[than] John[c] in borns
[=among those born]
of-women. So [=But]
the smaller [one] in the
kingdom of-god is greater
[than] him."

soft clothes, <like your>
rulers and your powerful
ones? They are dressed
in soft clothes, and they
cannot understand truth."

46 Jesus said, "From Adam
to John the Baptist, among
those born of women, no
one is so much greater
than John the Baptist
that his eyes should not
be averted. But I have
said that whoever among
you becomes a child will
recognize the <Father's>
kingdom and will become
greater than John."

[a] *what did-you-go-out to-see? prophet?* ℵ^{1} B* C D L Θ f^{1} f^{13} 33 1006 1506 𝔐 it vg sy cop^{sa}; *what prophet did-you-go-out to-see?* ℵ* B^{1} W Z 892 *pc.*

[b] *This* ℵ B D Z 892 it^{mss} sy^{s} sy^{c} cop^{bomss}; *For this* C L W Θ f^{1} f^{13} 33 1006 1342 1506 𝔐 it^{mss} vg sy^{p} cop.

[c] *John* 𝔭^{75} ℵ B L W Ξ f^{1} 579 *pc* cop^{sa}; *John the baptist* 33 565 *al* it cop^{samss}; *prophet John the baptist* A D Θ f^{13} 1006 1506 𝔐 it^{mss} vg sy^{p}; *prophet John* Ψ 700 893 1342 *pc* sy^{c}.

📖 Mt 11:10 – Mal 3:1; 📖 Lk 7:27 – Mal 3:1

124. Luke's Conclusion to Material on John

Luke 7:29-30

29 And all the whole-people [=all the people] and the tax-collectors, having-heard [this] was-righteous
[=glorified] god, having-been-baptized [with] the baptism of-John. 30 So [=But] the Pharisees and the
lawyers refused into [=for] themselves the council of-god no [=not] having-been-baptized under
[=by] him.

There are no variants in this pericope that appear in English.

125. John and the Prophets (→ §272)

Matt 11:12-15	Q 16:16	Luke 16:16
12“So from the days of-John the baptist until right-now the kingdom of-the heavens is-forced [=has been forced open] and forcefuls [=those who are forceful] plunder her.		
13For all the prophets and the law prophesied until John.	16“And the law and the prophets [were] until John [came]; from then the kingdom of-god is-forced [=has been forced open] and forcefuls [=those who are forceful] plunder her.”	16“The law and the prophets [were] to-the-point[b] [=until] of-John; from then the kingdom of-god is-proclaimed and all force [their way] into her.”
14And if you-wish to-receive [it], Elijah he [himself] is the [one] intending to-come. 15The [one] having ears[a] let-him-hear.”		

[a] *omit* B D 700 *pc* sy^{c}; *to-hear* ℵ C L W Z Θ f^{1} f^{13} 33 892 1006 1342 1506 𝔐 vg it^{mss} sy^{c} sy^{p} sy^{h} cop.
[b] *to-the-point* $\mathfrak{p}^{75}$ ℵ B L f^{1} f^{13} 205 579 892 2542 *pc*; *until* A D W Θ Ψ 1006 1342 1506 𝔐.
🕮 Mt 11:14 – Mal 4:5

126. The Parable of the Children in the Market

Matt 11:16-19	Q 7:31-35	Luke 7:31-35
16“So [=But] to-what will-I-compare this generation?	31“To-what will-I-compare this generation, and what is-it comparable-to?	31“Therefore, to-what will-I-compare the people of-this generation and what are-they comparable-to?
It-is comparable-to young-children sitting in the markets who, addressing the others, 17say,	32It-is comparable-to young-children sitting in the markets who, addressing the others, say,	32They-are comparable-to young-children sitting in [the] market and they-are-addressing one-another [during] which [one] says,
‘We-played-the-flute to-you and you-danced not; we-mourned and you-cut [=you lamented] not.’	‘We-played-the-flute to-you and you-danced not; we-mourned and you-wept not.’	‘We-played-the-flute to-you and you-danced not; we-mourned and you-wept not.’
18For John came not-even eating [and] not-even drinking, and they-say, ‘He-has [a] demon.’ 19The son of-the person came eating and drinking and they-say, ‘Look! [a] gluttonous and wine-drinking person, of-tax-collectors and sinfuls [=sinners a] friend.’ And wisdom was-made-righteous from [=by] her works.”	33For John the baptist came eating no bread [and] not-even drinking, and you-say, ‘He-has [a] demon.’ 34The son of-the person came eating and drinking and you-say, ‘Look! [a] gluttonous and wine-drinking person, of-tax-collectors and sinfuls [=sinners a] friend.’ 35And wisdom was-made-righteous from [=by] her descendants.”	33For John the baptist has-come eating no bread [and] not-even drinking wine[a], and you-say, ‘He-has [a] demon.’ 34The son of-the person has-come eating and drinking and you-say, ‘Look! [a] gluttonous and wine-drinking person, [a] friend of-tax-collectors and sinfuls [=sinners].’ 35And wisdom was-made-righteous from [=by] all her descendants.”

[a] *has-come eating no bread not-even drinking wine* B Ξ 1506 *pc*; *has-come eating not bread nor drinking wine* ℵ W 1342 *pc*; *has-come not-even eating bread not-even drinking wine* A D L Θ Ψ f^{1} f^{13} 33 892 1006 𝔐.

SYNOPTIC STUDY GUIDE 7

Farrer Hypothesis/Mark without Q

The Farrer Hypothesis is more widely known as the Farrer-Goulder Hypothesis, named for its two early champions, Austin Farrer (1904-1968) and Michael Goulder (1927-2010). It shares with the Two-Document Hypothesis Markan Priority, and that Matthew came next, relying on Mark. But it departs from the Two-Document Hypothesis over the question of Q, which it finds unnecessary. Farrer was troubled by the utter absence of any physical or literary evidence of Q's existence: it is not mentioned or described by any ancient author, and there is no surviving manuscript that could be it. In addition, its proponents see many instances where Matthew and Luke agree together in wording against Mark in Triple Tradition, exactly the sort of thing you would expect to find had the author of Luke used Matthew as a source. These agreements are known as the minor agreements (see Synoptic Study Guides 9 and 15). For critics of Q, these agreements are not so "minor." They may (in most but not all instances) comprise very small agreements, but their sheer volume renders the notion that the authors of Matthew and Luke wrote completely independently very problematic. This hypothesis has for this reason also been called "Mark without Q," since it maintains Markan priority but dispenses with Q.

One of the arguments commonly given to support the claim that the authors of Matthew and Luke wrote independently is that they never agree together on the placement of Double Tradition/Q material relative to the Gospel of Mark. Would you not expect, the argument goes, the author of Luke to agree with the Gospel of Matthew at least sometimes on the placement of Double Tradition material had he used Matthew? The Farrer Hypothesis argues that there *are* places where precisely this happens. The material about John the Baptizer (§16, §17, §19), the Temptation (§23), the location of Jesus in Nazareth at the start of his career (§25), the continuation of the Galilean mission after Matthew's and Luke's sermons (§89), the stories in which John questions Jesus from prison (§122) and in which Jesus praises John (§123), and finally the parable of the children in the market (§126) are all places where Matthew and Luke insert the same Double Tradition/Q story into the same place in Mark.

On the one hand, this is not many agreements in comparison to the entirety of the Double Tradition/Q; on the other hand, as with the minor agreements, it is fair to ask: if the writers of Matthew and Luke worked independently, why do they agree together against Mark as often as they do? In other words, at what point do the data cease to be circumstantial (e.g., they just *happen* to make the same decision) and when does one have to conclude that there was a direct literary relationship between Matthew and Luke?

The Farrer Hypothesis is a much stronger alternative to the Two-Document Hypothesis than the Griesbach Hypothesis, and thus has many more advocates today.

127. Woes on Galilean Cities (→ §202)

Matt 11:20-24	Q 10:13-15	Luke 10:13-15
20Then he-began to-denounce the cities in which most [of] his [signs of] powers happened, that [=because] they-repented not:		
21"Woe to-you Chorazin, woe to-you Bethsaida, that [=because] if the [signs of] powers having-happened in [=among] you happened in Tyre and Sidon, they-repented ever [=they would have repented] old-days [=long ago] in sack-cloth and ash.	13"Woe to-you Chorazin, woe to-you Bethsaida, that [=because] if the [signs of] powers having-happened in [=among] you were-happened [=were made to happen] in Tyre and Sidon, they-repented ever [=they would have repented] old-days [=long ago] in sack-cloth and ash.	13"Woe to-you Chorazin, woe to-you Bethsaida, that [=because] if the [signs of] powers having-happened in [=among] you were-happened[c] [=were made to happen] in Tyre and Sidon, they-repented ever [=they would have repented] old-days [=long ago] sitting in sack-cloth and ash.
22Nevertheless I-say to-you, it-will-be more-tolerable [in]	14Nevertheless it-will-be more-tolerable [in] Tyre	14Nevertheless it-will-be more-tolerable [in] Tyre

Tyre and Sidon in [=on the] day of-judgment or [=than] for-you. 23 And you, Capharnaum, will-you-be-exalted no [=not] until [=to] heaven? You-will-descend[a] until [=to] Hades; that [=because] if the [signs of] powers having-happened in [=among] you were-happened[b] [=were made to happen] in Sodoms, it-stayed ever [=they would have survived] to-the-point [=until] today. 24 Nevertheless I-say to-you that it-will-be more-tolerable [in the] land of-Sodoms in [=on the] day of-judgment or [=than] for-you."	and Sidon in [=at] the judgment or [=than] for-you. 15 And you, Capharnaum, will-you-be-exalted no [=not] until [=to] heaven? You-will-descend until [=to] the Hades."	and Sidon in [=at] the judgment or [=than] for-you. 15 And you, Capharnaum, will-you-be-exalted no [=not] until [=to] heaven? You-will-descend until [=to] the Hades[d]."

[a] *You-will-descend* B D W *pc* it vg sy^s sy^c cop^{sa}; *You-will-be-tossed-down* ℵ C L Θ f^1 f^{13} 33 892 1006 1342 1506 𝔐 sy^p cop^{bo}.
[b] *were-happened* ℵ B C D f^1 892 1424 *al*; *happened* L W Θ f^{13} 33 1006 1342 1506 𝔐.
[c] *were-happened* 𝔓^{45} 𝔓^{75} ℵ B D L Θ Ξ f^{13} 33 579 700 892 1342 1424 *pc*; *happened* A C W Ψ f^1 1006 1506 𝔐.
[d] *the Hades* 𝔓^{75} B L 1506 *pc*; *Hades* 𝔓^{45} ℵ A C D W Θ Ξ Ψ f^1 f^{13} 33 892 1006 1342 𝔐 cop.

128. Jesus Thanks the Father (→ §205)

Matt 11:25-27	Q 10:21-22	Luke 10:21-22	John 3:35; 7:29; 10:15a; 13:3a; 17:2a	Thomas 61
25 In that [=At the] proper-time, Jesus, having-answered, said, "I-acknowledge to-you, father, lord of-heaven and of-land, that you-hid these [things] from wises and intelligents [=wise and intelligent people] and you-revealed them [to] infants. 26 Yes, father, that [=because] thus happened [=was your] contentment in-front of-you. 27 All [things] were-delivered to-me under [=by] my father and no-one understands the son if no [=except] the father, nor [does] some [one] understand the	21 In [=At that time] he-said, "I-acknowledge to-you, father, lord of-heaven and of-land, that you-hid these [things] from wises and intelligents [=wise and intelligent people] and you-revealed them [to] infants. Yes, father, that [=because] thus happened [=was your] contentment in-front of-you. 22 All [things] were-delivered to-me under [=by] my father and no-one knows the son if no [=except] the father, nor [does] some [one] know	21 In it the [=same] hour, he-was-glad in the holy spirit[a] and[b] said, "I-acknowledge to-you, father, lord of-heaven and of-land, that you-hid-away these [things] from wises and intelligents [=wise and intelligent people] and you-revealed them [to] infants. Yes, father, that [=because] thus happened [=was your] contentment in-front of-you. 22 [c] All [things] were-delivered to-me under [=by] my father and no-one knows what [=who] the son is if no [=except] the father, and what [=who] is	3:35 "The father loves the son and has-given all [things] in [=into] his hand." 7:29 "I recognize him, that [=because] I-am along [=from] him, and-that [one] sent-off me. 10:15a "just-as the father knows me, I-too know the father" 13:3a "having-known that the father gave all [things] to-him into the [=his] hands" 17:2a "Just-as you [yourself] gave him authority [=over] all flesh"	Jesus said, "Two will recline on a couch; one will die, one will live." Salome said, "Who are you, mister? You have climbed onto my couch and eaten from my table as if you are from someone." Jesus said to her, "I am the one who comes from what is whole. I was granted from the things of my Father." "I am your disciple." "For this reason I say, if one is whole, one will be filled with light, but if one is divided, one will be filled with darkness."

father if no [=except] the son and to-whom if-ever the son might-want to-reveal.”	the father if no [=except] the son and to-whom if-ever the son might-want to-reveal.”	the father if no [=except] the son, and to-whom if-ever the son might-want to-reveal.”		

[a] *in the holy spirit* ℵ D L Ξ 33 *al* it; *in-the holy spirit* 𝔓[75] B C Θ *f*[1] 579 *al*; *in-the spirit* A W Ψ *f*[13] 1006 1342 1506 𝔐; *in the spirit* 𝔓[45] 892 2542 *pc*.
[b] *omit* 𝔓[45] 𝔓[75] ℵ B D Ξ *pc* it[mss] vg sy[s] sy[c] cop[sa]; *Jesus* A C W Ψ *f*[1] 892 1006 1342 1506 𝔐 it[mss] cop[bo].
[c] *omit* 𝔓[45] 𝔓[75] ℵ B D L X 070 *f*[1] *f*[13] 33 205 579 892 1342 1424 2542 *al* it[mss] vg sy[s] sy[c] cop; *And having-turned to the disciples he-said* A C W Θ Ψ 1006 1506 𝔐 it sy[p].

129. Matthew’s “Come to me”

Matt 11:28-30	Thomas 90
28“Come-on! to me all the laborings [=those who labor] and having-been-burdeneds [=those who have been burdened], I-too will-give-relief [to] you. 29Remove [=Take] my yoke upon you and learn from me, that [=because] I-am gentle and humble in-the heart and you-will-find relief [for] your souls. 30For my yoke is kind [=easy] and my burden insignificant.”	Jesus said, “Come to me, for my yoke is comfortable and my lordship is gentle, and you will find rest for yourselves.”

There are no variants in this pericope that appear in English.

130. Plucking Grain on the Sabbath (→ §69)

Matt 12:1-8	Mark 2:23-28	Luke 6:1-5
1In that proper-time [=season] Jesus traveled [on] the sabbaths through the grainfields; so [=and] his disciples hungered and they-began to-pluck ears-of-grain and to-eat [them].	23And it-happened him [=he happened once] in [=on] the sabbaths to-travel-by through the grainfields, and his disciples began plucking ears-of-grain to-do way [=as they were made their way along].	1So it-happened in [=on a] sabbath[d] him to-travel-through [=that he was going] through grainfields and his disciples were-plucking and were-eating the ears-of-grain, rubbing [them] in-the [=in their] hands.
2So the Pharisees, having-seen, said to-him, “Look! your disciples do [that] which is-permitted not to-do in [=on a] sabbath.”	24And the Pharisees were-saying to-him, “Look, what [=why] do-they-do [on] the sabbaths [that] which is-permitted not?”	2So [=But] some of-the Pharisees said, “What [=Why] do-you-do [that] which is-permitted not [on] the sabbaths?”
3So [=But] he-said to-them, “Did-you-read not what David did when he-hungered and the [ones] with him, 4how he-entered into the house of-god	25And he-says[b] to-them, “Never did-you-read what David did when he-had need and he [himself] hungered and the [ones] with him, 26how he-entered into the house of-god upon [=when] Abiathar [was] high-priest,	3And having-answered, Jesus said to them, “Nor did-you-read this, [that] which David did when he [himself] hungered and the beings [=those who are] with him, 4like [=when] he-entered into the house of-god, and having-taken the breads of-the presentation [=the show bread]
and they-ate[a] the breads of-the presentation [=the show bread], which was being-permitted not to-him to-eat nor to-the [ones] with him, if no [=only] to-the priests alone?	and he-ate the breads of-the presentation [=the show bread], which it-is-permitted not [to anyone] to-eat if no [=except] the priests, and he-gave and [=also] to-the beings [=those who are] together-with him?”	he-ate and gave to-the [ones] with him [that] which it-is-permitted not to-eat, if no [=except] alone the priests?”

Matt	Mark	Luke
[5]Or did-you-read not in the law that [on] the sabbaths the priests in the temple profane the sabbath and they-are blameless? [6]So I-say to-you that [something] greater of-the [=than the] temple is here. [7]So if you-had-known what 'I-WISH MERCY AND NOT SACRIFICE' is [=means], you-condemned [=you would have condemned] not ever the blamelesses [=those who are blameless].		
	[27]And he-was-saying to-them, "The sabbath happened through [=because of] the person and not the person through [=because of] the sabbath,	[5]And he-was-saying to-them,
[8]For [the] lord of-the sabbath is the son of-the person."	[28]with-the-result-that the son of-the person is lord and[c] [=even] of-the sabbath."	"[The] lord of-the sabbath, is the son of-the person."

[a] *they-ate* ℵ B *pc*; *he-ate* 𝔓[70] C D L W Θ *f*[1] *f*[13] 33 892[c] 1006 1506 𝔐 it vg sy cop; *he-took* 892*.
[b] *he-says* ℵ C L Θ *f*[13] 33 700 892 *pc*; *he was-saying* A *f*[1] 1006 1506 𝔐; *he says* 1424 *pc*; *having-answered he-said* D Θ 1342 it[mss]; *he-said* 𝔓[88] B 565 2427 cop[bo].
[c] *and* ℵ B C L Θ 13 2427; *omit* A *f*[1] *f*[13] 33 892 1006 1342 1506 𝔐 it[mss].
[d] *in sabbath* 𝔓[4] ℵ B L W *f*[1] 33 69* 205 579 2542 *pc* it sy[p] cop[sa] cop[bo]; *in next-to-last sabbath* A C D Θ Ψ *f*[13] 892 1006 1342 1506 𝔐 it[mss] vg.
🕮 Mt 12:3 – 1 Sam 21:6; 🕮 Mt 12:5 – Num 28:9,10; 🕮 Mt 12:7 – Hos 6:6; Mk 2:25 – 1 Sam 21:6

131. Healing the Withered Hand (→ §70)

Matt 12:9-14	Mark 3:1-6	Luke 6:6-11
[9]And having-headed-out from-there, he-went into their synagogue;	[1]And he-entered again[b] into the synagogue.	[6]So it-happened in [=on an] other sabbath to-enter him [=that he entered] into the synagogue and to-teach [=taught there].
[10]and look! [a] person having [=with a] withered hand[a].	And [a] person was there having the having-been-withered [=with a withered] hand.	And there-was [a] person there and his right hand was withered.
	[2]And they-were-watching-closely him [to see] if [on] the sabbaths he-will-heal him, in-order-that they-might-accuse him.	[7]So the scribes and the Pharisees were-watching-closely him [to see] if he-heals in [=on] the sabbath, in-order-that they-might-find [a way] to-accuse him[c].
And	[3]And he-says to-the person the withered hand having, "Rise [=Get up and come] into the middle."	[8]So [=But] he [himself] recognized their thoughts, so [=and] he-said to-the man having the withered hand, "Rise and stand into the middle." And having-gotten-up, he-stood [there].
they-questioned him saying, if "Is-it-permitted to-heal [on] the sabbaths?"	[4]And he-says to-them, "Is-it-permitted [on] the sabbaths to-do good or to-do-ill, to-save [a] soul or to-kill [it]?"	[9]So Jesus said to them, "I-question you if it-is-permitted [on] the sabbath to-do-good or to-do-ill, to-save [a] soul or to-destroy [it]?"

Matthew	Mark	Luke
in-order-that they-might-accuse him. [11]So [=But]	So [=But] they-were-being-silent.	
he-said to-them, "What person will-there-be out of-you who will-have one sheep and if-ever [on] the sabbaths this [sheep] might-fall-in into [a] ditch will-seize it indeed-not and raise [=lift it out]? [12]Therefore, how-great is-superior [=how much more superior is a] person [than a] sheep? With-the-result-that [=Therefore] it-is-permitted [on] the sabbaths to-do well."		
	[5]And having-looked-around [at] them with anger, being-grieved-deeply upon [=by] the obstinacy [of] their heart,	[10]And having-looked-around [at] all of-them,
[13]Then he-says to-the person, "Reach-out your hand." And he-stretched-out [it] and was-restored [=it was made] healthy, like the another [=other].	he-says to-the person, "Reach-out the [=your] hand." And he-stretched-out [it] and his hand was-restored.	he-said to-him, "Your hand reach-out." So he-did and his hand was-restored.
[14]So the Pharisees having-gone-out took [=made a] plot according-to [=against] him so-that they-might-destroy him.	[6]And the Pharisees, having-gone-out immediately gave [=made a] plot with the Herodians according-to [=against] him so-that they-might-destroy him.	[11]So they [themselves] were-filled [with] madness and were-talking-about to one-another what ever they-might-do to-Jesus.

[a] *person having withered hand* ℵ B C W 892 *pc* vg; *there-was person having the withered hand* 𝔐 it^{mss} vg^{mss}; *person was there having the withered hand* D L Δ Q f^{1} f^{13} 33 1006 1342 1424 1506 sy^{p}.

[b] *he-entered again* A C D L W Θ f^{1} f^{13} 33 892 1006 1342 1506 2427 𝔐 cop^{sa}; *omit* ℵ B.

[c] *they-might-find to-accuse him* 𝔓^{4} ℵ* B Q 0233 f^{1} 205 *al* cop^{sa}; *they-might-find accusation him* ℵ^{2} A L W f^{13} 33 1006 1342 1506 𝔐 cop^{bo}; *they-might-find to-accuse* (NB. Contains an alternate spelling of accuse) *him* D; *they-might-accuse him* Ψ *pc*.

132. Matthew's Jesus Heals Many

Matt 12:15-21

[15]So Jesus, having-known [this], retreated from-there. And many crowds followed him and he-healed them all, [16]and he-rebuked them in-order-that they-might-do [=they might make] him visible no [=not], [17]in-order-that the having-been-said [=what had been said] through Isaiah the prophet might-be-fulfilled saying, [18]"LOOK! MY CHILD WHOM I-SELECTED, MY BELOVED INTO [=with] WHOM MY SOUL WAS-CONTENT. I-WILL-PUT MY SPIRIT UPON HIM, AND HE-WILL-INFORM [=he will bring] JUDGMENT [=justice] TO-THE NATIONS. [19]HE-WILL-QUARREL NOT NOR WILL-HE-SCREAM NOR WILL-HEAR SOME [=will anyone hear] HIS VOICE IN THE WIDE-STREETS. [20]HE-WILL-PULVERIZE NOT [a] HAVING-BEEN-SHATTERED REED, AND HE-WILL-EXTINGUISH NOT [a] BEING-NEARLY-SMOTHERED WICK, UNTIL EVER HE-MIGHT-CAST-OUT [=bring] JUDGMENT [=justice] INTO VICTORY. [21]AND NATIONS WILL-HOPE [in] HIS NAME."

There are no variants in this pericope that appear in English.

📖 Mt 12:18-21 – Isa 42:1-4

133. Luke's Woman with the Ointment (→ §209, §345)

Luke 7:36-50

[36]So some [person] of-the Pharisees begged him in-order-that he-might-eat with him, and having-entered into the house of-the Pharisee, he-was-reclined-at-table[a]. [37]And look! [a] sinful woman whoever was in the city, and having-understood that he-lies-down in the home of-the Pharisee, having-obtained [an] alabaster-case, [38]and having-stood behind [him] along [=at] his feet weeping, began to-rain [on] his feet [with her] tears and she-was-drying [them with] the hairs [of] her head, and she-was-kissing his feet and was-smearing the ointment. [39]So the Pharisee the [one] having-called [=who had invited] him, having-seen, said in himself, saying, "If this [man] were [a] prophet, he-was-knowing ever [=he would have known] what [=who] and what-sort-of woman [this is] whoever is-touching him, that she-is sinful." [40]And having-answered Jesus said to him, "Simon, I-have some [thing] to-say to-you." So the [=Simon said], "Teacher, say [=speak]." [41]"There-were to-some loan-shark [=A money lender had] two needy-debtors; the one was-in-debt five-hundred denarii, so [=and] the other fifty. [42]Having no [=not] them to-give-over [=Since they could not repay him] he-gave-as-a-benefaction to-both [=he counted their debts as benefactions]. Therefore what [=which] of-them will-love him more?" [43]Simon having-answered said, "I-imagine that [=the one] to-whom he-gave-as-a-benefaction more." So he-said to-him, "You-judged correctly." [44]And having-turned to the woman, he-spoke to-Simon, "Do-you-look [=See] this woman? I-entered into your home, you-gave me not [any] water upon my feet, so [=but] this [woman] rained [on] my feet [with her] tears and dried [them with] her hairs. [45]You-gave me not [a] kiss; so [=but] this [woman] desisted-from kissing my feet not [=has not stopped kissing my feet] from which [=since] I [myself] entered. [46]You-smeared not my head [with] olive-oil; so [=but] this [woman] smeared my feet [with] ointment. [47]Of-which sake [=Therefore], I-say to-you, 'Her many sins have-been-excused, that [=since] she-loved many; so [=but] to-whom [a] little has-been-excused, he-loves [a] little.'" [48]So he-said to-her, "Your sins have-been-excused." [49]And the sitting-at-tables [=those who were sitting together] began to-say in themselves, "What [=Who] is this [=this man] who and [=even] excuses sins?" [50]So he-said to the woman, "Your loyalty has-saved you; travel into [=in] peace."

[a] *he-was-reclined-at-table* $\aleph^2$ B D L Ξ f^1 33 205 579 700 892 1342 *pc*; *he-reclined* ℵ*; *he-was-put-to-bed* A W Q Y f^{13} 1006 1506 𝔐.

134. Luke's Ministering Women

Luke 8:1-3

[1]And it-happened in the successively [=afterward that] and [=also] he [himself] was-going-on-through according-to [=each] city and village preaching and proclaiming the kingdom of-god, and the twelve together-with him, [2]and some women who were having-been-healed [=had been healed] from evil spirits and illnesses, Mary the [one] being-called [=also called] Magdalene from whom seven demons had-gone-out, [3]and Joanna woman [=wife] of-Chuza, steward of-Herod, and Suzanna and many others, whoever served them out of-the being-at-one's-disposals to-them [=from their belongings].

There are no variants in this pericope that appear in English.

135. Mark's Insane Jesus

Mark 3:20-21

[20]And he-comes[a] into house [=he went home]; and the crowd[b] comes-together again with-the-result-that them no [=not] to-be-able so-not to-eat bread [=so that they could not even eat]. [21]And the along him having-heard [=when his family heard], they-went-out to-seize him; for they-were-saying that he-was-surprised [=he was out of his mind].

[a] *he-comes* ℵ* B W 1342 1427 *pc* it^{mss} cop^{sa} cop^{bo}; *they-come* ℵ 2 A C L Q f^1 f^{13} 33 892 1006 1506 𝔐 vg it^{mss} sy^p; *they-enter* D.
[b] *the crowd* $\aleph^1$ A D L^C Δ Θ^C 565 892 1006 2427 2542 *pc* cop^{sa}; *crowd* ℵ* C L* W Θ* f^1 f^{13} 33 1342 1506 𝔐 cop^{bo}.

136. The Mute Demoniac (→ §101, §213)

Matt 9:34	**Mark 3:22**	Q 11:15	Luke 11:15	John 10:20; 8:48
34 So [=But] the Pharisees	22 And the scribes having-descended from Jerusalems,	15 So [=But] some	15 So [=But] some out of-them [=some of them]	10:20 So many out of-them [=many of them] were-saying, "He-has [a] demon and is insane. What [=Why do you] hear [=listen to] him?" 8:48 The Judeans answered and said to-him, "[Is it] not well [=right when] we [ourselves] say that 'You are [a] Samaritan and you-have [a] demon?'"
were-saying,	were-saying that "He-has Beelzebul[a]"	said,	said,	
"In [=By] the magistrate of-the demons he-casts-out the demons."	and that "In [=By] the magistrate of-the demons he-casts-out the demons."	"In [=By] Beelzebul, the magistrate of-the demons, he-casts-out the demons."	"In [=By] Beelzebul, the magistrate of-the demons, he-casts-out the demons."	

[a] *Beelzebul* ℵ A C D L W Θ Ψ f^1 f^{13} 33 892 1006 1342 1506 2427 𝔐 it vg^{mss} cop; *Beezebul* B; *Beelzebub* vg sy^s sy^p.

137. Matthew's Healing of the Blind Mute Demoniac (→ §101)

Matt 12:22-24

22 Then [a] blind and mute being-demon-possessed [=demoniac] was-offered to-him, and he-healed him, with-the-result-that the mute [was able] to-talk and to-look [=to see]. 23 And all the crowds were-being-surprised and were-saying, "Is this [man] surely-not the son of-David?" 24 So [=But] the Pharisees having-heard, said, "This [man] casts-out demons not if no [=only] in [=by] Beelzebul, magistrate of-the demons."

There are no variants in this pericope that appear in English.

138. A Kingdom Divided (→ §213, §214)

Matt 12:25-29	**Mark 3:23-27**	Q 11:17-20	Luke 11:17-21	Thomas 35
25 So, having-recognized[a] their deliberations, he-said to-them,	23 And having-summoned them he-was-saying [=he was speaking] to-them in parables. "How [is] adversary able to-cast-out adversary?	17 So having-recognized their ruminations, he-said to-them,	17 So [=But] he, having-recognized their ruminations, said to-them,	
"All [=Every] kingdom having-been-divided according-to [=against] itself is-made-desolate and all [=every] city or home having-been-divided according-	24 And if-ever [a] kingdom might-be-divided upon [=against] itself, that kingdom is-able not to-be-stood [=will not stand]. 25 And if-ever [a] home might-be-divided	"All [=Every] kingdom having-been-divided according-to [=against] itself is-made-desolate and all [=every] home having-been-divided according-	"All [=Every] kingdom having-been-divided-up upon [=against] itself is-made-desolate and house upon [=against] house falls.	

Q 7:35 (§126, p. 91)
Luke 8:3 (§134, p. 97)

to [=against] itself will-be-stood not [=will not stand].	upon [=against] itself, that home will-be-able not to-be-stood [=will not stand].	to [=against] itself will-be-stood not [=will not stand].		
26And if the adversary casts-out [an] adversary, he-was-divided [=he would be divided] upon [=against] itself.	26And if the adversary got-up upon [=rose against] itself, and was-divided	18And if the adversary was-divided-up upon [=against] itself,	18So and [=And also] if the adversary was-divided-up upon [=against] itself,	
Therefore how will-be-stood [=will stand] his kingdom?	he-is-able not to-stand, but has end [=would fall].	how his kingdom will-be-stood [=will his kingdom stand]?	how his kingdom will-be-stood [=will his kingdom stand]? That [=Because] you-say to-cast-out me [=that I cast out] the demons in [=by] Beelzebul.	
27And if I [myself] cast-out the demons in [=by] Beelzebul, in what [=by whose authority do] your sons cast-out [demons]? Through [=Because of] this they [themselves] will-be your judges. 28So [=But] if I [myself] cast-out the demons in [=by the] spirit of-god, consequently [=then] the kingdom of-god loomed upon [=over] you.		19And if I [myself] cast-out the demons in [=by] Beelzebul, in what [=by whose authority do] your sons cast-out [demons]? Through [=Because of] this they [themselves] will-be your judges. 20So [=But] if I [myself] cast-out the demons in [=by the] finger of-god, consequently [=then] the kingdom of-god loomed upon [=over] you."	19So if I [myself] cast-out the demons in [=by] Beelzebul, in what [=by whose authority do] your sons cast-out [demons]? Through [=Because of] this they [themselves] your judges will-be. 20So [=But] if I [myself] cast-out[b] the demons in [=by the] finger of-god, consequently [=then] the kingdom of-god loomed upon [=over] you.	
29Or how some is-able [=is it possible] to-enter into the home of-the strong and to-plunder his vessels, if-ever no [=unless] he-might-restrain first the strong [person]? And [only] then he-will-raid his home."	27But no-one, having-entered into the home of-the strong is-able not to-raid his vessels, if-ever no [=unless] he-might-restrain the strong [person] first and [only] then he-will-raid his home."		21Whenever the strong [person] having-been-fully-armed might-guard of-himself [=his very own] court-yard, his being-at-one's-disposals [=belongings] is in peace [=are safe]."	Jesus said, "One can't enter a strong person's house and take it by force without tying his hands. Then one can loot his house."

[a] *So having-recognized* ℵ* B cop^{sa}; *So Jesus, having-recognized* C L W Θ f^{1} f^{13} 1006 1342 1506 𝔐 vg it^{mss} sy^{p}; *So Jesus, seeing* 13 33 892^{C} *pc* cop^{bomss}; *So, seeing* 𝔓^{21} ℵ^{1} D 892* sy^{s} sy^{c} cop^{bo}.

[b] *I cast-out* 𝔓^{75} ℵ^{1} B C D L f^{13} 33 579 892 1342 *al* it cop; *I-cast-out* 𝔓^{45} ℵ* A W Θ Ψ f^{1} 1006 1506 𝔐 vg it^{mss}.

Q 7:35 (§126, p. 91)
Luke 8:3 (§134, p. 97)

139. Who Is Not with Me Is against Me (→ §215)

Matt 12:30	Q 11:23	Luke 11:23
[30]"The [one] no [=not] being with me is according-to [=against] me and the [one] no [=not] gathering with me disperses."	[23]"The [one] no [=not] being with me is according-to [=against] me and the [one] no [=not] gathering with me disperses."	[23]"The [one] no [=not] being with me is according-to [=against] me and the [one] no [=not] gathering with me disperses."

There are no variants in this pericope that appear in English.

140. Speaking against the Spirit and the Son of Man (→ §86, §231)

Matt 12:31-37	Mark 3:28-30	Q 12:10; 6:44-45	Luke 12:10; 6:44-45	Thomas 44; 45
[31]"Through this [=Therefore] I-say to-you, all sin and blasphemy will-be-excused [=will be forgiven] for-people,	[28]"Amen I-say to-you that all sinfulnesses and whatsoever if-ever [=any] blasphemies they-might-blaspheme will-be-excused for-the sons of-people.			[44]Jesus said, "Whoever blasphemes against the Father will be forgiven, and whoever blasphemes against the son will be forgiven, but whoever blasphemes against the holy spirit will not be forgiven, either on earth or in heaven."
so [=but] blasphemy of-the spirit will-be-excused not[a].	[29]So [=But] who ever might-blaspheme into [=against] the holy spirit has not remission [=will not be forgiven] into [=within] the eon, but is answerable [=guilty] of-eternal sinfulness[c]." [30]That [=Because] they-were-saying, "He-has [an] unclean spirit."			
[32]And who if-ever might-say [a] word according-to [=against] the son of-the person, it-will-be-excused for-him, so [=but] who ever might-say [=might speak] according-to [=against] the holy spirit it-will-be-excused for-him not in this eon neither in the intending [=age to come].		[12:10]"And who if-ever might-say [a] word into [=against] the son of-the person, it-will-be-excused for-him, so [=but] who ever might-say [a word] into [=against] the holy spirit it-will-be-excused for-him not."	[12:10]"And all who will-say [a] word into [=against] the son of-the person, it-will-be-excused for-him, so [=but] for-the [one] having-blasphemed into [=against] the holy spirit it-will-be-excused not."	

33Or [=Either] do [=make] the tree fine [=healthy] and its fruit fine, or do [=make] the tree rotten and its fruit rotten. For the tree is-known out of-the [=by its] fruit.		6:44"For the tree is-known out of-the [=by its] fruit. Surely-not are-picked out of-thorny-plants figs, or out of-thistles bunches-of-grapes?	6:44"For each tree is-known out [=by its] own fruit; for they-pick not figs out of-thorny-plants nor do-they-glean [a] bunch-of-grapes out [=from a] bramble-bush.	
34Offspring of-vipers, how are-you-able to-talk [=to say] good [things despite] being evil? For the mouth talks out of-the excess of-the heart[b]. 35The good person casts-out [=brings out] goods [=good things] out of-the good treasure-		45The good person out of-the good treasure-box casts-	45The good person out of-the good treasure-box of-the heart[c]	45Jesus said, "Grapes are not harvested from thorn trees, nor are figs gathered from thistles, for they yield no fruit. Good persons produce good from what they've stored up; bad persons produce evil from the wickedness they've stored up in their hearts, and say evil things. For from the overflow of the heart they produce evil."
box, and the evil person casts-out [=brings out] evils [=evil things] out of-the evil treasure-box.		out good [things], and the evil person out of-the evil treasure-box casts-out evil [things]. For out of-excess of-heart [=from the excess of the heart] his mouth talks."	produces the good, and the evil [person] out of-the evil [treasure box] produces the evil. For out of-excess of-heart [=from the excess of the heart] his mouth talks."	
36So I-say to-you that all idle speech which the people will-talk they-will-give-over around his word [=will have to be accounted for] in [=on the] day of-judgment; 37for you-will-be-made-righteous out [=by] your words and you-will-be-condemned out [=by] your words."				

[a] *omit* ℵ B f^1 205 1424 *pc* vg cop^{sa} cop^{bo}; *for-people* C D L W Θ f^{13} 33 1006 1342 1506 𝔐 it sy^{p}; *for-him* it^{mss} sy^{s} sy^{c} cop^{bomss}.
[b] *of-the heart* 𝔓^{75} ℵ B *pc*; *his heart* A C L W Θ Ξ Ψ f^1 f^{13} 33 893 1006 1342 1506 𝔐 cop.
[c] *sinfulness* ℵ B L Δ Θ 33 565 892* 2427; *judgment* A C^{2} f^1 892 1006 1342 1506 𝔐 vg^{mss} sy^{p}; *punishment* 348 1216 *pc*; *sins* C* D W f^{13}.

141. The Sign of Jonah (→ §173, §213, §218, §219)

Matt 12:38-42

[38]Then some of-the scribes and Pharisees answered him[a] saying, "Teacher, we-wish to-see [a] sign from you."
[39]So having-answered he-said to-them, "[An] evil and adulterous generation seeks [a] sign, and [=but a] sign will-be-given not to-it if no [=except] the sign of-Jonah the prophet. [40]For even-as Jonah was in the abdomen of-the large-sea-creature three days and three nights, thus the son of-the person will-be in the heart of-the land three days and three nights.
[41]Ninevite men will-get-up [=will rise] in [=at] the judgment with this generation and they-will-judge-against it, that [=because] they-repented into [=at] the preaching of-Jonah, and look! [a] more [=person greater than] Jonah [is] here. [42][The] queen [of the] south will-be-raised in [=at] the judgment with this generation, and she-will-judge-against it, that [=because] she-came out of-the edges of-the land [=from the ends of the earth] to-hear the wisdom of-Solomon, and look! [a] more [=person greater than] Solomon [is] here."

Q 11:16, 29-30, 32, 31

[16]So some were-searching [for a] sign along [=from] him.
[29]So he-said, "This generation is [an] evil generation; it-searches [for a] sign and [=but a] sign will-be-given not to-it if no [=except] the sign of-Jonah.
[30]For just-as Jonah happened [=became a] sign to-the Ninevites, thus and [=so too] will-be the son of-the person to-this generation.
[31][The] queen [of the] south will-be-raised in [=at] the judgment with this generation, and she-will-judge-against it, that [=because] she-came out of-the edges of-the land [=from the ends of the earth] to-hear the wisdom of-Solomon, and look! [a] more [=person greater than] Solomon [is] here. [32] Ninevite men will-get-up [=will rise] in [=at] the judgment with this generation and they-will-judge-against it, that [=because] they-repented into [=at] the preaching of-Jonah, and look! [a] more [=person greater than] Jonah [is] here."

Luke 11:16, 29-30, 32, 31

[16]So others, testing [him] were-searching [for a] sign out of-heaven along [=from] him. [29]So the crowds expanding [since the crowds were growing] he-began to-say, "This generation is [an] evil generation; it-searches[b] [for a] sign and [=but a] sign will-be-given not to-it if no [=except] the sign of-Jonah.
[30]For just-as Jonah happened [=became a] sign to-the Ninevites, thus and [=so too] will-be the son of-the person to-this generation.
[31][The] queen [of the] south will-be-raised in [=at] the judgment with the men [of] this generation, and she-will-judge-against them, that [=because] she-came out of-the edges of-the land [=from the ends of the earth] to-hear the wisdom of-Solomon, and look! [a] more [=person greater than] Solomon [is] here. [32]Ninevite men will-get-up [=will rise] in [=at] the judgment with this generation and they-will-judge-against it, that [=because] they-repented into [=at] the preaching of-Jonah, and look! [a] more [=person greater than] Jonah [is] here."

[a] *him* ℵ B C D L Θ f^{13} 33 892 1424 *al* vg it[mss] cop[sa] cop[bo]; *omit* W f^{1} 1006 1342 𝔐.
[b] *it-searches* 𝔓[45] 𝔓[75] ℵ B L Ξ 700 892 2542 *pc*; *it-seeks* C D W Θ Ψ f^{1} f^{13} 33 1006 1342 1506 𝔐.
🕮 Mt 12:40 – Jonah 1:17; 🕮 Mt 12:42 – 1 Kgs 10:1

142. Return of the Unclean Spirit (→ §216)

Matt 12:43-45

[43]"So whenever the unclean spirit might-go-out from the person, it-goes-through through [=it goes right through] waterless places searching [for] relief; and it-finds [it] not. [44]Then it-says, 'I-will-turn-back into [=I will return to] my house from-which I-went-out.' And having-come, it-finds [it already] being-unoccupied,[a] having-been-swept and having-been-adorned [=decorated].

Q 11:24-26

[24]"Whenever the unclean spirit might-go-out from the person, it-goes-through through [=it goes right through] waterless places searching [for] relief; and it-finds [it] not.
[44]Then it-says, 'I-will-turn-back into [=I will return to] my house from-which I-went-out.' [25]And having-come, it-finds [it] having-been-swept and having-been-adorned [=decorated].

Luke 11:24-26

[24]"Whenever the unclean spirit might-go-out from the person, it-goes-through through [=it goes right through] waterless places searching [for] relief and [=but] finding no [relief]. Then[b] it-says, 'I-will-return into [=I will return to] my house from-which I-went-out.' [25]And having-come, it-finds [it] having-been-swept and having-been-adorned [=decorated].

Q 7:35 (§126, p. 91)
Luke 8:3 (§134, p. 97)

[45]Then it-travels and takes-along with itself seven other spirits more-evil [than] itself and having-entered it-settles there. And the lasts [=last things] of-that person happen [=become] worse of-the firsts [=than the first things]. Thus it-will-be and [=also for] this evil generation."	[26]Then it-travels and takes-along with itself seven other spirits more-evil [than] itself and having-entered it-settles there. And the lasts [=last things] of-that person happen [=become] worse of-the firsts [=than the first things]."	[26]Then it-travels and takes-along other spirits more-evil [than] itself, seven, and having-entered it-settles there. And the lasts [=last things] of-that person happen [=become] worse of-the firsts [=than the first things]."

[a] *omit* B C^{2} D L W Z Θ f^{1} f^{13} 33 892 1006 1342 𝔐 vg it^{mss}; *and* ℵ C* 1424 1506 *al* it.
[b] *Then* $\mathfrak{P}^{75}$ $ℵ^{2}$ B L Θ Ξ 070 33 892 1342 *pc*; *omit* $\mathfrak{P}^{45}$ ℵ* A C D W Ψ f^{1} f^{13} 1006 1506 𝔐 vg it^{mss} sy^{s} sy^{c} sy^{p}.

143. True Family (→ §157)

Matt 12:46-50	**Mark 3:31-35**	Luke 8:19-21	John 15:14	Thomas 99
[46]Yet his [=While he was] talking to-the crowds, look! the [=his] mother and his brothers had-been-standing outside searching to-talk to-him.	[31]And his mother comes and his brothers and persevering outside they-sent-off to [=for] him calling him.	[19]So the [=his] mother arrived to him and his brothers and they-were-able not to-get-near-to him through the crowd.		
[47]So some [person] said to-him, "Look! your mother and your brothers outside have-stood searching to-talk to-you."[a]	[32]And [a] crowd was-sitting around him and they-say to-him, "Look! your mother and your brothers and your sisters outside search [for] you."	[20]So it-was-informed [=it was told] to-him,[d] "Your mother and your brothers have-stood outside wishing to-see you."		The disciples said to him, "Your brothers and your mother are standing outside."
[48]So having-answered he-said to-the sayings [=to those who were speaking] to-him, "What [=Who] is my mother and what [=who] are my brothers?"	[33]And having-answered he-says to-them, "What [=Who] is my mother and my[c] brothers?"	[21]So having-answered he-said to them,		He said to them, "Those here who do what my Father wants are my brothers and my mother. They are the ones who will enter my Father's kingdom."
[49]And having-reached-out his hand upon his disciples he-said, "Look! my mother and my brothers. [50]For whoever ever	[34]And having-looked-around [at] the sittings [=those who were sitting] among [=in a circle] around him, he-says, "Look [at] my mother and my brothers. [35]For who ever might-do			

might-do[b] the wish [of] my father in [the] heavens he is my brother and sister and mother."	the wish of-god, this [one] is my brother and sister and mother."	"My mother and my brothers are these hearings and doings [=those who hear and do] the word of-god."	14"You are my friends if-ever you-might-do [that] which I [myself] charge you."	

[a] *So some said to-him, "Look! your mother and your brothers outside have-stood searching to-talk to-you"* ℵ[1] ℵ[2] C D W Z Θ *f*[1] *f*[13] 33 892 1006 1342 1506 𝔐 vg it[mss] sy[p] cop[bo]; *omit verse* ℵ* B L 2542 *pc* it[mss] sy[s] sy[c] cop[sa].
[b] *whoever ever might-do* ℵ B Θ *f*[1] *f*[13] 33 892 1006 1342 1506 𝔐; *whoever does* D; *whoever ever will-do* L Z Q 579 1424 *al.*
[c] *my* ℵ A C L W Θ *f*[1] *f*[13] 33 892 1006 1342 1506 𝔐 vg it sy; *omit* B D.
[d] *omit* 𝔭[75] B W Δ *pc* vg; *that* ℵ D L Q *f*[1] 33 205 579 1342 *pc* it; *saying* A Ξ *f*[13] 1006 1506 𝔐; *saying that* Ψ 1424 *pc.*

144. The Parable of the Sower

Matt 13:1-9	Mark 4:1-9	Luke 8:4-8	Thomas 9
1In [=On] that day Jesus, having-gone-out the home[a] sat along the sea; 2and many crowds were-gathered to him with-the-result-that him to-sit [=he sits] having-embarked into [a] boat, and all the crowd had-stood upon the beach.	1And again he-began to-teach along the sea; and [a] most [=very great] crowd gathers[b] to him, with-the-result-that him to-sit [=he sits] having-embarked into [a] boat in the sea and all the crowd were upon the land to [=at the edge of] the sea.	4So many crowd being-with [=When a great crowd gathered] and the traveling-to to him according-to [a] city [=when each city went out to	
3And he-talked [=he was saying] to-them many [things] in parables, saying,	2And he-was-teaching them many [things] in parables and was-saying to-them in his instruction, 3"Hear [this].	him], he-said through [a] parable;	
"Look! the [one] sowing went-out to-sow.	Look! the [one] sowing went-out to-sow.	5"The [one] sowing went-out to-sow his seedling.	Jesus said, "Look, the sower went out, took a handful <of seeds>, and scattered <them>.
4And in the him to-sow [=when he was sowing], which for-one [=some seeds] fell along [=near] the way [=road],	4And it-happened in the to-sow [=when he was sowing], which for-one [=some seeds] fell along [=near] the way [=road],	And in the to-sow him [=when he was sowing], which for-one [=some seeds] fell along [=near] the way [=road] and it-was-tread-upon	Some fell on the road,
and the birds having-come consumed them.	and the birds came and consumed it.	and the birds of-heaven consumed it.	and the birds came and gathered them.
5So [=And] anothers [=other seeds] fell upon the rocky-grounds where it-was-having not many land [=they had not enough earth], and instantly they-sprouted-up through [=because] the to-have no [=it did not have] depth of-land. 6So [=But the] sun having-arisen [=when the sun rose] it-was-scorched	5So [=And] another fell upon the rocky-ground where it-was-having not many land [=they had not enough earth], and immediately they-sprouted-up through [=because] the to-have no [=it did not have] depth of-land. 6And when the sun arose it-was-scorched and	6And [an] other fell-down upon the rock and having-flourished it-was-withered through	Others fell on rock, and they didn't take root in the soil and didn't produce heads of grain.

Matt	Mark	Luke	Thomas
and through the to-have [=because it had] no root it-was-withered.	through the to-have [=because it had] no root it-was-withered.	the to-have [=because it had] no moisture.	
[7]So [=But] anothers [=others] fell upon the thorny-plants, and the thorny-plants ascended [=grew] and drowned [=choked] them.	[7]And another fell into the thorny-plants, and the thorny-plants ascended [=grew] and choked it, and it-gave not [any] fruit.	[7]And [an] other fell in [the] middle of-the thorny-plants and the thorny-plants having-flourished-with [it] suffocated it.	Others fell on thorns, and they choked the seeds and worms ate them.
[8]So [=But] anothers [=others] fell upon fine land and it-was-giving fruit, [some of] which for-one [produced] one-hundred, so [=but] which [=others produced] sixty, so [=but] which [=others] thirty. [9]The [one] having ears let-him-hear."	[8]And anothers [=others] fell into fine land and it-was-giving fruit, ascending and growing and one was-carrying [=was producing] thirty, and one sixty and one one-hundred." [9]And he-was-saying, "Who [ever] has ears to-hear, let-him-hear."	[8]And [an] other fell into good land and having-flourished did [=made] fruit [one] hundred-fold." Saying these [things] he-was-yelling, "The [one] having ears to-hear let-him-hear."	And others fell on good soil, and it produced a good crop: it yielded sixty per measure and one hundred twenty per measure."

[a] *the home* B Θ f^{1} f^{13} 1424 *pc*; *out of-the home* ℵ Z 33 892 1342 *pc*; *from the home* C L W 1006 1506 𝔐 vg it^{mss}; *omit* D it sys.
[b] *gathers* ℵ B C L Δ f^{13} 700 892 2427 2542 *pc*; *is-gathered* D W Θ 33 1006 1342 𝔐 it vg sy; *was-gathered* A 565 1506 *pc*; *comes-together* f^{1} 205.

145. The Reason for Speaking in Parables (→ §147, §206)

Matt 13:10-17	**Mark 4:10-12**	Q 10:23-24	**Luke 8:9-10;** 10:23-24	John 9:39b; 12:37-40	Thomas 62; 41; 17
	[10]And it-happened when according-to [=he was] alone, the [ones] around him together-				
[10]And the disciples having-approached said to-him, "Through what [=Why] do-you-talk to-them in	with the twelve were-begging him [=asked about] the		[8:9]So his disciples were-questioning him, "What may-be [=might mean] this		
parables?" [11]So having-answered he-said to-them[a],	parables. [11]And he-was-saying to-them,		parable?" [10]So he-said,		
"That [=Because] it-has-been-given to-you to know the mysteries of-the kingdom of-the heavens, so [=but] to-those [ones] it-has-	"The mystery of-the kingdom of-god has-been-given to-you; so [=but] to-those outside all [things] happen in parables,		"It-has-been-given to-you to-know the mysteries of-the kingdom of-god, so [=but] to-the remainders [=rest] in parables,		[62]Jesus said, "I disclose my mysteries to those <who are worthy> of <my> mysteries. Do not let your left hand know what your right

been-given not. 12For whoever has [something], it-will-be-given to-him, and it-will-be-exceeded; so [=but] whoever has not [something], and [=even that] which he-has will-be-removed from him. 13Through [=Because of] this I-talk to-them in parables, 'That looking they-

look [=they see] not, and hearing they-hear [=they understand] not, nor do-they-comprehend.'

14And the prophecy of-Isaiah is-borne-out for-them, the [one] saying, 'YOU-WILL-HEAR [a] RUMOR AND YOU-MIGHT-COMPREHEND NOT NO [=at all], AND LOOKING YOU-WILL-LOOK AND YOU-MIGHT-SEE NOT NO [=at all]. 15FOR THE HEART OF-THIS WHOLE-

---

12'In-order-that looking they-

might-look and they-might-see no [=not], and hearing they-will-hear and they-might-comprehend no [=not], lest they-might-turn-back and[b] it-might-be-excused [=it might be forgiven] for-them.'"

'In-order-that looking they-

might-look [=they might see] no [=not] and hearing they-might-comprehend no [=not].'"

9:39bI came into this world into verdict [=for judgment], in-order-that the lookings [=those who look] not might-look [=might see], and the lookings [=those who see] might-happen [=might become] blind.

12:37So his having-done [=although he did] so-many signs in-front of-them, they-were-believing into [=in] him not, 38in-order-that the word of-Isaiah the prophet might-be-fulfilled, which said, "Lord, what [=who] believed our rumor? And to-what [=to whom] was-revealed the arm [of the] lord?" 39Through [=Because of] this they-were-able not to-believe, that [=because] again Isaiah said, 40"He-has-

---

hand is doing."

41Jesus said, "Whoever has something in hand will be given more, and whoever has nothing will be deprived of even the little they have."

Matt	Q	Luke	Mark	Thomas
PEOPLE WAS-MADE-DULL AND THEY-HEARD IN-THE EARS DIFFICULTLY AND THEY-SHUT THEIR EYES, LEST THEY-MIGHT-SEE [with] THE EYES, AND THEY-MIGHT-HEAR [with] THE EARS AND THEY-MIGHT-COMPREHEND [with] THE HEART AND THEY-MIGHT-TURN-BACK [=they will repent] AND I-WILL-CURE THEM.'			blinded their eyes and he-hardened their heart, in-order-that the [=their] eyes might-see not and they-might-perceive [with] the heart and they-might-turn and I-will-cure them."	
		10:23 And having-been-turned to the disciples, he-said according-to own [=to each one],		
16 So, fortunate [are] your eyes that [=because] they-look [=they see] and your ears that [=because] they-hear.	23 "Fortunate [are] the eyes looking [=at that] which you-look [at],	"Fortunate [are] the eyes looking [=at that] which you-look [at],		17 Jesus said, "I will give you what no eye has seen, what no ear has heard, what no hand has touched, what has not arisen in the human heart."
17 For amen I-say to-you that many prophets and righteous [people] desired to-see [that]	24 for I-say to-you that many prophets and kings -ed* to-see [that] which	24 for I-say to-you that many prophets and kings wished to-see [that] which you [yourselves]		
which you-look [at] and [=but] saw not, and to-hear [that] which you-hear and [=but] heard not."	you-look [at] and [=but] saw not, and to-hear [that] which you-hear and [=but] heard not."	look [at] and [=but] saw not, and to-hear [that] which you-hear and [=but] heard not."		

[a] *to-them* B D L W Θ f^{1} f^{13} 33 1006 1342 1506 𝔐 vg it^{mss} sy cop^{sa}; *omit* ℵ C Z 892 *pc* it^{mss} cop^{bo}.
[b] *omit* ℵ B C L W f^{1} 205 892 2427 2542 *pc* cop^{bo}; *the sinfulness* A D Θ f^{13} 33 1006 1342 1506 𝔐 vg it^{mss} sy.
*IQP could only agree on the past tense of a verb here in Q, but could not agree on whether it was Matthew's 'desired' or Luke's 'wished.'
📖 Mt 13:14-15 – Isa 6:9-10; 📖 Mk 4:12 – Isa 6:9; 📖 Lk 8:10 – Isa 6:9

146. The Interpretation of the Parable of the Sower

Matt 13:18-23

18"Therefore you [yourselves] hear [=must understand] the parable of-the having-sown [=person who sowed]. 19All hearing [=When anyone hears] the word of-the kingdom and no [=not] comprehending [=does not comprehend], the evil [one] comes and plunders the having-been-sown [=what was sown] in his heart, this [seed] is the [one] having-been-sown along [=near] the way [=road]. 20So [=And] the [seed] having-been-sown upon the rocky-grounds, this is the [person] hearing the word and immediately taking it with joy, 21so it-has not [a] root in himself but is <u>temporary</u>, so distress or persecution having-happened through [=because of] the word he-is-caused-to-stumble immediately. 22So [=And] the [seed] having-been-sown into the thorny-plants, this is the [one] hearing the word and [=but] the worry of-the eon [=worries of the world] and the lure of-wealth chokes the word and it-happens [=it becomes] fruitless. 23So [=But] the [seed] <u>having-been-sown</u> upon <u>fine land</u>, this is the [one] hearing and comprehending the word, which indeed bears-fruit and [=some of] which for-one does [=makes] one-hundred [fold], so [=on the other hand] which [=others make] sixty, so [=on the other hand] which [=others make] thirty."

Mark 4:13-20

13And he-says to-them, "Have-you-recognized [=Have you understood] not this parable? And [=Then] how will-you-know all the parables? 14The [person] sowing sows the word. 15So these are the [seeds] along [=near] the way [=road], where the word is-sown, and whenever they-might-hear [the word], the adversary comes immediately[a] and removes the word having-been-sown into them[b]. 16And these are[c] the [seeds] being-sown upon the rocky-grounds, who whenever they-might-hear the word, they-take it immediately with joy, 17and [=but] they-have not [a] root in themselves but are temporary, moreover [when] distress or persecution having-happened through [=because of] the word they-are-caused-to-stumble immediately. 18And anothers [=others] are the being-sowns [=seeds that were sown] into the thorny-plants; these are the [seeds] having-heards [=that heard] the word, 19and [=but] the worries of-the eon [=world] and the lure of-wealth and the desires around [=concerning] the remainders [rest of things] traveling-in choke the word and it-happens [=it becomes] fruitless. 20And those are the [seeds] having-been-sown upon fine land, whoever [=who] hear the word and adopt [it] and they-bear-fruit, one thirty and one sixty and one one-hundred [fold]."

Luke 8:11-15

11"So the parable is this: the seedling is the word of-god. 12So [=And] the [seeds] along [=near] the way [=road] are the having-heards [=those who heard]. Moreover the devil comes and removes the word from their heart, in-order-that having-believed no [=not] they [themselves] might-be-saved. 13So the [seeds] upon the rock [are those] who whenever they-might-hear receive the word with joy, and these have not [a] root, which [=and they] believe to proper-time [=for a short time] and [=but] in [a] time of-test they-abandon [the faith]. 14So the [seed] having-fallen into the thorny-plants, these are the having-heards [=those who hear] and traveling [=as they go along], under [=by] worries and wealth and pleasures of-livelihood [=of life] they-are-choked and they-produce-mature-fruit not. 15So [=But] the [seeds] in <u>fine land</u>, these are whoever having-heard the word detain [=hold it secure] in [a] fine and good heart and they-bear-fruit in [=with] patience."

---

[a] *immediately* ℵ B C L W Δ f^{13} 33 892 2427 *pc*; *instantly* A D Θ 1006 1342 1506 𝔐; *omit* f^{1} 205 1542 *pc*.
[b] *into them* B W f^{1} f^{13} 205 2427 2542 *pc*; *in their hearts* D Θ 33 1006 1342 1506 𝔐 vg it^mss sy; *from their hearts* A; *in them* ℵ C L D 579 892 *pc*.
[c] *are* D W Θ f^{1} f^{13} 205 565 579 700 1005 2542 *pc* it sy^s sy^p cop^sa; *are comparable-to* ℵ A B C D L 33 892 1342 1506 2427 𝔐 vg it^mss.

Matt 13:23 (§146, p. 108)
Q 7:35 (§126, p. 91)

147. Listening Carefully (→ §50, 82, 145)

Matt 13:12

12 “For whoever has [something], it-will-be-given to-him, and it-will-be-exceeded; so [=but] whoever has not [something], and [=even that] which he-has will-be-removed from him.”

Mark 4:21-25

21 And he-was-saying to-them, “Surely-not[a] [is] the lantern comes [=brought in] in-order-that it-might-be-put under the bushel or under the stretcher? [Is it] not [rather brought in] in-order-that it-might-be-put upon the lamp-stand?

22 For not [=nothing] is hidden if-ever no [=except] in-order-that it-might-be-made-visible, nor did-it-happen [=was it] hidden-away but in-order-that it-might-come into [=it might become] visible.

23 If some [person] has ears to-hear, let-him-hear.”

24 And he-was-saying to-them, “Look [=Take heed of] what you-hear. In [=By] which measure you-measure, it-will-be-measured to-you and [more] will-be-added to-you.

25 For [the one] who has [more] will-be-given to-him, and [=but] [the one] who has not [anything], and [=even that] which he-has will-be-removed from him.”

Luke 8:16-18

16 “So no-one having-touched [=having lit a] lantern covers it [with a] vessel or puts[b] [it] beneath [a] <u>stretcher</u>, but he-puts [it] upon [a] lamp-stand in-order-that the traveling-ins [=ones who enter] might-look [at] the light.

17 For not [=nothing] is hidden which will-happen visible [=will become known] not, nor hidden-away which might-be-known not no [=at all] and into visible [light] it-might-come.

18 Therefore look [=pay attention to] how you-hear; for who ever might-have, [more] will-be-given to-him, and [=but] who ever might-have no [=nothing], and [=even that] which he-supposes [=he seems] to-have will-be-removed from him.”

Thomas 33; 5; 6; 41

33 Jesus said, “What you will hear in your ear, in the other ear proclaim from your rooftops. After all, no one lights a lamp and puts it under a basket, nor does one put it in a hidden place. Rather, one puts it on a lampstand so that all who come and go will see its light.”

5 Jesus said, “Know what is in front of your face, and what is hidden from you will be disclosed to you. For there is nothing hidden that will not be revealed. <And there is nothing buried that will not be raised.>”

6 His disciples asked him and said to him, “Do you want us to fast? How should we pray? Should we give to charity? What diet should we observe?” Jesus said, “Don’t lie, and don’t do what you hate, because all things are disclosed before heaven. After all, there is nothing hidden that will not be revealed, and there is nothing covered up that will remain undisclosed.”

41 Jesus said, “Whoever has something in hand will be given more, and whoever has nothing will be deprived of even the little they have.”

[a] *“Surely-not . . . ”* ℵ A C D W Θ f^{1} 33 1006 1342 1506 𝔐 it vg; *that “Surely-not . . . ”* B L 892 2427 sy; *“See surely-not . . . ”* f^{13} *pc.*
[b] *puts* $\mathfrak{P}^{75}$ ℵ B D F L Θ Ξ 070 205 579 892 1342 1424 2542; *places* A W Ψ 33 1006 1506 𝔐.

Q 7:35 (§126, p. 91)
Luke 8:18 (§147, p. 109)

148. Mark's Parable of the Independent Seed

Mark 4:26-29

[26]And he-was-saying, "Thus is the kingdom of-god like [a] person [who] might-throw the seedling
upon the land [27]and he-might-sleep and he-might-rise, night and day, and the seedling might-
germinate and might-bud, he [himself] recognizes [=knows] not like [=how]. [28]The land bears-fruit
automatically, first food [=a bud] moreover [=then an] ear-of-grain moreover [=then] full wheat in
the ear-of-grain. [29]So whenever the fruit might-deliver [=might be ready], immediately[a] he-sends-off
the [=he goes in with his] sickle, that [=because] the harvest has-been-present [=is ready]."

[a] *immediately* ℵ B C L 579 892 1342 2427; *instantly* A D Θ f^{13} 33 1006 1506 𝔐; *then* f^{1} 205; *omit* W it^{mss}.

149. Matthew's Parable of the Weeds in the Field

Matt 13:24-30	Thomas 57
[24]He-placed-before them another parable, saying "The kingdom of-the heavens was-compared [to a] person having-sown fine seed in his field. [25]So in the to-sleep the people [=while everyone slept], his enemy came and sowed-in-addition weeds up middle of-the [=among the] wheat and went-away. [26]So when the food [=plants] germinated and did [=made] fruit, then the weeds and [=also] were-appeared [=were made to appear]. [27]So the slaves of-the master-of-the-house having-approached said to-him, 'Lord, did-you-sow indeed-not fine seed in the to-your-own [=in your] field? Therefore from-where does-it-have weeds [=did the weeds come]?' [28]So he-spoke to-them, 'Enemy person [=An enemy] did this.' So the slaves say to-him, 'Therefore do-you-wish [that] having-gone-away we-might-pick them?' [29]So he-speaks[a], 'Not, lest [in] picking the weeds you-might-uproot the wheat in-unison-with them. [30]Excuse [=Allow] both to-grow-together until the harvest, and in [=at the] proper-time of-the harvest I-will-say to-the reapers: "Pick first the weeds and restrain them into [=in] bindings to [=in order] to-incinerate them, so [=and then] gather the wheat into my storehouse."'"	Jesus said, "The Father's kingdom is like a person who has <good> seed. His enemy came during the night and sowed weeds among the good seed. The person did not let the workers pull up the weeds, but said to them, 'No, otherwise you might go to pull up the weeds and pull up the wheat along with them.' For on the day of the harvest the weeds will be conspicuous, and will be pulled up and burned."

[a] *he-speaks* ℵ B C 892 *pc*; *he-spoke* L W f^{1} f^{13} 1006 1342 1506 𝔐; *he-spoke to-them* Θ *pc*; *he-says to-them* D 33 1424 *pc*.

150. The Parable of the Mustard Seed (→ §246)

Matt 13:31-32	Mark 4:30-32	Q 13:18-19	Luke 13:18-19	Thomas 20
[31]Another parable he-placed-before them, saying, "The kingdom of-the heavens	[30]And he-was-saying, "How might-we-compare the kingdom of-god or in what parable might-we-put it[a]?	[18]"What is the kingdom of-god comparable-to and to-what will-I-compare it?	[18]Therefore he-was-saying, "What is the kingdom of-god comparable-to and to-what will-I-compare it?	The disciples said to Jesus, "Tell us what Heaven's kingdom is like."

is comparable-to [a] tiny-seed of-mustard, which [a] person having-taken sowed in his field;	31[It is] like [a] tiny-seed of-mustard, <u>which</u> whenever it-might-be-sown upon the	19It-is comparable-to [a] tiny-seed of-mustard, which [a] person having-taken threw into his garden	19It-is comparable-to [a] tiny-seed of-mustard, which [a] person having-taken threw into of-himself [=his own] garden	He said to them, "It's like a mustard seed,
32which for-one is smaller of-all [=than all] of-the seeds, so [=but]	land, being smaller of-all [=than all] of-the seeds upon the land, 32and whenever it-might-	and	and	the smallest of all seeds, but when it falls on prepared soil,
whenever it-might-	be-sown, it-ascends [=it grows] and happens [=becomes]	it-grew and happened [=turned]	it-grew and happened [=turned]	it produces a large plant
grow it-is greater of-the [=than the] shrubs and happens [=becomes a] tree, with-the-result-that the birds of-heaven to-come [=come] and to-nest [=nest] in its branches."	greater of-all [=than all] of-the shrubs and does [=makes] great branches, with-the-result-that the birds of-heaven to-be-able [=are able] to-nest under its shade."	into [a] tree and the birds of-heaven nested in its branches."	into [a] tree[b] and the birds of-heaven nested in its branches."	and becomes a shelter for birds of the sky."

[a] *in what parable might-we-put it* ℵ B C* L Δ 892 1342 2427 *pc* cop^{bo}; *in what parable might-we-parable it* A C^{2} D Θ *f*^{1} 33 1006 1506 𝔐 vg it^{mss} sy; *in what parable might we give* W; *in what parable might-we-put it? We-parable it* *f*^{13}.

[b] *tree* 𝔭^{75} ℵ B D L 070 892 *pc* it sy^{s} sy^{c} cop^{sa} cop^{bomss}; *great tree* 𝔭^{45} A W Θ Ψ *f*^{1} *f*^{13} 33 1006 1506 𝔐 vg it^{mss} sy^{p} cop^{bomss}.

SYNOPTIC STUDY GUIDE 8

Mark-Q Overlaps

Recall that the idea of Q derived from the argument that Mark was the earliest written gospel, and that the authors of Matthew and Luke worked independently of one another: Q was the source that the authors of Matthew and Luke must have used for material they did not find in Mark but which they share. In other words, Triple Tradition material came from Mark, and Double Tradition material came from Q. Triple Tradition and Double Tradition by definition do not—cannot—overlap; something cannot be in only two and yet three gospels at the same time. How then is it possible for there to be a Mark-Q overlap?

Supporters of the Two-Document Hypothesis argue that it is not in the least far-fetched that Mark and Q might have shared some similar material. After all, Mark might be a primarily narrative source, but it has sayings of Jesus. But there are stronger reasons than this to admit the possibility of Mark-Q overlaps. Consider the Parables of the Mustard Seed and the Leaven (§150 and §151).

In the Mustard Seed, there are very few places in which Luke agrees with Mark against Matthew: the words "he-was-saying," "of-God," "it," that Jesus asks a question (which together make Luke's and Mark's parable introductions very similar), and finally the word "and" in the middle of Luke 3:19//Mark 4:32. There is, in other words, little evidence that the author of Luke's source for the Mustard Seed is Mark. Since Luke's source for the next parable is Q, then it is quite reasonable to think that Luke's source for the Mustard Seed might also be Q, not Mark.

Conversely, the author of Matthew appears to have used both sources and attempted to bring them together. This is suggested by the somewhat more significant number of agreements between Matthew and Mark against Luke (the choice of the verb "to sow," "smaller of-all of-the seeds," "whenever," "greater of-all the shrubs," "with-the-result-that," and "to-nest") and of Matthew and Luke against Mark ("comparable-to," the precise form of "which," "person having-taken,"

SYNOPTIC STUDY GUIDE 8

the choice of the verb "to grow," the choice of the verb "to happen," "tree," and "in its branches"). In other words, the direction of agreements suggests that the author of Matthew used Mark and Q, while the author of Luke used Q alone. Hence, both Mark and Q had parables of the Mustard Seed.

A Mark-Q overlap is not the only way to explain the pattern of agreements in these two parables. Critics of this hypothesis might argue that those ten words in the Parable of the Mustard Seed where Matthew and Luke agree against Mark *are* evidence that Luke took over Matthean additions to Mark! We do have evidence, they would argue, that the writer of Luke used Matthew for the Mustard Seed, and therefore for the Parable of the Leaven as well. No need for Q, and no Mark-Q overlap.

151. The Parable of the Leaven (→ §247)

Matt 13:33	Q 13:20-21	Luke 13:20-21	Thomas 96
33He-talked [=He said] another parable to-them, "The kingdom of-the heavens is comparable-to leaven, which [a] woman having-taken inserted into three satons [=measures] of-wheat-flour until which [time the] whole was- leavened."	20And again, "To-what will-I-compare the kingdom of-god? 21It-is comparable-to leaven, which [a] woman having-taken inserted into three satons [=measures] of-wheat-flour until which [time the] whole was- leavened."	20And he-said again, "To-what will-I-compare the kingdom of-god? 21It-is comparable- to leaven, which [a] woman having-taken inserted[a] into three satons [=measures] of-wheat-flour until which [time the] whole was-leavened."	Jesus <said>, "The Father's kingdom is like <a> woman. She took a little leaven, <hid> it in dough, and made it into large loaves of bread. Anyone here with two ears had better listen!"

[a] *inserted* $\mathfrak{P}^{75}$ ℵ A D W Θ Ψ 070 f^{13} 𝔐; *hid* B K L N 205 209 892 1342 1424 1506 2542 *al.*

152. Speaking Exclusively in Parables

Matt 13:34-35	Mark 4:33-34
34All these [things] Jesus talked to-the crowds in parables, and without [a] parable he-was-talking [=he would say] no-one[a] [=nothing] to-them, 35so-that the having-been-said [=what had been said] through [b] the prophet might-be-fulfilled, saying, "I-WILL-OPEN MY MOUTH IN PARABLES, I-WILL- DIVULGE HAVING-BEEN-HIDDENS [=things that were hidden] FROM [the] MOLDING [of the] WORLD."	33And he-was-talking to-them the word [in] many parables such-as-this, just-as they-were-able to- hear; 34so without parables he-was-talking [=he would speak] not to-them, so [=but] according- to own [=to each in private] he-explicated all [=everything] to-the [=to his] own disciples.

[a] *no-one* ℵ* B C W Δ f^{13} *al* cop^{sa} sy; *not* $ℵ^{2}$ D L Θ f^{1} 33 892 1006 1342 1506 𝔐 vg. it^{mss} cop^{bo}.
[b] *omit* $ℵ^{1}$ B C D L W 892 1006 1342 1506 𝔐 vg it^{mss} sy cop; *Isaiah* ℵ* Θ f^{1} f^{13} 33 *pc.*
📖 Mt 13:35 – Ps 78:2

153. Matthew's Interpretation of the Weeds in the Field

Matt 13:36-43

36Then having-excused [=after leaving] the crowds he-went in the home. And his disciples
approached him saying, "Explain to-us the parable of-the weeds of-the field." 37So having-
answered, he-said, "The [one] sowing the fine seed is the son of-the person, 38so [=and] the field is
the world, so [=and] the fine seed these are the sons of-the kingdom; so [=and] the weeds are the

sons of-evil, [39]so [=and] the enemy having-sown them is the devil, so [=and] the harvest is [the] conclusion [of-the] eon, so [=and] the reapers are announcers. [40]Therefore even-as [=just as] the weeds is-picked and is-incinerated[a] [with] fire thus it-will-be in the conclusion of-the eon. [41]The son of-the person will-send-off his announcers and they-will-pick out [of] his kingdom all the scandals [=scandalous things] and [those] doing [=promoting] lawlessness [42]and they-will-throw them into the oven of-fire. There-will-be wailing and gnashing of-the teeth there. [43]Then the righteous will-shine-forth like the sun in the kingdom [of] their father. The [one] having ears[b], let-him-hear."

[a] *is-incinerated* ℵ B f^1 892 *al*; *are-incinerated* D; *is-kindled* C L W Θ f^{13} 33 1006 1342 1506 𝔐.
[b] *omit* ℵ* B Θ 700 it^{mss}; *to-hear* ℵ^2 C D L W f^1 f^{13} 33 891 1006 1342 1506 𝔐 it vg sy cop.

154. Matthew's Parables of the Hidden Treasure and the Pearl

Matt 13:44-46

[44]"[a]The kingdom of-the heavens is comparable-to [a] treasure-box having-been-hidden in the field, which [a] person having-found hid [again], and from [=in] his joy leaves and sells all [=everything] whatsoever he-has and buys that field.

[45]Again, the kingdom of-the heavens is comparable-to [a] person, [a] merchant, searching [for] fine pearls. [46]So [=And] having-found one valuable pearl, [and] having-gone-away, has-peddled all whatsoever he-was-having [=everything he owned] and bought it."

Thomas 109; 76

[109]Jesus said, "The <Father's> kingdom is like a person who had a treasure hidden in his field but did not know it. And <when> he died he left it to his <son>. The son <did> not know about it either. He took over the field and sold it. The buyer went plowing, <discovered> the treasure, and began to lend money at interest to whomever he wished."
[76]Jesus said, "The Father's kingdom is like a merchant who had a supply of merchandise and found a pearl. That merchant was prudent; he sold the merchandise and bought the single pearl for himself. So also with you, seek his treasure that is unfailing, that is enduring, where no moth comes to eat and no worm destroys."

[a] *omit* ℵ B D 892 *pc* vg it^{mss} sy^s sy^c cop; *Again* C L W f^1 f^{13} 33 1006 1342 1506 𝔐 it^{mss} sy^p.

155. Matthew's Parable of the Dragnet

Matt 13:47-50

[47]"Again the kingdom of-the heavens is comparable-to [a] dragnet having-been-thrown into the sea and having-gathered out all [=every] type [of fish], [48]which when it-was-fulfilled [=it was filled and] having-pulled-up [it] upon the beach and having-sat-down they-picked [=they put] the fines [=those that were fine] into [a] container, so [=and] the rottens [=those that were rotten] they-threw outside. [49]Thus it-will-be in the conclusion of-the eon; the announcers [=angels] will-go-out [=will go out] and they-will-exclude the evil out middle [=from] the righteous [people] [50]and they-will-throw them into the oven of-fire. There-will-be wailing and gnashing of-the teeth there."

Thomas 8

And he said, "The person is like a wise fisherman who cast his net into the sea and drew it up from the sea full of little fish. Among them the wise fisherman discovered a fine large fish. He threw all the little fish back into the sea, and easily chose the large fish. Anyone here with two good ears had better listen!"

There are no variants in this pericope that appear in English.

156. Matthew's Parable of the New and Old Treasures

Matt 13:51-52

[51]"[a] Did-you-comprehended all these [things]?" They-say to-him, "Yes." [52]So he-said to-them, "Through this [=Therefore] all [=every] scribe being-a-disciple [for] the kingdom of-the heavens is comparable-to [a] person, [a] master-of-the-house, whoever casts-out [=who brings] out [from] his treasure-box news [=new things] and olds [=old things]."

[a] *omit* ℵ B D *pc* sy[s] cop[sa] cop[bo]; *Jesus says to-them* C L W Q *f*[1] *f*[13] 33 892 1996 1342 1506 𝔐 it[mss] sy[c] sy[p].

157. True Family (→ §143)

Matt 12:46-50	Mark 3:31-35	**Luke 8:19-21**	John 15:14	Thomas 99
[46]Yet his [=While he was] talking to-the crowds, look! the [=his] mother and his brothers had-been-standing outside searching to-talk to-him.	[31]And his mother comes and his brothers and persevering outside they-sent-off to [=for] him calling him.	[19]So the [=his] mother arrived to him and his brothers and they-were-able not to-get-near-to him through the		
	[32]And [a] crowd was-sitting around him	crowd.		
[47]So some [person] said to-him, "Look! your mother and your brothers outside have-stood searching to-talk to-you."[a]	and they-say to-him, "Look! your mother and your brothers and your sisters outside search [for] you."	[20]So it-was-informed [=it was told] to-him, [d] "Your mother and your brothers have-stood outside wishing to-see you."		The disciples said to him, "Your brothers and your mother are standing outside."
[48]So having-answered he-said to-the sayings [=to those who were speaking] to-him, "What [=Who] is my	[33]And having-answered he-says to-them, "What [=Who] is my	[21]So having-answered he-said to them,		He said to them, "Those here who do what my Father wants are my brothers and my mother. They are the ones who will enter my Father's kingdom."
mother and what [=who] are my brothers?"	mother and my[c] brothers?"			
[49]And having-reached-out his hand upon his disciples he-said, "Look! my mother and my brothers.	[34]And having-looked-around [at] the sittings [=those who were sitting] among [=in a circle] around him, he-says, "Look [at] my mother and my brothers.			

[50]For whoever ever might-do[b] the wish [of] my father in [the] heavens he is my brother and sister and mother."	[35]For who ever might-do the wish of-god, this [one] is my brother and sister and mother."	"My mother and my brothers are these hearings and doings [=those who hear and do] the word of-god."	[14]"You are my friends if-ever you-might-do [that] which I [myself] charge you."

[a] *So some said to-him, "Look! your mother and your brothers outside have-stood searching to-talk to-you"* ℵ[1] ℵ[2] C D W Z Θ *f*[1] *f*[13] 33 892 1006 1342 1506 𝔐 vg it[mss] sy[p] cop[bo]; *omit verse* ℵ* B L 2542 *pc* it[mss] sy[s] sy[c] cop[sa].
[b] *whoever ever might-do* ℵ B Θ *f*[1] *f*[13] 33 892 1006 1342 1506 𝔐; *whoever does* D; *whoever ever will-do* L Q Z 579 1424 *al.*
[c] *my* ℵ A C L W Θ *f*[1] *f*[13] 33 892 1006 1342 1506 𝔐 vg it sy; *omit* B D.
[d] *omit* 𝔭[75] B W Δ *pc* vg; *that* ℵ D L Q *f*[1] 33 205 579 1342 *pc* it; *saying* A Ξ *f*[13] 1006 1506 𝔐; *saying that* Ψ 1424 *pc*.

158. Stilling the Storm (→ §94)

Matt 8:23-27	**Mark 4:35-41**	**Luke 8:22-25**
[23]And having-embarked him [=when he had gotten] into the boat his disciples followed him.	[35]And he-says to-them in [=on] that day, evening having-happened, "Let-us-go-through into the beyond [=to the other side]." [36]And excusing [=leaving] the crowd they-take-along him in the boat like [=just as] he-was, and another [=other] boats were with him.	[22]So it-happened in [=on] one of-the days, and he [himself] embarked and his disciples into [a] boat and he-said to them, "Let-us-go-through into the beyond of-the harbor [=to the other side of the harbor], and they-were-led-up [=they launched the boat]."
[24]And look! [a] great earthquake happened in the sea, with-the-result-that the boat to-be-covered [=was covered] under the waves, so [=but] he [himself] was-sleeping.	[37]And [a] great squall of-wind happens and the waves were-throwing-on [=were being thrown] into the boat, with-the-result-that the boat already to-be-stuffed [=was filled]. [38]And he [himself] was in the stern sleeping upon the cushion.	[23]So their sailing [=while they were sailing] he-fell-asleep. And [a] squall of-wind descended into the harbor and they-were-being-swamped and they-were-being-endangered.
[25]And having-approached,[a] they-raised [=they awoke] him saying, "Lord, save[b]; we-are-destroying [=we are perishing]." [26]And he-says to-them, "What [=Why] are-you afraid, little-loyalties [=you of little faith]?" Then,	They-raise [=they wake] him and say to-him, "Teacher, is-it-of-concern not to-you that we-are-destroying [=we are perishing]?"	[24]So, having-approached they-awoke him saying, "Overseer, overseer, we-are-destroying [=we are perishing]."
having-been-raised [=having gotten up], he-rebuked the winds and the sea, and [a] great calm happened.	[39]And having-been-awoken, he-rebuked the wind and said to-the sea, "Be-silent, be-muzzled." And the wind ceased and [a] great calm happened. [40]And he-said to-them, "What [=Why] are-you afraid? Have-you not-yet [any] loyalty?[c]"	So having-been-awoken[d], he-rebuked the wind and the rough-waves of-the water. And they-stopped and [a] calm happened. [25]So he-said to-them, "Wheresoever [is] your loyalty?"
[27]So the people were-astonished	[41]And they-were-feared great fear	So having-been-feared [=being

saying, "What-sort-of [man] is this	[=they were very afraid] and were-saying to one-another, "What [=Who] consequently is this that and	afraid] they-were-astonished saying to one-another, "What [=Who] consequently is this that and [=even]
that and [=even] the winds and the sea obey him?"	[=even] the wind and the sea obeys him?"	he-presides-over the winds and the water and they-obey him?"

[a] *omit* ℵ B 33 892 it^{mss} vg cop^{sa} cop^{bo}; *the disciples* C^{2} L f^{13} 1005 1342 1506 𝔐; *his disciples* C* W Θ f^{1} 205 1424 it^{mss} sy.
[b] *omit* ℵ B C f^{1} f^{13} 33 205 892 pc cop^{bo}; *us* L W Θ 1006 1342 1506 𝔐 it vg sy.
[c] *What are-you afraid? Have-you not-yet loyalty?* ℵ B D L Δ Θ 565 579 700 892* 1424 1342 2427; *What are-you afraid thus? How have-you no loyalty?* A C 33 1006 1506 𝔐 sy^{p}; *What are-you afraid thus?* W; *What are-you thus afraid?* 𝔓^{45} f^{1} f^{13} 205 892^{C} 2542 *pc*.
[d] *having-been-awoken* 𝔓^{75} ℵ B L Q f^{13} 33 892; *having-been-raised* A D W Ψ f^{1} 1006 1342 1506 𝔐.

159. The Gerasene Demoniac (→ §95)

Matt 8:28-34	**Mark 5:1-20**	**Luke 8:26-39**
[28]And his having-come [=when he went] into the beyond [=across] into the region of-the Gadarenes[a] two extremely fierce being-demon-possesseds [=demoniacs] going-out	[1]And they-went into the beyond [=across] the sea into the region of-the Gerasenes[c].	[26]And they-sailed-along into the region of-the Gerasenes[e], whichever [=which] is opposite of-the Galilee.
out of-the tombs met him, with-the-	[2]And his having-gone-out [=when he got] out of-the boat, immediately [a] person in [=with] [an] unclean spirit met[d] him out of-the tombs,	[27]So having-gone-out him [=when he got out] upon the land, some man out [=from] the city having[f] demons met [him], and in-time fit [=for a long time] he-was-clothed not [with a] coat and was-staying not in [a] home but in the graves.
result-that no some [=one] to-have-the-strength [=was strong enough] to-pass-away [=to pass] through that way.	[3]who was-having [=had an] abode [=home] in the graves, and nor [=neither a] chain no-longer [=nor] no-one [=anyone] was-able to-restrain him, [4]through [=because] he [himself] to-have-been-restrained [=had been restrained] often [by] foot-shackles and chains and [=but] the chains to-have-been-broken-apart [=were broken apart] under [=by] him and the foot-shackles to-have-been-shattered [=were shattered], and no-one had-the-strength to-tame him. [5]And through all night and day in the graves and in the mountains he-was crying [out] and bruising himself [on] stones.	
[29]And look! they-cried [out]	[6]And having-seen Jesus from far-off he-ran and worshiped him [7]and having-cried [with a] great voice	[28]So having-seen Jesus, having-cried-out he-fell-to him and said
saying, "What to-us and to-you [=What have you to do with us], son of-god? Did-you-come here before [the] proper-time to-torment us?"	he-says, "What to-me and to-you [=What have you to do with me], Jesus son of-god the most-high? I-swear [to] you [by] god, [that] you-might-	[with a] great voice, "What to-me and to-you [=What have you to do with me], Jesus son of-god the most-high? I-implore you, [that] you-might-torment me no [=not]."

Matt 13:52 (§156, p. 114)
Q 7:35 (§126, p. 91)

30 So far-away from them [a] herd
of-many pigs was being-grazed. 31 So
the evil-spirits
were-exhorting him saying,
"If you-cast-out us, send-off us[b] into
the herd of-pigs."
32 And he-said to-them, "Leave." So
having-gone-out, they-went-away
into the pigs. And look! all the herd
rushed according-to [=down] the
steep-bank into the sea and they-
faced-death [=they died] in the
waters. 33 So the grazings [=the
herdsmen] fled and having-gone-
away into the city informed all
[=told everything] and the [report]
of-the being-demon-possesseds
[=demoniacs].
34 And look! all the city went-out
into [a] meeting [with] Jesus and
having-seen him they-exhorted him
so-that he-might-head-out from
their territories.

torment me no [=not]." 8 For he-was-
saying to-him, "Go-out, unclean
spirit out [=from] the person."
9 And he-was-questioning him,
"What [is] your name?" And he-says
to-him, "My name [is] Legion, that
[=because] we-are many." 10 And he-
was-exhorting him many [times] in-
order-that he-might-send-off them
no [=not] outside of-the region.
11 So [=Now] to [=on] the mountain
great [a] herd of-pigs was there
being-grazed. 12 And they-exhorted
him saying, "Send us into the pigs,
in-order-that we-might-enter into
them."
13 And he-allowed them. And the
unclean spirits, having-gone-out
[of the man], entered into the pigs,
and the herd rushed according-to
[=down] the steep-bank into the sea,
like [=about] two-thousand, and
they-drowned in the sea. 14 And
the grazings [=the herdsmen]
fled [from] them and informed
[=told of this] into [=in] the city and
into [=in] the fields [=countryside].
And they-went to-see what is the
having-happened [=had happened].
15 And they-come to Jesus and
they-catch-sight-of the being-
demon-possessed [=demoniac]
sitting, having-a-coat-on [=being
clothed] and being-sane, the [very
one] having-had the legion, and
they-were-feared [=they were afraid].
16 And the having-seens [=those who
saw it] narrated to-them how [=what]
happened to-the being-demon-
possessed [=demoniac] and around
[=concerning] the pigs.
17 And they-began to-
exhort him to-go-away
from their territories.

29 For he-enjoined the unclean spirit
to-go-out from the person. For
many times it-had-grabbed him and
he-was-being-bound in-chains and
foot-shackles [while] being-guarded
and [after] rending the bindings
[=his chains] he-was-being-driven
under [=by] the demon into the
deserteds [=deserted places].
30 So Jesus questioned him,
"What is your name?" So he-said,
"Legion" that [=because] many
demons entered into him." 31 And
they-were-exhorting him, in-order-
that he-might-preside-over them no
[=not] to-go-away into the abyss.
32 So [=Now a] fit [=large] herd of-pigs
was there being-grazed in [=on] the
mountain. And they-exhorted him
in-order-that he-might-allow them
to-enter into those [animals].
And he-allowed them. 33 So the
demons, having-gone-out from
the person, entered into the pigs,
and the herd rushed according-
to [=down] the steep-bank into
the harbor and it-was-suffocated
[=drowned]. 34 So the grazings [=the
herdsmen], having-seen the having-
happened [=what had happened], fled
and informed [=told of this] into
[=in] the city and into [=in] the fields
[=countryside]. 35 So they-went-out
[=they went out] to-see the having-
happened [=what had happened]
and they-went to Jesus and found
sitting the person from whom the
demons went-out having-a-coat-on
and being-sane along [=at] the feet
of-Jesus,
and they-were-feared [=they were
afraid]. 36 So the having-seens [=those
who saw it] informed them how the
having-been-demon-possessed
[=demoniac] was-saved.
37 And everyone [in] the multitude
[from] the surrounding-region of-the
Gerasenes begged him to-go-away
from them that [=because] they-
were-controlled [by a] great fear.

Matt 13:52 (§156, p. 114)
Q 7:35 (§126, p. 91)

18 And his embarking into the boat,
the having-been-demon-possessed
[=demoniac] was-exhorting him in-
order-that he-might-be [=he might
go] with him.
19 And he-excused him not [=he
did not allow it], but says to-him,
"Leave into your house, to your-
own [people], and inform them
whatsoever [=of all the things] the
lord has-done for-you and [how] he-
was-merciful [to] you."
20 And he-went-away and began to-
preach in the Decapolis whatsoever
Jesus did to-him,

and all were-being-astonished.

So having-embarked into [a] boat
he [himself] returned. 38 So the man
from whom the demons had-gone-
out implored him to-be together-
with him [=allowed to go along with
Jesus]. So [=But] he-released him

saying, 39 "Return into your house
and narrate whatsoever [=all the
things] god did for-you."

And he-went-away according-
to [=throughout] the whole city
preaching whatsoever [=about all the
things] Jesus did to-him.

[a] *Gadarenes* B C Δ Θ *al* sy^{s} sy^{p}; *Gerasenes* 892^{C} it vg cop^{sa}; *Gergesenes* ℵ^{2} L W f^{1} f^{13} 892* 1006 1342 1506 𝔐 cop^{bo}; *Gazarenes* ℵ*.
[b] *send-off us* ℵ B Θ f^{1} 22 205 892 *pc* it^{mss} vg sy^{s} cop; *allow us to-go-away* C L W f^{13} 1006 1342 1506 𝔐 it^{mss}.
[c] *Gerasenes* ℵ* B D it vg sy; *Gadarenes* A C f^{13} 1006 1342 1506 𝔐 sy^{p}; *Gergustenes* W; *Gergesenes* ℵ^{2} L Δ Θ f^{1} 33 205 565 700 782 1424 2427 2542 *al* sy^{s} cop^{bo}.
[d] *met* ℵ B C D G L Δ Θ f^{1} f^{13} 205 565 579 700 1342 1424 2542 *al*; *encountered* A W 33 892 1006 1506 𝔐.
[e] *Gerasenes* 𝔭^{75} B D it vg; *Gergesenes* ℵ L Θ Ξ f^{1} 33 205 579 700* 1342 *pc*; *Gadarenes* A W Y f^{13} 892 1006 1506 𝔐 sy.
[f] *having* 𝔭^{75} ℵ* B 579 1342 *pc*; *who was-having* ℵ^{2} A D L Θ f^{1} f^{13} 33 892 1006 1506 𝔐.

160. A Magistrate's Daughter and the Hemorrhaging Woman (→ §99)

Matt 9:18-26

18 His talking [=After he had said]
these [things] to-them

look!

one magistrate having-come

was-worshiping him saying that

"My daughter right-now expired
[=just died]. But having-come, place

your hand upon her, and she-will-
live."
19 And Jesus, having-risen,
and his disciples, followed him.

Mark 5:21-43

21 And the having-crossed-over of-
Jesus again into the beyond [=when
Jesus had gone back across the harbor a]
many [=great] crowd was-gathered
upon [=around] him, and he-was
along [=by] the sea.
22 And [c]

one of-the synagogue-leaders
comes, Jairus [by] name, and
having-seen him he-falls to [=at]
his feet 23 and exhorts him many
[=much], saying that "My little-

daughter has lastly [=finally died], in-
order-that having-come you-might-
place the [=your] hands [on] her,
in-order-that she-might-be-saved
and she-might-live."

24 And he-went-away with him. And
many [=a great] crowd was-following
him and was-pressing-upon him.

Luke 8:40-56

40 So [e] in the to-return Jesus
[=when Jesus was returning]

the crowd welcomed him,
for all were expecting him.

41 And look! [a] man, whose name
[was] Jairus, came and this [man]
was-being-at-one's-disposal [=was a]
magistrate of-the synagogue, and

having-fallen along the feet of-Jesus
he-was-exhorting him to-enter into
his house, 42 that [=because] there-
was to-him [=he had an] only-born
daughter like [=about] twelve years
[old] and she [herself] was-facing-
death.

So in the to-leave him [=while he was
leaving] the crowds were-choking
him.

Matt 13:52 (§156, p. 114)
Q 7:35 (§126, p. 91)

20 And look! [a] woman suffering-
chronic-bleeding [for] twelve years,

having-approached from-behind
touched the tassel [of] his coat. 21 For
she-was-saying in herself, "If-ever
only I-might-touch his coat, I-will-
be-saved."

22 So Jesus having-been-turned[a] and
having-seen her said, "Cheer-up,
daughter. Your loyalty has-saved
you." And the woman was-saved
from that hour.

25 And [a] woman being in [=with an]
issue of-blood [=having been bleeding
for] twelve years 26 and having-
suffered many [things] under many
physicians and having-spent all the
along her [=her wealth] and having-
been-achieved not-one [=having not
improved] but rather having-come
into worse [condition], 27 having-
heard[d] around [=concerning] Jesus,
having-come in the crowd from-
behind [him], she-touched his coat.
28 For she-was-saying that "If-ever
even-if [=If only] I-might-touch his
coats, I-will-be-saved."
29 And immediately the flow
[of] her blood was-withered [=was
dried up] and she-knew in-the body
that she-has-been-cured from the
scourge.
30 And immediately Jesus having-
understood in himself the power
having-gone-out out of-him,
having-turned in [=to] the crowd
was-saying, "What [=Who] touched
my coats?"

31 And his disciples were-saying
to-him, "You-look [at] the crowd
pressing-upon you, and you-say,
'What [=Who] touched me?'"
32 And he-was-looking-around to-
see the [woman] having-done this.

33 So [=But] the woman having-been-
feared [=being afraid] and trembling,
having-recognized which [=what]
happened to-her, came and fell-to
him and said to-him all the truth
[=told him everything].

34 So

he-said to-her, "Daughter, your
loyalty has-saved you. Leave into
[=Go in] peace and be-healthy [=be
free] from your scourge." 35 Yet his
talking [=while he was still talking]
they-come from the synagogue-
leader saying that, "Your daughter
faced-death [=has died]. What
[=Why] do-you-bother the teacher
yet [=still]?" 36 So [=But] Jesus
having-ignored the word being-

43 And [a] woman being in [=with an]
issue of-blood from [=for] twelve
years, whoever [=who despite]

having-expended the [=her] whole
livelihood [on] physicians had-the-
strength not from no-one to-be-
healed [=had not been healed by

anyone], 44 having-approached [from]
from-behind she-touched the tassel

[of] his coat and at-once the issue
[of] her blood stood [=stopped].

45 And Jesus

said, "What [=Who is] the [one]
having-touched me?" So [=But] all
denying [=when all denied it] Peter[f]
said,
"Overseer, the crowds control and
squeeze you."

46 So Jesus said, "Some [one] touched
me, for I [myself] knew [=felt]
power having-gone-out from me."
47 So the woman, having-seen that
she-remained-hidden not, came
trembling and having-fallen-to him
she-informed [=she told] in-the-sight
of-all the whole-people through
which reason [=why] she-touched
him and like [=how] she-was-cured
at-once. 48 So

he-said to-her, "Daughter, your
loyalty has-saved you. Travel into
[=in] peace."
49 Yet his [=while he was still] talking
some [person] comes along the
synagogue-leader saying that "Your
daughter has-died, bother the
teacher not-any-longer."

50 So [=But] Jesus having-heard,

Matt 13:52 (§156, p. 114)
Q 7:35 (§126, p. 91)

Matthew	Mark	Luke
	talked [=what was said], says to-the synagogue-leader, "Fear no [=not], only believe."	answered him[g], "Fear no [=not], only <u>believe</u>, and she-will-be-saved." 51 So having-come into the home he-excused [=he allowed] not some [=no one] to-enter together-with him if no [=except] Peter and John and James and the father of-the child and the
	37 And he-excused not no-one [=he would not let anyone] to-tag-along with him if no [=except] Peter and James and John the brother of-James. 38 And they-come into the house of-the synagogue-leader, and he-catches-sight-of [a] commotion and weeping and many [people] wailing-loudly, 39 and having-	mother. 52 So all were-weeping and were-cutting [=mourning] her.
23 And Jesus having-come into the home of-the magistrate and having-seen the flute-players and the crowd being-stirred-up 24 was-saying,	entered, he-says to-them, "What [=Why] are-you-stirred-up and do-you-weep?	So he-said,
"Retreat, for the girl faced-death not [=has not died] but sleeps." And they-were-laughing-heartily [at] him.	The young-child faced-death [=has died] not but sleeps." 40 And they-were-laughing-heartily [at] him.	"Weep no [=not], for she-faced-death not [=she has not died] but sleeps." 53 And they-were-laughing-heartily [at] him recognizing that she-faced-death [=she had died]. 54 So he, having-
25 So when the crowd was-cast-out,	So having-cast-out all [=everyone], he [himself] takes-along the father of-the young-child and the mother and the [ones] with him and travels-in where the young-child was.	
having entered, he-seized her hand	41 And having-seized the hand of-the young-child he-says to-her, "Talitha koum," which is being-translated, "Girl, I-say to-you, rise."	seized her hand, yelled saying, "Child, rise."
and the girl was-raised.	42 And immediately the girl got-up and was-walking-around; for she-was twelve years [old].	55 And her spirit turned-back [=returned to her] and she-got-up at-once
26 And this gossip[b] [=news] went-out into that whole land.		
		and he-appointed [=he asked for something] to-be-given to-her to-eat.
	And immediately they-were-surprised great ecstasy [=they are overcome with surprise].	56 And her parents were-surprised;
	43 And he-beseeched many [=emphatically of] them in-order-that not-one might-know [=they tell no one about] this and said [=asked for something] to-be-given to-her to-eat.	so he-enjoined them to-say to-not-one [=to no one] the having-happened [=what had happened].

[a] *having-been-turned* ℵ B f^{13} 33 205 892 *al*; *having-been-turned-to* C L W Θ f^{1} 1006 1442 1506 𝔐; *stood having-been-turned* D.
[b] *this gossip* B W Δ f^{13} 892 1006 1342 𝔐 it^{mss} vg sy; *her gossip* ℵ C Θ f^{1} 33 205 *pc* cop^{bo}; *his gossip* D 1424 1506 *pc* cop^{sa} cop^{bo}.
[c] *omit* ℵ B D L Δ 892 1342 2427 it^{mss} vg sy^{s} cop; *look!* 𝔭^{45} A C W f^{1} f^{13} 33 1006 1506 𝔐 it^{mss}.
[d] *omit* ℵ^{C} A C^{2} D L W Θ f^{1} f^{13} 33 892 1006 1342 1506 𝔐 sy cop; *the* ℵ* B C* Δ 2427 *pc*.
[e] *omit* 𝔭^{75} ℵ^{1} B L f^{1} 33 205 579 700* 1342 2542 pc sy^{s} sy^{p} cop^{sa}; *it-happened* ℵ* ℵ^{2} A C D W Θ Ψ f^{13} 892 1006 1506 𝔐 it vg.
[f] *omit* 𝔭^{75} B 700* *al* sy^{s} cop^{sa}; *and the together-with him* ℵ A C D L W Θ Ξ Ψ f^{1} f^{13} 33 892 1342 𝔐 it vg sy^{p} cop^{bo}; *and the with him* Ψ 1006 1506 𝔐.
[g] *him* 𝔭^{75} ℵ B L Ξ f^{1} 33 205 579 892 1342 1424 *pc* cop; *him saying* A C D W Θ Ψ f^{13} 1006 1506 𝔐 sy^{s}; *the father of-the child saying* 1229 it^{mss} vg sy^{p}.

Q 7:35 (§126, p. 91)
Luke 8:56 (§160, p. 120)

161. Jesus' Preaching at Nazareth (→ §25, §28, §102)

Matt 13:53-58; 9:35	**Mark 6:1-6**	Q 4:16	Luke 4:16-24	John 7:15; 6:42; 4:44	Thomas 31
		16 . . . Nazara . . .	16 And he-came into Nazara[c], which [=where] he-was nourished [=brought up] and		
53 And it-happened when Jesus completed these parables, he-took-leave from-there. 54 And having-come into his homeland	1 And he-went-out from-there and comes into his homeland and his disciples follow him.				
			according-to the having-been-accustomed for-him [=as was his custom] he-entered into the		
he-was-teaching them in their synagogue	2 And [when] sabbath having-happened [=started], he-began to-teach in the synagogue		synagogue in [=on] the day of-the sabbaths, and he-got-up to-read. 17 And [a] booklet of-the prophet Isaiah was-given-to him and having-unrolled[d] the booklet he-found the place which [=where] it-was having-been-written, 18 "[The] SPIRIT [of the] LORD [is] UPON ME BECAUSE OF-WHICH HE-ANOINTED		

			ME TO-PROCLAIM TO-POORS [=to poor people], HE-HAS-SENT-OFF ME TO-PREACH REMISSION [=release] TO-CAPTIVES AND RESTORATION-OF-SIGHT TO-BLINDS [=to blind people], TO-SEND-OFF HAVING-BEEN-OPPRESSEDS [=the oppressed] IN REMISSION [=freedom], [19]TO-PREACH [the] ACCEPTABLE ANNUM [=year of the] LORD." [20]And having-ravelled the booklet, [and] having-given-		
			over [it] to-the attendant, he-was-seated; and the eyes of-all in the synagogue were being-fixed on him. [21]so he-began to-say to them that "Today this writing has-been-fulfilled in your ears."	[7:15]Therefore the Judeans were-being-astonished, saying, "How [does] this [man] recognize letters [=writing], no [=despite never] having-been-learned [=having been trained]?"	
with-the-result-that they to-be-amazed [=were amazed] and	and many hearing were-being-amazed,		[22]And all were-testifying him and were-being-astonished upon [=by] the words of-benefaction [=of grace] traveling-out out [of] his mouth and were-saying,		
to-say [=said], "From-where [did] this [man get] this wisdom and the [=these] powers?	saying, "From-where [did] this [man get] these [things] and what [is] the wisdom having-				

Matt	Mark		Luke	John	Thomas
	been-given to-this[b] [man], and [what are] the powers such-as-these happening through his hands?			6:42 And they-were-saying, “Is this not Jesus the son of-Joseph, the father and the mother of-whom we [ourselves] recognize? Now how [does] he-say that, ‘I-have-descended out of-heaven’?”	
55 Is this not the son of-the carpenter? [Is] not his mother said [=called] Mary and his brothers James and Joseph[a] and Simon and Judah? 56 And are indeed-not his sisters all to [=with] us? Therefore from-where [did] this [man get] all these [abilities]?”	3 Is this not the carpenter, the son of-Mary and brother of-James and of-Joses and of-Judah and of-Simon? And are not his sisters here to [=with] us?”		“Is indeed-not this [a] son of-Joseph?”		
57 And they-were-being-caused-to-stumble [=they were offended] in [=by] him.	And they-were-being-caused-to-stumble [=they were offended] in [=by] him.				
So Jesus said to-them, “[A]	4 And Jesus was-saying to-them that, “[A]		23 And he-said to them, “By-all-means you-will-say this parable to-me, ‘Physician, heal yourself,’ [and] ‘Whatsoever we-heard having-happened into [=at] Capharnaum do and [=also] here in your homeland.’” 24 So he-said, “Amen I-say to-you that ‘No-one [=No prophet is acceptable in his	4:44 For Jesus he [himself] testified that [a] prophet has not honor in the [=his] own homeland.	Jesus said, “No prophet is welcome on his home turf; doctors don’t cure those who know them.”
prophet is not dishonorable if no [=except] in [his] homeland	prophet is not dishonorable if no [=except] in his homeland		homeland.’		

Matt	Mark	Luke	John	Other
	and in [=among] his kin			
and in his home.” 58 And he-did not many [works with his] powers there	and in his home.” 5 And he-was-being-able not to-do no-one [=any deeds of] power there, if no [=except] having-placed the hands [on them] he-healed [a] few unwell. 6 And he-was-being-astonished			
through [=because of] their disloyalty.	through [=by] their disloyalty.			
9:35 And Jesus was-leading-around all the cities and the villages teaching in their synagogues and preaching the proclamation of-the kingdom and healing all [=every] disease and all [=every] sickness.	And he-was-leading-around among the villages teaching.			

[a] *Joseph* ℵ^{2} B C Θ f^{1} 33 892 it^{mss} vg; *Joses* L W Δ 0106 f^{13} 565 1006 1342 1506 𝔐 it^{mss} cop^{sa}; *John* ℵ* D E G 579 1424 vg^{mss}.
[b] *to-this* ℵ B C L Δ 892 1342 cop^{samss} cop^{bo}; *to-him* A D W Θ f^{1} f^{13} 1006 1506 2427 𝔐 sy cop^{samss}.
[c] *Nazara* ℵ B* Δ Ξ 33 *pc* it^{mss}; *Nazaret* B^{2} F L 0233 205 209 565 579 892 1342 1424 1506 1582 2542; *Nazareth* D E G H W Ψ f^{1} f^{13} 788 1006 *pc*; *Nazarat* A Θ *pc*.
[d] *unrolled* ℵ D* K Δ Θ Ψ f^{1} f^{13} 28 565 700 𝔐 it vg; *opened* A B L W Ξ 33 579 892 1241 *pc* sy cop.
🕮 Lk 4:18 – Isa 61:1, 2

162. Commissioning the Twelve (→ §104, §106-108, §201)

Matt 10:5-6; 9-11, 14	**Mark 6:7-13**	**Luke 9:1-6**
5 These twelve Jesus sent-off	7 And he-summons the twelve and he-began to-send-off them two [by] two and he-was-giving authority to-them [over] the unclean spirits.	1 So having-called-together the twelve, he-gave power to-them and authority upon [=over] all the demons and to-heal diseases. 2 And he-sent-off them to-preach the kingdom of-god and to-cure the ills[d] [=those who are ill].

having-enjoined them
saying, "Might-you-go-away no
[=not] into way of-nations [=among
the Gentiles], and into [any] city
of-Samaritans might-you-enter no
[=not]. 6So [=But] travel rather to the
destroyed [=lost] sheep [of the] house
of-Israel."
9"Might-you-acquire no gold so-not
[=nor] silver so-not [=nor] copper
into your belts; 10no pouch into way
[=for the road] so-not [=nor] two
tunics so-not [=nor] sandals so-
not [=nor] staff[a], for the worker [is]
worthy [of] his nourishment.
11So into which ever city or village
you-might-enter, make-a-careful-
search [for] what [=who] in it is
worthy; and-there stay until ever
you-might-go-out.
14"And who ever might-receive no
[=not] you so-not [nor if] he-might-
hear your words, going-out outside
that home or city, shake-out the
dust [from] your feet."

8And he-enjoined them in-order-
that they-might-remove not-one
[=they might take nothing] into way
[=for their journey] if no [=except
a] staff only, no bread, no pouch,
[place], no copper into the belt,
9but having-worn little-sandals and
might-you-be-clothed no [not with]
two tunics.
10 And he-was-saying to-them,
"Where if-ever you-might-enter
into [a] home, stay there until ever
you-might-go-out from-there.
11And which ever place might-
receive you no [=not] so-not they-
might-hear [=so they will not hear]
you, traveling-out from-there shake-
out the dirt beneath your feet into
[=as] testimony to-them.[b]" 12And
having-gone-out they-preached[c]
in-order-that they-might-repent,
13and they-were-casting-out many
demons and they-were-smearing
[with] olive-oil many unwells [=sick
people] and they-were-healing
[them].

3And he-said to them,
"Remove not-one [=Take nothing]
into the way [=on the road] not-even
[a] staff, not-even [a] pouch, not-
even bread, not-even [a] silver coin,
not-even [=nor] to-have up two
[=two extra] tunics.
4And into which ever home you-
might-enter, stay there and go-out
from-there.
5And whatsoever [=where] ever
they-might-receive you no [=not],
going-out from that city the dust
from your feet shake-off into
[=as] testimony upon [=to] them."
6So, going-out, they-were-going-
through according-to [=each one
of] the villages proclaiming and
healing everywhere.

[a] *staff* ℵ B D Θ f^{1} 33 205 892 1424 *al* vg it^{mss} sy^{p} cop^{sa} cop^{bo}; *staffs* C L W f^{13} 1006 1342 1506 𝔐 it^{mss}.
[b] *omit* ℵ B C D L W Δ Θ 565 892 1342 2427 2542 *pc* vg it^{mss} sy^{s} cop^{sa}; *Amen I-say to-you, more-tolerable will-it-be Sodoms or Gomorrahs in day of-judgment or that city* A f^{1} f^{13} 33 1006 1506 𝔐 it^{mss} sy^{p} sy^{h}.
[c] *they-preached* ℵ B C D L Δ 892 1342 2427 *pc*; *they-were-preaching* A W Θ f^{1} f^{13} 33 1006 1506 𝔐.
[d] *the ills* ℵ A D L Ξ Ψ 070 f^{1} 33 205 579 *pc* it^{mss}; *the being-ills* C W Θ f^{13} 892 1006 1342 1506 𝔐 vg it^{mss}; *omit* B sy^{s} sy^{c}.

163. Some Opinions on Jesus' Identity

Matt 14:1-2

1In that proper-time Herod the
tetrarch heard the rumor of-Jesus,
2and he-said [to] his children
[=servants], "This is John the baptist;
he [himself] was-raised from the

Mark 6:14-16

14And king Herod heard, for his
name was-happening visible [=was
becoming known], and they-were-
saying[a] that "John the baptising
[one] has-been-raised out of-deads

Luke 9:7-9

7So Herod the tetrarch heard all
the happenings [=things that were
happening] and he-was-confused
through [=because] to-be-said [=it
was said] under [=by] some that
"John was-raised out of-deads
[=from the dead],"

deads [=dead people] and through
[=because of] this the powers
energize [=are at work] in him."

[=from the dead] and through
[=because of] this in-him the powers
energize [=are at work]."
15So [=But] anothers [=others] were-
saying that "He-is Elijah"; so [=but]
anothers [=others] were-saying that
"[=He is a] prophet like one of-
the prophets." 16So [=But] Herod,
having-heard, was-saying, "John
whom I [myself] beheaded, this [one]
was-raised."

8so [=but] under [=by] some
that "Elijah was-appeared [=had
appeared]," so [=but] anothers
[=others] that "Some prophet of-the
ancients got-up [=had risen]." 9So
[=But] Herod said, "I beheaded
John;
so what is this [person] around
[=concerning] whom I-hear[b] [things]
such-as-this?" And he-was-
searching to-see him.

[a] *they-were-saying* B D W 2427 *pc* it^{mss}; *he-was-saying* ℵ A C L Q f^{1} f^{13} 33 892 1006 1342 1506 𝔐 vg it^{mss} sy cop.
[b] *I-hear* $\mathfrak{p}^{75}$ ℵ B C* L Ξ 565 579 892 1342 1506 *pc* it^{mss}; *I hear* A C^{2} D W Θ Ψ f^{1} f^{13} 33 1006 𝔐 vg it^{mss}.

164. John's Imprisonment and Death (→ §20)

Matt 14:3-12

3For Herod, having-seized John,
restrained and deposited [him]
in prison through [=because of]
Herodias, the woman [=wife] of-
Philip his brother[a];
4for John was-saying to-him, "It-
is-permitted not for-you to-have
her." 5And [though] wishing to-kill
him, he-was-feared [=he feared] the
crowd, that [=because] they-were-
holding [=they thought of] him like
[a] prophet.
6So [the] birthdays of-Herod
having-happened, the daughter
of-Herodias danced in the middle
and pleased Herod 7from-which
[=so that]

Mark 6:17-29

17For Herod, having-sent-off
[soldiers], he [himself] seized John
and restrained him in prison
through [=because of] Herodias, the
woman [=wife] of-Philip his brother,
that [=because] he-married her;
18for John was-saying to-Herod that
"It-is-permitted not for-you to-have
the woman [=wife of] your brother."
19So [=But] Herodias was-being-
hostile to-him and she-wished to-
kill him and [=but] she-was-able not
[to do so]. 20For Herod was-fearing
John, having-recognized him [as a]
righteous and holy man, and he-
was-protecting him. And having-
heard him, he-was-uncertain many[c]
[=greatly] and [=but] gladly heard
[=listened to] him. 21And [=But
when the] opportune day having-
happened [=came] when Herod,
[on] his birthdays, did [=hosted a]
banquet [for] his people-of-high-
status and legion-leaders and [for]
the firsts [=leaders] of-the Galilee.
22And his daughter [by] Herodias[d],
having-entered and having-danced,
pleased Herod and the sitting-at-
tables [=his guests].

Luke 3:19-20

19So [=on the other hand] Herod the
tetrarch, being-exposed under [=by]
him around [=concerning] <u>Herodias</u>,
the woman [=wife of] his brother
and around [=concerning] all [the]
evils which Herod did, 20and added
this upon [=to it] all: he-shut-up
John in prison[f].

Matt 14:8-12

he-confessed with [a] sworn-oath
to-give her which if-ever [=whatever]
she-might-ask [for].

8 So, having-been-prompted under
[=by] her mother, she-speaks, "Give
me here upon [a] platter the head

of-John the baptist." 9 And the king

having-been-grieved through
[=because of] the sworn-oaths and
the sitting-at-tables [=his guests],

ordered [it] to-be-given, 10 and
having-sent, he-beheaded John in
the prison. 11 And his head was-
carried upon [a] platter and was-
given to-the girl and she-carried [it
to] her mother. 12 And his disciples,
having-approached, removed the
corpse and buried him[b]
and having-gone [away] they-
informed Jesus.

Mark 6:23-29

The king said to-the girl, "Ask me
[for that] which if-ever you-might-
wish, and I-will-give [it] to-you."
23 And he-vowed to-her[e], "Which
some if-ever [=Whatever] you-
might-ask I-will-give you, until [=as
much as] half my kingdom."
24 And having-gone-out she-said
[to] her mother, "What might-I-
ask [for]?" So she-said, "The head
of-John the baptizing [one]." 25 And
having-entered immediately with
haste to the king she-asked saying,
"I-wish in-order-that promptly you-
might-give me upon [a] platter the
head of-John the baptist." 26 And the
king, having-happened [=becoming]
very-grieved, wished not to-refuse
her through [=because of] the
sworn-oaths and the dinings [=his
guests]. 27 And immediately the king,
having-sent-off [for an] executioner,
presided-over [=commanded him] to-
carry his head [to him]. And having-
gone-away, he-beheaded him in the
prison, 28 and carried his head upon
[a] platter and gave it to-the girl, and
the girl gave it [to] her mother.
29 And his disciples, having-heard,
came and removed his corpse and
put it in [a] tomb.

[a] *Philip his brother* ℵ B C L W Z Δ Θ 0106 f^{1} f^{13} 28 33 𝔐 sy cop Origen; *his brother* D it vg Jer Aug.
[b] *him* ℵ B 0106; *it* C D L W Θ f^{1} f^{13} 𝔐 cop^{bo}.
[c] *he-was-uncertain many* ℵ B L Θ 2427 cop^{sa} cop^{bo}; *he-did many* A C D f^{1} 33 𝔐 it vg.
[d] *his daughter Herodias* ℵ B D L Δ 565; *the daughter of-Herodias herself* A C Θ f^{13} 28 33 𝔐 it vg; *the daughter of-Herodias* f^{1} 205 sy cop.
[e] *he-vowed to-her* ℵ A B Δ f^{13} 33 𝔐 it vg sy cop; *he-vowed many to-her* $𝔓^{45}$ D Θ 565 it.
[f] *in prison* $𝔓^{4}$ ℵ B D L Ξ 070 f^{1} 565; *in the prison* A W Θ Ψ f^{13} 33 892 1006 1342 𝔐.

165. The Apostles Report to Jesus

Mark 6:30-31

30 And the apostles were-gathered to [=around] Jesus and they-informed
him all whatsoever they-did and whatsoever they-taught. 31 And he-
says to-them, "Come-on! you they according-to own [=each one of you]
into [a] deserted place and be-given-relief [for a] little [while]." For many
were coming and leaving, and they-were-having-the-opportunity nor
[=not even] to-eat.

Luke 9:10a

10a And the apostles having-returned
narrated to-him whatsoever they-did.

There are no variants in this pericope that appear in English.

166. Five Thousand Fed

Matt 14:13-21	**Mark 6:32-44**	**Luke 9:10b-17**	John 6:1-13
13 So Jesus, having-heard, retreated from-there in [a] boat into [a] deserted place according-to own [=by himself].	32 And they-went-away in the boat into [a] deserted place according-to own [=by themselves].	10b And having-taken-along them, he-withdrew according-to own [=by himself] into [a] city being-called Bethsaida.	1 With [=After] these [things] Jesus went-away beyond the sea of-the Galilee [also called the sea] of-Tiberias.
And the crowds, having-heard, followed him by-foot from the cities.	33 And many saw them leaving and they-understood [=they recognized them] and they-ran-together there by-foot from all the cities and they-preceded them.	11 So [=But] the crowds having-known [this] followed him;	2 So [=But a] many [=great] crowd was-following him, that [=because] they-were-catching-sight-of the signs which he-was-doing upon the being-ills [=those who were ill]. 3 So Jesus went-up into the mountain and was-sitting with his disciples. 4 So [=Now] the passover was near, the feast of-the Judeans. 5 Therefore, Jesus, having-lifted-up the [=his] eyes, and having-noticed that many [=a great] crowd comes to him, says to Philip,
14 And having-gone-out [from the boat] he-saw many [=a great] crowd and had-pity upon [=for] them, and he-healed their unwells [=unwell people].	34 And having-gone-out [from the boat] he-saw many [=a great] crowd and had-pity upon [=for] them, that [=because] they-were like sheep having no shepherd, and he-began to-teach them many [things].	and having-welcomed them, he-was-talking to-them around [=concerning] the kingdom of-god, and the havings [=those who had] need of-healing he-was-curing.	
15 So evening having-happened, the disciples approached him saying, "The place is deserted and the hour already passed-away [=it is late]. Release the crowds, in-order-that having-gone-away into the [=their] villages they-might-buy sustenance for-themselves."	35 And already many hour having-happened [=when it had become late], his disciples, having-approached him were-saying that "The place is deserted and already [the] hour [is] many [=late]. 36 Release them in-order-that having-gone-away into the among [=surrounding] fields and villages they-might-buy themselves what [=something that] they-might-eat."	12 So the day began to-recline [=to end]; so the twelve, having-approached, said to-him, "Release the crowd in-order-that having-traveled into the among [=surrounding] villages and fields they-might-demolish [=they might find a place to stay] and they-might-find something-edible, that [=because] we-are in [a] deserted place here."	

16So [=But] Jesus said[a] to-them, “They-have not need to-go-away, you [yourselves] give [something] to-them to-eat.”

17So [=But] they-say to-him, “We-have not [=nothing] here if no [=except] five breads and two fishes.” 18So he-said, “Carry them here to-me.” 19And having-ordered the crowds to-be-stretched-out [=to recline] upon the food [=grass], [and]

having-taken the five breads and the two fishes, [and] having-looked-up into heaven, he-blessed [the food], and having-broken [some up] he-gave the breads to-the disciples, so [=and] the disciples [gave it] to-the crowds.

37So [=But] having-answered he-said to-them,

“You [yourselves] give them [something] to-eat.” And they-say to-him, “Having-gone-away might-we-buy [=are we to buy] bread [worth] two-hundred denarii and we-will-give [it] to-them to-eat?”

38So he-says to-them, “How-great [=How many] breads do-you-have? Leave, see[b].” And having-known [=having found out] they-say,

“Five, and two fishes.”

39And he-presided-over them to-stretch-out all parties parties [=he ordered them to be seated party by party] upon the green food [=grass]. 40And they-leaned [=they sat] groups groups [=group by group] according-to [=in groups of] one-hundred and according-to [=in groups of] fifty.

41And having-taken the five breads and the two fishes, [and] having-looked-up into heaven, he-blessed [the food], and he-broke-up the breads and was-giving [some to] his disciples in-order-that they-might-place-before them [the bread] and he-divided the two fishes

---

13So [=But] he-said to them,

“You [yourselves] give them [something] to-eat.” So [=But] they-said, “There-are not to-us [=We have no] more or [=than] five breads and two fishes, if surely-not [=unless] having-traveled we [ourselves] might-buy sustenance into [=for] all this whole-people.” 14For there-were as [=about] five-thousand men. So [=But] he-said to his disciples,

“Recline-at-table them [=Sit them down in] sections as[c] up [=of up to about] fifty.” 15And they-did thus and reclined-at-table [=sat down] everyone. 16So having-taken the five breads and the two fishes, [and] having-looked-up into heaven, he-blessed them and broke-up [the bread] and was-giving [it] to-the disciples to-place-before the crowd.

“From-where might-we-buy bread in-order-that these [people] might-eat?” 6So [=Now] he-was-saying this [as a way of] testing him, for he [himself] recognized [=he already knew] what he-was-intending to-do. 7Philip answered him, “Breads [worth] two-hundred denarii are-enough not [for] them in-order-that each might-take [a] little-bit.” 8One out [=of] his disciples, Andrew, the brother of-Simon Peter, says to-him, 9“Here is [a] little-boy who has five barley breads and two cooked-foods [=fish]. But what is [=are] these [=they] into [=among] so-many?” 10Jesus said, “Do [=Make] the people to-lean [=sit down].” So [=Now] there-was many [=much] food [=grass] in the place. Therefore the men leaned [=sat down], the number like [=numbering about] five-thousand. 11Therefore Jesus took the breads and having-given-thanks he-distributed [them] to-the dinings [=to those who were there], likewise and [=also] out of-the [=from the] cooked-foods, whatsoever they-were-wishing. 12So like [=when] they-were-satisfied, he-says [to] his disciples, “Gather the having-exceeded [=left over] fragments, in-order-that some no [=none of the food] might-be-destroyed.” 13Therefore they-gathered

[20]And all ate and were-fed, and they-removed the exceeding [=what was left over] of-the fragments, twelve baskets full. [21]So the eatings [=those who ate] were as [=about] five-thousand men without [=not including] women and young-children.	[among them] all. [42]And all ate and were-fed, [43]and they-removed [a] fullness of-twelve baskets [from] the fragments [of bread] and from the fishes. [44]And the having-eatens [=those who had eaten] the bread were five-thousand men.	[17]And they-ate and all were-fed, and the having-exceeded to-them [=what was left over] was-removed, twelve baskets of-fragments.	and stuffed twelve baskets of-fragments out of-the five barley breads which exceeded the having-been-devoureds [=what they had eaten].

[a] *Jesus said* ℵ^2 B C L W Θ f^1 f^{13} 33 892 1006 1342 1506 𝔐 vg it^{mss} cop^{samss}; *he-said* ℵ* D Z 579 1424 *pc* it^{mss} sy^s sy^p cop^{samss} cop^{bo}.
[b] *Leave, see* ℵ B D L W f^1 33 205 2427 2542 *pc* it^{mss} sy^s sy^p; *Leave and see* A Θ f^{13} 892 1006 1342 1506 𝔐.
[c] *as* ℵ B D C D L Ξ 33 579 892 1342 2542 *pc* cop^{sa}; *omit* A W Θ Ψ f^1 f^{13} 1006 1506 𝔐 vg it^{mss} sy^p cop^{bo}.

SYNOPTIC STUDY GUIDE 9

Problems with 2DH: Minor Agreements

Universal acceptance of Q among New Testament scholars is undermined most by the minor agreements (see also Synoptic Study Guide 15). The necessity of Q, according to the Two-Document Hypothesis, rests on the claim that the Gospels of Matthew and Luke were written independently, evidenced by the fact that in Triple Tradition they rarely agree together against Mark in wording. Had the author of Luke used Matthew, they suggest, there would be places where he follows Matthew against Mark, such as one finds in the extremely numerous instances in which Matthew and Mark agree against Luke, and Luke and Mark agree against Matthew. The problem is: Matthew and Luke *do* agree against Mark in Triple Tradition passages, it is just that the agreements are usually very minor.

The story of Five Thousand Fed (§166), has several positive minor agreements (agreeing on the *addition* of a word to Mark): Matt 14:13/Mark 6:33/Luke 9:11: followed him/—/followed him; Matt 14:15/Mark 6:35/Luke 9:12: So/And/So, crowds/them/crowd; Matt 14:17/Mark 6:37/Luke 9:13: So/And/So; Matt 14:18/Mark 6:38/Luke 9:14: he-said/he-says/he-said; Matt 14:19/Mark 6:41/Luke 9:16: crowds/them/crowd; Matt 14:20/Mark 6:42/Luke 9:17: exceeding/—/having-exceeded, of-the fragments/the fragments/of-the fragments. There are eight minor agreements in this single story, and this number could be doubled for this story, depending on how one defines "agreement." For example, Matthew and Luke (Matt 14:14/Luke 9:11) agree that Jesus healed the sick in the crowd, while in Mark he only taught them (Mark 6:34).

Negative agreements (agreeing on the *elimination* of a word or phrase from Mark) can be even harder to measure. For instance, Matthew and Luke agree on rejecting Mark's claim that the people followed Jesus because they recognized him (Matt 14:13/Mark 6:33/Luke 9:11), but they replace it differently. Is that a minor agreement against Mark? Also, Matthew and Luke agree on rejecting Mark's twofold repetition of how the people were made to sit down: party by party (Mark 6:39) and group by group (Mark 6:40).

By some counts, there are many hundreds of minor agreements, and this makes it extremely difficult for some scholars to accept the claim that the writer of Luke did not have access to the Gospel of Matthew. Incidentally, the minor agreements also offer the Griesbach Hypothesis support, since they suggest a relationship between Matthew and Luke. The issue of the minor agreements becomes even more pressing if you include Mark-Q overlaps here, rather than hiding them in their own category of agreements.

Supporters of the Two-Document Hypothesis contend that each of the minor agreements is consistent with the redactional patterns of Matthew or Luke, that they are simply coincidental changes, or sometimes that they are the result of scribal alterations done in the course of copying manuscripts, resulting in the appearance of agreements where there were none in the originals.

167. Jesus Walks on the Sea

Matt 14:22-33

22 And instantly he-compelled the disciples to-embark into the boat and to-lead-ahead [of] him into the beyond [=to the other side] until which he-might-release [=while he released] the crowds. 23 And having-released the crowds he-ascended into the mountain according-to own [=by himself] to-pray. So, evening having-happened [=when evening came] he-was there alone.

24 So [=Now] the boat received-in-full [=was] already many furlongs from the land being-tormented under [=by] the waves, for the wind was against [them]. 25 So [on the] fourth prison [=watch] of-the night, he-came to them walking-around upon the sea.
26 So the disciples having-seen him[a] walking-around upon the sea were-disturbed saying that "It-is [an] apparition," and they-cried from

the fear. 27 So immediately Jesus talked to-them saying,
"Cheer-up, I am [=it is me]; fear no [=not]."
28 So having-answered, Peter said to-him, "Lord, if you are [=if it is you], order me to-come to you upon the waters." 29 So he-said, "Come." And having-descended from the boat, Peter walked-around upon the waters and came to Jesus. 30 So [=But] looking [=seeing] the strong wind he-was-feared [=he was afraid], and having-begun to-sink he-cried saying, "Lord, save me." 31 So instantly Jesus, having-reached-out the hand, took-hold-of him and says to-him, "Little-loyalty [=You of little faith], into what [=why] did-you-doubt?" 32 And their having-ascended into the boat, the wind ceased.

Mark 6:45-52

45 And immediately he-compelled his disciples to-embark into the boat and to-lead-ahead into the beyond [=to the other side] to Bethsaida, until [=while] he [himself] releases the crowd. 46 And having-bid-goodbye to-them he-went-away into the mountain to-pray.
47 And evening having-happened [=when evening came] the boat was in [the] middle of-the sea, and he [himself was] alone upon the land.
48 And having-seen[b] them being-tormented in the to-drive [=by the oars], for the wind was against them, he-comes to them around [the time of the] fourth prison [=watch] of-the night, walking-around upon the sea and he-wished to-pass-away [=to pass by] them.
49 So [=But] having-seen him walking-around upon the sea, they-

supposed that "It-is [an] apparition,"[c] and they-cried-out. 50 For all saw him and were-disturbed. So immediately he-talked with them and says to-them, "Cheer-up, I am [=it is me]; fear no [=not]."

51 And he-ascended to them into the boat and the wind ceased, and they-were-surprised extremely in

John 6:16-21

16 So like [=when] evening happened, his disciples descended upon [=to] the sea 17 and having-embarked into [a] boat, were-going beyond [=across] the sea into Capharnaum.

And dark already had-happened and Jesus had-come to them not-yet. 18 Even the sea was-awakening,

[a] great wind heaving. 19 Therefore having-been-driven like [=about] twenty five or thirty furlongs [=three

or four miles] they-catch-sight-of Jesus walking-around upon the sea and happening [=coming] near the

boat, and they-were-feared [=they were afraid]. 20 So he-says to-them, "I am [=It is me]; be-feared no [=fear not]."

21 Therefore they-wished to-take him into the boat, and instantly the boat happened upon [=arrived at] the land into which they-left.

(Matt, continued)

33So the [ones] in the boat worshiped
him saying, "Truly you-are [a] son
of-god."

(Mark, continued)

themselves out of-excessive [=they
were utterly astonished].
52For they-comprehended not upon
[=about] the breads, but their heart
was hardened.

[a] *So the disciples having-seen him* $\aleph^{1}$ B D f^{13} *pc*; *So having-seen him* $\aleph^{*}$ Θ 700 *pc* it cop^{sa}; *And having-seen him* f^{1} 1424 *pc* vg cop^{bomss}; *And the disciples having-seen him* C L W 33 892 1006 1342 1506 𝔐.
[b] *having-seen* ℵ B D L W Δ Θ 579 892 1342 1424 2427 *pc* vg it^{mss}; *he-saw* $\mathfrak{P}^{45}$ A f^{1} f^{13} 33 1006 1506 𝔐.
[c] *they-supposed that "It-is apparition,"* ℵ B L Δ 33 579 892 *pc*; *they-supposed to-be apparition* $\mathfrak{P}^{45}$ A D W Θ f^{1} f^{13} 205 1006 1506 2427 2542 𝔐.

168. Healings at Gennesaret

Matt 14:34-36

34And having-crossed-over
they-came upon the land into
Gennesaret.
35And,
having-understood [=recognizing]
him, the men of-that place sent-off
[word of his arrival] into [=throughout]
that whole surrounding-region
and offered to-him all the havings
[=those who were sick] badly.
36And they-were-exhorting him
in-order-that they-might-touch
only the tassel [of] his coat; and
whatsoever [=whoever] touched [=it]
were-brought-safely-through [=were
healed].

Mark 6:53-56

53And having-crossed-over upon
[=to] the land they-came into
Gennesaret and they-were-moored
[there]. 54And their having-gone-
out [=when they had gotten] out
of-the boat, immediately having-
understood [=people recognized] him,
55that whole region they-ran-around
and began to-bring-around upon
mattresses the havings [=those who
were sick] badly where they-were-
hearing that he-is[a]. 56And where
ever he-was-traveling-in into
villages or into cities or into fields,
they-were-putting in the markets
the being-ills [=sick people] and
were-exhorting him in-order-that
they-might-touch even-if [=only] the
tassel [of] his coat, and whatsoever
ever [=whoever] touched him, they-
were-saved.

John 6:22-25

22[On] the next-day, the crowd
having-stood beyond [=on the other
side of] the sea saw that there-was
not another small-boat there if no
[=except] one and that Jesus entered-
with into the boat not [with] his
disciples but his disciples alone
went-away. 23But small-boats came
out of-Tiberias near the place where
they-ate the bread, having-given-
thanks of-the [=after giving thanks to]
lord. 24Therefore when the crowd
saw that Jesus is not there, nor his
disciples, they [themselves] embarked
into the small-boats and went into
Capharnaum searching [for] Jesus.
25And having-found him beyond
[=across] the sea they-said to-him,
"Rabbi, when had-you-happened
[=did you get] here?"

[a] *where they-were-hearing that he-is* ℵ B L Δ Θ 892 2427 vg it^{mss} sy^{p}; *where they-hear Jesus to-be* D it; *where they-hear that he-is there* A W f^{1} f^{13} 33 205 565 700 1006 1342 1506 𝔐.

169. On Purity (→ §83)

Matt 15:1-20

1Then Pharisees and
scribes approach
Jesus from
Jerusalems, saying,

Mark 7:1-23

1And the Pharisees
and some of-the
scribes, having-
come from
Jerusalems, gather
to him. 2And
having-seen some
[of] his disciples,
that they-eat bread
[with] common, this

Q 6:39

Luke 6:39

Thomas 14; 40; 34

[2]"Through what [=Why do] your disciples transgress the tradition of-the elders? For they-wash not their hands whenever they-might-eat

bread." [3]So having-answered he-said to-them, "And through what [=why do] you [yourselves] transgress the commandment of-god through your tradition?
[4]For god said[a], 'HONOR FATHER AND MOTHER' and 'THE [one] DAMNING FATHER OR

[=that] is unwashed, hands,— [3]for the Pharisees and all the Judeans they-eat not if-ever no [=unless] they-might-wash the hands [to the] wrist, seizing [=thus maintaining] the tradition of-the elders, [4]and if-ever no [=unless] they-might-baptize [=they clean things bought] from [a] market, they-eat [it] not, and there-is [=there are] many anothers [=others] which they-take-along to-seize [=many other traditions which they observe], [such as the] ritual-washings of-cups and of-pots and of-copper-bowls and of-stretchers [=beds],— [5]and the Pharisees and scribes question him, "Through what [=Why do] your disciples walk-around [=behave] not according-to the tradition of-the elders but eat bread [with] common hands?"
[6]So
he-said to-them[g],

[14]Jesus said to them, "If you fast, you will bring sin upon yourselves, and if you pray, you will be condemned, and if you give to charity, you will harm your spirits. When you go into any region and walk about in the countryside, when people take you in, eat what they serve

MOTHER LET-
HIM-EXPIRE IN-
DEATH.' 5So [=But]
you [yourselves] say
who ever might-
say to-father or
to-mother, 'Which
if-ever [=Whatever]
you-might-have-
achieved out
of-me [is a] gift,'
6he-will-honor
not no [=at all] his
father[b]; and you-
disregard the word[c]
of-god through
your tradition.
7Hypocrites, Isaiah
prophesied well
around [=concerning]
you, saying,

8"THIS THE
WHOLE-PEOPLE
HONORS ME [with]
THE [=their] LIPS,
SO [=but] THEIR
HEART RECEIVES-
IN-FULL [=stays]
FAR FROM ME;
9SO THEY-REVERE
ME VAINLY,
TEACHING
LESSONS [which are
the] PRECEPTS OF-
PEOPLE.'"

"Isaiah prophesied
well around
[=concerning]
you hypocrites,
like it-has-been-
written that[h] 'THIS
WHOLE-PEOPLE
HONORS ME [with]
THE [=their] LIPS,
SO [=but] THEIR
HEART RECEIVES-
IN-FULL [=stays]
FAR FROM ME;
7SO THEY-REVERE
ME VAINLY,
TEACHING
LESSONS [which are
the] PRECEPTS OF-
PEOPLE.'
8Having-excused
[=Having abandoned]
the commandment
of-god, you-seize
the tradition of-
people." 9And he-
was-saying to-them,
"You-refuse well
the commandment
of-god in-order-that
you-might-stand
[=you might keep]
your tradition.
10For Moses said,
'HONOR YOUR
FATHER AND
YOUR MOTHER'
and 'THE [one]

you and heal the
sick among them.
After all, what goes
into your mouth
will not defile you;
rather, it's what
comes out of your
mouth that will
defile you."
40Jesus said, "A
grapevine has been
planted apart from
the Father. Since it is
not strong, it will be
pulled up by its root
and will perish."

Matt 15:10-13	Mark 7:11-15
	DAMNING FATHER OR MOTHER, LET-HIM-EXPIRE IN-DEATH.’ 11 So [=But] you [yourselves] say, ‘If-ever [a] person might-say to-father or to-mother, “Which if-ever [=Whatever] you-might-have-achieved out of-me [is a] korban, which is [=means] gift,” 12 you-excuse [=you allow] him no-longer to-do no-one [=anything] for-father or for-mother, 13 disregarding the word of-god [for the sake of] your tradition which you-delivered; and you-do many [things] similar [to things] such-as-this.”
10 And having-summoned the crowd, he-said to-them, “Hear and comprehend; 11 the entering not [=it is not what enters] into the mouth, but the traveling-out [=what comes] out of-the mouth, this defiles the person.”	14 And having-summoned the crowd again he-was-saying to-them, “Hear me all [of you] and comprehend. 15 There-is no-one [=nothing] from-outside of-the person traveling-in into him which is-able to-defile him, but the [things] traveling-out out of-the person is [=are] the [things] defiling the person.”[i]
12 Then the disciples[d], having-approached say to-him, “Do-you-recognize that the Pharisees, having-heard the word, were-caused-to-stumble [=were offended]?” 13 So	

having-answered he-said,			6:39 And so he-said [a] parable to-them.	
“All [=Every] plant which my heavenly father planted not will-be-uprooted. 14 Excuse them [=Leave them alone], they-are blind escorts of-blind [people]; so if-ever [a] blind [person] might-escort [another] blind [person], they-will-fall both into [a] ditch.”		6:39 “Surely-not [is a] blind [person] able to-escort [another] blind [person]? Will-they-fall indeed-not both into [a] ditch?”	“Surely-not [is a] blind [person] able to-escort [another] blind [person]? Will-they-fall-in not both into [a] ditch?”	34 Jesus said, “If a blind person leads a blind person, both of them will fall into a hole.”
15 So having-answered Peter said to-him, “Interpret for-us the parable[e].”	17 And when he-entered into [his] house from the crowd, his disciples were-questioning him [about] the parable[j].			
16 So he-said[f], “And even-still are you [yourselves] unintelligent?	18 And he-says to-them, “Are you [yourselves] and [=also] unintelligent thus [=in this way]?			
17 Do-you-perceive not that all the [=anything] entering into the mouth accepts [=goes] into the abdomen and is-cast-out into [the] latrine?”	Do-you-perceive not that all the [=anything] from-outside traveling-in into the person is-able not to-defile him, 19 that [=because] it-travels-in not into his heart but into the abdomen, and travels-out into the latrine?”			
	[Thus he was] purifying all sustenances [=food].			
18 The [things] traveling-out out of-the mouth go-out [=come] out of-the heart, and-those defiles the person. 19 For evil thoughts,	20 So he-was-saying that “The traveling-out [Whatever comes] out of-the person, that [is what] defiles the person. 21 For the bad thoughts travel-out out of-the hearts			

murders, adulteries,
fornications, thefts,
false-witness-
testimonies,
blasphemies go-out
out of-the heart.
[20]These is the
defilings [=These
are what defile] the
person, so [=but] to-
eat [with] unwashed
hands defiles not the
person."

of-the people, from-
within: fornications,
thefts, murders,
[22]adulteries,
covetousnesses,
evilnesses, cunning,
indecency, evil
eye, blasphemy,
arrogance, folly. [23]All
these evil [things]
travel-out from-
within and defiles
the person."

[a] *god said* $ℵ^{1}$ B D Θ f^{1} f^{13} 579 700 892 *pc* vg it^{mss} sy^{s} sy^{c} sy^{p} cop; *god charged saying* ℵ* $ℵ^{2}$ C L W 33 1006 1342 1506 𝔐 sy^{h}.
[b] *omit* ℵ B D *pc* it^{mss} sy^{c} cop^{sa}; *or his mother* C L W Θ f^{1} 1006 1342 1506 𝔐 it^{mss} sy^{p} sy^{h}; *and his mother* 565 *pc* it^{mss} cop^{bo}; *or mother* f^{13} 33 579 700 892 *pc* it^{mss}.
[c] *the word* $ℵ^{1}$ B D Θ 579 700 892 *pc* it sy^{s} sy^{c} sy^{p} cop; *the commandment* L W f^{1} 33 1006 1342 1506 𝔐 vg it^{mss} sy^{h}; *the law* ℵ* $ℵ^{2}$ C f^{13} *pc*.
[d] *the disciples* ℵ B D Θ f^{13} 579 700 892 1506 *pc*; *his disciples* C L W f^{1} 33 1006 1342 𝔐 vg it^{mss} sy.
[e] *the parable* ℵ B f^{1} 579 700 892 vg^{mss} cop; *this parable* C D L W Θ f^{13} 33 1006 1342 1506 𝔐 it^{mss} vg sy.
[f] *he-said* ℵ B D Z 0233 33 579 892 1424 *pc* vg it^{mss} sy^{s} sy^{c} sy^{p} cop; *Jesus said* C L W Θ f^{1} f^{13} 1006 1342 1506 it^{mss} sy^{h}.
[g] *omit* ℵ B L Δ Θ 33 579 1342 2427 *pc* sy^{s} sy^{p}; *that* $𝔭^{45}$ A D W f^{1} f^{13} 892 1006 1506 𝔐 it^{mss} sy^{h}.
[h] *that* ℵ B L 0274 892 1342 2427 *pc*; *omit* A D W Θ f^{1} f^{13} 33 1006 1506 𝔐 vg it sy^{h}.
[i] *omit* ℵ B L Δ 0274 1342 2427 cop^{samss} cop^{bomss}; [16]*if some has ears to-hear, let-him-hear* A D W Θ f^{1} f^{13} 33 892 1006 1506 𝔐 vg it sy cop^{samss} cop^{bomss}.
[j] *the parable* ℵ B D L Δ 33 579 892 1342 2427 vg it^{mss}; *around the parable* A W Θ f^{1} f^{13} 1006 1506 𝔐 cop^{samss}.
🕮 Mt 15:4 – Exod 20:12; 21:17; Deut 5:16; Lev 20:9; Prov 20:20; 🕮 Mt 15:8 – Isa 29:13; 🕮 Mk 7:6 – Isa 29:13; 🕮 Mk 7:10 – Exod 20:12; 21:17; Deut 5:16; Prov 20:20

170. The Foreign Woman Bests Jesus

Matt 15:21-28

[21]And having-gone-out from-there, Jesus retreated into
the parts [=region] of-Tyre and Sidon.

[22]And look! [a] Canaanite woman from those territories
having-gone-out was-crying[a] saying, "Be-merciful

[to] me, lord, son of-David; my daughter is-demon-
possessed badly."
[23]So [=But] he-answered [he said] not [a] word to-her.
And his disciples having-approached, were-begging[b]
him saying, "Release [=Get rid of] her, that [=for] she-
cries from-behind us." [24]So having-answered he-said,
"I-was-sent-off not if no into [=I was sent only for] the
destroyed [=lost] sheep [of the] house of-Israel." [25]So
[=But] having-come, she-was-worshiping[c] him saying,
"Lord, help me."

Mark 7:24-30

[24]So having-gotten-up, he-went-away from-there
into the territories of-Tyre[d]. And having-entered
into [a] home, he-wished no-one to-know, and [=but]
he-was-abled [he was enabled] not to-remain-hidden.
[25]But immediately [a] woman, who her [=whose] little-
daughter was-having [an] unclean spirit, having-heard
around [=about] him, [and] having-come, fell-to to
his feet. [26]So [=Now] the woman was [a] Hellene, [a]
Syrophoenician [by] type [=race]; and she-was-begging
him in-order-that he-might-cast-out the demon out [of]
her daughter.

26 So having-answered he-said, "It-is not fine to-take the bread of-the descendants and to-throw [it] to-the house-dogs." 27 So [=But] she-said, "Yes lord, for and [=even] the house-dogs eat from the scraps-of-food falling from the table [of] their lords."

28 Then having-answered Jesus said to-her, "Oh woman, great [is] your loyalty; let-it-happen for-you like you-wish."
And her daughter was-cured from that hour.

27 And he-was-saying to-her, "Excuse [=Allow] the descendants to-be-fed first, for it-is not fine to-take the bread of-the descendants and to-the house-dogs to-throw [it]." 28 So [=But] she-answered and says to-him, "Lord, and [=even] the house-dogs beneath the table eat from the scraps-of-food of-the young-children."
29 And he-said to-her, "Through [=Because of] this word, leave; the demon has-gone-out out [=from] your daughter." 30 And having-gone-away into her house, she-found the young-child having-been-thrown [=lying] upon the stretcher and the demon having-gone-out.

[a] *was-crying* ℵ^{2} B D Θ f^{1} 579 892 *pc*; *cried* ℵ* Z f^{13} 1506 *pc*; *was-screaming* M *pc*; *screamed* C L W 1006 1342 1506 𝔐.
[b] *were-begging* ℵ B C D 579 *pc*; *having-begged* L W Θ f^{1} f^{13} 33 892 1006 1342 1506 𝔐; *begged* 0106 1424 *pc*.
[c] *she-was-worshiping* ℵ* B D Θ f^{1} f^{13} 33 579 700 1424 *al* it; *she-worshiped* ℵ^{2} C L W 892 1006 1342 1506 𝔐 vg it^{mss} cop^{bo}.
[d] *omit* D L W Δ Θ 565 *pc* it sy^{s}; *and Sidon* ℵ A B f^{1} f^{13} 33 892 1006 1342 1506 𝔐 vg it^{mss} sy^{p} cop.

171. Healings around Tyre and Sidon

Matt 15:29-31

29 And having-headed-out from-there, Jesus went along [=near] the sea of-the Galilee, and having-ascended into [=up] the mountain, he-sat there. 30 And many crowds approached him having with themselves lames [=people who were lame], blinds [=people who were blind], maimeds [=people who were maimed], deafs [=people who were deaf], and many others and they-tossed them along [=at] his feet, and he-healed them,

31 with-the-result-that the crowd[a] to-be-astonished [=was astonished] looking [=seeing the] mutes talking, maimeds healthy, and lames walking-around and blinds looking; and they-glorified the god of-Israel.

Mark 7:31-37

31 And again having-gone-out out of-the territories of-Tyre he-went through Sidon[b] into [=to] the sea of-the Galilee up [the] middle of-the territories [of the] Decapolis. 32 And they-carry to-him [a person who is] mute [=deaf] and scarcely-able-to-talk

and they-exhort him in-order-that he-might-place the hand [on] him. 33 And having-received-back [=having escorted] him from the crowd according-to own [=to a private place], he-threw [=he put] his fingers into his ears and having-spit he-touched his tongue, 34 and having-looked-up into the heaven he-groaned and says to-him, "Ephphatha," which is [=means] open-up. 35 And instantly his rumors [=ears] were-opened, and the binding [of] his tongue was-loosed and he-was-talking correctly. 36 And he-beseeched them in-order-that they-might-say [=they might speak] to-not-one [=to no one]; so [=but] whatsoever he-was-beseeching [of] them, rather they [themselves] preached more-excessive [=all the more].
37 And they-were-being-amazed over-excessively saying, "He-has-done [=He has made] all [things] well, and the mutes [=deaf people] he-does [=he makes] to-hear and the speechlesses to-talk."

[a] *crowd* ℵ C D Δ Θ f^{1} f^{13} 33 579 700 892 1424 *al*; *crowds* B L W 1006 1342 1506 𝔐 vg it^{mss} sy^{c} sy^{p}.
[b] *of-Tyre he-went through Sidon* ℵ B D L Δ Θ 33 565 700 892 1342 2427 vg it^{mss} cop^{samss} cop^{bo}; *of-Tyre and Sidon he-went* 𝔓^{45} A W f^{1} f^{13} 1006 1506 𝔐 sy cop^{samss}.

172. Four Thousand Fed

Matt 15:32-39

32 So Jesus having-summoned his disciples said, "I-have-pity upon [=for] the crowd, that [=because] already three days they-stay-with me and they-have not what [=anything] they-might-eat; and I-wish not to-release [=to send away] them hungry, lest they-might-faint in the way [=on the road]."

33 And the disciples say to-him, "From-where in [this] deserted-place [are we to get] so-many [=enough] breads with-the-result-that to-feed so-many [=so great a] crowd?" 34 And Jesus says to-them, "How-great [=How many] breads have-you?" So they-said, "Seven and [a] few small-fishes." 35 And having-enjoined the crowd to-lean [=to sit] upon the land [=ground], 36 he-took the seven breads and the fishes and having-given-thanks he-broke [it] and was-giving[a] [it] to-the disciples, so [=and] the disciples to-the crowds.

37 And all ate and were-fed. And the exceeding [=what was left over] of-the fragments they-removed, seven large-baskets full. 38 So the eatings [=those who were eating] were four-thousand men without women and young-children. 39 And having-released the crowds, he-embarked into the boat and went into the territories of-Magadan[b].

Mark 8:1-10

1 In those days again many [=a great] crowd being [=was there], and having no [=not] what [=anything that] they-might-eat, having-summoned the disciples, he-says to-them, 2 "I-have-pity upon [=for] the crowd, that [=because] already three days they-stay-with me and they-have not what [=anything] they-might-eat; 3 and if-ever I-might-release [=I might send away] them hungry into their house, they-will-be-fainted [=they will faint] in the way [=on the road]. And some of-them have-pressed-forward [=have come] from far-off."
4 And his disciples answered him that "From-where [=How] will-be-able some [=someone] to-feed breads [to] these [people] here upon [=in this] deserted-place?"
5 And he-begged them, "How-great [=How many] have-you breads?" So they-said, "Seven." 6 And he-enjoins the crowd to-lean [=to sit] upon the land [=ground], and having-taken the seven breads, [and] having-given-thanks, he-broke [it] and was-giving [it to] his disciples in-order-that they-might-place-before [=they might distribute them], and the disciples placed-before [=placed the breads before] the crowd. 7 And they-were-having [a] few small-fishes; and having-blessed them he-said and these [=that these too] to-place-before [=should be distributed]. 8 And they-ate and were-fed, and they-removed excesses [=what was left over of the] fragments, seven large-baskets.

9 So they-were[c] like four-thousand. And he-released them. 10 And immediately having-embarked into the boat with his disciples he-went into the parts of-Dalmanoutha.

[a] *was-giving* ℵ B D Θ f^{13} 33 579 700 892 1582 *pc*; *gave* C L W f^{1} 1006 1342 1506 𝔐.
[b] *Magadan* ℵ* B D; *Magdala* C L Q W f^{1} f^{13} 33 565 892 1006 1342 1506 𝔐; *Magedan* $ℵ^{2}$ vg it^{mss} cop^{sa}.
[c] *they-were* ℵ B L D 33 579 892 1342 1424 2427 *pc* cop^{samss} cop^{bomss}; *the eatings were* A C D W Θ f^{1} f^{13} 1006 1506 𝔐 vg it sy cop^{samss} cop^{bomss}.

173. Searching for Signs (→ §141)

Matt 16:1-4

1 And the Pharisees and Sadducees, having-approached, [and] testing questioned him to-point-out to-them [a] sign out of-the [=from] heaven. 2 So having-answered he-said to-them, [a]
4 "[An] evil and adulterous generation seeks [a] sign, and [=but a] sign will-be-

Mark 8:11-13

11 And the Pharisees went-out and began to-discuss [=to argue with] him, searching [for a] sign from the heaven along [=from] him, testing him. 12 And having-groaned-loudly [in] his spirit, he-says, "What [=Why does] this generation searches[c] [for a] sign? Amen

John 6:30

30 Therefore they-said to-him, "What sign therefore [do] you do, in-order-that we-might-see and we-might-believe in-you? What [wonder] are-you-working?"

given not to-it if no [=except] the sign
of-Jonah[b]."
And having-quit [=having left] them he-
went-away.

I-say to-you if [=no] sign will-be-given
to-this generation."
13And having-excused them, [and]
again having-embarked, he-went-away
into the beyond [=across the sea].

[a] *omit* ℵ B X Γ *f*[13] 579 *al* sy[c] sy[s] cop[sa] cop[bomss]; 3*"Evening having-happened you-say, 'Pleasant, for the heaven is-fiery'; 3and early, 'Today stormy, for the heaven is-fiery looking-gloomy.' You-know for-one to-evaluate the face of-the heaven, so you-are-able not the signs of-the proper-times?"* C D L W Θ Π *f*[1] 33 𝔐 it[mss] sy[p] cop[bomss].
[b] *of-Jonah* ℵ B D L 579 700 vg it[mss] cop[sa]; *of-Jonah the prophet* C W Θ *f*[1] *f*[13] 33 892 1006 1342 1506 𝔐 it sy cop[bo].
[c] *searches* ℵ B C D L Δ Θ *f*[1] 33 205 579 892 2426 2542 *pc; asks* 𝔭[45]; *seeks* A W *f*[13] 1006 1506 𝔐.
📖 Mt 16:4 – Jonah 1:17

174. The Leaven of the Pharisees (→ §226)

Matt 16:5-12

5And having-come into the beyond
[=to the other side], the disciples[a]
neglected to-take breads.

6So Jesus said to-them,
"See [=Watch] and pay-close-
attention from [=beware of]
the leaven of-the Pharisees and
Sadducees." 7So they-were-
pondering in themselves saying
that "We-took not [any] breads." 8So
[=But] Jesus, having-known [this],
said, "What [=Why] do-you-ponder
in themselves [=yourselves], little-
loyalties [=you of little faith], that
you-have not [any] breads? 9Do-
you-perceive not-yet, nor recall the
five breads [for] the five-thousand
and how-great [=how many] baskets
you-took [away]? 10Nor the seven
breads [for] the four-thousand and
how-great [=how many] large-baskets
you-took [away]?

11How do-you-perceive not that
I-said [=I spoke] to-you not around
[=concerning] breads? So pay-
close-attention from [=beware
of] the leaven of-the Pharisees

Mark 8:14-21

14And they-neglected to-take
breads and they-had not [any]
with themselves in the boat if no
[=except] one bread. 15And he-was-
beseeching [=he was warning] them
saying,
"See, look [away] from the

leaven of-the Pharisees and the
leaven of-Herod." 16And they-
were-pondering to one-another[b]
that they-have not [any] breads.
17And having-known [this], he-
says to-them, "What [=Why] do-
you-ponder that you-have not
[any] breads? Do-you-perceive
not-yet, nor do-you-comprehend?
Do-you-have your heart having-
been-hardened [=hardened hearts]?
18Having eyes do-you-look not and
having ears do-you-hear not? And
do-you-recall not 19when I-broke
the five breads into five-thousand[c],
how-great [=how many] baskets full
of-fragments you-removed?" They-
say to-him, "Twelve." 20"When [I
broke] the seven into four-thousand,
how-great [=how many] large-baskets
[in their] fullness of-fragments
you-removed?" And they-say to-
him, "Seven." 21And he-was-saying
to-them, "Do-you-comprehend
not-yet?"

Luke 12:1

1In which [=When] the crowd
of-many-thousands having-been-
collected [=had been gathered], with-
the-result-that to-tread-upon [=they
trampled] one-another, he-began to-
say [=to speak] to his disciples first,
"Pay-close-attention themselves
from [=You yourselves be careful to
avoid] the leaven, whoever [=which]
is hypocrisy, of-the Pharisees."

and Sadducees." [12]Then they-comprehended that he-said not to-pay-close-attention from [=to beware of] the leaven of-the breads but from [=to beware of] the instruction of-the Pharisees and Sadducees.

[a] *the disciples* ℵ B C Θ f^{13} 205 209 892 *pc*; *his disciples* L W f^{1} 33 1006 1506 𝔐 vg it^{mss} sy cop^{bo}; *omit* Δ *pc*.
[b] *omit* $\mathfrak{P}^{45}$ ℵ B D W f^{1} 205 565 700 1342 2427 2542 *pc* it cop^{sa}; *saying* A C L Θ f^{13} 33 892 1006 1506 𝔐 it^{mss} vg sy cop^{bo}.
[c] *five-thousand* $\mathfrak{P}^{45}$ A B L W f^{13} 892 1006 1342 1506 2427 𝔐 sy^{p} cop^{bo}; *five-thousand and* ℵ C D Θ f^{1} 33 205 565 579 1424 2542 *al* sy^{s}; *five-thousand people and* Δ it cop^{samss}.

175. Mark's Blind Man from Bethsaida

Mark 8:22-26

[22]And they-come into Bethsaida. And they-carry to-him [a] blind [man] and they-exhort him
in-order-that he-might-touch him. [23]And having-taken-hold-of the hand of-the blind [man]
he-brought-out[a] him outside of-the village and having-spit into his eyeballs, [and] having-placed
the hands [on] him, he-was-questioning him, "If you-look some [=Can you see anything]?" [24]And
having-looked-up he-was-saying, "I-look [=I see] people that I-see walking-around like trees."
[25]Moreover again he-placed the hands upon his eyes, and he-looked-through [=he saw clearly] and
he-restored [=his sight was restored] and he-beheld everyone clearly. [26]And he-sent-off him into his
house saying, "Might-you-enter so-not [=not even] into the village[b]."

[a] *he-brought-out* $\mathfrak{P}^{45}$ ℵ B C L Δ Θ 33 892 1342 2427 *pc*; *he-led-out* A D W f^{1} f^{13} 1006 1506 𝔐.
[b] *"Might-you-enter so-not into the village"* ℵ B L Δ f^{1} 205 2427 pc sy^{s} cop^{sa}; *"Leave into your house and speak not-one into the village"* D; *"Leave into your house and if-ever you-might-enter into the village speak so-not to-not-one"* Θ f^{13} 565 2542 *pc* vg it^{mss}; *"Might-you-enter so-not into the village, speak so-not to-some in the village"* A C 33 892 1006 1342 1506 𝔐 sy^{p}.

176. Jesus Asks for Confirmation

Matt 16:13-20	**Mark 8:27-30**	**Luke 9:18-21**	John 6:67-69	Thomas 13
[13]So Jesus, having-come into the parts [=region] of-Caesarea of-Philip [=of Caesarea Philippi], was-	[27]And Jesus and his disciples went-out into the villages of-Caesarea of-Philip [=of Caesarea Philippi], and in [=on] the way he-was-questioning	[18]And it-happened in the to-be him [=while he was] praying according-to [=all] alone, [that] the disciples were-with [=approached] him, and he-questioned them	[67]Therefore Jesus said to-the twelve, "No and wish you to-leave [=Do you too wish to leave]?"	
begging his disciples saying, "What [=Who do] the people say the son of-the person	his disciples saying to-them, "What [=Who do] the people say me	saying, "What [=Who do] the crowds say me		Jesus said to his disciples, "Compare me to something and tell me what I am like." Simon Peter said to him, "You are like a just messenger." Matthew said to him, "You are like a
to-be [=is]?" [14]So	to-be [=that I am]?"	to-be [=that I am]?" [19]So having-		
they-said,	[28]So they-said to-him saying[c] that	answered they-said,		
"John the baptist, for-one, so [=and] anothers [=others	"John the baptist, and anothers [=others say] Elijah,	"John the baptist, so [=and] anothers [=others say] Elijah,		

say] Elijah, so [=and]
others Jeremiah
or one of-the
prophets."

15 He-says to-them,
"So what [=who do]
you [yourselves] say
me to-be [=that I
am]?" 16 So having-
answered, Simon
Peter said, "You are
the anointed-one,
the son of-the living
god."
17 So having-
answered[a], Jesus said
to-him, "Fortunate
are-you, Simon
Bar-Jonah, that
[=because] flesh
and blood revealed
[this] not to-you but
my father in the
heavens. 18 So I-too
say to-you that you
[yourself] are Peter,
and upon this rock
I-will-build my
assembly and [the]
gates of-Hades will-
over-power it not.
19 I-will-give to-you
the keys of-the
kingdom of-the
heavens, and who
if-ever [=whosoever]
you-might-
restrain upon
the land [=earth]
will-be having-
been-restrained
[=restrained] in the
heavens, and who
if-ever [=whosoever]
you-might-loose
upon the land
[=earth] will-be
having-been-loosed
[=will be released] in
the heavens."

so [=and] anothers
[=others say] that
[you are] one of-the
prophets."

29 And he [himself]
was-questioning
them, "So what
[=who do] you
[yourselves] say me
to-be [=that I am]?"
Having-answered[d],
Peter says to-him,
"You are the
anointed-one."

so [=and] anothers
[=others say] that
some prophet of-the
ancients got-up
[=was resurrected]."
20 So he-said to-
them, "What [=Who
do] you [yourselves]
say me to-be [=that
I am]?"
So Peter having-
answered said, "The
anointed-one of-
god."

68 Simon Peter
answered him,
"Lord, to what
[=whom] will-we-
go-away? You-have
speeches [=the
words] of-eternal life.
69 And we [ourselves]
have-believed and
have-known that
you [yourself] are the
holy [one]
of-god."

wise philosopher."
Thomas said to him,
"Teacher, my mouth
is utterly unable to
say what you are
like." Jesus said, "I
am not your teacher.
Because you have
drunk, you have
become intoxicated
from the bubbling
spring that I have
tended." And he
took him, and
withdrew, and spoke
three sayings to him.
When Thomas came
back to his friends
they asked him,
"What did Jesus say
to you?" Thomas
said to them, "If I
tell you one of the
sayings he spoke to
me, you will pick up
rocks and stone me,
and fire will come
from the rocks and
devour you."

Matt	Mark	Luke		
[20]Then he-beseeched the disciples in-order-that they-might-say not-one [=they might tell no one] that[b] he [himself] is the anointed-one.	[30]And he-rebuked them in-order-that they-might-say not-one [=nothing] around [=concerning] him.	[21]So having-rebuked them, he-enjoined [them] to-say this [to] not-one [person].		

[a] *having-answered* ℵ B D Θ f^1 f^{13} 33 579 1424 *pc* vg it^{mss} cop^{sa} cop^{bo}; *And having-answered* C L W 892 1006 1342 1506 𝔐 it^{mss} sy^h; *omit* sy^c.
[b] *omit* ℵ* B L Δ Θ f^1 f^{13} 565 700 1342 1424 *al* it^{mss} sy^c sy^p cop^{samss}; *Jesus* ℵ^2 C D W 892 1006 1506 𝔐 vg it^{mss} sy^h cop^{samss} cop^{bo}.
[c] *they-said to-him saying* ℵ B C L Δ 579 892 1342 2427 *pc*; *they-answered* A f^1 1006 1506 𝔐 sy^h; *they-answered him saying* D W Θ f^{13} 33 565 *pc* vg it^{mss}.
[d] *Having-answered* B L 579 *pc* it^{mss} vg sy^p sy^h cop^{samss}; *So, having-answered* ℵ C D W Θ f^1 f^{13} 1006 𝔐 it^{mss} cop^{samss}; *And having-answered* A 33 892 1342 1424 2427 *pc* it.

177. The Rebuke of Peter

Matt 16:21-23	Mark 8:31-33	Luke 9:22
[21]From then Jesus began to-show his disciples that it-is-necessary [for] him to-go-away into Jerusalems and to-suffer many [things] from [=by] the elders and high-priests and scribes and to-be-killed and to-be-raised [on] the third day. [22]And having-taken-aside him Peter began to-rebuke him saying[a], "Propitious to-you [=God forbid], lord, this will-be not no [=will never happen] to-you." [23]So having-turned, he-said to-Peter, "Leave [=Get] behind me, adversary. You-are my scandal [=stumbling block], that [=because] you-consider not the [things] of-god but the [things] of-the people."	[31]And he-began to-teach them that it-is-necessary [for] the son of-the person to-suffer many [things] and to-be-rejected under [=by] the elders and the high-priests and the scribes and to-be-killed and to-get-up [=to rise again] with [=after] three days. [32]And he-was-talking the word [=about all this] in-boldness [=boldly]. And Peter, having-taken-aside him, began to-rebuke him. [33]So having-turned-back and having-seen his disciples he-rebuked Peter and says, "Leave [=Get] behind me, adversary, that [=because] you-consider not the [things] of-god but the [things] of-the people."	[22] . . . having-said that it-is-necessary [for] the son of-the person to-suffer many [things] and to-be-rejected from [=by] the elders and high-priests and scribes and to-be-killed and to-be-raised [on] the third day.

[a] *began to-rebuke him saying* ℵ C L W 892 1006 1342 1506 𝔐 sy^h; *began him to-rebuke saying* Θ f^1 f^{13} 13 565 700 1424 *pc*; *began him to-rebuke and to-say* D it; *says to-him rebuking* B *pc*.

178. A Model of Discipleship

Matt 16:24-28	Mark 8:34-9:1	Luke 9:23-27	John 12:25	Thomas 55
[24]Then Jesus said [to] his disciples, "If some [one] wishes	[34]And having-summoned the crowd together-with his disciples he-said to-them, "If some [one] wishes	[23]So he-was-saying to all, "If some [one] wishes to-come		Jesus said, "Whoever does not hate father and

Matt	Mark	Luke		
to-come [=to follow] behind me, let-him-disown himself and let-him-remove [=let him take up] his cross	to-follow behind me, let-him-disown himself and let-him-remove [=let him take	[=to follow] behind me, let-him-deny[c] himself and let-him-remove [=let him take up] his cross according-to the		mother cannot be my disciple, and whoever does not hate brothers and sisters, and carry the cross as I do, will not be worthy of me.”
and let-him-follow me. [25]For who if-ever [=whosoever] might-wish to-save his soul will-destroy it. So [=But] who ever might-destroy his soul because-	up] his cross and let-him-follow me. [35]For who if-ever [=whosoever] might-wish to-save his soul will-destroy it. So [=But] who ever will-destroy his soul because-of me and the proclamation	[=every] day and let-him-follow me. [24]For who ever might-wish to-save his soul will-destroy it. So [=But] who ever might-destroy his soul because-of	[25]“The [one] liking his soul destroys it, and the [one] hating his soul in this world will-guard it into eternal life.”	
of me will-find it. [26]For what will-be-achieved if-ever [a] person might-gain the whole world so [=but] his soul	will-save it. [36]For what achieves[b] [how does it benefit a] person to-gain the whole world and his	me, this [one] will-save it. [25]For what person achieves [=does a person achieve] having-gained the whole world so [=but] having-destroyed himself or having-been-forfeited?		
might-be-forfeited? Or what [a] person will-give [in] exchange [for] his soul?	soul to-be-forfeited? [37]For what [a] person might-give [in] exchange [for] his soul?			
	[38]For who if-ever [=whosoever] might-be-ashamed-of me and my-own words in this adulterous and sinful generation, the son of-the person	[26]For who ever might-be-ashamed-of me and my-own words, this [one] the son of-the person		
	will-be-ashamed of him and [=also] whenever he-might-come in the glory [of] his father with the announcers [=angels] holy.”	will-be-ashamed-of whenever he-might-come in the glory of-him and of-the father and of-the holy announcers [=angels].		
[27]For the son of-the person intends to-come in the glory [of] his father with his announcers [=angels], and then he-will-give-over to-each according-to his deed.				

Matt 16:28	Mark 9:1	Luke 9:27		
[28]Amen I-say to-you that[a] there-are some of-the having-stoods [=those who are standing] here whoever [=who] might-taste not no [=will never taste] death until ever they-might-see the son of-the person coming in his kingdom."	[9:1]And he-was-saying to-them, "Amen I-say to-you that there-are some of-the having-stoods [=those who are standing] here whoever [=who] might-taste not no [=will never taste] death until ever they-might-see the kingdom of-god having-come in power."	[27]So I-say to-you truly, there-are some of-the having-stoods [=those who are standing] of-him [=here] who might-taste not no [=will never taste] death until ever they-might-see the kingdom of-god."		

[a] *that* ℵ B L Θ f^{13} 33 579 700 1424 *al* it; *omit* C D W f^{1} 892 1006 1342 1506 𝔐 vg it^{mss}.
[b] *achieves* ℵ B L W 892 1424 2427; *will-achieve* A C D Θ f^{1} f^{13} 1006 1342 1506 𝔐 cop; *will-be-achieved* 33 579 *pc*.
[c] *let-him-deny* ℵ A B^{2} D L Θ Ξ f^{13} 33 579 1342 *pc*; *let-him-disown* $\mathfrak{P}^{75}$ B* C W Ψ f^{1} 892 1006 1506 𝔐.

179. The Transfiguration

Matt 17:1-9	**Mark 9:2-10**	**Luke 9:28-36**	John 12:28-30
		[28]So it-happened with these words as eight days [=Eight days after these sayings], and having-taken-along Peter and John and James he-ascended into the mountain to-pray.	
[1]And with [=after] six days Jesus takes-along Peter and James and John his brother and brings-up them into [a] high mountain according-to own [=by themselves]. [2]And he-was-metamorphized in-front of-them, and his face shone like the sun, so [=and] his coats happened [=became] white like the light.	[2]And with [=after] six days Jesus takes-along Peter and James and John and brings-up them into [a] high mountain according-to own alone [=all by themselves], and he-was-metamorphized in-front of-them, [3]and his coats happened [=became] extremely glistening white, such-as [a] bleacher upon the land is-able not to-make-white thus [=such as no human could bleach white].	[29]And it-happened in the to-pray him [=while he was praying], the form [of] his face other [=became different] and his apparel [=became] white, flashing-like-lightning.	[28]"Father, glorify your name." Therefore [a] voice came out of-the heaven, and [said] "I-glorified and I-will-glorify again." [29]Therefore the crowd having-stood and having-heard were-saying to-have-happened thunder [=that it was thunder], anothers [=others] were-saying, "[An] announcer [=angel] has-talked to-him." [30]And having-answered, Jesus said, "This voice has-happened [=came] not through [=for] me but through [=for] you."
[3]And look! Moses was-seen [by] them and Elijah talking-with with him[a].	[4]And Elijah together-with Moses was-seen [by] them and they-were talking-with Jesus.	[30]And look! two men were-talking-with him, whoever [=who] were Moses and Elijah, [31]who having-been-seen in glory were-saying [were speaking about] his exodus, which he-was-intending to-fulfill in Jerusalem. [32]So [=But] Peter and the [ones] together-with him were	

Matt 17:4-9	Mark 9:5-9	Luke 9:33-36	
		having-been-weighed-down [with] sleep; so having-woken-up they-saw his glory and the two men having-stood-with him. 33And it-happened in the to-depart them from him [=as they were leaving	
4So Peter having-answered said to-Jesus, "Lord, it-is fine [for] us to-be here; if you-wish, I-will-do [=I will make] three tents here, [for] you one, and [for] Moses one, and [for] Elijah one."	5And Peter having-answered says to-Jesus, "Rabbi, it-is fine [for] us to-be here; and [=so] might-we-do [=let us make] three tents, [for] you one, and [for] Moses one, and [for] Elijah one."	him that] Peter said to Jesus, "Overseer, it-is fine [for] us to-be here, and [=so] might-we-do [=let us make] three tents, one [for] you, and one [for] Moses, and one [for] Elijah," no	
	6For he-recognized not what he-might-answer[c], for they-were-happening [=they were becoming] terrified[d].	having-recognized which he-says [=not realizing what he was saying].	
5Yet him talking [=While he was still talking] look! [a] cloud full-of-light overshadowed them, and	7And [a] cloud happened [=arrives] overshadowing	34So these his saying [=as he was saying these things], [a] cloud happened [=came] and was-overshadowing them; so they-were-feared [=they were afraid] in the to-enter them [=as they were entering] into the cloud.	
look! [a] voice [comes] out of-the cloud saying, "This is my son the beloved, in whom I-was-content. Hear him."	them, and [a] voice happened [=came] out of-the cloud, "This is my son the beloved, hear him."	35And [a] voice happened [=came] out of-the cloud saying, "This is my son the having-been-chosen[e] [=chosen one], him hear."	
6And the disciples having-heard fell upon their face and were-feared very [=were very scared]. 7And Jesus approached and having-touched them said, "Be-raised [=Get up] and fear no [=not]." 8So having-lifted-up their eyes they-saw no-one if no [=except] Jesus him [=himself] alone.	8And all-of-a-sudden having-looked-around they-saw no-longer no-one but Jesus alone with themselves.	36And in the to-happen the voice [=after the voice finished], Jesus was-found alone.	
9And their descending out of-the mountain [=As they were going down the mountain] Jesus charged them saying, "Might-you-say not-one [=thing about] the sight until which [time] the son of-the person might-be-raised[b] out of-deads [=from the dead]."	9And their descending out of-the mountain [=as they were going down the mountain] he-beseeched them in-order-that they-might-narrate not-one [thing about] which they-saw, if no [=except] whenever the son of-the person might-get-up out of-deads [=from the dead].	And they were-quiet and they-informed no-one in those days no-one [=nothing of that] which they-have-seen.	

	[10]And they-seized the word to themselves discussing what is the [meaning of] to-get-up out of-deads [=from the dead]?		

[a] *Moses was-seen by-them and Elijah talking-with with him* 𝔭[44] ℵ B D Θ *f*[13] 33 579 1342 vg it[mss] sy[c]; *Moses and Elijah were-seen by-them talking-with with him* C L W *f*[1] 892 1006 1506 𝔐 it[mss] sy[p] sy[h].
[b] *might-be-raised* B D; *might-get-up* ℵ C L W Z Θ *f*[1] *f*[13] 33 892 1342 1506 𝔐.
[c] *he-might-answer* B C* L Δ Ψ *f*[1] 33 205 565 579 700 892 1342 2427 2542 *pc*; *he-was-talking* Θ sy[s]; *he-talks* 𝔭[45] W cop[sa]; *he-will-talk* A C[3] *f*[13] 1006 1506 𝔐.
[d] *for they-were-happening terrified* ℵ B C D L Δ Θ Ψ 33 565 579 892 1342 1424 2427 *pc* it; *for they-were terrified* 𝔭[45] A W *f*[1] *f*[13] 1006 1506 𝔐 vg it[mss] sy[p] sy[h].
[e] *the having-been-chosen* 𝔭[45] 𝔭[75] ℵ B L Ξ 579 892 1342 1582* *pc* it[mss] sy[s]; *the beloved* A C* W *f*[13] 33 1006 1506 𝔐 it vg[mss] sy[p] sy[h] sy[c]; *the beloved in whom I-was-content* C[3] D Ψ *pc* cop[bomss].

180. The Coming of Elijah

Matt 17:10-13	Mark 9:11-13
[10]And the disciples questioned him saying, "What therefore [=Why do] the scribes say that 'It-is-necessary [for] Elijah to-come first'?" [11]So having-answered he-said[a], "Elijah for-one comes [=is indeed coming] and he-will-restore all [things].	[11]And they-were-questioning him saying, "That [=Why do] the scribes say that 'It-is-necessary [for] Elijah to-come first'?" [12]So he-spoke[b] to-them, "Elijah for-one, having-come first, restores all [things].
	And how has-it-been-written upon [=about] the son of-the person in-order-that he-might-suffer many [things] and might-be-treated-contemptuously?
[12]So I-say to-you that Elijah came already and they-understood [=they recognized] him not but they-did in [=to] him whatsoever they-wished; and thus the son of-the person intends to-suffer under them [=at their hands]." [13]Then the disciples comprehended that he-said [=he was speaking] to-them around [=about] John the baptist.	[13]But I-say to-you and [=also] that Elijah has-come and they-did to-him whatsoever they-were-wishing, just-as it-has-been-written upon [=about] him."

[a] *he-said* ℵ B D L W Z *f*[1] 33 579 892 1424 *pc* vg it[mss] sy[c] cop; *Jesus said* C Θ *f*[13] 1006 1342 1506 𝔐 it[mss] sy[p] sy[h].
[b] *he-spoke* ℵ B C L Δ Ψ 579 892 1342 2427 *pc* sy[p] cop; *having-answered he-said* A D W Θ *f*[1] *f*[13] 33 1006 1506 𝔐 vg it[mss] sy[s] sy[h].
🕮 Mt 17:10 – Mal 4:5; 🕮 Mk 9:11 – Mal 4:5

181. A Mute Boy Is Healed (→ §279)

Matt 17:14-21	Mark 9:14-29	Luke 9:37-43a	Thomas 48; 106
[14]And having-come [=When they came] to	[14]And having-come [=When they came] to the disciples they-saw many [=a great] crowd around them and scribes discussing to [=things with] them. [15]And immediately all the crowd having-seen him were-greatly-surprised and having-run-to [him] greeted him.	[37]So it-happened [on] the following day their having-gone-down [=as they were descending] from the mountain many [=a great] crowd met-with him. [38]And look! [a] man shouted[c] from the crowd	

the crowd [a] person approached him kneeling [before] him 15and saying,	16And he-questioned them, "What do-you-discuss to [=are you arguing about with] them?" 17And one out of-the crowd answered him[b],		
"Lord, be-merciful [to] my son, that [=because] he-is-epileptic and he-suffers badly, for often he-falls into the fire and often into the water.	"Teacher, I-carried my son, having [a] speechless spirit, to you.	saying, "Teacher, I-implore you to-look-upon upon my son, that [=because] he-is [the] only-born to-me,	
	18And where if-ever it-might-grasp him, it-devastates him, and he-froths and grinds the [=his] teeth and is-withered,	39and look! [a] spirit takes him and suddenly it-cries [out] and convulses him with froth; and it-withdraws-back scarcely[d] from him shattering him.	
16And I-offered him [to] your disciples and they-were-abled [they were enabled] not to-heal him." 17So having-answered	And I-said [=I spoke] [to] your disciples in-order-that they-might-cast-out it, and they-had-the-strength not." 19So having-answered he-says to-them,	40And I-implored your disciples in-order-that they-might-cast-out it, and they-were-abled [they were enabled] not." 41So having-answered Jesus	
Jesus said, "Oh disloyal and having-been-distorted generation, until when will-I-be with you? Until when will-I-put-up-with you? Carry him here to-me."	"Oh disloyal generation, until when to [=with] you will-I-be? Until when will-I-put-up-with you? Carry him to me."	said, "Oh disloyal and having-been-distorted generation, until when will-I-be to [=with] you and will-I-put-up-with you? Lead-to here your son.	
	20And they-carried him to him. And having-seen him immediately the spirit thrashed him, and having-fallen upon the land [=ground] he-was-rolling-around frothing. 21And he-questioned his father, "How-great time [How long] is-it like [=since] this has-happened to-him?" So he-said, "Out [=From] childhood. 22And often it-threw him and [=both] into fire and into water in-order-that it-might-destroy him, but if you-might-be-able [to do] some [=something], help us, having-had-pity upon	42So yet [=while he was] approaching him, the demon devastated and thrashed him.	

18 And Jesus
rebuked it and the demon
went-out from him and
the child was-healed from
that hour. 19 Then the
disciples having-
approached Jesus
according-to own [=in
private] said, "Through
what [=Why] we [ourselves]
were-able [were enabled]
not to-cast-out it?"
20 So he-says to-them,
"Through [=Because of]
your littleness-of-loyalty;
for amen I-say to-you,
if-ever you-might-have
loyalty like [a] tiny-seed
of-mustard, you-will-say
to-this mountain, 'Head-
out from-this-place [to]
there' and it-will-head-

[=for] us." 23 So Jesus said
to-him, "'If you-might-
be-able,'; all [things are]
possible to-the believing
[person]." 24 Immediately
the father of-the young-
child having-cried [out]
was-saying, "I-believe;
help my disloyalty." 25 So
Jesus, having-seen that the
crowd closes-in rebuked
the unclean spirit saying
to-it, "Speechless and
mute spirit, I [myself]
preside-over you, go-out
out of-him and might-
you-enter into him
not-any-longer." 26 And
having-cried [out] and
having-convulsed many
[times], it-went-out.
And he-happened as [=he
appeared] dead with-the-
result-that the many
to-say [=were saying] that
"He-faced-death [=He
died]." 27 So Jesus having-
seized his hand raised
him, and he-got-up.
28 And his having-entered
[=when he had entered] into
[the] house, his disciples
were-questioning him
according-to own [=in
private], "That [=Why]
we [ourselves] were-abled
[were enabled] not to-cast-
out it?"
29 And he-said to-them,
"This type is-able to-go-
out in no-one [=by no
means] if no in [=except by]
prayer."

So Jesus
rebuked the unclean spirit
and cured the child and
gave-over him [to] his
father. 43a So all were-
being-amazed upon [=by]
the majesty of-god.

48 Jesus said, "If two make
peace with each other in a
single house, they will say
to the mountain, 'Move
from here!' and it will
move."
106 Jesus said, "When you
make the two into one,
you will become children

out. And no-one [=nothing] will-be-impossible for-you."[a]			of Adam, and when you say, 'Mountain, move from here!' it will move."

[a] *omit* ℵ* B Θ 33 579 788 892* *pc* sy^{s} sy^{c} sa; [21]*"So this type travels-out not if no in prayer and fasting."* ℵ^{2} C D L W f^{1} f^{13} 892 1006 1342 𝔐 it Origen.
[b] *one out of-the crowd answered him* ℵ B D L Δ Ψ 33 579 1342 2427 *pc* it cop^{bo}; *having-answered one out of-the crowd to-him* A C W f^{1} f^{13} 205 565 892 1006 1506 𝔐 vg sy^{h}; *one out of-the crowd answered and said to-him* Θ.
[c] *shouted* 𝔭^{45} 𝔭^{75} ℵ B C D L Ψ f^{13} 579 700 892 1342 1506 2524 *pc*; *shouted-out* A W Θ f^{1} 33 1006 𝔐.
[d] *scarcely* 𝔭^{75} ℵ A C D L Ψ f^{13} 33 892 1006 1342 𝔐 cop; *hardly* B W Θ f^{1} 205 700 1424 *pc*.

182. Second Passion Prediction

Matt 17:22-23	Mark 9:30-32	Luke 9:43b-45	John 7:1
		[43b]So all being-astonished [=while everyone was astonished] upon [=by] all [the things] which he-was-doing[c],	
[22]So their [=as they were] being-marshaled[a] in the	[30]And-from-there having-gone-out, they-were-traveling-by through the Galilee, and he-was-wishing not in-order-that some might-know [=he wanted no one to know].		
Galilee, Jesus	[31]For he-was-teaching his disciples and was-	he-said to his disciples,	
said to-them,	saying to-them that		
		[44]"[May] you [yourselves] put into your ears these	[1]And with [=after] these [things] Jesus was-walking-around in the Galilee, for he-was-wishing not to-walk-around in Judea, that [=because] the Judeans were-searching [for] him [in order] to-kill [him].
"The son of-the person intends to-be-delivered into [the] hands of-people, [23]and they-will-kill him,	"The son of-the person is-delivered into [the] hands of-people, and they-will-kill him and having-been-killed with [=after] three	words, for the son of-the person intends to-be-delivered into [the] hands of-people."	
and [on] the third day he-will-be-raised." And they-were-grieved very [=deeply].	days[b] he-will-get-up."		
	[32]So they-were-being-ignorant [concerning] the	[45]So they-were-being-ignorant [concerning] this speech, and it-was having-been-shrouded from them in-order-that they-might-deduce it no [=not], and	
	speech, and were-fearing [=were afraid] to-question him.	they-were-fearing [=they were afraid] to-beg [=to ask] him around [=about] this speech.	

[a] *being-marshaled* ℵ B f^{1} 579 892 vg it^{mss} cop^{sa}; *being-turned-up* C D L W Θ f^{13} 33 1006 1342 1506 𝔐 cop^{samss} cop^{bo}.
[b] *with three days* ℵ B C* D L Δ Ψ 579 1342 2427 *pc* it cop; *the third day* A C^{3} W Θ f^{1} f^{13} 1006 1506 𝔐 vg sy.
[c] *he-was-doing* 𝔭^{75} ℵ B D L Ξ f^{1} 205 579 700 1342 2542 *pc* vg it^{mss} sy^{s} sy^{c} cop; *Jesus was-doing* A C Θ Ψ f^{13} 33 892 *al*; *Jesus did* W 1006 1506 𝔐.

Q 7:35 (§126, p. 91)

183. Matthew's Payment of the Temple Tax

Matt 17:24-27

[24]So their having-come [=when they had come] into Capharnaum the takings [=those who take]
the didrachmas approached Peter and they-said, "[Does] your teacher not complete [=pay] the
didrachmas?" [25]He-says, "Yes." And having-come[a] into the home [=when Peter arrived home] Jesus
anticipated it, saying, "What [do] you [yourself] suppose, Simon? From what [people do] the kings
of-the land take ends [=tributes] or tax? From their sons or from foreigners [=others]?" [26]So having-
said "From foreigners [=others]," Jesus spoke to-him, "The sons consequently in-effect are free, [27]so
in-order-that we-might-cause-to-stumble them no [=not], having-traveled into [=to the] sea throw
[a] fish-hook and remove the first ascending fish, and having-opened his mouth, you-will-find [a]
four-drachma; having-taken that give [it] to-them in-place of-me and of-you."

[a] *having-come* ℵ[1] B f[1] 892; *having-entered* ℵ* D Θ f[13] 33 sy[c] 579; *when they-came* C *al* sy[c]; *when he-entered* L W 1006 1342 1506 𝔐.

184. Who Is Greater?

Matt 18:1-5	Mark 9:33-37	Luke 9:46-48	John 3:3, 5; 13:20	Thomas 22
[1]In that hour the disciples approached Jesus saying,	[33]And he-went into Capharnaum. And having-happened [=having arrived] in the home he-was-questioning them,	[46]So thought entered in [=an argument arose among] them,		
"What [=Who] consequently is	"What were-you-pondering in [=on] the way?" [34]So [=But] they-were-being-silent; for to one-another in [=on] the way they-dialogued [concerning] what [=who of them is]	the [issue of] what [=who] ever of-them might-be [the]		
greater in the kingdom of-the heavens?"	greater.	greater.		
	[35]And having-been-seated he-yelled [at] the twelve and says to-them, "If some [=someone] wishes to-be first he-will-be last of-all and servant of-all."	[47]And Jesus, having-recognized the thought [of] their	[3:3]Jesus answered and said to-him, "Amen amen I-say to-you, if-ever some might-be-begotten no from-the-start [=if someone is not born from above] he-is-able not to-see the kingdom of-god."	
[2]And having-summoned [a] young-child, he-stood it in [the] middle of-them	[36]And having-taken [a] young-child, he-stood it in [the] middle of-them and having-embraced it said to-them,	heart, having-taken-hold-of [a] young-child, stood it along [=before] himself	[5]Jesus answered, "Amen amen I-say to-you, if-ever some might-be-begotten no out [=if someone is not born] of-water	Jesus saw some babies nursing. He said to his disciples, "These nursing babies are like those who enter the <Father's>

3and said, "Amen I-say to-you, if-ever no [=unless] you-might-be- turned and might- happen [=might become] like the young-children, you-might-enter not no [=at all] into the kingdom of-the heavens. 4Therefore whoever will-humble himself like this young- children, this [one] is the greater in the kingdom of-the heavens. 5And who if-ever may-receive one young-children such-as-this upon [=in] my name, he- receives me."		48and he-said to-	and spirit, he-is-able not to-enter into the kingdom of-god."	kingdom." They said to him, "Then shall we enter the <Father's> kingdom as babies?" Jesus said to them, "When you make the two into one, and when you make the inner like the outer and the outer like the inner, and the upper like the lower, and when you make male and female into a single one, so that the male will not be male nor the female be female, when you make eyes in place of an eye, a hand in place of a hand, a foot in place of a foot, an image in place of an image, then you will enter <the kingdom>."
	37"Who ever may- receive one of-the young- children such-as- these upon [=in] my name receives me. And who ever might-receive me receives not me but the [one] having- sent-off me."	them, "Who if-ever may-receive this young-child upon [=in] my name receives me; and who ever may- receive me receives the [one] having- sent-off me. For the smaller [one] being- at-one's-disposals [=existing] in [=among] all of-you, this [one] is[a] great."	13:20"Amen amen I-say to-you, the ever taking some I-might-send takes me [=who ever receives someone that I send receives me], so [=and] the [one] taking [=receiving] me takes [=receives] the [one] having- sent me."	

[a] *is* 𝔭45 𝔭75 א B C L Ξ Ψ f^1 33 205 579 700 1342 2542 *pc* vg it[mss] cop; *will-be* A D W Θ Ψ f^{13} 892 1006 1506 𝔐.

185. Unsanctioned Miracles (→ §120)

Matt 10:42	**Mark 9:38-41**	**Luke 9:49-50**
	38John spoke[a] to-him, Teacher, we- saw some [=someone] casting-out demons in your name, and we- were-hindering him that [=because] he-was-following <u>us</u> not. 39So [=But] Jesus said, "Hinder him no [=not]. For [there] is no-one who will-do [deeds of] power upon [=in] my name and will-be-able quickly to- damn me. 40For who is [=acts] not according-to [=against] us is [=acts] on-behalf of-us.	49So having-answered, John said, "Overseer, we-saw some [=someone] casting-out demons in[c] your name, and we-were-hindering him that [=because] he-follows with <u>us</u> not." 50So [=But] Jesus said to him, "Hinder no [=them not]; for who is [=acts] not according-to [=against] you is [=acts] on-behalf of-you."

Matt 18:6-8

42 “And who ever might-give-a-drink [of] only [=even a] cup of-cold [=water to] one of-these smalls [=little ones] into [=in the] name [of a] disciple, amen I-say to-you might-he-destroy [=might he lose] not no [=at all] his wages.”

Mark 9:41-45

41 For who ever might-give-a-drink [of a] cup of-water [to] you that [=because] you-are in [you bear the] name[b] [of the] Anointed-one, amen I-say to-you that might-he-destroy [=might he lose] not no [=at all] his wages.”

[a] *spoke* ℵ B L Δ Θ Ψ 0274 579 892 1342 2427 *pc* sy[p]; *having-answered spoke* C; *and having-answered said* W *f*[13] 565 700 *pc*; *answered and said* D *f*[1] 205 *pc* it cop[bomss]; *so answered saying* A 1006 1506 𝔐 sy[h].
[b] *name* ℵ[2] B C* L Ψ *f*[1] 205 579 892 1342 1424 2427 *al* sy; *my name* ℵ* D W Δ Θ *f*[13] 1006 1506 𝔐 it vg cop.
[c] *in* 𝔭[45] 𝔭[75] ℵ B L Δ Θ Ξ Ψ *f*[1] *f*[13] 33 205 579 700 892 1342 2542 *pc*; *upon* A C D W Θ 1006 1506 𝔐.

186. Solutions to Stumbling Blocks (→ §276)

Matt 18:6-9

6 “So who ever might-cause-to-stumble one of-these smalls [=little ones] believing into [=in] me, it-is-profitable for-him in-order-that [a] donkey [=great] mill-stone might-be-hung around his neck and [that] he-might-be-sunk in the deep-part of-the sea. 7 Woe to-the world from [=because of] scandals [=stumbling blocks].

For [it is] inevitable [for] scandals to-come, nevertheless woe to-the person[a] through whom the scandal comes.
8 So if your hand or your foot causes-to-stumble you, cut-off it and throw [it] from you; it-is fine [=better] for-you to-enter into life maimed or lame or [=than] having two hands or two feet [only] to-be-thrown into the eternal fire.

Mark 9:42-48

42 “And who ever might-cause-to-stumble one of-these smalls [=little ones] believing into [=in] me, it-is fine [=better] for-him rather if [a] donkey [=great] mill-stone is-laid-around around his neck and he-has-been-thrown into the sea.

43 And if-ever your hand might-cause-to-stumble you, cut-away it; it-is fine [=better for] you to-enter into life maimed or [=than] having two hands [only] to-go-away into Gehenna, into the unquenchable fire. [b]

45 And if-ever your foot might-cause-to-stumble you, cut-away it; it-is fine [=better for] you to-enter into life lame or [=than] having two feet [only] to-be-thrown into Gehenna. [c]

Q 17:2, 1

2 “It-is-advantageous for-him if [a] stone [from a] milling-stone is-laid-around around his neck and [if] he-has-been-tossed into the sea or [=than] in-order-that he-might-cause-to-stumble one of-these smalls [=little ones].

1 [It is] inevitable [for] scandals to-come, nevertheless woe [to the one] through whom it-comes.”

Luke 17:2, 1

2 “It-is-advantageous for-him if [a] stone [from a] milling-stone is-laid-around around his neck and [if] he-has-been-tossed into the sea or [=than] in-order-that he-might-cause-to-stumble one of-these smalls [=little ones].”

1 So he-said to his disciples, “It-is not-possible [for] scandals to-come no [=not], nevertheless woe [to the one] through whom it-comes.”

9 And if your eye causes-to-stumble you, pull-out it and throw [it] from you. It-is fine [=better] for-you to-enter into life one-eyed [than] having two eyes [only] to-be-thrown into the Gehenna of-fire."	47 And if-ever your eye might-cause-to-stumble you, cast-out it; it-is fine [=better for] you to-enter into the kingdom of-god one-eyed or [=than] having two eyes [only] to-be-thrown into Gehenna, 48 where their worm expires not and the fire is-extinguished not."		

[a] *to-the person* ℵ D L f[1] 571 892 *pc* sy cop[samss] cop[bo]; *to-that person* B W Θ f[13] 1006 1506 𝔐 it cop[samss].
[b] *omit* ℵ B C L W Δ Ψ 0274 f[1] 28 565 892 2427 *pc* sy[s] cop; [44]*where their worm expires not and the fire is-extinguished not* A D Θ f[13] 1006 1342 1506 𝔐 it[mss] sy[p] sy[h].
[c] *omit* ℵ B C L W Δ Ψ 0274 f[1] 28 565 892 2427 *pc* sy[s] cop; [46]*where their worm expires not and the fire is-extinguished not* A D Θ f[13] 1006 1342 1506 𝔐 it[mss] sy[p] sy[h].
📖 Mk 9:48 – Isa 66:24

187. The Parable of the Salt (→ §32, §263)

Matt 5:13	**Mark 9:49-50**	Q 14:34-35	Luke 14:34-35
13 "You are the salt of-the land; so [=but] if-ever the salt might-become-tasteless, in what [=how] will-it-be-made-salty?	49 "For all will-be-made-salty [by] fire[b]. 50 The salt [is] fine, so [=but] if-ever the salt might-happen [=becomes] unsalty, in what will-you-flavor it [=will you use it as flavoring]? Have salt in themselves [=yourselves] and be-at-peace in [=with] one-another."	34 "The salt [is] fine so if-ever the salt might-become-tasteless, in what will-it-be-flavored [=will it be used as flavoring]?	34 "Therefore[c] the salt [is] fine, and so[d] if-ever the salt might-become-tasteless, in what will-it-be-flavored [=will it be used as flavoring]?
It-has-the-strength into no-one [=It is good for nothing] yet if no [=except], having-been-thrown[a] outside, to-be-tread-upon under [=by] the people."		35 Neither into [=for the] land neither [=nor] into [=for the] dung-heap is-it usable; they-throw it outside."	35 Neither into [=for the] land neither [=nor] into [=for the] dung-heap is-it usable; they-throw it outside. The [one] having ears to-hear, let-him-hear."

[a] *having-been-thrown* 𝔭[86] ℵ B C f[1] 33 205 892 *pc*; *to-be-thrown* D W Θ f[13] 1006 1342 1506 𝔐.
[b] *For all will-be-made-salty fire* ℵ B L Δ 0274 f[1] f[13] 205 565 700 1006 2427 *pc* sy[s] cop; *For all sacrifice will-be-made-salty salt* D it; *For all will-be-made-salty fire and all sacrifice will-be-made-salty salt* A C Θ Ψ 892 1506 𝔐 it[mss] vg sy[p].
[c] *Therefore* 𝔭[75] ℵ B L Θ f[13] 579 892 *pc*; *omit* A D W Ψ f[1] 1006 1506 𝔐 it vg sy cop[samss].
[d] *so* ℵ B D L Θ Ψ 0233 579 *pc* it[mss] sy[p] cop[samss]; *omit* 𝔭[75] A W f[1] f[13] 892 1006 1342 1506 𝔐 it[mss] vg sy[s] sy[c] cop.

188. The Parable of the Lost Sheep (→ §265, §277)

Matt 18:10-14	Q 15:4-5a, 7	Luke 15:3-7	Thomas 107
10 "See [that] you-might-despise no [=not] one of-these smalls [=little ones], for I-say to-you that their		3 So he-said to them this parable, saying,	

announcers [=angels] in [the] heavens look [upon] the face [of] my father in [the] heavens through all [=continuously].[a]			
12What [=How] supposes [=does it seem] to-you?	4"What person out of-you	4"What person out of-you	Jesus said, "The <Father's> kingdom is like a shepherd who had a hundred sheep. One of them, the largest, went astray. He left the ninety-nine and looked for the one until he found it. After he had toiled, he said to the sheep, 'I love you more than the ninety-nine.'"
If-ever one-hundred sheep might-happen [=might belong] to-some person and one out of-them might-be-deceived [=might wander off], will-he-excuse indeed-not [=would he not leave] the ninety nine upon the mountains and having-traveled [would he not] search [for] the [one] being-deceived?	having one-hundred sheep might-happen [=might belong] to-some person and one out of-them might-be-deceived [=might wander off], will-he-excuse indeed-not [=would he not leave] the ninety nine upon the mountains and having-traveled [would he not] search [for] the [one] having-been-destroyed [=having been lost]?	having one-hundred sheep and having-destroyed [=losing] out of-them one, quits [=leaves] not the ninety nine in the deserted [place] and travels upon [=goes after] the [one] having-been-destroyed [=having been lost] until he-might-find it?	
13And if-ever he-might-happen to-find it, amen	5aAnd if-ever he-might-happen	5And having-found [it] places [it] upon his shoulders rejoicing? 6And having-come into the house he-calls-together the [=his] friends and next-door-neighbors saying to-them, 'Be-rejoiced-with [=Be made happy with] me, that [=for] I-found my having-been-destroyed [=lost] sheep.'	
I-say to-you that he-rejoices upon [=over] it rather or [=more than]	to-find it, 7I-say to-you that he-rejoices upon [=over] it rather or [=more than] upon [=for] the	7I-say to-you that thus there-will-be [more] joy in heaven upon [=for] one sinful [person] repenting or [=than] upon [=for]	
upon [=for] the ninety nine no [=not] having-been-deceived.	ninety nine no [=not] having-been-deceived."	ninety nine righteouses [=righteous people] whoever [=who] have no need [=for] repentance."	
14Thus is not [the] wish in-front [=of] your father in [the] heavens in-order-that [=that] one of-these smalls [=little ones] might-be-destroyed."			

[a] *omit* ℵ B L* Θ* f^{1} f^{13} 33 892 *pc* sy^{s} cop^{sa}; 11*For the son of-the person came to-save the having-been-destroyed* D L^{C} W $Θ^{C}$ 1006 1342 1506 𝔐 vg it^{mss} sy^{c} sy^{p} sy^{h}.

Mark 9:50 (§187, p. 154) Q 7:35 (§126, p. 91)
Luke 9:50 (§185, p. 152)

189. On Reproving Those Close to You (→ §276, §278)

Matt 18:15-18

15“So if-ever your brother might-sin[a], leave [and] expose him between you and him alone. If-ever he-might-hear you, you-gained [back] your brother. 16So [=But] if-ever he-might-hear you no [=not], take-along with you yet one or two, in-order-that all speech [=every word] might-be-stood upon mouth [=might be confirmed by] two or three witnesses. 17So if-ever he-might-ignore them, say [so] to-the assembly; so [=but] if-ever he-might-ignore and [=even] the assembly, let-him-stand [=let him be] to-you even-as the Gentile or the tax-collector. 18Amen I-say to-you, whatsoever if-ever you-might-restrain upon the land, it-will-be having-been-restrained in heaven[b], and whatsoever if-ever you-might-loose upon the land, it-will-be having-been-loosed in heaven[c].”

Q 17:3

3“So if-ever your brother might-sin, rebuke him, and if-ever he-might-repent, excuse [=forgive] him.”

Luke 17:3

3“Pay-close-attention to-themselves [=Be on your guard]. If-ever your brother might-sin, rebuke him, and if-ever he-might-repent, excuse [=forgive] him.”

John 20:23

23“[If] ever you-might-excuse the sins of-some [=of someone], they-have-been-excused for-them, [and if] ever you-might-seize [=you might hold onto the sins] of-some [=of someone], they-have-been-seized.”

[a] *omit* ℵ B f^{1} 579 *pc* cop^{sa}; *into you* D L W Θ 1078 f^{13} 33 𝔐 vg it sy.
[b] *in heaven* B Θ f^{13} *pc*; *in the heavens* ℵ D^{C} L 33 579 892 *pc* vg^{mss} cop; *in the heaven* W f^{1} 1006 1342 1506 𝔐.
[c] *in heaven* ℵ B Θ f^{13} *pc*; *in the heavens* D L 33 579 *pc* vg^{mss} cop; *in the heaven* W f^{1} 892 1006 1342 1506 𝔐.
📖 Mt 18:15 – Lev 19:17; 📖 Mt 18:16 – Lev 19:15; Deut 19:15; 📖 Lk 17:3 – Lev 19:17

190. Matthew's Agreeing in Numbers

Matt 18:19-20

19“Again amen[a] I-say to-you that if-ever two out of-you might-agree upon the land around [=concerning] all [=every] event which if-ever they-might-ask, it-will-happen to-them along [=before] my father in [the] heavens. 20For which [=where] there-are two or three having-been-gathered into [=in] my-own name, there I-am in [the] middle of-them.”

Thomas 30; 77

30Jesus said, “Where there are three deities, they are divine. Where there are two or one, I am with that one.” 77Jesus said, “I am the light that is over all things. I am all: from me all came forth, and to me all attained. Split a piece of wood; I am there. Lift up the stone, and you will find me there.”

[a] *Again amen* B Θ f^{13} 33 1006 1342 1506 𝔐 it sy^{s} sy^{c} cop^{sa}; *So again* W Δ *pc* sy^{h}; *Again* ℵ D L f^{1} 579 892 *al* vg it^{mss} sy^{p} cop^{bo}.

191. On Forgiveness (→ §278)

Matt 18:21-22	Q 17:4	Luke 17:4
[21]Then Peter having-approached said to-him, "Lord, how-often will-sin my brother into [=against] me and will-I-excuse [=forgive] him? Until [=as many as] seven-times?" [22]Jesus says to-him, "I-say to-you not until seven-times but until seventy-times seven [=seventy-seven times]."	[4]"And if-ever seven-times he-might-sin into [=against] you and [=then] seven-times you-will-excuse [=you will forgive] him."	[4]"And if-ever seven-times of-the [=per] day he-might-sin into [=against] you and [=then] seven-times[a] might-turn-back to you[b] saying, 'I-repent,' you-will-excuse [=you will forgive] him."

[a] *seven-times* ℵ B D L Ψ 892 2542 *pc* it sy^{s} sy^{c} cop^{bomss}; *seven-times of-the day* A W Θ f^{1} f^{13} 1006 1342 1506 𝔐 vg it^{mss} sy^{p} sy^{h} cop^{sa} cop^{bomss}.
[b] *to you* ℵ A B D L Ψ f^{1} 205 579 892 2542 *al* vg it^{mss} sy; *omit* W Θ f^{13} 1006 1342 1506 𝔐.

192. Matthew's Parable of the Unforgiving Servant

Matt 18:23-35

[23]"Through this [=Therefore] the kingdom of-the heavens was-compared [to a] person, [a] king,
who wished to-discharge [=to settle] word [=accounts] with his slaves. [24]So his having-begun [=when
he was starting] to-discharge [the debts], one debtor of-ten-thousand talants [=5 million denarii]
was-offered to-him. [25]So [=But] his no having to-give-over [=when he could not repay] the lord[a]
ordered him and the woman [=his wife] and the [=his] descendants and all whatsoever he-has[b]
to-be-peddled [=to be sold off]. [26]Therefore the slave[c] having-fallen [on his face] was-worshiping him
saying, '[d] Be-patient upon [=with] me, and I-will-give-over all [I will repay everything] to-you.' [27]So
the lord of-that slave having-had-pity released him and excused [=erased] the loan for-him. [28]So
having-gone-out, that slave found one [of] his fellow-slaves who was-owing him one-hundred
denarii and having-seized him he-was-drowning [=he was choking him] saying, 'Give-over some if
[=whatever] you-are-in-debt.' [29]Therefore his fellow-slave having-fallen [on his face] [e] was-exhorting
him saying, 'Be-patient upon [=with] me, and I-will-give-over [I will repay] to-you [what I owe].' [30]So
[=But] he-wished not [to be merciful] but [rather] having-gone-away he-threw him into prison until[f]
he-might-give-over the being-in-debt [=what he owed]. [31]Therefore, his fellow-slaves having-seen
the having-happeneds [=the things that had happened] were-having-been-grieved very and having-
gone they-explained to-the lord of-themselves [=to their lord] all the having-happeneds [=all that
had happened]. [32]Then having-summoned him, his lord says to-him, 'Evil slave, I-excused all that
debit for-you, as-a-result-of [=because] you-exhorted me; [33]was-it-necessary not and [=also for] you
to-be-merciful [toward] your fellow-slave, like I-too was-merciful [toward] you?' [34]And his lord
having-been-angered delivered him to-the tormenters until which [time] he-might-give-over all
the being-in-debt [=that he owed][g]. [35]Thus and [=also] my heavenly father will-do to-you, if-ever
each [of] you-might-excuse no [=not] his brother[h] from your hearts."

[a] *the lord* ℵ B D L 579 vg it^{mss}; *his lord* W Θ f^{13} 33 892 1006 1342 1506 𝔐 it sy^{p} sy^{h} cop; *omit* f^{1} 700 sy^{s} sy^{c}.
[b] *he-has* B Θ f^{1} 1506 *pc*; *he-was-having* ℵ D L W f^{13} 33 892 1005 𝔐.
[c] *the slave* ℵ* B W f^{1} f^{13} 1005 1342 1506 𝔐 cop^{sa}; *that slave* ℵ^{2} D L Δ Θ 33 579 892 *al* vg it^{mss} sy cop^{bo}.
[d] *omit* B D Θ 700 *pc* vg it^{mss} sy^{s} sy^{c}; *Lord* ℵ L W f^{1} f^{13} 33 892 1006 1342 1506 𝔐 it sy^{p} sy^{h} cop.
[e] *omit* ℵ B C* D G L Θ 058 f^{1} 570 700 892 1424 *al* vg it^{mss} sy^{s} sy^{c} cop; *into his feet* C^{2} W f^{13} 33 1006 1342 𝔐 sy^{p} sy^{h}; *was-worshiping him and* 28.
[f] *omit* ℵ B C L 892; *which* D W Θ f^{1} f^{13} 33 1006 1342 𝔐.
[g] *omit* ℵ^{1} B D Θ f^{13} 700 1424 *pc* vg it sy^{s} sy^{c} cop; *to-him* ℵ* ℵ^{2} C L W f^{1} 33 892 1006 1342 1506 𝔐 sy^{p} sy^{h}.
[h] *omit* ℵ B D L Θ f^{1} 700 892 *pc* vg it^{mss} sy^{s} sy^{c} cop; *their wrongdoings* C W f^{13} 33 1006 1342 1506 𝔐 sy^{p} sy^{h}.

SYNOPTIC STUDY GUIDE 10

Special Matthew

Special Matthew refers to material unique to Matthew. Typically, this does not refer to unique words or phrases scattered throughout Matthew, but to whole stories or other blocks of material. All solutions to the Synoptic Problem agree that the source of this material cannot be known. On the Griesbach Hypothesis, it is simply part of Matthew's initial composition. On the Farrer Hypothesis, Special Matthew is material Matthew added to Mark that Luke did not take over, but its origin is unknowable. Conversely, some people call the Two-Document Hypothesis the *Four-Document* Hypothesis. For them, the four documents are Mark, Q, M (Special Matthew), and L (Special Luke). But neither M nor L is likely to have been a *document*, so Four-Document Hypothesis is not an ideal name. M (and L as well) lacks any coherence; it lacks the feel of having derived from a single written source. It is also significant that Special M has a higher degree of vocabulary style that is unique to Matthew: it makes it appear strongly that this material was composed by Matthew, not derived from a document with its own style. The same can be said of Special Luke and Luke's style. The material that makes up Special Matthew likely came from a number of places, including the author's community, the author's own imagination, long-standing oral tradition, written sources or partial sources, and the Hebrew Bible.

The following list does not exhaust what is unique to the Gospel of Matthew, but it offers a sample of Special Matthew material: Birth of Jesus (§7), Herod, the Magi, and the Infant Jesus (§9), Flight to and Return from Egypt (§12), the Law and the Prophets (§34), the Parable of the Weeds in the Field (§149) and its interpretation (§153), the Hidden Treasure and the Pearl (§154), the Dragnet (§155), the New and Old Treasures (§156), the Unforgiving Servant (§192), the Laborers in the Vineyard (§296), the Two Sons (§313), the Ten Virgins (§340), "Whoever Does This to the Least" (§342), the Interpretation of the Death of Judas (§366), the Sealing of Jesus' Tomb (§381), the Report of the Guard (§384), and the Great Commission (§387).

193. Leaving the Galilee

Matt 19:1-2	Mark 10:1	Luke 9:51
[1]And it-happened when Jesus completed these words, he-took-leave from the Galilee and went into the territories of-Judea, beyond the Jordan. [2]And many crowds followed him and he-healed them there.	[1]And having-gotten-up from-there he-goes into the territories of-Judea and beyond[a] the Jordan, and again crowds travel-together-with to [=gather around] him, and like he-had-been-accustomed [to doing], he-taught them again.	[51]So it-happened in the to-be-swamped the days [of] his transportation [=The days were drawing near for his being taken up], and he [himself] made-firm the [=set his] face to-travel into Jerusalem.

[a] *and beyond* ℵ B C* L Ψ 0274 892 2427 *pc* cop; *through the beyond* A 1006 1506 𝔐 sy^h; *beyond* C2 D G W Δ Θ f^1 f^{13} 579 656 1342 2542 *al* vg it sy^s sy^p.

Luke's Journey toward Jerusalem

194. Luke's Jesus in a Samaritan Village

Luke 9:52-56

52And he-sent-off announcers before his face [=in front of him]. And having-traveled they-entered into [a] village of-Samaritans like[a] [=in order] to-make-ready for-him. 53And they-received him not, that [=because] he-was traveling [=setting] his face into [=toward] Jerusalem. 54So [=But] the disciples James and John, having-seen [this], said, "Lord, do-you-wish [that] we-might-say [=we might command] fire to-descend from the heaven and to-annihilate them[b]?" 55So [=But] having-been-turned, he-rebuked them. 56And they-traveled into other [=another] village.

[a] *like* $\mathfrak{P}^{45}$ $\mathfrak{P}^{75}$ ℵ* B it; *with-the-result-that* $ℵ^{2}$ A C D L W Θ Ξ Ψ f^{1} f^{13} 33 892 1006 1342 1506 𝔐 cop^{bo}.
[b] *omit* $\mathfrak{P}^{45}$ $\mathfrak{P}^{75}$ ℵ B L Ξ 579 700* *pc* vg it^{mss} sy^{s} sy^{c} cop^{sa} cop^{bomss}; *like Elijah and did* A C D W Θ Ψ f^{1} f^{13} 33 892 1006 1506 𝔐 it sy^{p} sy^{h} cop^{bomss}.

195. On Following Jesus (→ §93)

Matt 8:19-22	**Q 9:57-60**	**Luke 9:57-62**	Thomas 86
		57And their traveling [=while they were traveling] in [=on] the way [=road]	
19And one scribe, having-approached, said to-him, "Teacher, I-will-follow you where if-ever you-might-go-away."	57And some [one] said to-him, "I-will-follow you where if-ever you-might-go-away."	some [one] said to him, "I-will-follow you where if-ever you-might-go-away[a]."	
20And Jesus says to-him, "The foxes have holes and the birds of-the heaven [have] nests, so [=but] the son of-the person has not [a place] wheresoever he-might-recline the [=his] head."	58And Jesus said to-him, "The foxes have holes and the birds of-the heaven [have] nests, so [=but] the son of-the person has not [a place] wheresoever he-might-recline the [=his] head."	58And Jesus said to-him, "The foxes have holes and the birds of-the heaven [have] nests, so [=but] the son of-the person has not [a place] wheresoever he-might-recline the [=his] head."	Jesus said, "<Foxes have> their dens and birds have their nests, but human beings have no place to lay down and rest."
		59So he-said to-other [=to another disciple], "Follow me."	
21So [=But an] other [of] his disciples said to-him, "Lord, first allow me to-go-away and to-bury my father." 22So [=But] Jesus says to-him, "Follow me and excuse [=leave] the dead to-bury the dead themselves."	59So [=but an] other said to-him, "Lord, first allow me to-go-away and to-bury my father." 60So [=But] he-says to-him, "Follow me and excuse [=leave] the dead to-bury the dead themselves."	So [=But] he-said, "Lord[b], allow me, having-gone-away, first to-bury my father." 60So [=But] he-said to-him, "Excuse [=Leave] the dead to bury the dead themselves,	

so [=but] you, having-gone-away, give-notice [about] the kingdom of-god." 61 So [=But an] other said, "I-will-follow you, lord; so [=but] first allow me to-bid-goodbye to-the [ones] into [=in] my house [=family]." 62 So Jesus said to him, "No-one having-thrown-on the [=putting his] hand upon [a] plow and looking into the behind [=back] is usable in-the kingdom of-god."

[a] *omit* 𝔭^{45} 𝔭^{75} ℵ B D L Ξ *f*^{1} 205 1342 pc it^{mss} vg sy^{s} sy^{c} cop^{sa}; *lord* A C W Θ Ψ *f*^{13} 33 892 1006 1506 𝔐 it^{mss} cop^{bo}.
[b] *Lord* 𝔭^{45} 𝔭^{75} ℵ A B^{2} C L W Θ Ξ Ψ 0181 *f*^{1} *f*^{13} 33 8921006 1342 1506 𝔐 it sy^{c} sy^{p} cop; *omit* B* D pc sy^{s}.

196. Luke's Sending of the Seventy-Two

Luke 10:1

1 So with [=after] these [things] the lord commissioned seventy two[a] others and sent-off them up two two[b] [=in pairs] before his face into all [=every] city and place [to] which he [himself] was-intending to-go.

[a] *seventy two* 𝔭^{75} B D 0181 *pc* vg it^{mss} sy^{s} sy^{c} cop^{sa}; *seventy* ℵ A C L W Θ Ξ Ψ *f*^{1} *f*^{13} 892 1006 1342 1506 𝔐 sy^{p} sy^{h} cop^{bo}.
[b] *two two* B Θ *f*^{13} 565 *al* sy^{h}; *two* ℵ A C D L W Ξ Ψ 0181 *f*^{1} 33 892 1006 1342 1506 𝔐.

197. Too Great a Harvest (→ §102)

Matt 9:37-38	**Q 10:2**	**Luke 10:2**	John 4:35	Thomas 73
37 Then he-says [to] his disciples, "The harvest for-one [=on the one hand] many [=is great], so [=but] the workers little [=are few]. 38 Therefore implore the lord of-the harvest so-that he-might-cast-out [=he might send] workers [out] into his harvest."	2 He-says [to] his disciples, "The harvest for-one [=on the one hand] many [=is great], so [=but] the workers little [=are few]. Therefore implore the lord of- the harvest so-that he-might-cast-out [=he might send] workers [out] into his harvest."	2 So he-was-saying to them, "The harvest for-one [=on the one hand] many [=is great], so [=but] the workers little [=are few]. Therefore implore the lord of- the harvest so-that workers he-might-cast-out[a] [=he might send out] into his harvest."	35 "[Do] you [yourselves] not say that 'It-is four-month yet [four months to go] and [then] the harvest comes'? Look! I-say to-you, lift-up your eyes and notice the regions that are white to harvest [=that are ready for the harvest]."	Jesus said, "The crop is huge but the workers are few, so beg the harvest boss to dispatch workers to the fields."

[a] *workers he-might-cast-out* 𝔭^{75} B D 0181 700; *he-might-cast-out workers* ℵ A C L W Θ Ξ Ψ *f*^{1} *f*^{13} it^{mss} vg.

198. Sheep and Wolves (→ §110)

Matt 10:16	Q 10:3	Luke 10:3	Thomas 39
[16]"Look! I [myself] send- off you like sheep in [the] middle of-wolves; therefore happen [=be] sensible like the snakes and guileless like the doves."	[3]"Leave. Look! I-send- off[a] you like sheep in [the] middle of-wolves."	[3]"Leave. Look! I-send-off[a] you like sacrificial-lambs in [the] middle of-wolves."	Jesus said, "The Pharisees and the scholars have taken the keys of knowledge and have hidden them. They have not entered nor have they allowed those who want to enter to do so. As for you, be as sly as snakes and as simple as doves."

[a] *I-send-off* 𝔓^{75} ℵ A B 579 *pc* cop^{samss}; *I send-off* C D L W Θ Ξ 0181 f^{1} f^{13} 33 892 1006 1506 𝔐 vg it^{mss} cop^{samss} cop^{bo}.

199. Missionary Provisions (→ §106)

Matt 10:9-10a	Q 10:4	Luke 10:4
[9]"Might-you-acquire no gold so-not [=nor] silver so-not [=nor] copper into your belts; [10a]no pouch into way [=for the road] so-not [=nor] two tunics so-not [=nor] sandals so-not [=nor] staff[a] . . . "	[4]"Bear no [=not] [a] moneybag, no pouch, no sandals, no staff and might-you-greet not-one [person] according-to [=along] the way."	[4]"Bear no [=not] [a] moneybag, no pouch, no sandals, and might-you-greet not-one [person] according-to [=along] the way."

[a] *staff* ℵ B D Θ f^{1} 33 205 892 1424 *al* vg it^{mss} sy^{p} cop^{sa} cop^{bo}; *staffs* C L W f^{13} 1006 1342 1506 𝔐 it^{mss}.
📖 Lk 10:4 – 2 Kgs 4:29

200. Dealing with Supporters and Opponents (→ §105, §107)

Matt 10:12-13, 10b-11, 7	Mark 6:10	Q 10:5-9	Luke 10:5-9	Thomas 14
[12]"So entering into the home, greet it. [13]And if-ever for-one the home might-be worthy, let-come your peace upon it; so [=but] if-ever it-might-be no [=not] worthy, let-be-turned-back your peace to you."		[5]"So into which ever home you-might-enter, first say, 'Peace to-this house.' [6]And if-ever for-one [a] son of-peace might-be there, let-come your peace upon him; so [=but] if no, let-turn-back your peace upon you. [7]So stay in the it [=same] home eating and drinking the along of-them [=whatever they place	[5]"So into which ever home you-might-enter, first say, 'Peace to-this house.' [6]And if-ever [a] son of-peace might-be there, upon him your peace will-be-rested; so [=but] if no in-effect [=on the other hand], it-will-head-back upon you. [7]So stay in it [=the same] home eating and drinking the along of-them [=whatever they place	Jesus said to them, "If you fast, you will bring sin upon yourselves, and if you pray, you will be condemned, and if you give to charity, you will harm your spirits.

10b“for the worker [is] worthy [of] his nourishment.”		before you]; for the worker [is] worthy [of] his wages. Head-out no [=not] out of-home into [another] home.	before you]; for the worker [is] worthy [of] his wages. Head-out no [=not] out of-home into [another] home.	When you go into any region and walk about in the countryside, when people take you in, eat what they serve you and heal the sick among them. After all, what goes into your mouth will not defile you; rather, it’s what comes out of your mouth that will defile you.”
11“So into which ever city or village you-might-enter, make-a-careful-search [for] what [=who] in it is worthy; and-there stay until ever you-might-go-out.”	10And he-was-saying to-them, “Where if-ever you-might-enter into [a] home, stay there until ever you-might-go-out from-there.”	8And into which ever city you-might-enter, and they-might-receive you, eat the being-placed-befores [=the things put before] you.	8And into which ever city you-might-enter, and they-might-receive you, eat the being-placed-befores [=the things put before] you.	
7“So traveling, preach saying that ‘The kingdom of-the heavens has-neared.’”		9And heal the being-ills in it [=those who are ill] and say to-them, ‘The kingdom of-god has-neared upon you.’”	9And heal the ills in it [=those who are ill] and say to-them, ‘The kingdom of-god has-neared upon you.’”	

There are no variants in this pericope that appear in English.

201. Responding to Inhospitable Cities (→ §108, §109, §162)

Matt 10:14-15	Mark 6:11	**Q 10:10-12**	**Luke 10:10-12**
14“And who ever might-receive no [=not] you so-not [nor if] he-might-hear	11“And which ever place might-receive you no [=not] so-not they-might-hear [=so they will not hear]	10“So into which ever city you-might-enter and they-might-receive you no	10“So [=But] into which ever city you-might-enter and they-might-receive
your words, going-out outside that home or city,	you, traveling-out from-	[=not], going-out outside	you no [=not], having-gone-out into its wide-streets say, 11‘And [=Even]
shake-out the dust [from]	there shake-out the dirt	that city 11shake-out the	the dust out [of] your city having-been-clung to-us
your feet.	beneath your feet into [=as] testimony to-them.[a]”	dust [from] your feet.	into the feet [=sticking to our feet], we-wipe-off [our feet] to-you; nevertheless, know this, that the kingdom of-god has-neared[b].
15Amen I-say to-you, more-tolerable will-it-be [in the] land of-Sodoms and of-		12I-say to-you that it-will-be more-tolerable in-Sodoms	12I-say to-you that in-Sodoms

Matt	Q	Luke
Gomorrahs in [=on the] day of-judgment or [=than in] that city.”	in [=on] that day or [=than in] that city.”	in [=on] that day it-will-be more-tolerable or [=than in] that city.”

[a] *omit* ℵ B C D L W Δ Θ 565 892 1342 2427 2542 *pc* vg it^{mss} sy^{s} cop^{sa}; *Amen I-say to-you, more-tolerable will-it-be Sodoms or Gomorrahs in day of-judgment or that city* A f^{1} f^{13} 33 1006 1506 𝔐 it^{mss} sy^{p} sy^{h}.
[b] *omit* 𝔓^{45} 𝔓^{75} ℵ B D L Ξ 0181 33 579 1342 1424 1582 2542 *pc* vg it^{mss} sy^{s} sy^{c} cop^{bo}; *upon you* A C W Θ Ψ f^{13} 1006 1506 𝔐 sy^{p} sy^{h} cop^{sa}.

202. Woes on Galilean Cities (→ §127)

Matt 11:21-23b	**Q 10:13-15**	**Luke 10:13-15**
21“Woe to-you Chorazin, woe to-you Bethsaida, that [=because] if the [signs of] powers having-happened in [=among] you happened in Tyre and Sidon, they-repented ever [=they would have repented] old-days [=long ago] in sack-cloth and ash. 22Nevertheless I-say to-you, it-will-be more-tolerable [in] Tyre and Sidon in [=on the] day of-judgment or [=than] for-you. 23bAnd you, Capharnaum, will-you-be-exalted no [=not] until [=to] heaven? You-will-descend[a] until [=to] Hades . . . ”	13“Woe to-you Chorazin, woe to-you Bethsaida, that [=because] if the [signs of] powers having-happened in [=among] you were-happened [=were made to happen] in Tyre and Sidon, they-repented ever [=they would have repented] old-days [=long ago] in sack-cloth and ash. 14Nevertheless it-will-be more-tolerable [in] Tyre and Sidon in [=at] the judgment or [=than] for-you. 15And you, Capharnaum, will-you-be-exalted no [=not] until [=to] heaven? You-will-descend until [=to] the Hades.”	13“Woe to-you Chorazin, woe to-you Bethsaida, that [=because] if the [signs of] powers having-happened in [=among] you were-happened[b] [=were made to happen] in Tyre and Sidon, they-repented ever [=they would have repented] old-days [=long ago] sitting in sack-cloth and ash. 14Nevertheless it-will-be more-tolerable [in] Tyre and Sidon in [=at] the judgment or [=than] for-you. 15And you, Capharnaum, will-you-be-exalted no [=not] until [=to] heaven? You-will-descend until [=to] the Hades[c].”

[a] *You-will-descend* B D W *pc* it vg sy^{s} sy^{c} cop^{sa}; *you-will-be-tossed-down* ℵ C L Θ f^{1} f^{13} 33 892 1006 1342 1506 𝔐 sy^{p} cop^{bo}.
[b] *were-happened* 𝔓^{45} 𝔓^{75} ℵ B D L Θ Ξ f^{13} 33 579 700 892 1342 1424 *pc*; *happened* A C W Ψ f^{1} 1006 1506 𝔐.
[c] *the Hades* 𝔓^{75} B L 1506 *pc*; *Hades* 𝔓^{45} ℵ A C D W Θ Ξ Ψ f^{1} f^{13} 33 892 1006 1342 𝔐 cop.

203. On Rewards (→ §119)

Matt 10:40	**Q 10:16**	**Luke 10:16**	John 13:20
40“The [one] receiving you receives me and the [one] receiving me receives the [one] having-sent-off me.”	16“The [one] receiving you receives me and the [one] receiving me receives the [one] having-sent-off me.”	16“The [one] hearing you hears me and the [one] refusing me refuses the [one] having-sent-off me.”	20“Amen amen I-say to-you, the [one] taking [=who receives] ever some [=whoever] I-will-send takes [=receives] me, so [=and] the [one] taking [=receiving] me takes [=receives] the [one] having-sent me.”

There are no variants in this pericope that appear in English.

204. Luke's Return of the Seventy-Two

Luke 10:17-20

17 So the seventy two[a] returned with joy saying, "Lord, and [=even] the demons submit to-us in
your name." 18 So he-said to-them, "I-was-catching-sight-of the adversary having-fallen out of-the
heaven like [a] flashing-light. 19 Look! I-have-given[b] you authority to-tread above [=upon] snakes
and scorpions and upon [=over] all the power of-the enemy, and no-one might-be-unrighteous[c]
[to] you not no [=at all]. 20 Nevertheless, rejoice in this no [=not] that the spirits submit to-you, so
[=but] rejoice that your names have-been-written in the heavens."

[a] *seventy two* 𝔓[45] 𝔓[75] B D *pc* vg it[mss] sy[s] cop[sa] cop[bomss]; *seventy* ℵ A C L W Θ Ξ Ψ *f*[1] *f*[13] 33 892 1006 1342 1506 𝔐 sy[p] sy[c] sy[h] cop[bomss].

[b] *I-have-given* 𝔓[75] ℵ B C* L W *f*[1] 205 579 700 892 1342 1424 2542 *pc* vg it[mss] cop[sa] cop[bo]; *I-give* 𝔓[45] A C[3] D Θ Ψ *f*[13] 33 1006 1506 𝔐 sy.

[c] *might-be-unrighteous* 𝔓[45] 𝔓[75] B C Ψ *f*[13] 892 1006 1342 1605 𝔐; *will-be-unrighteous* ℵ A D E L W Θ 1 33 543 983 *al.*

205. Jesus Thanks the Father (→ §128)

Matt 11:25-27	**Q 10:21-22**	**Luke 10:21-22**	John 3:35; 7:29; 10:15a; 13:3a; 17:2a	Thomas 61
25 In that [=At the] proper-time, Jesus, having-answered, said, "I-acknowledge to-you, father, lord of-heaven and of-land, that you-hid these [things] from wises and intelligents [=wise and intelligent people] and you-revealed them [to] infants. 26 Yes, father, that [=because] thus happened [=was your] contentment in-front of-you. 27 All [things] were-delivered to-me under [=by] my father and no-one understands the son if no [=except] the father, nor [does] some [one] understand the	21 In [=At that time] he-said, "I-acknowledge to-you, father, lord of-heaven and of-land, that you-hid these [things] from wises and intelligents [=wise and intelligent people] and you-revealed them [to] infants. Yes, father, that [=because] thus happened [=was your] contentment in-front of-you. 22 All [things] were-delivered to-me under [=by] my father and no-one knows the son if no [=except] the father, nor [does] some [one] know the	21 In it the [=same] hour, he-was-glad in the holy spirit[a] and[b] said, "I-acknowledge to-you, father, lord of-heaven and of-land, that you-hid-away these [things] from wises and intelligents [=wise and intelligent people] and you-revealed them [to] infants. Yes, father, that [=because] thus happened [=was your] contentment in-front of-you. 22[c] All [things] were-delivered to-me under [=by] my father and no-one knows what [=who] the son is if no [=except] the father, and what [=who]	3:35 "The father loves the son and has-given all [things] in [=into] his hand." 7:29 "I recognize him, that [=because] I-am along [=from] him, and-that [one] sent-off me." 10:15a "just-as the father knows me, I-too know the father" 13:3a "having-known that the father gave all [things] to-him into the [=his] hands" 17:2a "Just-as you [yourself] gave him authority [=over] all flesh"	Jesus said, "Two will recline on a couch; one will die, one will live." Salome said, "Who are you, mister? You have climbed onto my couch and eaten from my table as if you are from someone." Jesus said to her, "I am the one who comes from what is whole. I was granted from the things of my Father." "I am your disciple." "For this reason I say, if one is whole, one will be filled with light, but if one is divided, one

father if no [=except] the son and to-whom if-ever the son might-want to-reveal.”	father if no [=except] the son and to-whom if-ever the son might-want to-reveal.”	is the father if no [=except] the son, and to-whom if-ever the son might-want to-reveal.”		will be filled with darkness.”

[a] *in the holy spirit* ℵ D L Ξ 33 *al* it; *in-the holy spirit* 𝔓^{75} B C Θ *f* ^{1} 579 *al*; *in-the spirit* A W Ψ *f* ^{13} 1006 1342 1506 𝔐; *in the spirit* 𝔓^{45} 892 2542 *pc*.
[b] *omit* 𝔓^{45} 𝔓^{75} ℵ B D Ξ *pc* it^{mss} vg sy^{s} sy^{c} cop^{sa}; *Jesus* A C W Ψ *f* ^{1} 892 1006 1342 1506 𝔐 it^{mss} cop^{bo}.
[c] *omit* 𝔓^{45} 𝔓^{75} ℵ B D L X 070 *f* ^{1} *f* ^{13} 33 205 579 892 1342 1424 2542 *al* it^{mss} vg sy^{s} sy^{c} cop; *And having-turned to the disciples he-said* A C W Θ Ψ 1006 1506 𝔐 it sy^{p}.

206. The Fortunate Disciples (→ §145)

Matt 13:16-17	**Q 10:23-24**	**Luke 10:23-24**	Thomas 17
		[23] And having-been-turned to the disciples, he-said according-to own [=to each one],	Jesus said, “I will give you what no eye has seen, what no ear has heard, what no hand has touched, what has not arisen in the human heart.”
[16]“So, fortunate [are] your eyes that [=because] they-look [=they see] and your ears that [=because] they-hear.	[23]“Fortunate [are] the eyes looking [=at that] which	“Fortunate [are] the eyes looking [=at that] which you-look [at],	
[17]For amen I-say to-you that many prophets and righteous [people]	you-look [at], [24]for I-say to-you that many prophets and kings	[24]for I-say to-you that many prophets and kings	
desired to-see [that] which you-look [at] and [=but] saw not, and to-hear [that] which you-hear and [=but] heard not.”	-ed* to-see [that] which you-look [at] and [=but] saw not, and to-hear [that] which you-hear and [=but] heard not.”	wished to-see [that] which you [yourselves] look [at] and [=but] saw not, and to-hear [that] which you-hear and [=but] heard not.”	

*IQP could not decide which, if either, of Matthew’s ‘desired’ or Luke’s ‘wished’ was original to Q.
There are no variants in this pericope that appear in English.

207. The Greatest Commandments (→ §318)

Matt 22:34-40	Mark 12:28-34	**Luke 10:25-28**
[34]So the Pharisees, having-heard that he-muzzled the Sadducees, were-gathered upon [=because of] it. [35]And one out of-them, [a] lawyer, testing him questioned,	[28]And one of-the scribes, having-approached, [and] having-heard them discussing, [and] having-seen that he-answered them well,	[25]And look! some lawyer got-up trying him [c] saying, “Teacher, having-done what will-I-inherit [=what must I do to inherit] eternal
[36]“Teacher, what-kind-of [=which] commandment in the law [is] great [=the greatest]?” [37]So he-spoke to-him,	questioned him, “What-kind-of [=Which] commandment is first of-all?” [29]Jesus answered[a] that “[The] first is, ‘HEAR, ISRAEL, THE LORD OUR GOD [the] LORD IS ONE.’ [30]And	life?” [26]So he-said to him, “What has-been-written in the law? How do-you-read [that]?”

"‘YOU-WILL-LOVE [the] LORD YOUR GOD IN [=with] YOUR WHOLE HEART AND IN [=with] YOUR WHOLE SOUL AND IN [=with] YOUR WHOLE MIND.’

38 This is the great [=greatest] and first commandment. 39 So [=And a] second [is] comparable-to it: ‘YOU-WILL-LOVE YOUR NEIGHBOR LIKE YOURSELF.’ 40 The whole law and the prophets is-hung in [=on] these two commandments."

‘YOU-WILL-LOVE THE LORD YOUR GOD OUT [=with] YOUR WHOLE HEART AND OUT [=with] YOUR WHOLE SOUL AND OUT [=with] YOUR WHOLE MIND, AND OUT [=with] YOUR WHOLE MIGHT.’ [b] 31 This [is the]

second, ‘YOU-WILL-LOVE YOUR NEIGHBOR LIKE YOURSELF.’ There-is not another commandment greater [than] these." 32 And the scribe said to-him, "Well [said], teacher, you-said upon [=you spoke with] truth that he-is one and there-is not another nevertheless [=besides] him, 33 and to-love him out [=with] the whole heart and out [=with] the whole comprehension and out [=with] the whole might and to-love the neighbor like oneself is more-excessive [than] all the burnt-offerings and sacrifices." 34 And Jesus having-seen that he-was-answered intelligently said to-him, "You-are not far-away from the kingdom of-god." And no-one no-longer was-daring to-question him.

27 So having-answered he-said, "YOU-WILL-LOVE [the] LORD YOUR GOD OUT [=with] YOUR WHOLE HEART AND IN [=with] YOUR WHOLE SOUL AND IN [=with] YOUR WHOLE MIGHT, AND IN [=with] YOUR WHOLE

MIND, AND YOUR NEIGHBOR LIKE YOURSELF."

28 So he-said to-him, "You-answered correctly; do this and you-will-live."

[a] *Jesus answered* ℵ B L Δ Ψ 33 579 1342; *So Jesus answered him* A C 1006 𝔐 vg sy^{h}; *So having-answered he-said to-him* D W Θ f^{1} f^{13} 205 565 1506 *pc* cop^{bo}.

[b] *omit* ℵ B E L Δ Ψ 1342 2427 *pc* cop^{sa}; *This first commandment* A D W Θ f^{1} f^{13} 33 1006 892 1506 𝔐 vg it^{mss} sy cop^{bomss}.

[c] *omit* ℵ B L Ξ 579 *pc*; *and* A C D W Θ Ψ f^{1} f^{13} 33 892 1006 1342 1506 𝔐 vg it^{mss}.

📖 Mt 22:37 – Deut 6:5; 📖 Mt 22:39 – Lev 19:18; 📖 Mk 12:29 – Deut 6:4, 5; 📖 Mk 12:33 – 1 Sam 15:22; 📖 Lk 10:27 – Deut 6:5; Lev 19:18; 📖 Lk 10:28 – Lev 18:5

208. Luke's Parable of the Good Samaritan

Luke 10:29-37

29 So [=But] wishing to-be-righteous himself he-said to Jesus, "And what [=who] is my neighbor?"
30 Having-imagined [=Answering], Jesus said, "Some person was-descending from Jerusalem into
Jericho and bandits ambushed [him], who and [=also] having-stripped him and having-placed
blows [=laid a beating upon him] they-went-away excusing [=leaving him] half-dead. 31 So [=But]
according-to [=by] chance, some priest was-descending in [=along] that way and having-seen
him passed-by-on-the-other-side. 32 So likewise [a] Levite and [=also] having-come according-to
[=past] the place and having-seen [him] passed-by-on-the-other-side. 33 So [=But] some venturing
Samaritan came according-to [=upon] him and having-seen [a] had-pity, 34 and having-approached
he-bandaged his wounds pouring-on olive-oil and wine, so [=and] having-put-upon [=having put]
him upon the [=his] own animal he-led him into [an] inn and took-care of-him. 35 And upon the
tomorrow [=the next day], having-cast-out [b] [=taking out some money] he-gave two denarii to-the
inn-keeper and said, ‘Take-care of-him, and which some ever [=whatever] you-might-overspend

I [myself] will-give-over to-you in me to-come-back-through [=when I pass by here again].' [36]What [=Which] of-these three [do] you [yourself] suppose to-have-happened [=to have been a] neighbor of-the [man] having-fallen-in into [=who fell into the hands of] the bandits?" [37]So he-said, "The [one] having-done [=having] mercy with [=on] him." So [c] Jesus said to-him, "Travel [=Go] and you [yourself] do likewise."

[a] *omit* 𝔓45 𝔓75 ℵ B L Ξ f^1 33 205 700 892 1342 *pc* it; *him* A C D W Θ Ψ f^{13} 1006 1506 𝔐 vg it[mss] sy cop[sa].
[b] *having-cast-out* 𝔓45 𝔓75 ℵ B D Ξ f^1 33 205 892 1342 *pc* it sy[s] sy[c] sy[p]; *having-gone-out* A C* W Θ Ψ f^{13} 1006 1506 𝔐 sy[h].
[c] *omit* 𝔓45 𝔓75 ℵ B L Ξ Ψ 070 f^1 205 892 1342 *pc* cop[sa]; *therefore* A C D W Θ f^{13} 33 1006 1506 𝔐 sy[p] sy[h] cop[bo].

209. Luke's Anecdote about Mary and Martha (→ §133, §345)

Luke 10:38-42

[38]So in[a] the to-travel them [=as they moved on] he [himself] entered into some village; so [=and] some woman [by the] name Martha hailed him [b]. [39]And there-was [a] sister to-such [=of this woman] being-called Mary, and having-been-seated-near to the feet of-the lord she-heard [=she listened to] his word [=what he was saying]. [40]So [=But] Martha was-being-distracted around [=concerning] many service [=tasks]. So having-stood-by [=approaching] she-said, "Lord is-it-of-concern not to-you that my sister quit [=left] me to-serve alone? Therefore say to-her in-order-that she-might-assist me." [41]So [=But] having-answered the lord said to-her, "Martha, Martha, you-worry and are-distracted around [=about] many [things], [42]so [=but] there-is one need. For Mary chose the good portion whichever will-be-taken-away [from] her not."

John 11:1; 12:1-3

[11:1]So there-was some [man] being-ill, Lazarus from Bethany, out of-the [=from the] village of-Mary and of-Martha her sister.
[12:1]Therefore six days before the passover Jesus went into Bethany where Lazarus was, whom Jesus raised out [=from the] dead. [2]Therefore they-did [=they made a] banquet for-him there, and Martha was-serving, so [=and] Lazarus was one out of-the dinings [=one of those dining] together-with him. [3]Therefore Mary, having-taken [a] liter of-valuable ointment of-liquid nard, smeared the feet of-Jesus and dried his feet [with] her hairs. So the home was-fulfilled [=was filled] out [=by] the fragrance of-the ointment.

[a] *So in* 𝔓45 𝔓75 ℵ B L Ξ 33 579 892 1342 2542 pc sy[s] sy[c] cop; *So it-happened in* A C D W Θ Ψ f^1 f^{13} 1006 1506 𝔐 vg it sy[p] sy[h].
[b] *omit* 𝔓45 𝔓75 B cop[sa]; *into the home* ℵ* ℵ[2] C L Ξ 33 579 *pc*; *into her home* ℵ[1] C[3]; *into her house* A D W Θ Ψ 070 f^1 f^{13} 892 1006 1342 1506 𝔐 vg it[mss] sy cop[bo].

210. The Lord's Prayer (→ §43)

Matt 6:7-13

[7]"So, praying you-might-babble no [=not] even-as the Gentiles, for they-suppose that in their wordiness they-will-be-paid-attention-to. [8]Therefore, be-compared no [=not] to-them, for your father recognizes [that] of-which you-have need before you [yourselves] to-ask [=ask] him. [9]Therefore you [yourselves must] pray thus: 'Our father in the heavens, let-be-made-holy your name, [10]let-come your kingdom,

Q 11:2-4

[2]"Whenever you-might-pray say, 'Father, let-be-made-holy your name, let-come your kingdom,

Luke 11:1-4

[1]And it-happened in the to-be him [=while he was] in some place praying, like [=when] he-stopped, some [=one of] his disciples said to him, "Lord, teach us to-pray, just-as and [=even] John taught his disciples." [2]So he-said to-them,

"Whenever you-might-pray say, 'Father, let-be-made-holy your name, let-come your kingdom, [b]

Matt	Q	Luke
let-happen your wish like in heaven and [=also] upon land [=earth]. 11 Give to-us today our bread [for] the coming-day, 12 and excuse us our debts, like and [=also] we [ourselves] excused our debtors. 13 And might-you-bring us no [=not] into [a] test, but rescue us from the evil [one] [a].'"	3 give to-us today our bread [for] the coming-day, 4 and excuse us our debts, like and [=also] we [ourselves] excused our debtors; and might-you-bring us no [=not] into [a] test.'"	3 <u>give</u> to-us according-to [a] day [=every day] our bread [for] the coming-day, 4 and excuse us our sins, for and [=even] we [ourselves] excuse all [those] being-in-debt to-us; and might-you-bring us no [=not] into [a] test [c].'"

[a] *omit* א B D Z f^1 205 *pc* it^{mss} vg; *that the kingdom and the power and the power and the glory is yours into the ages. Amen.* L W Θ f^{13} 33 892 1006 1342 1506 𝔐 it^{mss} sy cop^{sa}; *that the kingdom of-the father and the son and the holy spirit is yours into the ages. Amen.* 1253 *pc.*

[b] *omit* 𝔭^{75} B L f^1 f^{13}42 *pc* vg sy^s sy^c; *let-happen your wish like in heaven and upon land* א A C D W Θ Ψ f^{13} 33 892 1006 1506 𝔐 it cop^{bomss}; *let-happen your wish* vg^{mss} cop^{sa} cop^{bomss}.

[c] *omit* 𝔭^{75} א* B L f^1 700 vg sy^s cop^{sa}; *but rescue us from the evil* A C D W Θ Ψ f^{13} 33 892 1006 1506 𝔐 it vg^{mss} sy^c sy^p.

211. Luke's Parable of the Persistent Friend

Luke 11:5-8

5 And he-said to them, "What [=Who] out of-you will-have [a] friend and will-travel to him [at] midnight and might-say to-him, 'Friend, lend me three breads, 6 since my friend arrived to me out way [=from a journey] and I-have not which [=anything] I-will-place-before him.' 7 And-that [person] having-answered from-within might-say, 'Present me no troubles [=Don't bother me]; the door has-been-locked already and my young-children are with me into [=in] the bed. I-am-able not having-gotten-up to-give you [anything].' 8 I-say to-you, and [=even] if he-will-give to-him not having-gotten-up through [=because] to-be [=he is] his friend, in-effect [=indeed] through [=because of] his shameless-persistence having-been-raised he-will-give him whatsoever he-needs."

There are no variants in this pericope that appear in English.

212. God's Answering of Prayer (→ §53)

Matt 7:7-11	**Q 11:9-13**	**Luke 11:9-13**	John 16:24; 14:13-14; 15:7	Thomas 92; 94; 2
7 "Ask and it-will-be-given to-you, search and you-will-find, knock and it-will-be-opened to-you; 8 for all [=each one] asking takes [=receives], and the [one] searching finds, and to-the [one] knocking it-will-be-opened. 9 Or what person is [there] out of-you,	9 "I-say to-you, ask and it-will-be-given to-you, search and you-will-find, knock and it-will-be-opened to-you; 10 for all [=each one] asking takes [=receives], and the [one] searching finds, and to-the [one] knocking it-will-be-opened. 11 What person is [there] out of-you,	9 "I-too say to-you, ask and it-will-be-given to-you, search and you-will-find, knock and it-will-be-opened to-you; 10 for all [=each one] asking takes [=receives], and the [one] searching finds, and to-the [one] knocking it-is-opened[b]. 11 So what father out of-you [when] the	16:24 "Until right-now you-asked not no-one [=for anything] in my name; ask and you-will-take in-order-that your joy might-be having-been-fulfilled." 14:13 "And [if] ever you-might-ask some which [=for anything at all] in my name, I-will-do this, in-	92 Jesus said, "Seek and you will find. In the past, however, I did not tell you the things about which you asked me then. Now I am willing to tell them, but you are not seeking them." 94 Jesus <said>, "One who seeks will find, and for <one who knocks> it will be opened."

who [when] his son will-ask [for] bread will-give-to him [a] stone no [=instead]? [10]Or and [=And if] he-will-ask[a] [for a] fish will-he-give-to him [a] snake no [=instead]?	who [when] his son will-ask [for] bread will-give-to him [a] stone no [=instead]? [12]Or and [=And if] he-will-ask[a] [for a] fish will-give-to him [a] snake no [=instead]?	son will-ask [for a] fish, and in-place of-fish will-give-to him [a] snake? [12]Or and [=And if] he-will-ask [for an] egg he-will-give-to him [a] scorpion?	order-that the father might-be-glorified in the son. [14]If-ever you-might-ask me [for] some [thing] in my name, I [myself] will-do [it]." [15:7]"If-ever you-might-stay [=you might remain] in me and my speech [=words] might-stay [=might remain] in you, ask which if-ever [=for whatever] you-might-wish, and it-will-happen for-you."	[2]Jesus said, "Those who seek should not stop seeking until they find. When they find, they will be disturbed. When they are disturbed, they will marvel, and will reign over all. <And after they have reigned they will rest.>"
[11]Therefore, if you,	[13]Therefore, if you,	[13]Therefore, if you, being-at-one's-disposals [=being by nature]		
being evil, recognize [how] to-give good presents [to] your descendants, how-great rather [=how much more] your father in the heavens will-give good [things] to-the askings [=to those who ask] him."	being evil, recognize [how] to-give good presents [to] your descendants, how-great rather [=how much more] the father out of-heaven will-give good [things] to-the askings [=to those who ask] him."	evil, recognize [how] to-give good presents [to] your descendants, how-great rather [=how much more] the father out of-heaven will-give [the] holy spirit to-the askings [=to those who ask] him."		

[a] *he-will-ask* ℵ* B C Θ it[mss] sy[c] sy[p]; *if-ever he-might-ask* ℵ[1] L W *f*[1] *f*[13] 33 892 1006 1506 𝔐 it[mss] vg it.
[b] *it-is-opened* 𝔓[75] B D; *it-will-be-opened* 𝔓[45] ℵ C L Θ Ψ *f*[1] *f*[13] 3 579 700 892 1241 2542 *pm*; <u>*it-will-be-opened*</u> A K W G Δ 565 1424 *pm*.

213. Charges of Magic (→ §101, §136, §138, §218)

Matt 9:32-34; 12:25-28	Mark 3:22-26	**Q 11:14-15, 16, 17-20**	**Luke 11:14-20**	John 7:20; 10:20; 8:48, 52a
[9:32]So their going-out [=when they were leaving], look! they-offered [=they brought] to-him [a] mute person[a] being-demon-possessed [=a mute demoniac].				[7:20]"The crowd answered, "You-have [a] demon. What searches [=Who is trying] to-kill you?"
[33]And the demon having-been-cast-		[14]And he-cast-out [a] mute demon. And the demon having-been-cast-out the	[14]And he-was casting-out [a] demon and it was mute. So it-happened the demon having-	[10:20]So many out of-them [=many of them] were-saying, "He-has [a] demon and is-insane. What [=Why do you] hear [=listen to] him?"

out the mute [person] talked. And the crowds were-astonished saying, “Thus [=The likes of this] never appeared in Israel.”		mute [person] talked and the crowds were-astonished.	gone-out [=when the demon came out that] the mute [person] talked and the crowds were-astonished.	8:48The Judeans answered and said to-him, “[Is it] not well [=right when] we [ourselves] say that ‘You are [a] Samaritan and you-have [a] demon?’”
34So [=But] the Pharisees were-saying, “In [=By] the magistrate of-the demons he-casts-out the demons.”	22And the scribes having-descended from Jerusalems, were-saying that “He-has Beelzebul[c]” and that “In [=By] the magistrate of-the demons he-casts-out demons”	15So [=But] some said, “In [=By] Beelzebul, the magistrate of-the demons, he-casts-out the demons.	15So [=But] some out of-them [=some of them] said, “In [=By] Beelzebul, the magistrate of-the demons, he-casts-out the demons.”	52aTherefore the Judeans said to-him, “Now we-have-known that you-have [a] demon.”
		16So some were-searching [for a] sign along [=from] him.	16So others, testing [him], were-searching [for a] sign along [=from] him.	
12:25So, having-recognized[b] their deliberations, he-said to-them,	23And having-summoned them he-was-saying [=he was speaking] to-them in parables. “How [is] adversary able to-cast-out adversary?	17So having-recognized their ruminations, he-said to-them,	17So [=But] he, having-recognized their ruminations, said to-them,	
“All [=Every] kingdom having-been-divided according-to [=against] itself is-made-desolate and all [=every] city or home having-been-divided according-to [=against] itself will-be-stood not [=will not stand].	24And if-ever [a] kingdom might-be-divided upon [=against] itself, that kingdom is-able not to-be-stood [=will not stand]. 25And if-ever [a] home might-be-divided upon [=against] itself, that home will-be-able not to-be-stood [=will not stand].	“All [=Every] kingdom having-been-divided according-to [=against] itself is-made-desolate and all [=every] home having-been-divided according-to [=against] itself will-be-stood not [=will not stand].	“All [=Every] kingdom having-been-divided-up upon [=against] itself is-made-desolate and house upon [=against] house falls.	
26And if the adversary casts-out [an] adversary, he-was-divided [=he would be divided] upon [=against] itself.	26And if the adversary got-up upon [=rose against] itself, and was-	18And if the adversary was-divided-up upon	18So and [=And also] if the adversary was-divided-up upon [=against] itself,	
Therefore how will-be-stood [=will stand] his kingdom?	divided he-is-able not to-stand, but has end [=would fall].”	[=against] itself, how his kingdom will-be-stood [=will his kingdom stand]?	how his kingdom will-be-stood [=will his kingdom stand]? That [=Because]	

27 And if I [myself] cast-out the demons in [=by] Beelzebul, in what [=by whose authority do] your sons cast-out [demons]? Through [=Because of] this they [themselves] will-be your judges. 28 So [=But] if I [myself] cast-out the demons in [=by the] spirit of-god, consequently [=then] the kingdom of-god loomed upon [=over] you."		19 And if I [myself] cast-out the demons in [=by] Beelzebul, in what [=by whose authority do] your sons cast-out [demons]? Through [=Because of] this they [themselves] will-be your judges. 20 So [=But] if I [myself] cast-out the demons in [=by the] finger of-god, consequently [=then] the kingdom of-god loomed upon [=over] you."	you-say to-cast-out me [=that I cast out] the demons in [=by] Beelzebul. 19 So if I [myself] cast-out the demons in [=by] Beelzebul, in what [=by whose authority do] your sons cast-out [demons]? Through [=Because of] this they [themselves] your judges will-be. 20 So [=But] if I [myself] cast-out[d] the demons in [=by the] finger of-god, consequently [=then] the kingdom of-god loomed upon [=over] you."	

[a] *person* C D L W Θ f^{1} 33 1006 1342 𝔐 it vg; *omit* ℵ B f^{13} 892 *pc* sy^{s} sy^{p} cop.
[b] *having-recognized* ℵ* B cop^{sa}; *So Jesus, having-recognized* C L Q W f^{1} f^{13} 1006 1342 1506 𝔐 vg it^{mss} sy^{p}; *So Jesus, seeing* 13 33 892^{C} *pc* cop^{bomss}; *So, seeing* 𝔭^{21} ℵ^{1} D 892* sy^{s} sy^{c} cop^{bo}.
[c] *Beelzebul* ℵ A C D L W Θ Ψ f^{1} f^{13} 33 892 1006 1342 1506 2427 𝔐 it vg^{mss} cop; *Beezebul* B; *Beelzebub* vg sy^{s} sy^{p}.
[d] *I cast-out* 𝔭^{75} ℵ^{1} B C D L f^{13} 33 579 892 1342 *al* it cop; *I-cast-out* 𝔭^{45} ℵ* A W Θ Ψ f^{1} 1006 1506 𝔐 vg it^{mss}.

214. Robbing the Strong (→ §138)

Matt 12:29	Mark 3:27	**Luke 11:21-22**	Thomas 35
29 "Or how some is-able [=is it possible] to-enter into the home of-the strong and to-plunder his vessels, if-ever no [=unless] he-might-restrain first the strong [person]? And [only] then he-will-raid his home."	27 "But no-one, having-entered into the home of-the strong is-able not to-raid his vessels, if-ever no [=unless] he-might-restrain the strong [person] first and [only] then he-will-raid his home."	21 "Whenever the strong [person] having-been-fully-armed might-guard of-himself [=his very own] courtyard, his being-at-one's-disposals [=belongings] is in peace [=are safe]. 22 So [=But] as-soon-as his stronger [someone stronger than him] having-come-upon [=attacks him] he-might-defeat him [=and defeats him], he-removes his armor upon which he-had-persuaded [=he trusted], and he-distributes his spoils."	Jesus said, "One can't enter a strong person's house and take it by force without tying his hands. Then one can loot his house."

There are no variants in this pericope that appear in English.

215. The One Not with Me (→ §139)

Matt 12:30

30“The [one] no [=not] being with me
is according-to [=against] me and the
[one] no [=not] gathering with me
disperses.”

Q 11:23

23“The [one] no [=not] being with me
is according-to [=against] me and the
[one] no [=not] gathering with me
disperses.”

Luke 11:23

23“The [one] no [=not] being with me
is according-to [=against] me and the
[one] no [=not] gathering with me
disperses.”

There are no variants in this pericope that appear in English.

216. Return of the Unclean Spirit (→ §142)

Matt 12:43-45

43“So whenever the unclean spirit
might-go-out from the person, it-
goes-through through [=it goes right
through] waterless places searching
[for] relief; and it-finds [it] not.
44Then it-says, ‘I-will-turn-back into
[=I will return to] my house from-
which I-went-out.’
And having-come, it-finds [it
already] being-unoccupied,[a]
having-been-swept and having-
been-adorned [=decorated]. 45Then
it-travels and takes-along with itself
seven other spirits more-evil [than]
itself and having-entered it-settles
there. And the lasts [=last things] of-
that person happen [=become] worse
of-the firsts [=than the first things].
Thus it-will-be and [=also for] this
evil generation.”

Q 11:24-26

24“Whenever the unclean spirit
might-go-out from the person, it-
goes-through through [=it goes right
through] waterless places searching
[for] relief; and it-finds [it] not. Then
it-says, ‘I-will-turn-back into [=I
will return to] my house from-which
I-went-out.’
25And having-come, it-finds [it]
having-been-swept and having-
been-adorned [=decorated].
26Then it-travels and takes-along
with itself seven other spirits more-
evil [than] itself and having-entered
it-settles there. And the lasts [=last
things] of-that person happen
[=become] worse of-the firsts [=than
the first things].”

Luke 11:24-26

24“Whenever the unclean spirit
might-go-out from the person, it-
goes-through through [=it goes right
through] waterless places searching
[for] relief and [=but] finding no
[relief]. Then[b] it-says, ‘I-will-return
into [=I will return to] my house
from-which I-went-out.’
25And having-come, it-finds [it]
having-been-swept and having-
been-adorned [=decorated].
26Then it-travels and takes-along
other spirits more-evil [than] itself,
seven, and having-entered it-settles
there. And the lasts [=last things] of-
that person happen [=become] worse
of-the firsts [=than the first things].”

[a] *omit* B C^{2} D L W Z Θ f^{1} f^{13} 33 892 1006 1342 𝔐 vg it^{mss}; *and* ℵ C* 1424 1506 *al* it.

[b] *Then* 𝔓^{75} ℵ^{2} B L Θ Ξ 070 33 892 1342 *pc*; *omit* 𝔓^{45} ℵ* A C D W Ψ f^{1} f^{13} 1006 1506 𝔐 vg it^{mss} sy^{s} sy^{c} sy^{p}.

217. Luke’s Saying about True Blessedness

Luke 11:27-28

27So it-happened in the to-say him [=while he was saying]
these [things], some woman having-lifted-up [her] voice
out of-the crowd said to-him, “Fortunate the abdomen
[=womb] having-borne you and [the] breasts which
you-nursed.” 28So he [himself] said, “On-the-contrary[a],
fortunate [are those] hearing the word of-god and
guarding [it].”

Thomas 79

A woman in the crowd said to him, “Lucky are the womb that bore you and the breasts that fed you.” He said to <her>, “Lucky are those who have heard the word of the Father and have truly kept it. For there will be days when you will say, ‘Lucky are the womb that has not conceived and the breasts that have not given milk.’”

[a] *On-the-contrary* 𝔓^{75} ℵ B* L W Δ Ξ *pc*; *On-the-contrary in-effect* B^{2} C D Θ Ψ 070 f^{1} f^{13} 33 𝔐.

218. The Sign of Jonah (→ §141, §213)

Matt 12:38-40

[38]Then some of-the scribes and Pharisees answered him[a] saying, "Teacher, we-wish to-see [a] sign from you."
[39]So having-answered

he-said to-them, "[An] evil and adulterous generation seeks [a] sign, and [=but a] sign will-be-given not to-it if no [=except] the sign of-Jonah the prophet. [40]For even-as Jonah was in the abdomen of-the large-sea-creature three days and three nights, thus the son of-the person will-be in the heart of-the land three days and three nights."

Q 11:16, 29-30

[16]So some were-searching

[for a] sign along [=from] him.

[29]So

he-said, "This generation is [an] evil generation; it-searches [for a] sign and [=but a] sign will-be-given not to-it if no [=except] the sign of-Jonah. [30]For just-as Jonah happened [=became a] sign to-the Ninevites, thus and [=so too] will-be the son of-the person to-this generation."

Luke 11:16, 29-30

[16]So others, testing [him] were-searching
[for a] sign out of-heaven along [=from] him.
[29]So the crowds expanding [since the crowds were growing] he-began to-say, "This generation is [an] evil generation; it-searches[b] [for a] sign and [=but a] sign will-be-given not to-it if no [=except] the sign of-Jonah. [30]For just-as Jonah happened [as a] sign to-the Ninevites, thus and [=so too] will-be the son of-the person to-this generation."

[a] *him* ℵ B C D L Θ f^{13} 33 892 1424 *al* vg it^{mss} cop^{sa} cop^{bo}; *omit* W f^{1} 1006 1342 𝔐.
[b] *it-searches* ℵ B C D L Δ Θ f^{1} 33 205 579 892 2426 2542 *pc*; *it-asks* 𝔓^{45}; *it-seeks* A W f^{13} 1006 1506 𝔐.
🕮 Mt 12:40 – Jonah 1:17 🕮 Lk 11:30 – Jonah 1:17; 3:1-10; 4:1-11

219. Jonah and the Ninevites (→ §141)

Matt 12:41-42

[41]"Ninevite men will-get-up [=will rise] in [=at] the judgment with this generation and they-will-judge-against it, that [=because] they-repented into [=at] the preaching of-Jonah, and look! [a] more [=person greater than] Jonah [is] here.
[42][The] queen [of the] south will-be-raised in [=at] the judgment with this generation, and she-will-judge-against it, that [=because] she-came out of-the edges of-the land [=from the ends of the earth] to-hear the wisdom of-Solomon, and look! [a] more [=person greater than] Solomon [is] here."

Q 11:31-32

[31]"[The] queen [of the] south will-be-raised in [=at] the judgment with this generation, and she-will-judge-against it, that [=because] she-came out of-the edges of-the land [=from the ends of the earth] to-hear the wisdom of-Solomon, and look! [a] more [=person greater than] Solomon [is] here. [32] Ninevite men will-get-up [=will rise] in [=at] the judgment with this generation and they-will-judge-against it, that [=because] they-repented into [=at] the preaching of-Jonah, and look! [a] more [=person greater than] Jonah [is] here."

Luke 11:31-32

[31]"[The] queen [of the] south will-be-raised in [=at] the judgment with the men [of] this generation, and she-will-judge-against them, that [=because] she-came out of-the edges of-the land [=from the ends of the earth] to-hear the wisdom of-Solomon, and look! [a] more [=person greater than] Solomon [is] here. [32]Ninevite men will-get-up [=will rise] in [=at] the judgment with this generation and they-will-judge-against it, that [=because] they-repented into [=at] the preaching of-Jonah, and look! [a] more [=person greater than] Jonah [is] here."

There are no variants in this pericope that appear in English.
🕮 Mt 12:42 – 1 Kgs 10:1; 🕮 Lk 11:31 – 2 Kgs 10:1

220. The Parable of the Light (→ §33)

Matt 5:15	**Q 11:33**	**Luke 11:33**	Thomas 33
15“nor do-they-kindle [a] lantern and put it under the bushel but upon the lamp-stand and it-shines for-all the [ones who are] in the home.”	33“No-one kindles [a] lantern and puts it into [a] cellar but upon the lamp-stand it-shines for-all the [ones who are] in the home.”	33“No-one having-touched [=having lit a] lantern puts [it] into [a] cellar nor under the bushel[a] but upon the lamp-stand, in-order-that the traveling-ins [=those who enter] might-look [at] the light.”	Jesus said, “What you will hear in your ear, in the other ear proclaim from your rooftops. After all, no one lights a lamp and puts it under a basket, nor does one put it in a hidden place. Rather, one puts it on a lampstand so that all who come and go will see its light.”

[a] *nor under the bushel* ℵ A B C D W Θ Ψ f^{13} 𝔐 it vg sy^{c} sy^{p}; *omit* 𝔓^{45} 𝔓^{75} L Γ Ξ 070 f^{1} 700* 1241 2542 *pc* sy^{s} cop^{sa}.

221. The Healthy Eye (→ §47)

Matt 6:22-23	**Q 11:34-35**	**Luke 11:34-36**	Thomas 24
22“The lantern of-the body is the eye. Therefore, if-ever your eye might-be unencumbered[a] [=functioning properly], your whole body will-be full-of-light. 23So [=But] if-ever your eye might-be evil, your whole body will-be darksome. Therefore, if the light [which is] in you is darkness, how-great [must be] the darkness?”	34“The lantern of-the body is the eye. If-ever your eye, unencumbered [=functioning properly] might-be your whole body is full-of-light. So [=But] ever your eye might-be evil, your whole body and [=also is] darksome. 35Therefore, if the light [which is] in you is darkness, how-great [must be] the darkness?”	34“The lantern of-the body is your eye. [b] Whenever your eye unencumbered [=functioning properly] might-be, and [=also] your whole body is full-of-light. So [=But] as-soon-as it-might-be evil, your body and [=also is] darksome. 35Therefore be-concerned no [=not lest] the light in you is [actually] darkness. 36Therefore, if your whole body [is] full-of-light, no [=not] having some part darksome, [then the] whole will-be full-of-light like whenever the lantern might-illumine you in-the flashing-light.”	His disciples said, “Show us the place where you are, for we must seek it.” He said to them, “Anyone here with two ears had better listen! There is light within a person of light, and it shines on the whole world. If it does not shine, it is dark.”

[a] *if-ever your eye might-be unencumbered* ℵ B W 1342 *pc* it^{mss} vg; *if-ever unencumbered might-be your eye* L Θ f^{1} f^{13} 33 892 1005 1506 𝔐 it.
[b] *omit* 𝔓^{45} 𝔓^{75} ℵ B D L W 070 579 *pc*; *Therefore* A C Θ Ψ f^{1} f^{13} 33 892 1006 1342 1506 𝔐 sy.

222. Denouncing of Pharisees and Lawyers (→ §321)

Matt 23:23, 25-26, 6-7, 27	**Q 11:42, 39b, 41, 43-44**	**Luke 11:37-44**	Thomas 89
		37So in the to-talk [=while he was speaking, a] Pharisee[a] begs him so-that he-might-have-lunch along [=with] him. So having-entered, he-leaned [=he reclined at table]. 38So the Pharisee, having-seen, was-astonished that [=because] he-was-baptized not first before the meal. 39So the lord said to him,	
23:23"Woe to-you scribes and Pharisees, hypocrites, that [=because] you-tithe mint and dill and cumin and you-excused [=you forgot] the more-weighty [=more important things] of-the law: the judgment and the mercy and the loyalty. So [=But] it-was-necessary to-do these [things] and-those [things] to-excuse no [=without neglecting the others]."	42"Woe to-the Pharisees, that [=because] you-tithe mint and dill and cumin and you-excused [=you forgot] the judgment and the mercy and the loyalty. So [=But] it-was-necessary to-do these [things] and-those [things] to-excuse no [=without neglecting the others]."		
25"Woe to-you scribes and Pharisees, hypocrites, that [=because] you-purify the cup and the plate from-outside, so [=but] from-within [=the insides] are-full out [=of] violent-greed and self-indulgence.	39b"Woe to-you Pharisees, that [=because] you-purify the cup and the plate from-outside, so [=but] the from-within [=the insides] are-full out [=of] violent-greed and self-indulgence.	"Now you Pharisees purify the from-outside [=outside] of-the cup and of-the platter, so [=but] your from-within [=inside] is-full of-violent-greed and of-evilness. 40Simpletons, not the having-done the from-outside and did the from-within [=did the one who made the outside not also make the inside]?	Jesus said, "Why do you wash the outside of the cup? Don't you understand that the one who made the inside is also the one who made the outside?"

Matt	Q	Luke	
26 Blind Pharisee, first <u>purify</u> the inside of-the cup, in-order-that its outer [part] and might-happen [=might also become] pure.”	41 Purify the inside of-the cup, and its outer [part] might-happen [=might become] pure.	41 Nevertheless, give [as] almsgiving the being-insides [=the things that are inside you], and look! all is pure for-you. 42 But woe to-you Pharisees, that [=because] you-tithe mint and scented-herb and all [=every] shrub and you-pass-away [=you neglect] the judgment and love of-god. So [=But] it-was-necessary to-do these [things] and-those [things] to-lose-sight-of no [=without neglecting the others].	
6 “So [=But] they-like the place-of-honor in the banquets and the seats-of-honor in the synagogues 7 and the greetings in the markets and to-be-called rabbi under [=by] the people.”	43 Woe to-you Pharisees that [=because] you-like place-of-honor in the banquets and the seat-of-honor in the synagogues and the greetings in the markets.	43 Woe to-you Pharisees that [=because] you-love the seat-of-honor in the synagogues and the greetings in the markets.	
27 “Woe to-you scribes and Pharisees, hypocrites, that [=because] you-resemble sepulchers having-been-white-washed, whoever [=which] from-outside for-one appear lovely, so [=but] from-within are-full of-bones of-deads [=of dead people] and of-all [=of every] uncleanliness.”	44 Woe to-you Pharisees, that [=because] you-are like the unmarked tombs and the people walking-around above recognize [it] not.”	44 Woe to-you, [b]that [=because] you-are like the unmarked tombs and the people walking-around above recognize [it] not.”	

[a] *Pharisee* $\mathfrak{P}^{45}$ $\mathfrak{P}^{75}$ א B L 070 f^{1} f^{13} 205 579 700 2542 *pc*; *some Pharisee* A C D W Θ Ψ 33 892 1006 1342 1506 vg it sy^{p}.
[b] *omit* $\mathfrak{P}^{45}$ $\mathfrak{P}^{75}$ א B C L f^{1} 33 205 2542 *pc* vg it^{mss} sy^{s} sy^{c} cop^{sa} cop^{bomss}; *scribes and Pharisees hypocrites* A D W Θ Ψ f^{13} 892 1006 1342 1506 𝔐 it sy^{p} sy^{h} cop^{bomss}.

223. Locking the Kingdom and Killing the Prophets (→ §225, §321)

Matt 23:4, 13, 29-32	**Q 11:46b, 52, 47-48**	**Luke 11:45-46, 52, 47-48**
4 “So		45 So, some [man from among] the lawyers, having-answered, says to-him, “You-insult us and [=also by] saying these [things].” 46 So he

Matt	Q	Luke
they-bind weighty and awkward[a] burdens and they-place [them] upon the shoulders of-the people, so [=but] they [themselves] wish not [to	46b“And woe to-you lawyers, that [=because] you-bind burdens and you-place [them] upon the shoulders of-the people, so [=but] they you-wish [=you yourselves wish] not [to	[himself] said, “And to-you lawyers woe, that [=because] you-burden
		the people [with] awkward burdens and they [=you] lend-a-hand to-the burdens not [with] one [of] your
lift] their finger to-move them.”	lift] your finger to-move them.	fingers.”
13“So woe to-you, scribes and Pharisees, hypocrites, that [=because] you-lock the kingdom of-the heavens in-front [=from] the people; for you [yourselves] enter not nor excuse [=allow] the enterings [=those wishing to enter] to-enter.”	52Woe to-you lawyers, that [=because] you-lock the kingdom of-god in-front [=from] the people; you entered not nor excuse [=allow] the enterings [=those wishing to enter] to-enter.	52“Woe to-you lawyers, that [=because] you-removed the keys of-knowledge; they you-entered [=you yourselves entered] not and you-hindered enterings [=those wishing to enter].”
29“Woe to-you scribes and Pharisees, hypocrites, that [=because] you-build the sepulchers of-the prophets and you-adorn the tombs of-the righteous, 30and you-say, ‘If we-were [there] in the days [of] our fathers, not ever we-were [=we would never have been] their companions in [shedding] the blood of-the prophets.’	47Woe to-you that [=because] you-build the tombs of-the prophets, so [=but] your	47“Woe to-you that [=because] you-build the tombs of-the prophets, so [=but] your
	fathers killed them.	fathers killed them.
31With-the-result-that you-testify themselves [=yourselves] that you-are sons of-the having-murdereds [=those who murdered] the prophets.	48You-testify themselves [=yourselves]	48Consequently, you-are witnesses[b] and you-approve the works [of]
32And fulfill, you, the measure [of] your fathers.”	that you-are sons [of] your fathers.”	your fathers that [=because] they for-one killed them, so [on the other hand] you-build [their tombs] [c].”

[a] *weighty and awkward* B D W Θ f^{13} 33 1006 1342 1506 𝔐 vg it^{mss} sy^{h} cop^{sa}; *weighty* L f^{1} 205 892 *pc* it sy^{s} sy^{c} sy^{p} cop^{bo}; *great weight* א.
[b] *you-are witnesses* א B L 700* 892 2542 sy; *you-testify* 𝔭^{75} A C D W Θ Ψ f^{1} f^{13} 33 1006 1506 𝔐 vg it^{mss}.
[c] *omit* 𝔭^{75} א B D L 579 *pc* it sy^{s} sy^{c} cop^{sa} cop^{bo}; *their sepulchers* f^{1} f^{13} 205 2542 *pc* vg; *their graves* A C W Θ Ψ 33 892 1006 1342 𝔐.

224. Pursuing the Prophets (→ §321)

Matt 23:34-36	**Q 11:49-51**	**Luke 11:49-51**
34“Through this [=Therefore] look! I send-off prophets and wise [people]	49“Through this [=Therefore] and [=also] the wisdom said, ‘I-will-send	49“Through this [=Therefore] and [=also] the wisdom of-god said, ‘I-will-send-off prophets and apostles
and scribes to you. [Some] out of-them you-will-kill and will-crucify,	prophets to them and [=some] out of-them they-will-kill and will-	into [=among] them and [=some] out of-them they-will-kill and will-
and you-will-scourge [some] out of-them in your synagogues and you-will-pursue [them] from city into city, 35so-that all righteous	pursue, 50in-order-that it-might-be-sought-out [=this generation might be charged	pursue,’ 50in-order-that it-might-be-sought-out [=this generation might be charged
blood being-shed upon the land might-come upon you, from the	for] the blood of-all the prophets having-been-poured-out[a] from	for] the blood of-all the prophets having-been-poured-out[a] from

blood of-righteous Abel until the blood of-Zachariah son of-Barachiah, whom you-murdered between the sanctuary and the sacrificial-altar. [36]Amen I-say to-you, all these [things] will-press-forward [=will come] upon this generation."	the molding of-the world from [=by] this generation, [51]from [the] blood of-Abel until [the] blood of-Zachariah the [one] having-been-destroyed between the sacrificial-altar and the house [=sanctuary]. Yes I-say to-you, it-will-be-sought-out from [=it will be charged against] this generation."	the molding of-the world from [=by] this generation, [51]from [the] blood of-Abel until [the] blood of-Zachariah the [one] having-been-destroyed between the sacrificial-altar and the house [=sanctuary]. Yes I-say to-you, it-will-be-sought-out from [=it will be charged against] this generation."

[a] *having-been-poured-out* 𝔓45 B 0233 *f* 13 33 *pc* vg it mss; *being-shed* 𝔓75 ℵ A C D L W Θ Ψ *f* 1 892 1006 1342 1506 𝔐.
📖 Mt 23:35 – Gen 4:8; 2 Chr 24:21, 22; 📖 Lk 11:51 – Gen 4:8; 2 Chr 24:21, 22

225. The Authorities Begin Plotting (→ §223, §321)

Matt 23:13	Q 11:52	**Luke 11:52-54**	Thomas 39; 102
[13]"So woe to-you, scribes and Pharisees, hypocrites, that [=because] you-lock the kingdom of-the heavens in-front [=from] the people; for you [yourselves] enter not nor excuse [=allow] the enterings [=those wishing to enter] to-enter."	[52]"Woe to-you lawyers, that [=because] you-lock the kingdom of-god in-front [=from] the people; you [yourselves] entered not nor excuse [=allow] the enterings [=those wishing to enter] to-enter."	[52]"Woe to-you lawyers, that [=because] you-removed the keys of-knowledge; they you-entered [=you yourselves entered] not and you-hindered enterings [=those wishing to enter]." [53]And-from-there his having-gone-out[a] [=when he left], the scribes and the Pharisees began to-be-hostile [to him] terribly and to-attack-with-questions him around [=concerning] more [things], [54]plotting-against him to-pounce-on some [thing that might come] out [of] his mouth[b].	[39]Jesus said, "The Pharisees and the scholars have taken the keys of knowledge and have hidden them. They have not entered nor have they allowed those who want to enter to do so. As for you, be as sly as snakes and as simple as doves." [102]Jesus said, "Damn the Pharisees! They are like a dog sleeping in the cattle manger: the dog neither eats nor <lets> the cattle eat."

[a] *And-from-there his having-gone-out* 𝔓45 𝔓75 ℵ B C L 33 579 *pc* cop; *So his saying these to them* A D W Θ Ψ *f* 1 *f* 13 892 1006 1342 1506 𝔐 vg it sy.
[b] *omit* 𝔓45 𝔓75 ℵ B L 579 892 2542 *pc* cop; *in-order-that they-might-accuse him* A C D W Θ Ψ *f* 1 *f* 13 33 1006 1342 1506 𝔐 vg sy p sy h.

226. The Leaven of the Pharisees (→ §174)

Matt 16:5-6	Mark 8:14-15	**Luke 12:1**
[5]And having-come into the beyond [=to the other side], the disciples[a] neglected to-take breads.	[14]And they-neglected to-take breads and they-had not [any] with themselves in the boat if no [=except] one bread. [15]And he-was-demanding [=he was warning] them saying,	[1]In which [=When] the crowd of-many-thousands having-been-collected [=had been gathered], with-the-result-that to-tread-upon [=they trampled] one-another, he-began to-say [to speak] to his disciples first,

6“So Jesus said to-them, “See [=Watch] and pay-close-attention from [=beware of] the leaven of-the Pharisees and Sadducees.”	“See, look [away] from the leaven of-the Pharisees and the leaven of-Herod.”	“Pay-close-attention themselves from [=You yourselves be careful to avoid] the leaven, whoever [=which] is hypocrisy, of-the Pharisees.”

[a] *the disciples* ℵ B C Θ f^{13} 205 209 892 *pc*; *his disciples* L W f^{1} 33 1006 1506 𝔐 vg it^{mss} sy cop^{bo}; *omit* Δ *pc*.

227. Fearless Confession (→ §113)

Matt 10:26-27	**Q 12:2-3**	**Luke 12:2-3**	Thomas 5; 33
26“Therefore might-you-be-feared no [=fear not] them, for no-one is having-been-covered [=nothing is hidden] which will-be-revealed not and [nothing is] hidden which will-be-known not.	2“No-one having-been-covered is [=Nothing is hidden] which will-be-revealed not and [nothing is] hidden which will-be-known not.	2“So no-one [=nothing] is having-been-concealed which will-be-revealed not and [nothing is] hidden which will-be-known not. 3In-place of-which [=Therefore] whatsoever you-said in the dark will-be-heard in the light, and [that] which you-talked [=you whispered] to the ear in the private-rooms will-be-preached upon [=from] the housetops.”	5Jesus said, “Know what is in front of your face, and what is hidden from you will be disclosed to you. For there is nothing hidden that will not be revealed. <And there is nothing buried that will not be raised.>”
27Which [=What] I-say to-you in the dark, say in the light and which [=what] you-hear [whispered] into the ear preach upon [=from] the housetops.”	3Which [=What] I-say to-you in the dark, say in the light and which [=what] you-hear into the ear [=whispered] preach upon [=from] the housetops.”		33Jesus said, “What you will hear in your ear, in the other ear proclaim from your rooftops. After all, no one lights a lamp and puts it under a basket, nor does one put it in a hidden place. Rather, one puts it on a lampstand so that all who come and go will see its light.”

There are no variants in this pericope that appear in English.

228. Killing the Body but Not the Soul (→ §114)

Matt 10:28	**Q 12:4-5**	**Luke 12:4-5**
28“And fear[a] no [=not] from the killings [=those who kill] the body, so [=but] being-able no [=not] to-kill the soul.	4“And fear no [=not] from the killings [=those who kill] the body, so [=but] being-able no [=not] to-kill the soul.	4“So I-say to-you, [to] my friends, might-you-be-feared no from [=fear not] the killings [=those who kill] the body, and with these no having some to-do [=but cannot do] more-excessive [=more than this].
So [=But] rather fear[b] the [one] being-able to-destroy and [=both] soul and body in Gehenna.”	5So [=But] fear the [one] being-able to-destroy and [=both] soul and body in the Gehenna.”	5So I-will-display to-you what you-might-be-fear [=you should fear]. Might-you-be-feared [=You should fear] the [one] having [the] authority to-throw-in [people] into the Gehenna with to-kill [=after he has killed them]. Yes, I-say to-you fear this [one].”

[a] *fear* ℵ C K L Γ Δ f^{13} 565 579 700 *pm*; *might-you-be-feared* B D N W Θ f^{1} 33 892 1424 *pm*.
[b] *fear* ℵ B C W 892 *pc*; *might-you-be-feared* D L Θ f^{1} f^{13} 33 𝔐.

229. Even the Birds Are Cared For (→ §115)

Matt 10:29-31	**Q 12:6-7**	**Luke 12:6-7**
[29]"Two sparrows is-sold [for an] assarion, indeed-not [=are they not]? And not one out of-them will-fall upon the land apart [from the will of] your father. [30]So and [=even] the hairs [on that] head [of] yours are all having-been-counted. [31]Therefore fear no [=not], you [yourselves] are-superior [=are worth more than] many sparrows."	[6]"Five sparrows are-sold [for] two assarions, indeed-not [=are they not]? And not one out of-them will-fall upon the land apart [from the will of] your father. [7]So and [=even] the hairs [on that] head [of] yours are all having-been-counted. Fear no [=not], you [yourselves] are-superior [=are worth more than] many sparrows."	[6]"Five sparrows are-sold[a] [for] two assarions, indeed-not [=are they not]? And not one out of-them is having-been-neglected in-the-sight of-god. [7]But and [=even] all the hairs [of] your head have-been-counted. Fear no[b] [=not]; you-are-superior [=you are worth more than] many sparrows."

[a] *are-sold* 𝔭75 ℵ B Θ Ψ *f* 13 892 1241 2542 *pc*; *is-sold* 𝔭45 D L W 070 *f* 1 33 𝔐.
[b] *Fear no* 𝔭45 𝔭75 B L 070 579 *pc* it; *Therefore fear no* ℵ A D W Θ Ψ *f* 1 *f* 13 33 892 1006 1342 1506 𝔐 vg it[mss] sy.

230. Confessing the Son of Man (→ §116)

Matt 10:32-33	**Q 12:8-9**	**Luke 12:8-9**
[32]"Therefore all whoever will-confess in me in-front of-the people, I-too will-confess in him in-front [of] my father in the heavens[a]. [33]So [=But] whoever ever might-deny me in-front of-the people, I-too will-deny him in-front [of] my father in the heavens[b]."	[8]"All who ever might-confess in me in-front of-the people, and [=even] the son of-the person will-confess in him in-front of-the announcers [=angels]. [9]So [=But] who ever might-deny me in-front of-the people will-be-denied in-front of-the announcers [=angels]."	[8]"So I-say to-you, all who ever might-confess in me in-front of-the people, and [=even] the son of-the person will-confess in him in-front of-the announcers [=angels] of-god. [9]So [=But] the [one] having-denied me in-the-sight of-the people will-be-disowned in-the-sight of-the announcers [=angels] of-god."

[a] *in the heavens* B *f* 13 579 892 1424 *al*; *in heavens* 𝔭19 ℵ C D L W Θ *f* 1 1006 1342 𝔐.
[b] *in the heavens* B C *f* 13 579 892 1506 *al*; *in heavens* 𝔭19 ℵ D L W Θ *f* 1 1006 1342 𝔐.

231. Blaspheming the Spirit (→ §140)

Matt 12:32	**Q 12:10**	**Luke 12:10**	Thomas 44
[32]"And who if-ever might-say [a] word according-to [=against] the son of-the person, it-will-be-excused for-him, so [=but] who ever might-say [=might speak] according-to [=against] the <u>holy spirit</u> it-will-be-excused for-him not in this eon neither in the intending [=age to come].	[10]"And who if-ever might-say [a] word into [=against] the son of-the person, it-will-be-excused for-him, so [=but] who ever might-say [a word] into [=against] the holy spirit it-will-be-excused for-him not."	[10]"And all who will-say [a] word into [=against] the son of-the person, it-will-be-excused for-him, so [=but] for-the [one] having-blasphemed into [=against] the holy spirit it-will-be-excused not."	Jesus said, "Whoever blasphemes against the Father will be forgiven, and whoever blasphemes against the son will be forgiven, but whoever blasphemes against the holy spirit will not be forgiven, either on earth or in heaven."

There are no variants in this pericope that appear in English.

232. Guidance of the Holy Spirit (→ §111, §326)

Matt 10:19-20	Mark 13:11	**Q 12:11-12**	**Luke 12:11-12**
9“So whenever they-might-deliver[a] you, you-	11“And whenever they-might-lead you, delivering	11“Whenever they-might-bring-into you [=When they bring you] into the synagogues, you-might-	11“Whenever they-might-bring-into[b] you [=When they bring you] upon [=before] the synagogues, and the beginnings [=rulers], and the authorities, you-might-
might-worry no [=not]	[you], worry-ahead-of-	worry no [=not] how or	worry no [=not] how or
how or what you-might-	time no [=not] what you-might-talk [=you might	what you-might-say,	[with] what you-might-defend [yourself] or what
talk [=you might say]. For what you-might-talk will-be-given to-you in that hour. 20For you-are not the talkings [=those ones doing the talking] but the spirit [of] your father [who is] talking in you.”	say], but talk [=say] this which if-ever [=whatever] might-be-given to-you in that hour, for you-are not the talkings [=those ones doing the talking] but the holy spirit.”	12for the holy spirit will-teach you what you-might-say in the [=that] hour.”	you-might-say. 12For the holy spirit will-teach you in it [=in that very] hour [that] which it-is-necessary to-say.”

[a] *they-might-deliver* ℵ B *f*[1] 205 892 *pc*; *they-will-deliver* D G L W 33 579 1424 1596 *al* vg it[mss]; *they-give* C Θ *f*[13] 1006 1342 𝔐.
[b] *they-might-bring-into* 𝔭[45] 𝔭[75] ℵ B L 070 *f*[1] 33 579 700 892 2542 *pc* it[mss] vg; *they-might-offer* A W Θ Ψ *f*[13] 1006 1342 1506 𝔐 it[mss]; *they-might-bring* D it[mss].

233. Treasures (→ §46, §237)

Matt 6:19-21	**Q 12:33-34**	Luke 12:33-34	Thomas 76
		33“Sell your being-at-one's-disposals [=belongings] and give almsgiving;	Jesus said, “The Father's kingdom is like a merchant who had a supply of merchandise and found a pearl.
19“Store-treasure no [=not] to-you [in] treasure-boxes upon the land [=earth], where moth and rust disfigures [it] and where thieves break-in and steal [it], 20so [=but] store-treasure to-you	33“Store-treasure no [=not] to-you [in] treasure-boxes upon the land [=earth], where moth and rust disfigures [it] and where thieves break-in and steal [it], so [=but] store-treasure to-you		
		do [=make] for-themselves [=for yourselves] moneybags [that are] no [=not] becoming-old, [a]	That merchant was prudent; he sold the merchandise and bought the single pearl for himself. So also with
[in] treasure-boxes in heaven where neither moth neither [=nor] rust disfigures and where thieves break-in not nor steal [it].	[in] treasure-boxes in heaven where neither moth neither [=nor] rust disfigures and where thieves break-in not neither [=nor] steal [it].	never-decreasing treasure-box in the heavens where thief nears not nor moth corrupts;	you, seek his treasure that is unfailing, that is enduring, where no moth comes to eat and no worm destroys.”

[21]For where [ever] your
treasure-box is, there will-
be and [=also] your heart."

[34]For where [ever] your
treasure-box is, there will-
be and [=also] your heart."

[34]for where <u>your</u> treasure-
box is, there and [=also]
<u>your</u> heart will-be."

There are no variants in this pericope that appear in English.

234. Luke's Lesson about Covetousness

Luke 12:13-15

[13]So some [one] out of-the crowd said to-him, "Teacher, say [to] my
brother to-divide the inheritance with me." [14]So [=But] he-said to-him,
"Person [=Man], what [=who] established me [as] judge or arbitrator[a]
upon [=over] you?" [15]So he-said to them, "See and guard from [=against]
all covetousness, that [=because] not in the to-exceed to-what is his
life out of-the being-at-one's-disposals to-him [=a person's life does not
consist in the abundance of possessions]."

Thomas 72

A <person said> to him, "Tell my brothers to divide my father's possessions with me." He said to the person, "Mister, who made me a divider?" He turned to his disciples and said to them, "I'm not a divider, am I?"

[a] *judge or arbitrator* 𝔓[75] ℵ B L 070 *f*[1] *f*[13] 33 205 579 700 892 2542 *pc*; *judicator and arbitrator* A W Θ Ψ 1006 1342 1506 𝔐; *judge* D; *judicator* 28 *pc*.

235. Luke's Parable of the Rich Fool

Luke 12:16-21

[16]So [=Then] he-said [a] parable to them saying, "The region of-some wealthy
person produced-good-crops. [17]And he-was-pondering in himself saying,
'What will-I-do, that [=because] I-have not [a place] wheresoever I-will-gather
my fruits [=harvest]?' [18]And he-said, 'I-will-do this: I-will-bring-down my
storehouses and I-will-build greaters [=bigger ones], and there I-will-gather
all the wheat and my goods[a], [19]and I-will-say [to] my soul, "Soul, you-have
many goods laying into [=stored up for] many years; give-relief [=relax], eat,
drink, be-merry."' [20]So [=But] god said to-him, 'Simpleton, [on] this night
they-demand-back[b] your soul from you, so [=and] which [things] you-made-
ready, to-what [=whose] will-it-be? [21]Thus [it is with] the [one] storing-treasure
[for] himself and no [=not] being-wealthy into [=toward] god.'"

Thomas 63

Jesus said, "There was a rich person who had a great deal of money. He said, 'I shall invest my money so that I may sow, reap, plant, and fill my storehouses with produce, that I may lack nothing.' These were the things he was thinking in his heart, but that very night he died. Anyone here with two ears had better listen!"

[a] *all the wheat and my goods* 𝔓[75] ℵ[2] B L 070 *f*[1] *f*[13] 205 579 892 *pc* cop; *all my produce* ℵ* D it sy[s] sy[c]; *my fruits* it[mss]; *all my produce and my goods* A W Θ Ψ 1006 1342 1506 𝔐 vg sy[p] sy[h].
[b] *they-demand-back* ℵ A D W Θ Ψ *f*[1] *f*[13] 892 1006 1506 𝔐; *they-ask* 𝔓[75] B L Q 070 33 579 *pc*.

236. Anxiety (→ §49)

Matt 6:25-34

[25]"Through [=Because of]
this, I-say to-you, worry
no [=not about] your soul
[=life] what you-might-eat,
or what you-might-drink[a],
so-not [=nor for] your
body, [in] what you-
might-be-clothed.

Q 12:22-31

[22]"Through [=Because of]
this I-say to-you, worry
no [=not about] your soul
[=life], what you-might-
eat, so-not [=nor for] your
body, [in] what you-
might-be-clothed.

Luke 12:22-32

[22]So he-said to his
disciples[d], "Through
[=Because of] this I-say to-
you, worry no [=not about]
the soul[e] [=life], what you-
might-eat, so-not [=nor
for] the body, [in] what
you-might-be-clothed.

Thomas 36

Jesus said, "Do not fret, from morning to evening and from evening to morning, <about your food—what you're going to eat, or about your clothing—> what you are going to wear.

Is indeed-not the soul [=life] more [than] nourishment and the body [more than] clothes? 26 Behold into [=Look at] the birds of-heaven, that they-sow not nor do-they-harvest nor do-they-gather into storehouses, and your heavenly father nourishes them.	23 Is indeed-not the soul [=life] more [than] nourishment and the body [more than] clothes? 24 Think-about the crows, that they-sow not nor do-they-harvest, nor do-they-gather into storehouses, and god nourishes them.	23 For the soul [=life] is more [than] nourishment and the body [more than] clothes. 24 Think-about the crows, that they-sow not nor do-they-harvest, to-whom there-is not [a] private-room nor storehouse, and god nourishes them.	
Are-superior rather not you of-them [=Are you not more important than them]?	Are-superior rather not you of-the birds [=How much more superior must you be than the birds]?	How-great rather you are-superior of-the birds [=How much more superior must you be than the birds]?	
27 So what [=who] out of-you, worrying, is-able to-add one cubit [=day] upon his age?	25 So what [=who] out of-you, worrying, is-able to-add [a] cubit [=day] upon his age?	25 So what [=who] out of-you, worrying, is-able [a] cubit [=day] to-add upon his age? 26 Therefore, if you-are-able [to change] nor [=not even the] least, what [=why] do-you-worry around [=concerning] the remainders [=rest]?	
28 And what [=why] do-you-worry around [=concerning] clothes? Observe the lilies of-the field, how they-grow; they-labor not nor do-they-spin[b].	26 And what [=why] do-you-worry around [=concerning] clothes? 27 Observe the lilies, how it-grows, it-labors not nor spins.	27 Think-about the lilies, how it-grows, it-labors not nor spins.	<You're much better than the lilies, which neither card nor spin. As for you, when you have no garment, what will you put on? Who might add to your stature?
29 So I-say to-you that, nor [=not even] Solomon, in all his glory, was-arrayed like one of-these. 30 So if god thus dresses the food [=plants] of-the field, today being [alive] and tomorrow being-thrown into [a] furnace, not rather by-many you [=will he not dress you all the more], little-loyalties [you of little faith]? 31 Therefore, you-might-worry no [=not], saying 'What might-we-eat?' or 'What might-we-drink?' or 'What [=How] might-we-be-arrayed? 32 For the nations seek all these [things]; for your heavenly father recognizes that you-need everyone	So I-say to-you, nor [=not even] Solomon, in all his glory, was-arrayed like one of-these. 28 So if god thus dresses the food [=plants] in [the] field, being [alive] today and tomorrow being-thrown into [a] furnace, not rather by-many you [=will he not dress you all the more], little-loyalties [you of little faith]? 29 Therefore, you-might-worry no [=not], saying 'What might-we-eat?' or 'What might-we-drink?' or 'What [=How] might-we-be-arrayed? 30 For the nations seek all these [things]; for your father recognizes that you-need everyone of-these	So I-say to-you, nor [=not even] Solomon, in all his glory, was-arrayed like one of-these. 28 So if god thus attires the food [=plants] in [the] field, being [alive] today and tomorrow being-thrown into [a] furnace, how-great rather you [=how much more will he dress you], little-loyalties [you of little faith]? 29 And you, search no [=not for] what you-might-eat and what you-might-drink and be-of-doubtful-mind not. 30 For the nations of-the world seek all these [things]; so [=but] your father recognizes that you-need these [things].	

Matt	Q	Luke	Thomas
of-these [things]. 33So, search [for] his kingdom and righteousness[c] first and all these [things] will-be-added to-you. 34Therefore, you-might- worry no [=not] into tomorrow, for tomorrow will-worry [about] itself; the wickedness of-it [is] enough [for this] day."	[things]. 31So, search [for] his kingdom and all these [things] will-be-added to-you."	31Nevertheless, search [for] his kingdom[f] and these [things] will-be-added to-you. 32Fear no [=not], small fold, that [=because] your father was-content to-give to-you the kingdom."	That very one will give you your garment.>"

[a] *or what you-might-drink* B W f^{13} 33 205 209 1342 it cop^{samss} cop^{bo}; *and what you-might-drink* L Θ 1006 1506 𝔐 sy^{p}; *omit* ℵ f^{1} 892 *pc* it^{mss} sy^{s} cop^{samss}.
[b] *they-grow; they-labor not nor do-they-spin* ℵ^{1} Θ f^{1} 205 sy^{s}; *it-grows; it-labors not nor spins* L f^{13} 892 1006 1342 𝔐.
[c] *his kingdom and righteousness* ℵ it^{mss} cop^{sa} cop^{bo}; *his righteousness and kingdom* B; *the kingdom of-god and his righteousness* L W Θ f^{1} f^{13} 33 892 1006 1342 1506 𝔐 it^{mss} vg sy.
[d] *his disciples* 𝔭^{75} B *pc* it^{mss}; *the disciples* ℵ A D L W Θ Ψ f^{1} f^{13} 892 1006 1342 1506 𝔐 it^{mss} vg sy cop.
[e] *the soul* 𝔭^{75} ℵ A B D L Q W Θ f^{1} 700 2542 it^{mss} vg sy^{s}; *your soul* 𝔭^{45} Ψ f^{13} 33 892 1006 1342 𝔐 it^{mss} sy^{s} sy^{p} cop.
[f] *his kingdom* ℵ B D* L Ψ 579 892 *pc* it^{mss} cop; *the kingdom* 𝔭^{75}; *the kingdom of-god* 𝔭^{45} A D^{1} W Θ f^{1} f^{13} 33 1006 1342 1506 𝔐 it sy.

237. Treasures (→ §46, §233)

Matt 6:19-21	**Q 12:33-34**	**Luke 12:33-34**	Thomas 76
19"Store-treasure no [=not] to-you [in] treasure- boxes upon the land [=earth], where moth and rust disfigures [it] and where thieves break-in and steal [it], 20so [=but] store-treasure to-you [in] treasure-boxes in heaven where neither moth neither [=nor] rust disfigures and where thieves break-in not nor steal [it]. 21For where [ever] your treasure-box is, there will- be and [=also] your heart."	33"Store-treasure no [=not] to-you [in] treasure- boxes upon the land [=earth], where moth and rust disfigures [it] and where thieves break-in and steal [it], so [=but] store-treasure to-you [in] treasure-boxes in heaven where neither moth neither [=nor] rust disfigures and where thieves break-in not neither [=nor] steal [it]. 34For where [ever] your treasure-box is, there will- be and [=also] your heart."	33"Sell your being-at-one's- disposals [=belongings] and give almsgiving; do [=make] for-themselves [=for yourselves] moneybags [that are] no [=not] becoming-old, [a] never-decreasing treasure- box in the heavens where thief nears not nor moth corrupts; 34for where <u>your</u> treasure- box is, there and [=also] <u>your</u> heart will-be."	Jesus said, "The Father's kingdom is like a merchant who had a supply of merchandise and found a pearl. That merchant was prudent; he sold the merchandise and bought the single pearl for himself. So also with you, seek his treasure that is unfailing, that is enduring, where no moth comes to eat and no worm destroys."

There are no variants in this pericope that appear in English.

238. Luke on Being Prepared

Luke 12:35-38

[35]Let-be having-been-garbed [=Let be dressed] your waists and the lanterns being-kindled [36]and
you [be] comparable-to people waiting-for the lord themselves when he-might-retire out of-the
[=return from the] weddings, in-order-that having-come and having-knocked they-might-open
to-him instantly. [37]Fortunate [are] those slaves whom, having-come, the lord will-find staying-
awake. Amen I-say to-you that he-will-be-garbed and he-will-stretch-out them [=he will seat them
at the table], and having-passed-away [=arriving] he-will-serve them. [38]Even-if [=And if] in [=on] the
second even-if [=or if] in [=on] the third prison [=watch], he-might-come and might-find [them]
thus, fortunate are those [ones][a].

[a] *those* 𝔓[75] ℵ[1] B D L sy[s] sy[c] cop[bomss]; *those slaves* A W Θ Ψ *f*[1] *f*[13] 33 892 1006 1342 1506 𝔐 vg it[mss] sy[p] sy[h] cop[sa] cop[bomss]; *omit* ℵ* it.

239. Being On Guard (→ §338)

Matt 24:43-44	**Q 12:39-40**	**Luke 12:39-40**	Thomas 21
[43]"So know that: that if the master-of-the-house recognized what-kind-of [=on what] prison [=watch] the thief comes, he-stayed-awake ever [=he would have stayed awake] and he-conceded not ever [=he would not have permitted] his home to-be-broken-in. [44]Through this [=Therefore] you [=yourselves] and [=also] happen [=must be] ready that [=because] you-suppose [=you know] not in-which hour the son of-the person comes."	[39]"So know that: that if the master-of-the-house recognized what-kind-of [=on what] prison [=watch] the thief comes, he-conceded not ever [=he would not have permitted] his house to-be-broken-in. [40]you [=yourself] and [=also] happen [=must be] ready that [=because] you-suppose [=you know] not in-which hour the son of-the person comes."	[39]"So know this: that if the master-of-the-house recognized what-kind-of [=at what] hour the thief comes, he-excused not ever[a] [=he would not have permitted] his house to-be-broken-in. [40]And [b] you [=yourselves also] happen [=must be] ready that [=because] in-which hour you-suppose [=you know] not [when] the son of-the person comes."	Mary said to Jesus, "What are your disciples like?" He said, "They are like little children living in a field that is not theirs. When the owners of the field come, they will say, 'Give us back our field.' They take off their clothes in front of them in order to give it back to them, and they return their field to them. For this reason I say, if the owners of a house know that a thief is coming, they will be on guard before the thief arrives and will not let the thief break into their house <their domain> and steal their possessions. As for you, then, be on guard against the world. Prepare yourselves with great strength, so the robbers can't find a way to get to you, for the trouble you expect will come. Let there be among you a person who understands. When the crop ripened, he came quickly carrying a sickle and harvested it. Anyone here with two good ears had better listen!"

[a] *he-excused not ever* 𝔓[75] ℵ* D sy[s] sy[c] cop[samss]; *he-stayed-awake ever and he-excused not* ℵ[1] A B L W Θ Ψ *f*[1] *f*[13] 33 892 1006 1342 1506 𝔐 vg it[mss] sy[p] sy[h] cop[samss] cop[bo].
[b] *omit* 𝔓[75] ℵ B L Q Θ Ψ 070 579 2542 *pc* vg it[mss] sy[s] sy[c] cop; *therefore* A D W *f*[13] 33 892 1006 1342 1506 𝔐 sy[p] sy[h].

240. The Loyal and Disloyal Slave (→ §339)

Matt 24:45-51

45“What [=Who] consequently is
the loyal and sensible slave whom
the lord[a] established upon [=over]
his household[b] to-give them
nourishment in [=at the] proper-
time?
46Fortunate [is] that slave whom, his
lord having-come,
will-find [him] thus doing.
47Amen I-say to-you that he-
will-establish him upon [=over]
all his being-at-one's-disposals
[=belongings]. 48So [=But] if-ever that
bad slave might-say in his heart,
‘My lord delays,’ 49and he-might-
begin to-hit his fellow-slaves, so and
[=also] he-might-eat and he-might-
drink with being-drunks [=those
who are drunk], 50the lord of-that
slave will-press-forward [=will come]
in [=on a] day which he-expects
not and in [=at an] hour which
he-knows not, 51and he-will-bisect
him and will-put his part with the
hypocrites.
There-will-be wailing and gnashing
of-the teeth there.”

Q 12:42-46

42“What [=Who] consequently is the
loyal and sensible slave whom the
lord established upon [=over] his
household to-give them in [=at the]
proper-time nourishment?
43Fortunate [is] that slave whom,
his lord having-come, will-find
[him] thus doing. 44Amen I-say
to-you that he-will-establish him
upon [=over] all his being-at-one's-
disposals [=belongings]. 45So [=But]
if-ever that slave might-say in his
heart, ‘My lord delays’ and he-
might-begin to-hit his fellow-slaves,
so and [=and also] might-eat and
might-drink with being-drunks
[=those who are drunk],
46 the lord of-that slave will-press-
forward [=will come] in [=on a] day
which he-expects not and in [=at an]
hour which he-knows not, and he-
will-bisect him and will-put his part
with the disloyal.”

Luke 12:42-48

42And the lord said,
“What [=Who] consequently is the
loyal, the sensible, manager whom
the lord will-establish upon [=over]
his healing [=servants] <u>to-give</u> [a]
ration in [=at the] proper-time?
43Fortunate [is] that slave whom, his
lord having-come,
will-find [him] doing thus.
44Truly I-say to-you that he-
will-establish him upon [=over]
all his being-at-one's-disposals
[=belongings]. 45So [=But] if-ever that
slave might-say in his heart, ‘My
lord delays to-come,’ and might-
begin to-hit the children and the
slave-girls, and even to-eat and to-
drink and to-get-drunk,
46the lord of-that slave will-press-
forward [=will come] in [=on a] day
which he-expects not and in [=on
an] hour which he-knows not, and
he-will-bisect him and will-put his
part with the disloyal.

47So [=But] that slave having-known
the wish [of] his lord and no [=not]
having-made-ready or having-done
[=having conformed] to his wish will-
be-beaten many [times]. 48So [=But]
the [one] having-known no [=not],
so [=and] having-done [something]
worthy of-blows will-be-beaten few
[=lightly]. So to-all to-whom many
[=much] was-given many [=much]
will-be-searched [for] along [=from]
him. And [the one] to-whom they-
placed-before many [=much], they-
will-ask much-more [from] him.”

[a] *the lord* ℵ B D L f^1 33 205 *pc* it; *his lord* W Θ f^{13} 892 1006 1342 1506 𝔐 sy[h] cop.
[b] *his household* B L W Δ Θ f^{13} 33 *al* vg it[mss] sy[p] sy[h]; *his home* ℵ 565 579 892 *al*; *his healing* D f^1 1006 1342 1506 𝔐 sy[s].

Matt 19:2
Mark 10:1 (§193, p. 158)

241. Casting Disunity and Divisions (→ §117)

Matt 10:34-36	Q 12:51, 53	Luke 12:49-53	Thomas 10; 16
		[49]"I come to-throw fire upon the land and what [=how] I-wish if it-was-enflamed already. [50]So I-have [a] baptism to-be-baptized, and how I-am-controlled [=I am consumed with it] until whoever [=whenever] it-might-be-completed.	[10]Jesus said, "I have cast fire upon the world, and look, I'm guarding it until it blazes."
[34]"You-might-think no [=Do not think] that I-came to-throw [=to bring] peace upon the land. I-came not to-throw [=to bring] peace but [the] sword.	[51]"Do-you-suppose that I-came to-throw [=to bring] peace upon the land? I-came not to-throw [=to bring] peace but [the] sword.	[51]Do-you-suppose that I-arrived to-give peace in the land? Indeed-not, I-say to-you, but or [=rather] disunity. [52]For from the now [=from now on] five in one house will-be having-been-divided-up, three upon [=against] two and two upon [=against] three,	[16]Jesus said, "Perhaps people think that I have come to cast peace upon the world. They do not know that I have come to cast conflicts upon the earth: fire, sword, war. For there will be five in a house: there'll be three against two and two against three, father against son and son against father, and they will stand alone."
[35]For I-came to-slice [=to separate a] person according-to [=from] his father and	[53]For I-came to-slice [=to separate a] son according-to [=from] father,	[53]they-will-be-divided-up father upon [=from] son and son upon [=from] father,	
daughter according-to [=from] her mother, and	daughter according-to [=from] her mother, and	mother upon [=from] the daughter and daughter upon [=from] the mother,	
bride according-to [=from] her mother-in-law, [36]and enemies of-the person [will be] his house-members."	bride according-to [=from] her mother-in-law."	mother-in-law upon [=from] her bride and bride upon [=from] the[a] mother-in-law."	

[a] *the* 𝔭[45] 𝔭[75] ℵ* B D L 579 892 *pc*; *her* ℵ[2] A W Θ Ψ *f*[1] *f*[13] 33 1006 1342 1506 𝔐 it[mss] vg sy cop[sa] cop[bo].

242. Searching for Signs (→ §173)

Luke 12:54-56	Thomas 91
[54]So he-was-saying and [=also] to-the crowds, "Whenever you-might-see [a] cloud arising upon [=in the] west, instantly you-say that '[A] shower is-coming,' and thus it-happens. [55]And whenever [there is a] south [wind] heaving, you-say that 'There-will-be scorching-heat,' and it-happens. [56]Hypocrites, you-recognize [=you know how] to-examine the face of-the land and of-the heaven [=sky], so [=but] this proper-time you-recognize not how to-examine?"	They said to him, "Tell us who you are so that we may believe in you." He said to them, "You examine the face of heaven and earth, but you have not come to know the one who is in your presence, and you do not know how to examine the present moment."

There are no variants in this pericope that appear in English.

243. Resolving Conflicts with Opponents (→ §35)

Matt 5:25-26	**Q 12:58-59**	**Luke 12:57-59**
		57“And so what [=why] do-you-judge not from themselves [=for yourselves] the [=what is] righteous?
25“Be making-friends quickly [with] your opponent until whoever [=while] you-are with him in [=on]	58“Until whoever [=While you are] with your opponent in [=on] the way [to court], give [an] effort to-be-resolved from [=to settle the case with] him,	58For like [=when] you-leave with your opponent upon [=to go to the] magistrate, in [=on] the way [to court] give [an] effort to-be-resolved
the way [to court], lest the opponent might-deliver you to-the judge and the judge[a] to-the attendant, and you-will-be-thrown into prison. 26Amen I-say to-you, you-might-go-out not no [=at all] from-there until ever you-might-give-over the last quadrans.”	lest your opponent might-deliver you to-the judge, and the judge to-the attendant, and the attendant will-throw you into prison. 59I-say to-you, you-might-go-out not no [=at all] from-there until the last quadrans you-might-give-over.”	from [=to settle the case with] him, lest he-might-drag you to the judge, and the judge will-deliver[b] you to-the bailiff and the bailiff will-throw you into prison. 59I-say to-you, you-might-go-out not no [=at all] from-there until and [=even] the last lepton you-might-give-over.”

[a] *omit* 𝔓[64] ℵ B *f*[1] *f*[13] 205 892 *pc*; *might-deliver you* D L W Θ 33 1006 1342 1506 𝔐 it[mss] vg sy[c] sy[p].
[b] *will-deliver* 𝔓[45] ℵ A B D E *f*[13] 579 2427 *pc*; *might-deliver* L W Ψ *f*[1] 33 892 1006 1342 1506 𝔐.

244. Luke's Parable of the Fig Tree

Luke 13:1-9

1So some were-being-there in the it proper-time [=at that very time] informing him around
[=concerning] the Galileans, the blood of-whom Pilate mixed with their sacrifices. 2And having-
answered[a] he-said to-them, “Do-you-suppose that these Galileans happened sinfuls [=were sinful
people] along [=beyond] all the Galileans that [=because] they-have-suffered these [things]? 3Indeed-
not, I-say to-you, but if-ever no [=unless] you-might-repent all [of] you-will-be-destroyed likewise[b].
4Or those eighteen upon whom the tower fell in Siloam and killed them, do-you-suppose that
they [themselves] happened [=were] debtors along [=beyond] all people settling [in] Jerusalem?
5Indeed-not, I-say to-you, but if-ever no [=unless] you-might-repent all [of] you-will-be-destroyed
in-the-same-way.” 6So he-was-saying this parable: “Some [person] was-having [a] fig-tree having-
been-planted in his vineyard, and he-came searching [for] fruit in [=on] it and found not [=none].
7So he-said to the vine-dresser, ‘Look! three years from which I-come [=for three years I have come]
searching [for] fruit in [=on] this fig-tree and I-find not [=none]. Therefore[c] cut-off it [=cut it down];
and for-what-reason [=tell me why] it-uses-up the land?’ 8So having-answered he-says to-him,
‘Lord, excuse it and this year [=leave it for one more year] until whichever I-might-dig around it and
I-might-throw [down some] dung, 9even-if [=and if] for-one it-might-do [=it might make] fruit into
the intending [=in the next year, fine]; so [=but] if no in-effect, you-will-cut-off it [=then cut it down].’”

[a] *omit* 𝔓[75] ℵ B L 070 *pc* vg it[mss] cop[samss]; *Jesus* A D W Θ Ψ *f*[1] *f*[13] 33 892 1006 1342 1506 𝔐 it sy cop[samss] cop[bo].
[b] *likewise* 𝔓[75] ℵ B D L Θ 070 *f*[1] *f*[13] 33 205 579 892 2542 *al*; *in-the-same-way* A W Ψ 1006 1342 1506 𝔐.
[c] *Therefore* 𝔓[75] A L Θ Ψ 0233 *f*[13] 33 579 892 *al* vg it[mss] sy[h] cop; *omit* ℵ B D W *f*[1] 1006 1342 1506 𝔐 sy[c] sy[p].

Matt 19:2
Mark 10:1 (§193, p. 158)

245. Luke's Healing of the Hunched Woman on the Sabbath

Luke 13:10-17

10 So he-was teaching in one of-the synagogues in [=on] the sabbaths. 11 And look! [a] woman having
[a] spirit of-illness [for] eighteen years and she-was bending-over and being-able to-straighten-
up no [=not] into the completely [=fully]. 12 So having-seen her, Jesus addressed and said to-her,
"Woman, you-have-been-released [from] your illness." 13 And he-placed the hands [on] her, and
at-once she-was-straightened-up and was-glorifying god. 14 So the synagogue-leader having-
answered, being-indignant that [=because] Jesus healed [on] the sabbath, was-saying to the crowd,
"That[a] [=Because] there-are six days in which it-is-necessary to-work, therefore coming in [=on]
them[b] be-healed, and no [=but not] [on] the day of-the sabbath." 15 So the lord answered him and
said, "Hypocrites, does-one-loose not his ox or ass from the feeding-trough [on] the sabbath and
having-led-away [it] does-one-give-a-drink-of-water [to it], each of-you? 16 So [=And] this [woman]
being [a] daughter of-Abraham, whom the adversary restrained, look!, for ten and eight years,
it-is-necessary not [for her] to-be-loosed from this binding [on] the day of-the sabbath?" 17 And his
saying these of-him [=when he had said these things], all the [ones] opposing him were-being-put-to-
shame and all the crowd was-rejoicing upon [=at] all the glorious happenings under [=being done
by] him.

[a] *That* 𝔓^{75} ℵ B L Θ 579 892 *pc*; *omit* 𝔓^{45} A D W f^1 f^{13} 1006 1342 1506 𝔐 sy.
[b] *them* 𝔓^{45} 𝔓^{75} ℵ B L W Ψ 070 0233 f^1 f^{13} 205 579 892 *al*; *these* D Θ 1006 1342 1506 𝔐.

246. The Parable of the Mustard Seed (→ §150)

Matt 13:31-32	Mark 4:30-32	**Q 13:18-19**	**Luke 13:18-19**	Thomas 20
31 Another parable he-placed-before them, saying, "The kingdom of-the heavens	30 And he-was-saying, "How might-we-compare the kingdom of-god or	18 "What is the kingdom of-god	18 Therefore he-was-saying, "What is the kingdom of-god	The disciples said to Jesus, "Tell us what Heaven's kingdom is like." He said to them,
	in what parable might-we-put it[a]?	comparable-to and to-what will-I-compare it?	comparable-to and to-what will-I-compare it?	
is comparable-to [a] tiny-seed of-mustard, which [a] person having-taken sowed in his field;	31 [It is] like [a] tiny-seed of-mustard, which whenever it-might-be-sown upon the land,	19 It-is comparable-to [a] tiny-seed of-mustard, which [a] person having-taken threw into his garden	19 It-is comparable-to [a] tiny-seed of-mustard, which [a] person having-taken threw into of-himself [=his own] garden	"It's like a mustard seed, the smallest of all seeds, but when it falls on prepared
32 which for-one is smaller of-all [=than all] of-the seeds,	being smaller of-all [=than all] of-the seeds			
so [=but] whenever it-might-grow it-is	upon the land, 32 and whenever it-might-be-sown, it-ascends [=it grows] and happens [=becomes]	and it-grew and happened [=turned]	and it-grew and happened [=turned]	soil, it produces
greater of-the [=than the] shrubs and happens [=becomes	greater of-all [=than all] of-the shrubs and does [=makes]			

a] tree, with-the-result-that the birds of-heaven to-come [=come] and to-nest [=nest] in its branches."	great branches, with-the-result-that the birds of-heaven to-be-able [=are able] to-nest under its shade."	into [a] tree and the birds of-heaven	into [a] tree[b] and the birds of-heaven	a large plant and becomes a shelter for birds of the sky."
		nested in its branches."	nested in its branches."	

[a] *in what parable might-we-put it* ℵ B C* L Δ 892 1342 2427 *pc* cop^{bo}; *in what parable might-we-parable it* A C^{2} D Θ *f*^{1} 33 1006 1506 𝔐 vg it^{mss} sy; *in what parable might we give* W; *in what parable might-we-put it? We-parable it* *f*^{13}.
[b] *tree* 𝔭^{75} ℵ B D L 070 892 *pc* it sy^{s} sy^{c} cop^{sa} cop^{bomss}; *great tree* 𝔭^{45} A W Θ Ψ *f*^{1} *f*^{13} 33 1006 1506 𝔐 vg it^{mss} sy^{p} cop^{bomss}.

247. The Parable of the Leaven (→ §151)

Matt 13:33	**Q 13:20-21**	**Luke 13:20-21**	Thomas 96
[33]He-talked [=He said] another parable to-them,	[20]And again, "To-what will-I-compare the kingdom of-god?	[20]And he-said again, "To-what will-I-compare the kingdom of-god?	Jesus <said>, "The Father's
"The kingdom of-the heavens is comparable-to leaven, which [a] woman having-taken inserted into three satons [=measures] of-wheat-flour until which [time the] whole was-leavened."	[21]It-is comparable-to leaven, which [a] woman having-taken inserted into three satons [=measures] of-wheat-flour until which [time the] whole was-leavened."	[21]It-is comparable-to leaven, which [a] woman having-taken inserted[a] into three satons [=measures] of-wheat-flour until which [time the] whole was-leavened."	kingdom is like <a> woman. She took a little leaven, <hid> it in dough, and made it into large loaves of bread. Anyone here with two ears had better listen!"

[a] *inserted* 𝔭^{75} ℵ A D W Θ Ψ 070 *f*^{13} 𝔐; *hid* B K L N 205 209 892 1342 1424 1506 2542 *al.*

248. The Ones Who Seek the Narrow Door (→ §55, §57, §340)

Matt 7:13-14; 25:10-12; 7:22-23	**Q 13:24-27**	**Luke 13:22-27**
		[22]And he-was-traveling-through according-to [=each of the] cities and villages teaching and doing [=making his] journey into Jerusalems.[23]So some [person] said to-him, "Lord, if [=are] the being-saveds [=those who will be saved] few?" So he-said to them,
[7:13]"Enter through the narrow gate;	[24]"Enter through the narrow gate	[24]"Struggle to-enter through the narrow door[b], that [=because]
that [=because it is a] wide gate and roomy way [=road] leading-away into destruction and many are the enterings [=those who enter] through it. [14]What[a] [=How] narrow [is] the gate and having-been-pressed-against [=really narrow is] the way	that [=because] many will-search	many, I-say to-you, will-search
leading-away into life and few are the findings [=those who find] it."	to-enter and few are the enterings [=those who enter] through it.	to-enter and [=but] they-will-have-the-strength not.
[25:10]"So their going-away [=when they had gone away] to-buy [it], the bridegroom came and the readies	[25]From which ever [=When] the master-of-the-house might-be-raised [=might be awoken] and might-	[25]From which ever [=When] the master-of-the-house might-be-raised [=might be awoken] and might-

[=those who were ready] with him into the weddings and the door was-locked. [11]Afterward, the remainders [= rest of the] virgins come and [=also] saying, 'Lord, lord, open [the door] to-us.'" [12]So having-answered he-said, "Amen I-say to-you, I-recognize you not."	lock-up the door and [when] you-might-begin to-stand outside and to-knock [on] the door saying, 'Lord, open [the door] to-us,' and having-answered he-will-say to-you, 'I-recognize you not.'	lock-up the door and [when] you-might-begin to-stand outside and to-knock [on] the door saying, 'Lord[c], open [the door] to-us,' and having-answered he-will-say to-you, 'I-recognize you not [nor] from-where you-are.'
[7:22]"Many will-say to-me in [=on] that day, 'Lord, lord, we-prophesied not [=did we not prophesy] in your-own name, and we-casted-out [=did we not cast out] demons in your-own name and did-we [not do] many powers [=miracles] in your-own name?'	[26]Then you-will-begin to-say, 'We-ate and we-drank in-the-sight of-you and you-taught in our wide-streets.'	[26]Then you-will-begin to-say, 'We-ate and we-drank in-the-sight of-you and you-taught in our wide-streets.'
[23]And then I-will-confess to-them that I-knew you never; draw-back from me the workings [=you who work] lawlessness."	[27]And he-will-say, saying to-you, 'I-recognize you not. Abandon from [=Leave] me the workings [=you who work] lawlessness.'"	[27]And he-will-say, saying to-you, 'I-recognize you not [nor] from-where you-are[d]. Abandon from [=Leave] me all [you] workers of-unrighteousness[e].'"

[a] *What* $\aleph^2$ C L W Θ f^1 f^{13} 892 1006 1506 𝔐 it^{mss} vg sy; *And* 205 209; *That* $\aleph^*$ 700^c *pc* cop^{samss} cop^{bo}; *So that* B* cop^{samss}.
[b] *door* $\mathfrak{p}^{75}$ ℵ B D L Θ f^1 205 892 2542 *pc* cop^{bo}; *gate* A W Ψ f^{13} 1006 1342 1506 𝔐 cop^{sa}.
[c] *Lord* $\mathfrak{p}^{75}$ ℵ B L 892 1241 *pc* it^{mss} vg sy^s cop^{sa} cop^{bomss}; *Lord, lord* A D W Θ Ψ f^1 f^{13} 𝔐 it sy^c sy^p cop^{bomss}.
[d] *I-recognize you not from-where you-are* ℵ A W Θ Ψ f^1 f^{13} 𝔐 it^{mss} vg sy; *I-recognize not from-where you-are* $\mathfrak{p}^{75}$ B L 070 1241 2542 *pc* it^{mss}; *I-recognized you never* D.
[e] *of-unrighteousness* $\mathfrak{p}^{75}$ ℵ A B L W Θ Ψ 070 f^1 f^{13} 892 𝔐; *of-lawlessness* D 1424 cop^{bomss}.
🕮 Mt 7:23 – Ps 6:8; 🕮 Lk 13:27 – Ps 6:8

249. Many Will Come (→ §89, 251)

Matt 8:11a	**Q 13:29**	Luke 13:29
[11a]"So I-say to-you that many will-press-forward [=will come] from easts [=east] and wests [=west] and will-be-stretched-out [=will recline at table] . . . "	[29]"And many will-press-forward [=will come] from easts [=east] and wests will-press-forward and will-be-stretched-out [=will recline at table] . . . "	[29]"And they-will-press-forward from easts [=east] and wests [=west] and from north and south and they-will-be-stretched-out in the kingdom of-god."

There are no variants in this pericope that appear in English.

250. But They Will Be Rejected (→ §89)

Matt 8:11b-12	**Q 13:28**	Luke 13:28
[11b]". . . with Abraham and Isaac and Jacob in the kingdom of-the heavens, [12]so [=but] the sons of-the kingdom will-be-cast-out into the outermost darkness. There-will-be wailing and gnashing of-the teeth there."	[28]". . . with Abraham and Isaac and Jacob in the kingdom of-god, so [=but] you [yourselves] will-be-cast-out into the outermost darkness. There-will-be wailing and gnashing of-the teeth there."	[28]"There will-be wailing and grinding of-teeth whenever you-might-see Abraham and Isaac and Jacob and all the prophets in the kingdom of-god, so [=but] you being-cast outside."

There are no variants in this pericope that appear in English.

251. Many Will Come (→ §89, §249)

Matt 8:11a	Q 13:29	**Luke 13:29**
11a“So I-say to-you that many will-press-forward [=will come] from easts [=east] and wests [=west] and will-be-stretched-out [=will recline at table] . . . ”	29“And many will-press-forward [=will come] from easts [=east] and wests will-press-forward and will-be-stretched-out [=will recline at table] . . . ”	29“And they-will-press-forward from easts [=east] and wests [=west] and from north and south and they-will-be-stretched-out in the kingdom of-god.”

There are no variants in this pericope that appear in English.

252. The First and the Last (→ §297)

Matt 20:16	**Q 13:30**	**Luke 13:30**	Thomas 4
16“Thus the lasts will-be firsts and the firsts lasts.[a]”	30“The lasts will-be firsts and the firsts lasts.”	30“And look! [those] who will-be firsts are lasts and [those] who will-be lasts [ones] are firsts.”	Jesus said, “The person old in days won’t hesitate to ask a little child seven days old about the place of life, and that person will live. For many of the first will be last, and will become a single one.”

[a] *omit* ℵ B L Z 085 892 1342 *pc* cop^{sa}; *for many are called, so few chosen-ones* C D W Θ f^1 f^{13} 33 892 1006 1506 𝔐 it vg sy.

253. Luke’s Warning about Herod

Luke 13:31-33

31In it the [=At that very] hour[a] some Pharisees approached saying to-him, “Go-out and travel
from-here, that [=because] Herod wishes to-kill you.” 32And he-said to-them, “Having-traveled, say
to-this fox, ‘Look! I-cast-out demons and I-accomplish[b] cures today and tomorrow and [on] the
third I-am-finished. 33Nevertheless, it-is-necessary [for] me today and tomorrow and the having
[=the next day] to-travel that [=because] it-is-imaginable not for [a] prophet to-be-destroyed outside
of-Jerusalem.’”

[a] *hour* 𝔭^{75} ℵ A B* D L f^1 f^{13} 205 579 700 892 *pc* cop^{samss}; *day* B^1 W Θ Ψ 1006 1342 1506 𝔐 vg it^{mss} sy^s sy^c cop^{samss} cop^{bo}.
[b] *I-accomplish* 𝔭^{75} ℵ B L 33 *pc*; *accomplishing* D; *I-perform* A W Θ Ψ f^1 f^{13} 892 1006 1342 1506 𝔐; *doing and* 𝔭^{45} sy^p.

254. Lament for Jerusalem (→ §322)

Matt 23:37-39	**Q 13:34-35**	**Luke 13:34-35**
37“Jerusalem, Jerusalem, the [one] killing the prophets and stoning the having-been-sent-offs [=those who were sent] to her; how-often did-I-wish to-collect your descendants which manner [=like a] hen collects her young-birds under the [=her] wings, and [=but] you-wished not. 38Look! your house is-excused [=is left] to-you deserted[a]. 39For I-say to-you, you-might-see me not no	34“Jerusalem, Jerusalem, the [one] killing the prophets and stoning the having-been-sent-offs [=those who were sent] to her; how-many-times did-I-wish to-collect your descendants which manner [=like a] hen collects her young-birds under the [=her] wings, and [=but] you-wished not. 35Look! your house is-excused [=is left] to-you. I-say to-you you-might-see me not no [=ever	34“Jerusalem, Jerusalem, the [one] killing the prophets and stoning the having-been-sent-offs [=those who were sent] to her; how-many-times did-I-wish to-collect your descendants which manner [=like a] hen herself [=does with her own] brood under the [=her] wings, and [=but] you-wished not. 35Look! your house is-excused [=is left] to-you. So[b] I-say you-might-see me not

[=ever again] from right-now until [the time when] ever you-might-say, 'Having-been-blessed [is] the [one] coming in [the] name [of the] lord.'"

again] until [the time] will-press-forward [=will come] when you-might-say, 'Having-been-blessed [is] the [one] coming in [the] name [of the] lord."

until [the time] will-press-forward [=will come] when you-might-say, 'Having-been-blessed [is] the [one] coming in [the] name [of the] lord."

[a] *deserted* ℵ C D W Θ f^1 f^{13} 33 892 1006 1341 1506 𝔐 vg it[mss] sy[p] sy[h]; *omit* B L sy[s] cop[sa].
[b] *So* 𝔭[75] ℵ[2] A B D W Θ Ψ f^1 f^{13} 892 1006 1342 1506 𝔐 vg it[mss] sy[p] sy[h] cop[bo]; *omit* 𝔭[45] ℵ* L 2542 *pc* it sy[c] cop[sa].
🕮 Mt 23:38 – Ps 69:25; Jer 12:7; 22:5; 🕮 Mt 23:39 – Ps 118:26; 🕮 Lk 13:35 – Ps 118:26; Jer 12:7; 22:5

255. Luke's Jesus Heals a Person with Dropsy on the Sabbath

Luke 14:1-6

[1]And it-happened in the to-come him [=once he went] into the house of-some [=of one] of-the magistrates of-the Pharisees [on the] sabbath to-eat bread and they [themselves] were watching-closely him. [2]And look! some person suffering-from-dropsy was in-front of-him. [3]And having-answered, Jesus said to the lawyers and Pharisees saying, "[a] Is-it-permitted [on] the sabbath to-heal or not?" [4]So [=But] the [lawyers and Pharisees] were-unresponsive. And having-taken-hold-of him he-cured him and released [him]. [5]And[b] he-said to them, "[If] some [one] of-you [had a] son or [an] ox will-fall [=who fell] into [a] pit, will-he-draw-out it not instantly and [=also] in [=on a] day of-the sabbath?" [6]And they-had-the-strength not to-answer-back to these [things].

[a] *omit* 𝔭[75] ℵ B D L Θ Ψ 892 2542 *pc*; *if* 𝔭[45] A W f^1 f^{13} 1006 1342 1506 𝔐 vg it[mss] sy.
[b] *omit* 𝔭[45] 𝔭[75] ℵ[1] B D L f^1 69 205 788 892 2542 *al* it sy[s] sy[c] sy[p] cop; *having-answered* ℵ* ℵ[2] A W Θ Ψ f^{13} 1006 1342 1506 𝔐 vg sy[h].

256. Luke's Teaching about Seats of Honor

Luke 14:7-10

[7]So, monitoring how they-were-choosing the places-of-honor, he-was-saying [a] parable to the having-been-calleds [=invited guests], saying to them, [8]"Whenever you-might-be-called under [=by] some [person] into [=to] weddings, might-you-recline-at-table no into [=you should not take] the place-of-honor, lest [someone] more-honored [than] you might-have-been having-been-called under [=by] him, [9]and having-come, the [one] having-called you and him will-say to-you, 'Give [the] place to-this [man]' and then you-might-begin to-detain [=to move to] the last place with shame. [10]But whenever you-might-be-called, having-traveled lean into [=sit in] the last place in-order-that whenever the [one] having-called you might-come he-will-say[a] to-you, 'Friend, move-up higher', then glory will-be [ascribed] to-you in-the-sight of-all[b] the sitting-at-tables [=those sitting with] you."

[a] *he-will-say* 𝔭[75] 𝔭[97] ℵ B L Θ 579 892 *pc*; *he-might-say* A D W Ψ f^1 f^{13} 33 1006 1506 𝔐.
[b] *of-all* 𝔭[75] ℵ A B L Θ f^1 f^{13} 33 205 579 892 *al* sy[c] sy[p] sy[h]; *omit* 𝔭[97] D W Ψ 1006 1342 1506 𝔐 vg it[mss] sy[s].
🕮 Lk 14:8 – Prov 25:6

257. Honor Reversal (→ §321)

Matt 23:12	Q 14:11	Luke 14:11
[12]"So whoever will-exalt himself will-be-humbled, and whoever will-humble himself will-be-exalted."	[11]"The all [=each person] exalting himself will-be-humbled, and the [one] humbling himself will-be-exalted."	[11]"That [=Because] the all [=each person] exalting himself will-be-humbled, and the [one] humbling himself will-be-exalted."

There are no variants in this pericope that appear in English.

258. Luke's Teaching about Honor Reciprocity

Luke 14:12-14

12 So [=But] he-was-saying and [=also] to-the [one] having-called him, "Whenever you-might-
do [=you might have a] meal or [a] banquet yell no [=do not call] your friends so-not [=nor] your
brothers so-not [=nor] your kindreds so-not [=nor] wealthy next-door-neighbors, lest they
[themselves] and [=too] might-invite-in-return you and repayment might-happen [=might be
made to] you. 13 But whenever you-might-do [=you might have a] dinner, call poors [=poor people],
crippleds [=crippled people], lames [=lame people], blinds [=blind people]. 14 And you-will-be
fortunate that [=because] they-have not to-repay you, for you-will-be-repaid in [=at] the rise of-the
righteouses [=righteous people]."

There are no variants in this pericope that appear in English.

259. The Parables of the Great Supper (→ §315)

Matt 22:1-14	**Q 14:16-18, 21, 23**	**Luke 14:15-24**	Thomas 64
1 And having-answered Jesus said [=spoke] again in parables to-them saying,		15 So having-heard these [things] some [person] of-the sitting-at-tables [=of the guests] said to-him, "Fortunate [is] whoever will-eat bread in the kingdom of-god." 16 So [=But] he-said to-him,	
2 "The kingdom of-the heavens was-compared [to a] person, [a] king, whoever [=who] did [=gave] weddings [=a wedding feast] to-his son. 3 And he-sent-off his slaves to-call the having-been-calleds [=those who were invited] into the weddings [=wedding feast], and they-were-wishing not to-come. 4 Again, he-sent-off another [group of] slaves saying, 'Say to-the having-been-calleds [=those who	16 "Some person was-doing [=was giving a] great banquet and he-called many 17 and he-sent-off his slave at-the hour of-the banquet to-say to-the having-been-calleds [=those who had been invited],	"Some person was-doing[c] [=was giving a] great banquet and he-called many, 17 and he-sent-off his slave at-the hour of-the banquet to-say to-the having-been-calleds [=those who had been	Jesus said, "A person was receiving guests. When he had prepared the dinner, he sent his slave to invite the guests. The slave went to the first and said to that one, 'My master invites you.' That one said, 'Some merchants owe me money; they are coming to me tonight. I have to go and give them instructions. Please excuse
were invited]: "Look! my meal I-have-made-ready[a], my bulls and the fattened-calves having-been-slaughtered and all [things being] ready. Come-on into the weddings [=wedding feast].'"	'Come that [=because] it-is ready already.'	invited], 'Come that [=because] it-is ready already.'	me from dinner.' The slave went to another and said to that one, 'My master has invited you.' That one said to the slave, 'I have bought a house, and I have been called away for a day. I shall have no time.'
5 So the having-rebuffeds [=those who refused the invitation] went-away, who for-one [=one of whom went] into		18 And they-began from one all [=one and all] to-make-apologies. The first said to-him, 'I-bought [a]	The slave went to another and said to that one, 'My master invites you.' That one said to the slave, 'My

the [=his] own field, who so [=and the other] upon [=to] his business, 6 so [=while] the remainders [=rest] having-seized his slaves insulted and killed [them].	18 . . . field . . .	field and I-have inevitable [=I need] having-gone-out to-see it. I-beg you, have me having-made-apologies [=accept my regrets].' 19 And [an] other said, 'I-bought five pairs of-oxen and I-travel to-examine them. I-beg you, have me having-made-apologies [=accept my regrets].' 20 And [an] other said, 'I-married [a] woman and through this [=because of this] I-am-able not to-come.'	friend is to be married, and I am to arrange the banquet. I shall not be able to come. Please excuse me from dinner.' The slave went to another and said to that one, 'My master invites you.' That one said to the slave, 'I have bought an estate, and I am going to collect the rent. I shall not be able to come. Please excuse me.'
	21 And the slave . . .	21 And the slave having-arrived [back home]	The slave returned and said to his master, 'Those
7 So [=Now] the king[b] was-angered and having-sent his troops he-destroyed those murderers and burned-down their city.	his lord [of] these [things]. Then the master-of-the-house having-been-angered said [to] his	informed his lord [of] these [things]. Then the master-of-the-house having-been-angered	whom you invited to dinner have asked to be excused.' The master said to his slave,
8 Then he-says [to] his slaves, 'The wedding [feast], for-one, is ready, so [=but] the having-been-calleds [=those who were invited] were not worthy.	slave, 23 'Go-out into	said [to] his slave,	
		'Go-out without-delay into the wide-streets and laneways of-the city and lead-in the poors [=poor people] and crippleds [=crippled people] and blinds [=blind people] and lames [=lame people].' 22 And the slave said, 'Lord, which [=what] you-presided-over [=you commanded] has-happened, and there-is yet [=still] place [=room].'	'Go out on the streets and bring back whomever you find to have dinner.' Buyers and merchants [will] not enter the places of my Father."
9 Therefore travel upon the passages of-the ways [=main roads] and call whatsoever if-ever [=whoever] you-might-find into the weddings [=wedding feast].'	the ways [=roads] and call whatsoever if-ever [=whoever] you-might-find in-order-that my house might-be-filled-up.'"	23 And the lord said to the slave, 'Go-out into the ways [=roads] and hedges and compel [them] to-enter, in-order-that my house might-be-stuffed.	
		24 For I-say to-you that no-one of-those men having-been-called [=who were invited] will-taste my banquet.'"	

10 And those slaves,
having-gone-out into the
ways [=roads], gathered
all whom they-found,
[the] evil and even [the]
good. And the wedding
was-filled of-dinings
[=with diners]. 11 So [=But]
the king, having-entered
to-notice [=to observe]
the dinings [=diners],
saw there [a] person not
having-been-clothed
[wearing] wedding clothes,
12 and he-says to-him,
'Comrade, how did-
you-enter here no [=not]
having wedding clothes?'
So [=But] he-was-muzzled
[=he was speechless].
13 Then the king said
to-the servants, 'Having-
restrained his feet and
hands, cast-out him into
the outermost darkness,
there-will-be wailing and
gnashing of-the teeth
there. 14 For many are
called, so [=but there are]
few chosen-ones.'"

[a] *I-have-made-ready* ℵ B C* D L 085 *f*^{1} 33 205 700 1424 2542 *pc*; *has-been-made-ready* 1342 *al*; *I-made-ready* C^{3} W *f*^{13} 892 1006 1506 𝔐.
[b] *So the king* ℵ B L 085 *f*^{1} 205 700 892 *pc* sy^{s} sy^{c} cop^{sa} cop^{bomss}; *So the king having-heard* Θ *f*^{13} vg it^{mss} sy^{p} cop^{bomss}; *And that king having-heard* C D W 1006 1342 1506 𝔐 it^{mss} sy^{h}.
[c] *was-doing* 𝔭^{75} ℵ B *f*^{1} *pc*; *did* A D L W Θ Ψ *f*^{13} 892 1006 1342 1506 𝔐.

260. Loving Mother and Father (→ §118)

Matt 10:37-38	**Q 14:26-27**	**Luke 14:25-27**	Thomas 55; 101
		25 So many crowds were- traveling-together-with him, and having-been- turned he-said to them,	
37 "The [one] liking father or mother on-behalf [=more than] me is not worthy of-me, and the [one] liking son or daughter on-behalf [=more	26 "Who hates not the father and the mother is-able not to-be my	26 "If some [one] comes to me and hates not the father himself[a] [=his very own father] and the mother and the woman [=wife] and the descendants	55 Jesus said, "Whoever does not hate father and mother cannot be my disciple, and whoever does not hate brothers and sisters, and carry the cross

than] me is not worthy of- me. 38And who [ever] takes not his cross and follows behind me is not worthy of-me.”	disciple and who hates not the son and the daughter is-able not to-be my disciple.” 27“Who takes not his cross and follows behind me is-able not to-be my disciple.”	and the brothers and the sisters and yet even and [=also] the soul himself [=his very own life], he-is-able not to-be my disciple. 27Whoever bears not the cross himself [=his very own cross] and comes behind me is-able not to-be my disciple.”	as I do, will not be worthy of me.” 101“Whoever does not hate <father> and mother as I do cannot be my <disciple>, and whoever does <not> love <father and> mother as I do cannot be my <disciple>. For my mother < . . . >, but my true <mother> gave me life.”

[a] *the father himself* 𝔓^{75} B L Ψ *pc*; *his father* 𝔓^{45} ℵ A D W Θ *f*^{1} *f*^{13} 892 1006 1342 𝔐; *the father* 579 1506 2542.
📖 Lk 14: 26 – Mic 7:6

261. Luke's Making Plans and Sacrifices

Luke 14:28-33

28“For what [person] out of-you [=among you] wishing to-build [a] tower having-been-seated
indeed-not he-estimates first the expense, if he-has into [=whether you have enough for] completion?
29In-order-that lest [=Otherwise] his having-put [=when he has laid down a] foundation and having-
the-strength no [=not being unable] to-finish-off, all the catching-sight-ofs [=those who see him]
might-begin to-mock him, 30saying that ‘This person began to-build and had-the-strength not
[=was unable] to-finish-off.’ 31Or what king traveling to-mull-over [=to consider whether to meet
an] other king into [=in] battle, having-been-seated will-plan[a] indeed-not first if it-is possible in
[=with] ten thousand to-meet [to fight] the [king] coming upon him with twenty thousand? 32So if
no in-effect [=If he cannot], yet his being far [=while the other is still far away], having-sent-off [an]
embassy-of-elders begs to [=for] peace. 33Thus therefore all [=each] out of-you who [does] not bid-
goodbye to-all being-at-one's-disposals himself [=give up his very own belongings] is-able not to-be
my disciple.”

[a] *will-plan* 𝔓^{75} ℵ B Θ *pc* it; *plans* A D L W Ψ *f*^{1} *f*^{13} 892 1006 1342 1506 𝔐 vg it^{mss}.

262. Finding and Losing One's Life (→ §118, §287)

Matt 10:39	**Q 17:33**	Luke 17:33	John 12:25
39“The [one] having-found his soul [=life] will-destroy [=will lose] it and the [one] having-destroyed his soul [=life] because-of me will-find it.”	33“The [one] having-found his soul [=life] will-destroy [=will lose] it and the [one] having-destroyed his soul [=life] because-of me will-find it.”	33“Who if-ever might-search to-make-secure his soul[a] will-destroy it, so [=but] who ever might-destroy [their life] will-give-life [to] it.”	25“The [one] liking his soul [=life] destroys it and the [one] hating his soul [=life] in this world will-guard it into eternal life.”

[a] *Who if-ever might-search to-make-secure his soul* 𝔓^{75} B L 579; *Who if-ever might-search to-save his soul* ℵ A W Θ Ψ *f*^{1} *f*^{13} 892 1006 1342 1506 𝔐 it^{mss} vg; *Who ever might-wish to-give-life his soul* D sy^{s} sy^{p} cop^{sa}.

263. The Parable of the Salt (→ §32, §187)

Matt 5:13	Mark 9:50	**Q 14:34-35**	**Luke 14:34-35**
13"You are the salt of-the land; so [=but] if-ever the salt might-become-tasteless, in what [=how] will-it-be-made-salty?	50"The salt [is] fine, so [=but] if-ever the salt might-happen [=becomes] unsalty, in what will-you-flavor it [=will you use it as flavoring]? Have salt in themselves [=in yourselves] and be-at-peace in [=with] one-another."	34"The salt [is] fine so if-ever the salt might-become-tasteless, in what will-it-be-flavored [=will it be used as flavoring]?	34"Therefore[b] the salt [is] fine, and so[c] if-ever the salt might-become-tasteless, in what will-it-be-flavored [=will it be used as flavoring]?
		35Neither into [=for the] land neither [=nor] into [=for the] dung-heap is-it usable;	35Neither into [=for the] land neither [=nor] into [=for the] dung-heap is-it usable;
It-has-the-strength into no-one [=It is good for nothing] yet if no [=except], having-been-thrown[a] outside, to-be-trod-upon under [=by] the people."		they-throw it outside."	they-throw it outside.
			The [one] having ears to-hear, let-him-hear."

[a] *having-been-thrown* $\mathfrak{P}^{86}$ ℵ B C f^{1} 33 205 892 *pc*; *to-be-thrown* D W Θ f^{13} 1006 1342 1506 𝔐.
[b] *Therefore* $\mathfrak{P}^{75}$ ℵ B L Θ f^{13} 579 892 *pc*; *omit* A D W Ψ f^{1} 1006 1506 𝔐 it vg sy cop^{samss}.
[c] *so* ℵ B D L Θ Ψ 0233 579 *pc* it^{mss} sy^{p} cop^{samss}; *omit* $\mathfrak{P}^{75}$ A W f^{1} f^{13} 892 1006 1342 1506 𝔐 it^{mss} vg sy^{s} sy^{c} cop.

264. Loyalty to Two Masters (→ §48, §270)

Matt 6:24	**Q 16:13**	Luke 16:13	Thomas 47
24"No-one [a] is-able to-be-a-slave [for] two lords; for or [=either] he-will-hate the one, and he-will-love the other, or he-will-hold-fast [to the] one and he-will-despise the other. You-are-able not to-be-a-slave to-god and to-money."	13"No-one is-able to-be-a-slave [for] two lords; for or [=either] he-will-hate the one, and he-will-love the other, or he-will-hold-fast [to the] one and he-will-despise the other. You-are-able not to-be-a-slave to-god and to-money."	13"No-one [=No] house-servant is-able to-be-a-slave [for] two lords; for or [=either] he-will-hate the one, and he-will-love the other, or he-will-hold-fast [to the] one and he-will-despise the other. You-are-able not to-be-a-slave to-god and to-money."	Jesus said, "A person cannot mount two horses or bend two bows. And a slave cannot serve two masters, otherwise that slave will honor the one and offend the other. Nobody drinks aged wine and immediately wants to drink young wine. Young wine is not poured into old wineskins, or they might break, and aged wine is not poured into a new wineskin, or it might spoil. An old patch is not sewn onto a new garment, since it would create a tear."

[a] *omit* ℵ B D f^{1} f^{13} 33 892 1006 1342 1506 𝔐 vg; *house-servant* L Δ 1242 *pc*.

Matt 19:2 Mark 10:1 (§193, p. 158)
Q 16:13 (§264, p. 198)

265. The Parable of the Lost Sheep (→ §188, §277)

Matt 18:12-14

12 "What [=How] supposes
[=does it seem] to-you? If-
ever one-hundred sheep
might-happen [=might
belong] to-some person
and one out of-them
might-be-deceived [=might
wander off], will-he-excuse
indeed-not [=would he
not leave] the ninety nine
upon the mountains and
having-traveled [would he
not] search [for] the [one]
being-deceived? 13 And
if-ever he-might-happen
to-find it, amen
I-say to-you that he-
rejoices upon [=over] it
rather or [=more than]

Q 15:4-5a, 7

4 "What person out of-you
having one-hundred
sheep might-happen
[=might belong] to-some
person and one out of-
them might-be-deceived
[=might wander off],
will-he-excuse indeed-
not [=would he not leave]
the ninety nine upon the
mountains and having-
traveled [would he not]
search [for] the [one]
having-been-destroyed
[=having been lost]? 5a And
if-ever he-might-happen
to-find it,
7 I-say to-you that he-
rejoices upon [=over] it
rather or [=more than]

Luke 15:1-7

1 So all the tax-collectors
and the sinfuls [=sinners]
were nearing him to-
hear him. 2 And even[a]
[=both] the Pharisees
and the scribes were-
grumbling-loudly saying
that "This [person] waits-
for [=welcomes] sinfuls
[=sinners] and eats-with
them." 3 So he-said to
them this parable, saying,
4 "What person out of-you
having one-hundred
sheep and having-
destroyed [=losing] out of-
them one, quits [=leaves]
not the ninety nine in the
deserted [place] and travels
upon [=goes after] the [one]
having-been-destroyed
[=having been lost] until he-
might-find it? 5 And
having-found [it] places
[it] upon his shoulders
rejoicing?
6 And having-come into
the house he-calls-
together the [=his] friends
and next-door-neighbors
saying to-them, 'Be-
rejoiced-with [=Be made
happy with] me, that [=for]
I-found my having-been-
destroyed [=lost] sheep.'
7 I-say to-you that thus
there-will-be [more] joy
in heaven upon [=for] one
sinful [person] repenting
or [=than] upon [=for]

Thomas 107

Jesus said, "The <Father's> kingdom is like a shepherd who had a hundred sheep. One of them, the largest, went astray. He left the ninety-nine and looked for the one until he found it. After he had toiled, he said to the sheep, 'I love you more than the ninety-nine.'"

upon [=for] the ninety nine no [=not] having-been-deceived [=having wandered off]. [14]Thus is not [the] wish in-front [=of] your father in [the] heavens in-order-that [=that] one of-these smalls [=little ones] might-be-destroyed."	upon [=for] the ninety nine no [=not] having-been-deceived [=having wandered off]."	ninety nine righteouses [=righteous people] whoever [=who] have no need [=for] repentance."	

[a] *even* 𝔭[75] א B D L Θ 892 *pc*; *omit* A W Ψ f^1 f^{13} 1006 1342 𝔐 cop.

266. Luke's Parable of the Lost Coin

Luke 15:8-10

[8]"Or what woman having ten drachmas if-ever she-might-destroy [=she might lose] one drachma indeed-not touches [=lights a] lantern and sweeps the home and searches [for it] carefully until which [time] she-might-find [it]? [9]And having-found it she-calls-together the [=her] friends and next-door-neighbors saying, 'Be-rejoiced-with [=Be made happy with] me, that [=because] I-found the drachma which I-destroyed [=I lost].' [10]Thus I-say to-you, 'Joy happens[a] in-the-sight of-the announcers [=angels] of-god upon [=because of] one sinful [person] repenting.'"

[a] *Joy happens* 𝔭[75] א B L 33 579 *pc*; *There-will-be joy* D f^{13} 2542 *pc* vg it cop[bomss].

SYNOPTIC STUDY GUIDE II

Special Luke

Special Luke (designated 'L' by the Two-Document Hypothesis) refers to material unique to Luke. As with Special Matthew, this refers to whole stories or other blocks of material, not individual words or phrases unique to Luke. And as with Special Matthew, the explanation concerning the origin of this is the same: Luke's imagination (for example, that Quirinius was governor at the time of Jesus' birth), or written sources in addition to Mark and Q that Luke had access to, either whole or partial. But Luke also claims to have investigated everything thoroughly (so perhaps some of his unique stories came from that as well). Beyond that it would be difficult to trace: if someone gave Luke a story of Jesus, did that story come from that person's community or imagination, or did it come from further back than that?

The following material is not *all* of Special Luke, but only a sampling of that interesting material: the Promise of the Birth of John the Baptist (§2), the Annunciation (§3), Mary and Elizabeth (§4), the Birth of John the Baptist (§5), the Birth of Jesus (§10), Jesus Circumcised and Presented at the Temple (§11), Jesus as a Boy in the Temple (§15), the Widow's Son at Nain (§90), the parables of the Good Samaritan (§208), the Persistent Friend (§211), the Fig Tree (§244), the Lost Coin (§266), the Prodigal Son (§267), the Unrighteous Manager (§268), the Rich Man and Lazarus (§275), the Unjust Judge (§289), the Pharisee and the Tax Collector (§290), the Healing of the Hunched Woman on the Sabbath (§245), the Healing of a Person with Dropsy on the Sabbath (§255), the Cleansing of Ten Lepers (§281), Jesus' Weeping over Jerusalem (§305), the Decision of Pilate (§369), the Appearance of Jesus on the Road to Emmaus (§385).

267. Luke's Parable of the Prodigal Son

Luke 15:11-32

[11]So he-said, "Some person was-having two sons. [12]And the fresher [=younger one] of-them said to-the father, 'Father, give me the throwing-on part [=my share] of-the property.' So he-split the livelihood [=his property between] them. [13]And not many days with [=after], having-gathered all[a] [his things], the fresher [=younger] son left-home into [=for a] far-away region and there he-scattered [=he squandered] his property [by] living recklessly. [14]So his having-spent [=When he had spent] all [=everything], strong [=a serious] famine happened according-to [=throughout] that region, and he [himself] began to-be-deficient. [15]And having-traveled, he-clung to-one of-the citizens of-that region, and he-sent him into his fields to-graze pigs, [16]and he-was-desiring [=he would have liked] to-be-fed[b] out of-the [=from the] pods which the pigs were-eating, and [=but] no-one was-giving [anything] to-him. [17]So [=But] having-come into himself, he-spoke [=he said], 'How-many wage-laborers [of] my father exceed breads [=have more than enough food], so [=but] here I [myself] am-being-destroyed [by] famine. [18]Having-gotten-up I-will-travel to my father and I-will-say to-him, "Father, I-sinned into [=against] heaven and in-the-sight of-you. [19]I-am no-longer worthy to-be-called your son. Do [=Treat] me like one [of] your wage-laborers."' [20]And having-gotten-up, he-went to his father himself. So yet his receiving-in-full far-away [=But while he was still far away], his father saw him and had-pity and having-run he-assailed upon [=threw his arms around] his neck and kissed him. [21]So [=And] the son said to-him, 'Father, I-sinned into [=against] heaven and in-the-sight of-you. I-am no-longer worthy to-be-called your son.'[c] [22]So [=But] the father said to his servants, 'Bring-out the first [=best] robe quickly[d] and clothe him, and give [=put a] ring into his hand and sandals into [=on] the [=his] feet, [23]and carry the fattened calf, slaughter [it], and having-eaten [it] let-us-be-merry, [24]that [=because] this son of-me [=of mine] was dead and [=but] lived-again, had-been-destroyed [=had been lost] and [=but] was-found.' And they-began to-be-merry. [25]So [=Now] his elder son was in [the] field and like [=when he was] coming he-neared the home, he-heard music and dancings [=dancing people]. [26]And having-summoned one of-the children, he-was-inquiring what ever might-be these [=what was going on]. [27]So he-said to-him that 'Your brother presses-forward [=has come home] and your father slaughtered the fattened calf, that [=because] he-received-back him being-healthy.' [28]So [=Now] he-was-angered and was-wishing not to-enter, so [=but] his father having-gone-out was-exhorting him. [29]So [=and] having-answered [=answering] he-said [to] his father, 'Look! so-many years I-am-a-slave to-you, and never passed-away [=disobeyed] your commandment and never you-gave me [a] goat in-order-that I-might-be-merry with my friends. [30]So [=But] when this son of-you [=of yours] came [back], the [one] having-consumed your livelihood [=property] with fornicators, you-slaughtered [a] fattened calf for-him.' [31]So he-said to-him, 'Descendant, you [yourselves] are always with me, and all [=everything of] my-own is your-own. [32]So [=But] it-was-necessary to-be-merry and to-rejoice, that [=because] this brother of-you [=of yours] was dead and lived, having-been-destroyed [=was lost] and [=but] was-found.'"

[a] *all* 𝔓[75] B D 2542 *pc*; *everyone* ℵ A L W Θ Ψ *f*[1] *f*[13] 892 1006 1506 𝔐.
[b] *to-be-fed* 𝔓[75] ℵ B D L *f*[1] *f*[13] 579 2542 *pc* sy[c] cop[sa]; *to-fill-up his abdomen* A Θ Ψ 892 1006 1342 1506 𝔐 vg it[mss] sy[s] sy[p] sy[h] cop[bo]; *to-fill-up the abdomen and to-be-feed* W.
[c] *omit* 𝔓[75] A L W Θ Ψ *f*[1] *f*[13] 𝔐 vg it[mss] sy[s] sy[c] sy[p] cop; *'Do me like one of-your wage-laborers'* ℵ B D 33 700 1241 *pc* vg[mss] sy[h].
[d] *quickly* 𝔓[75] ℵ B D L *f*[13] 579 892 pc vg it sy[s] sy[c] sy[h] cop[samss] cop[bo]; *omit* A W Θ Ψ *f*[1] 1006 1342 1506 𝔐 sy[p] cop[samss].

268. Luke's Parable of the Unrighteous Manager

Luke 16:1-9

[1]So he-was-saying and [=also] to the[a] disciples, "Some person was wealthy who was-having [=had a] manager, and charges-were-brought to-him like [=that] this [person] was-scattering [=was squandering] his being-at-one's-disposals [=belongings]. [2]And having-yelled [for] him he-said to-him, 'What [is] this I-hear around [=concerning] you? Give-over the word [=Account for] your management, for you-are-able not yet [=no longer] to-manage [for me].' [3]So the manager said in

himself, 'What will-I-do, that [=because] my lord takes-away the [position of] management from
me? I-have-the-strength not to-dig, [and] I-am-ashamed to-ask-for-alms. 4I-knew what I-would-
do, in-order-that whenever I-might-have-been-banished out [=from] the [position of] management,
[people] might-receive me into their houses.' 5And having-summoned each one of-the needy-
debtors of-the lord himself [=of his own lord], he-was-saying to-the first, 'How-great [=How much]
are-you-in-debt my lord?' 6So he-said, 'One-hundred vats of-olive-oil.' So he-said to-him, 'Receive
your letters[b] [=Take your bills] and having-been-seated without-delay write fifty.' 7Later he-said
[to an] other, 'So [=And] how-great [=how much] are-in-debt you?' So he-said, 'One-hundred cors
of-wheat.' He-says to-him, 'Receive your letters [=Take your bills] and write eighty.' 8And the lord
commended the manager of-unrighteousness, that [=because] he-did [=he had acted] sensibly. That
[=For] the sons of-this eon are more-sensible into [=with] themselves [=their own] generation on-
behalf [=than are] the sons of-light. 9And I [myself] say to-you, 'Do [=Make] themselves [=yourselves]
friends out [=from] the money of-unrighteousness in-order-that whenever it-might-fail they-
might-receive you into the eternal tents [=homes].'"

[a] *to the* 𝔓75 ℵ B D L 69 579 788 2542 *pc*; *to his* A W Θ Ψ f^1 f^{13} 892 1006 1342 𝔐 vg it[mss] sy cop[sa].
[b] *letters* 𝔓75 ℵ B D L Ψ 579 788 *pc* cop[bo]; *letter* A W Θ f^1 f^{13} 33 892 1006 1342 𝔐 cop[sa].

269. Luke's Lesson Concerning Loyalty

Luke 16:10-12

10"The [one who is] loyal in least [=with little] is and [=also] loyal in many [=with much], and the
[one who is] unrighteous in least [=with little] is and [=also] unrighteous in many [=with much].
11Therefore, if you-happened [=if you were] not loyal in [=with] the unrighteous money, what [=who]
will-believe [=will entrust] to-you the genuine? 12And if you-happened [=if you were] not loyal in
[=with] the foreigner [=other people's belongings], what [=who] will-give to-you the [things that are]
y'all's-own[a]?"

[a] *y'all's-own* 𝔓75 ℵ A D W Θ Ψ f^1 f^{13} 892 1006 1342 1506 𝔐 vg it[mss] sy cop; *our-own* B L *pc*; *my-own* 157 it[mss]; *genuine* 33 *pc*.

270. Loyalty to Two Masters (→ §48, 264)

Matt 6:24	Q 16:13	**Luke 16:13**	Thomas 47
24"No-one a is-able to-be-a-slave [for] two lords; for or [=either] he-will-hate the one, and he-will-love the other, or he-will-hold-fast [to the] one and he-will-despise the other. You-are-able not to-be-a-slave to-god and to-money."	13"No-one is-able to-be-a-slave [for] two lords; for or [=either] he-will-hate the one, and he-will-love the other, or he-will-hold-fast [to the] one and he-will-despise the other. You-are-able not to-be-a-slave to-god and to-money."	13"No-one [=No] house-servant is-able to-be-a-slave [for] two lords; for or [=either] he-will-hate the one, and he-will-love the other, or he-will-hold-fast [to the] one and he-will-despise the other. You-are-able not to-be-a-slave to-god and to-money."	Jesus said, "A person cannot mount two horses or bend two bows. And a slave cannot serve two masters, otherwise that slave will honor the one and offend the other. Nobody drinks aged wine and immediately wants to drink young wine. Young wine is not poured into old wineskins, or they might break, and aged wine is not poured into a new wineskin, or it might spoil. An old patch is not sewn onto a new garment, since it would create a tear."

[a] *omit* ℵ B D f^1 f^{13} 33 892 1006 1342 1506 𝔐 vg; *house-servant* L Δ 1242 *pc*.

271. Luke's Pharisees Shamed

Luke 16:14-15

14So, the Pharisees, being-at-one's-disposals [=who were] money-lovers, were-hearing all these [things] and were-making-fun-of him. 15And he-said to-them, "You are the being-righteouses [=those make righteous] themselves [=yourselves] in-the-sight-of-the people, so [=but] god knows your hearts, that [=because] the high [prize] in [=among] people [is an] abomination in-the-sight of-god."

There are no variants in this pericope that appear in English.

272. John and the Prophets (→ §125)

Matt 11:12-13	**Q 16:16**	**Luke 16:16**
12"So from the days of-John the baptist until right-now the kingdom of-the heavens is-forced [=has been forced open] and forcefuls [=those who are forceful] plunder her. 13For all the prophets and the law prophesied until John."	16"And the law and the prophets [were] until John [came]; from then the kingdom of-god is-forced [=has been forced open] and forcefuls [=those who are forceful] plunder her."	16"The law and the prophets [were] to-the-point [=until][a] of-John; from then the kingdom of-god is-proclaimed and all force [their way] into her."

[a] *to-the-point* 𝔓75 ℵ B L f^1 f^{13} 205 579 892 2542 *pc*; *until* A D W Θ Ψ 1006 1342 1506 𝔐.

273. The Law and the Prophets (→ §34)

Matt 5:18	**Q 16:17**	**Luke 16:17**
18"For amen I-say to-you, until ever might-pass-away the heaven and the land, no [=not] one iota or one stroke [=hook of a letter] might-pass-away not from the law, until ever all [this] might-happen."	17"So, it is easier [for] the heaven and the land to-pass-away or [=than for] one stroke [=hook of a letter] of-the law to-fall."	17"So, it-is easier [for] the heaven and the land to-pass-away or [=than for] one stroke [=hook of a letter] of-the law to-fall."

There are no variants in this pericope that appear in English.

274. Adultery, Divorce, and Stumbling (→ §37)

Matt 5:32	**Q 16:18**	**Luke 16:18**
32"So [=But] I [myself] say to-you that all the [=every person] releasing his woman [=wife] except-for [the] word [=matter] of-fornication does [=causes] her to-commit-adultery, and who if-ever might-marry [a] having-been-released [=divorcée] becomes-an-adulterer."	18"All the [=every person] releasing his woman [=wife] and marrying another commits-adultery, and the [one] marrying [a] having-been-released [=divorcée] commits-adultery."	18"All the [=every person] releasing his woman [=wife] and marrying [an] other commits-adultery, and the[a] [one] marrying [a] having-been-released [=divorcée] from [a] man commits-adultery."

[a] *the* 𝔓75 B D L 69 788 983 2542 *pc* vg it^{mss} sy^s cop; *all the* ℵ A W Θ Ψ f^1 f^{13} 892 1006 1342 1506 𝔐 sy^p sy^h.

275. Luke's Rich Man and Lazarus

Luke 16:19-31

19“So some person was wealthy, and he-was-having-on [=he was wearing a] purple-cloth and flax-
linen being-merry [=celebrating] sumptuously according-to [=each] day. 20So [=But] some poor
[person], Lazarus [by] name, had-been-thrown [=was lying] to [=at] his gateway having-been-
covered-with-sores 21and desiring to-be-fed from[a] the fallings [=what fell] from the table of-the
wealthy [person], but and [=even] the dogs coming were-licking his sores. 22So it-happened [that]
the poor [person] to-face-death [=died] and him to-be-carried-away [=he was carried away] under
[=by] the announcers [=angels] into the bosom of-Abraham. So [=And] the wealthy [person] and
[=also] faced-death [=died] and was-buried. 23And in Hades, having-lifted-up his eyes, being-at-
one's-disposal [=being] in torments, he-sees Abraham from far-off and Lazarus in his bosoms.
24And he, having-yelled, said, ‘Father Abraham, be-merciful [with] me and send Lazarus in-order-
that he-might-dunk the tip [of] his finger [into] water and might-cool my tongue that [=because] I-
am-fretting [=I am in agony] in this flame.’ 25But Abraham said, ‘Descendant, remember that in your
life you-received-back your good [things] and Lazarus likewise the bad [things]. So now here he-is-
exhorted [=he is comforted] so [=but] you-fret [=you are in agony]. 26And in all these [things], between
us and you [a] great chasm has-been-made-firm [=has been put in place] so-that the wishings [=those
who wish] to-go-over from-this-place to you might-be-able no [=not], so-not [=so that] they-
might-cross-over [=not] from-there to us.’ 27So he-said, ‘Therefore, I-beg you, Father, in-order-that
you-might-send him into my father's house, 28for I-have five brothers, so-that he-might-alert them
in-order-that they [themselves] and [=too] might-come no [=not] into this place of-torment.’ 29So
Abraham says[b], ‘They-have Moses and the prophets; let-them-hear them.’ 30So [=But] he [himself]
said, ‘Indeed-not, father Abraham, but if-ever some [one] from deads [=dead people] might-travel to
them they-will-repent.’ 31So he-said to-him, ‘If they-hear not Moses and the prophets, nor will-
they-be-persuaded if-ever [=even if] some [person] out of-deads [=from the dead] might-get-up.’”

[a] *omit* 𝔓75 ℵ* B L it sy^s cop^sa; *scraps-of-food* ℵ2 A D W Θ Ψ (*f* 1) *f* 13 33 892 1006 1342 1506 𝔐 vg it^mss sy^p sy^h.
[b] *omit* 𝔓75 ℵ B L 579 892 2542 *pc* it^mss sy^s cop^bomss; *to-him* A D W Θ Ψ *f* 1 *f* 13 1006 1342 1506 𝔐 vg it^mss sy^p sy^h cop.

276. Solutions to Stumbling Blocks (→ §186)

Matt 18:7, 6

7“Woe to-the world from [=because of] scandals [=stumbling blocks]. For [it is] inevitable [for] scandals to-come, nevertheless woe to-the person[a] through whom the scandal comes.” 6“So who ever might-cause-to-stumble one of-these smalls [=little ones] believing into [=in] me, it-is-profitable for-him in-order-that [a] donkey [=great] mill-stone might-be-hung around his neck and [that] he-might-be-sunk in the deep-part of-the sea.”

Mark 9:42

42“And who ever might-cause-to-stumble one of-these smalls [=little ones] believing into [=in] me, it-is fine [=better] for-him rather if [a] donkey [=great] mill-stone is-laid-around around his neck and he-has-been-thrown into the sea.”

Q 17:1-2

1“[It is] inevitable [for] scandals to-come, nevertheless woe [to the one] through whom it-comes. 2It-is-advantageous for-him if [a] stone [from a] milling-stone is-laid-around around his neck and [if] he-has-been-tossed into the sea or [=than] in-order-that he-might-cause-to-stumble one of-these smalls [=little ones].”

Luke 17:1-3a

1So he-said to his disciples, “It-is not-possible [for] scandals to-come no [=not], nevertheless woe [to the one] through whom it-comes. 2It-is-advantageous for-him if [a] stone [from a] milling-stone is-laid-around around his neck and [if] he-has-been-tossed into the sea or [=than] in-order-that he-might-cause-to-stumble one of-these smalls [=little ones].

3aPay-close-attention to-themselves [=to yourselves].”

[a] *to-the person* ℵ D L f^{1} 579 892 *pc* sy cop^{samss} cop^{bo}; *to-that person* B W Θ f^{13} 33 1006 1506 𝔐 it cop^{samss}.
📖 Lk 17:3 – Lev 19:17

277. The Lost Sheep (→ §188, §265)

Matt 18:12-13

12“What [=How] supposes [=does it seem] to-you? If-ever one-hundred sheep might-happen [=might belong] to-some person and one out of-them might-be-deceived [=might wander off], will-he-excuse indeed-not [=would he not leave] the ninety nine upon the mountains and having-traveled [would he not] search [for] the [one] being-deceived [=wandering off]? 13And if-ever he-might-happen to-

find it, amen I-say to-you that he-rejoices upon [=over] it rather or [=more than] upon [=for] the

ninety nine no [=not] having-been-deceived [=having wandered off].”

Q 15:4-5a, 7

4“What person out of-you having one-hundred sheep might-happen [=might belong] to-some person and one out of-them might-be-deceived [=might wander off], will-he-excuse indeed-not [=would he not leave] the ninety nine upon the mountains and having-traveled [would he not] search [for] the [one] having-been-destroyed [=having been lost]? 5aAnd if-ever he-might-happen

to-find it, 7I-say to-you that he-rejoices upon [=over] it rather or [=more than] upon [=for] the

ninety nine no [=not] having-been-deceived [=having wandered off].”

Luke 15:4-5a, 7

4“What person out of-you having one-hundred sheep and having-destroyed [=losing] out of-them one, quits [=leaves] not the ninety nine in the deserted [place] and travels upon [=goes after] the [one] having-been-destroyed [=having been lost] until

he-might-find it? 5aAnd having-found [it] places [it] upon his shoulders rejoicing? 7I-say to-you that thus there-will-be [more] joy in heaven upon [=for] one sinful [person] repenting or [=than] upon [=for] ninety nine righteouses [=righteous people] whoever [=who] have no need [=for] repentance.”

Thomas 107

Jesus said, “The <Father’s> kingdom is like a shepherd who had a hundred sheep. One of them, the largest, went astray. He left the ninety-nine and looked for the one until he found it.

After he had toiled, he said to the sheep, ‘I love you more than the ninety-nine.’”

There are no variants in this pericope that appear in English.

278. On Forgiveness (→ §189, §191)

Matt 18:15a, 21b-22

15a“So if-ever your brother might-sin[a], leave [and] expose him between you and him alone. If-ever he-might-hear you, you-gained [back] your brother.”

Q 17:3-4

3“So if-ever your brother might-sin,

rebuke him, and if-ever he-might-repent, excuse [=forgive] him.

Luke 17:3b-4

3b“If-ever your brother might-sin,

rebuke him, and if-ever he-might-repent, excuse [=forgive] him.

21b“Lord, how-many-times will-sin my brother into [=against] me and will-I-excuse [=forgive] him? Until [=as many as] seven-times?” 22Jesus says to-him, “I-say to-you not until seven-times but until seventy-times seven [=seventy-seven times].”	4And if-ever seven-times he-might-sin into [=against] you and [=then] seven-times you-will-excuse [=you will forgive] him.”	4And if-ever seven-times of-the [=per] day he-might-sin into [=against] you and [=then] seven-times[b] might-turn-back to you[c] saying, ‘I-repent,’ you-will-excuse [=you will forgive] him.”

[a] *omit* ℵ B f^{1} 579 *pc* cop^{sa}; *into you* D L W Θ 1078 f^{13} 33 𝔐 vg it sy.
[b] *seven-times* ℵ B D L Ψ 892 2542 *pc* it sy^{s} sy^{c} cop^{bomss}; *seven-times of-the day* A W Θ f^{1} f^{13} 1006 1342 1506 𝔐 vg it^{mss} sy^{p} sy^{h} cop^{sa} cop^{bomss}.
[c] *to you* ℵ A B D L Ψ f^{1} 205 579 892 2542 *al* vg it^{mss} sy; *omit* W Θ f^{13} 1006 1342 1506 𝔐.
🕮 Mt 18:15 – Lev 19:17

279. Faith like a Mustard Seed (→ §181)

Matt 17:20	**Q 17:6**	**Luke 17:5-6**	Thomas 48; 106
20So he-says to-them, “Through [=Because of] your littleness-of-loyalty; for amen I-say to-you, if-ever you-might-have loyalty like [a] tiny-seed of-mustard, you-will-say to-this mountain, ‘Head-out from-this-place [to] there’ and it-will-head-out. And no-one [=nothing] will-be-impossible for-you.”	6“If you-have loyalty like [a] tiny-seed of-mustard and ever you-were-saying to-the[a] mulberry-tree, ‘Be uprooted and be-planted in the sea,’ and it-obeyed ever [=it would obey] you.”	5And the apostles said to-the lord, “Add loyalty to-us.” 6So the lord said, “If you-have loyalty like [a] tiny-seed of-mustard and ever you-were-saying to-the[a] mulberry-tree, ‘Be uprooted and be-planted in the sea,’ and it-obeyed ever [=it would obey] you.”	48Jesus said, “If two make peace with each other in a single house, they will say to the mountain, ‘Move from here!’ and it will move.” 106Jesus said, “When you make the two into one, you will become children of Adam, and when you say, ‘Mountain, move from here!’ it will move.”

[a] *to-the* $\mathfrak{P}^{75}$ ℵ D L 579 *pc* sy^{c} cop^{bo}; *to-this* A B W Θ Ψ f^{1} f^{13} 892 1006 1342 1506 𝔐 vg it^{mss} sy^{s} sy^{p} cop^{sa}.

280. Luke on the Status of Servants

Luke 17:7-10

7“So what [person] out of-you having [a] slave plowing or shepherding, who will-say to-him having-entered out of-the field, ‘Instantly having-passed-away, lean’ [=Come immediately and recline at the table]? 8But indeed-not, he-will-say to-him, ‘Make-ready [=Prepare] what I-might-banquet-on and having-been-garbed serve me until [=while] I-might-eat and drink, and with [=after] these [things] you [yourself] will-eat and will-drink.’ 9You-have no benefaction [=gratitude] to-the slave that [=because] he-did the [things] having-been-appointed, [do you]? 10And thus you, whenever you-might-do all the [things] having-been-appointed to-you, say that ‘We-are worthless slaves, who were-owing [=we were obligated] to-do [what] we-have-done.’”

There are no variants in this pericope that appear in English.

281. Luke's Cleansing of Ten Lepers

Luke 17:11-19

[11]And it-happened in the to-travel into [=as they went to] Jerusalem and he [himself] was-going-
through through [the] middle [between] Samaria and Galilee. [12]And his entering [=when he entered]
into some village, ten leprous men, who stood at-a-distance, encountered him[a]. [13]And they-
removed [=they raised] voice [=their voices] saying, "Jesus, overseer, be-merciful [to] us." [14]And
having-seen [this] he-said to-them, "Having-traveled, point-out themselves [=yourselves] to-the
priests." And it-happened in them to-leave [=when they went away] they-were-purified. [15]So [=But]
one out of-them, having-seen that he-was-cured, returned glorifying god with [a] great voice.
[16]And he-fell upon [his] face along [=before] his feet, giving-thanks to-him. And he [himself] was
Samaritan. [17]So having-answered, Jesus said, "Ten were-purified, indeed-not [=were they not]? So
wheresoever [are] the [other] nine? [18]Were-they-found not having-returned to-give glory to-god
if no [=except] this foreign-born [person]?" [19]And he-said to-him, "Having-gotten-up, travel. Your
loyalty has-saved you."

[a] *encountered him* A W Ψ 33 1006 1342 1506 𝔐 vg it[mss] sy[p] cop; *encountered* 𝔓[75] B L pc it; *met him* ℵ L Θ *f*[1] *f*[13] 205 579 892 2542 *al*; *encountered him where they were* D it.

282. Luke's Inner Kingdom of God (→ §329)

Matt 24:23	Mark 13:21	**Luke 17:20-21**	Thomas 3
[23]"Then if-ever some [person] might-say to-you, 'Look! here [is] the anointed-one' or 'Here,' might-you-believe [it] no [=not]."	[21]"And then if-ever some [person] might-say to-you, 'Look here [is] the anointed-one, look there,' believe [it] no [=not]."	[20]So having-been-questioned under [=by] the Pharisees when the kingdom of-god comes [=will come], he-answered them and said, "The kingdom of-god comes not with observable-signs, [21]nor will-they-say, 'Look! here,' or 'There'[a] For look! the kingdom of-god is inside of-you."	Jesus said, "If your leaders say to you, 'Look, the <Father's> kingdom is in the sky,' then the birds of the sky will precede you. If they say to you, 'It is in the sea,' then the fish will precede you. Rather, the <Father's> kingdom is within you and it is outside you. When you know yourselves, then you will be known, and you will understand that you are children of the living Father. But if you do not know yourselves, then you live in poverty, and you are the poverty."

[a] *'Look! here,' or 'There'* 𝔓[75] ℵ B L 2542 pc it[mss] sy[s]; *'Look! here' or 'Look! there'* A D W Ψ *f*[1] *f*[13] 892 1006 1342 1506 𝔐 vg it[mss] sy[c] sy[p]; *'Look! here, there'* Θ.

283. The Day of the Son of Man (→ §330)

Matt 24:26-27	**Q 17:23-24**	**Luke 17:22-25**
[26]"Therefore, if-ever they-might-say to-you: 'Look! he-is in the deserted	[23]"If-ever they-might-say to-you: 'Look! he-is in the deserted [place],'	[22]So he-said to the disciples, "Days will-come when you-will-desire to-see one of-the days of-the son of-the person, and you-will-see not. [23]And they-will-say to-you, 'Look! there,' or 'Look! here.' Might-you-

[place],' might-you-go-out [=might you go out there] no [=not]; 'Look! in the private-rooms,' might-you-believe [it] no [=not].
[27]For even-as the flashing-light [=lightning] goes-out from [=comes out of] easts [=the east], and appears until wests [=as far as the west], thus will-be the presence of-the son of-the person."

might-you-go-out [there] no [=not]; 'Look! in the private-rooms,' might-you-pursue [=follow them] no [=not].

[24]For even-as the flashing-light [=lightning] goes-out from [=comes out of] the east [=east], and appears until [=as far as the] west, thus will-be the son of-the person in [=on] his day."

go-away no [=not] so-not [=nor] might-you-pursue [=follow them].

[24]For even-as the flashing-light [=lightning] flashing shines out under heaven into under heaven [=from one side of the sky to the other] thus will-be the son of-the person in [=on] his day[a].
[25]So [=But] first it-is-necessary [for] him to-suffer many [things] and to-be-rejected from this generation."

[a] *in his day* ℵ A L W Θ Ψ f^1 f^{13} 892 1006 1342 1506 𝔐 vg it[mss] sy cop[bo]; *omit* 𝔭[75] B D it cop[sa].

284. Eagles and a Corpse (→ §288, §331)

Matt 24:28

[28]"Where if-ever the corpse might-be, there the eagles will-be-gathered."

Q 17:37

[37]"Where the corpse [is], there the eagles will-be-gathered."

Luke 17:37

[37]And having-answered, they-say to-him, "Wheresoever, lord?" So he-said to-them, "Where the body [is], there and [=also] the eagles will-be-collected[a]."

[a] *will-be-collected* ℵ B L 892 *pc*; *will-be-gathered* A D W Θ Ψ f^1 f^{13} 1342 1506 𝔐 cop[sa] cop[bo].

285. The Judgment of Noah (→ §335)

Matt 24:37-39

[37]"For even-as the days of-Noah [were], thus will-be the presence of-the son of-the person. [38]For like[a] [=as] in those days before the flood they-were chewing and drinking, marrying and giving-in-marriage[b], till which day Noah entered into the ark, [39]and they-knew not [=nothing] until the flood came, and it-removed everyone;

Q 17:26-27, 30

[26]"Just-as it-happened in the days of-Noah, thus it-will-be and [=also] in [=on] the day of-the son of-the person. [27]For like in those days they-were chewing and drinking, marrying and giving-in-marriage, till which day Noah entered into the ark, and the flood came, and it-removed everyone.

Luke 17:26-30

[26]"And just-as it-happened in the days of-Noah, thus it-will-be and [=also] in the days of-the son of-the person. [27]They-were-eating, they-were-drinking, they-were-marrying, they-were-being-given-in-marriage, till which day Noah entered into the ark and the flood came and destroyed all[c] [things].

[28]Likewise just-as it-happened in the days of-Lot: they-were-eating, they-were-drinking, they-were-buying, they-were-selling, they-were-planting, they-were-building.
[29]So [on] the day Lot went-out from Sodoms, fire and sulfur rained from heaven and destroyed all [things].

thus and [=also] will-be the presence of-the son of-the person."	30Thus and [=also] it-will-be [on] which [=on that] day the son of-the person is-revealed."	30It-will-be according-to them [=just like this on] which [=on that] day the son of-the person is-revealed."

[a] *like* ℵ B L 33 892; *even-as* D W Θ f^{1} f^{13} 1006 1342 1506 𝔐.
[b] *giving-in-marriage* ℵ D 33 1006 *pc*; *giving-in-wedlock* B *pc*; *giving-away-in-wedlock* W 1424 *pc*; *marrying-off* L Θ f^{1} 1506 𝔐; *bringing-in-for-marriage* f^{13} 892 1342 *al.*
[c] *all* $\mathfrak{P}^{75}$ B D L Θ 579 892 *pc*; *everyone* ℵ A W Ψ f^{1} f^{13} 33 1006 1342 1506 𝔐.
🕮 Mt 24:37 – Gen 7:4; 🕮 Lk 17:27 – Gen 7:7; 🕮 Lk 17:29 – Gen 19:16

286. Futility of Possessions (→ §328)

Matt 24:17-18	Mark 13:15-16	**Luke 17:31-32**
17"Let-him-descend no [=not] the [person] upon the housetop to-remove the [things] out [of] his home. 18and [whoever is] in the field let-him-turn-back no behind [=let him not go back] to-remove his coat."	15"So [=And] let-him-descend[a] no [=not] the [person] upon the housetop so-not [=nor] let-him-enter to-remove some [things] out [of] his home, 16and [whoever is] in the field let-him-turn-back no into the behind [=let him not go back] to-remove his coat."	31"In [=On] that day, who [ever] will-be upon the housetop and his vessels [=belongings are] in the home, let-him-descend no [=not] to-remove them, and likewise [whoever is] in the field, let-him-turn-back into the behind no [=let him not turn back to it]. 32Recall the woman [=wife] of-Lot."

[a] *omit* ℵ B L Ψ 892 1342 2427 *pc* sy^{p} cop; *into the home* A D W Θ f^{1} f^{13} 1006 1506 𝔐 vg it^{mss} sy^{s}.
🕮 Lk 17:32 – Gen 19:26

287. Saving Your Life (→ §118, §262)

Matt 10:39	Q 17:33	**Luke 17:33**	John 12:25
39"The [one] having-found his soul [=life] will-destroy [=will lose] it and the [one] having-destroyed his soul [=life] because-of me will-find it."	33"The [one] having-found his soul [=life] will-destroy [=will lose] it and the [one] having-destroyed his soul [=life] because-of me will-find it."	33"Who if-ever might-search to-make-secure his soul[a] will-destroy it, so [=but] who ever might-destroy [his life] will-give-life [to] it."	25"The [one] liking his soul [=life] destroys it and the [one] hating his soul [=life] in this world will-guard it into eternal life."

[a] *Who if-ever might-search to-make-secure his soul* $\mathfrak{P}^{75}$ B L 579; *Who if-ever might-search to-save his soul* ℵ A W Θ Ψ f^{1} f^{13} 892 1006 1342 1506 𝔐 it^{mss} vg; *Who ever might-wish to-give-life his soul* D sy^{s} sy^{p} cop^{sa}.

288. One Taken, One Left Behind (→ §284, §331, §336)

Matt 24:40-41, 28	**Q 17:34-35**, 37	**Luke 17:34-37**
40"Then two [men] there-will-be in the field, one is-taken-along [=is taken] and one is-excused [=is left].	34"I-say to-you, there-will-be two [men] in the field, one is-taken-along [=is taken] and one is-excused [=is left].	34"I-say to-you, [on] this night, there-will-be two [men] upon one stretcher [=bed]; the one will-be-taken-along [=will be taken] and the other will-be-excused [=will be left behind].
41Two grinding-grains [=women are grinding grain] in [=on] the mill-stone, one is-taken-along [=is taken]	35Two grinding-grains [=women are grinding grain] in [=on] the mill-stone, one is-taken-along [=is taken]	35There-will-be two grinding-grains [=women grinding grain] upon the it [=at the same place]; the one will-be-

and one is-excused [=is left]."	and one is-excused [=is left]."	taken-along [=will be taken] so the other will-be-excused [=will be left behind]."[a] 37And having-answered, they-say to-him, "Wheresoever, lord?" So he-said to-them, "Where the body [is], there and [=also] the eagles will-be-collected[b]."
28"Where if-ever the corpse might-be, there the eagles will-be-gathered."	37"Where the corpse [is], there the eagles will-be-gathered."	

[a] *omit vs 36* $\mathfrak{p}^{75}$ ℵ A B K L W X Θ Π Ψ f^{1} 28 33 565 892 cop; [36]*There there-will-be two in the field, one will-be-taken-along and the other will-be-excused* D f^{13} 700 1006 *al* vg it^{mss} sy.
[b] *will-be-collected* ℵ B L 892 *pc*; *will-be-gathered* A D W Θ Ψ f^{1} f^{13} 1342 1506 𝔐 cop^{sa} cop^{bo}.

289. Luke's Parable of the Unjust Judge

Luke 18:1-8

1So he-was-saying [a] parable to-them to to-be-necessary [=in order to show that it is necessary for]
them always to-pray and to-become-discouraged no [=not], 2saying, "There-was some judge in
some city no [=not] fearing god and no [=not] being-respected [by a single] person. 3So [=Now],
there-was [a] widow in that city, and she-was-coming to him saying, 'Adjudicate-for me from
[=against] my opponent.' 4And he-was-wishing not upon [=at that] time, so with these [=but later]
he-said in [=to] himself, 'If and [=Even though] I-fear not god nor am-respected [by a single] person,
5through in-effect [=because] this widow to-present [=keeps giving] me trouble, I-will-adjudicate-
for her, in-order-that no [=lest] coming into end [=by continually coming] she-might-give-a-black-
eye [to] me.'" 6So the lord said, "Hear what the judge of-unrighteousness says; 7so god might-do
adjudication not no [=will not god grant adjudication for] his chosen-ones shouting to-him[a] day and
night, and is-he-patient upon them [=will he make them wait]? 8I-say to-you that he-will-do their
adjudication in speed [=with haste]. Nevertheless, the son of-the person having-come, will-he-find
consequently [=will he find] loyalty upon [=in] the land?"

[a] *to-him* $\mathfrak{p}^{75}$ ℵ B L Q T Ψ 892 *pc*; *to him* A W Θ f^{13} 33 1006 1342 1506 𝔐 vg it^{mss}; *their shouting* D.

290. Luke's Parable of the Pharisee and the Tax Collector

Luke 18:9-14

9So he-said and [=also] this parable to some [who were] having-been-persuaded upon [=trusting
in] themselves that they-are righteous and viewing-with-disdain the remainders [=rest]. 10"Two
people ascended into the temple to-pray, the one [a] Pharisee and the other [a] tax-collector. 11The
Pharisee having-stood was-praying these [things] to himself, 'God, I-give-thanks to-you that I-am
not even-as [=like] the remainders [=rest] of-the people: ravenous, unrighteous, adulterers, or and
[=also] like this tax-collector; 12I-fast twice of-the sabbath [=twice a week], I-tithe[a] all [the things]
whatsoever I-acquire.' 13So the tax-collector having-stood far-off, was-wishing not nor [=even] to-
lift-up [his] eyes into heaven, but was-hitting his chest saying, 'God, deal-mercifully-with me the
sinful [one].' 14I-say to-you, this [man] descended into his house having-been-made-righteous along
that [=as opposed to the other one], that [=because] all [=every one] exalting himself will-be-humbled,
so [=but] the [one] humbling himself will-be-exalted."

[a] *I-tithe* $ℵ^{2}$ A D L W Θ Ψ f^{1} f^{13} 892 1006 1342 1506 𝔐; *I-tenth* $\mathfrak{p}^{75}$ ℵ* B T.

Q 17:35 (§288, p. 209)
Luke 18:14 (§290, p. 210)

Jesus' Ministry in Judea

291. Jesus' Teaching on Divorce

Matt 19:3-9

3And[a] Pharisees approached him testing him and saying [=asking] if it-is-permitted [for a] person[b] to-release his woman [=wife] according-to all [=for any] reason? 4So having-answered he-said, "Did-you-read not that the [one] having-created from [the] beginning 'HE-DID [=He made] THEM MALE AND FEMALE'?" 5And he-said, "BECAUSE-OF THIS [a] PERSON WILL-QUIT [=will leave] FATHER AND MOTHER AND WILL-BE-CLUNG [=will be joined to] HIS WOMAN [=wife], AND THE TWO WILL-BE [made] INTO ONE FLESH. 6With-the-result-that [=Therefore] they-are no-longer two but one flesh. Therefore, [that] which god brought-together let-separate no person." 7They-say to-him, "What [=Why] therefore did-charge Moses to-give booklet of-bill-of-divorce [=a certificate of divorce] and to-release her[c]?" 8He-says to-them that, "Moses allowed you to-release your women to [=because of] your hardness-of-heart, so [=but] it-has-happened thus not [it has not been this way] from [the] beginning. 9So [=But] I-say to-you that who ever might-release his woman [=wife] no upon [=except for] fornication and might-marry another becomes-an-adulterer.[d]"

Mark 10:2-12

2And Pharisees having-approached were-questioning him if it-is-permitted [for a] man to-release [=divorce a] woman, testing him. 3So having-answered he-said to-them, "What did-charge Moses to-you?" 4So they-said, "Moses allowed [us] to-write booklet of-bill-of-divorce [=a certificate of divorce] and to-release [her]." 5So Jesus said[e] to-them, "He-wrote this commandment for-you to [=because of] your hardness-of-heart. 6So [=But] from [the] beginning of-creation[f] 'HE-DID [=He made] THEM MALE AND FEMALE.' 7'BECAUSE-OF THIS [a] PERSON WILL-QUIT [=will leave] HIS FATHER AND MOTHER[g], 8AND THE TWO WILL-BE [made] INTO ONE FLESH; WITH-THE-RESULT-THAT [=therefore] THEY-ARE NO-LONGER TWO BUT ONE FLESH.' 9Therefore, [that] which god brought-together let-separate no person." 10And into the home [=in the house] the disciples were-questioning him again around [=concerning] this. 11And he-says to-them, "Who ever might-release his woman [=wife] and might-marry another becomes-an-adulterer upon [=against] her. 12And if-ever, having-released her man [=husband], she [herself] might-marry another, she-becomes-an-adulterer."

[a] *omit* $\mathfrak{p}^{25}$ B C L W Δ Θ f^1 f^{13} 33 565 579 700 892 *al* cop^{samss} cop^{bo}; *the* ℵ D 1006 1342 1506 𝔐 cop^{samss}.
[b] *person* ℵ^2 C D W Θ 087 f^1 f^{13} 33 892 1006 1342 1506 𝔐 it vg; *omit* ℵ* B L 579 700 1424 *pc*; *man* 1424^C *pc*.
[c] *her* B C W 087 f^{13} 33 892 1006 1342 1506 𝔐 it^{mss} sy^p sy^h cop^{bomss}; *omit* ℵ D L Z Θ f^1 579 700 *pc* it^{mss} vg.
[d] *omit* ℵ C^3 D L 69 209* *pc* it sy^s sy^c cop^{bomss}; *and the marrying having-been-released becomes-an-adulterer* B C* W Z Θ f^1 f^{13} 33 892 1006 1342 1506 𝔐 vg it^{mss} sy^p sy^h cop^b; *and in-the-same-way the marrying having-been-released becomes-an-adulterer* $\mathfrak{p}^{25}$ it^{mss}.
[e] *So Jesus said* ℵ B C L Δ Θ Ψ 579 892 1342 2427 *pc* cop; *and having-answered said* A D W f^1 f^{13} 1006 1506 𝔐 it^{mss} vg sy^s sy^p.
[f] *omit* ℵ B C L Δ 579 1342 2427 *pc* cop; *god* D W *pc* it; *god himself* A Θ Ψ f^1 f^{13} 892 1006 1506 𝔐 it^{mss} vg sy.
[g] *omit* ℵ B Ψ 892 2427 sy^s; *and will-be-clung-to to his woman* A C D L N W Δ Θ f^1 f^{13} 579 𝔐 vg it^{mss} sy^p sy^h cop.
📖 Mt 19:4 – Gen 1:27; 📖 Mt 19:5 – Gen 2:24; Deut 19:15; 📖 Mt 19:7 – Deut 24:1; 📖 Mk 10:4 – Deut 24:1; 📖 Mk 10:6 – Gen 1:27; 📖 Mk 10:7 – Gen 2:24

292. Matthew's Teaching on Celibacy

Matt 19:10-12

10His disciples say to-him, "If the reason [=relationship of a] person with his woman [=wife] is thus [=like this], is-it profitable [=better] not to-marry?" 11So [=But] he-said to-them, "Not all accept this word but [only those] to-whom it-has-been-given. 12For there-are eunuchs whoever were-begotten thus [=like this] out [=from] the abdomen [of a] mother, and there-are eunuchs whoever were-made-into-a-eunuch under [=by] people, and there-are eunuchs whoever made-into-a-eunuch themselves through [=because of] the kingdom of-the heavens. Let-accept [this] the [he who is] being-able to-accept.

There are no variants in this pericope that appear in English.

293. Jesus Blesses Children

Matt 19:13-15

13 Then young-children
were-offered to-him
in-order-that he-might-
place the hands [on] them
and might-pray; so [=but]

the disciples rebuked
them. 14 So [=But] Jesus

said,
"Excuse [=Leave] the
young-children and hinder
them no [=not] to-come to
me, for the kingdom of-the
heavens is [=belongs to]
such-as-these."

15 And

having-placed the hands
[upon] them he-traveled
from-there.

Mark 10:13-16

13 And they-were-offering
young-children to-him
in-order-that he-might-

touch them; so [=but] the

disciples rebuked them.
14 So [=But] Jesus having-
seen was-indignant
and said to-them,
"Excuse [=Leave] the
young-children to-come
to me, hinder them no
[=not], for the kingdom
of-god is [=belongs to]
such-as-these.
15 Amen I-say to-you, who
ever might-receive no
[=not] the kingdom of-god
like [a] young-child, he-
might-enter into it not no
[=at all]."
16 And having-embraced
them he-was-blessing-
greatly [them] putting the
hands upon them.[a]

Luke 18:15-17

15 So [=Now] they-were-
offering and the [=even]
babies to-him in-order-
that he-might-touch
them; so [=but] the
disciples having-seen
were-rebuking them. 16 So
Jesus summoned

them saying,
"Excuse [=Leave] the
young-children to-come
to me and hinder them no
[=not], for the kingdom
of-god is [=belongs to]
such-as-these.
17 Amen I-say to-you, who
ever might-receive no
[=not] the kingdom of-god
like [a] young-child, he-
might-enter into it not no
[=at all]."

Thomas 22

Jesus saw some babies nursing. He said to his disciples, "These nursing babies are like those who enter the <Father's> kingdom." They said to him, "Then shall we enter the <Father's> kingdom as babies?" Jesus said to them, "When you make the two into one, and when you make the inner like the outer and the outer like the inner, and the upper like the lower, and when you make male and female into a single one, so that the male will not be male nor the female be female, when you make eyes in place of an eye, a hand in place of a hand, a foot in place of a foot, an image in place of an image, then you will enter <the kingdom>."

[a] *he-was-blessing-greatly putting the hands upon them* ℵ B C L Δ Θ Ψ 579 892 1342 1424 2427; *he-was-putting the hands upon them and blesses them* D W it; *putting the hands upon them he-blesses them* A f^1 f^{13} 1006 1506 𝔐 it^{mss} vg.

294. The Young Man with Many Possessions

Matt 19:16-22

16 And look!
one having-approached him
said,
"Teacher[a], what good might-I-do
in-order-that I-might-have eternal
life?" 17 So he-said to-him, "What
[=Why] do-you-beg me around [=
concerning] the good? One [alone] is
good[b]. So [=But] if you-wish to-enter

into life keep the commandments."
18 He-says to-him, "What-kind-
of [=Which ones]?" So Jesus said,
"YOU-WILL-MURDER NOT, YOU-
WILL-COMMIT-ADULTERY

Mark 10:17-22

17 And his traveling-out [=when he
went out] into [the] way one having-
run-to [him] and having-knelt [to]
him was-questioning him, "Good
teacher, what might-I-do in-order-
that I-might-inherit eternal life?"
18 So Jesus said to-him, "What
[=Why] do-you-say [=do you call]
me good? No-one [is] good if no
[=except] god one [=alone]. 19 You-
recognize the commandments:

'YOU-MIGHT-MURDER NO
[=not], YOU-MIGHT-COMMIT-

Luke 18:18-23

18 And
some magistrate
questioned him saying,
"Good teacher, having-done what
might-I-inherit eternal life?" 19 So
said to-him Jesus, "What [=Why]
do-you-say [=do you call] me good?
No-one [is] good if no [=except] god
one [=alone].

20 You recognize the
commandments:

'YOU-MIGHT-MURDER NO
[=not], YOU-MIGHT-COMMIT-

NOT, YOU-WILL-STEAL NOT,
YOU-MIGHT-TESTIFY-FALSELY
NOT, 19HONOR FATHER AND
MOTHER, AND YOU-WILL-
LOVE YOUR NEIGHBOR LIKE
YOURSELF.”
20The young-man says to-him,
“I-guarded [=I kept] all these
[things]. What am-I-deficient
[of] yet [=still]?”
21Jesus spoke to-him, “If you-wish
to-be perfect, leave, sell your being-
at-one’s-disposals [=belongings]
and give [it all] to-the poor, and
you-will-have [a] treasure-box in
[the] heavens; and [then] come-here
follow me.” 22So the young-man
having-heard the word went-away
being-grieved, for he-was having
many possessions.

ADULTERY NO [=not], YOU-
MIGHT-STEAL NO [=not], YOU-
MIGHT-TESTIFY-FALSELY NO
[=not], YOU-MIGHT-DEFRAUD
NO [=not]; HONOR YOUR
FATHER AND MOTHER.’”
20So he-spoke to-him[c],
“Teacher, I-guarded [=I kept] all
these [things] out my youth [=for all
of my young life].” 21So Jesus having-
beheld him loved him and said to-
him, “One [thing] is-deficient [for]
you: leave, sell whatsoever you-have
and give [it all] to-the poor, and you-
will-have [a] treasure-box in heaven;
and [then] come-here follow me.”
22So [=But] having-looked-gloomy
upon the word [=by what he heard]
he-went-away, being-grieved, for
he-was having many possessions.

ADULTERY NO [=not], YOU-
MIGHT-STEAL NO [=not], YOU-
MIGHT-TESTIFY-FALSELY NO
[=not],
HONOR FATHER AND
MOTHER.”
21So he-said,
“I-guarded [=kept] all these
[commandments] out of-youth [=for
all of my young life].” 22So Jesus,
having-heard[d], said to-him, “One
[thing] lacks [in] you yet: sell all
whatsoever you-have and distribute
[to the] poor, and you-will-have [a]
treasure-box in [the] heavens, and
[then] come-here follow me.”
23So [=But] having-heard
these [things], he-was-happened [=he
was made] very-grieved, for he-was
very wealthy.

[a] *Teacher* ℵ B D L f^{1} 892 *pc* it^{mss}; *Good teacher* C W Θ f^{13} 33 1006 1342 1506 𝔐 it^{mss} vg sy cop^{sa}.
[b] *What do-you-beg me around the good? One is good* ℵ B D L Θ f^{1} 700 892 *pc* it^{mss} vg; *Why do-you-say me good? No-one good if no god one* C W f^{13} 1006 1342 1506 𝔐 it^{mss} sy^{p} sy^{h} cop^{sa}.
[c] *he-spoke to-him* ℵ B Δ Ψ 0274 579 892 1342 2427 *pc* cop; *having-answered he-said* A D W Θ f^{1} f^{13} 1006 1506 𝔐 it vg sy; *having-answered he-spoke* C.
[d] *omit* ℵ B D L f^{1} 33 69 205 579 892 *pc* sy^{s} sy^{c} cop; *these* A W Θ Ψ f^{13} 1006 1342 1506 𝔐 sy^{p} sy^{h}.
🕮 Mt 19:18 – Exod 20:12; 🕮 Mt 19:19 – Lev 19:18; 🕮 Mk 10:19 – Exod 20:12, 13, 14; 🕮 Lk 18:20 – Exod 20:12; Deut 5:17, 18

295. Who Will Enter the Kingdom? (→ §352)

Matt 19:23-30

23So Jesus said [to] his disciples,
“Amen I-say to-you that [a] wealthy
[person] will-enter into the kingdom
of-the heavens not-easily.

24So again, I-say to-you,

It-is easier [for a] camel to-go-
through through [an] eyelet [of
a] needle or [=than for a] wealthy
[person] to-enter into the kingdom
of-god.” 25So [=But] the[a] disciples
having-heard were-being-amazed
very [much] saying,
“What [=Who] consequently
is-able to-be-saved?” 26So [=But]

Mark 10:23-31

23And having-looked-around
Jesus says [to] his disciples, “How
not-easily [will it be for] the havings
[=those who have many] goods [when]
they-will-enter into the kingdom
of-god.” 24So his disciples were-
being-astounded upon [=at] his
words. So having-answered again
Jesus says to-them, “Descendants,
how not-easy it-is to-enter into the
kingdom of-god. 25It-is easier [for a]
camel to-go-through through [an]
opening [of a] needle or [=than for a]
wealthy [person] into the kingdom
of-god to-enter.” 26So they-were-
being-amazed excessively [=greatly]
saying to themselves,
“And what [=Who then] is-able to-
be-saved?” 27Jesus, having-beheld

Luke 18:24-30

24So having-seen him
Jesus said, “How not-easily [will it
be for] the havings [=those who have
many] goods [when] they-will-enter
into the kingdom of-god.

25For it-is easier [for a] camel to-
enter through [an] aperture [of
a] sewing-needle or [=than for a]
wealthy [person] into the kingdom
of-god to-enter.” 26So, the having-
heards [=those who heard this]
said,
“And what [=who then] is-able

Matthew

Jesus, having-beheld [them], said
to-them, "Before [=For] people this
is impossible, so [=but] along [=for]
god all [things are] possible."
[27]Then Peter having-answered
said to-him,
"Look! we [ourselves] excused all
[=left everything] and we-followed
you. What consequently will-be
to-us [=will we get]?" [28]So Jesus
said to-them, "Amen I-say to-you
that you having-followeds [=who
have followed] me, in the next-
generation whenever the son of-the
person might-be-seated upon his
throne of-glory, you [yourselves] and
[=also] will-sit upon twelve thrones
judging the twelve tribes of-Israel.
[29]And all whoever excuse [=leave]
homes or brothers or sisters or
father or mother or descendants or
fields because-of my name will-take
[=will receive a] hundred-fold and
will-inherit eternal life.
[30]So, many firsts will-be lasts and
lasts firsts."

Mark

them, says, "Before [=For] people
[this is] impossible, but not along
[=for] god, for all [things are] possible
along [=for] god."
[28]Peter began
to-say to-him,
"Look! we [ourselves] excused all
[=left everything] and we-have-
followed you."
[29]Jesus spoke[b],
"Amen I-say to-you,
there-is no-one who excused [=left]
home or brothers or sisters or
mother or father or descendants or
fields because-of me and because-
of the proclamation, [30]if-ever
he-might-take [=he might receive]
no [=not a] hundred-fold now
in this proper-time: homes and
brothers and sisters and mothers
and descendants and fields with
persecutions, and in the coming eon
eternal life. [31]So, many firsts will-be
lasts and the[c] lasts firsts."

Luke

to-be-saved?" [27]So he-said, "The
impossible along [=for] people is
possible along [=for] god."
[28]So Peter
said,
"Look! we, having-excused [=having
left] own [things],
we-followed you."
[29]So he-said to-them.
"Amen I-say to-you that
there-is no-one who excused [=left]
home or woman [=wife] or brothers
or parents or descendants because-
of the kingdom of-god, [30]who
indeed-not no might-receive-back
[=will not receive] many-times-more
in this proper-time and in the
coming eon eternal life."

[a] *the* ℵ B C D L Z Δ Θ *f*[13] 33 565 579 700 892 *al* it[mss] vg sy[s] sy[p] sy[h] cop; *his* W *f*[1] 1006 1342 1506 𝔐 sy[c].
[b] *Jesus spoke* B Δ 892 1342 2427 *pc* cop[bo]; *Jesus spoke to-him* ℵ *pc*; *And having-answered them Jesus said* A C E F G H W Θ *f*[1] *f*[13] 205 565 700 1006 1506 2542 it[mss] vg sy[h]; *So having-answered Jesus said* D 1424 it.
[c] *the* B C N Γ *f*[13] 892 2427 cop[sa]; *omit* ℵ A D K L W Δ Θ Ψ *f*[1] 28 565 579 700 1241 1424 2542 cop[bo].
📖 Mt 19:26 – Jer 32:17

296. Matthew's Parable of the Laborers in the Vineyard

Matt 20:1-15

[1]"For the kingdom of-the heavens is comparable-to [a] person, [a] master-of-the-house, whoever
[=who] went-out in-unison-with early [=early in the morning] to-hire workers into [=for] his
vineyard. [2]So having-agreed with the workers out [=at a] denarius [for] the day he-sent-off them
into his vineyard. [3]And having-gone-out around [the] third hour he-saw anothers [=others] having-
stood idle in the market. [4]And he-said to-those, 'You and [=also] leave into [=for] the vineyard,
and I-will-give you which if-ever might-be righteous [=what is fair].' [5]So they-went-away. So again[a]
having-gone-out around [the] sixth and ninth hour he-did in-the-same-way. [6]So around the
eleventh [hour] having-gone-out he-found anothers [=others] having-stood[b] and he-says to-them,
'What [=Why] have-you-stood here the whole day idle?' [7]They-say to-him, 'That [=Because] no-one
hired us.' He-says to-them, 'You and [=also] leave into [=for] the vineyard[c].' [8]So, evening having-
happened the lord of-the vineyard says [to] his steward, 'Call the workers and give-over to-them
the [=their] wages having-begun from the lasts until the firsts.' [9]And the having-comes [=those who

came] around the eleventh hour took [=received a] denarius up [=each]. [10]And the firsts [=the first
ones hired] having-come, thought that they-will-take more, and [=but] they-took [=they received a]
denarius up [=each], they and [=too]. [11]So having-taken [=when they received their pay] they-were-
grumbling according-to [=against] the master-of-the-house, [12]saying, 'These lasts did [=worked] one
hour and you-did [=you made] them equal to-us, to-the having-bornes [=those who bore] the weight
of-the day and the scorching-heat.' [13]So having-answered he-said to-one of-them, 'Comrade, I-am-
unrighteous [to] you not; indeed-not did-you-agree [=did you not agree with] me [for a] denarius?
[14]Remove your-own [things] and leave. So I-wish to-give to-this last [person hired] like and [=also I
gave] to-you. [15]Is-it-permitted not for-me to-do which [=what] I-wish in [=with] my-owns [=my own
things]? Or is your eye evil that [=because] I [myself] am good?'"

[a] *So again* ℵ C D L 33 579 892 1006 *pc* it^{mss} vg sy^{h} cop^{sa}; *Again* B W Θ 085 f^1 f^{13} 1342.
[b] *omit* ℵ B C* D L Θ 085 33 579 700 892 it^{mss} vg sy^{s} sy^{c} cop; *idle* C^{2} W f^1 f^{13} 1006 1342 1506 𝔐 it^{mss} sy^{p} sy^{h}.
[c] *the vineyard* ℵ B L Θ f^1 579 892 it^{mss} vg cop^{bo}; *my vineyard* C^{3} D Z 565 it vg sy^{s} cop^{sa} Cyril; *the vineyard and you-will take what if-ever might-be righteous* C* W f^{13} 33 892 1506 𝔐 sy^{c} sy^{p} sy^{h}; *my vineyard and you-will take what if-ever might-be righteous* 346 565 *al* it^{mss}.

297. The First and the Last (→ §252)

Matt 20:16	Q 13:30	Luke 13:30	Thomas 4
[16]"Thus the lasts will-be firsts and the firsts lasts.[a]"	[30]"The lasts will-be firsts and the firsts lasts."	[30]"And look! [those] who will-be firsts are lasts and [those] who will-be lasts are firsts."	Jesus said, "The person old in days won't hesitate to ask a little child seven days old about the place of life, and that person will live. For many of the first will be last, and will become a single one."

[a] *omit* ℵ B L Z 085 892 1342 *pc* cop^{sa}; *for many are called, so few chosen-ones* C D W Θ f^1 f^{13} 33 892 1006 1506 𝔐 it vg sy.

298. The Third Passion Prediction

Matt 20:17-19	Mark 10:32-34	Luke 18:31-34
[17]And Jesus, <u>ascending</u> into Jerusalems,	[32]So they-were in [=on] the way ascending into Jerusalems, and Jesus was leading-ahead [of] them, and they-were-being-astounded, so [=and] the followings [=those who followed] were-fearing. And	[31]So
took-along the twelve disciples[a] according-to own [=by themselves] and in [=on] the way said to-them,	having-taken-along [=taking aside] the twelve again and he-began to-say to-them the intendings [=the things that were about] to-come-about to-him,	having-taken-along [=taking aside] the twelve he-said to them,
[18]"Look! we-ascend into Jerusalems	[33]that [=saying] "Look! we-ascend into Jerusalems and	"Look! we-ascend into Jerusalems and all the having-been-writtens [=that has been written] through the prophets will-be-completed in-the son of-the person.
and the son of-the person will-be-delivered to-the high-priests and scribes, and they-will-judge-against	the son of-the person will-be-delivered to-the high-priests and to-the scribes, and they-will-judge-	

[=they will sentence] him to-death[b],
[19]and they-will-deliver him to-the
nations [=Gentiles] into [=in order]

to-mock and to-scourge and to-
crucify [him], and [on] the third day
he-will-be-raised."

against [=they will sentence] him
to-death, and they-will-deliver him
to-the nations [=Gentiles] [34]and they-
will-mock him and they-will-spit-

on him and they-will-scourge him
and they-will-kill [him], and with
[=after] three days[c] he-will-get-up."

[32]For he-will-be-delivered to-the
nations [=Gentiles] and he-will-be-
mocked and he-will-be-insulted and
he-will-be-spat-on [33]and having-
scourged [him] they-will-kill him
and [on] the third day he-will-get-
up."
[34]And they [themselves]
comprehended no-one [=none] of-
these [things], and this speech was
having-been-hidden from them and
they-were-knowing the sayings not.

[a] *the twelve disciples* B C W 085 33 1006 𝔐 it^{mss} vg sy^{h} cop^{samss}; *the twelve* ℵ D L Θ f^{1} f^{13} 892 *pc* sy^{s} sy^{c} cop^{bo}; *his twelve disciples* 13 346 543 1342 1424 *pc* it vg^{mss} sy^{p} cop^{samss}.
[b] *to-death* C D L W Z Θ 085 f^{1} f^{13} 33 892 1006 1342 𝔐; *into death* ℵ 700; *omit* B.
[c] *with three days* ℵ B C D L Δ Ψ 892 1342 2427 *pc* it cop; *the third day* A W Θ f^{1} f^{13} 1006 𝔐 vg sy.

299. The Sons of Zebedee

Matt 20:20-23

[20]Then the mother of-the sons of-Zebedee approached
him with her sons worshiping and asking some [thing]
from him.

[21]So he-said to-her, "What do-you-wish?"
She-says to-him, "Say in-order-that [=Declare that]
these my two sons might-be-seated one out [=to] your
right and one out [=to] your left in your kingdom." [22]So
having-answered
Jesus said, "You-recognize not what you-ask. Are-
you-able to-drink the cup what [=which] I-intend to-
drink?"[a]
They-say to-him, "We-are-able."
[23]He-says to-them, "You-will-drink my cup for-one,
[b]

so [=but] to-be-seated out [=to] my right and out [=to
my] left, this is not my-own to-give, but to-whom it-
has-been-made-ready
under [=by] my father."

Mark 10:35-40

[35]And James and John the sons of-Zebedee traveled-
toward him saying to-him, "Teacher, we-wish in-order-
that which [=what] if-ever we-might-ask you you-
might-do [for] us."
[36]So he-said to-them, "What do-you-wish me to-do
[for] you?" [37]So they-said to-him, "Give us in-order-
that we-might-be-seated one out [=to] your right and
one out [=to your] left-hand in your glory." [38]So Jesus
said to-them, "You-recognize not what you-ask. Are-
you-able to-drink the cup which I-drink or to-be-
baptized [with] the baptism [with] which I [myself]

am-baptized?" [39]So they-said to-him, "We-are-able."
So [=But] Jesus said to-them, "The cup which I [myself]
drink you-will-drink and the baptism what [=which] I
[myself] am-baptized you-will-be-baptized, [40]so [=but]
to-be-seated out [=to] my right or out [=to my] left, is
not my-own to-give, but to-whom[c] it-has-been-made-
ready."

[a] *omit* ℵ B D L Z Θ 085 f^{1} f^{13} 2542 *pc* it^{mss} vg sy^{s} sy^{c} cop^{sa}; *or to-be-baptized the baptism what I-am-baptized?* C W 33 892 1006 1342 1506 𝔐 sy^{p} sy^{h}.
[b] *omit* ℵ B D L Z 085 f^{1} f^{13} *pc* it^{mss} vg sy^{s} sy^{c}; *and the baptism what I am-baptized you-will-be-baptized* C W 33 892 1006 1342 1506 𝔐 sy^{p} sy^{h}.
[c] *to-whom* A B^{2} Θ Ψ f^{1} f^{13} 892 1006 1342 1506 𝔐 sy^{p} sy^{h} cop^{bo}; *for-anothers* 225 it cop^{samss}; *so for-anothers* sy^{s}.

300. A Dispute among the Disciples (→ §351)

Matt 20:24-28	Mark 10:41-45	Luke 22:24-27	John 13:4-5, 12-17
24 And the ten having-heard were-indignant around [=concerning] the two brothers.	41 And the ten having-heard began to-be-indignant around [=concerning] James and John.	24 So [a] dispute and [=also] happened in [=among] them, the what [=which one] of-them does-he-suppose to-be greater.	. . . 4 he-rises out of-the banquet [=from the table] and puts the [=his] coats [aside] and having-taken [a] towel encloaked himself; 5 moreover, he-throws water into the wash-basin and he-began to-wash the feet of-the disciples and to-dry [them with] the towel in-which he-was having-been-encloaked.
25 So [=But] Jesus having-summoned them said "You-recognize that	42 And having-summoned them Jesus says to-them, "You-recognize that the supposings [=those who are supposed] to-begin [=to rule]	25 So he-said to-them, "The	
the magistrates of-the nations act-as-lord-over them and the greats [=tyrants] rule-over them.	the nations act-as-lord-over them and their greats [=tyrants] rule-over them.	kings of-the nations act-as-lord of-them and the havings-authority-over [=those who have authority over] them are-called workers-of-kindness [=benefactors].	12 Therefore when he-washed their feet and took his coats and leaned [=reclined at the table] again, he-said to-them, "Do-you-know what I-have-done for-you?
26 It-will-be not thus [=this way] in [=with] you, but who if-ever might-wish to-happen [=to become] great in [=among] you will-be your servant,	43 So [=But] it-is not thus [=this way] in [=with] you, but who ever might-wish to-happen [=to become] great in [=among] you will-be your servant,	26 So [=But it is] not thus [=this way for] you. But the greater in [=among] you let-happen [=let him be] like the newer [=younger], and the ruling [one] like the [one] serving.	13 You yell [=You call] me 'Teacher' and 'lord' and you-speak well [=correctly], for I-am. 14 Therefore if I, the lord and the teacher, washed your feet, you [yourselves] and [=also] owe one-another to-wash the feet.
27 and who ever in [=among] you might-wish to-be first will-be your slave. 28 Even-as the son of-the person came not to-be-served but to-serve and to-give his soul [=life as] ransom in-place of-many."	44 and who ever in [=among] you might-wish to-be[a] first will-be slave of-all, 45 for and [=even] the son of-the person came not to-be-served but to-serve and to-give his soul [=life as] ransom in-place of-many."		15 For I-gave you [an] example in-order-that just-as I [myself] did for-you, you [yourselves] might-do [for each other] and [=also]. 16 Amen amen I-say to-you, [a] slave is not greater [than] his lord nor [an] apostle greater [than] the [one] having-sent him.
		27 For what [=who is] greater, the [one] dining or the [one] serving? [Is it] indeed-not the [one] dining? So [=But] I [myself] am in [the] middle of-you like the [one] serving."	17 If you-recognize these [things] you-are fortunate if-ever you-might-do them."

[a] *who ever in you might-wish to-be* ℵ B C* L Δ Θ Ψ 579 700 892 1342 1424 2427 *pc*; *who ever of-you might-wish to-be* D W f^1 205 565 2543 *pc*; *who ever of-you might-wish to-happen* A C³ f^{13} 1006 𝔐.

301. Healing a Blind Man (→ §100)

Matt 20:29-34	Mark 10:46-52	Luke 18:35-43
29 And their traveling-out from [=as they were leaving] Jericho, many [=a great] crowd followed him. 30 And look! two blinds [=two blind people] sitting along [=by] the way [=road]	46 And they-come into Jericho. And his traveling-out from [when he was leaving] Jericho and his disciples and [a] fit [=large] crowd, Bartimaeus the son of-Timaeus, [a] blind panhandler, sat along [=by] the way [=road].	35 So it-happened in the to-near him into [=as he was nearing] Jericho some blind [person] sat along [=by] the way [=road] asking-for-alms[c]. 36 So having-heard [a] crowd traveling-through he-was-inquiring what this may-be. 37 So they-informed him that Jesus the Nazarite passes-away [=passes by].
having-heard that Jesus passes-by cried saying, "Be-merciful [to] us lord, son of-David."	47 And having-heard that it-is Jesus the Nazarene, began to-cry and to-say, "Son of-David, Jesus, be-merciful [to] me."	38 And he-shouted saying, "Jesus son of-David be-merciful [to] me."
31 So the crowd rebuked them in-order-that they-might-be-silent. So [=But] they-cried[a] greater [=more loudly] saying, "Be merciful [to] us lord, son of-David." 32 And Jesus, having-stood [=having stopped], he-yelled [to] them and said,	48 And many were-rebuking him in-order-that he-might-be-silent. So [=but] rather he-was-crying many [=more loudly], "Son of-David, be-merciful [to] me." 49 And Jesus, having-stood [=having stopped] said, "Yell [=Call to] him." And they-yell [=they call to] the blind [person] saying to-him,	39 And the leading-aheads [=those who were out in front] were-rebuking him in-order-that he-might-be-quiet, so [=but] rather he [himself] cried many [=more loudly], "Son of-David, be-merciful [to] me." 40 So Jesus having-been-stood [=having been stopped] ordered him to-be-led [to] him. So having-neared him he-questioned him,
	"Cheer-up, rise, he-yells [=he calls for] you." 50 So having-thrown-off his coat [and] having-jumped-up he-went to Jesus. 51 And having-answered him Jesus said,	
"What do-you-wish I-might-do to-you?" 33 They-say to-him, "Lord, in-order-that our eyes might-be-opened." 34 So Jesus, having-had-pity touched their eyeballs; and instantly they-looked-up [=they could see] and followed him.	"What do-you-wish I-will-do [for] you?" So the blind [person] said to-him, "Rabbouni, in-order-that I-might-look-up [=I might see again]." 52 And Jesus said to-him, "Leave. Your loyalty has-saved you." And immediately[b] he-looked-up [=he saw again] and was-following him in the way [=on the road].	41 "What do-you-wish I-will-do for-you?" So he-said "Lord, in-order-that I-might-look-up [=I might see again]." 42 And Jesus said to-him, "Look-up. Your loyalty has-saved you." 43 And he-looked-up at-once and was-following him glorifying god. And all the whole-people, having-seen, gave praise to-god.

[a] *they-cried* ℵ B D L Z 085 700 892 *pc*; *they-were-crying* C W f^{1} 33 1006 1342 1506 𝔐; *they-were-screaming* Θ f^{13}; *they-screamed* 𝔭[45].
[b] *immediately* ℵ B L 892 1342 2427; *instantly* A C D Θ f^{1} f^{13} 1006 1506 𝔐.
[c] *asking-for-alms* ℵ B D L T 579 *pc*; *panhandling* A W Θ Ψ f^{1} f^{13} 33 892 1006 1342 1506 𝔐 cop[sa].

SYNOPTIC STUDY GUIDE 12

Redaction Criticism

Redaction Criticism is interested in how an author edits his sources, for the gospel authors were not simply creating stories from nothing but were using sources they altered here and there. As a method of reading the gospels, Redaction Criticism is distinct from Source Criticism, yet it has particular application to the Synoptic Problem. For many scholars, it is possible to understand how an author might edit a source, especially if close analysis reveals a *pattern* of similar editing throughout. One such pattern is the drive among early Christian writers to improve upon Mark's sometimes troubling depiction of Jesus. Consider the Baptism of Jesus (§21). The combination of Mark 1:4 + 1:9 creates something of a theological problem: why would the Son of God receive a baptism of repentance for the forgiveness of sins? What had Jesus done that qualified as sin and required repentance? This problem does not exist in Matthew or Luke. Matthew contains a short conversation (replete with vocabulary and themes typical of Matthew) in which Jesus commands the baptism without admitting sin (Matt 3:14-15), and the writer of Luke makes Jesus' baptizer a mystery, since he has John imprisoned before the baptism and then does not actually name Jesus' baptizer! For most scholars, this is evidence of direction of dependence, since it is more likely that Mark wrote first and that Matthew and Luke worked to resolve the theological problem (and each doing so differently, also illustrating their independence from each other), than it is that Mark used Matthew and Luke and introduced a theological problem where none existed.

Plenty of other examples exist. Mark 1:32-33 (§62) relates that "all" the sick and demon-possessed were brought to Jesus, and that "many of them" were healed. Why did Jesus not heal *all* of them? Matthew does not have this problem, for in his version "many" were brought and "all" were healed! In Jesus' preaching at Nazareth (§28), the Gospel of Mark says that Jesus was unable to do more than a few healings. In the same story, Matthew's gospel lacks the implication that Jesus was rendered incapable and says instead that Jesus *did not do* many miracles (in other words, he chose not to!). Finally, Mark's Jesus curses a fig tree for not producing figs (§308) even though its author says it was not the season for figs (Mark 11:13). The Gospel of Matthew's version of the story lacks the comment about the wrong season, thereby rendering Jesus' indignation perfectly rational. After all, who in his right mind would curse a tree for not producing fruit out of season?

How do these examples relate to the Synoptic Problem? They point to Markan Priority. It is after all more likely that Matthew and Luke corrected problems in Mark's gospel to make Jesus look better than it is that Mark introduced theological problems into his gospel where Matthew and Luke had things right, or that Mark made the Son of God look more fallible than the one found in his sources.

302. Luke's Story of Zacchaeus the Tax Collector

Luke 19:1-10

1 And having-entered he-was-going-through Jericho. 2 And look! [a] man being-called [by] name
Zacchaeus and he [himself] was [a] tax-chief and he [himself was] wealthy[a]. 3 And he-was-searching
[for] to-see what [=who] Jesus is and he-was-able not from [=because of] the crowd, that [=because]
he-was small by-age [=he was too short]. 4 And having-run-ahead into the in-front [=in front of
Jesus] he-ascended upon [a] sycamore-tree in-order-that he-might-see him that [=because] he-
was-intending to-go-through that [way]. 5 And like [=when] he-came upon the place, Jesus having-
looked-up[b] said to him, "Zacchaeus, having-hurried, descend, for today it-is-necessary [for] me
to-stay in your house." 6 And having-hurried, he-descended and hailed him rejoicing. 7 And all
having-seen [this] were-grumbling-loudly saying that "He-entered to-demolish [=He has gone to be a
guest] along [=of a] sinful man." 8 So Zacchaeus, having-been-stood, said to the lord, "Look! half [of]
my being-at-one's-disposals [=belongings] lord, I-give to-the poor, and if I-blackmailed [=I have ever
defrauded] some [one] of-some [=of something] I-give-over [=I will pay them back] four-fold." 9 So Jesus
said to him that, "Today salvation happened in-this house on-account-that [=because] he [himself]
and [=too] is [a] son of-Abraham, 10 for the son of-the person came to-search [for] and to-save the
having-been-destroyed [=the lost]."

[a] *tax-chief and he wealthy* B T f^{1} f^{13} 579 2542 *al* it^{mss} vg; *tax-chief and he was wealthy* Θ *pc* it vg^{mss}; *tax-chief and this was wealthy* A W 1006 1342 1506 𝔐; *tax-chief and he-was wealthy* ℵ L 892 *pc* cop^{bo}; *wealthy tax chief* D cop^{sa}.

[b] *omit* ℵ B L T Θ f^{1} 205 579 2542 *pc* sy^{s} sy^{c} sy^{p} cop; *saw him and* A D W Ψ f^{13} 33 892 1006 1342 1506 𝔐 it vg sy^{h}.

303. The Parable of the Evil Slave (→ §341)

Matt 25:14-30	**Q 19:12-13, 15-24, 26**	**Luke 19:11-27**
		11So their hearing [=while they were listening to] these [things] having-added he-said [=he went on to tell a] parable through [=because] him to-be [=he was] near Jerusalem and to-suppose them [=because they supposed] that the kingdom of-god intends to-be-brought-into-sight [=was to appear] at-once. 12Therefore he-said,
14“For even-as [=it is as if a] person	12“Some person, [on] leaving-home,	“Some noble person traveled into [a] distant region to-take [for] himself [a] kingdom and to-return.
[on] leaving-home called the [=his] own slaves and delivered to-them his being-at-one’s-disposals [=belongings], 15and to-whom for-one [=to one of them] he-gave five talants, so to-whom [= and to another] two, so to-whom [=and to another] one, to-each according-to the own power [=his ability], and he-left-home instantly. 16The [one] having-taken [=having received] the five talants, having-traveled, worked in [=with] them and gained[a] another five. 17In-the-same-way, the [one who received] the two [talants] gained another two. 18So [=But] the [one] having-taken [=who received] the one [talant] having-gone-away dug-a-hole [in the] land and hid the silver-coin [of] his lord.	13called ten slaves [for] himself, he-gave them ten minas and said to-them, ‘Invest [it] in [=until] which I-come [back].’	13So having-called ten slaves [for] himself, he-gave them ten minas and said to them, ‘Invest [it] in [=until] which I-come [back].’
		14So [=But] his citizens were-hating him and they-sent-off [an] embassy-of-elders behind [=after] him saying, ‘We-wish not [for] this [man] to-be-king upon [=over] us.’
19So with many [=after much] time	15With many [=After much] time	15And it-happened in the to-come-back-through him [=when he returned], having-taken the kingdom, and he-said [for] these slaves to-whom he-had-given the silver-coin to-be-yelled [=to be called] to-him in-order-that he-might-know what [=how] they-profited.
the lord of-those slaves comes and discharges word [=settles accounts] with them.	the lord of-those slaves comes and discharges word [=settles accounts] with them.	
20And having-approached the [one] having-taken [=having received] the five talants offered another five talants saying, ‘Lord, you-delivered to-me five talants; look, I-gained[b] another five talants.’	16And the first came saying, ‘Lord, your mina yielded ten minas.’	16So the first arrived saying, ‘Lord, your mina yielded ten minas.’

21 His lord spoke to-him, 'Splendidly
[done], slave good and loyal;
you-were loyal upon [=over a]
few [things], I-will-establish you
[=I will give you authority] upon
[=over] many [things]. Enter into
the joy [of] your lord.' 22 So having-
approached and [=also], the [one
having received] the two talants, said
'Lord, you-delivered to-me two
talants; look, I-gained another two
talants.' 23 His lord spoke to-him,
'Splendidly [done], slave good and
loyal; you-were loyal upon [=over a]
few [things], I-will-establish you [=I
will give you authority] upon [=over]
many [things]. Enter into the joy
[of] your lord.' 24 And so having-
approached, the [one] having-taken
[=having received] the one talant, said
'Lord, I-knew that you [yourself]
are [a] hard person, harvesting
where you-sowed not and gathering
from-which [place] you-scattered
[seed] not, 25 and having-been-feared
[=being afraid and] having-gone-away
I-hid your talant in the land; look,
you-have [what is] your-own.' 26 So
his lord, having-answered, said to-
him,
'Evil slave and lazy, you-recognized

that I-harvest where I-sowed not
and I-gather from-which [places]
I-scattered [seed] not?
27 Therefore it-was-necessary [for]
you [yourself] to-throw [=to take]
my silver-coins to-the bankers and
having-come [back] I [myself would
have] obtained [what] ever [was] my-
own together-with interest.

28 Therefore, remove the talant from
him and give [it] to-the [one] having

[=who has] ten talants.
29 For to-the [one] having [=who has]
all [more] will-be-given and he-will-
be-exceeded [=he will be rich], so
[=but from] the [one] having no
[=nothing] and [=even that] which he-
has will-be-removed from him.

17 And he-said to-him, 'Splendidly
[done], good slave. You-were
loyal upon [=over a] few [things],
I-will-establish you [=I will give
you authority] upon [=over] many
[things].'
18 And the second came

saying, 'Lord, your mina did
[=made] five minas.'

19 He-said to-him, 'Splendidly [done],
good slave. You-were loyal upon
[=over a] few [things], I-will-establish
you [=I will give you authority] upon
[=over] many [things].'

20 And the other came saying,

'Lord, 21 I-knew that you [yourself]
are [a] hard person, harvesting
where you-sowed not and gathering
from-which [place] you-scattered
[seed] not, and having-been-feared
[=being afraid and] having-gone-away
I-hid your mina in the land; look,
you-have [what is] your-own.' 22 He-
says to-him,

'Evil slave, you-recognized that

I-harvest where I-sowed not and
I-gather from-which [places] I-
scattered [seed] not?
23 Therefore it-was-necessary [for]
you [yourself] to-throw [=to take]
my silver-coins to-the bankers and
having-come [back] I [myself would
have] obtained [what] ever [was] my-
own together-with interest.

24 Therefore, remove the mina from
him and give [it] to-the [one] having

[=who has] ten minas.
26 For to-the [one] having [=who has]

all [more] will-be-given, so [=but
from] the [one] having no [=nothing]
and [=even that] which he-has will-
be-removed from him.'"

17 And he-said to-him, 'Bravo[c] good
slave, that [=because] you-happened
[=you were] loyal in [the] least, be
having authority above [=take charge
over] ten cities.'

18 And the second came

saying, 'Your mina,
lord, did [=made] five minas.'

19 And so he-said to-this [one],

'And you, happen [=rule] above five
cities.'

20 And the other came saying,

'Lord, look! your mina which I-had
wrapped-up in cloth, 21 for I-was-
fearing you, that [=because] you-are
[a] harsh person; you-remove [that]
which you-put not [=you did not
deposit] and harvest [that] which
you-sowed not.'

22 He-says to-him, 'I-will-judge
you out your mouth [=by your own
words], evil slave. You-recognized
that I [myself] am [a] harsh person
removing [that] which I-put not
[=I did not deposit] and harvesting

[that] which I-sowed not?
23 And through what [=why] did-
you-give not my silver-coin upon
table [=to a bank]? I-too [=Then I]
having-come practiced [=could
have collected] it together-with ever
[=whatever] interest.'
24 And to-the being-presents [=to the
bystanders] he-said,
'Remove from him the mina and
give [it] to-the [one] having ten
minas.' 25 And they-said to-him,
'Lord, he-has ten minas.'
26 'I-say to-you that to-the [one]
having [=who has] all [more] will-
be-given, so [=but] from the [one]
having no [=nothing] and [=even that]
which he-has will-be-removed [=will
be taken away].

30 And cast-out the worthless slave
into the outermost darkness; there-
will-be wailing and gnashing of-the
teeth there.'"

27 Nevertheless these my enemies
having-wished me no [=not] to-be-
king upon [=over] them, lead [them]
here and slay them in-front of-me.'"

[a] *gained* ℵ^{2} B C D L Θ f^{1} f^{13} 33 205 892 1424 1506 *al* vg it^{mss} sy^{p} cop^{sa}; *did* ℵ* A^{C} W 1006 1342 𝔐 sy^{h}.
[b] *I-gained* ℵ B L 33 892 *pc* it^{mss} cop; *I-gained-in-addition upon them* A C W f^{1} f^{13} 1006 1342 1506 𝔐 sy^{p} sy^{h}.
[c] *Bravo* B D 892 vg it^{mss}; *Splendidly* ℵ A L W Θ Ψ f^{1} f^{13} 1006 1342 1506 𝔐.

304. Jesus' Final Entry into Jerusalem

Matt 21:1-9

1 And when they-
neared into Jerusalems
and they-went into
Bethphage into [=onto]
the mountain of-the
olives, then Jesus sent-
off two disciples, 2 saying
to-them, "Travel into the
village ahead[a] of-you, and
instantly you-
will-find [an] ass
having-been-restrained
and [a] colt with it.
Having-loosed [it] lead
[it] to-me. 3 And if-ever
some [one] might-say
some [thing] to-you, you-
will-say that their
lord has need [of the
animals]. So immediately[b]
he-will-send-off them."
4 So this has-happened
in-order-that the having-
been-said [=what had
been said] through the
prophet might-be-
fulfilled, saying 5 "SAY
TO-THE DAUGHTER
OF-ZION, LOOK! YOUR
KING COMES TO-YOU
GENTLE AND HAVING-
MOUNTED UPON [an]
ASS AND UPON [a]
COLT[c], SON [=offspring of
a] BEAST-OF-BURDEN."

Mark 11:1-10

1 And when they-
near into Jerusalems, into
Bethphage and Bethany,
to the mountain of-the
olives, he-sends-off two
[of] his disciples 2 and says
to-them, "Leave, into the
village ahead of-you, and
traveling-in into it
immediately you-will-
find [a] colt upon which
no-one of-people not-yet
sat [=that no one has ever
ridden] having-been-
restrained.
Loose and carry [=bring]
it. 3 And if-ever some [one]
might-say to-you,
'What [=Why] are-you-
doing this?' say
'Its lord has need [of it],
and immediately he-will-
send-off it here again.'"

Luke 19:28-40

28 And having-said these
[things] he-was-traveling
in-front [of them]
ascending into Jerusalems.
29 And it-happened like
[=as] he-neared into
Bethphage and Bethany, to
the mountain being-called
of-olives, he-sent-off two
of-the disciples 30 saying,
"Leave [=Go] ahead into
the village, in which
traveling-in you-will-
find [a] colt upon which
no-one of-people at-any-
time sat [=that no one has
ever ridden] having-been-
restrained, and having-
loosed lead it [here]. 31 And
if-ever some [one] might-
beg you,
'Through what [=Why] do-
you-loose?' you-will-say
thus, that 'Its lord has
need [of it].'"

John 12:12-15

12 [On] the next-day the
many [=great] crowd
having-come into the
feast, having-heard
that Jesus comes into
Jerusalems,

Matt 21:6-9	Mark 11:4-9	Luke 19:32-38	
6So the disciples, having-traveled and having-done	4And they-went-away	32So having-gone-away the having-been-sent-offs [=those who had been sent off] found	
	and they-found [a] colt having-been-restrained to [a] door outside upon the roadway and they-loose it.		
just-as Jesus directed them,		just-as he-said to-them.	
	5And some of-the having-stoods [=of those standing] there were-saying to-them, "What are-you-doing loosing the colt?" 6So they-said to-them just-as Jesus said, and they-excused them [=they let them go].	33So their loosing [=when they loosed] the colt, its lords said to them, "What [=Why] do-you-loose the colt?" 34So they-said, "Its lord has need [of it]."	
	7And they-carry[d] [=they lead] the colt to Jesus and throw-on it their coats,	35And they-led it to Jesus, and having-tossed-on their coats	
7they-led the ass and the colt and they-placed upon them the [=their] coats,			
and he-sat-upon above [=he sat on] them.	and he-sat upon it.	upon the colt they-put-upon [=they placed] Jesus [on it].	
8So [=And] the most crowd [=the majority of the crowd]	8And many	36So his traveling [=when he left],	
spread-out the coats of-themselves in the way [=on the road], so [=and] anothers [=others] were-cutting branches from the trees and were-spreading-out [them] in the way [=road].	spread-out their coats into the way [=onto the road] so [=and] anothers [=others] leafy-branches having-cut [=which they cut] out of-the fields.	they-were-spreading-right-out their coats in the way [=on the road].	13took palm-branches of-the palm-tree and went-out into [the] meeting [with] him and were-screaming,
9So the crowds leading-ahead [of] him and the followings [=those who followed] were-	9And the leading-aheads [=those who went ahead] and the followings [=those who followed]	37So	
		his nearing [=when he approached], already to the slope of-the mountain of-the olives, the everyone [=the whole] multitude of-the disciples began to-praise god [with a] great voice rejoicing around [=concerning] all [the] powers which they-had-seen, 38saying,	

crying saying, “Hosanna to-the son of-David, HAVING-BEEN-BLESSED [is] THE [one] COMING IN [the] NAME [of the] LORD.	were-crying, “Hosanna, HAVING-BEEN-BLESSED [is] THE [one] COMING IN [THE] NAME [of the] LORD.	“HAVING-BEEN-BLESSED [is] THE [one] COMING, THE KING IN [the] NAME [of the] LORD. Peace in heaven and glory in [the] most-high.”	“Hosanna; HAVING-BEEN-BLESSED [is] THE [one] COMING IN [the] NAME [of the] LORD, the king of-Israel.” 14So Jesus having-found [a] young-donkey was-seated upon it, just-as is having-been-written, 15“FEAR NO [=not] DAUGHTER OF-ZION, LOOK! YOUR KING COMES, SITTING UPON [the] COLT [of an] ASS.”
Hosanna in the most-high.”	10Having-been-blessed [is] the coming kingdom [of] our father David. Hosanna in the most-high.”		
		39And some of-the Pharisees from the crowd said to-him, “Teacher, rebuke your disciples.” 40And having-answered, he-said, “I-say to-you, if ever these will-be-silent, the stones will-cry [out].”	

[a] *ahead* ℵ B C D L Z Θ f^{13} 33 70 892 *al*; *across-from* W f^{1} 1006 1342 1506 𝔐.
[b] *So immediately* ℵ B L Θ 700 788 892 *pc*; *And instantly* D 33 579 *pc*; *So instantly* C W f^{1} f^{13} 1006 1342 1506 𝔐.
[c] *colt* ℵ B L f^{1} 700 2542 *pc* sy cop^{sa}; *omit* C D W Θ f^{13} 33 892 1006 1342 1506 𝔐 it vg cop^{bo}.
[d] *they-carry* ℵ^{2} B L Δ Ψ 892 2427 *pc*; *they-led* A D 1006 1506 𝔐 sy; *they-lead* ℵ* C W Θ f^{1} f^{13} 205 1342 2542 *pc*.
🕮 Mt 21:5 – Zech 9:9; 🕮 Mt 21:9 – Ps 118:26; 🕮 Mk 11:9 – Ps 118:26; 🕮 Lk 19:38 – Ps 118:26; 🕮 Jn 12:13 – Ps 118:26; 🕮 Jn 12:15 – Zech 9:9

305. Luke's Jesus Weeping over Jerusalem

Luke 19:41-44

41And like [=when] he-neared the city, having-seen [=and saw it], he-wept upon [=over] it, 42saying
that “If [only] you-knew in [=on] this day, and [=even] you, the [things that lead] to peace[a]; so [=but]
now they-are-hidden from your eyes. 43That [=For the] days will-press-forward [=will come] upon
you and your enemies will-throw-up [a] rampart [around] you and they-will-surround you and
they-will-control you from-everywhere [=from all sides], 44and they-will-flatten you and your
descendants in [=with] you and they-will-excuse [=they will leave] not stone upon stone in [=among]
you, in-place of-which [=because] you-knew not the proper-time [of] your visitation.”

[a] *to peace* ℵ B L Θ 579 *pc* cop^{sa}; *to your peace* A W Ψ f^{1} 892 1006 1342 1506 𝔐 sy cop^{bo}; *to peace in-you* D f^{13} *pc* vg it^{mss}.

Jesus in Jerusalem

306. Mark's Temple Preview by Jesus

Mark 11:11

11And he-entered into Jerusalems into the temple, and having-looked-around all [=at everything], [it] being late already of-the hour, he-went-out into Bethany with the twelve.

There are no variants in this pericope that appear in English.

Mark 11:11 (§306, p. 224) Q 17:35 (§288, p. 209)
Luke 19:44 (§305, p. 224)

307. The Temple Scene (→ §309)

Matt 21:10-17	Mark 11:15-19	Luke 19:45-48	John 2:13-17
10 And his having-entered [=when he entered] into Jerusalems all the city was-shaken saying, "What [=Who] is this?" 11 So the crowds were-saying, "This is the prophet Jesus from Nazareth of-the Galilee."	15 And they-come into Jerusalems.		13 And the passover of-the Judeans was near, and Jesus ascended into Jerusalems.
12 And Jesus entered into the temple and cast-out all the sellings and buyings [=those who were selling and buying] in the temple[a], and the tables of-the money-changers he-over-turned and the seats of-the sellings [=those who were selling] the doves.	And having-entered into the temple, he-began to-cast-out the sellings [=those who were selling] and the buyings [=those who were buying] in the temple, and the tables of-the money-changers and the seats of-the sellings [=those who were selling] the doves he-over-turned, 16 and he-excused not in-order-that some might-be-superior [=he did not allow anyone to carry a] vessel through the temple.	45 And having-entered into the temple he-began to-cast-out the sellings[b] [=those who were selling],	14 And in the temple he-found the sellings [=those who were selling] oxen and sheep and doves and [he found] the cash-changers sitting [there]. 15 And having-done [=having made a] whip out of-ropes he-cast-out all out of-the temple, even the sheep and the oxen and he-poured-out the cash of-the money-changers and he-flipped the tables.
13 And he-says to-them, "It-has-been-written, 'MY HOUSE WILL-BE-CALLED [a] HOUSE OF-PRAYER,' so [=but] it you [yourselves] do [=make into a] cave of-bandits." 14 And blinds [=blind people] and lames [=lame people] approached him in the temple and he-healed them.	17 And he-was-teaching and was-saying to-them, "It-has-been-written not [=Is it not written] that 'MY HOUSE WILL-BE-CALLED [a] HOUSE OF-PRAYER IN-ALL THE NATIONS'? so [=but] you [yourselves] have-made it [a] cave of-bandits."	46 saying to-them, "It-has-been-written, 'AND MY HOUSE WILL-BE [a] HOUSE OF-PRAYER,' so [=but] you [yourselves] did [=made] it [a] cave of-bandits."	16 And to-the sellings [=to those who were selling] the doves he-said, "Remove these from-here; do [=make] no [=not] the house [of] my father [a] house of-merchandise." 17 His disciples remembered that it-is having-been-written, "THE ZEAL [of] YOUR HOUSE WILL-CONSUME ME."
15 So [=But] the high-priests and the scribes, having-seen the wonderfuls [=wonderful things] which he-did and the children crying	18 And the high-priests and the scribes heard and	47 And he-was teaching according-to [=each] day in the temple. So [=But] the high-priests and the scribes	

[out] in the temple and [having-heard them] saying, "Hosanna to-the son of-David," were-indignant 16 and they-said to-him, "Do-you-hear what these [people] say?" So [=But] Jesus says to-them, "Yes. Never did-you-read that 'OUT OF-MOUTHS OF-INFANTS AND OF-NURSINGS [=of nursing babies] YOU-MENDED [=you brought forth] PRAISE'?"	they-were-searching [for] how they-might-destroy him,	were-searching to-destroy him and [so too] the firsts [=leaders] of-the whole-people,	
	for they-were-fearing him, for all the crowd were-amazed upon [=by] his instruction.	48 and they-were-finding not what they-might-do, for everyone [of the] whole-people were-being-spell-bound hearing him.	
17 And having-quit [=having left] them, he-went-out outside of-the city into Bethany and he-camped-out there.	19 And whenever it-happened [=when it became] late-in-the-day, they-were-traveling-out outside of-the city.		

[a] *the temple* ℵ B L Θ f^{13} 33 700 892 1424 *al* cop; *the temple of-god* C D W f^{1} 1006 1342 1506 𝔐 it^{mss} vg sy.
[b] *the sellings* ℵ B L f^{1} 205 579 *pc* cop; *the sellings in it and buying* A C W Θ Ψ f^{13} 33 892 1006 1342 𝔐 vg sy; *the sellings in it and the buyings, and was-pouring-out the tables of-the money-changers and the seats of-the sellings doves* D *pc* it sy^{h}.
🕮 Mt 21:13 – Isa 56:7; Jer 7:11; 🕮 Mt 21:16 – Ps 8:2; 🕮 Mk 11:17 – Isa 56:7; Jer 7:11; 🕮 Lk 19:46 – Isa 56:7; Jer 7:11; 🕮 Jn 2:17 – Gen 28:12

308. The Cursing of the Fig Tree

Matt 21:18-19	Mark 11:12-14
18 So putting-out[a] [=leaving] early[b] into [=for] the city, he-hungered [=he was hungry].	12 And [on] the next-day their having-gone-out [=when they had left] from Bethany, he-hungered [=he was hungry].
19 And having-seen one fig-tree upon the way [=at the side of the road] he-went	13 And having-seen [a] fig-tree from far-off having leaves [=in leaf], he-went consequently [to see]
upon [=to] it and found no-one in [=nothing on] it if no [=except] only leaves;	if he-will-find some [fruit] in it, and having-gone upon [=up to] it he-found no-one [=nothing] if no [=except] leaves,
	for it-was not the proper-time of-figs [=season for figs].
and he-says to-it, "Let-happen [=Let there come] out of-you fruit not-any-longer into the eon [=for ever more]."	14 And having-answered he-said to-it, "Not-any-longer into the eon not-one might-eat fruit out of-you [=Let no one ever eat fruit from you again]."
And the fig-tree was-withered at-once.	And his disciples were-hearing [=heard him].

[a] *putting-out* $ℵ^{2}$ B^{1} C Θ f^{1} f^{13} 892 1006 1342 1506 𝔐; *having-put-out* ℵ* B* L; *passing-by* D it sy^{c}; *leaving* W.
[b] *early* ℵ* B D Θ *pc*; *in-the-morning* $ℵ^{2}$ C L W f^{1} f^{13} 892 1006 1342 1506 𝔐.

309. The Temple Scene (→ §307)

Matt 21:10-17	**Mark 11:15-19**	**Luke 19:45-48**	John 2:13-17
10 And his having-entered [=when he entered] into	15 And they-come		13 And the passover of-the Judeans was near, and Jesus ascended into Jerusalems.
Jerusalems all the city was-shaken saying, “What [=Who] is this?” 11 So the crowds were-saying, “This is the prophet Jesus from Nazareth of-the Galilee.”	into Jerusalems.		
12 And Jesus entered into the temple and cast-out all the sellings and buyings [=those who were selling and buying] in the temple[a], and the tables of-the money-changers he-over-turned and the seats of-the sellings [=those who were selling] the doves.	And having-entered into the temple, he-began to-cast-out the sellings [=those who were selling] and the buyings [=those who were buying] in the temple, and the tables of-the money-changers and the seats of-the sellings [=those who were selling] the doves he-over-turned, 16 and he-excused not in-order-that some might-be-superior [=he did not allow anyone to carry a] vessel through the temple.	45 And having-entered into the temple he-began to-cast-out the sellings[b] [=those who were selling],	14 And in the temple he-found the sellings [=those who were selling] oxen and sheep and doves and [he found] the cash-changers sitting [there]. 15 And having-done [=having made a] whip out of-ropes he-cast-out all out of-the temple, even the sheep and the oxen and he-poured-out the cash of-the money-changers and he-flipped the tables.
13 And he-says to-them, “It-has-been-written,	17 And he-was-teaching and was-saying to-them, “It-has-been-written not [=Is it not written] that	46 saying to-them, “It-has-	16 And to-the sellings [=to those who were selling] the doves he-said, “Remove these from-here; do [=make] no [=not] the house [of] my father [a] house of-merchandise.” 17 His disciples remembered that it-is having-been-written, “THE ZEAL [of] YOUR HOUSE WILL-CONSUME ME.”
‘MY HOUSE WILL-BE-CALLED [a] HOUSE OF-PRAYER,’ so [=but] it you [yourselves] do [=make into a] cave of-bandits.”	‘MY HOUSE WILL-BE-CALLED [a] HOUSE OF-PRAYER IN-ALL THE NATIONS’? so [=but] you [yourselves] have-made it [a] cave of-bandits.”	been-written, ‘AND MY HOUSE WILL-BE [a] HOUSE OF-PRAYER,’ so [=but] you [yourselves] did [=made] it [a] cave of-bandits.”	
14 And blinds [=blind people] and lames [=lame people] approached him in the temple and he-healed them.			
	18 And	47 And he-was teaching according-to [=each] day in the temple. So [=But]	
15 So [=But] the high-priests and the scribes, having-seen the wonderfuls [=wonderful things] which he-did	the high-priests and the scribes heard and	the high-priests and the scribes	

and the children crying [out] in the temple and [having-heard them] saying, "Hosanna to-the son of-David," were-indignant	they-were-searching [for] how they-might-destroy him,	were-searching to-destroy him and [so too] the firsts [=leaders] of-the whole-people,	
[16]and they-said to-him, "Do-you-hear what these [people] say?" So [=But] Jesus says to-them, "Yes. Never did-you-read that 'OUT OF-MOUTHS OF-INFANTS AND OF-NURSINGS [=of nursing babies] YOU-MENDED [=you brought forth] PRAISE'?"			
	for they-were-fearing him, for all the crowd were-amazed upon [=by] his instruction.	[48]and they-were-finding not what they-might-do, for everyone [of the] whole-people were-being-spell-bound hearing him.	
[17]And having-quit [=having left] them, he-went-out outside of-the city into Bethany and he-camped-out there.	[19]And whenever it-happened [=when it became] late-in-the-day, they-were-traveling-out outside of-the city.		

[a] *the temple* ℵ B L Θ f^{13} 33 700 892 1424 *al* cop; *the temple of-god* C D W f^{1} 1006 1342 1506 𝔐 it[mss] vg sy.
[b] *the sellings* ℵ B L f^{1} 205 579 *pc* cop; *the sellings in it and buying* A C W Θ Ψ f^{13} 33 892 1006 1342 𝔐 vg sy; *the sellings in it and the buyings, and was-pouring-out the tables of-the money-changers and the seats of-the sellings doves* D *pc* it sy[h].
🕮 Mt 21:13 – Isa 56:7; Jer 7:11; 🕮 Mt 21:16 – Ps 8:2; 🕮 Mk 11:17 – Isa 56:7; Jer 7:11; 🕮 Lk 19:46 – Isa 56:7; Jer 7:11; 🕮 Jn 2:17 – Gen 28:12

310. Having Enough Faith to Move Mountains

Matt 21:20-22	**Mark 11:20-24**	Thomas 48; 106
[20]And the disciples having-seen	[20]And traveling-by [in the] early [=morning], they-saw the fig-tree having-been-withered out of-roots [=to its very roots].	
were-astonished saying, "How was-withered the fig-tree at-once?"	[21]And Peter, having-been-reminded, says to-him, "Rabbi, look, the fig-tree which you-cursed has-been-withered."	
[21]So having-answered, Jesus said to-them, "Amen I-say to-you, if-ever you-might-have loyalty and you-might-be-evaluated no [=you might not have any doubt] you-will-do not only the [=what has been done] to-the fig-tree, but even-if you-might-say to-this	[22]And having-answered, Jesus says to-them, "Have [the] loyalty of-god. [23]Amen I-say to-you that who ever might-say to-this	[48]Jesus said, "If two make peace with each other in a single house, they will say to the mountain, 'Move from here!' and it will move." [106]Jesus said, "When you make the two into one, you will become children of Adam, and when you say, 'Mountain, move from here!' it will move."
mountain, 'Be-removed and be-thrown into the sea,' it-will-happen.	mountain, 'Be-removed and be-thrown into the sea' and might-be-	

22And all whatsoever ever you-
might-ask believing in prayer, you-
might-take [=you will receive]."

evaluated [=if he doubts] no [=not]
in his heart but might-believe that
[that] which he-talks [=he says]
happens, it-will-be [it will happen]
for-him. 24Through this [=Therefore]
I-say to-you, all whatsoever you-
pray and ask [for], believe that
you-took[a] [you have received it] and
it-will-be [=it will come] to-you."

[a] *you-took* ℵ B C L W Δ Ψ 892 1342 2427 *pc* cop[samss] cop[bomss]; *you-take* A *f*[13] 33 1006 1506 𝔐; *you-will-take* D Θ *f*[1] 205 565 700 *pc* vg it.

311. The Conditions for Prayer (→ §44)

Matt 6:14-15

14"For if-ever you-might-excuse [=you might forgive] the
people their wrongdoings, your heavenly father will-
excuse [=will forgive] and [=also] you; 15so [=but] if-ever
you-might-excuse no [=not] the people, nor [=neither]
your father will-excuse your wrongdoings."

Mark 11:25-26

25"And whenever you-persevere praying, excuse
[=forgive] if you-have some [=anything] according-to
[=against] some [=anyone], in-order-that and [=also]
your father in the heavens, might-excuse you your
wrongdoings."[a]

[a] *omit* ℵ B L W Δ Ψ 205 565 700 892 2427 *pc* it[mss] sy[c] cop[sa]; 26*So if you excuse not, nor your father in the heavens, will-excuse your wrongdoings.* A C D Θ *f*[1] *f*[13] 33 1342 1506 𝔐 it[mss] vg sy[p].

312. Challenging Jesus' Authority

Matt 21:23-27

23And his having-come
[=when he entered]
into the temple, the high-priests
and the elders of-the whole-people
approached him [while he was]
teaching, saying, "In [=By] what-
kind-of authority do-you-do these
[things]? And what [=who] gave to-
you this authority?"
24So Jesus having-answered said to-
them, "I-too will-beg [=will ask] you
one word [=question], which if-ever
you-might-say [=you might answer]
me I-too will-say to-you in [=by]
what-kind-of authority I-do these
[things]?
25From-where was the baptism of-
John? Out of-heaven or out [=from]
people?" So they-were-pondering
in [=among] themselves saying, "If-
ever we-might-say 'Out of-heaven'

Mark 11:27-33

27And again they-come into
Jerusalems. And his walking-around
[=while he was walking around]
in the temple, the high-priests and
the scribes and the elders come to
him 28and they-were-saying to-him,
"In [=By] what-kind-of authority
do-you-do these [things]? Or what
[=who] gave to-you this authority
in-order-that you-might-do these
[things]?"
29So Jesus said to-them, "I-will-
question [=I will ask] you one word
[=question], and answer me and I-
will-say to-you in [=by] what-kind-
of authority I-do these [things].
30Was the baptism of-John out
of-heaven or out [=from] people?
Answer me." 31And they-were-
pondering to themselves saying, "If-
ever we-might-say 'Out of-heaven'

Luke 20:1-8

1And it-happened in [=on] one
of-the days[b], his [=while he was]
teaching and proclaiming [to]
the whole-people in the temple,
the high-priests and the scribes
together-with the elders stood-by,
2and they-said to him saying,
"Say to-us in [=by] what-kind-of
authority do-you-do these [things],
or what [=who] is the [one] having-
given to-you this authority?"
3So having-answered he-said to
them, "I-too will-beg [=will ask] you
[a] word [=will ask you one question],
and say to-me:
4Was the baptism of-John out of-
heaven or out [=from] people?" 5So
they-were-arguing to themselves
[=among themselves] saying that "If-
ever we-might-say 'Out of-heaven'

Matt	Mark	Luke
he-will-say to-us 'Therefore through what [=why] did-you-believe him not?' [26]So [=But] if-ever we-might-say 'Out [=From] people' we-fear the	he-will-say 'Through what [=Why] did-you-believe him not?' [32]But might-we-say 'Out [=From] people'?" They-were-fearing the	he-will-say 'Through what [=Why] did-you-believe him not?' [6]So [=But] if-ever we-might-say 'Out [=from] people' everyone [of] the whole-people will-kill-by-stoning us,
crowd, for all have [=hold] John like [=as a] prophet."	crowd[a], for everyone was-having [=was holding] that John was definitely [a] prophet.	for to-be having-been-persuaded [=they are convinced that] John is [a] prophet."
[27]And having-answered, they-said to-Jesus, "We-recognize not [=We don't know]."	[33]And having-answered they-say to-Jesus, "We-recognize not [=We don't know]."	[7]And they-answered no to-recognize from-where [=that they did not know where it came from].
And he [himself] spoke to-them, "Nor [=Neither will] I [myself] say to-you in [=by] what-kind-of authority I-do these [things]."	And Jesus says to-them, "Nor [=Neither will] I [myself] say to-you in [=by] what-kind-of authority I-do these [things]."	[8]And Jesus said to-them, "Nor [=Neither will] I [myself] say to-you in [=by] what-kind-of authority I-do these [things]."

[a] *the crowd* ℵ B C 33 579 1342 1424 2542 *pc* cop^{sa} cop^{bo}; *the people* A D L W Θ Ψ *f*$^{1\ 13}$ 892 1006 1506 𝔐 vg it^{mss} sy^{h}.
[b] *one of-the days* ℵ B D L Q Ψ 205 579 2542 *pc* vg it^{mss} sy^{s} sy^{c} sy^{p} cop^{bo}; *one of-those days* A C W Θ *f*^{13} 33 892 1006 1342 1506 𝔐 sy^{h}.

313. Matthew's Parable of the Two Sons

Matt 21:28-32

[28]"So what it-supposes [=how does it seem] to-you? [A] person was-having two descendants. And[a] having-approached he-said to-the first, 'Descendant, leave today [and] work in the vineyard.' [29]So [=But] having-answered he-said, 'I-wish not [to],' so [=but] afterward having-been-sorry he-went-away [into the vineyard]. [30]So [=And] having-approached he-said to-the other in-the-same-way [=likewise]. So [=And] having-answered he-said, 'I [will go], lord,' and he-went-away [to work] not. [31]What [=Which one] out of-the two did the wish of-the father?" They say "The first." Jesus says-to-them, "Amen I-say to-you that the tax-collectors and the fornicators lead-ahead [of] you into the kingdom of-god. [32]For John came to you in [the] way of-righteousness, and you-believed him not, so [=but] the tax-collectors and the fornicators believed him, so [=but] you, having-seen, nor were-sorry [were not even sorry enough] afterward to-believe in-him."

[a] *And* B C D W Θ *f*$^{1\ 13}$ 33 892 1006 1342 1506 𝔐 vg it^{mss} sy^{p} sy^{h}; *omit* ℵ L Z it^{mss} sy^{s} sy^{c} cop.

314. The Parable of the Tenants

Matt 21:33-46	Mark 12:1-12	Luke 20:9-19	Thomas 65; 66
[33]"Hear another parable:	[1]And he-began to-talk to-them in parables.	[9]So he-began to-say to the whole-people this parable:	[65]He said, "A < . . . >
There-was [a] person, [a] master-of-the-house,	"[A] person	"Some person	person owned a vineyard and rented it to some farmers, so they could work it and he could collect its crop from them.
whoever [=who] planted [a] vineyard and put-around it [a] hedge and dug-a-hole in it [for a] wine-press and built [a]	planted [a] vineyard and put-around [a] hedge and dug-a-hole [as a] wine-press-pit, and he-built [a]	planted [a] vineyard,	
tower and leased it to-farmers and left-home.	tower and he-leased it to-farmers and left-home.	and he-leased it to-farmers and he-left-home fit times [=for a while].	

Matt 21:34-40	Mark 12:2-8	Luke 20:10-15	
34 So when the proper-time of-the fruits [=harvest time] neared, he-sent-off his slaves to the farmers to-take his fruits.	2 And he-sent-off [a] slave to the farmers [at] the proper-time in-order-that he-might-take along [=from] the farmers from [=his share] of-the fruits of-the vineyard.	10 And [at the] proper-time he-sent-off [a] slave to the farmers in-order-that they-will-give[e] him from [=his share of] the fruit of-the vineyard.	He sent his slave so the farmers would give him the vineyard's crop.
35 And the farmers, having-taken his slaves whom for-one [=one] they-beat, so whom [=and another] they-killed, so whom [=and another] they-stoned.	3 And having-taken him, they-beat [him] and sent-off [him] empty [=with nothing].	So [=But] the farmers sent-forth him, having-beaten [him], empty [=with nothing].	They grabbed him, beat him, and almost killed him, and the slave returned and told his master. His master said, 'Perhaps he didn't know them.'
36 Again he-sent-off another [=other] slaves, more of-the [=than at] first, and they-did to-them [=they treated them] in-the-same-way.	4 And again he-sent-off to them another slave. And-that [one][c] they-beat-on-the-head and treated-dishonorably.	11 And he-added [=he proceeded] to-send [an] other slave. So and-that [=But that one], having-beaten and having-treated-dishonorably, they-sent-forth empty [=with nothing].	He sent another slave, and the farmers beat that one as well. Then the master sent his son and said,
	5 And he-sent-off another. And-that [one] they-killed and many anothers [=others] whom for-one beating [=some of whom they beat] whom so killing [=others of whom they killed].	12 And he-added [=he proceeded] to-send [a] third. So [=But] this [one] and [=also] they-cast-out, having-wounded [him].	
37 So afterward he-sent-off to them his son saying, 'They-will-respect my son.'	6 He-was-having one yet [=He had one more], [a] son beloved[d]. He-sent-off him to them last saying that 'They-will-respect my son.'	13 So the lord of-the vineyard said, 'What will-I-do? I-will-send my beloved son. Perhaps they-will-respect this [one].'	'Perhaps they'll show my son some respect.'
38 So [=But] the farmers, having-seen the son said in [=to] themselves, 'This is the inheritor; come-on! we-might-kill him and we-might-have[a] his inheritance,'	7 So [=But] those farmers said to themselves that 'This is the inheritor; come-on! we-might-kill him and the inheritance will-be ours.'	14 So [=But] having-seen him, the farmers pondered to one-another saying, 'This is the inheritor; we-might-kill him in-order-that the inheritance might-happen [=might become] ours.'	Because the farmers knew that he was the heir to the vineyard,
39 and having-taken him they-cast-out [him] outside of-the vineyard and they-killed [him].	8 And having-taken [him] they-killed him and they-cast-out him outside of-the vineyard.	15 And having-cast-out him outside of-the vineyard they-killed [him].	they grabbed him and killed him. Anyone here with two ears had better listen!"
40 Therefore, whenever the lord of-the vineyard			

Matt 21:41-45	Mark 12:9-12	Luke 20:16-19	
might-come, what will-he-do to-those farmers?”	9 What will-do the lord of-the vineyard?	What therefore will-do to-them the lord of-the vineyard?	
41 They-say to-him, “He-will-destroy them bad badly [=very severely] and he-will-lease the vineyard to-another [=to other] farmers, whoever will-give-over to-him the fruits in their proper-times.”	He-will-come and he-will-destroy the farmers and will-give the vineyard to-anothers [=to others].	16 He-will-come and will-destroy these farmers and will-give the vineyard to-anothers [=to others].”	
		So [=But] having-heard they-said, “May-it-happen no [=not].”	
42 Jesus says to-them, “Never did-you-read in the writings:	10 Nor [=Neither] did-you-read this writing:	17 So having-beheld [them], he-said to-them, “What therefore is the [meaning of] this having-been-written [=piece of writing]:	
‘[A] STONE WHICH THE BUILDINGS [=those building] REJECTED, THIS WAS-HAPPENED [=was made] INTO HEAD OF-CORNER [=the cornerstone]; THIS HAPPENED ALONG [=with the sanction of the] LORD AND IT-IS AMAZING IN OUR EYES’?	‘[A] STONE WHICH THE BUILDINGS [=those building] REJECTED, THIS WAS-HAPPENED [=was made] INTO HEAD OF-CORNER [=the cornerstone]; 11 THIS HAPPENED ALONG [=with the sanction of the] LORD AND IT-IS AMAZING IN OUR EYES’?”	‘[A] STONE WHICH THE [ones doing the] BUILDING REJECTED, THIS HAPPENED INTO HEAD OF-CORNER [=became the cornerstone]?	66 Jesus said, “Show me the stone that the builders rejected: that is the keystone.”
43 Through [=Because of] this I-say to-you that the kingdom of-god will-be-removed from you and it-will-be-given [to the] nation doing [=making] her [=the kingdom of God’s] fruit.			
44 And the [one] having-fallen upon this stone will-be-broken-to-pieces; so [=and] upon whom ever it-might-fall it-will-crush him[b].”		18 ALL [=EVERY ONE] HAVING-FALLEN UPON THAT STONE WILL-BE-BROKEN-TO-PIECES; SO [=AND] UPON WHOM EVER IT-MIGHT-FALL, IT-WILL-CRUSH HIM.’”	
45 And the high-priests and the Pharisees, having-heard his parables, knew that he-says around [=he was speaking concerning] them.		19 And the scribes and the high-priests	
46 And searching [for a way]	12 And they-were-searching [for a way] to-seize him and [=but]	searching [for a way] to-throw-on upon the hands [=to get their hands on] him in the it hour [=at that	

to-seize him, they-were-feared [=they feared] the crowds, as-a-result-of [=because] they-were-holding him into [=as a] prophet.	they-were-feared [=they were afraid of] the crowd, for they-knew that he-said the parable to [=against] them, and having-excused [=having left] him they-went-away.	very hour], and they-were-feared [=they feared] the whole-people, for they-knew that he-said this parable to [=against] them.	

[a] *we-might-have* ℵ B D L Z Θ f^{1} *pc* vg it^{mss} sy^{s} sy^{c}; *we-might-detain* C W f^{13} 892 1006 1342 1506 𝔐 sy^{p} sy^{h}.
[b] *And the having-fallen upon this stone will-be-broken-to-pieces; so upon whom ever it-might-fall it-will-crush him* ℵ B C L W Z f^{1} f^{13} 892 1006 1506 𝔐 vg it^{mss} sy^{c} sy^{p} sy^{h} cop; *omit* D 33 it sy^{s}.
[c] *omit* ℵ B D L W Δ Ψ f^{1} 33 205 565 579 700 1342 2427 *pc* vg it cop; *having-stoned* A C Θ f^{13} 892 1006 1506 𝔐.
[d] *son beloved* ℵ B C D L Δ Ψ 565 700 892 1342 2427 *pc* vg it^{mss} sy^{s} sy^{p} cop^{samss} cop^{bo}; *his beloved son* 𝔓^{45} A W f^{1} f^{13} 33 1006 1506 𝔐 sy^{h} cop^{samss}.
[e] *they-will-give* ℵ A B L Q f^{13} 33 579 892 1506 2542 *al*; *they-might-give* C D W Θ Ψ f^{1} 1006 1342 𝔐.
🕮 Mt 21:33 – Isa 5:1; 🕮 Mt 21:42 – Ps 118:22, 23; 🕮 Mt 21:44 – Isa 8:14; Zech 12:3; Dan 2:34, 35, 44; 🕮 Mk 12:1 – Isa 5:1; 🕮 Mk 12:10 – Ps 118:22,23; 🕮 Lk 20:9 – Isa 5:1; 🕮 Lk 20:17 – Ps 118:22, 23; 🕮 Lk 20:18 – Isa 8:14; Zech 12:3; Dan 2:44; Deut 25:5

SYNOPTIC STUDY GUIDE 13

Gospel of Thomas and the Synoptics

The relationship of the Gospel of Thomas (GT) to the Synoptic Gospels is complicated by several issues. The first is language: though a few Greek fragments of GT exist, most of what we have is a Coptic translation. It is possible to see where this text might share sayings with the canonical gospels, but even so, it is difficult to argue for shared wording.

The second issue has to do with date: how old is GT? The Coptic text that we have was likely written out about 350 CE. But there are Greek fragments of GT from as early as 200 CE. There are enough textual variants among these surviving fragments of the Coptic version of GT to suggest a long history of copying. And then there is the thorny question of theology.

GT was found in a library of Gnostic texts, so the working assumption is often that GT is a Gnostic gospel. And it is true that some sayings from GT are very Gnostic: they denigrate the physical/material world and carry a stark dualism. But other sayings lack evidence of Gnostic editing. No less, they can even be said to lack the theology that is abundantly present in the synoptic editing of parallel sayings. Of GT's 114 sayings, 68 of them have parallels with the Synoptic Gospels; some of these sayings appear to predate the synoptic versions of those same sayings, and some definitely derive from a later, more Gnostic period. So clearly a date in the fourth century does not tell the whole story of GT's history.

Consider the Parable of the Tenants (§314). The version of the parable in Mark demands to be read allegorically. By opening with an illusion to Isaiah 5:1-17, it becomes impossible *not* to read Mark's vineyard as Israel, the owner as God, and the servants as the prophets, the son of the owner as the son of God, Jesus. This son is killed by the evil tenants (the Israelites) who are ultimately destroyed, and the killed son becomes the favored one. The allegory—of evil Israel killing its own Messiah and in turn being rejected by God—is a favorite one among Christians of the first two centuries. Contrast Mark's version with that found in GT, where we find a much more straightforward story in which a landowner leases a vineyard to tenants and later sends servants to collect the crop but they are abused by the resentful tenants. The owner sends his son, thinking the tenants must have misunderstood the origin of the servants, and his son is killed. The end. With no allusions to Isaiah, and with no vindication of the son, there is none of Mark's allegorical theology found in GT.

This suggests that perhaps a more fruitful way of thinking about the date of GT is not to focus on the date of the work as we have it (which is likely very late) but on the date of the individual sayings. I would suggest that for *this* story, the GT story is more original (earlier, less theologized) than the earliest synoptic version (Mark). Other GT stories are extremely Gnostic and therefore must be much later, and less historically reliable than the Synoptic Gospels. But in the end, one should proceed saying by saying, rather than making untenable pronouncements on the early date of the entirety.

315. The Parables of the Great Supper (→ §259)

Matt 22:1-14	Q 14:16-18, 21, 23	Luke 14:15-24	Thomas 64
1 And having-answered Jesus said [=spoke] again in parables to-them saying,		15 So having-heard these [things] some [person] of-the sitting-at-tables [=of the guests] said to-him, “Fortunate [is] whoever will-eat bread in the kingdom of-god.” 16 So [=But] he-said to-him,	
2 “The kingdom of-the heavens was-compared [to a] person, [a] king, whoever [=who] did [=gave] weddings [=a wedding feast] to-his son. 3 And he-sent-off his slaves to-call the having-been-calleds [=those who were invited] into the weddings [=wedding feast], and they-were-wishing not to-come.	16 Some person was-doing [=was giving a] great banquet and he-called many 17 and he-sent-off his slave at-the hour of-the banquet to-say to-the having-been-calleds [=those who had been invited],	“Some person was-doing[c] [=was giving a] great banquet and he-called many, 17 and he-sent-off his slave at-the hour of-the banquet to-say to-the having-been-calleds [=those who had been invited],	Jesus said, “A person was receiving guests. When he had prepared the dinner, he sent his slave to invite the guests. The slave went to the first and said to that one, ‘My master invites you.’ That one said, ‘Some merchants owe me money; they are coming to me tonight. I have to go and give them instructions. Please excuse me from dinner.’ The slave went to another and said to that one, ‘My master has invited you.’ That one said to the slave, ‘I have bought a house, and I have been called away for a day. I shall have no time.’ The slave went to another and said to that one, ‘My master invites you.’ That one said to the slave, ‘My friend is to be married, and I am to arrange the banquet. I shall not be able to come. Please excuse me from dinner.’ The slave went to another and said to that one, ‘My master invites you.’ That one said to the slave, ‘I have bought an estate, and I am going to collect the rent. I shall not be able to come. Please excuse me.’
4 Again, he-sent-off another [group of] slaves saying, ‘Say to-the having-been-calleds [=those who were invited]: “Look! my meal I-have-made-ready[a], my bulls and the fattened-calves having-been-slaughtered, and all [things being] ready. Come-on into the weddings [=wedding feast].’”	“Come that [=because] it-is ready already.”	‘Come that [=because] it-is ready already.’	
5 So the having-rebuffeds [=those who refused the invitation] went-away, who for-one [=one of whom went] into the [=his] own field, who so [=and the other] upon [=to] his business, 6 so [=while] the remainders [=rest] having-seized his slaves insulted and killed [them].	18 . . . field . . .	18 And they-began from one all [=one and all] to-make-apologies. The first said to-him, ‘I-bought [a] field and I-have inevitable [=I need] having-gone-out to-see it. I-beg you, have me having-made-apologies [=accept my regrets].’ 19 And [an] other said, ‘I-bought five pairs of-oxen and I-travel [now] to-examine them. I-beg you, have me having-made-apologies [=accept my regrets].’ 20 And [an] other said, ‘I-married [a] woman and through this	

		[=because of this] I-am-able not to-come.’	
	21And the slave . . .	21And the slave having-arrived [back home]	The slave returned and said to his master, ‘Those whom you invited to dinner have asked to be excused.’ The master said to his slave,
7So [=Now] the king[b] was-angered and having-sent his troops he-destroyed those murderers and burned-down their city.	his lord [of] these [things]. Then the master-of-the-house having-been-	informed his lord [of] these [things]. Then the master-of-the-house having-been-angered	
8Then he-says [to] his slaves, ‘The wedding [feast], for-one, is ready, so [=but] the having-been-called [=those who were invited] were not worthy.	angered said [to] his slave,	said [to] his slave,	
		‘Go-out without-delay into the wide-streets and laneways of-the city and lead-in the poors [=poor people] and crippleds [=crippled people] and blinds [=blind people] and lames [=lame people].’ 22And the slave said, ‘Lord, which [=what] you-presided-over [=you commanded] has-happened, and there-is yet [=still] place [=room].’ 23And the lord said to the slave,	‘Go out on the streets and bring back whomever you find to have dinner.’ Buyers and merchants [will] not enter the places of my Father.”
9Therefore travel upon the passages of-the ways [=main roads] and call whatsoever if-ever [=whoever] you-might-find into the weddings [=wedding feast].’	23‘Go-out into the ways [=roads] and call whatsoever if-ever [=whoever] you-might-find in-order-that my house might-be-filled-up.	‘Go-out into the ways [=roads] and hedges and compel [them] to-enter, in-order-that my house might-be-stuffed.	
		24For I-say to-you that no-one of-those men having-been-called [=who were invited] will-taste my banquet.’”	
10And those slaves, having-gone-out into the ways [=roads], gathered all whom they-found, [the] evil and even [the] good. And the wedding was-filled of-dinings [=with diners]. 11So [=But] the king, having-entered to-notice [=to observe]			

the dinings [=diners], saw there [a] person not having-been-clothed [wearing] wedding clothes, 12 and he-says to-him, ‘Comrade, how did-you-enter here no [=not] having wedding clothes?’ So [=But] he-was-muzzled [=he was speechless]. 13 Then the king said to-the servants, ‘Having-restrained his feet and hands, cast-out him into the outermost darkness, there-will-be wailing and gnashing of-the teeth there. 14 For many are called, so [=but there are] few chosen-ones.’”			

[a] *I-have-made-ready* ℵ B C* D L 085 f^{1} 33 205 700 1424 2542 *pc*; *has-been-made-ready* 1342 *al*; *I-made-ready* C[3] W f^{13} 892 1006 1506 𝔐.
[b] *So the king* ℵ B L 085 f^{1} 205 700 892 *pc* sy[s] sy[c] cop[sa] cop[bomss]; *So the king having-heard* Θ f^{13} vg it[mss] sy[p] cop[bomss]; *And that king having-heard* C D W 1006 1342 1506 𝔐 it[mss] sy[h].
[c] *was-doing* 𝔭[75] ℵ B f^{1} *pc*; *did* A D L W Θ Ψ f^{13} 892 1006 1342 1506 𝔐.

316. A Question about Roman Taxes

Matt 22:15-22	Mark 12:13-17	Luke 20:20-26	Thomas 100
15 Then the Pharisees, having-traveled, took plot [=counseled together]	13 And they-send-off to him some of-the Pharisees and of-the Herodians	20 And having-watched-closely they-sent-off spies pretending to-be righteous themselves,	
so-that they-might-entrap him in word [=by his words].	in-order-that they-might-ensnare him [by his] word.	in-order-that they-might-take-hold-of his word with-the-result-that to-deliver [=so that they might deliver] him to-the beginning [=jurisdiction] and to-the authority of-the ruler.	
16 And they-send-off to-him their disciples with the Herodians saying,	14 And having-come they-	21 And they-questioned him saying,	
“Teacher, we-recognize that you-are true and you-teach the way of-god in truth, and it-is-of-concern not to-you around no-one [=you show deference to no one], for you-look not into	say to-him, “Teacher, we-recognize that you-are true and it-is-of-concern not to-you around no-one [=you show deference to no one], for you-look not into	“Teacher, we-recognize that you-say [=you speak] and teach correctly and	
face of-people [=you do not treat people with partiality].	face of-people [=you do not treat people with partiality],	take face not [=show deference to no one], but	

Matt	Mark	Luke	Thomas
	but you-teach the way of-god upon [=in] truth.	you-teach the way of-god upon [=in] truth.	
17 Therefore say to-us what it-supposes [=how it seems] to-you: is-it-permitted to-give tax to-Caesar or not?"	Is-it-permitted to-give tax to-Caesar or not? Might-we-give or might-we-give no [=not]?"	22 Is-it-permitted [for] us to-give [the] tribute to-Caesar or not?"	
18 So [=But] Jesus having-known their evilness said, "What [=Why] do-you-test me, hypocrites?	15 So [=But] having-recognized their hypocrisy he-said to-them, "What [=Why] do-you-test me?	23 So having-thought-about their craftiness he-said to them, [c]	
19 Point-out to-me [a] coin of-tax."	Carry to-me [a] denarius in-order-that I-might-see [it]."	24 "Show to-me [a] denarius.	They showed Jesus a gold coin and said to him, "The Roman emperor's people demand taxes from us."
So they-offered him [a] denarius. 20 And he-says to-them, "The image and inscription of-what [person is] this?"	16 So they-carried [=they brought one]. And he-says to-them, "The image and inscription of-what [person is] this?"	[The] image and inscription of-what [person] does-it-have?"	
21 They-say to-him[a], "Of-Caesar."	So they-said to-him, "Of-Caesar."	So they-said, "Of-Caesar."	
Then he-says to-them, "Therefore give-over the [things] of-Caesar to-Caesar and the [things] of-god to-god."	17 So Jesus said to-them[b], "The [things] of-Caesar give-over to-Caesar and the [things] of-god to-god."	25 So he-said to them, "So-now give-over the [things] of-Caesar to-Caesar and the [things] of-god to-god."	He said to them, "Give the emperor what belongs to the emperor, give God what belongs to God, and give me what is mine."
22 And having-heard they-were-astonished and having-excused him they-went-away.	And they-were-completely-astonished upon [=at] him.	26 And they-had-the-strength not to-take-hold-of his speech [=they were not able to trap him by what he said] ere of-the [=in the sight of] the whole-people, and having-been-astonished upon [=by] his answer they-were-quiet.	

[a] *to-him* D L W Z Θ f^1 f^{13} 33 892 1006 1342 1506 𝔐 vg it sy[s] sy[c] sy[h] cop; *omit* ℵ B sy[p].
[b] *So Jesus said to-them* ℵ B F L Δ Ψ 33 579 892 1342 2427 *pc* sy[p] cop[sa] cop[bo]; *And having-answered Jesus said* A D f^1 f^{13} 1006 1506 𝔐 vg it[mss] sy[s] sy[h]; *And having-answered he-said* W Θ 565; *And he-says* 1424.
[c] *omit* ℵ B L f^1 205 579 892 1424 2542 *pc* cop; *What do-you-test me?* A D W Θ Ψ f^{13} 33 1006 1342 1506 𝔐 vg it[mss] sy; *What do-you-test me, hypocrites?* C *pc*.

317. Questions about the Resurrection

Matt 22:23-33	Mark 12:18-27	Luke 20:27-40
23 In [=On] that day Sadducees, saying to-be no rise [=who say there is no resurrection] approached him and questioned him 24 saying,	18 And Sadducees, whoever [=who] say no rise to-be [=there is no resurrection], come to him and they-were-questioning him saying,	27 So some of-the Sadducees, saying no rise to-be [=who say there is no resurrection], having-approached, questioned him 28 saying,

"Teacher, Moses said, 'IF-EVER SOME [person] MIGHT-FACE-DEATH HAVING NO

DESCENDANTS, HIS BROTHER WILL-WED HIS WOMAN [=wife] AND HE-WILL-GET-UP [=he will raise] SEED [=a descendent for] HIS BROTHER.' 25So [=Now] there-were seven brothers along [=among] us, and the first having-married[a] expired [=died], and having no seed [=offspring] he-excused [=he left] his woman [=wife to] his brother.
26Likewise and [=also] the second

and the third until the seven

[=seventh]. 27So [=And] afterward [=last] of-all the woman faced-death.
28Therefore in the rise [=resurrection] of-what [of which] of-the seven [men] will-she-be woman [=wife], for all

had her?"
29So having-answered Jesus said to-them, "You-are-deceived having-recognized [=having understood] no [=neither] the writings so-not [=nor] the power of-god. 30For in

the rise [=resurrection] neither do-they-marry neither [=nor] are-they-given-in-marriage[b],

but like announcers [=angels] in the heaven they-are.

31So around [=concerning] the rise [=resurrection] of-the deads [=of dead people] did-you-read not the having-been-said [=what had been said] to-you under [=by] god, saying,

32'I AM THE GOD OF-ABRAHAM AND THE GOD OF-ISAAC AND THE GOD OF-JACOB'? He-is not

19"Teacher, Moses wrote to-us that 'IF-EVER [the] BROTHER OF-SOME [person] MIGHT-FACE-DEATH AND MIGHT-QUIT [=might leave a] WOMAN AND MIGHT-EXCUSE [=might leave] NO [=not a] DESCENDANT, [=let it be] IN-ORDER-THAT HIS BROTHER MIGHT-TAKE [=might marry] THE[c] WOMAN [=widow] AND HE-MIGHT-BRING-UP SEED [=a descendant for] HIS BROTHER.'
20There-were seven brothers; and the first took [a] woman [=wife] and facing-death, he-excused not seed [=he left no offspring].
21And the second took her and faced-death quitting [=leaving] no seeds [=no offspring]. And the third in-the-same-way. 22And [all of] the seven[d] excused [=left] not seed [=no offspring]. Last of-all the woman and [=also] faced-death.
23In the rise [=resurrection] of-what [of which] of-them will-she-be woman [=wife], for the seven

had her [as] woman [=wife]?"
24Jesus spoke to-them, "[Is it] not through [=because of] this [that] you-are-deceived, having-recognized no [=having understood neither] the writings so-not [=nor] the power of-god. 25For whenever they-might-get-up out of-deads [=from the dead] neither do-they-marry neither [=nor] are-they-given-in-marriage but they-are

like announcers [=angels] in the heavens.

26So [=Now] around [=concerning] the deads [=dead people], that they-are-raised, did-you-read not in the book of-Moses upon [=about] the bramble-bush, how god said

to-him saying, 'I [am] THE GOD OF-ABRAHAM AND THE GOD OF-ISAAC AND THE GOD OF-

"Teacher, Moses wrote to-us, 'IF-EVER [the] BROTHER OF-SOME [person] MIGHT-FACE-

DEATH HAVING [a] WOMAN [=wife], AND THIS [MAN] MIGHT-BE[e] DESCENDANTLESS, [=let it be] IN-ORDER-THAT HIS BROTHER MIGHT-TAKE [=might marry] THE WOMAN [=the widow] AND MIGHT-BRING-UP SEED [=a descendant for] HIS BROTHER.'
29Therefore, there-were seven brothers, and the first, having-taken [the] woman, faced-death descendantless.
30And the second

31and the third took her, so [=but] in-the-same-way and [=also all] the seven quit not [=left no] descendants and faced-death. 32And afterward the woman faced-death.
33Therefore, in the rise [=resurrection] the woman [=wife] of-what [=of which] of-them does-happen woman [=will the woman be], for the seven had her [as] woman [=wife]?"
34And[f] Jesus said to-them, "The sons of-this eon marry and are-given-in-wedlock 35so [=but] the having-been-counted-worthies [=those who are worthy] to-attain that eon and the rise [=resurrection] out

of-deads [=from the dead] neither do-they-marry neither [=nor] are-they-given-in-marriage. 36For nor they-are-able to-face-death yet [=any more], for they-are announcer-likes [=like angels] and they-are sons of-god, being sons of-the rise [=resurrection].
37So, that the deads [=dead people]

are-raised, Moses and [=also] disclosed upon [=in the story] of-the bramble-bush, like [=where] he-says [=he speaks of] the lord god of-Abraham and god of-Isaac and god of-Jacob.

the god of-deads [=of dead people] but [of the] living."

33 And having-heard, the crowds were-amazed upon [=at] his instruction.

JACOB'? 27 He-is not god of-deads [=of dead people] but of-livings [=of living people]. You-are-deceived many [=greatly]."

38 So god is not of-deads [=of dead people] but of-livings [=of the living], for all live in-him."
39 So having-answered, some of-the scribes said, "Teacher, you-said [=you spoke] well." 40 For they-were-daring no-longer to-question him no-one [=about anything].

[a] *having-married* ℵ B L Θ f^{1} 33 205 700 892 *pc*; *having-married* D W f^{13} 1006 1342 1506 𝔐; *omit* sy^{s}.
[b] *are-they-given-in-marriage* ℵ B D f^{1} 892 1424 *al*; *are-they-married-off* 1006 1342 1506 𝔐; *are-they-given-in-wedlock* W Θ 33 700 *pc*.
[c] *the* ℵ B C L W Δ Θ Ψ f^{1} 205 565 700 892 1342 2427 2542 *pc* cop^{bo}; *his* A D f^{13} 33 1006 1506 𝔐 vg it^{mss} sy^{p} sy^{h} cop^{sa}.
[d] *And the third in-the-same-way.* 22 *And the seven* ℵ B C L W Δ Ψ f^{13} 33 579 892 1342 2427 *pc*; *And in-the-same-way the seven took her* D it^{mss}; *the third in-the-same-way and took her. And the seven* Θ f^{1} 205 565 700 2542; *the third in-the-same-way; and the seven took her and* A 1006 𝔐 vg it^{mss} sy.
[e] *might-be* ℵ B L Ψ f^{1} 33 205 579 892 2542 *pc* vg it^{mss} cop; *might-face-death* A W Θ f^{13} 1006 1342 𝔐 it^{mss} sy.
[f] *omit* ℵ B D L 579 892 *pc* vg it^{mss} sy^{c} sy^{p} cop; *having-answered* A W Θ Ψ f^{1} f^{13} 33 1006 1342 𝔐 sy^{h}.
📖 Mt 22:24 – Deut 25:5; 📖 Mt 22:32 – Exod 3:6; 📖 Mk 12:19 – Deut 25:5; 📖 Mk 12:26 – Exod 3:6; 📖 Lk 20:37 – Exod 3:6

318. The Greatest Commandments (→ §207)

Matt 22:34-40

34 So the Pharisees, having-heard that he-muzzled the Sadducees, were-gathered upon [=because of] it. 35 And one out of-them, [a] lawyer, testing him questioned, 36 "Teacher, what-kind-of [=which] commandment in the law [is] great [=the greatest]?"
37 So he-spoke to-him,

"'YOU-WILL-LOVE [the] LORD YOUR GOD IN [=with] YOUR WHOLE HEART AND IN [=with] YOUR WHOLE SOUL AND IN [=with] YOUR WHOLE MIND.'

38 This is the great [=greatest] and first commandment. 39 So [=And a] second [is] comparable-to it: 'YOU-WILL-LOVE YOUR NEIGHBOR LIKE YOURSELF.' 40 The whole law and the prophets is-hung in [=on] these two commandments."

Mark 12:28-34

28 And one of-the scribes, having-approached, [and] having-heard them discussing, [and] having-seen that he-answered them well,

questioned him, "What-kind-of [=Which] commandment is first of-all?"
29 Jesus answered[a] that "[The] first is, 'Hear, Israel, the lord our god [the] lord is one.' 30 And

'YOU-WILL-LOVE THE LORD YOUR GOD OUT [=with] YOUR WHOLE HEART AND OUT [=with] YOUR WHOLE SOUL AND OUT [=with] YOUR WHOLE MIND, AND OUT [=with] YOUR WHOLE MIGHT.'[b]
31 This [is the] second, 'YOU-WILL-

LOVE YOUR NEIGHBOR LIKE YOURSELF.' There-is not another commandment greater [than] these."
32 And the scribe said to-him, "Well [said], teacher, you-said upon [=you spoke with] truth that he-is one and there-is not another nevertheless

Luke 10:25-28

25 And look! some lawyer got-up trying him[c] saying, "Teacher, having-done what will-I-inherit [=what must I do to inherit] eternal

life?" 26 So he-said to him, "What has-been-written in the law? How do-you-read [that]?"

27 So having-answered he-said, "YOU-WILL-LOVE [the] LORD YOUR GOD OUT [=with] YOUR WHOLE HEART AND IN [=with] YOUR WHOLE SOUL AND IN [=with] YOUR WHOLE MIGHT, AND IN [=with] YOUR WHOLE

MIND, AND YOUR NEIGHBOR LIKE YOURSELF."

Mark

[=besides] him, [33]and to-love him out [=with] the whole heart and out [=with] the whole comprehension and out [=with] the whole might and to-love the neighbor like oneself is more-excessive [than] all the burnt-offerings and sacrifices." [34]And Jesus having-seen that he-was-answered intelligently said to-him, "You-are not far-away from the kingdom of-god." And no-one no-longer was-daring to-question him.

Luke

[28]So he-said to-him, "You-answered correctly; do this and you-will-live."

[a] *Jesus answered* ℵ B L Δ Ψ 33 579 1342; *So Jesus answered him* A C 1006 𝔐 vg sy[h]; So *having-answered he-said to-him* D W Θ f[1] f[13] 205 565 1506 *pc* cop[bo].
[b] *omit* ℵ B E L Δ Ψ 1342 2427 *pc* cop[sa]; *This first commandment* A D W Θ f[1] f[13] 33 892 1006 1506 𝔐 vg it[mss] sy cop[bomss].
[c] *omit* ℵ B L Ξ 579 *pc*; *and* A C D W Θ Ψ f[1] f[13] 33 892 1006 1342 1506 𝔐 vg it[mss].
📖 Mt 22:37 – Deut 6:5; 📖 Mt 22:39 – Lev 19:18; 📖 Mk 12:29 – Deut 6:4, 5; 📖 Mk 12:33 – 1 Sam 15:22; 📖 Lk 10:27 – Deut 6:5; Lev 19:18; 📖 Lk 10:27 – Lev 18:5

319. How Can the Messiah Be the Son of David?

Matt 22:41-46

[41]So, the Pharisees having-gathered, Jesus questioned them, [42]saying

"What does-it-suppose to-you around [=do you think about] the anointed-one? Of-what [=Whose] son is-he?" They-say to-him, "Of-David."

[43]He-says to-them, "Therefore how in spirit David calls [=does David call] him lord saying [44]'[The] LORD SAID [to] MY LORD, "SIT OUT [=to] MY RIGHT UNTIL EVER I-MIGHT-PUT YOUR ENEMIES BENEATH[a] YOUR FEET." ' [45]Therefore if David calls him lord, how is-he his son?"

[46]And no-one was-being-able to-answer him [a] word nor [did] some dare from that day to-question him no-longer [=any longer].

Mark 12:35-37a

[35]And Jesus having-answered was-saying, teaching in the temple,

"How [do] the scribes say that the anointed-one is [the] son of-David?

[36]David he [=himself] said in the holy spirit, '[THE] LORD SAID [to] MY LORD, "SIT OUT [=to] MY RIGHT UNTIL EVER I-MIGHT-PUT YOUR ENEMIES BENEATH YOUR FEET." '

[37a]David he [=himself] says [=calls] him lord, and [so] from-where [=how] is-he his son?"

Luke 20:41-44

[41]So he-said to them,

"How do-they-say the anointed-one to-be [=is the] son of-David?

[42]For David he [=himself] says in [the] book of-Psalms '[The] LORD SAID [to] MY LORD, "SIT OUT [=to] MY RIGHT [43]UNTIL EVER I-MIGHT-PUT YOUR ENEMIES [as a] FOOTSTOOL [for] YOUR FEET." '

[44]Therefore David calls him lord, and [so] how is-he his son?"

[a] *beneath* ℵ B D G L Z Θ f[13] 579 892 1006 *al* it cop[sa] cop[bo]; *footstool* W f[1] 33 1342 1506 𝔐 vg it[mss].
📖 Mt 22:44 – Ps 110:1; 📖 Mk 12:36 – Ps 110:1; 📖 Lk 20:42 – Ps 110:1

320. Criticism of the Scribes

Mark 12:37b-40

[37b]And the many [=large] crowd heard him gladly. [38]And in his instruction he-was-saying[a], "Look from [=Beware] of-the the scribes wishing in robes to-walk-around and greetings in the markets [39]and seats-of-honor in the synagogues and places-of-honor in the banquets, [40]consuming the homes of-the widows and praying distant [=at length] for-show. These will-take excessive verdict [=They will receive the greater condemnation]."

Luke 20:45-47

[45]So [=While] all the whole-people [were] hearing, he-said [to] his disciples[b], [46]"Pay-close-attention from [=Beware] of-the scribes wishing to-walk-around in robes and liking greetings in the markets and seats-of-honor in the synagogues and places-of-honor in the banquets, [47]who consume the homes of-the widows and praying distant [=at length] for-show. These will-take excessive verdict [=They will receive the greater condemnation]."

[a] *And in his instruction he-was-saying* ℵ B L Δ Ψ 1342 2427; *And he-was-saying to-them in his instruction* A W f^1 f^{13} 1006 1505 𝔐 vg sy^h cop^{samss}; *So teaching in-unison-with he-was-saying to-them* D Θ 565 sy^s.

[b] *his disciples* ℵ A L W Θ Ψ f^1 f^{13} 33 892 1006 1342 vg it^{mss} sy cop; *to-the disciples* B D 2542; *to them* Q.

321. Woes against the Scribes and Pharisees (→ §222, §223, §224, §225, §257)

Matt 23:1-36	Q 11:46b, 43; 14:11; 11:52, 42, 39b, 41, 44, 47-51	Luke 11:46b, 43; 14:11; 11:52, 42, 39, 41, 44, 47-51	Thomas 39; 89
[1]Then Jesus talked to-the crowds and [to] his disciples, [2]saying, "The scribes and the Pharisees sat upon the seat of-Moses; [3]therefore do and keep all whatsoever if-ever they-might-say to-you, so [=but] do no according-to [=not imitate] their works, for they-say [=they command] and [=but] do not [do it].			
[4]So they-bind weighty and awkward[a] burdens and they-place [them] upon the shoulders of-the people, so [=but] they wish not [to lift] their finger to-move them.	[46b]"And woe to-you lawyers, that [=because] you-bind burdens and you-place [them] upon the shoulders of-the people, so [=but] they you-wish [=you yourselves wish] not [to lift] your finger to-move them."	[46]So he [himself] said, "And to-you lawyers woe, that [=because] you-burden the people [with] awkward burdens and they [=you] lend-a-hand to-the burdens not [with] one [of] your fingers."	
	[43]"Woe to-you Pharisees	[43]"Woe to-you Pharisees	
[5]So [=But] they-do all their works to [=in order] to-be-noticed by-the people, for they-widen their phylacteries and magnify the tassels. [6]So [=But] they-like the place-of-honor in the banquets	that [=because] you-like place-of-honor in the	that [=because] you-love	

and the seats-of-honor in the synagogues 7and the greetings in the markets and to-be-called rabbi under [=by] the people. 8So [=But] you [yourselves] might-be-called no [=do not let yourselves be called] rabbi, for your teacher is one, so [=but] you [yourselves] are all brothers. 9And you-might-call no [=do not call anyone] upon the land your father, for your heavenly father is one. 10So-not [=Nor] might-you-be-called instructors, that [=because] your instructor is one, the Anointed-one. 11So [=For] the greater of-you will-be your servant.	banquets and the seat-of-honor in the synagogues and the greetings in the markets."	the seat-of-honor in the synagogues and the greetings in the markets."	
12So [=And] whoever will-exalt himself will-be-humbled and whoever will-humble himself will-be-exalted.	14:11"The all [=each person] exalting himself will-be-humbled, and the [one] humbling himself will-be-exalted."	14:11"That [=Because] the all [=each person] exalting himself will-be-humbled, and the [one] humbling himself will-be-exalted."	
13So woe to-you, scribes and Pharisees, hypocrites, that [=because] you-lock the kingdom of-the heavens in-front [=from] the people; for you [yourselves] enter not nor excuse [=allow] the enterings [=those wishing to enter] to-enter.	11:52"Woe to-you lawyers, that [=because] you-lock the kingdom of-god in-front [=from] the people; you [yourselves] entered not nor excuse [=allow] the enterings [=those wishing to enter] to-enter.	11:52"Woe to-you lawyers, that [=because] you-removed the keys of-knowledge; they you-entered [=you yourselves entered] not and you-hindered enterings [=those wishing to enter]."	39Jesus said, "The Pharisees and the scholars have taken the keys of knowledge and have hidden them. They have not entered nor have they allowed those who want to enter to do so. As for you, be as sly as snakes and as simple as doves."
b 15Woe to-you, scribes and Pharisees, hypocrites, that [=because] you-lead-around the sea and the withered [=dry land] to-do [=to make] one proselyte and whenever it-might-happen you-do [=you make] him [a] son of-Gehenna double [as much as] you. 16Woe to-you, blind escorts saying, 'Who ever might-vow in [=by] the sanctuary, he-is [obligated to] no-one,			

Mark 12:40 (§320, p. 241) Q 17:35 (§288, p. 209)
Luke 20:47 (§320, p. 241)

so [=but] who ever
might-vow in [=by] the
gold of-the sanctuary,
he-is-in-debt [=he is
obligated].' 17 Moronics
and blinds [=Foolish and
blind men], for what is
greater, the gold or the
sanctuary having-made-
holy the gold? 18 And
'Who ever might-vow
in [=by] the sacrificial-
altar, he-is [obligated to]
no-one, so [=but] who
ever might-vow in [=by]
the gift [=offering] above
[=upon] it, he-is-in-debt
[=he is obligated].' 19 Blinds
[=Blind men], for what
[is] greater, the gift or the
sacrificial-altar making-
holy the gift? 20 Therefore
the [one] having-vowed
in [=by] the sacrificial-
altar vows in [=by] it and
in [=by] all [that is] above
[=upon] it. 21 And the [one]
having-vowed in [=by]
the sanctuary vows in
[=by] it and in [=by] the
[one] settling [in] it. 22 And
the [one] having-vowed
in [=by] heaven vows in
[=by] the throne of-god
and in [=by] the [one]
sitting above [=upon] it.
23 Woe to-you scribes and
Pharisees, hypocrites,
that [=because] you-tithe
mint and dill and cumin
and you-excused [=you
forgot] the more-weighty
[=more important things]
of-the law: the judgment
and the mercy and the
loyalty. So [=But] it-was-
necessary to-do these
[things] and-those [things]
to-excuse no [=without
neglecting the others].
24 Blind escorts, filtering-
out the gnat, so [=but]
drinking-down the camel.
25 Woe to-you scribes and

42 Woe to-the Pharisees,
that [=because] you-tithe
mint and dill and cumin
and you-excused [=you
forgot] the judgment and
the mercy and the loyalty.
So [=But] it-was-necessary
to-do these [things]
and-those [things] to-
excuse no [=without
neglecting the others]."

42 But woe to-you
Pharisees, that [=because]
you-tithe mint and
scented-herb and all
[=every] shrub and you-
pass-away [=you neglect]
the judgment and love
of-god. So [=But] it-
was-necessary to-do
these [things] and-
those [things] to-lose-
sight-of no [=without
neglecting the others]."
39 So the lord said to him,

Pharisees, hypocrites, that [=because] you-purify the cup and the plate from-outside, so [=but] from-within [=the insides] are-full out [=of] violent-greed and self-indulgence. 26Blind Pharisee, first purify the inside of-the cup, in-order-that its outer [part] and might-happen [=might also become] pure.	39b"Woe to-you Pharisees, that [=because] you-purify the cup and the plate from-outside, so [=but] the from-within [=the insides] are-full out [=of] violent-greed and self-indulgence." 41Purify the inside of-the cup, and its outer [part] might-happen [=might become] pure."	"Now you Pharisees purify the from-outside [=outside] of-the cup and of-the platter, so [=but] your from-within [=inside] is-full of-violent-greed and of-evilness." 41Nevertheless, give [as] almsgiving the being-insides [=the things that are inside you], and look! all is pure for-you."	89Jesus said, "Why do you wash the outside of the cup? Don't you understand that the one who made the inside is also the one who made the outside?"
27Woe to-you scribes and Pharisees, hypocrites, that [=because] you-resemble sepulchers having-been-white-washed, whoever [=which] from-outside appear lovely, so [=but] from-within are-full of-bones of-deads [=of dead people] and of-all [=of every] uncleanliness. 28And thus you for-one from-outside appear righteous	44"Woe to-you Pharisees, that [=because] you-are like the unmarked tombs	44"Woe to-you, that [=because] you-are like the unmarked tombs	
to-the people, so [=but] from-within you-are over flowing [with] hypocrisy and lawlessness.	and the people walking-around above recognize [it] not."	and the people walking-around above recognize [it] not."	
29Woe to-you scribes and Pharisees, hypocrites, that [=because] you-build the sepulchers of-the prophets and you-adorn the tombs of-the righteous, 30and you-say, 'If we-were [there] in the days [of] our fathers,	47"Woe to-you that [=because] you-build the tombs of-the prophets,	47"Woe to-you that [=because] you-build the tombs of-the prophets,	
not ever we-were [=we would never have been] their companions in [shedding] the blood of-the prophets.'	so [=but] your fathers killed them.	so [=but] your fathers killed them.	
31With-the-result-that you-testify themselves [=yourselves] that you-are sons of-the having-murdereds [=those who murdered] the prophets.	48You-testify themselves [=yourselves] that you-are	48Consequently, you-are witnesses[c] and you-approve the works	
32And fulfill, you, the measure [of] your fathers. 33Snakes, offspring of-vipers, how might-you-flee from the judgment of-Gehenna?	sons [of] your fathers.	[of] your fathers that [=because] they for-one killed them, so [on the other hand] you-build[d] [their tombs].	

34Through this [=Therefore]	49Through this [=Therefore] and [=also] the wisdom said, ‘I-will-send prophets to them and [=some] out of-them they-will-kill and	49Through this [=Therefore] and [=also] the wisdom of-god said, ‘I-will-send-off prophets and apostles into [=among] them and [=some] out of-them they-
look! I send-off prophets and wise [people] and scribes to you. [Some] out of-them you-will-kill and will-crucify, and you-will-scourge [some] out of-them in your synagogues and you-will-pursue [them] from city into city,	will-pursue,	will-kill and will-pursue,’
35so-that all righteous blood being-shed upon the land might-come	50in-order-that it-might-be-sought-out [=this generation might be charged for] the blood of-all the prophets having-been-poured-out from the molding of-the world from [=by] this generation,	50in-order-that it-might-be-sought-out [=this generation might be charged for] the blood of-all the prophets having-been-poured-out[e] from the molding of-the world from [=by] this generation,
upon you, from the blood of-righteous Abel until the blood of-Zachariah son of-Barachiah, whom you-murdered between the sanctuary and the sacrificial-altar. 36Amen I-say to-you, all these [things] will-press-forward [=will come] upon this generation.”	51from [the] blood of-Abel until [the] blood of-Zachariah the [one] having-been-destroyed between the sacrificial-altar and the house [=sanctuary]. Yes I-say to-you, it-will-be-sought-out from [=it will be charged against] this generation.”	51from [the] blood of-Abel until [the] blood of-Zachariah the [one] having-been-destroyed between the sacrificial-altar and the house [=sanctuary]. Yes I-say to-you, it-will-be-sought-out from [=it will be charged against] this generation.”

[a] *weighty and awkward* B D W Θ f^{13} 33 1006 1342 1506 𝔐 vg it^{mss} sy^{h} cop^{sa}; *weighty* L f^{1} 205 892 *pc* it sy^{s} sy^{c} sy^{p} cop^{bo}; *great weight* ℵ.
[b] *omit* ℵ B D L Z Θ f^{1} 33 205 892 *pc* it^{mss} sy^{s} cop^{sa}; *14Woe to-you scribes and Pharisees, hypocrites, that you-consume the homes of-the widows praying distant for-show. These will-take excessive verdict* f^{13} *pc* it sy^{c} cop; *same verse but placed after vs. 12* W 1006 1342 1506 𝔐 sy^{p} sy^{h}.
[c] *you-are witnesses* ℵ B L 700* 892 2542 sy; *you-testify* 𝔭^{75} A C D W Θ Ψ f^{1} f^{13} 33 1006 1506 𝔐 vg it^{mss}.
[d] *omit* 𝔭^{75} ℵ B D L 579 *pc* it sy^{s} sy^{c} cop^{sa} cop^{bo}; *their sepulchers* f^{1} f^{13} 205 2542 *pc* vg; *their graves* A C W Θ Ψ 33 892 1006 1342 𝔐.
[e] *having-been-poured-out* 𝔭^{45} B 0233 f^{13} 33 *pc* vg it^{mss}; *being-shed* 𝔭^{75} ℵ A C D L W Θ Ψ f^{1} 892 1006 1342 1506 𝔐.
🕮 Mt 23:35 – Gen 4:8; 2 Chr 24:21, 22; 🕮 Lk 11:51 – Gen 4:8; 2 Chr 24:21, 22

322. Lament for Jerusalem (→ §254)

Matt 23:37-39	Q 13:34-35	Luke 13:34-35
37“Jerusalem, Jerusalem, the [one] killing the prophets and stoning the having-been-sent-offs [=those who were sent] to her; how-often did-I-wish to-collect your descendants which manner [=like a] hen collects her young-birds under the [=her] wings, and [=but] you-wished not. 38Look! your house is-excused [=is left] to-you deserted[a]. 39For I-say	34“Jerusalem, Jerusalem, the [one] killing the prophets and stoning the having-been-sent-offs [=those who were sent] to her; how-many-times did-I-wish to-collect your descendants which manner [=like a] hen collects her young-birds under the [=her] wings, and [=but] you-wished not. 35Look! your house is-excused [=is left] to-you. I-say to-	34“Jerusalem, Jerusalem, the [one] killing the prophets and stoning the having-been-sent-offs [=those who were sent] to her; how-many-times did-I-wish to-collect your descendants which manner [=like a] hen herself [=does with her own] brood under the [=her] wings, and [=but] you-wished not. 35Look! your house is-excused [=is left] to-you.

to-you, you-might-see me not no
[=ever again] from right-now until
[the time when] ever you-might-say,
'Having-been-blessed [is] the [one]
coming in [the] name [of the] lord.'"

you you-might-see me not no [=ever
again] until [the time] will-press-
forward [=will come] when you-
might-say, 'Having-been-blessed [is]
the [one] coming in [the] name [of
the] lord."

So[b] I-say you-might-see me not
until [the time] will-press-forward
[=will come] when you-might-say,
'Having-been-blessed [is] the [one]
coming in [the] name [of the] lord."

[a] *deserted* ℵ C D W Θ *f*[1] *f*[13] 33 892 1006 1341 1506 𝔐 vg it[mss] sy[p] sy[h]; *omit* B L sy[s] cop[sa].
[b] *So* 𝔓[75] ℵ[2] A B D W Θ Ψ *f*[1] *f*[13] 892 1006 1342 1506 𝔐 vg it[mss] sy[p] sy[h] cop[bo]; *omit* 𝔓[45] ℵ* L 2542 *pc* it sy[c] cop[sa].
🕮 Mt 23:38 – Ps 69:25; Jer 12:7; 22:5; 🕮 Mt 23:39 – Ps 118:26; 🕮 Lk 13:35 – Ps 118:26; Jer 12:7; 22:5

323. The Generous Widow

Mark 12:41-44

[41]And having-been-seated[a] ahead of-the [=across from
the] treasury, he-was-catching-sight-of how the crowd
throws copper into the treasury. And many wealthies
[=weathy people] were-throwing many [=a lot]. [42]And one
poor widow, having-come threw two leptons, which
is [worth a] quadrans. [43]And having-summoned his
disciples, he-said to-them, "Amen I-say to-you that this
poor widow threw [in] more [than] all of-the throwings
[=of those throwing money] into the treasury. [44]For all
threw [=contributed] out of-the exceeding to-them
[=from their abundance], so [=but] this [woman] out [of]
her deficit threw [in] all whatsoever she-was-having
[=all she had], the whole [of] her livelihood."

Luke 21:1-4

[1]So, having-looked-up he-saw the wealthy throwing
their gifts into the treasury, [2]so [=but] he-saw some

destitute widow throwing two leptons there.

[3]And he-said, "Truly I-say to-you that this poor widow
threw [in] more [than] all.
[4]For these [people] all threw into the gifts[b] out of-the
exceeding to-them [=from their abundance], so [=but]
this [woman] out [of] her deficiency threw [in] all the
livelihood which she-was-having."

[a] *And having-been-seated* ℵ B L Δ Ψ 892 1342 2427 *pc* cop[bo]; *Jesus, having-been-seated* A 33 1006 1506 𝔐 vg it[mss] sy[p] sy[h] cop[samss]; *Jesus, sitting* D; *Jesus, having-stood* W Θ *f*[1] *f*[13] 205 565 2542 *pc*.
[b] *omit* ℵ B L *f*[1] 205 579 2542 *pc* sy[s] sy[c]; *of-god* A D W Θ Ψ *f*[13] 33 892 1006 1342 𝔐 vg it sy[p] sy[h].

324. A Prediction against the Temple

Matt 24:1-2

[1]And Jesus, having-gone-out
from the temple, and his disciples
approached to-point-out to-him the

buildings of-the temple.

[2]So, having-answered he-said to-
them,
"Do-you-look [=Do you see] not all
these [things]? Amen I-say to-you,
not no stone upon stone [=a single
stone] here might-be-excused
not [=will be left], which will-be-
demolished not."

Mark 13:1-2

[1]And his [=while he was] traveling-
out out of-the temple, one [of] his
disciples says to-him, "Teacher,
look, what-sort-of [=at what
awesome] stones and what-sort-of
[=what awesome] buildings [these
are]."
[2]And Jesus said to-him[a],

"Do-you-look [=Do you see]
these great buildings? Not no
stone upon stone [=a single stone]
here might-be-excused not [=will
be left alone], which might-be-
demolished not no [=at all]."

Luke 21:5-6

[5]And
[when] some [were] saying [=talking]
around [=concerning] the temple,
that it-had-been-adorned [with]
fine stones and votive-gifts,

he-said,

[6]"These [things] which you-catch-
sight-of, days will-come in which
stone upon stone will-be-
excused [=will be left alone] not,
which will-be-demolished not."

[a] *And Jesus said to-him* ℵ B L Ψ 33 579 892 1342 2427 *pc* sy[s] sy[p] cop[samss] cop[bo]; *And Jesus, having-answered, said to-him* A D *f*[1] *f*[13] 205 1006 1506 2542 𝔐 vg it[mss] cop[samss] sy[h]; *And having-answered, he-said to-him* W Θ 565 700.

325. Signs of the End

Matt 24:3-8

3So his [=while he was] sitting upon the mountain of-the olives, the disciples approached him according-to own [=in private] saying, "Say to-us, when will-be these [things] and what [will be] the sign of-your-own presence and conclusion of-the eon?"

4And having-answered Jesus said to-them, "Look [=Beware that] some [person] might-deceive you no [=not]; 5for many will-come upon [=in] my name saying, 'I am the anointed-one,' and they-will-deceive many.

6So [=And] you-will-intend [=you are about] to-hear [of] battles and rumors of-battles; see [that you] be-startled no [=not]. For it-is-necessary[a] [for this] to-happen; but the end is not-yet.

7For nation will-be-raised upon [=against] nation and kingdom upon [=against] kingdom and there-will-be famines and earthquakes according-to [=in different] places. 8So [=But] all these [things are the] beginning of-birth-pains."

Mark 13:3-8

3And his [while he was] sitting into [=upon] the mountain of-the olives ahead of-the [=across from the] temple, Peter and James and John and Andrew were-questioning him according-to own [=in private], 4"Say to-us, when will-be these [things] and what [will be] the sign all whenever these [=when things] it-might-intend [=are about] to-be-concluded?"

5So Jesus began to-say to-them[b], "Look [=Beware that] some [person] might-deceive you no [=not]; 6many will-come upon [=in] my name saying, 'I am,' and they-will-deceive many.

7So whenever you-might-hear [about] battles and rumors of-battles, be-startled no [=not]. It-is-necessary [for this] to-happen; but the end [is] not-yet.

8For nation will-be-raised upon [=against] nation and kingdom upon [=against] kingdom, there-will-be earthquakes according-to [=in different] places, there-will-be famines. These [things are the] beginning of-birth-pains."

Luke 21:7-11

7So they-questioned him saying, "Teacher, when therefore will-be these [things] and what [will be] the sign whenever these [=when things] it-might-intend [=are about] to-happen?"

8So he-said, "Look [=Beware that] you-might-be-deceived no [=not]; for many will-come upon [=in] my name saying[c] 'I am,' and 'The proper-time has-neared.' Might-you-travel no [=not] behind them.

9So whenever you-might-hear [about] battles and chaoses, might-you-be-alarmed no [=not]. For it-is-necessary [for] these [things] to-happen first, but the end [will follow] not instantly." 10Then he-was-saying to-them, "Nation will-be-raised upon [=against] nation and kingdom upon [=against] kingdom, 11even great earthquakes and famines according-to [=in different] places and plagues will-there-be, even fearful-events and great signs from heaven will-there-be."

---

[a] *omit* ℵ B D L Θ f^{1} 33 205 892 *pc* cop; *all* C W f^{13} 1006 1342 𝔐 sy^{p} sy^{h}; *these* 565 1506 *pc* it^{mss} vg sy^{s}; *all these* 544 1241 *pc.*

[b] *So Jesus began to-say to-them* ℵ B L Ψ 33 579 892 1342 2427 *pc* sy^{p} cop^{samss} cop^{bo}; *So Jesus, having-answered them, began to-say* A 1006 1506 𝔐 sy^{h} cop^{samss}; *And having-answered, Jesus said to-them* D Θ 565 700 1424 2542 *pc*; *and having-answered them Jesus began to-say* G W f^{1} f^{13} 205 *pc.*

[c] *omit* ℵ B L 579 2542 *pc*; *that* A D W Θ Ψ f^{1} f^{13} 33 892 1006 1342 𝔐 it^{mss} vg sy^{h}.

🕮 Mk 13:5 – Jer 29:8

326. The Fate of the Disciples (→ §111, §232)

Matt 10:17-23	**Mark 13:9-13**	Q 12:11-12	**Luke 21:12-19;** 12:11-12
17"So pay-close-attention from the [=be aware of] people, For they-will-	9"So you themselves [=yourselves] look [=beware];[b] they-will-		12"So [=But] before all these [things] they-will-throw-on their hands upon [=they will beat] you and they-will-pursue [you], delivering [you] into the synagogues and prisons, being-led-away upon [=before] kings and rulers because-of my name. 13It-will-get-out to-you into [=This will be your chance to offer] testimony.
deliver you into Sanhedrins and in their synagogues they-will-scourge you. 18And upon [=before] <u>rulers</u> so and [=and also] kings you-will-be-led because-of me into [=as] testimony to-them and to-the	deliver you into Sanhedrins and into synagogues you-will-be-beaten and upon [=before] rulers and kings you-will-be-stood [=you will be put] because-of me into [=as] testimony to-them.		
nations [=Gentiles].	10And it-is-necessary [for] the proclamation to-be-preached first into all the nations.		
			14Therefore, put in your hearts no [=not] to-prepare-ahead-of-time to-defend [yourself]; 15for I-will-give you [a] mouth and wisdom which everyone [of] the opposings [=those who oppose] you will-be-able not to-resist or to-refute. 16So you-will-be-delivered and [=even] under [=by] parents and brothers and kins and friends and they-will-put-to-death out [=some] of-you. 17And you-will-be being-hated under [=by] all through [=because of] my name. 18And [a] hair out [of] your head might-be-destroyed not no [=at all]. 19In your patience acquire your souls."
19So whenever they-might-deliver[a] you,	11And whenever they-might-lead you, delivering	11"Whenever they-might-bring-into you [=When they bring you] into the synagogues,	12:11"So whenever they-might-bring-into[c] you [=when they bring you] upon [=before] the synagogues, and the beginnings [=rulers], and the authorities,
you-might-worry no	[you], worry-ahead-of-	you-might-worry no	you-might-worry no [=not] how or [with]

[=not] how or what you-might-talk [=you might say]. For what you-might-talk will-be-given to-you in that hour.

[20]For you-are not the talkings [=the ones doing the talking] but the spirit [of] your father [who is] talking in you.
[21]So brother will-deliver brother into death and father descendant, and descendants will-turn-against upon parents, and they-will-put-to-death them. [22]And you-will-be being-hated under [=by] all through [=because of] my name. So [=But] the having-stayed-behind [=the one who perseveres] into [the] end, this [one] will-be-saved.
[23]So whenever they-might-pursue you in this city, flee into the other, for amen I-say to-you, you-might-complete not no [=at all] the cities of-Israel until ever the son of-the person might-come."

time no [=not] what you-might-talk [=you might say], but talk [=say] this which if-ever [=whatever] might-be-given to-you

in that hour, for you-are not the talkings [=the ones doing the talking] but the holy spirit.

[12]And brother will-deliver brother into death and father descendant, and descendants will-turn-against upon parents, and they-will-put-to-death them. [13]And you-will-be being-hated under [=by] all through [=because of] my name. So [=But] the having-stayed-behind [=the one who perseveres] into [the] end, this [one] will-be-saved."

[=not] how or what you-

might-say, [12]for the holy spirit will-teach you what you-might-say in the [=that] hour."

what you-might-defend [yourself] or what you-might-say.
[12]For the holy spirit will-teach you in it [=in that very] hour [that] which it-is-necessary to-say."

[a] *they-might-deliver* ℵ B f^{1} 205 892 *pc*; *they-will-deliver* D G L W 33 579 1424 1596 *al* vg it^{mss}; *they-give* C Θ f^{13} 1006 1342 𝔐.
[b] *omit* B L Ψ 2427 *pc* cop^{samss} cop^{bo}; *for* ℵ A f^{13} 33 892 1006 1342 1506 𝔐 it^{mss} vg sy^{p} cop^{samss}; *and* W f^{1} *pc* sy^{s}; *moreover* D Θ 565 700 it.
[c] *they-might-bring-into* 𝔓^{45} 𝔓^{75} ℵ B L 070 f^{1} 33 579 700 892 2542 *pc* it^{mss} vg; *they-might-offer* A W Θ Ψ f^{13} 1006 1342 1506 𝔐 it^{mss}; *they-might-bring* D it^{mss}.
🕮 Mk 13:12 – Mic 7:6

327. Matthew's Admonition to Remain Loyal (→ §111)

Matt 24:9-14

[9]"Then they-will-deliver you into distress and they-will-kill you, and you-will-be being-hated under [=by] all the nations through [=because of] my name. [10]And then many will-be-caused-to-stumble and they-will-deliver one-another and they-will-hate one-another. [11]And many false-prophets will-be-raised and they-will-deceive many. [12]And through [=because of] to-be-multiplied [=the increase of] lawlessness, the love of-the many will-grow-cold. [13]So [=But] the [one] having-stayed-behind into [the] end, this [one] will-be-saved. [14]And this proclamation of-the kingdom will-be-preached in-the whole inhabited-earth into [=as] testimony to-all the nations and then the end will-press-forward [=will come]."

There are no variants in this pericope that appear in English.

328. The Sacking of Jerusalem (→ §286)

Matt 24:15-22	Mark 13:14-20	**Luke 21:20-22**; 17:31-32; **21:23-24**
15“Therefore whenever you-might-see the abomination of-the	14“So whenever you-might-see the	20“So whenever you-might-see Jerusalem being-circled under [=by] foot-soldiers, then know that its desolation has-neared.
desolation the having-been-said [=which had been said] through Daniel the prophet having-stood in [the] holy place—let-perceive the reading [person]— 16then let-flee the [people] in Judea into the mountains.	abomination of-the desolation having-been-stood where it-is-necessary [=it ought] not [to stand],—let-perceive the reading [person]— then let-flee the [people] in Judea into the mountains.	21Then the [ones] in Judea let-flee into the mountains, and the [ones] in [the] middle of-it let-escape, and the [ones] in the [surrounding] regions let-enter into it no [=not], 22that [=because] these are days of-adjudication, of-the to-be-filled [=as the fulfillment of] all the [things] having-been-written.
17Let-him-descend no [=not] the [person] upon the housetop to-remove the [things] out [of] his home. 18and [whoever is] in the field let-him-turn-back no behind [=let him not go back] to-remove his coat.	15So [=And] let-him-descend[a] no [=not] the [person] upon the housetop so-not [=nor] let-him-enter to-remove some [things] out [of] his home, 16and [whoever is] in the field let-him-turn-back no into the behind [=let him not go back] to-remove his coat.	17:31In [=On] that day, who [ever] will-be upon the housetop and his vessels [=belongings are] in the home, let-him-descend no [=not] to-remove them, and likewise [whoever is] in the field, let-him-turn-back into the behind no [=let him not turn back to it]. 17:32Recall the woman [=wife] of-Lot.
19So woe to-the havings in stomach [=to those who are pregnant] and to-the nursings [=to those nursing] in those days. 20So pray in-order-that your flight might-happen no [=not] of-stormy [=in winter] so-not [=nor on the] sabbath. 21For there-will-be great distress then such-as had-happened not from [the] beginning [of the] world until the now nor might-happen not no [=ever].	17So woe to-the havings in stomach [=to those who are pregnant] and to-the nursings [=to those nursing] in those days. 18So pray in-order-that it-might-happen no [=not] of-stormy[b] [=in winter]. 19For those days will-be [days of] distress such-as such-as-this had-happened not from [the] beginning of-creation which god created until the now and might-happen not no [=ever].	21:23Woe to-the havings in stomach [=to those who are pregnant] and to-the nursings [=to those nursing] in those days, for there-will-be great inevitable [=pressure] upon the land and anger [against] this whole-people.
22And if those days were-shortened no [=not], all flesh was-saved not ever [=no one would have been saved]; so [=but] through [=because of] the chosen-ones those days will-be-shortened.”	20And if [the] lord shortened the days no [=not], all flesh was-saved not ever [=no one would have been saved], but through [=because of] the chosen-ones whom he-chose he-shortened the days.”	

		[24]And they-will-fall [by the] mouth [=edge of the] sword and they-will-be-taken-captive into all the nations and Jerusalem being-tread [upon] under [=by] nations till which [the] proper-times [of the] nations might-be-fulfilled."

[a] *omit* ℵ B L Ψ 892 1342 2427 *pc* sy^{p} cop; *into the home* A D W Θ f^{1} f^{13} 1006 1506 𝔐 vg it^{mss} sy^{s}.
[b] *it-might-happen no of-stormy* ℵ* B W 083 2427 sy^{s} cop^{bomss}; *they-might-happen no of-stormy* D; *these might-happen no of-stormy* Θ f^{13} 565 *pc* it^{mss}; *these happen no of-stormy or sabbath* L *al* cop^{samss} cop^{bomss}; *your flight might-happen no of-stormy* ℵ^{2} A Ψ f^{1} 892 1006 1342 1506 𝔐 sy^{p} sy^{h} cop.
🕮 Mt 24:15 – Dan 9:27; 8:13; 11:31; 12:11; 🕮 Mt 24:21 – Jer 30:7; 🕮 Mk 13:14 – Dan 8:13; 9:27; 11:31; 12:11

329. Signs and False Leaders (→ §282)

Matt 24:23-25	**Mark 13:21-23**	Luke 17:21	Thomas 3
[23]"Then if-ever some [person] might-say to-you, 'Look! here [is] the anointed-one' or 'Here,' might-you-believe [it] no [=not]. [24]For falsely-anointed-ones and false-prophets will-be-raised and they-will-give great signs and omens with-the-result-that [=in order] to-deceive, if possible, and [=even] the chosen-ones. [25]Look! I-have-told-before [these things] to-you."	[21]"And then if-ever some [person] might-say to-you, 'Look here [is] the anointed-one, look there,' believe [it] no [=not]. [22]For falsely-anointed-ones and false-prophets will-be-raised and they-will-give signs and omens to the [=in order] to-deceive-thoroughly, if possible, the chosen-ones. [23]So [=But] you [yourselves] look [out]; I-have-told-before all [these things] to-you."	[21]"nor will-they-say, 'Look! here,' or 'There'[a] For look! the kingdom of-god is inside of-you."	Jesus said, "If your leaders say to you, 'Look, the <Father's> kingdom is in the sky,' then the birds of the sky will precede you. If they say to you, 'It is in the sea,' then the fish will precede you. Rather, the <Father's> kingdom is within you and it is outside you. When you know yourselves, then you will be known, and you will understand that you are children of the living Father. But if you do not know yourselves, then you live in poverty, and you are the poverty."

[a] *'Look! here!' or 'There'* 𝔓^{75} ℵ B L 2542 pc it^{mss} sy^{s}; *'Look! here!' or 'Look! there!'* A D W Ψ f^{1} f^{13} 892 1006 1342 1506 𝔐 vg it^{mss} sy^{c} sy^{p}; *'Look! here, there'* Θ.

330. The Day of the Son of Man (→ §283)

Matt 24:26-27	Q 17:23-24	Luke 17:22-25
		[22]So he-said to the disciples, "Days will-come when you-will-desire to-see one of-the days of-the son of-the person, and you-will-see not.
[26]"Therefore, if-ever they-might-say to-you: 'Look! he-is in the deserted	[23]"If-ever they-might-say to-you: 'Look! he-is in the deserted [place],'	[23]And they-will-say to-you, 'Look! there,' or 'Look! here.' Might-you-

Matt	Mark	Luke
[place],' might-you-go-out [there] no [=not]; 'Look! in the private-rooms,' might-you-believe [it] no [=not]. 27 For even-as the flashing-light [=lightning] goes-out from [=comes out of] easts [=the east], and appears until wests [=as far as the west], thus will-be the presence of-the son of-the person."	might-you-go-out [=might you go out there] no [=not]; 'Look! in the private-rooms,' might-you-pursue [=follow them] no [=not]. 24 For even-as the flashing-light [=lightning] goes-out from [=comes out of] the east [=east], and appears until [=as far as the] west, thus will-be the son of-the person in [=on] his day."	go-away no [=not] so-not [=nor] might-you-pursue [=follow them]. 24 For even-as the flashing-light [=lightning] flashing shines out under heaven into under heaven [=from one side of the sky to the other] thus will-be the son of-the person in [=on] his day.[a] 25 So [=But] first it-is-necessary [for] him to-suffer many [things] and to-be-rejected from this generation."

[a] *in his day* ℵ A L W Θ Ψ f^1 f^{13} 892 1006 1342 1506 𝔐 vg it[mss] sy cop[bo]; *omit* 𝔓[75] B D it cop[sa].

331. Eagles and a Corpse (→ §284, §288)

Matt 24:28	Q 17:37	Luke 17:37
		37 And having-answered, they-say to-him, "Wheresoever, lord?" So he-said to-them,
28 "Where if-ever the corpse might-be, there the eagles will-be-gathered."	37 "Where the corpse [is], there the eagles will-be-gathered."	"Where the body [is], there and [=also] the eagles will-be-collected[a]."

[a] *will-be-collected* ℵ B L 892 *pc*; *will-be-gathered* A D W Θ Ψ f^1 f^{13} 1342 1506 𝔐 cop[sa] cop[bo].

332. Heavenly Signs Attend the Son of Man

Matt 24:29-31	**Mark 13:24-27**	**Luke 21:25-28**
29 "So immediately with [=after] the distress of-those days the sun will-be-darkened and the moon will-give her lustre not and the stars will-fall	24 "But in those days with [=after] that distress the sun will-be-darkened and the moon will-give its lustre not 25 and the stars will-be falling out	25 "And there-will-be signs in [the] sun and moon and constellations and upon the land [the] anxiety of-nations in confusion [at the] noise of-sea and of-swells, 26 people losing-heart from fear and [from the] imminent-judgment of-the [=of what is] coming-upon the inhabited-earth,
from heaven and the powers of-the <u>heavens</u> will-be-shaken-up.	of-heaven[a] and the powers in the heavens will-be-shaken-up.	for the powers of-the heavens will-be shaken-up.
30 And then the sign of-the son of-the person will-be-appeared [=will be made to appear] in heaven and then all the tribes of-the land will-cut [=will mourn] and	26 And then	27 And then
they-will-see the son of-the person coming upon the clouds of-heaven with power and many [=much] glory.	they-will-see the son of-the person coming in clouds with many [=much] power and glory.	they-will-see the son of-the person coming in [a] cloud with power and many [=much] glory.

[31]And he-will-send-off his announcers [=angels] with [a] great trumpet-blast and they-will-collect his chosen-ones out [=from] the four winds, from tips of-heavens until their tips [=from one end of heaven to the other]."

[27]And then he-will-send-off the announcers[b] [=angels] and he-will-collect his chosen-ones out [=from] the four winds, from tip of-land until tip of-heaven [=from the ends of heaven and earth]."

[28]So [with] these [things] beginning to-happen, straighten-up and lift-up your heads, through-that [=because] your deliverance nears."

[a] *will-be falling out of-heaven* ℵ B C Θ Ψ 892 1424 *pc*; *will-be falling-out of-heaven* L f^1 1506 𝔐 vg sy[h]; *the will-be falling out of-heaven* D f^{13} 2542 *pc*; *having-fallen out of-heaven* W 565 579 700 2427; *will-be falling-out out of-heaven* A 1006.

[b] *the announcers* B D L W 1506 2427 it; *his announcers* ℵ A C Θ Ψ f^1 f^{13} 892 1006 1342 𝔐 vg it[mss] sy cop.

📖 Mt 24:29 – Isa 13:9, 10; Joel 2:10; 3:15; Ezek 32:7; 📖 Mk 13:24 – Isa 13:9, 10; Joel 3:15

333. The Parable of the Fig Tree

Matt 24:32-36

[32]"So learn the parable from the fig-tree: whenever already [=as soon as] her branch might-happens [=might become] ready-to-bear-fruit and might-extend the leaves, you-know that the summer [is] near. [33]And thus you, whenever you-might-see all these [things], you-know that he-is near, upon [=at the] doors.
[34]Amen I-say to-you that[a] this generation might-pass-away not no [=ever] until ever [=the time when] all these [things] might-happen. [35]Heaven and land will-pass-away, so [=but] my words might-pass-away not no [=ever].
[36]So around [=concerning] that day and hour no-one recognizes [=knows], nor [=neither] the announcers [=angels] of-the heavens nor the son, if no [=except] the father alone."

Mark 13:28-32

[28]"So learn the parable from the fig-tree: whenever already [=as soon as] its branch ready-to-bear-fruit might-happen [=might become], and the leaves might-extend, you-know that the summer is near. [29]And thus you, whenever you-might-see these [things] happening, you-know that he-is near, upon [=at the] doors.
[30]Amen I-say to-you that this generation might-pass-away not no [=ever] to-the-point [=until] which [time] all these [things] might-happen. [31]Heaven and land will-pass-away, so [=but] my words will-pass-away not no [=ever].
[32]So around [=concerning] that day or the hour no-one recognizes [=knows], nor [=neither] the announcers [=angels] in heaven nor the son, if no [=except] the father."

Luke 21:29-33

[29]And he-said [a] parable to-them, "See the fig-tree and all the trees. [30]Whenever they-might-put-forward [leaves] already, looking from themselves [=for yourselves] you-know that the summer is already near. [31]And thus you, whenever you-might-see these [things] happening, you-know that the kingdom of-god is near.

[32]Amen I-say to-you that this generation might-pass-away not no [=ever] until ever [=the time when] all [these things] might-happen. [33]Heaven and land will-pass-away, so [=but] my words will-pass-away[b] not no [=ever]."

Thomas 11

Jesus said, "This heaven will pass away, and the one above it will pass away. The dead are not alive, and the living will not die. During the days when you ate what is dead, you made it come alive. When you are in the light, what will you do? On the day when you were one, you became two. But when you become two, what will you do?"

[a] *that* B D F L Θ f^1 f^{13} 33 205 700 892 1424 *al* vg it; *omit* ℵ W 1006 1342 1506 𝔐.

[b] *will-pass-away* ℵ B D L W T 33 892 *pc*; *might-come* A C Θ Ψ f^1 f^{13} 1006 1342 𝔐.

334. Luke's Warning to Remain Alert

Luke 21:34-36

34“So pay-close-attention to-themselves [=to yourselves], lest your hearts might-be-weighed-down
in [=by] debauchery and drunkenness and daily worries and that day might-stand-by [=might fall]
upon you unexpectedly 35like [a] trap[a]; for it-will-come-in-upon upon all the sittings [those who
dwell] upon [the] face of-all the land [=earth]. 36So, remain-alert in all proper-time [=at all times]
imploring [=praying] in-order-that you-might-over-power [=you might have the strength] to-flee-
away [from] all these [things] intending [=that are about] to-happen, and to-stand in-front of-the son
of-the person.”

[a] *unexpectedly like trap* ℵ B D *pc* it cop; *unexpectedly; for it-will-come-upon like trap* A C W Θ Ψ f^1 f^{13} 33 892 1006 1342 1506 𝔐 vg it[mss] sy.

335. The Judgment of Noah (→ §285)

Matt 24:37-39

37“For even-as the days of-Noah
[were], thus will-be the presence
of-the son of-the person. 38For
like[a] [=as] in those days before
the flood they-were chewing and
drinking, marrying and giving-
in-marriage[b], till which day Noah
entered into the ark, 39and they-
knew not [=nothing] until the flood
came, and it-removed everyone;

thus and [=also] will-be the presence
of-the son of-the person.”

Q 17:26-27, 30

26“Just-as it-happened in the days
of-Noah, thus it-will-be and [=also]
in [=on] the day of-the son of-the
person. 27For like in those days
they-were chewing and drinking,
marrying and giving-in-marriage,
till which day Noah entered into
the ark, and the flood came, and it-
removed everyone.

30Thus and [=also] it-will-be [on]
which [=on that] day the son of-the
person is-revealed.”

Luke 17:26-30

26“And just-as it-happened in the
days of-Noah, thus it-will-be and
[=also] in the days of-the son of-the
person. 27They-were-eating, they-
were-drinking, they-were-marrying,
they-were-being-given-in-marriage,
till which day Noah entered into
the ark and the flood came and
destroyed all[c] [things].

28Likewise just-as it-happened in
the days of-Lot: they-were-eating,
they-were-drinking, they-were-
buying, they-were-selling, they-
were-planting, they-were-building.
29So [on] the day Lot went-out from
Sodoms, fire and sulfur rained from
heaven and destroyed all [things].
30It-will-be according-to them [=just
like this on] which [=on that] day the
son of-the person is-revealed.”

[a] *like* ℵ B L 33 892; *even-as* D W Θ f^1 f^{13} 1006 1342 1506 𝔐.
[b] *giving-in-marriage* ℵ D 33 1006 *pc*; *giving-in-wedlock* B *pc*; *giving-away-in-wedlock* W 1424 *pc*; *marrying-off* L Θ f^1 1506 𝔐; *bringing-in-for-marriage* f^{13} 892 1342 *al.*
[c] *destroyed all* 𝔭[75] B D L Θ 579 892 *pc*; *everyone* ℵ A W Ψ f^1 f^{13} 33 1006 1342 1506 𝔐.
🕮 Mt 24:37 – Gen 7:4; 🕮 Lk 17:27 – Gen 7:7; 🕮 Lk 17:29 – Gen 19:16

336. One Taken, One Left Behind (→ §288)

Matt 24:40-41

40“Then two [men] there-will-be in
the field, one is-taken-along [=is
taken] and one

Q 17:34-35

34“I-say to-you, there-will-be
two [men] in the field, one is-taken-
along [=is taken] and one

Luke 17:34-36

34“I-say to-you, [on] this night,
there-will-be two [men] upon one
stretcher [=bed]; the one will-be-
taken-along [=will be taken] and

is-excused [=is left].
[41]Two grinding-grains [=women are grinding grain] in [=on] the mill-stone, one is-taken-along [=is taken] and one is-excused [=is left]."

is-excused [=is left].
[35] Two grinding-grains [=women are grinding grain] in [=on] the mill-stone, one is-taken-along [=is taken] and one is-excused [=is left]."

the other will-be-excused [=will be left behind]. [35]There-will-be two grinding-grains [=women grinding grain] upon the it [=at the same place]; the one will-be-taken-along [=will be taken] so the other will-be-excused [=will be left behind]." [a]

[a] *omit* 𝔓[75] ℵ A B K L W X Θ Π Ψ *f*[1] 28 33 565 892 cop; [36]*There there-will-be two in the field, one will-be-taken-along and the other will-be-excused* D *f*[13] 700 1006 *al* vg it[mss] sy.

337. Mark's Parable of the Watchful Slaves

Matt 24:42

[42]"Therefore stay-awake. That [=because] you-recognize not what-kind-of [=on which] day your lord comes."

Mark 13:33-37

[33]"Look, remain-alert [a]; for you-recognize not when the proper-time is. [34][It is] like [a] person away-from-home, having-excused [=having left] his home and having-given authority [to] his slaves, to-each his work, and he-charged the door-keeper in-order-that he-might-stay-awake. [35]Therefore stay-awake. For you-recognize not when the lord of-the home comes, or [=whether] late-in-the-day or [at] midnight or rooster-sound [=dawn] or early, [36]no [=lest] having-come [home] suddenly he-might-find you sleeping. [37]So [=Now that] which I-say to-you I-say to-all: stay-awake."

[a] *omit* B D 2427; *and-pray* ℵ A C L W Θ Ψ *f*[1] *f*[13] 892 1006 1342 1506 𝔐 vg it[mss] sy cop.

338. Being on Guard (→ §239)

Matt 24:43-44

[43]"So know that: that if the master-of-the-house recognized what-kind-of [=on what] prison [=watch] the thief comes, he-stayed-awake ever [=he would have stayed awake] and he-conceded not ever [=he would not have permitted] his home to-be-broken-in. [44]Through this [=Therefore] you [=yourselves] and [=also] happen [=must be] ready that [=because] you-suppose [=you know] not in-which hour the son of-the person comes."

Q 12:39-40

[39]"So know that: that if the master-of-the-house recognized what-kind-of [=on what] prison [=watch] the thief comes, he-conceded not ever [=he would not have permitted] his house to-be-broken-in.

[40]you [=yourself] and [=also] happen [=must be] ready that [=because] you-suppose [=you know] not in-which hour the son of-the person comes."

Luke 12:39-40

[39]"So know this: that if the master-of-the-house recognized what-kind-of [=at what] hour the thief comes, he-excused not ever[a] [=he would not have permitted] his house to-be-broken-in.

[40]And [b] you [=yourselves also] happen [=must be] ready that [=because] in-which hour you-suppose [=you know] not [when] the son of-the person comes."

Thomas 21

Mary said to Jesus, "What are your disciples like?" He said, "They are like little children living in a field that is not theirs. When the owners of the field come, they will say, 'Give us back our field.' They take off their clothes in front of them in order to give it back to them, and they return their field to them. For this reason I say, if the owners of a house know that a thief is coming, they will be on guard before the thief arrives and will not let the thief break into their house <their domain> and steal their possessions. As for you, then, be on guard against the world. Prepare yourselves with great strength, so the robbers can't find a way to get to you, for the trouble you expect will come.

Let there be among you a person who understands. When the crop ripened, he came quickly carrying a sickle and harvested it. Anyone here with two good ears had better listen!"

[a] *he-excused not ever* 𝔓[75] ℵ* D sy[s] sy[c] cop[samss]; *he-stayed-awake ever and he-excused not* ℵ[1] A B L W Θ Ψ *f*[1] *f*[13] 33 892 1006 1342 1506 𝔐 vg it[mss] sy[p] sy[h] cop[samss] cop[bo].
[b] *omit* 𝔓[75] ℵ B L Q Θ Ψ 070 579 2542 *pc* vg it[mss] sy[s] sy[c] cop; *therefore* A D W *f*[13] 33 892 1006 1342 1506 𝔐 sy[p] sy[h].

339. The Loyal and Disloyal Slave (→ §240)

Matt 24:45-51

45"What [=Who] consequently is the loyal and sensible slave whom the lord[a] established upon [=over] his household[b] to-give them nourishment in [=at the] proper-time? 46Fortunate [is] that slave whom, his lord having-come, will-find [him] thus doing. 47Amen I-say to-you that he-will-establish him upon [=over] all his being-at-one's-disposals [=belongings]. 48So [=But] if-ever that bad slave might-say in his heart, 'My lord delays,' 49and he-might-begin to-hit his fellow-slaves, so and [=also] he-might-eat and he-might-drink with being-drunks [=those who are drunk], 50the lord of-that slave will-press-forward [=will come] in [=on a] day which he-expects not and in [=at an] hour which he-knows not, 51and he-will-bisect him and will-put his part with the hypocrites.
There-will-be wailing and gnashing of-the teeth there."

Q 12:42-46

42"What [=Who] consequently is the loyal and sensible slave whom the lord established upon [=over] his household to-give them in [=at the] proper-time nourishment? 43 Fortunate [is] that slave whom, his lord having-come, will-find [him] thus doing. 44Amen I-say to-you that he-will-establish him upon [=over] all his being-at-one's-disposals [=belongings]. 45So [=But] if-ever that slave might-say in his heart, 'My lord delays' and he-might-begin to-hit his fellow-slaves, so and [=and also] might-eat and might-drink with being-drunks [=those who are drunk], 46 the lord of-that slave will-press-forward [=will come] in [=on a] day which he-expects not and in [=at an] hour which he-knows not, and he-will-bisect him and will-put his part with the disloyal."

Luke 12:42-46

42And the lord said, "What [=Who] consequently is the loyal, the sensible, manager whom the lord will-establish upon [=over] his healing [=servants] to-give [a] ration in [=at the] proper-time? 43Fortunate [is] that slave whom, his lord having-come, will-find [him] doing thus. 44Truly I-say to-you that he-will-establish him upon [=over] all his being-at-one's-disposals [=belongings]. 45So [=But] if-ever that slave might-say in his heart, 'My lord delays to-come,' and might-begin to-hit the children and the slave-girls, and even to-eat and to-drink and to-get-drunk, 46the lord of-that slave will-press-forward [=will come] in [=on a] day which he-expects not and in [=on an] hour which he-knows not, and he-will-bisect him and will-put his part with the disloyal."

[a] *the lord* ℵ B D L *f*[1] 33 205 *pc* it; *his lord* W Θ *f*[13] 892 1006 1342 1506 𝔐 sy[h] cop.
[b] *his household* B L W Δ Θ *f*[13] 33 *al* vg it[mss] sy[p] sy[h]; *his home* ℵ 565 579 892 *al*; *his healing* D *f*[1] 1006 1342 1506 𝔐 sy[s].

340. Matthew's Parable of the Ten Virgins (→ §248)

Matt 25:1-13

1The the kingdom of-the heavens will-be-compared [to] ten unmarried-girls, whoever [=who] having-taken the lamps of-themselves went-out into a meeting of-the [=with the] bridegroom. 2So [=Now] five out of-them were moronics and five sensibles. 3For

Q 13:25

Luke 13:25

the moronics [=morons] having-taken their lamps
took not [any] olive-oil with themselves. 4So [=But] the
wises [=the wise girls] took olive-oil in the flasks[a] with
the lamps of-themselves. 5So [while] the bridegroom
[was] delaying, all [of them] became-drowsy and were-
sleeping. 6So [in the] middle [of the] night [a] scream
has-happened. 'Look! the bridegroom [b], go-out into
encounter [=in order to meet] him.' 7Then all those
unmarried-girls were-raised and adorned [=trimmed]
the lamps of-themselves. 8So [=And] the moronics
[=morons] said to-the wises [=wise girls], 'Give us out
[=some of] your olive-oil, that [=because] our lamps
are-extinguished.' 9So the wises [=wise girls] answered
saying, 'No [=at all] lest there-might-be-enough not
for-us and for-you.' 10So their going-away [=when
they had gone away] to-buy [it], the bridegroom came
and the readies [=those who were ready] with him into
the weddings and the door was-locked. 11Afterward,
the remainders [=rest of the] virgins come and
[=also] saying, "Lord, lord, open [the door] to-us."
12So having-answered he-said, "Amen I-say to-you,
I-recognize you not." 13Therefore, stay-awake, that
[=because] you-recognize not the day nor the hour."

25"From which ever [=When] the master-of-the-house might-be-raised [=might be awoken] and might-lock-up the door and [when] you-might-begin to-stand outside and to-knock [on] the door saying, 'Lord, open [the door] to-us,' and having-answered he-will-say to-you, 'I-recognize you not.'"

25"From which ever [=When] the master-of-the-house might-be-raised [=might be awoken] and might-lock-up the door and [when] you-might-begin to-stand outside and to-knock [on] the door saying, 'Lord[c], open [the door] to-us,' and having-answered he-will-say to-you, 'I-recognize you not [nor] from-where you-are.'"

[a] *in the flasks* ℵ B D L Z Θ f^1 205 700 *pc* sy^s sy^p; *in their flasks* C W f^{13} 1006 1342 1506 𝔐 vg it^{mss} sy^h.
[b] *omit* ℵ B C D L Z 700 892 pc cop^{samss}; *comes* W Θ f^1 f^{13} 1006 1342 1506 𝔐 vg it^{mss} sy cop^{samss}.
[c] *Lord* 𝔭^{75} ℵ B L 892 1241 *pc* it^{mss} vg sy^s cop^{sa} cop^{bomss}; *Lord, lord* A D W Θ Ψ f^1 f^{13} 𝔐 it sy^c sy^p cop^{bomss}.

341. The Parable of the Evil Slave (→ §303)

Matt 25:14-30

14"For even-as [=it is as if a] person [on] leaving-home called the [=his] own slaves and delivered to-them his being-at-one's-disposals [=belongings], 15and to-whom for-one [=to one of them] he-gave five talants, so to-whom [=and to another] two, so to-whom [=and

Q 19:12-13, 15-24, 26

12"Some person, [on] leaving-home, 13called ten slaves [for] himself, he-gave them ten minas and said to-them, 'Invest [it] in [=until] which I-come [back].'

Luke 19:11-27

11So their hearing [=while they were listening to] these [things] having-added he-said [=he went on to tell a] parable through [=because] him to-be [=he was] near Jerusalem and to-suppose them [=because they supposed] that the kingdom of-god intends to-be-brought-into-sight [=was to appear] at-once. 12Therefore he-said, "Some noble person traveled into [a] distant region to-take [for] himself [a] kingdom and to-return. 13So having-called ten slaves [for] himself, he-gave them ten minas and said to them, 'Invest [it] in [=until] which I-come [back].'

to another] one, to-each according-
to the own power [=his ability], and
he-left-home instantly. 16 The [one]
having-taken [=having received]
the five talants, having-traveled,
worked in [=with] them and gained[a]
another five. 17 In-the-same-way, the
[one who received] the two [talants]
gained another two. 18 So [=But] the
[one] having-taken [=who received]
the one [talant] having-gone-away
dug-a-hole [in the] land and hid the
silver-coin [of] his lord.

19 So with many [=after much] time

the lord of-those slaves comes and
discharges word [=settles accounts]
with them.

20 And having-approached the [one]
having-taken [=having received] the
five talants offered another five
talants saying, 'Lord, you-delivered
to-me five talants; look, I-gained[b]
another five talants.'
21 His lord spoke to-him, 'Splendidly
[done], slave good and loyal; you-
were loyal upon [=over a] few
[things], I-will-establish you [=I
will give you authority] upon [=over]
many [things]. Enter into the joy [of]
your lord.' 22 So having-approached
and [=also], the [one having received]
the two talants, said 'Lord, you-
delivered to-me two talants; look,
I-gained another two talants.' 23 His
lord spoke to-him, 'Splendidly
[done], slave good and loyal; you-
were loyal upon [=over a] few
[things], I-will-establish you [=I will
give you authority] upon [=over] many
[things]. Enter into the joy [of] your
lord.' 24 And so having-approached,
the [one] having-taken [=having
received] the one talant, said
'Lord, I-knew that you [yourself] are
[a] hard person, harvesting where

---

15 With many [=After much] time

the lord of-those slaves comes and
discharges word [=settles accounts]
with them.

16 And the first came saying, 'Lord,
your mina yielded ten minas.'

17 And he-said to-him, 'Splendidly
[done], good slave. You-were
loyal upon [=over a] few [things],
I-will-establish you [=I will give
you authority] upon [=over] many
[things].'
18 And the second came

saying, 'Lord, your mina did

[=made] five minas.' 19 He-said to-
him, 'Splendidly [done], good slave.
You-were loyal upon [=over a] few
[things], I-will-establish you [=I will
give you authority] upon [=over] many
[things].'
20 And the other came saying,

'Lord, 21 I-knew that you [yourself]
are [a] hard person, harvesting

---

14 So [=But] his citizens were-hating
him and they-sent-off [an] embassy-
of-elders behind [=after] him saying,
'We-wish not [for] this [man] to-be-
king upon [=over] us.'
15 And it-happened in the to-
come-back-through him [=when
he returned], having-taken the
kingdom, and he-said [for] these
slaves to-whom he-had-given the
silver-coin to-be-yelled [=to be
called] to-him in-order-that he-
might-know what [=how] they-
profited. 16 So the first arrived saying,
'Lord, your mina yielded ten minas.'

17 And he-said to-him,
'Bravo[c] good slave, that [=because]
you-happened [=you were] loyal in
[the] least, be having authority above
[=take charge over] ten cities.'

18 And the second came

saying, 'Your mina,
lord, did [=made] five minas.'

19 And so he-said to-this [one],

'And you, happen [=rule] above five
cities.'

20 And the other came saying,

'Lord, look! your mina which I-had
wrapped-up in cloth, 21 for I-was-

you-sowed not and gathering from-which [place] you-scattered [seed] not, [25]and having-been-feared [=being afraid and] having-gone-away I-hid your talant in the land; look, you-have [what is] your-own.'
[26]So his lord, having-answered, said

to-him, 'Evil slave and lazy, you-

recognized that I-harvest where I-sowed not and I-gather from-which [places] I-scattered [seed] not?
[27]Therefore it-was-necessary [for] you [yourself] to-throw [=to take] my silver-coins to-the bankers and having-come [back] I [myself would have] obtained [what] ever [was] my-own together-with interest.

[28]Therefore, remove the talant from him and give [it] to-the [one] having

[=who has] ten talants.
[29]For to-the [one] having [=who has] all [more] will-be-given and he-will-be-exceeded [=he will be rich], so [=but from] the [one] having no [=nothing] and [=even that] which he-has will-be-removed from him.

[30]And cast-out the worthless slave into the outermost darkness; there-will-be wailing and gnashing of-the teeth there.'"

where you-sowed not and gathering from-which [place] you-scattered [seed] not, and having-been-feared [=being afraid and] having-gone-away I-hid your mina in the land; look, you-have [what is] your-own.'
[22]He-says to-him,

'Evil slave, you-recognized that

I-harvest where I-sowed not and I-gather from-which [places] I-scattered [seed] not?
[23]Therefore it-was-necessary [for] you [yourself] to-throw [=to take] my silver-coins to-the bankers and having-come [back] I [myself would have] obtained [what] ever [was] my-own together-with interest.

[24]Therefore, remove the mina from him and give [it] to-the [one] having

[=who has] ten minas.
[26]For to-the [one] having [=who has]

all [more] will-be-given, so [=but from] the [one] having no [=nothing] and [=even that] which he-has will-be-removed from him.'"

fearing you, that [=because] you-are [a] harsh person; you-remove [that] which you-put not [=you did not deposit] and harvest [that] which you-sowed not.'

[22]He-says to-him, 'I-will-judge you out your mouth [=by your own words], evil slave. You-recognized that I [myself] am [a] harsh person removing [that] which I-put not [=I did not deposit] and harvesting [that]

which I-sowed not?
[23]And through what [=why] did-you-give not my silver-coin upon table [=to a bank]? I-too [=Then I] having-come practiced [=could have collected] it together-with ever [=whatever] interest.'
[24]And to-the being-presents [=to the bystanders] he-said,
'Remove from him the mina and give [it] to-the [one] having ten minas.' [25]And they-said to-him,
'Lord, he-has ten minas.'
[26]'I-say to-you that to-the [one] having [=who has] all [more] will-

be-given, so [=but] from the [one] having no [=nothing] and [=even that] which he-has will-be-removed [=will be taken away].
[27]Nevertheless these my enemies having-wished me no [=not] to-be-king upon [=over] them, lead [them] here and slay them in-front of-me.'"

[a] *gained* ℵ[2] B C D L Θ f^1 f^{13} 33 205 892 1424 1506 *al* vg it[mss] sy[p] cop[sa]; *did* ℵ* A[C] W 1006 1342 𝔐 sy[h].
[b] *I-gained* ℵ B L 33 892 *pc* it[mss] cop; *I-gained-in-addition upon them* A C W f^1 f^{13} 1006 1342 1506 𝔐 sy[p] sy[h].
[c] *Bravo* B D 892 vg it[mss]; *Splendidly* ℵ A L W Θ Ψ f^1 f^{13} 1006 1342 1506 𝔐.

342. Matthew's "Whoever Does This to the Least"

Matt 25:31-46

[31]"So whenever the son of-the person might-come in his glory and all the[a] announcers [=angels]
with him, then he-will-sit upon [the] his throne of-glory. [32]And all the nations will-be-gathered in-
front of-him, and he-will-exclude [=he will separate] them from one-another, even-as the shepherd
excludes [=separates] the sheep from the goats. [33]And he-will-stand the sheep, for-one, out [=to] his
right, so [=but] the young-goats out [=to the] left. [34]Then the king will-say to-the [ones] out [=on]
his right, 'Come-on! [you] having-been-blessed [by] my father, inherit the kingdom having-been-
made-ready for-you from [=since the] molding [of the] world. [35]For I-hungered and you-gave me
[something] to-eat, I-was-thirsty and you-gave-a-drink [to] me, I-was [a] stranger and you-gathered

me, [36]naked and you-were-arrayed [=you dressed] me, I-was-ill and you-cared-for me, I-was in
prison and you-came to me.' [37]Then the righteouses [=righteous people] will-be-answered [=will
answer] him saying, 'Lord, when did-we-see you hungering and [when] did-we-nourish [you] or
being-thirsty and [when] did-we-give-a-drink [to you]? [38]So [=And] when did-we-see you [as a]
stranger and [when] did-we-gather [you], or naked and [when] were-we-arrayed [=did we dress you]?
[39]So [=And] when did-we-see you being-ill[b] or in prison and [when] did-we-come to you?' [40]And
having-answered, the king will-say to-them, 'Amen I-say to-you, upon whatsoever [=whatever]
you-did [to] one of-the least of-these my brothers, you-did to-me.' [41]Then he-will-say and [=also]
to-the [ones] out [=on] his left, 'TRAVEL FROM ME, HAVING-BEEN-CURSEDS [=you who were
cursed], into the eternal fire having-been-made-ready [by] the devil and his announcers [=angels].
[42]For I-hungered and you-gave me not [anything] to-eat, I-was-thirsty and you-gave-a-drink [to]
me not, [43]I-was [a] stranger and you-gathered me not, and naked and you-were-arrayed [=you
clothed] me not, ill and in prison and cared-for me not.' [44]Then they [themselves] will-be-answered
[=will answer] and [=also] saying, 'Lord, when did-we-see you hungering or being-thirsty or [being a]
stranger or naked or ill or in prison and [when] did-we-serve you not?' [45]Then he-will-be-answered
[=he will answer] them saying, 'Amen I-say to-you, upon whatsoever [=whatever] you-did not [do for]
one of-the least of-these [people], nor did-you-do [for] me.' [46]And these [people] will-go-away into
eternal punishment, so [=but] the righteouses [=righteous people will go] into eternal life."

[a] *omit* ℵ B D L Θ f^{1} 33 205 565 *pc* vg it^{mss} cop^{sa}; *holy* A W f^{13} 892 1006 1342 1506 𝔐 sy^{p} sy^{h}.
[b] *being-ill* B D Θ *pc*; *ill* ℵ A L W f^{1} f^{13} 33 892 1006 1342 1506 𝔐.
📖 Mt 25:41 – Ps 6:8

343. Luke's Conclusion to the Apocalyptic Discourse

Luke 21:37-38	John 8:1-2
[37]So he-was teaching in the temple [during] the days, so [=but during] the nights going-out [of the city] he-was-camping-out into [=on] the mountain being-called Of-Olives. [38]And all the whole-people were-early [coming] to him in the temple to-hear him.	[1]So Jesus traveled into [=onto] the mountain of-olives. [2]So early-in-the-morning again he-arrived into [=at] the temple and all the whole-people were-coming to-him, and having-sat he-was-teaching them.

There are no variants in this pericope that appear in English.

The Passion Narratives

344. The Decision to Kill Jesus

Matt 26:1-5	**Mark 14:1-2**	**Luke 22:1-2**	John 11:47-53
[1]And it-happened when Jesus completed all these words, he-said [to] his disciples, [2]"You-recognize that with [=after] two days, passover happens, and the son of-the person is-delivered into the [=in order] to-be-crucified."	[1]So [=Now] passover and the days-of-unleavened-bread was with [=in] two days.	[1]So the feast of-the days-of-unleavened-bread, being-said [=called] passover, was-nearing.	[47]Therefore the high-priests and the Pharisees gathered [=the] Sanhedrin and were-saying, "What do-we-do [now], that [=because] this person does many signs? [48]If-ever we-might-excuse [=we might ignore] him thus, all will-believe into [=in] him, and the Romans will-come and will-remove [=will destroy] and [=both] our place and the
[3]Then the high-priests[a] and the elders of-the	And the high-priests	[2]And the high-priests	nation." [49]So [=But] some one

whole-people were-gathered into the court-yard of-the high-priest, being-said [=named] Caiaphas, [4]and they-advised [=they conspired] in-order-that [in] cunning they-might-seize and might-kill Jesus.	and the scribes were-searching [for] how, having-seized him in-cunning, they-might-kill [him].	and the scribes were-searching [for] how they-might-abolish [=they might destroy] him,	out of-them, Caiaphas, being high-priest of-that annum, said to-them, "You recognize not no-one [=You know nothing], [50]nor do-you-take-into-account that it-is-profitable [=it is better for] you in-order-that one person might-face-death on-behalf of-the whole-people and no [=rather than] the whole nation might-be-destroyed." [51]So [=Now] he-said this not from himself, but being high-priest of-that annum, he-prophesied that Jesus intended [=was destined] to-face-death on-behalf of-the nation, [52]and not on-behalf of-the nation only but in-order-that and [=also] he-might-gather the descendants of-god having-been-scattered into one [group]. [53]Therefore, from that day, they-planned in-order-that they-might-kill him.
[5]So [=But] they-were-saying, "No [=Not] in the feast, in-order-that commotion [=a riot] might-happen no [=not] in [=among] the whole-people."	[2]For they-were-saying, "No [=Not] in the feast, lest there-will-be [a] commotion of-the whole-people."	for they-were-fearing the whole-people.	

[a] *omit* 𝔭[45] ℵ B D L Θ *f*[1] *f*[13] 205 565 700 892 1424 al vg it[mss] sy[s] cop; *and the scribes* 1006 1342 1506 𝔐 it sy[p] sy[h]; *and the Pharisees* W.

345. The Woman with the Ointment (→ §133, §209)

Matt 26:6-13	**Mark 14:3-9**	John 12:1-8
[6]So Jesus having-happened [=While Jesus was] in Bethany in [the] home of-Simon the leprous, [7][a] woman approached him having [=holding an] alabaster-case of-precious ointment and she-poured-over [it] upon his head [while he was] dining.	[3]And his being [=While he was] in Bethany in the home of-Simon the leprous, his lying-down [=and as he was reclining a] woman came having [=holding an] alabaster-case of-costly ointment of-liquid nard, having-shattered[b] the alabaster-case she-poured-over [it over] his head.	[1]Therefore six days before the passover Jesus went into Bethany where Lazarus was, whom Jesus raised out [=from the] dead. [2]Therefore they-did [=they made a] banquet for-him there, and Martha was-serving, so [=and] Lazarus was one out of-the dinings [=one of those dining] together-with him. [3]Therefore Mary, having-taken [a] liter of-valuable ointment of-liquid nard, smeared the feet of-Jesus and dried his feet [with] her hairs. So the home was-fulfilled [=was filled] out [=by] the fragrance of-the ointment.
[8]So the disciples[a], having-seen, were-indignant saying, "Into what [=Why] this destruction [=waste]? [9]For she-was-able to-peddle this [=she could have sold it] many [=for much] and to-be-given [=given it] to-poors [=to poor people]."	[4]So [=Now] there-were some being-indignants [=people thinking indignantly] to themselves, "Into what [=Why] has-happened this destruction of-the ointment? [5]For she-was-able to-peddle [=she could have sold] this ointment [for] above three-hundred denarii and to-be-given [=given it] to-the poors [=poor people]." And they-were-censuring her.	[4]So Judas the Iscariot one out [of] his disciples, the [one] intending to-deliver him, says, [5]"Through what [=Why] this ointment was-peddled not [for] three-hundred denarii and [the proceeds] given to-poor [people]?"
[10]So [=But] Jesus, having-known, said to-them, "What [=Why] do-	[6]So [=But] Jesus said, "Excuse her [=Leave her alone]. What [=Why]	[6]So [=Now] he-said

you-present troubles to-the [=do you trouble the] woman? For she-worked fine work [=she did a good deed] into [=for] me. [11]For you-have the poors [=poor people] always with themselves [=yourselves], so [=but] you-have not me always. [12]For this [woman], having-thrown [=having poured] this ointment upon my body, did [this] to me to-prepare-for-burial. [13]Amen I-say to-you, where if-ever this proclamation might-be-preached in the whole world, [that] which this [woman] did will-be-talked [=will be spoken] and [=also] into her memory."

do-you-present troubles to-her [=do you trouble her]? She-worked fine work [=She did a good deed] in [=for] me. [7]For you-have the poors [=poor people] always with themselves [=yourselves], and whenever you-might-wish you-are-able to-do splendidly [=to do good] for-them, so [=but] you-have not me always. [8]She-did which she-had [=what she could]; she-took-before [=she undertook] to-pour-perfume-on my body in [=for] burial. [9]So amen I-say to-you, where if-ever the proclamation might-be-preached into the whole world, and [=also that] which she [herself] did will-be-talked [=will be spoken] into her memory."

this not that [=because] around the poor was-being-of-concern [=the poor were any concern] to-him but that [=because] he-was [a] thief and having the money-box he-was-bearing the being-throwns [=he kept the common purse and stole from what they were given]. [7]Therefore Jesus said, "Excuse her, in-order-that she-might-keep it into [=for] the day [of] my burial. [8]For you-have always the poors [=poor people] with themselves [=yourselves], so [=but] you-have not me always."

[a] *the disciples* $\mathfrak{p}^{45}$ $\mathfrak{p}^{64}$ ℵ B D L Θ 089 *f* ^{13} 33 700 892 *pc* vg it^{mss} cop; *his disciples* A W *f* ^{1} 1006 1342 1506 $\mathfrak{M}$ it^{mss} sy cop^{sa}.
[b] *having-shattered* ℵ B L Ψ 2427; *and having-shattered* A C W *f* ^{1} *f* ^{13} 892 1006 1342 1506 $\mathfrak{M}$ sy^{c}; *having-repressed* D Θ 565.

SYNOPTIC STUDY GUIDE 14

John's Relationship to the Synoptics

Readers of the New Testament have always been aware of how different the Gospel of John is from the other gospels: John's Jesus is explicit about his identity (the "I am" statements), while in the synoptics, Jesus is evasive and coy; the synoptic Jesus speaks in parables, and short witty sayings, while the Johannine Jesus delivers long speeches; the cleansing of the temple is the inaugural event in Jesus' ministry in John, but it is one of his final public acts in the synoptics; Jesus dies in the afternoon of Passover in the synoptics, but in John he dies the afternoon before the Passover supper, and is thereby executed with all the other "lambs" that day.

These differences have long invited readers to question John's relationship to the Synoptic Gospels. Had its author ever read one or any of the other gospels? Did he use them at all in the creation of his own gospel? Perhaps the easiest way to explain John's differences is to conclude that its author wrote independently of the Synoptic Gospels, and even independently of synoptic *tradition*. In other words, not only was the writer of the Gospel of John not familiar with any one of the canonical gospels, he was not even aware of their depiction of Jesus as a coy speaker of parables who runs a one-year mission. (Since only one Passover occurs in the Synoptic Gospels, it is reasonable to conclude that Jesus' career there covers at most one year, probably less.) There are after all very few episodes in the life of Jesus upon which John and the synoptics agree, and those they agree upon can easily be chalked up to the oral transmission of Jesus stories (e.g., Five Thousand Fed [§166], The Temple Scene [§307], and much of John 18-19 [§355-§380]). A simple glance at these and other parallels, however, reveals very few agreements in wording.

And yet, it is never that simple. There *are* a few places where John and one of the synoptics (usually Mark or Luke) share *wording* in a shared story, which is the sort of thing we expect to find when there is a direct literary relationship. For example, in §345, John and Mark are the only Gospels to mention that the ointment used by the woman was "ointment of-liquid nard"; John and Luke alone share the detail that the woman used her hair on Jesus' feet (in Luke 7:38 to dry them of her tears, in John 12:3 to apply the ointment). If these were details that all three Synoptic Gospels shared, it would be easier to argue that oral tradition alone brought those details to the author of John (such as happens with John's phrase "Rise, remove your mattress and walk-around" in §96). If it is the case that John did have direct access to one or more of the Synoptic Gospels, then the question of John's uniqueness becomes all the more interesting because it means he *knew* the other version of the Jesus story but deliberately and considerably altered that tradition.

346. Introduction of Judas Iscariot

Matt 26:14-16	Mark 14:10-11	Luke 22:3-6	John 13:2, 27; 6:70-71
14 Then one of-the twelve, being-said [=called] Judas Iscariot,	10 And Judas Iscariot, one of-the twelve,	3 So [the] adversary entered into Judas, being-called [=called] Iscariot, being out of-the number [=who was one] of-the twelve.	2 And [while a] banquet [was] happening, the devil already having-thrown [=put the plan] into the heart [of] Judas [son] of-Simon Iscariot, in-order-that he-might-deliver him 27 And with [=after he received] the small-bit-of-bread, then the adversary entered into that [man]. Therefore, Jesus says to-him, “[That] which you-are-doing, do quickly.” 6:70 Jesus answered them, “I-choose you, the twelve, [did] I not? And [yet] one out of-you is [a] devil.” 71 So [=Now] he-was-saying [this about] Judas [son] of-Simon Iscariot; for this [person], one out of-the twelve, was-intending to-deliver him.
having-traveled to the high-priests, 15 said, “What do-you-wish to-give to-me [if] I-too will-deliver him to-you?”	went-away to the high-priests in-order-that he-might-	4 And having-gone-away he-talked-with the high-priests and [with the] generals how	
	deliver him to-them.	he-might-deliver him to-them.	
So they-stood [=they offered] thirty silver-coins to-him.	11 So [=And] having-heard, they-rejoiced and they-promised to-give him silver-coin.	5 And they-rejoiced and they-elected to-give him silver-coin.	
16 And from then he-was-searching [for an] opportune-time in-order-that he-might-deliver him.	And he-was-searching [for an] opportunity how [=when] he-might-deliver him.	6 And he-acknowledged [he accepted] and he-was-searching [for an] opportune-time to-deliver him apart-from [the] crowd to-them[a].	

[a] *apart-from crowd to-them* $\mathfrak{p}^{75}$ ℵ A B C L Ψ 579 892 *pc*; *to-them apart-from crowd* W Θ f^{1} 1006 1342 1506 𝔐 it cop^{samss}; *apart-from crowd* D vg it^{mss} cop^{samss}; *to-them* f^{13} *pc* cop^{samss}.

347. Preparation for Passover

Matt 26:17-20	Mark 14:12-17	Luke 22:7-14
17 So [on] the first of-the days-of-unleavened-bread, the	12 And [on] the first day of-the days-of-unleavened-bread, when they-were-slaughtering the passover	7 So the day of-the days-of-unleavened-bread came, in [=on] which the passover [lamb] was-necessary [=had] to-be-slaughtered. 8 And he-sent-off Peter and John having-said, “Having-traveled, make-ready for-us the passover in-order-that we-might-eat.”
disciples approached Jesus saying, “Wheresoever do-you-wish [that] we-might-make-ready for-you to-	[lamb], his disciples say to-him, “Wheresoever, having-gone-away [=after we have gone], do-you-wish [that] we-might-make-ready in-order-that you-might-eat the passover?”	9 So they-said to-him, “Wheresoever do-you-wish [that] we-might-
eat the passover?” 18 So he-said, “Leave into the city to so-and-so, and say to-him,	13 And he-sends-off two [of] his disciples and says to-them, “Leave into the city and [a] person bearing [a] clay-jar of-water will-	make-ready?” 10 So he-said to-them, “Look! your having-entered [=when you have entered] into the city, [a] person bearing [a] clay-jar of-water

Matt	Mark	Luke
	encounter you; follow him. 14And where if-ever he-might-enter, say to-the master-of-the-house that	will-meet-with you. Follow him into the home into which he-travels-in, 11and you-will-say to-the master-of-the-house of-the home,
'The teacher says, "My proper-time is near, to [=with] you I-do the passover with my disciples."'"	'The teacher says, "Wheresoever is my guest-room where I-might-eat the passover with my disciples?"' 15And he [himself] will-show you [a] great upstairs-room having-been-spread-out ready [=fully furnished], and make-ready for-us there."	'The teacher says to-you, "Wheresoever is the guest-room where I-might-eat the passover with my disciples?"' 12And-that [person] will-show you [a] great upstairs-room having-been-spread-out [=fully furnished]. Make-ready [for us] there.
19And the disciples did like Jesus directed them and they-made-ready the passover. 20So evening having-happened, he-was-dining with the twelve.	16And the disciples went-out and went into the city and found just-as he-said to-them and they-made-ready the passover. 17And evening having-happened, he-comes with the twelve.	13So, having-gone-away they-found just-as he-had-said to-them and they-made-ready the passover. 14And when the hour happened, he-leaned [=he reclined at the table] and the apostles[a] together-with him.

[a] *the apostles* 𝔭⁷⁵ ℵ* B D *pc* it cop^samss; *the twelve* ℵ¹ L *pc* cop^samss; *the twelve apostles* ℵ² A C W Θ *f*¹ *f*¹³ 892 1006 1342 1506 𝔐 vg it^mss sy^p sy^h cop^bo; *his disciples* sy^s sy^c.

348. Jesus Predicts His Betrayal (→ §350)

Matt 26:21-25	Mark 14:18-21	Luke 22:21-23	John 13:21-30
21And their [=as they were] eating he-said, "Amen I-say to-you that one out of-you will-deliver me." 22And being-grieved very [=greatly] they-began to-say to-him	18And their dining and [=As they were] eating, Jesus said, "Amen I-say to-you that one out of-you eating with me will-deliver me." 19They-began to-be-grieved and to-say to-him one according-to one [=each one of them],	21"Nevertheless look! the hand of-the [one] delivering me [is] with me upon [=at] the table.	21Having-said these [things], Jesus was-disturbed in-the spirit and he-testified and said, "Amen amen I-say to-you that one out of-you, will-deliver me." 22The disciples were-looking into [=at] one-another being-uncertain around [=concerning] what he-says. 23One out [of] his disciples, whom Jesus was-loving, was dining [=reclining] in the bosom of-Jesus. 24Therefore, Simon Peter nods to-this [person] to-inquire what ever it-might-be around [=concerning] which [that] he-speaks. 25Therefore, that [one] having-leaned thus upon the chest of-Jesus says to-him, "Lord, what [=who] is it?" 26Jesus answers, "That [one] is to-whom I [myself] will-dip the small-bit-of-bread and I-will-give to-him." Therefore having-dipped the small-bit-of-bread he-takes and gives [it] to-Judas [son] of-Simon Iscariot. 27And with [=after receiving] the small-bit-of-bread, then the adversary entered into
each one, "Surely-not am I [the one], lord?"	"Surely-not I[a]?"		
23So having-answered he-said, "The [one] having-dipped the hand in the dish with me, this [one] will-deliver me.	20So he-said to-them, "One of-the twelve, dipping with me into the <u>dish</u>.		
24The son of-the person for-one leaves just-as it-has-been-written around [=concerning]	21That [=Because] the son of-the person for-one leaves just-as it-has-been-written around [=concerning] him, so	22That [=Because] the son for-one of-the person travels according-to the having-been-decided [=what has been foreordained],	
him, so woe to-that person through whom the son of-the person is-	woe to-that person through whom the son of-the person is-	nevertheless woe to-that person through whom he-is-delivered."	

delivered. It-was-being
[=It would have been] fine
[=better] for-him if that
person was-begotten
not."
25 So having-answered
Judas, the [one]
delivering him, said,
"Surely-not am I [the
one], rabbi?" He-says to-
him, "You said [it]."

delivered. It-was-being
[=would have been] fine
[=better] for-him if the
person was-begotten
not."

23 And they [themselves]
began to-discuss to
[=among] themselves
consequently what
[=who] might-be the
[one] out of-them
intending to-practice
[=about to do] this.

that [person]. Therefore Jesus
says to-him, "[That] which
you-do do more-quickly." 28 So
no-one of-the dinings [=of those
who were dining] knew what
[=why] he-said this to him.
29 For some were-supposing,
as-a-result-of [=because] Judas
was-having [=held] the money-
box, that Jesus says to-him "Buy
[that] which we-have need into
[=for] the feast," or in-order-that
he-might-give some to-the poor.
30 Therefore having-taken the
small-bit-of-bread that [person]
went-out immediately. So [=And]
it-was night.

[a] *Surely-not I* ℵ B C L W Δ Ψ 1342 1506 2427 *pc* vg it^{mss} sy cop; *Surely-not I. And another, surely-not I* D Θ f^{1} 1006 𝔐 it; *Surely-not am I, rabbi. And another, surely-not I* A *pc*; *Surely-not am I, lord. And another, surely-not I* 892 1424 *pc*; *Surely-not am I. And another, surely-not I* f^{13}.

349. The Last Supper

Matt 26:26-29

26 So their [=While they are]
eating, Jesus, having-taken
bread[a] and having-blessed
[it] he-broke [it], and
having-given [it] to-the
disciples he-said[b], "Take,
eat, this is my body." 27 And
having-taken [a] cup and
having-given-thanks he-
gave [it] to-them saying,
"Drink out of-him [=from
it], all [of you], 28 for this is
my blood of-the[c] covenant
being-shed around [=on
behalf] of-many into [=for
the] remission of-sins.
29 So I-say to-you, might-I-
drink out of-this produce
of-the vine not no from
right-now [=never again]
until that day whenever
I-might-drink it new
[=again] with you in the
kingdom [of] my father."

Mark 14:22-25

22 And their [=While they
are] eating, [d] having-taken
bread [and] having-blessed
[it] he-broke [it] and gave
[it] to-them and said,
"Take, this is my body."
23 And having-taken [a]
cup, [and] having-given-
thanks, he-gave [it]
to-them and all drank out
of-him [=from it]. 24 And
he-said to-them, "This is
my blood of-the covenant
being-shed on-behalf of-
many.

25 Amen I-say to-you that
no-longer might-I-drink
not no [=ever again] out of-
the produce of-the vine
until that day whenever
I-might-drink it new
[=again] in the kingdom
of-god."

Luke 22:15-20

15 And he-said to-them,
"I-desired in-desire
[=strongly] to-eat this
passover with you before
me to-suffer [=I suffer].
16 For I-say to-you that
I-might-eat it not no
[=ever again] until whoever
[=everything] is-fulfilled
in the kingdom of-god."
17 And having-received
[a] cup, [and] having-
given-thanks, he-said,
"Take this and divide-up
into [=divide it up among]
themselves [=yourselves].
18 For I-say to-you that
might-I-drink not no
from the now [=never
again] from the produce
of-the vine until which
[time] the kingdom of-
god might-come." 19 And
having-taken bread, [and]
having-given-thanks,
he-broke [it] and gave [it]
to-them saying,

John 6:51-56

51 "I am the living bread
having-descended out
of-heaven. If-ever some
might-eat out [=some]
of-this bread, he-will-live
into the eon [=eternity]
and so the bread which
I [myself] will-give on-
behalf of-the life of-
the world is my flesh."
52 Therefore the Judeans
were-confronting to
[=were arguing with] one-
another saying, "How
is-able this [person] to-
give us his flesh to-eat?"
53 Therefore, Jesus said to-
them, "Amen amen I-say
to-you, if-ever you-might-
eat no [=not] the flesh
of-the son of-the person
and might-drink his
blood, you-have not life in
themselves [=yourselves].
54 The [one] chewing my
flesh and drinking my
blood has eternal life,

"This is my body, being-given on-behalf of-you. Do this into [=in] my-own remembrance." 20 And [with] the cup [he acted] in-the-same-way with to-banquet-on [=after supper], saying, "This cup [is] the new covenant in my blood being-shed on-behalf of-you."

I-too will-get-up [=will raise] him [on] the last day. 55 For my flesh is true rust [=food] and my blood is true potion. 56 The [one] chewing my flesh and drinking my blood stays in me [and] I-too in him."

a *bread* $\mathfrak{p}^{45}$ ℵ B C D G L Z Θ f^{1} 33 205 579 700 892 1424 *al* cop; *the bread* A W f^{13} 1006 1342 1506 𝔐.
b *having-given to-the disciples he-said* $\mathfrak{p}^{37}$ $\mathfrak{p}^{45}$ $ℵ^{1}$ B D L Z Θ f^{1} f^{13} 33 205 700 892 1424 *al*; *gave to-the disciples and said* ℵ* A C W 1006 1342 1506 𝔐.
c *omit* $\mathfrak{p}^{37}$ ℵ B L Z Θ 33 *pc*; *new* A C D W f^{1} f^{13} 892 1006 1342 1506 𝔐 vg it sy cop.
d *omit* $ℵ^{1}$ B D W f^{13} 565 1427 it sy^{s} cop^{sa}; *Jesus* ℵ* ℵ2 A C L Θ Ψ f^{1} 69 892 983 1006 1342 1506 𝔐 vg it^{mss} sy^{p} sy^{h} cop^{bo}.

350. Jesus Predicts His Betrayal (→ §348)

Matt 26:21-25

21 And their [=as they were] eating he-said, "Amen I-say to-you that one out of-you will-deliver me." 22 And being-grieved very [=greatly] they-began to-say to-him each one, "Surely-not am I [the one], lord?" 23 So having-answered he-said, "The [one] having-dipped the hand in the dish with me, this [one] will-deliver me. 24 The son of-the person for-one leaves just-as it-has-been-written around [=concerning] him, so woe to-that person through whom the son of-the person is-delivered. It-was-being [=It would have been] fine [=better] for-him if that person was-begotten not."

Mark 14:18-21

18 And their dining and [=As they were] eating, Jesus said, "Amen I-say to-you that one out of-you eating with me will-deliver me." 19 They-began to-be-grieved and to-say to-him one according-to one [=each one of them], "Surely-not I[a]?" 20 So he-said to-them, "One of-the twelve, dipping with me into the dish. 21 That [=Because] the son of-the person for-one leaves just-as it-has-been-written around [=concerning] him, so woe to-that person through whom the son of-the person is-delivered. It-was-being [=would have been] fine [=better] for-him if the person was-begotten not."

Luke 22:21-23

21 "Nevertheless look! the hand of-the [one] delivering me [is] with me upon [=at] the table. 22 That [=Because] the son for-one of-the person travels according-to the having-been-decided [=what has been foreordained], nevertheless woe to-that person through whom he-is-delivered."

John 13:21-30

21 Having-said these [things], Jesus was-disturbed in-the spirit and he-testified and said, "Amen amen I-say to-you that one out of-you, will-deliver me." 22 The disciples were-looking into [=at] one-another being-uncertain around [=concerning] what he-says. 23 One out [of] his disciples, whom Jesus was-loving, was dining [=reclining] in the bosom of-Jesus. 24 Therefore, Simon Peter nods to-this [person] to-inquire what ever it-might-be around [=concerning] which [that] he-speaks. 25 Therefore, that [one] having-leaned thus upon the chest of-Jesus says to-him, "Lord, what [=who] is it?" 26 Jesus answers, "That [one] is to-whom I [myself] will-dip the small-bit-of-bread and I-will-give to-him." Therefore having-dipped the small-bit-of-bread he-takes and gives [it] to-Judas [son] of-Simon Iscariot. 27 And with [=after receiving] the small-bit-of-bread, then the adversary entered into that [person]. Therefore Jesus says to-him, "[That] which you-do do more-quickly." 28 So no-one of-the dinings [=of those

25 So having-answered Judas, the [one] delivering him, said, "Surely-not am I [the one], rabbi?" He-says to-him, "You said [it]."

23 And they [themselves] began to-discuss to [=among] themselves consequently what [=who] might-be the [one] out of-them intending to-practice [=about to do] this.

who were dining] knew what [=why] he-said this to him. 29 For some were-supposing, as-a-result-of [=because] Judas was-having [=held] the money-box, that Jesus says to-him "Buy [that] which we-have need into [=for] the feast," or in-order-that he-might-give some to-the poor. 30 Therefore having-taken the small-bit-of-bread that [person] went-out immediately. So [=And] it-was night.

[a] *Surely-not I* ℵ B C L W Δ Ψ 1342 1506 2427 *pc* vg it^{mss} sy cop; *Surely-not I. And another, surely-not I* D Θ *f*^{1} 1006 𝔐 it; *Surely-not am I, rabbi. And another, surely-not I* A *pc*; *Surely-not am I, lord. And another, surely-not I* 892 1424 *pc*; *Surely-not am I. And another, surely-not I f*^{13}.

351. A Dispute among the Disciples (→ §300)

Matt 20:24-28

24 And the ten having-heard were-indignant around [=concerning] the two brothers. 25 So [=But] Jesus having-summoned them said "You-recognize that the magistrates of-the nations act-as-lord-over them and the greats [=tyrants] rule-over them.

26 It-will-be not thus [=this way] in [=with] you, but who if-ever might-wish to-happen [=to become] great in [=among] you will-be your servant,

27 and who ever in [=among] you might-wish to-be first will-be your slave. 28 Even-as the son of-the person came not to-be-served but to-serve and to-give his soul [=life as] ransom in-place of-many."

Mark 10:41-45

41 And the ten having-heard began to-be-indignant around [=concerning] James and John.
42 And having-summoned them Jesus says to-them, "You-recognize that the supposings [=those who are supposed] to-begin [=to rule] the nations act-as-lord-over them and their greats [=tyrants] rule-over them.

43 So [=But] it-is not thus [=this way] in [=with] you, but who ever might-wish to-happen [=to become] great in [=among] you will-be your servant,

44 and who ever in [=among] you might-wish to-be[a] first will-be slave of-all, 45 for and [=even] the son of-the person came not to-be-served but to-serve and to-give his soul [=life as] ransom in-place of-many."

Luke 22:24-27

24 So [a] dispute and [=also] happened in [=among] them, the what [=which one] of-them does-he-suppose to-be greater.
25 So he-said to-them, "The kings of-the nations act-as-lord of-them and the having-authority-overs [=those who have authority over] them are-called workers-of-kindness [=benefactors].
26 So [=But it is] not thus [=this way for] you. But the greater in [=among] you let-happen [=let him be] like the newer [=younger], and the ruling [one] like the [one] serving.

John 13:4-5, 12-17

. . . 4 he-rises out of-the banquet [=from the table] and puts the [=his] coats [aside] and having-taken [a] towel encloaked himself; 5 moreover, he-throws water into the wash-basin and he-began to-wash the feet of-the disciples and to-dry [them with] the towel in-which he-was having-been-encloaked. 12 Therefore when he-washed their feet and took his coats and leaned [=reclined at the table] again, he-said to-them, "Do-you-know what I-have-done for-you? 13 You yell [=You call] me 'Teacher' and 'lord' and you-speak well [=correctly], for I-am. 14 Therefore if I, the lord and the teacher, washed your feet, you [yourselves] and [=also] owe one-another to-wash the feet. 15 For I-gave you [an] example in-order-that just-as I [myself] did for-you, you [yourselves] might-do [for each other]

Matt	Mark	Luke	John
		27 For what [=who is] greater, the [one] dining or the [one] serving? [Is it] indeed-not the [one] dining? So [=But] I [myself] am in [the] middle of-you like the [one] serving."	and [=also]. 16 Amen amen I-say to-you, [a] slave is not greater [than] his lord nor [an] apostle greater [than] the [one] having-sent him. 17 If you-recognize these [things] you-are fortunate if-ever you-might-do them."

a *who ever in you might-wish to-be* ℵ B C* L Δ Θ Ψ 579 700 892 1342 1424 2427 *pc*; *who ever of-you might-wish to-be* D W f^{1} 205 565 2542 *pc*; *who ever of-you might-wish to-happen* A C^{3} f^{13} 1006 𝔐.

352. The Judgment of the Twelve Tribes/The End of Q (→ §295)

Matt 19:28	**Q 22:28, 30**	**Luke 22:28-30**
28 So Jesus said to-them, "Amen I-say to-you that you having-followeds [=who have followed] me, in the next-generation whenever the son of-the person might-be-seated upon his throne of-glory, you and [=also] will-sit upon twelve thrones judging the twelve tribes of-Israel."	28 "You having-followeds [=who have followed] me, 30 will-sit upon twelve thrones judging the twelve tribes of-Israel."	28 "So you are the having-remaineds [=those who remained] with me in my tests. 29 I-too confer [upon] you, just-as my father conferred to-me, [a] kingdom, 30 in-order-that you-might-eat and you-might-drink upon [=at] my table in my kingdom, and you-will-sit upon thrones judging the twelve tribes of-Israel."

There are no variants in this pericope that appear in English.

353. Peter's Denial Predicted

Matt 26:30-35	**Mark 14:26-31**	**Luke 22:31-34**	John 13:36-38
30 And having-sung-a-hymn, they-went-out into the mountain of-the olives. 31 Then Jesus says to-them, "You all will-be-caused-to-stumble in [=because of] me in [=on] this night, for it-has-been-written, 'I-WILL-STRIKE-DOWN THE SHEPHERD AND WILL-BE-SCATTERED THE SHEEP OF-THE FLOCK.' 32 So with [=after] the to-be-raised me [=I have been raised] I-will-lead-ahead [of] you into the Galilee."	26 And having-sung-a-hymn, they-went-out into the mountain of-the olives. 27 And Jesus says to-them that "All [of] you-will-be-caused-to-stumble, that [=because] it-has-been-written, 'I-WILL-STRIKE-DOWN THE SHEPHERD AND THE SHEEP WILL-BE-SCATTERED.' 28 But with [=after] the to-be-raised me [=I have been raised] I-will-lead-ahead [of] you into the Galilee."		

Matt 26:33-35	Mark 14:39-31	Luke 22:31-38	John
		31 a "Simon Simon, look! the adversary requested to-sift [all of] you like wheat, 32so [=but] I [myself] was-implored [=prayed] around [=for] you in-order-that your loyalty might-fail no [=not]. And you, sometime having-turned-back [=whenever you have returned], make-firm [=strengthen] your brothers."	36Simon Peter says to-him, "Lord, where are-you-leaving [for]?" Jesus answered him, "Where I-leave [for] you-are-able not to-follow me now, so [=but] you-will-follow afterward."
33So having-answered, Peter said to-him, "If all will-be-caused-to-stumble in [=because of] you, I [myself] never will-be-caused-to-stumble."	29So Peter spoke to-him, "And if [=Maybe] all will-be-caused-to-stumble, but not I."	33So he-said to-him, "Lord, I-am ready to-travel with you and [=both] into prison and into death."	37Peter says to-him, "Lord, through what [=why] am-I-able not to-follow you right-now? I-will-put my soul on-behalf [=I will give my life to] you."
34Jesus spoke to-him, "Amen I-say to-you that in [=on] this night, prior-to rooster to-yell [=before the rooster crows] three-times you-will-disown me."	30And Jesus says to-him, "Amen I-say to-you that you, today, [on] this night, prior-to or rooster to-yell [=before the rooster crows] twice, you-will-disown me three-times."	34So he-said, "I-say to-you, Peter, [a] rooster will-yell [=will crow] not today until you-might-disown to-recognize [=you deny knowing] me three-times."	38Jesus answers, "You-will-put your soul on-behalf [=You will give your life to] me? Amen amen I-say to-you, [a] rooster might-yell [=might crow] not no [=ever] until which [time] you-might-disown me three-times."
35Peter says to-him, "Even-if it-might-be-necessary [for] me to-face-death together-with you, I-will-disown you not no [=ever]." And all the disciples said likewise.	31So he-was-talking emphatically, "If-ever it-might-be-necessary [for] me to-face-death-with you, I-will-disown you not no [=ever]." And so all were-saying in-the-same-way [=the same thing].		

[a] *omit* 𝔓75 B L T *pc* sy[s] cop; *So the lord said* ℵ A D W Θ Ψ *f* [1] *f* [13] 892 1006 1342 1506 𝔐 vg it sy[c] sy[p] sy[h].
🕮 Mt 26:31 – Zech 13:7; 🕮 Mk 14:27 – Zech 13:7

354. Luke's Two Swords

Luke 22:35-38

35And he-said to-them, "When I-sent-off you apart-from [=without a] moneybag and [a] pouch and
sandals, you-were-in-need no some [=you did not need anything, did you]?" So they-said, "Nothing."
36So he-said to-them, "But now the [one] having [a] moneybag, let-him-remove [=he must take it
along] and likewise [the one having a] pouch; and the [one] having no sword, let-him-sell his coat
and let-him-buy [one]. 37For I-say to-you that this having-been-written [=scripture] is-necessary
to-be-completed [=must be fulfilled] in me: 'AND HE-WAS-TAKEN-INTO-ACCOUNT WITH [=he
was included among] LAWLESSES [=those who are lawless]'; and for the around me has end [=for what
has been written about me is being fulfilled]." 38So they-said, "Lord, look! here [are] two swords." So he-
said to-them, "It-is fit [=sufficient]."

There are no variants in this pericope that appear in English.
🕮 Lk 22:37 – Isa 53:12

355. Jesus and the Disciples in Gethsemane

Matt 26:36-46	**Mark 14:32-42**	**Luke 22:39-46**	John 18:1; 12:27
36 Then Jesus comes with them into [a] small-region being-said [=called]	32 And they-go into [a] small-region which [had] the name	39 And having-gone-out he-traveled according-to the custom into the mountain of-the olives, and so the disciples followed him.	18:1 Jesus, having-said these [things] went-out together-with his disciples beyond the winter-stream of-the Kidron where there-was [a] garden, into which he entered and his disciples.
Gethsemane and he-says to-the disciples[a], "Be-seated his [=here] until having-gone-away there I-might-pray."	Gethsemane and he-says [to] his disciples, "Be-seated here until [=while] I-might-pray."		
		40 So having-happened upon the place he-said to-them, "Pray to-enter no [=Pray that you might not enter] into test [=a time of trial]."	12:27 "Now my soul has-been-disturbed, and what might-I-say? Father, save me out [=from] this hour? But [it is] through [=because of] this [that] I-came into this hour."
37 And having-taken-along Peter and the two sons of-Zebedee he-began to-be-grieved and to-be-agitated. 38 Then he-says to-them, "My soul is very-grieved, until [=even to] death. Stay here and stay-awake with me."	33 And he-takes-along Peter and James and John with him and he-began to-be-greatly-surprised [=to be very distressed] and to-be-agitated. 34 And he-says to-them, "My soul is very-grieved, until [=even to] death. Stay here and stay-awake."		
39 And having-preceded[b] [a] small [distance] he-fell upon his face praying and saying, "My father, if it-is possible, let-pass-away from me this cup; nevertheless, not like [=as] I [myself] wish but like [=as] you [wish]."	35 And having-preceded [a] small [distance] he-was-falling upon the land [=on the ground] and was-praying in-order-that, if it-is possible, the hour might-pass-away from him. 36 And he-was-saying, "Abba, father, all [things are] possible for-you, carry-from [=remove] from me this cup; but not what I wish but what you [wish]."	41 And he-drew-away from them as [=about a] throw [of a] stone [away], and having-put the [=his] knees [on the ground] he-was-praying, 42 saying, "Father, if you-want, carry-from [=remove] from me this cup; nevertheless, let-happen no [=not] my wish but your-own." [e]	
40 And he-comes to the disciples and finds them sleeping, and he-says to-Peter, "<u>You-had-the-strength</u> not thus to-stay-awake with me one	37 And he-comes and finds them sleeping, and he-says to-Peter, "Simon, are-you-sleeping? You-had-the-strength not to-stay-awake one hour?	45 And having-gotten-up from the prayer, [and] having-come to the disciples, he-found them perishing from the grief. 46 And he-said to-them, "What [=Why] are-you-sleeping?	

hour? [41]Stay-awake and pray in-order-that you-might-enter no [=not] into test [=a time of trial]. The spirit for-one [is] willing, so [=but] the flesh [is] ill [=weak]."	[38]Stay-awake and pray in-order-that you-might-come no [=not] into test [=a time of trial]. The spirit for-one [is] willing, so [=but] the flesh [is] ill [=weak]."	Having-gotten-up, pray in-order-that you-might-enter no [=not] into test [=a time of trial]."	
[42]Again having-gone-away out [=a] second [time], he-prayed saying, "My father, if it-is-able not [=for] this[c] to-pass-away if-ever no [=unless] I-might-drink it, let-happen your wish."	[39]And again having-gone-away he-prayed having-said the it [=same] word.		
[43]And having-come again he-found them sleeping, for their eyes were having-been-weighed-down [=heavy].	[40]And again, having-come he-found them[d] sleeping, for their eyes were being-very-heavy, and they-recognized [=they knew] not what [=how] they-might-answer him.		
[44]And having-excused [=having left] them again, [and] having-gone-away, he-prayed having-said again the it [=same] word out [=for a] third [time].			
[45]Then he-comes to the disciples and says to-them, "Are-you-sleeping the remainder [of the night] and are-you-giving-relief [=are you resting]?	[41]And he-comes [for] the third-time and says to-them, "Are-you-sleeping the remainder [of the night] and are-you-giving-relief [=are you resting]? It-receives-in-full [=That's enough]! The hour came.		
Look! the hour has-neared and the son of-the person is-delivered into [the] hands of-sinfuls [=of sinners]. [46]Rise, let-us-lead [=let us go]. Look! has-neared the [one] delivering me."	Look! the son of-the person is-delivered into the hands of-the sinfuls [=of sinners]. [42]Rise, let-us-lead [=let us go]. Look! the [one] delivering me has-neared."		

[a] *to-the disciples* B L 33 892 1006 1342 1506 𝔐 vg^{mss} cop^{samss}; *to-them* Θ f^{13} *pc*; *his disciples* ℵ A C D f^{1} 205 1424 *al* vg it^{mss} sy cop^{samss} cop^{bo}.
[b] *having-preceded* 𝔓^{37} 𝔓^{45} B 892 1424 1582 2542 *al* vg it^{mss} sy^{s} sy^{p} cop; *having-approached* 𝔓^{53} ℵ A C D L W Θ f^{1} f^{13} 33 1006 1342 1506 𝔐 sy^{h}.
[c] *omit* 𝔓^{37} ℵ A B C L W Δ 067 f^{1} 33 205 565 *pc* sy^{h} cop^{samss}; *cup* D Θ f^{13} 892 1006 1342 1506 𝔐 vg it^{mss} sy^{s} sy^{p} cop^{bo}.
[d] *And again, having-come, he-found them* ℵ B D L Ψ 083 892 1342 2427 *pc* sy^{s} cop; *And having-returned he-found them again* A C W Θ f^{1} f^{13} 1006 1506 𝔐 sy^{p} sy^{h}.
[e] *omit* 𝔓^{69} 𝔓^{75} ℵ^{1} A B T W 13* 579 *pc* sy^{s} cop^{sa}; [43]*So announcer from heaven, giving-strength him, was-seen to-him.* [44]*And having-happened in agony he-was-praying more-persistently, and his perspiration happened as drops of-blood descending upon the land* ℵ* ℵ^{2} D L Θ Ψ f^{1} 892 1006 1342 1506 𝔐 vg it^{mss} sy^{c} sy^{p} sy^{h}.

356. The Handing Over of Jesus

Matt 26:47-56	**Mark 14:43-52**	**Luke 22:47-53**	John 18:2-11
47And his yet [=while he was still] talking, look!	43And immediately his yet [=while he was still] talking,	47Yet his [While he was still] talking, look! [a] crowd, and the [one] being-said [=called] Judas, one of-the twelve, was-preceding them and neared Jesus	2And so Judas, the [one] delivering him, recognized the place, that [=because] Jesus often was-gathered there with his disciples. 3Therefore, Judas, having-taken the cohort and out [=some] attendants of-the high-priests and out [=some] of-the Pharisees, comes there with torches and lamps and weapons. 4Therefore Jesus having-recognized all the comings [=having seen all those coming] upon him went-out and says to-them "What are-you-searching?" 5They-answered him, "Jesus the Nazarite." He-says to-them, "I am." And so Judas, the [one] delivering him, had-stood with them. 6Therefore, like [=when] he-said to-them, "I am," they-went-away into the behind [=they stepped back] and fell groundward. 7Therefore again he-questioned them, "What are-you-searching?" So they-said, "Jesus the Nazarite." 8Jesus answered, "I-said to-you that I am. If therefore you-are-searching [for] me, excuse [=let] these [others] to-leave, 9in-order-that the word which he-said might-be-fulfilled, that 'I-destroyed not no-one out of-them whom you-had-given to-me.'" 10Therefore, Simon Peter, having [a] sword, hauled it [out] and struck the slave of-the high-priest and cut-away his right little-ear. So [=Now the] name [of] the slave was Malchus.
Judas, one of-the twelve,	Judas arrives, one of-the		
came			
and with him many [=a great] crowd from the high-priests and elders of-the whole-people with swords and clubs. 48So the [one] delivering him gave them [a] sign saying, "Whom ever I-might-like [=The one I kiss] is he; seize him."	twelve, and with him [a] crowd with swords and clubs along [=from] the high-priests and the scribes and the elders. 44So the [one] delivering him had-given [a] signal to-them saying, "Whom ever I-might-like [=The one I kiss] is he; seize him and lead-away [him] securely."	to-like [=to kiss] him.	
49And instantly, having-approached Jesus he-said, "Rejoice [=Greetings] rabbi," and he-kissed him. 50So Jesus said to-him, "Comrade, you-are-there upon which [=do what you came to do]." Then having-approached,	45And immediately having-come [and] having-approached him he-says, "[a] Rabbi," and he-kissed		
they-threw-on the hands upon [=they grabbed] Jesus and seized [=arrested] him.	him. 46So they-threw-on the hands [=they grabbed] him and they-seized [=they arrested] him.		
51And look!	47So [=But]	48So Jesus said to-him, "Judas, [is it with a] kiss [that] you-deliver the son of-the person [=of a man]?" 49So [=But] the [ones] around him, having-seen the being [=what was about to happen] said, "Lord, if will-we-strike-down [them] in [=with a] sword?" 50And some one out of-	
one of-the [ones] with Jesus having-reached-out the hand drew-away his sword and having-struck-down the slave of-the high-priest took-away his	some one of-the having-been-presents[b] [=of those who were present], having-drawn the sword struck the slave of-the high-priest and took-away his little-ear. 48And having-answered Jesus said to-them,	them struck-down the slave of-the high-priest and took-away his right ear. 51So [=But] having-answered Jesus said,	
outer-ear. 52Then Jesus says to-him, "Turn-away [=Return] your sword into its place, for all the			

having-takens [=those who
take up] the sword will-
destroy in [=will perish by
the] sword. 53 Or do-you-
suppose that I-am-able
not to-exhort my father
and he-will-be-present
[with] me right-now
[with] more [than] twelve
legions of-announcers
[=of angels]. 54 Therefore
how might-be-fulfilled
the writings [=scriptures]
that [say] it-is-necessary
[for it] to-happen thus."
55 In that hour Jesus said
to-the crowds, "Did-you-
go-out with swords and
clubs to-grip me like [you
would] upon [a] bandit?
According-to [=Day after]
day I-was-seating-myself
in the temple teaching
and you-seized me not.
56 So [=But] this whole
[thing] has-happened
in-order-that the writings
of-the prophets might-
be-fulfilled." Then all the
disciples having-excused
[=having left] him fled.

"Did-you-go-out with
swords and clubs to-grip
me like [you would] upon
[a] bandit? 49 According-to
[=Day after] day I-was-
being to [=I was among]
you in the temple teaching
and you-seized me not.
But
in-order-that the writings
[=scriptures] might-be-
fulfilled."
50 And having-excused
[=having left] him all
[=everyone] fled. 51 And some
young-man was-tagging-
along [with] him, having-
been-arrayed [=having been
dressed with only a] linen-
sheet upon [=over his] naked
[=nakedness], and they-seize
him, 52 so [=but] the [one]
having-quit [=having left
behind] the linen-cloth fled
naked[c].

"Permit until [=No more]
of-this." And having-
touched the outer-ear, he-
cured it. 52 So [=Then] Jesus
said to the high-priests
and generals of-the temple
and [the] elders having-
arrived upon him,
"Did-you-go-out with
swords and clubs like [you
would] upon [a] bandit?
53 According-to [=Day
after] day being me [=when
I was] with you in the
temple you-stretched-
out the [=you laid your]
hands upon me not, but
this is your hour and the
authority of-the darkness."

11 Therefore Jesus said
to-Peter, "Throw [=Put]
the sword into the sheath.
The cup which the father
has-given to-me, might-I-
drink it not no [=ever]?"

[a] *omit* ℵ B C* D L Θ Δ 579 1342 2427 pc vg it^{mss} sy^{s} cop^{bo}; *Rejoice* C^{2} W *f*^{1} *f*^{13} 205 565 892 1424 2542 *pc* cop^{sa}; *Rabbi* A 1006 1506 𝔐 sy^{p} sy^{h}.
[b] *So some one of-the having-been-presents* B C Θ Ψ *f*^{13} 33 892 1006 1342 1506 2427 𝔐 vg sy^{h}; *so one of-the having-been-presents* ℵ A L 579 700 *al* sy^{p}; *and some* D it; *and some one of-the having-been-presents* W *f*^{1} 205.
[c] *omit* ℵ B C L Ψ 892 2427 *pc* sy^{p} cop; *from them* A D W Θ *f*^{1} *f*^{13} 1006 1342 1506 𝔐 vg it^{mss} sy^{s} sy^{h}.

357. The Arrest of Jesus

Matt 26:57-58	**Mark 14:53-54**	**Luke 22:54-55**	John 18:12-16
57So the having-seizeds [=those who seized] Jesus led-away [him] to Caiaphas the high-priest, where the scribes and the elders were-gathered.	53And they-led-away Jesus to the high-priest, and all the high-priests and the elders and the scribes come-together.	54So having-gripped him they-led [him away] and led-in [him] into the home of-the high-priest.	12Therefore, the cohort and the legion-leader and the attendants of-the Judeans gripped Jesus and restrained him. 13And they-led [him] to Annas first; for he-was father-in-law of-Caiaphas, who was high-priest of-that annum. 14So [=Now] Caiaphas was the [one] having-advised the Judeans that it-is-profitable [=it is better for] one person to-face-death on-behalf of-the whole-people.
58So [=And] Peter was-following him from far-off until [=as far as] the courtyard of-the high-priest and having-entered within he-was-sitting with the attendants to-see the end.	54And Peter from far-off followed him until within into [=he was inside] the courtyard of-the high-priest, and he-was sitting-together with the attendants and staying-warm to the light [=at the fire].	So [=And] Peter was-following [from] far-off. 55So [=And] having-ignited[a] [a] fire in [the] middle of-the courtyard and having-been-seated-together[b] [around it], Peter sat [in the] middle of-them.	15So [=And] Simon Peter and another disciple was-following Jesus. So [=Now] that disciple was [an] acquaintance [of] the high-priest, and he-entered-with Jesus into the courtyard of-the high-priest, 16so [=but] Peter had-stood to [=at] the door [=gate] outside. Therefore the another [=other] disciple the acquaintance of the high-priest went-out and said [=spoke] to-the [female] door-keeper and he-led-in Peter.

[a] *having-ignited* 𝔓75 ℵ B L T 070 579 1506 *pc*; *having-touched* A D W G Θ Ψ *f*1 *f*13 205 892 1006 1342 2542 𝔐.
[b] *having-been-seated-together* 𝔓75 ℵ B L T 070 579 1506 *pc*; *their having-been-seated-together* A W Θ Ψ *f*1 *f*13 892 1006 1342 𝔐; *having-sat-around* D G 205 209 1582 2542 *pc*.

358. Peter's Denial (→ §364)

Matt 26:69-75	Mark 14:66-72	**Luke 22:56-62**	John 18:17, 25-27
69So Peter was-sitting outside in the courtyard,	66And Peter being [=while Peter was] below in the	56So having-seen him sitting to [=at] the light [=fire] and having-fixed-on [=looking closely at] him, some slave-girl	
and one slave-girl	courtyard, one of-the slave-girls of-the high-priest comes,		17Therefore the door-keeper slave-girl
approached him	67and having-seen Peter staying-warm, [and] having-beheld him, says,		
saying, "And you [=You also] were with-being Jesus	"You and [=also] were-being with the Nazarene,	said, "And this [person] was together-with him."	says to-Peter, "Are you [yourself] no [=not] and out [=also one] of-the disciples of-this person?" That [person] says, "I-am not."
the Galilean." 70So [=But] he-denied [it] in-front of-all saying, "I-recognize not what you-say."	Jesus." 68So [=But] he-denied [it] saying, "Neither do-I-recognize neither [=nor]	57So [=But] he-denied [it] saying, "I-recognize him not, woman."	

Matthew

71 So having-gone-out[a] into the gateway [=porch]
another [girl] saw him and says to-the [ones] there,
"This [person] was with Jesus the Nazarite."
72 And again he-denied with [a] sworn-oath that "I-recognize not the person." 73 So with small [=after a short time], the having-stoods [=those who were standing around],
having-approached, said to-Peter, "Truly you are and [=also] out [=one] of-them, for and [=even] your talk does [=makes] you obvious." 74 Then he-began to-call-curses and to-vow that "I-recognize not the person."
And instantly [a]
rooster yelled [=crowed]. 75 And
Peter remembered the speech having-been-said [by] Jesus that "Prior-to rooster to-yell [=Before a rooster crows] three-times you-will-disown me." And having-gone-out outside
he-wept bitterly.

Mark

fathom what you say." And he-went-out outside into the forecourt, and [a] rooster yelled [=crowed]. 69 And the slave-girl, having-seen him, began again to-say[b] to-the having-been-presents [=to those who were standing around] that "This [person] is out [=one] of-them."
70 So [=But] again he-was-
denying [it]. And with small [=after a short time], again the having-been-presents [=those who were standing around] were-saying to-Peter, "Truly you-are out [=one] of-them, for you-are and [=also] Galilean."
71 So [=But] he-began to-bind-himself-by-curses and <u>to-vow</u> that "I-recognize not this person [of] whom you-speak." 72 And immediately out of-second [=for a second time a] rooster yelled [=crowed]. And
Peter was-reminded [of] the <u>speech</u> like [=when] Jesus said to-him that "Prior-to rooster to-yell [=Before a rooster crows] twice, three-times you-will-disown me."
62 And having-thrown-on [=having thrown himself to the ground] he-was-weeping.

Luke

58 And with [=after a] little-bit, [an] other having-seen him spoke,
"And you [=You yourself also] are out [=one] of-them."
So [=But] Peter spoke[c], "Person, I-am not."
59 And as [=about] one hour having-passed, another some [=person] was-
insisting saying, "Upon truth [=Very truly] this [person] was and [=also] with him, for he-is and [=also] Galilean."
60 So [=But] Peter said, "Person, I-recognize not [that] which you-say."
And at-once his yet [while he was still] talking [a] rooster yelled [=crowed]. 61 And the lord, having-turned, beheld Peter, and Peter was-remind-about the speech of-the lord like [=when] he-said to-him that "Prior-to rooster to-yell [=Before a rooster crows] today, you-will-disown me three-times." 62 And having-gone-out outside
he-wept bitterly.

John

25 So Simon Peter was having-stood and staying-warm. Therefore they-said to-him,
"And are no you [=Are you yourself not also] out [=one of] his disciples?" That [person] denied [it] and said, "I-am not."
26 One of-the slaves of-the high-priest, being [a] kin of-whom [=of the person whose] outer-ear Peter cut-away, says "I saw you not [=Didn't I see you] with him in the garden?"
27 Therefore again Peter denied [it], and instantly
[a] rooster yelled [=crowed].

[a] *So having-gone-out* ℵ B L Z 13 33 892 1006 *pc*; *so having-gone-out him* A C W Θ f^{1} f^{13} 1342 1506 𝔐; *so his having-gone-out* D *pc* vg it^{mss}.
[b] *began again to-say* ℵ C L Δ Ψ 892 1342 1424 *pc*; *began to-say* D W Θ 565 579 700 2542 vg it sy^{s} sy^{p}; *again began to-say* A f^{1} f^{13} 33 1006 1506 𝔐 sy^{h}; *said* B 2427 *pc* cop.
[c] *Peter spoke* $\mathfrak{p}^{75}$ ℵ B L T 070 f^{13} *al*; *he-said* $\mathfrak{p}^{69}$ D sy^{s}; *he said* sy^{c}; *Peter said* A W Θ Ψ f^{1} 892 1006 1342 1506 𝔐.

359. Who Is It That Struck You? (→ §363)

Matt 26:67-68	Mark 14:65	**Luke 22:63-65**
[67]Then they-spat-on into his face and they-harassed him, so [=and] they-slapped [him] [68]saying, "Prophesy to-us, anointed-one, what [=who] is the [one] having-struck you?"	[65]And some began to-spit-on him and to-cloak his face and to-harass him and to-say to him, "Prophesy,"	[63]And the men controlling him[a] were-mocking him [and] beating [him] [64]and having-cloaked him[b] they-were-questioning [him] saying, "Prophesy, what [=who] is the [one] having-struck you?"
	and the attendants took him slaps [=in order to beat him].	[65]And blaspheming, they-were-saying many other [things] into [=against] him.

[a] *him* 𝔓[75] ℵ B D L T 070 579 2542 *al* vg it[mss] sy[s]; *Jesus* A W Θ Ψ *f* [1] *f* [13] 892 1006 1342 1506 𝔐 sy[c] sy[p] sy[h].
[b] *him* 𝔓[75] ℵ B L T *al* cop[bo]; *him they-were-hitting his face and* A* D W Θ Ψ *f* [13] 892 1006 1342 1506 𝔐 vg it[mss] sy[h]; *his face* 070 *f* [1] *pc* sy[s] sy[c] sy[p] cop[sa].
🕮 Mt 26:67 – Isa 50:6

SYNOPTIC STUDY GUIDE 15

Problems with 2DH: Major Minor Agreements?

Recall from Synoptic Study Guide 9 that places where Matthew and Luke agree together against Mark in Triple Tradition material (the "minor agreements") are a problem for the Two-Document Hypothesis. This is because these passages could be evidence that the author of Luke used Matthew, which would eliminate the necessity of Q. Recall also that the minor agreements really are minor: they are almost always single and insignificant words. But there are some minor agreements that are not so minor at all. These might be thought of as "major minor agreements."

One such agreement can be seen in §359. When the guards are mocking Jesus, Mark has them command Jesus to "Prophesy." Matthew and Luke on the other hand go on from there: "what is the having-struck you?" An agreement of five consecutive verbatim words is not in itself enough to require a direct literary relationship, but it certainly requires an explanation. How could Matthew and Luke agree on this if they wrote independently?

Could they have found the phrase in Q? Anything is possible, since we do not know the precise contents of the original Q; but this is not a solution supporters of the Two-Document Hypothesis want to pursue. To ascribe minor agreements to Q would erode some of the logic behind Q, part of which derives from the coherence of the Double Tradition; if one were to start adding words or passages like the minor agreements to Q, then Q would begin to lose its coherence, and with it likely its persuasiveness.

Most New Testament scholars are not convinced that the minor agreements, or even "major" minor agreements, are enough to posit a direct literary relationship between the gospels of Matthew and Luke. For them, phenomena like this suggest that the *real* relationship among the Synoptic Gospels is infinitely more complicated than these three simple hypotheses can possibly reflect. For example, the Two-Document and Farrer Hypotheses presuppose, for the sake of theoretical simplicity, that the copy of Mark available to the authors of Matthew and Luke was the very same. The Griesbach Hypothesis presupposes that the copy of Matthew available to the writers of Mark and Luke was the very same. Yet, given the testimony of the thousands of surviving manuscripts of the New Testament, which present hundreds of thousands of textual variants, this presupposition is extremely unreasonable. And aside from changes made by copyists, what if there were different editions of the gospels circulating, an early Mark and a late Mark, for example? And what if there were even scribal changes in circulating copies of these two versions of Mark? As you can see, the complexity rises exponentially once we depart from our simple hypotheses, which likely explains why scholars continue to favor them even though they recognize them as overly simplified.

360. Leading Jesus to the Sanhedrin (→ §365)

Matt 27:1	Mark 15:1a	**Luke 22:66**
[1]So morning having-happened, all the high-priests and the elders of-the whole-people took plot [=held a council] according-to [=against] Jesus with-the-result-that to-put-to-death him [=in order that they put him to death].	[1a]And immediately early[a] [=when day first broke], the high-priests having-done plot [=held a consultation] with the elders and scribes and the whole Sanhedrin. . . .	[66]And like [=when] day happened, the council-of-elders of-the whole-people, even high-priests and scribes, was-gathered, and they-led-away[b] him into their Sanhedrin.

[a] *early* ℵ B C D L Θ Ψ 565 892 1342 2427 2542 *pc*; *upon the early* A E W *f*[1] *f*[13] 33 346 543 700 1006 1506 𝔐 sy[h]; *early happened* 1424.
[b] *they-led-away* 𝔓[75] ℵ B D T *f*[13] 579 892 *pc*; *they-led-up* A L W Θ Ψ *f*[1] 1006 1342 1506 𝔐 sy; *they-led* N 28 *pc*.

361. False Testimony against Jesus

Matt 26:59-61	**Mark 14:55-59**	Thomas 71
[59]So the high-priests[a] and the Sanhedrin whole were-searching [for] false-witness-testimony according-to [=against] Jesus so-that they-might-put-to-death him, [60]and they-found not [=none out] of-many false-witnesses having-approached. So afterward two, having-approached, [61]said, "This [person] spoke [=said], 'I-am-able to-demolish the sanctuary of-god and through [=after] three days to-build [it again].'"	[55]So the high-priests and the whole Sanhedrin were-searching [for] witness-testimony according-to [=against] Jesus into [=in order] to-put-to-death him, and they-were-finding[b] not [=none]. [56]For many were-testifying-falsely according-to [=against] him and the witness-testimonies were not equal [=did not agree with each other]. [57]And some, having-gotten-up were-testifying-falsely according-to [=against] him, saying [58]that "We heard him saying that 'I will-demolish this sanctuary made-by-hand and through [=after] three days I-will-build another not-made-by-hand.'" [59]And their witness-testimony was equal nor thus [=did not agree even on this point].	Jesus said, "I will destroy <this> house, and no one will be able to build it < . . . >."

[a] *omit* ℵ B D L Θ *f*[13] 893 1506 *pc* vg it[mss] cop; *and the elders* A C W *f*[1] 33 1006 1342 𝔐 sy[p] sy[h].
[b] *they-were-finding* B D L W Δ Ψ *f*[1] 205 579 *pc*; *finding* ℵ A C Θ *f*[13] 892 1342 1506 2427 𝔐.

362. The Verdict against Jesus

Matt 26:62-66	**Mark 14:60-64**	**Luke 22:67-71**
[62]And the high-priest, having-gotten-up, said to-him, "Do-you-answer no-one [=Have you no answer for] what these [people] testify-against you?" [63]So [=But] Jesus was-being-silent. And the high-priest	[60]And the high-priest, having-gotten-up into middle [=before them], questioned Jesus saying, "Do-you-answer not no-one [=at all] what these [people] testify-against you?" [61]So [=But] he-was-being-silent and answered not no-one [=at all]. Again the high-priest was-	

Matt	Mark	Luke
said to-him, "I-swear-under-oath you according-to [=before] the living god in-order-that you-might-say to-us if you [yourself] are the anointed-one, the son of-god."	questioning him and says to-him, "Are you [yourself] the anointed-one, the son of-the blessed [one]?"	67 saying, "If you [yourself] are the anointed-one, say [so] to-us." So [=But] he-said to-them, "If-ever I-might-say [so] to-you, you-might-believe [it] not no [=at all]. 68 So [=And] if-ever I-might-beg [an answer from you], you-might-answer not no [=at all]. 69 So
64 Jesus says to-him, "You said [it].	62 So Jesus said, "I am,	
Nevertheless, I-say to-you, from right-now [=now on] you-will-see the son of-the person sitting out [=to the] right of-power and coming upon the clouds of-heaven."	and you-will-see the son of-the person out [=to the] right of-power sitting and coming with the clouds of-heaven."	from the now [=now on] the son of-the person will-be sitting out [=to the] right of-the power of-god."
		70 So all said, "Are you [yourself] therefore the son of-god?" So [=But] he-spoke to them, "You say that I am."
65 Then the high-priest rent his coats saying[a], "He-blasphemed. What yet [=further] need have-we of-witnesses? Look, now you-heard the blasphemy.	63 So the high-priest having-rent his tunics says, "What yet [=further] need have-we of-witnesses? 64 You-heard the blasphemy.	71 So [=But] they-said, "What yet [=further] need of-witness [=of testimony] have-we? For we-heard they [=it ourselves] from his mouth."
66 What suppose you [=is your verdict]?" So having-answered they-said, "He-is answerable [=deserving] of-death."	What [=How] does-it-appear to-you?" So all judged-against him to-be answerable [=deserving] of-death."	

[a] *saying* ℵ^2 B C^2 D L Z Θ 33 700 892 *pc* vg it; *saying that* A C* W f^1 f^{13} 1006 1342 1506 𝔐; *saying, "Look"* ℵ* sy^p.

363. Who Is It That Struck You? (→ §359)

Matt 26:67-68	**Mark 14:65**	Luke 22:63-65
67 Then they-spat-on into his face and they-harassed him, so [=and] they-slapped [him] 68 saying, "Prophesy to-us, anointed-one, what [=who] is the [one] having-struck you?"	65 And some began to-spit-on him and to-cloak his face and to-harass him and to-say to him, "Prophesy," and the attendants took him slaps [=in order to beat him].	63 And the men controlling him[a] were-mocking him [and] beating [him] 64 and having-cloaked him[b] they-were-questioning [him] saying, "Prophesy, what [=who] is the [one] having-struck you?" 65 And blaspheming, they-were-saying many other [things] into [=against] him.

[a] *him* 𝔓^{75} ℵ B D L T 070 579 2542 *al* vg it^{mss} sy^s; *Jesus* A W Θ Ψ f^1 f^{13} 892 1006 1342 1506 𝔐 sy^c sy^p sy^h.
[b] *him* 𝔓^{75} ℵ B L T *al* cop^{bo}; *him they-were-hitting his face and* A* D W Θ Ψ f^{13} 892 1006 1342 1506 𝔐 vg it^{mss} sy^h; *his face* 070 f^1 *pc* sy^s sy^c sy^p cop^{sa}.
📖 Mt 26:67 – Isa 50:6

Q 17:35 (§288, p. 209)
Luke 22:71 (§362, p. 278)

364. Peter's Denial (→ §358)

Matt 26:69-75	**Mark 14:66-72**	Luke 22:56-62	John 18:17, 25-27
69 So Peter was-sitting outside in the courtyard,	66 And Peter being [=While Peter was] below in the	56 So having-seen him sitting to [=at] the light [=fire] and having-fixed-on [=looking closely at] him,	
and one slave-girl	courtyard, one of-the slave-girls of-the high-priest comes,	some slave-girl	17 Therefore the door-keeper slave-girl
approached him	67 and having-seen Peter staying-warm, [and]		
saying, "And you [=You also] were with-being Jesus the Galilean."	having-beheld him, says, "You and [=also] were-being with the Nazarene, Jesus."	said, "And this [person] was together-with him."	says to-Peter, "Are you [yourself] no [=not] and out [=also one] of-the disciples of-this person?"
70 So [=But] he-denied [it] in-front of-all saying, "I-recognize not what you-say."	68 So [=But] he-denied [it] saying, "Neither do-I-recognize neither [=nor] fathom what you say."	57 So [=But] he-denied [it] saying, "I-recognize him not, woman."	That [person] says, "I-am not."
71 So having-gone-out[a] into the gateway [=porch]	And he-went-out outside into the forecourt, and [a] rooster yelled [=crowed].		
another [girl] saw him and says to-the [ones] there,	69 And the slave-girl, having-seen him, began again to-say[b] to-the having-been-presents [=to those who were standing around] that	58 And with [=after a] little-bit, [an] other having-seen him spoke,	25 So Simon Peter was having-stood and staying-warm. Therefore they-said to-him,
"This [person] was with Jesus the Nazarite."	"This [person] is out [=one] of-them."	"And you [=You yourself also] are out [=one] of-them."	"And are no you [=Are you yourself not also] out [=one of] his disciples?"
72 And again he-denied with [a] sworn-oath that "I-recognize not the person."	70 So [=But] again he-was-denying [it].	So [=But] Peter spoke[c], "Person, I-am not."	That [person] denied [it] and said, "I-am not."
73 So with small [=after a short time], the having-stoods [=those who were standing around], having-approached, said to-Peter, "Truly you are and [=also] out [=one] of-them, for and [=even] your talk does [=makes] you obvious."	And with small [=after a short time], again the having-been-presents [=those who were standing around] were-saying to-Peter, "Truly you-are out [=one] of-them, for you-are and [=also] Galilean."	59 And as [=about] one hour having-passed, another some [person] was-insisting saying, "Upon truth [=Very truly] this [person] was and [=also] with him, for he-is and [=also] Galilean."	26 One of-the slaves of-the high-priest, being [a] kin of-whom [=of the person whose] outer-ear Peter cut-away, says "I saw you not [=Didn't I see you] with him in the garden?"
74 Then he-began to-call-curses and to-vow that "I-recognize not the person."	71 So [=But] he-began to-bind-himself-by-curses and to-vow that "I-recognize not this person [of] whom you-speak."	60 So [=But] Peter said, "Person, I-recognize not [that] which you-say."	27 Therefore again Peter denied [it],
And instantly [a] rooster yelled [=crowed].	72 And immediately out of-second [=for a second time a] rooster yelled [=crowed].	And at-once his yet [while he was still] talking [a] rooster yelled [=crowed].	and instantly [a] rooster yelled [=crowed].

75 And Peter remembered the speech having-been-said [by] Jesus that "Prior-to rooster to-yell [=Before a rooster crows] three-times you-will-disown me." And having-gone-out outside he-wept bitterly.	And Peter was-reminded [of] the speech like [=when] Jesus said to-him that "Prior-to rooster to-yell [=Before a rooster crows] twice, three-times you-will-disown me." And having-thrown-on [=having thrown himself to the ground] he-was-weeping.	61 And the lord, having-turned, beheld Peter, and Peter called-to-mind the speech of-the lord like [=when] he-said to-him that "Prior-to rooster to-yell [=Before a rooster crows] today, you-will-disown me three-times." 62 And having-gone-out outside he-wept bitterly.	

[a] *So having-gone-out* ℵ B L Z 13 33 892 1006 *pc*; *so having-gone-out him* A C W Θ f^{1} f^{13} 1342 1506 𝔐; *so his having-gone-out* D *pc* vg it^{mss}.
[b] *began again to-say* ℵ C L Δ Ψ 892 1342 1424 *pc*; *began to-say* D W Θ 565 579 700 2542 vg it sy^{s} sy^{p}; *again began to-say* A f^{1} f^{13} 33 1006 1506 𝔐 sy^{h}; *said* B 2427 *pc* cop.
[c] *Peter spoke* 𝔭^{75} ℵ B L T 070 f^{13} *al*; *he-said* 𝔭^{69} D sy^{s}; *he said* sy^{c}; *Peter said* A W Θ Ψ f^{1} 892 1006 1342 1506 𝔐.

365. Jesus Is Taken to Pilate (→ §360)

Matt 27:1-2	**Mark 15:1**	**Luke** 22:66; **23:1**	John 18:28
1 So morning having-happened, all the high-priests and the elders of-the whole-people took plot [=held a council] according-to [=against] Jesus with-the-result-that to-put-to-death him [=in order that they put him to death]. 2 And having-restrained him they-led-away [him] and delivered [him] to-Pilate[a] the ruler.	1 And immediately early[b] [=when day first broke], the high-priests having-done plot [=held a consultation] with the elders and scribes and the whole Sanhedrin [and] having-restrained Jesus they-carried-away and delivered [him] to-Pilate.	66 And like [=when] day happened, the council-of-elders of-the whole-people, even high-priests and scribes, was-gathered, and they-led-away[c] him into their Sanhedrin. 23:1 And having-gotten-up, everyone [of] the multitude of-them, they-led him upon [=to] Pilate.	28 Therefore, they-lead Jesus from Caiaphas into the praetorium. So [=Now] it-was early [in the morning]. And they [themselves] entered not into the praetorium, in-order-that they-might-be-contaminated no [=not] but might-eat the passover [meal].

[a] *to-Pilate* ℵ B L 33 *pc* sy^{s} sy^{p} cop; *to-Pontius Pilate* A C W Θ f^{1} f^{13} 892 1006 1342 1506 𝔐 vg it sy^{h}.
[b] *early* ℵ B C D L Θ Ψ 565 892 1342 2427 2542 *pc*; *upon the early* A E W f^{1} f^{13} 33 346 543 700 1006 1506 𝔐 sy^{h}; *early happened* 1424.
[c] *they-led-away* 𝔭^{75} ℵ B D T f^{13} 579 892 *pc*; *they-led-up* A L W Θ Ψ f^{1} 1006 1342 1506 𝔐 sy; *they-led* N 28 *pc*.

366. Matthew's Interpretation of the Death of Judas

Matt 27:3-10

3 Then Judas, the [one] delivering[a] him, having-seen that he-was-judged-against, having-been-sorry turned [=returned] the thirty silver-coins to-the high-priests and elders, 4 saying, "I-sinned having-delivered [=by delivering] innocent blood." So [=But] they-said, "What [is that] to us? You [yourself]

will-see [to it]." [5]And having-tossed the silver-coins into the sanctuary he-retreated, and having-
gone-away he-hanged-himself. [6]So [=But] the high-priests, having-taken the silver-coins, said,
"It-is-permitted not to-throw them into the temple-treasury, as-a-result-of [=because] it-is honor
of-blood [=blood money]." [7]So having-taken plot [=after conferring], they-bought out [=with] them
the field of-the potter into [=as a] burial-place of-the strangers [=for foreigners]. [8]For-this-reason
that field was-called field of-blood until [=even still] today. [9]Then the having-been-said [=what had
been said] through [=by] Jeremiah the prophet was-fulfilled, saying, "AND THEY-TOOK THE
THIRTY SILVER-COINS, THE HONOR OF-THE HAVING-BEEN-HONORED [=the price that
was set] WHICH THEY-HONORED FROM [the] SONS OF-ISRAEL, [10]AND THEY-GAVE THEM
INTO THE FIELD OF-THE POTTER JUST-LIKE [the] LORD DIRECTED ME."

[a] *delivering* B L 33 *pc* cop; *having-delivered* ℵ A C W Θ *f*[1] *f*[13] 1006 1342 1506 𝔐.
📖 Mt 27:9 – Zech 11:13; Jer 32:6-16; Jer 18:1-3

367. Jesus' Trial before Pilate

Matt 27:11-14	Mark 15:2-5	Luke 23:2-5	John 18:29-38
		[2]So they-began to-accuse him saying, "We-found this [person] distorting our nation and hindering [=encouraging people not] to-give tributes to-Caesar and saying [that he] himself to-be [=is the] anointed-one, [a] king."	[29]Therefore Pilate went-out outside to them and speaks, "What accusation do-you-carry according-to [=against] this person?" [30]They-answered and said to-him, "If no [=Unless] this [person] was doing bad [things], we-delivered him not ever [=we would never have delivered him] to-you."
[11]So Jesus was-stood[a] in-front of-the ruler; and the ruler questioned him saying, "Are you [yourself] the king of-the Judeans?" So [=But] Jesus spoke[b], "You say [so]." [12]And in the to-be-accused him [=when he was being accused] under [=by] the high-priests and elders, he-answered no-one.	[2]And Pilate questioned him, "Are you [yourself] the king of-the Judeans?" So [=But] having-answered he-says to-him, "You say [so]." [3]And the high-priests were-accusing him [of] many [things].	[3]So Pilate begged him saying, "Are you [yourself] the king of-the Judeans?" So having-answered he-spoke to-him, "You say [so]."	[31]Therefore Pilate said to-them, "You [yourselves] take him and judge him according-to your law." The Judeans said to-him, "It-is-permitted not for-us to-kill no-one [=anyone]," [32]in-order-that the word of-Jesus might-be-fulfilled which he-said indicating what-kind-of death he-was-intending to-face-death [=what sort of death he was to die].
[13]Then Pilate says to-him, "Do-you-hear not how-great [=how much] they-testify-against you?"	[4]So Pilate was-questioning him again saying, "You-answer no-one not [=at all]? Look how-great [=how much] they-accuse you."	[4]So Pilate said to the high-priests and the crowds, "I-find no-one [=no] blame in this person." [5]So [=But] they-were-urging [him]	[33]Therefore Pilate entered again into the praetorium and yelled [=called to] Jesus and said to-him, "Are you [yourself] the king of-the Judeans?" [34]Jesus answered, "You say this from yourself or did-say anothers [=did others say this] to-you around [=concerning] me?" [35]Pilate answered, "Surely-not, am I Judean? Your-own nation and the high-priests delivered you to-me. What did-you-do?" [36]Jesus answered, "My-own kingdom is not out of-this [=is not from this] world.

Matthew	Mark	Luke	John
[14]And he-answered him not nor to one speech [=any of the charges], with-the-result-that to-be-astonished extremely [=it exceedingly surprised] the ruler.	[5]But Jesus no-longer answered no-one [=anyone] with-the-result-that to-be-astonished [=it astonished] Pilate.	saying that "He-incites the whole-people teaching according-to [=throughout] the whole of-Judea, and[c] having-begun from [=starting in] the Galilee until [=and as far as] here."	If my-own kingdom was out of-this [=from this] world, my-own attendants were-struggling [=would be fighting] in-order-that I-might-be-delivered no [=not] to-the Judeans. So [=But] now my-own kingdom is not from-here." [37]Therefore Pilate said to-him, "So-then you [yourself] are [a] king?" Jesus answered, "You say that I-am [a] king. I [myself] have-been-begotten into [=for] this and into [=for] this I-have-come into the world, in-order-that I-might-testify to-the truth. All the being out [=Everyone who belongs to] the truth hears my voice." [38]Pilate says to-him, "What is truth?" And having-said this again he-went-out to the Judeans and says to-them, "I find in him no-one [=no] reason [to arrest him]."

[a] *was-stood* ℵ B C L Θ f[1] 33 *pc*; *stood* A W f[13] 892 1006 1342 1506 𝔐.
[b] *omit* ℵ L 33 700 892 *pc* cop[sa] cop[bo]; *to-him* A B W Θ f[1] f[13] 1006 1342 506 𝔐 vg it[mss] sy.
[c] *and* ℵ B L T 070 *pc* sy; *omit* 𝔭[75] A D W Θ Ψ f[1] f[13] 892 1006 1506 𝔐 it.

368. Luke's Trial before Herod Antipas

Luke 23:6-12

[6]So Pilate, having-heard [this], questioned [him] if the person is Galilean. [7]And having-understood
that he-is out [=under] the authority of-Herod he-sent-up him to Herod, being him [=who was]
and [=also] in Jerusalems in these days. [8]So Herod, having-seen Jesus, rejoiced extremely, for
he-was wishing to-see him out fit times [=for a long time] through the to-hear [=because of what
he had heard][a] around [=concerning] him and he-was-hoping to-see some sign happening [=being
performed] under [=by] him. [9]So he-was-questioning him in fit words [=at length], so [=but] he
[himself] answered him no-one [=not]. [10]So the high-priests and the scribes had-stood vigorously
accusing him. [11]So Herod together-with his troops, having-viewed-with-disdain him and having-
mocked [and] having-arrayed [him in] sumptuous raiment sent-up him to-Pilate. [12]So even Herod
and Pilate happened [=became] friends with one-another in the it [=on that same] day, for they-
were-existing-previously being in enmity to them [=each other].

[a] *omit* 𝔭[75] ℵ B D L T Θ f[1] 205 579 2542 *al* sy[s] sy[c] cop; *many* A W Ψ f[13] 892 1006 1506 𝔐 vg it[mss] sy[p] sy[h].

369. Luke's Decision of Pilate

Luke 23:13-16

13 So Pilate having-called-together the high-priests and the magistrates and the whole-people, 14 said
to them, "You-offered this person to-me like [=as one] turning-away the whole-people, and look!
having-assessed [him] in-the-sight of-you I [myself] found in this person nothing [=no] blame of
which you-accuse according-to [=against] him. 15 But nor [did] Herod, for he-sent-up him [back] to
us, and look! no-one [=nothing] worthy of-death is having-been-practiced [=has been done by] him.
16 Therefore, having-disciplined him, I-will-release [him]."

There are no variants in this pericope that appear in English.

370. Jesus or Barabbas?

Matt 27:15-23	Mark 15:6-14	Luke 23:17-23	John 18:39-40
15 So [=Now] according-to [=at each] feast, the ruler had-been-accustomed to-release one prisoner to-the crowd, whom [ever] they-were-wishing.	6 So [=Now] according-to [=at each] feast he-was-releasing [=he would release] to-them one prisoner whom they-were-making-apologies [=they were defending].	17 d	39 "So there-is [a] habit to-you [=among you] in-order-that I-might-release to-you one [prisoner] in [=on] the passover.
16 So then [=Now at that time], they-were-having [=they had a] notorious prisoner being-said [=who was called] [a] Barabbas.	7 So [=Now] there-was the [one] being-said [=who was called] Barabbas, having-been-restrained with the insurrectionists, whoever [=someone who] had-done [=had committed] murder in the insurrection.	18 So they-cried-out all-together saying, "Remove this [man], so [=but] release Barabbas to-us," 19 whoever [=who] was having-been-thrown [=thrown] in prison through [=because of an] insurrection what having-happened [=which happened] in the city and [because of] murder.	
17 Therefore, their having-been-gathered [=when they had been gathered], Pilate said to-them, "What [=Who] do-you-wish [that]	8 And the crowd, having-ascended[b], began to-ask [him to do] just-as he-was-doing for-them. 9 So [=But] Pilate answered them saying, "Do-you-wish		

Matt 27:18-23	Mark 15:10-14	Luke 23:20-23	John
I-might-release to-you, Barabbas or Jesus the being-said [=one who is called the] anointed-one?" 18 For he-recognized that they-delivered him through envy.	[that] I-might-release to-you the king of-the Judeans?" 10 For he-was-knowing that the high-priests had-delivered him through envy.		Therefore do-you-want [that] I-might-release to-you the king of-the Judeans?"
19 So his [=while he was] sitting upon the judicial-bench, his woman [=wife] sent-off [word] to him saying, "Not-one to-you and [=Have nothing to do with] that righteous [man], for I-suffered many [things] today according-to [=because of a] dream through [=concerning] him."			
20 So [=Now] the high-priests and the elders persuaded the crowds in-order-that they-might-ask [for] Barabbas, so they-might-destroy Jesus. 21 So [=But] having-answered, the ruler said to-them, "What [=Who] from the two do-you-wish [that] I-might-release to-you?"	11 So [=But] the high-priests incited the crowd in-order-that he-might-release Barabbas to-them rather [=instead].	20 So again Pilate, wishing to-release Jesus, addressed them.	
So they-said, "Barabbas." 22 Pilate says to-them, "What therefore might-I-do [with] Jesus the being-said [=who is called the] anointed-one?"	12 So [=But] Pilate having-answered again was-saying[c] to-them, "What therefore do-you-wish [that] I-might-do [with the one] whom you-say [=you call] the king of-the Judeans?"		40 Therefore they-screamed again, "No this [=Not person], but Barabbas." So [=Now] Barabbas was [a] bandit.
All [of them] say, "Let-him-be-crucified."	13 So again they-cried, "Crucify him."	21 So [=But] they-were-yelling-out saying, "Crucify, crucify him."	
23 So he-spoke, "For what bad [thing] did-he-do?"	14 So [=But] Pilate was-saying to-them, "For what did-he-do [that was] bad?"	22 So he-said to them [for a] third [time], "For what bad [thing] did-do this [person]? I-found in him no-one [=no] blame [worthy] of-death. Therefore, having-disciplined him, I-will-release [him]."	
So [=But] they-were-crying excessively [=even more loudly] saying,	So [=But] they-cried excessively [=even more loudly],	23 So [=But] they-were-laying-upon [=they were insisting with] great voices asking [for]	

"Let-him-be-crucified."	"Crucify him."	him to-be-crucified, and their voices were-over-powering.	

[a] *omit* א A B D L W f^{13} 892 1006 1342 1506 𝔐 vg it sy^{p} sy^{h} cop; *Jesus* Θ f^{1} 700 *pc* sy^{s}.
[b] *having-ascended* א* B D 892 2427 vg it^{mss} cop; *having-shouted-out* $א^{2}$ A C W Θ f^{1} f^{13} 𝔐 sy.
[c] *having-answered again was-saying* א B C 1342 2427 *pc* vg it^{mss}; *having-answered again said* A Ψ f^{1} f^{13} 33 892 1006 1506 𝔐; *having-answered said* D W 13 69 1424 *pc*; *answered again* Θ 565 700.
[d] *omit* $𝔓^{75}$ A B L T 070 892 *pc* vg^{mss} cop^{sa}; *[17]So he-was-having inevitable to-release one according-to feast* א D W Θ Ψ f^{1} f^{13} 1006 1342 1506 𝔐 vg it^{mss} sy^{p} sy^{h}.

371. The Sentencing of Jesus

Matt 27:24-26	**Mark 15:15**	**Luke 23:24-25**
[24]So Pilate, having-seen that he-achieves no-one [=he was achieving nothing], but rather [that] commotion happens [=a riot was starting], [and] having-taken water washed-off the [=his] hands across-from[a] [=in front of] the crowd saying, "I-am innocent from the blood of-this [man]. You [yourselves] will-see." [25]And all the whole-people, having-answered, said, "His blood [be] upon us and upon our descendants."	[15]So Pilate, wanting to-do fit [=right with] the crowd,	[24]And Pilate passed-sentence [for] their demand to-happen.
[26]Then he-released Barabbas to-	released Barabbas to-them,	[25]So he-released the [one] having-been-thrown into prison through [=because of] insurrection and murder [for] whom they-were-asking,
them, so [=but] having-whipped Jesus, he-delivered [him] in-order-that he-might-be-crucified.	and having-whipped [him], he-delivered Jesus in-order-that he-might-be-crucified.	so [=but] he-delivered Jesus [according to] their wish.

[a] *across-from* א A L W Θ f^{1} f^{13} 33 892 1006 1342 1506 𝔐; *ahead* B D.

372. The Mocking of Jesus

Matt 27:27-31a	**Mark 15:16-20a**	John 19:2-3
[27]Then the soldiers of-the ruler, having-taken-along Jesus into the praetorium, gathered the whole cohort upon [=around] him. [28]And having-stripped him they-put-around him [a] scarlet soldier's-robe.	[16]So the soldiers led-away him within the courtyard, which is [the] praetorium, and they-call-together the whole cohort. [17]And they-have-on [=they dress] him [in a] purple-	[2]And the soldiers
[29]And having-woven [a] crown out of-thorny-plants, they-placed [it] upon his head and [placed a] reed in his right [hand],	cloth and having-woven [a] thorny crown, they-put-around [=they put it on] him.	having-woven [a] crown out of-thorny-plants, they-placed [it upon] his head and arrayed him [in a] purple coat.

Matthew

and having-knelt in-front of-him
they-mocked[a] him saying, "Rejoice,
king[b] of-the Judeans." 30 And having-
spat-on into him they-took the reed
and were-hitting [him] into [=on] his
head.
31a And when [=after] they-mocked
him, they-stripped him [of] the
soldier's-robe and clothed him [in]
his coats . . .

Mark

18 And they-began to-greet him,
"Rejoice, king of-the Judeans." 19 And
they-were-hitting his head [with a]
reed and were-spitting-on him and
putting the knees [to the ground]
they-were-worshiping him.
20a And when [=after] they-mocked
him, they-stripped him [of] the
purple-cloth and clothed him [in]
his coats.

John

3 And they-were-coming to him and
were-saying, "Rejoice, the king of-
the Judeans," and they-were-giving
him slaps.

[a] *they-mocked* ℵ B D L 33 892 *pc*; *they-were-mocking* A W Θ f^1 f^{13} 1006 1342 1506 𝔐 vg it^{mss}.
[b] *king* B D Δ Θ 0250 f^1 205 *al*; *the king* ℵ A L W f^{13} 33 892 1006 1342 1506 𝔐.

373. The Enlisting of Simon the Cyrenian

Matt 27:31b-32

31b . . . and they-led-away
him into the [=in order]
to-crucify [him].
32 So going-out they-found
[a] Cyrenian person,
Simon [by] name; they-
enlisted this [person]
in-order-that
he-might-remove [=he
might carry] his cross.

Mark 15:20b-21

20b And they-lead-out
him in-order-that they-
might-crucify him.
21 And they-enlist some
passing-by [=passerby],
Simon, [a] Cyrenian,
coming from [a] field, the
father of-Alexander and
of-Rufus, in-order-that
he-might-remove [=he
might carry] his cross.

Luke 23:26

26 And like [=when] they-
led-away him,
having-taken-hold-of
Simon, some Cyrenian
coming from [a] field,
they-placed the cross [on]
him to-carry from-behind
[=behind] Jesus.

John 19:16-17a

16 Therefore then
they-delivered him
to-them in-order-that
he-might-be-crucified.
Therefore they-took-along
Jesus,
17a and bearing the cross
himself . . .

There are no variants in this pericope that appear in English.

374. Luke's "Daughters of Jerusalem"

Luke 23:27-31

27 So many [=a great] multitude of-the whole-people, and of-women
who were-cutting [=were beating their breasts] and mourning, were-
following him. 28 So [=But] Jesus, having-turned to them, said,
"Daughters of-Jerusalem, weep no [=not] upon [=over] me, nevertheless
[=but rather] weep upon themselves [=for yourselves] and upon [=for]
your descendants. 29 That [=Because] look! days come in which they-
will-say, 'Fortunate [are] the sterile and the abdomens [=wombs] which
begat not and the breasts which nourished[a] not.' 30 THEN THEY-
WILL-BEGIN TO-SAY TO-THE MOUNTAINS, 'FALL UPON US'
AND TO-THE HILLS, 'COVER US.' 31 That [=Because] if they-do these
[things] in the verdant club [=when the tree is green], what might-happen
in [=when] the [tree is] withered?"

Thomas 79

A woman in the crowd said to him, "Lucky are the womb that bore you and the breasts that fed you." He said to <her>, "Lucky are those who have heard the word of the Father and have truly kept it. For there will be days when you will say, 'Lucky are the womb that has not conceived and the breasts that have not given milk.'"

[a] *nourished* 𝔓^{75} ℵ B C* L 070 892 1582 2542* *pc*; *breast-fed* C^2 D Θ Ψ f^1 205 579 2542^C *pc*; *nursed* A W f^{13} 33 1006 1342 1506 𝔐 vg.
🕮 Lk 23:29 – Isa 54:1; 🕮 Lk 23:30 – Hos 10:8

375. The Crucifixion of Jesus

Matt 27:33-38	Mark 15:22-28	Luke 23:32-34	John 19:17b-24
		32 So and [=also] two other criminals[c] were-being-led together-with him to-be-abolished [=to be executed].	17 b . . . he-went-out into the being-said [=what is called] the Place [of a] Skull, which in-Hebrew is-said [=is called] Golgotha, 18 where they-crucified him, and with him two anothers [=others] from-here and from-here [=one on either side of him], so [=and] Jesus [in the] middle. 19 So Pilate and [=also] wrote [a] notice and put [it] upon the cross. [On it] was having-been-written [=written], "Jesus the Nazarite the king of-the Judeans." 20 Therefore many of-the Judeans read this notice, that [=because] the place where Jesus was-crucified was near the city. And it-was having-been-written in-Hebrew, in-Roman-letters, [and] in-Greek-letters. 21 Therefore the high-priests of-the Judeans were-saying to-Pilate, "Write no [=not], 'The king of-the Judeans,' but that 'That [man] said, I am king of-the Judeans.'" 22 Pilate answered, "[That] which I-have-written, I-have-written." 23 Therefore the soldiers, when they-crucified Jesus, took his coats and did [=divided them into] four parts, [a] part to-each soldier, and the tunic. So [=Now] the tunic was seamless, interwoven out from-the-start through whole [=woven in one piece from top to bottom]. 24 Therefore they-said to one-another, "Let-us-rip it no [=not] but let-us-have-as-one's-lot [=let us draw straws] around [=concerning] of-what [=whose] it-will-be, in-order-that the writing might-be-fulfilled, "THEY-DIVIDED-UP MY COATS [among] THEMSELVES, AND UPON [=over] MY APPAREL THEY THREW [=drew a] STRAW." Therefore for-one the soldiers did these [things].
33 And having-come into [a] place being-said [=which is called] Golgotha, which is being-said [=means] Place [of a] Skull, 34 they-gave him wine to-drink having-been-mixed with bitter-gall, and having-tasted [it] he-wished not to-drink [it]. 35 So having-crucified him	22 And they-carry him upon [=up to] the place [called] Golgotha, which is being-translated Place [of a] Skull. 23 And they-were-giving him wine having-been-flavored-with-myrrh, so [=but] which he-took not. 24 And they-crucify him	33 And when they-came upon the place being-called [=which is called] The Skull, there they-crucified him and the criminals [one of] which for-one out [=was to the] right so [=and the other] which out [=was on the] left-hand [side].	
they-divided-up his coats [by] throwing [=drawing a] straw.	and[a] divide-up his coats throwing [=drawing a] straw upon [=over] them [to decide] what [=who] might-remove [=might take] what. 25 So [=Now] it-was [the] third hour [=nine a.m.] and they-crucified him.	34 d So dividing-up his coats they-threw [=they drew] straws [over them].	
36 And sitting they-were-keeping [watch over] him there. 37 And above his head they-placed his reason [=charge] having-been-written [=on which was written], "This is Jesus the king of-the Judeans." 38 Then two bandits are-crucified together-with him, one out [=to the] right and one out [=to the] left.	26 And there-was the inscription [of] his reason [=charge] having-been-inscribed [with the words], "The king of-the Judeans." 27 And they-crucify two bandits together-with him, one out [=to the] right and one out [=on] his left. [b]		

[a] *they-crucify him and* B L Ψ 92 2427 it; *and having-crucified him* ℵ A C D Θ f^1 f^{13} 33 1006 1342 1506 𝔐 sy[h].

Continued

[b] *omit* ℵ A B C D Ψ 2427 *pc* sy[s] cop; [28]*And the writing was-fulfilled saying, "He-was-taken-into-account with the lawlesses"* L Θ 083 *f*[1] *f*[13] 892 1006 1342 1506 𝔐 vg it[mss] sy[p] sy[h].
[c] *two other criminals* 𝔭[75] ℵ B; *others, two criminals* A C D L W Θ Ψ *f*[1] *f*[13] 33 892 1006 1342 1506 𝔐.
[d] *omit* 𝔭[75] ℵ[1] B D* W Θ 070 579 *pc* sy[s] cop[sa]; *So Jesus was-saying, "Father, excuse them, for they-recognize not what they-do."* ℵ* ℵ[2] A C D[2] L Ψ *f*[1] *f*[13] 33 892 1006 1506 𝔐 vg it[mss] sy[s] sy[p] sy[h].
🕮 Mt 27:35 – Ps 22:18; 🕮 Mk 15:28 – Isa 53:12; 🕮 Jn 19:24– Ps 22:18

376. Jesus Is Mocked by Passersby

Matt 27:39-43	Mark 15:29-32a	Luke 23:35-38
[39]So the traveling-bys [=those who	[29]And the traveling-bys [=those who	[35]And the whole-people had-stood [there] catching-sight-of [=watching], so and [=and even] the magistrates
were passing by] were-blaspheming him, moving [=shaking] their heads, [40]and saying, "The [one] demolishing the sanctuary and in three days building [it again], save yourself, if you-are the son of-god, descend from the cross." [41]And likewise the high-priests, mocking [him] with the scribes and elders[a], were-saying, [42]"He-saved anothers [=others], he-is-able not to-save himself. He-is[b] [the] king of-Israel, let-him-descend now from the cross and we-will-believe upon [=in] him. [43]He-has-persuaded upon [=He trusts in] god, let-him-rescue him now if he-wishes, for he-said that of-god I-am son.'"	were passing by] were-blaspheming him, moving [=shaking] their heads, and saying, "Ha. The [one] demolishing the sanctuary and building [it again] in three days, [30]save yourself, having-descended from the cross." [31]And likewise the high-priests, mocking [him] to one-another, with the scribes, were-saying, "He-saved anothers [=others], he-is-able not to-save himself. [32a]The anointed-one, the king of-Israel, let-him-descend now from the cross in-order-that we-might-see and we-might-believe."	were-making-fun-of [him] saying, "He-saved anothers [=others], let-him-save himself, if this is the anointed-one of-god, the chosen-one."
		[36]So approaching, the soldiers and [=also] mocked him offering him sour-wine, [37]and saying, "If you [yourself] are the king of-the Judeans, save yourself." [38]So [=Now] there-was and [=also an] inscription upon [=above] him[c], "This [is] the king of-the Judeans."

[a] *the scribes and elders* A B L Θ *f*[1] *f*[13] 33 205 700 892 *al* vg it[mss] cop[sa] cop[bo]; *the scribes and Pharisees* D W 1424 *pc* it sy[s]; *the scribes and elders and Pharisees* 1006 1342 1506 𝔐 sy[p] sy[h] cop[bo]; *the scribes* Γ *pc*; *the elders and scribes* ℵ.
[b] *He-is* ℵ B D L 33 892 *pc* cop[sa]; *If he-is* A W Θ *f*[1] *f*[13] 1006 1342 1506 𝔐 vg it[mss] sy cop[bo].
[c] *inscription upon him* 𝔭[75] ℵ[1] B L 070 *pc* cop[sa] cop[bo]; *inscription having-been-written upon him* C* sy[s] sy[c] cop[samss]; *inscription having-been-written upon him in-greek and in-latin and in-hebraic letters* C[3] W Θ Ψ *f*[1] *f*[13] 33 892 1006 1342 1506 𝔐 vg it sy[p] sy[h] cop[bo]; *inscription upon him in-hebraic letters* ℵ* ℵ[C]; *inscription having-been-inscribed upon him in-hebraic letters* D; *inscription having-been-inscribed upon him in-greek and in-latin and in-hebraic letters* A Q.
🕮 Mt 27:43 – Ps 22:7, 8, 9

377. Jesus and the Bandits

Matt 27:44

[44]So the it [=in the same way] the bandits having-been-crucified-with together-with him[a] were-denouncing and [=also] him.

Mark 15:32b

[32b]And the having-been-crucified-withs [=those who were crucified] together-with him[b], were-denouncing him [as well].

Luke 23:39-43

[39]So one of-the criminals having-been-hung [=who had also been crucified] was-blaspheming him saying, "Are you [yourself] indeed-not the anointed-one? Save yourself and us." [40]So [=But] the other having-answered rebuking him spoke[c], "Do-fear you nor [=not even] god, that [=since] you-are in the it [=under the same] verdict? [41]And we [ourselves] for-one [suffer] justifiably, for we-are-receiving-back worthy [=equal to that] which we-practiced [=we did wrong]; so [=but] this [person] practiced no-one [=did nothing] improper." [42]And he-was-saying, "Jesus remember me whenever you-might-come into your kingdom." [43]And he-said to-him, "Amen I-say to-you, today you-will-be with me in paradise[d]."

[a] *together-with him* ℵ B D L Θ 892; *with him pc*; *him* A C W f^1 f^{13} 33 1006 1342 1506 𝔐.
[b] *together-with him* ℵ B L Θ 579 892 2427 *pc*; *him* A C f^1 f^{13} 33 1006 1506 𝔐; *with him* Ψ; *omit* D 1424.
[c] *rebuking him spoke* 𝔓[75] ℵ B C* L 070 579 892 *pc*; *rebuked him saying* A C[2] D W Θ Ψ f^1 f^{13} 33 1006 1342 1506 𝔐 vg it sy[h].
[d] *And he-was-saying, "Jesus remember me whenever you-might-come into your kingdom." And he-said to-him, "Amen I-say to-you, today you-will-be with me in paradise"* 𝔓[75] B L cop[sa] cop[bo]; *And he-was-saying, "Jesus remember me whenever you-might-come in your kingdom." And he-said to-him, "Amen I-say to-you, today you-will-be with me in paradise"* ℵ C*; *And he-was-saying to-Jesus, "Remember me lord whenever you-might-come in your kingdom." And Jesus said to-him, "Amen I-say to-you, today you-will-be with me in paradise."* A C[2] W Θ Ψ f^1 f^{13} 33 892 1006 1342 1506 vg it[mss] sy; *Having-turned to the lord he-said to-him, "Remember me in the day of-your second-coming." So having-answered, Jesus said reprimanding him, "Cheer-up."* D.

378. The Death of Jesus

Matt 27:45-54

[45]So from sixth hour [=from noon] until ninth hour [=three in the afternoon] darkness happened upon all the land.

[46]So around the <u>ninth hour</u> Jesus shouted-out [with a] great voice saying, "ĒLI ĒLI, LEMA SABACHTHANI[a]?" This is, "My <u>god</u>, my <u>god</u>, for-what-reason did-you-forsake me?" [47]So some of-the having-stoods [=of those standing]

Mark 15:33-39

[33]And sixth hour having-happened [=from noon] until ninth hour [=three in the afternoon] darkness happened upon all the land.

[34]And [on] the ninth hour, Jesus shouted [with a] great voice, "ELŌI ELŌI, LEMA SABACHTHANI?" which is-translated, "My god, my god, into what [=why] did-you-forsake me?" [35]And some of-the being-presents [=those

Luke 23:44-48

[44]And it-was already as [=about the] sixth hour [=noon] until [the] ninth hour [=three in the afternoon] and darkness happened upon the whole land, [45]the sun having-failed, so [=and] the curtain of-the sanctuary was-ripped [up the] middle.

[46]And having-yelled [with a] great voice, Jesus said,

"Father, INTO YOUR HANDS I-PLACE-BEFORE [=I commend] MY SPIRIT."

John 19:28-30

[28]With [=After] this, Jesus having-recognized that already all [things] have-been-completed, in-order-that the writing might-be-finished [=might be fulfilled], says, "I-am-thirsty."

there, having-heard,
were-saying that "This
[person] yells [for] Elijah."
48 And instantly one out
of-them having-run and
having-taken [a] sponge,
[and] having-filled [it]
even [with] sour-wine
and having-put-around
[=having put it on] reed
[=a stick], was-giving-a-
drink [to] him [with it].
49 So [=But] the remainders
[=rest] were-saying,
"Excuse [=Leave him alone],
let-us-see if Elijah comes
saving him.[b]
50 "So [=But]
Jesus again having-cried
[out in a] great voice,
excused [=gave up] the
spirit.
51 And look! the
curtain of-the sanctuary
was-ripped from from-
the-start until below
[=from top to bottom] into
two and the land was-
shaken and the rocks
were-ripped [=were split],
52 and the tombs were-
opened and many bodies
of-holies [=of saints]
having-perished were-
raised,
53 and having-gone-
out out of-the tombs with
[=after] his resurrection
they-entered into the
holy city and were-made-
apparent [=appeared]
to-many.
54 So [=Now] the officer
and the keepings [=those
guarding] Jesus with him,

having-seen the
earthquake and the
having-happeneds [=things
that had happened], were-
feared very [=were very
afraid], saying, "Truly
this [person] was [a] son
of-god."

who were there], having-
heard, were-saying, "Look,
he-yells [for] Elijah."
36 So
some [person] having-run
and having-stuffed [a]
sponge [with] sour-wine,
[and] having-put-around
[=having put it on] reed
[=a stick], was-giving-a-
drink [to] him [with it]

saying, "Excuse [=Wait!],
let-us-see if Elijah comes
to-bring-down him."
37 So [=But] Jesus, having-
excused [=having let out
a] great voice [=cry],

stopped-breathing.
38 And the curtain of-the
sanctuary was-ripped into
two from from-the-start
until below [=from top to
bottom].

39 So, the centurion,

having-been-present out
against [standing out in
front] of-him [and] having-

seen that he-stopped
breathing thus [=in this
way], said, "Truly this
person was [a] son of-
god."

So [=And] having-said
this he-stopped-

breathing.

47 So the officer,

having-seen
the having-happened
[=thing that had happened]
was-glorifying[c] god

saying, "This person
was definitely righteous
[=innocent]."
48 And all the
crowds having-happened-
to-come-together upon

29 [A] vessel overflowing
[with] sour-wine was-
lying [nearby]. Therefore,
[a] sponge overflowing
[with] the sour-wine
[and] having-put-around
[=having put it on a]
hyssop-branch, they-
offered [it to] his mouth.
30 Therefore, when Jesus
took the sour-wine,
he-said, "It-has-been-
completed," and having-
laid-down [=having
dropped] the [=his] head
he-delivered the [=his]
spirit.

		[=for] this spectacle, having-caught-sight-of the having-happeneds [=things that had happened], were-returning [to their homes and] hitting their chests [in grief].	

a *lema sabachthani* ℵ L 33 700 2542 *pc*; *lama zaphthani* D* it^{mss}; *lama sabachthani* Θ *f*^{1} *pc* vg; *lima sabachthani* A W *f*^{13} 1006 1342 1506 𝔐; *lema sabakthani* B 892 *pc* vg it^{mss} cop^{bo}.
b *omit* A D W Θ *f*^{1} *f*^{13} 33 892 1006 1342 1506 𝔐 vg it^{mss} sy cop; *So another, having taken spear, pierced his side and water and blood went-out* ℵ B C L pc vg^{mss}.
c *was-glorifying* 𝔭^{75} ℵ B D L Ψ 070 892 *pc*; *glorified* A C W Θ *f*^{1} *f*^{13} 33 1006 1506 1342 𝔐.
🕮 Mt 27:46 – Ps 22:1; 🕮 Mk 15:34 – Ps 22:1; 🕮 Lk 23:46 – Ps 31:5; 🕮 Jn 19:28 – Ps 69:21

379. Witnesses of the Crucifixion

Matt 27:55-56	**Mark 15:40-41**	**Luke 23:49**	John 19:25-27
55 So many women, whoever [=who] followed Jesus from the Galilee serving him, were there catching-sight-of	40 So there-were and [=also] women catching-sight-of	49 So all the acquaintances to-him had-stood	25 So [=But] his mother and the sister [of] his mother, Mary the [wife of] Clopas and Mary the Magdalene, had-stood before the cross of-Jesus. 26 Therefore, Jesus having-seen the mother and disciple having-been-present whom he-was-loving, he-says to-the mother, "Woman, look, your son." 27 Then he-says to-the disciple, "Look, your mother." And from that hour the disciple took her into the own [=his home].
[=watching] from far-off.	[=watching] from far-off,	[watching] from far-off	
56 In whom [=Among them] was Mary the Magdalene, and Mary the mother of-James and of-Joseph and the mother of-the sons of-Zebedee.	in [=among] whom [were] and Mary the Magdalene and Mary the mother of-James the small [=younger] and of-Joses and Salome,	and women tagging-	
	41 who when he-was in the Galilee were-following him and were-serving him and many anothers [=other women] having-ascended-together-with him into Jerusalems.	along [with] him from the Galilee seeing these [things].	

There are no variants in this pericope that appear in English.

380. The Burial of Jesus

Matt 27:57-61	**Mark 15:42-47**	**Luke 23:50-56**	John 19:38-42
57 So evening having-happened, [a] wealthy person came from Arimathea, the-name-of-	42 And evening already having-happened, [and] as-a-result-of [=because] it-was preparation-day, which is [the day] before-the-sabbath,		
whom [was] Joseph, and who he [=himself] was-discipled[a] to-Jesus. [=had been made a disciple of Jesus]	43 Joseph from Arimathea, [a] respectable	50 And look! [a] man [by the] name [of] Joseph, being-at-one's-disposal [=who was a] council-member, a good and righteous man 51—this [person] was not having-	38 So with [=after] these [things] Joseph from Arimathea, being [a] disciple of-Jesus, so having-been-hidden [=but a secret one] through [=because of his] fear of-the

Matt 27:58-61	Mark 15:44-47	Luke 23:52-56	
	council-member, and who he [=himself] was waiting-for the kingdom of-god, having-come [and] having-dared,	consented [=did not agree with] the council and their deed—from Arimathea, [a] city of-the Judeans, who was-waiting-for the kingdom of-god.	
58 This [person] having-approached Pilate asked [for] the body of-Jesus.	entered to [=before] Pilate and asked [for] the body of-Jesus.	52 This [person], having-approached Pilate, asked [for] the body of-Jesus.	Judeans, begged Pilate in-order-that he-might-remove the body of-Jesus.
	44 So [=But] Pilate was-astonished [=wondered] if already he-has-died and having-summoned the centurion questioned him if he-faced-death old-days [=whether Jesus had been dead long]. 45 And having-known [=having learned the facts] from the centurion,		
Then Pilate ordered [it] to-be-given-over[b]. 59 And having-taken the body,	he-bestowed the corpse[c] to-Joseph. 46 And having-bought [a] linen-sheet [and] having-brought-	53 And having-brought-	And Pilate allowed [it]. Therefore, he-came and
Joseph wrapped it in pure [a] linen-sheet. 60 And he-put it in his new tomb, which he-hewed in the	down [it] he-bundled it [=the corpse] in-the linen-sheet and put it in [the] tomb which was having-been-hewed out of-rock	down [it] he-wrapped it [in a] linen-sheet and put it [=the corpse] in [a] rock-hewn grave which [=where] no-one was not not-yet lying [=had yet been laid].	removed his body. 39 So Nicodemus, the [one] having-come to him [at] first [by] night, and [=also] came bringing [a] mixture of-myrrh and aloe, like [=about] one-hundred liters. 40 Therefore they-took the body of-Jesus
rock and having-rolled [a] great stone to-the door of-the tomb he-went-away. 61 So [=And] Mary the Magdalene and the another [=other] Mary were there sitting across-from the sepulcher.	and he-rolled [a] stone upon [=against] the door of-the tomb. 47 So [=And] Mary the Magdalene and Mary the [mother] of-Joses[d] were-catching-sight-of wheresoever he-was-put.		and they-restrained [=they wrapped] it in-wrappings with fragrant-spices, just-as is [the] custom to-prepare-for-burial [of] the Judeans. 41 So [=Now] there-was [a] garden in
		54 And it-was [the] day of-preparation-day and sabbath was-dawning. 55 So [=And] the women[e], having-followed-after, whoever [=who] were having-come-together [=having followed] him out of-the Galilee, noticed the tomb and like [=how] his body was-put [in it]. 56 So having-returned, they-made-ready fragrant-spices and	the place where he-was-crucified, and in the garden [there was a] new tomb in which no-one was not-quite-yet having-been-put [=no one had ever been laid]. 42 Therefore through [=because it was] the preparation-day of-the Judeans, [and] that [=because] the tomb was near, he-put Jesus there.

ointments. And they-were-unresponsive [=they rested on] the sabbath for-one according-to the commandment.

[a] *was-discipled* ℵ C D Θ f^{1} 33 205 700 892 *pc*; *was-a-disciple* A B L W f^{13} 1006 1342 1506 𝔐.
[b] *ordered to-be-given-over* ℵ B L f^{1} 33 205 892 1506 *pc* cop^{bo}; *ordered the body to-be-given-over* A C D W Θ f^{13} 1006 1342 𝔐 vg it^{mss} sy^{p} sy^{h}; *ordered the body of-Jesus to-be-given-over* Σ pc vg^{mss}; *ordered the body to-be-given-over to-Joseph* 1424; *ordered to-be-given-over to-him* 237 cop^{sa}.
[c] *the corpse* ℵ B L Θ 565 2427; *the body* A C W Ψ 083 f^{1} f^{13} 33 892 1006 1342 1506 𝔐 vg it^{mss} sy^{p} sy^{h} cop; *his corpse* D sy^{s}.
[d] *of-Joses* ℵ^{2} B L Δ Ψ 083 2427 *pc* cop^{samss} cop^{bo}; *of-James* D 1342 *pc* it vg^{mss} sy^{s}; *of-James and of-Joses* Θ f^{13} 565 2542 *pc*; *of-Jose* C W Ψ^{C} 33 892 1006 1506 𝔐 cop^{samss}; *of-Joseph* A *pc* vg.
[e] *the women* 𝔭^{75} B L Θ Ψ 070 f^{1} f^{13} 33 205 579 892 2542 *al*; *two women* D it vg^{mss}; *women* ℵ A C W 1006 1342 1506 𝔐.

381. Matthew's Sealing of Jesus' Tomb

Matt 27:62-66

62So [on] the next-day, whoever [=which] is with [=after] the preparation-day, the high-priests and
the Pharisees were-gathered to [=before] Pilate, 63saying, "Lord, we-were-remembered [=we were
reminded] that that deceiver said yet [=while he was still] living, 'With [=After] three days I-am-
raised.' 64Therefore order [someone] to-secure the sepulcher until the third day, lest, his disciples[a],
having-come, might-steal him and might-say to-the whole-people, 'He-was-raised from the deads
[=dead people],' and the last deception will-be worse [than] the first." 65Pilate spoke to-them, "You-
have [a] custodia; leave, secure [it] like you-recognize [=you know how]." 66So having-traveled with
the custodia they-secured the sepulcher [by] sealing the stone.

[a] *his disciples* A C D L W Θ f^{1} f^{13} 33 892 1006 1342 1506 𝔐 vg it sy cop; *the disciples* ℵ B.

Resurrection Narratives

382. The Empty Tomb

Matt 28:1-8

1So late-in-the-day of-sabbaths [=after the sabbath], in-the dawning into one of-sabbaths [=on the first day of the week], Mary the Magdalene and the another [=other] Mary came to-catch-sight-of the sepulcher

Mark 16:1-8

1And the sabbath having-elapsed, Mary the Magdalene and Mary the [mother] of-James and Salome bought fragrant-spices in-order-that having-come they-might-smear him. 2And extremely early [on] the one [=first day] of-the sabbaths [=week], the sun having-arisen, they-come upon the tomb. 3And they-were-saying to themselves, "What [person] will-roll-away for-us the stone out of-the

Luke 24:1-12

1So [on] the one [=first day] of-the sabbaths [=week], deep [in the] early-morning, they-came upon the grave carrying fragrant spices which they made-ready.

John 20:1-13

1So [on] the one [=first day] of-the sabbaths [=week], Mary the Magdalene comes into the tomb early yet being [=while it is still] dark, and looks [at] the stone having-been-removed out [=from] the tomb. 2Therefore she-runs and comes to Simon Peter and to the another [=other] disciple whom Jesus was-liking and says to-them, "They removed the lord out of-the tomb and we-recognize not wheresoever they-put him."

2 And look! [a] great
earthquake happened; for
[an] announcer [=angel
of the] lord having-
descended out of-heaven
and having-approached
rolled-away the stone[a]
and sat above it.

3 So his appearance was
like flashing-light and
his clothes [were] white

like snow. 4 So [=And] the
keepings [=those guarding]
were-shaken from the
fear of-him and were-
happened [=became] like
dead [people]. 5 So [=But]
the announcer, having-
answered, said to-the
women, "You [yourselves]
fear no [=must fear not]
for I-recognize that you-
search [for] Jesus the [one]
having-been-crucified.
6 He-is not here, for he-
was-raised just-as he-said.
Come-on! See the place
where he-was-laid[b].

door of-the tomb?" 4 And
having-looked-up they-
catch-sight-of [=they see]
that the stone has-been-
rolled-away; for it-was
very great. 5 And having-
entered into the tomb

they-saw [a] young-man
sitting in [=on] the right,
having-been-arrayed [in
a] white robe, and they-
were-greatly-surprised.

6 So

he-says to-them, "Be-
greatly-surprised no
[=not]; you-are-searching
[for] Jesus the Nazarene,
the [one] having-been-
crucified.
He-was-raised; he-is not
here.
Look, the place where
they-put him.

7 But leave, say [to] his
disciples and [to] Peter
that he-leads-ahead [of]
you into the Galilee. You-
will-see him there, just-as
he-said to-you.'"

2 So [=But] they-found
the stone having-been-
rolled-away from the

tomb, 3 so [=but] having-
entered they-found not
the body of-the lord Jesus.
4 And it-happened in the
to-be-uncertain them
[=while they were confused]
around [=concerning]
this, and look! two men
stood-by them in flashing
[=bright] raiment.

5 So their having-happened
[=when they became]
frightened and reclining
the faces into the land
[=put their faces to the

ground], they-said to them,
"What [=Why] are-you-
searching [for] the living
with the deads [=dead]?

6 He-is not here, but he-
was-raised.

Remember like [=how]
he-talked to-you yet being
[=when he was still] in the
Galilee, 7 saying that it-is-
necessary [for] the son of-
the person to-be-delivered
into [the] hands of-sinful
people and to-be-crucified
and to-get-up [=to rise on]
the third day." 8 And they-
remembered his speeches.

3 Therefore Peter and the
another [=other] disciple
went-out and they-were-
going into the tomb. 4 So
the two were-running
close-by [=together] and
the another [=other]
disciple ran-ahead more-
quickly [than] Peter and
he-went first into the
tomb. 5 And having-bent-
down he-looks [at] the
wrappings lying [there];
however he-entered not.
6 And therefore Simon
Peter comes following
him and entered into the
tomb and he-catches-
sight-of the wrappings
lying [there]. 7 And the
cloth which was upon his
head [was] not with the
wrappings lying [there],
but without [=was apart]
having-been-wrapped
[=having been rolled] into
one place. 8 Therefore
then the another [=other]
disciple, the [one] having-
come first and [=also]
entered into the tomb, and
he-saw and believed. 9 For
they-recognized [=they
understood] not-quite-yet
the writing that [says]
it-is-necessary [for]
him to-get-up out of-
deads [=from the dead].
10 Therefore the disciples
went-away again to them
[=their homes]. 11 So [=But]
Mary had-stood outside
weeping to [=at] the
tomb. Therefore like [=as]
she-was-weeping, she-
bent-down into the tomb,
12 and catches-sight-of two
announcers [=angels] in
white seating-themselves,
one to [=at] the head and
one to [=at] the feet, where
the body of-Jesus was-

Matt	Mark	Luke	John
7 And having-traveled quickly, say [to] his disciples that 'He-was-raised from the deads [=dead people], and look! he-leads-ahead [of] you into the Galilee; you-will-see him there.' Look! I-said [this] to-you."			lying. 13 And those [angels] say to-her, "Woman, what [=why] do-you-weep?" She-says to-them that "They-removed my lord and I-recognize not wheresoever they-put him."
8 And having-gone-away quickly from the tomb with fear and great joy they-ran to-inform his disciples.	8 And having-gone-out they-fled from the tomb, for tremor and ecstasy was-having [=had gripped] them; and they-said no-one [=nothing] to-no-one, for they-were-fearing [=they were afraid]. [c]	9 And having-returned from the tomb they-informed the eleven and all the remainders [=rest] all these [things].	
		10 So [=Now] they-were the Magdalene Mary, and Joanna and Mary the [mother] of-James and the remainders [=rest] together-with them. They-were-saying these [things] to the apostles. 11 And these[d] speeches appeared in-the-sight of-them as nonsense and they-were-being-disloyal to-them. 12 So Peter, having-gotten-up, ran upon [=to] the tomb and having-bent-down looks [=sees] the wrappings alone, and he-went-away to himself [=his home] being-astonished [at] the having-happened [=what had happened].	

[a] *omit* ℵ B D 700 892 *pc* vg it^{mss} sy^{s} cop^{sa}; *from the door* A C G H W Δ 69 579 1342 1424 1506 1542 *pm* sy^{p}; *from the door of-the tomb* E F L Θ *f*^{1} *f*^{13} 33 205 565 1006 *pm* sy^{h} cop^{bo}.

[b] *he-was-laid* ℵ B Θ 33 892* *pc* sy^{s} cop; *the lord was-laid* A C D L W *f*^{1} *f*^{13} 892^{C} 1006 1342 1506 𝔐 vg it^{mss} sy^{p} sy^{h}; *the body of-the lord was-laid* 1424 *pc*; *Jesus was-laid* Φ.

[c] *omit* ℵ A B C D W Θ *f*^{1} *f*^{13} 33 892 1006 1342 1506 2427 𝔐 vg it^{mss} sy cop^{samss} cop^{bo}; the shorter ending of Mark: *So they-declared briefly all the having-been-enjoineds to-the around Peter. And so with these Jesus he sent-forth from east till dusk the sacred and imperishable preaching of-eternal salvation. Amen.* it. (For the longer ending of Mark, see Synoptic Study Guide 17.)

[d] *these* p^{75} ℵ B L Ψ 070 *pc* vg it^{mss} sy^{s} sy^{c} sy^{p} cop; *their* A W Θ *f*^{1} *f*^{13} 33 892 1006 1342 𝔐 sy^{h}.

📖 Jn 20:9 – Ps 16:10

SYNOPTIC STUDY GUIDE 16

Problems with the Farrer Hypothesis

The Farrer Hypothesis has many things going for it: the extreme likelihood of Markan Priority and not having to rely on a hypothetical source like Q. It is a common objection to Q's existence that apparently it was respected deeply by Matthew and Luke (evidenced by how closely they follow its wording) and yet not respected enough by anyone else to ensure its survival. No less, it was not even transmitted broadly enough for a single early Christian writer to know of its existence and to refer to it. In other words, there is not a single piece of evidence outside of Matthew and Luke for the existence of Q.

However, each of the levels of tradition (Triple, Double, and Single) presents different problems for the Farrer Hypothesis. In the Triple Tradition, the evidence connecting Matthew and Luke is tenuous. There are none of the extensive agreements between Matthew and Luke that there are between Matthew and Mark or between Mark and Luke. These sorts of agreements leave no doubt that there *is* a direct literary relationship between those other gospels. If there is a direct literary relationship between the Gospels of Matthew and Luke, why does the evidence of that relationship look so different from the evidence of the literary relationship between Matthew and Mark, and Luke and Mark? (The same issue plagues the Two-Document Hypothesis, since there Matthew and Luke agree with Q much more thoroughly than they do with Mark; see Synoptic Study Guide 3).

The Double Tradition presents a problem, too: if the author of Luke took that material from Matthew, then it appears that although he respected Matthew enough to take over that material verbatim more often than not (Luke does not do this as often with Mark), he so disrespected Matthew's arrangement of this material that he rearranged almost all of it. In other words, Luke's *respect* for Matthew's wording of the Double Tradition is as high as his *disrespect* for its order, and this strikes critics of the Farrer Hypothesis as very strange. By the counting of pericopae in this synopsis, Luke follows Matthew in the placement of Q material in only 9/84 places.

But it is the Single Tradition, particularly the beginning and ending of Matthew, that is most troubling for the Farrer Hypothesis. If the author of Luke had seen Matthew's infancy narrative, why did he reject practically everything in it? The Gospel of Matthew has Jesus born in Bethlehem because Mary and Joseph live there in a house; Matthew has Magi from the East visit the infant Jesus; Matthew has the family flee into Egypt from a tyrannical Herod the Great; when Matthew has the family finally settle in Nazareth, it is clear they have never been there before. Conversely, Luke has Jesus born in Bethlehem because Mary and Joseph were there for a census that cannot have happened when its author says it did; Luke has shepherds visit the infant Jesus; Luke has the family go to the temple for the ritual purification on their way *home* to Nazareth. What compelled Luke to respect Matthew for many sayings of Jesus, but so completely reject the infancy material? And to do so as well for the resurrection narratives at the end of Matthew, which the author of Luke also wholly rejects (with the possible exception of three words: "all the nations," which can be found in Luke 24:47 and Matt 28:19).

383. Matthew's First Appearance of Jesus

Matt 28:9-10

[9] [a] And look! Jesus met[b] them
saying, "Rejoice." So having-
approached they-seized his feet
and worshiped him. [10]Then Jesus
says to-them, "Fear no [=not].
Leave, inform my brothers in-
order-that they-might-go-away
into the Galilee, and-there they-
will-see me."

John 20:14-18

[14]Having-said these [things] she-was-turned into the behind [=Mary
Magdalene turned around] and catches-sight-of Jesus having-stood, and she-
recognized not that it-is Jesus. [15]Jesus says to-her, "Woman, what [=why]
do-you-weep? What are-you-searching?" That [woman], supposing that he-is
the gardener says to-him, "Lord, if you [yourself] bore him [somewhere], say
to-me wheresoever you-put him; I-too will-remove him." [16]Jesus says to-her,
"Mary." Having-turned, that [woman] says to-him in-Hebrew, "Rabbouni,"
which is-said [=means] "Teacher." [17]Jesus says to-her, "Touch me no [=not],
for not-yet have-I-ascended to the father. So [=But] travel to my brothers and
say to-them, 'I-ascend to my father and your father and my god and your
god.'" [18]Mary the Magdalene comes announcing to-the disciples that "I-
have-seen the lord" and he-said these [things] to-her.

[a] *omit* ℵ B D W Θ f^{13} 33 700 892 1506 *al* vg it[mss] sy[p] cop; *So like they-were-traveling to-inform his disciples* A C L f^{1} 1006 1342 𝔐 sy[h].

[b] *met* ℵ* B C Θ f^{1} f^{13} 205 565 700 892 1424 *al*; *encountered* ℵ[2] A D L W 33 1006 1342 1506 𝔐.

🕮 Jn 20:17 – Ps 22:22

Mark 16:8 (§382, p. 295)
Q 17:35 (§288, p. 209)

384. Matthew's Report of the Guard

Matt 28:11-15

[11]So their [while they were] traveling, look! some of-the custodia having-come into the city informed
the high-priests everyone the having-happeneds [=everything that had happened]. [12]And having-
been-gathered with the elders, even having-taken [=having devised a] plot [in which] they-gave fit
[=many] silver-coins to-the soldiers, [13]saying, "Say that his disciples having-come [in the] night stole
him our perishing [=while we slept]. [14]And if-ever this might-be-heard upon [=by] the ruler, we
[ourselves] will-persuade him[a] and we-will-do [=we will keep] you without-worry." [15]So having-taken
the silver-coins they-did like they-were-taught. And this word was-spoken-out along [=by the]
Judeans to-the-point of-the today[b] [=even into the present day].

[a] *him* A C D L W f^{1} f^{13} 892 1006 1342 1506 𝔐 vg it^{mss} sy; *omit* ℵ B Θ 33.
[b] *to-the-point of-the today* ℵ A W f^{1} f^{13} 33 892 1006 1342 1506 𝔐; *to-the point of-the day today* B D L Θ *pc* vg it^{mss}.

385. Luke's Appearance of Jesus on the Road to Emmaus

Luke 24:13-35

[13]And look! two out of-them in the it [=on the same] day were traveling into [a] village sixty furlongs
receiving-in-full [=distant] from Jerusalem, whose name [was] Emmaus. [14]And they [themselves]
were-conversing to one-another around [=concerning] all these having-come-abouts [=things
that had come about]. [15]And it-happened in the to-converse and to-discuss them [=while they were
conversing and discussing], and Jesus he [=himself] having-neared was-traveling-together-with them,
[16]so [=that] their eyes were-being-seized the no [=were being kept from] to-understand [=recognizing]
him. [17]So he-said to them, "What [are] these words which you-swap to [=with] one-another [while]
walking-around?" And they-were-stood [=they stood still looking] gloomy. [18]So having-answered,
one [by the] name Cleopas[a] said to him, "You alone visit Jerusalem and knew not the having-
happeneds [=things that have occurred] in it in these days?" [19]And he-said to-them, "What-kind-
of [things]?" So they-said to-him, "The [things] around [=concerning] Jesus the Nazarene[b], who
happened [=was a] man prophet possible [=mighty] in work [=deed] and word ere [=in the sight of]
god and all the whole-people, [20]even so-that our high-priests and magistrates delivered him into
[a] verdict of-death and crucified him. [21]So [=But] we [ourselves] were-hoping[c] that he [himself] is
the [one] intending to-set-free Israel. But in-effect and together-with all these [=what is worse is
that] this [is the] third day leads from which [=since] these [things] happened. [22]But and [=also] some
women out [=among] us surprised us. Having-happened [=Having arrived] early-in-the-day upon
the tomb [23]and having-found no [=not] his body, they-came saying and [=also] to-have-seen [=that
they had seen a] vision of-announcers [=of angels], who say him to-live [=that he is alive]. [24]And some
of-the [ones] together-with us went-away upon [=to] the tomb and found thus [=it was true] and
just-as the women said, so [=but] they-saw him not." [25]And he [himself] said to them, "Oh foolishes
[=foolish people] and slows in-the heart [=slow of heart] to-believe upon [=in] all which the prophets
talked [=said]. [26]Was-it-necessary indeed-not [for] the anointed-one to-suffer these [things] and
to-enter into his glory?" [27]And having-begun from Moses and from all the prophets he-deciphered
for-them the [things] around [=concerning] himself in all the writings [=scriptures]. [28]And they-
neared into the village [to] which they-were-traveling, and he [himself] gave-the-impression
to-travel [=that he would be traveling] farther. [29]And they-entreated him saying, "Stay with us, that
[=because] it-is [coming on] to late-afternoon and already the day has-reclined [=is nearly over]."
And he-entered to-stay together-with them. [30]And it-happened in the him to-be-reclined-at-table
[=while he was dining] with them, having-taken the bread he-blessed [it] and having-broken [it] he-
gave-to them [some of it]. [31]So their eyes were-opened-up and they-understood [=they recognized]
him; and he-happened [=he became] invisible from them. [32]And they-said to one-another, "Was
our heart indeed-not being-kindled in us like [=when] he-talked to-us in [=on] the way [here], like
[=when] he-was-opening-up the writings to-us?" [33]And having-gotten-up they-returned into

Jerusalem the it hour [=in that same hour], and they-found the eleven and the [ones] together-with them having-been-assembled, [34]saying that the lord definitely was-raised and was-seen by-Simon. [35]And they [themselves] were-describing the [things that happened] in [=on] the way [=road] and like [=how] he-was-made-known to-them in the breaking of-the bread.

[a] *one name Cleopas* $\mathfrak{P}^{75}$ א B D L Ψ f^1 205 *al*; *the one name Cleopas* A W 892 1006 1342 𝔐; *one out of-them name Cleopas* Θ f^{13} 33 579 2542 *pc* it sy cop^{sa}.
[b] *Nazarene* $\mathfrak{P}^{75}$ א B L vg it^{mss}; *Nazarite* A D W Θ Ψ f^1 f^{13} 33 892 1006 1342 𝔐 cop^{sa}.
[c] *were-hoping* A B D L W Ψ f^1 f^{13} 892 1006 1342 𝔐 vg it^{mss} sy^h cop^{samss} cop^{bomss}; *had-hoped* $\mathfrak{P}^{75}$; *we-are-hoping* א Δ Θ *al* cop^{samss} cop^{bomss}.

386. Luke's Resurrected Jesus Eats

Luke 24:36-43

[36]So their [While they were] talking [about] these [things], he [himself] stood[a] in [the] middle of-them, and he-says to-them, "Peace [be on] you." [37]So, having-been-alarmed and having-happened [=having become] frightened, they-were-supposing to-catch-sight-of [=that they were seeing a] spirit. [38]And he-said to-them, "What [=Why] are-you being-disturbed, and through what [=why do] thoughts [=doubts] ascend in your heart? [39]See my hands and my feet, that I am he. Handle [=Touch] me and see, that [for the] spirit has not flesh and bones just-as you-catch-sight-of [=you see] me having." [40]And having-said this he-showed them the hands and the [=his] feet. [41]So yet their [while they were still] being-disloyal from the joy and being-astonished he-said to-them, "Do-you-have some [thing] edible in-here?" [42]So they-gave-to him part [of a] broiled fish[b]. [43]And having-taken [it] he-ate [it] in-the-sight of-them.

John 20:19-23

[19]Therefore, being [when it was] evening [on] that day, the one of-sabbaths [=on the first day of the week], and the doors having-been-locked where the disciples were [hiding] through fear of-the Judeans, Jesus came and stood into the middle
and says to-them, "Peace [be on] you."
[20]And having-said this he-showed the hands and the [=his] side to-them. Therefore, the disciples, having-seen the lord, were-rejoiced [=were overjoyed]. [21]Therefore he-said to-them again, "Peace [be on] you. Just-as the father has-sent-off me, I-too send you." [22]And having-said this, he-breathed-upon and says to-them, "Take [the] holy spirit." [23][If] ever you-might-excuse the sins of-some, they-have-been-excused to-them, [and if] ever you-might-seize [=you might retain the sins] of-some, they-have-been-seized [=they have been retained]."

[a] *he stood* $\mathfrak{P}^{75}$ א B D L *pc* it sy^s sy^c cop^{sa}; *Jesus stood* A W Θ Ψ f^1 f^{13} 33 892 1342 1506 𝔐 sy^p sy^h.
[b] *omit* $\mathfrak{P}^{75}$ א B G H L f^1 33 205 579 892 983 *al*; *and from honey-comb of-bees* W Θ Ψ f^{13} 1006 1342 𝔐.

387. Matthew's Great Commission

Matt 28:16-20

[16]So the eleven disciples traveled into the Galilee, into the mountain [to] which Jesus consigned them. [17]And having-seen him, they-worshiped [him], so [=but] they-doubted. [18]And having-approached, Jesus talked to-them saying, "All authority in heaven and upon land [=on earth] was-given to-me. [19]Therefore[a], having-traveled, be-disciple [=make disciples of] all the nations, baptizing them into the name of-the father and of-the son and of-the holy spirit, [20]teaching them to-keep all whatsoever I-charged you. And look! I am with you all the days until the conclusion of-the eon.[b]"

[a] *Therefore* B W Δ Θ f^1 33 205 543 565 892 *al* vg it^{mss} sy cop^{samss}; *Now* D it; *omit* א A f^{13} 1006 1342 1506 𝔐 cop^{samss}.
[b] *omit* א A* B D W f^1 33 1006 *pc* vg it^{mss} cop^{sa}; *Amen* A^C Θ f^{13} 892 1342 1506 𝔐 it vg^{mss} sy.
🕮 Mt 28:18 – Dan 7:14

SYNOPTIC STUDY GUIDE 17

The End of Mark

The Gospel of Mark originally ended with "they-said no-one to-no-one, for they-were-fearing," and it seems no one except Mark was satisfied with that. Even today, some scholars assume or argue that a longer ending of Mark was lost. They argue that it is unlikely that a whole work would end in as weak a word as *gar* (for). The manuscript tradition does not support this argument. The scribes who copied Mark felt the same way about the ending as apparently Matthew and Luke did (who each add resurrection narratives to Mark): the manuscripts of Mark attest three different endings! There is a two-sentence ending found in one Old Latin manuscript (see textual variant c at the end of §382), and another ending that combines this short ending plus the longer ending that follows below (L Y 083 099 579). These two variants can be eliminated from consideration outright because of their poor manuscript support.

The two serious options for how Mark ended are the longer ending (below) and the "no-ending" (that it ended at 16:8). Here is the longer ending:

> [9]So having-gotten-up early [on the] first [day] of-sabbath [=of the week] he-was-appeared [=was seen] first [by] Mary the Magdalene, along [=from] whom he-had-cast-out seven demons. [10]That [woman] having-traveled informed the having-happeneds [=those who were] with him [while they were] lamenting and weeping. [11]And-those, having-heard that he-lives and was-noticed under [=was seen by] her disbelieved. [12]So with [=after] these [things] he-was-made-visible in [an] other shape to-two out of-them walking-around traveling into [a] field. [13]And-those having-gone-away informed the remainders [=rest], [but] nor did-they-believe those [ones]. [14]So afterward he-was-made-visible to-the eleven to-them [themselves while there were] dining and he-denounced their lack-of-faith and hardness-of-heart, that [=because] they-believed not the having-noticeds [=those who saw] him having-been-raised. [15]And he-said to-them, "Having-traveled into the everyone [=whole] world, preach the proclamation to-all creation. [16]The [one] having-believed and having-been-baptized will-be-saved, so [=but] the having-disbelieveds [=those who do not believe] will-be-judged-against. [17]So these signs will-attend the having-believeds [=those who believe]: they-will-cast-out demons in my name, they-will-talk in-new tongues, [18]and in the [=their] hands they-will-remove [=they will carry] snakes, [and] even-if they-might-drink some deadly-poison, it-might-harm them not no [=at all], they-will-place hands upon the unwell and they-will-have [=they will become] well." [19]Therefore for-one, the lord Jesus, with to-talk [=after he had talked] to-them, he-was-transported into heaven is-seated out [=to the] right of-god. [20]So those having-gone-out preached everywhere, working-with the lord and confirming the word through the signs following-upon [=attending it].

The manuscripts that contain this longer, more theologically pleasing ending are extremely numerous: they include uncials (A C D W Θ), minuscule families (f^{1} f^{13}), strong minuscules (33 892 1006 1342 1506 2427), and the testimony of the majority of Byzantine witnesses (𝔐); they also include translations, some of excellent quality (vg sy^{c} sy^{p} sy^{h} cop^{bo}), and some of lesser quality (it^{mss}). In all, this insertion enjoys wide geographical distribution, and some old and good-quality manuscripts. Nonetheless, the fact that this longer ending is missing from manuscripts that are both (a) the oldest and (b) in Greek (א B) speaks very loudly against this longer ending being original. As well, the absence of this longer ending is attested in some Byzantine minuscules (*pc*) as well as some old translations (sy^{s} cop^{samss}). All this suggests that the longer ending of Mark was added by scribes who found theologically troubling Mark's lack of a narrativized, explicit resurrection for Jesus, and the failure of the women to broadcast what they saw. Notice also that this longer scribal ending is actually a conflation of the other gospel resurrection narratives: Jesus appears to two walking along (with the Gospel of Luke), then to the remaining eleven (with the Gospels of Matthew, Luke, and John), followed by the commission (with the Gospel of Matthew). There are also stylistic and theological features of the longer ending that are not compatible with the rest of Mark's style and theology, as we know it.

388. Luke's Final Instruction

Luke 24:44-53

44So he-said to them, "These [are] my words which I-talked [=I spoke] to you yet being [=when I was
still] together-with you, that it-is-necessary to-be-fulfilled all the having-been-writtens [=that has
been written] in the law of-Moses and the prophets and psalms around [=concerning] me." 45Then
he-opened-up their intellect to-comprehend the writings [=scriptures] 46and said to-them that "It-
has-been-written thus, [that] the anointed-one [is] to-suffer and to-get-up [=to rise] out of-deads
[=from the dead on] the third day, 47and [that] repentance into [=for the] remission of-sins [is] to-
be-preached upon [=in] his name into all the nations, having-begun from Jerusalem. 48You [are]
witnesses of-these [things]. 49And I [myself] send-off the promise [of] my father upon you. So you
be-seated [=stay] in the city until which you-might-be-clothed [with] power out height [=from on
high]." 50So he-led-out them until to [=as far as] Bethany and having-lifted-up his hands he-blessed
them. 51And it-happened in the to-bless him them [=while he was blessing them] he-passed [=he
disappeared] from them and was-being-brought-up into heaven. 52And they, having-worshiped
him, returned into Jerusalem with great joy, 53and they [themselves] were through all [=continually]
in the temple blessing[a] god. [b]

[a] *blessing* $\mathfrak{p}^{75}$ ℵ B C* L sy^{s}; *praising* D it; *praising and blessing* A C^{2} W Θ Ψ f^{1} f^{13} 33 892 1006 1342 𝔐 vg it^{mss} sy^{p} sy^{h}.
[b] *omit* $\mathfrak{p}^{75}$ ℵ C* D L W 1 33 1582 *pc* it sy^{s} cop; *Amen* A B C^{2} Θ Ψ f^{13} 892 1006 1342 𝔐 vg it^{mss} sy^{p} sy^{h} cop^{bomss}.

How To Use This Vocabulary Key

This vocabulary key lists in English alphabetical order all the words that appear in the synopsis. It is not a complete list of words that appear in the whole New Testament, but only those words that appear in this synopsis. Keep in mind that there are many translation options for every word; for this synopsis, one English word has been chosen to render each Greek word. This key tells you which Greek word stands behind the English word you see in the synopsis.

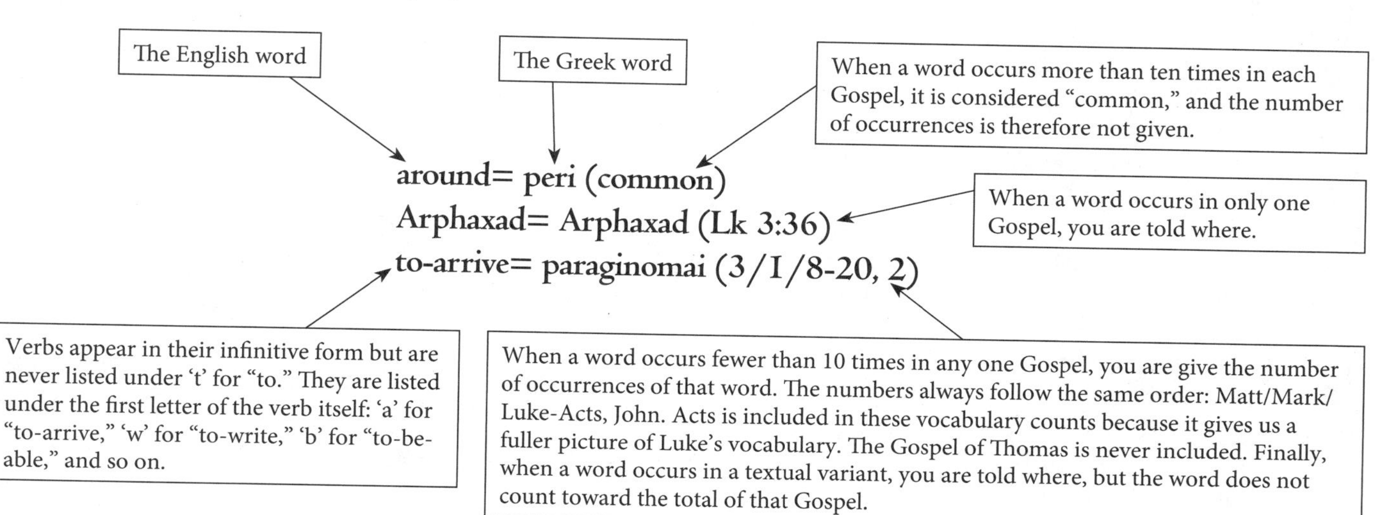

The English word
The Greek word
When a word occurs more than ten times in each Gospel, it is considered "common," and the number of occurrences is therefore not given.
around= peri (common)
Arphaxad= Arphaxad (Lk 3:36)
to-arrive= paraginomai (3/1/8-20, 2)
When a word occurs in only one Gospel, you are told where.
Verbs appear in their infinitive form but are never listed under 't' for "to." They are listed under the first letter of the verb itself: 'a' for "to-arrive," 'w' for "to-write," 'b' for "to-be-able," and so on.
When a word occurs fewer than 10 times in any one Gospel, you are give the number of occurrences of that word. The numbers always follow the same order: Matt/Mark/Luke-Acts, John. Acts is included in these vocabulary counts because it gives us a fuller picture of Luke's vocabulary. The Gospel of Thomas is never included. Finally, when a word occurs in a textual variant, you are told where, but the word does not count toward the total of that Gospel.

Some Greek letters have a direct parallel in English (e.g., a, b, g, m, n, etc.), but some do not. Here is how I have rendered those Greek letters in English for this key: ch = chi (χ); ē = eta (η); ō = omega (ω); ph = phi (φ); ps = psi (ψ); th = theta (Θ); u = upsilon (υ); and x = xi (ξ).

A

Aaron= Aarōn (Lk 1:5)
to-abandon= aphistēmi (0/0/4-6, 0)
Abba= Abba (Mk 14:36)
abdomen= koilia (3/1/8-2, 2)
Abel= Abel (1/0/1-0, 0)
Abiathar= Abiathar (Mk 2:26)
Abijah= Abia (2/0/0-0, 0)
Abilene= Abilēnē (Lk 3:1)
Abiud= Abioud (2/0/0-0, 0)
abode= katoikēsis (Mk 3:5)
to-abolish= anaireō (1/0/2-19, 0)
abomination= bdelugma (1/1/1-0, 0)
above= epanō (8/1/5-0, 1)
Abraham= Abraam (6/1/15-7, 11)
abyss= abussos (Lk 8:31)
to-accept= chōreō (3/1/0-0, 3)
acceptable= dektos (0/0/2-1, 0)
to-accomplish= apoteleō (Lk 13:32)
according-to= kata (common)
accurately= akribōs (1/0/1-5, 0)
accusation= katēgoria (Jn 18:29)
to-accuse= katēgoreō (2/3/4-9, 2)
to-achieve= ōpheleō (3/3/1-0, 1)
Achim= Achim (2/0/0-0, 0)
to-acknowledge= exomologeō (2/1/2-1, 0)
acquaintance= gnōstos (0/0/2-10, 2)
to-acquire= ktaomai (1/0/2-3, 0)
across-from= apenanti (2/0/0-2, 0)
to-act-as-lord= kurieuō (Lk 22:25)
to-act-as-lord-over= katakurieuō (1/1/0-1, 0)
Adam= Adam (Lk 3:38)
to-add= prostithēmi (2/1/7-6, 0)
Addi= Addi (Lk 3:28)
to-address= prosphōneō (1/0/4-2, 0)
to-adjudicate-for= ekdikeō (0/0/2-0, 0)
adjudication= ekdikēsis (0/0/3-1, 0)
Admin= Admin (Lk 3:33)
to-adopt= paradechomai (0/1/0-3, 0)
to-adorn= kosmeō (3/0/2-0, 0)
adulterer= moichos (Lk 18:11)
adulterous= moichalis (2/1/0-0, 0)
adultery= moicheia (1/1/0-0, 1)
to-advance= probainō (1/1/3-0, 0)
adversary= satanas (4/6/5-2, 1)
to-advise= sumbouleuō (1/0/0-1, 1)
afraid= deilos (1/1/0-0, 0)
afterward= husteros (7/1/1-0, 1)
again= palin (17/28/3-5, 44)
against= enantios (1/2/0-0, 0)
age= hēlikia (1/0/3-0, 2)
agedness= gēras (Lk 1:36)
to-aggravate= enochleō (Lk 6:18)
agony= agōnia (Lk 22:44)
to-agree= sumphōneō (3/0/1-2, 0)
ah= ea (Lk 4:34)
Ahaz= Achaz (2/0/0-0, 0)
ahead= katenanti (1/3/1-0, 0)

to-aid= antilambanō (0/0/1-1, 0)
alabaster-case= alabastros (1/2/1-0, 0)
to-alert= diamarturomai (0/0/1-9, 0)
Alexander= Alexandros (0/1/0-3, 0)
all= pas (common)
all-of-a-sudden= exapina (Mk 9:8)
to-allow= epitrepō (2/2/4-5, 1)
all-together= pamplēthei (Lk 18:23)
almsgiving= eleēmosunē (3/0/2-8, 0)
aloe= aloē (Jn 19:39)
alone= monos (7/4/9-0, 10)
along= para (common)
Alpheus= Halphaios (1/2/1-1, 0)
already= ēdē (7/8/10-3, 15)
always= pantote (2/2/2-0, 7)
amazing= thaumastos (1/1/0-0, 1)
to-ambush= peripiptō (0/0/1-1, 0)
amen= amēn (31/13/6-0, 50)
Aminadab= Aminadab (1/0/1-0, 0)
Amon= Amōn (Mt 1:10)
among= kuklō (0/3/1-0, 0)
Amos= Amōs (1/0/1-0, 0)
and= kai (common)
and-from-there= kakeithen (0/1/1-8, 0)
Andrew= Andreas (2/4/1-1, 5)
and-that= kakeinos (0/4/3-1, 3)
and-there= kakei (3/1/0-5, 1)
and-those= kakeinoi (2/0/1-2, 2) (two more appear in textual variants at Mk 16:11, 13)
and-yet= kaitoige (Jn 4:2)
anger= orgē (1/1/2-0, 1)
animal= ktēnos (0/01-1, 0)
Anna= Hanna (Lk 2:36)
Annas= Hannas (0/0/1-1, 2)
to-annihilate= analoō (Lk 9:54)
to-announce= aggellō (Jn 20:18)
announcer= aggelos (20/6/26-21, 3)
announcer-like= isaggelos (Lk 20:36)
annum= eniautos (0/0/1-2, 3)
to-anoint= chriō (0/0/1-2, 0)
anointed-one= christos (common)
another= allos (common)
answer= apokrisis (0/0/2-0, 2)
to-answer= apokrinomai (common)
answerable= enochos (5/2/0-0, 0)
to-answer-back= antapokrinomai (Lk 14:6)
to-anticipate= prophthanō (Mt 17:25)
anxiety= sunochē (Lk 21:25)
apart= aneu (Mt 10:29)
apart-from= ater (0/0/2-0, 0)
aperture= trēma (Lk 18:25)
apostle= apostolos (1/2/6-28, 1)
apparel= himatismos (0/0/2-1, 1)
apparition= phantasma (1/1/0-0, 0)
to-appear= phainō (13/2/2-0, 2)
appearance= eidea (Mt 28:3)
to-appoint= diatassō (1/0/4-5, 0)
to-apprehend= piazō (0/0/0-2, 8)
to-approach= proserchomai (51/5/10-10, 1)
to-approve= suneudokeō (0/0/1-2, 0)
Aram= Aram (1/0/1-0, 0)
arbitrator= meristēs (Lk 12:14)
ancient= archaios (2/0/2-3, 0)
Archelaus= Archelaus (Mt 2:22)
to-argue= sullogizomai (Lk 20:5)
Arimathea= Arimathaia (1/1/1-0, 1)
to-arise= anatellō (3/2/1-0, 0)
ark= kibōtos (1/0/1-0, 0)
arm= brachiōn (0/0/1-1, 1)
armor= panoplia (Lk 11:22)
Arni= Arni (Lk 3:33)
around= peri (common)
Arphaxad= Arphaxad (Lk 3:36)
to-arrive= paraginomai (3/1/8-20, 2)
arrogance= huperēphania (Mk 7:22)
arrogant= huperēphanos (Lk 1:51)
as= hōsei (3/1/9-6, 0)
Asa= Asa (2/0/0-0, 0)
Asaph= Asaph (2/0/0-0, 0)
as-a-result-of= epei (3/1/1-0, 2)
to-ascend= anabainō (9/9/9-19, 16)
to-ascend-together-with= sunanabainō (0/1/0-1, 0)
to-ascertain= akriboō (2/0/0-0, 0)
ash= spodos (1/0/1-0, 0)
Asher= Asēr (Lk 2:36)
to-ask= aiteō (14/9/11-10, 10)
to-ask-for-alms= epaiteō (0/0/2-0, 0)
ass= onos (3/0/1-0, 1)
to-assail= epipiptō (0/1/2-6, 0)
assarion= assarion (1/0/1-0, 0)
to-assemble= athroizō (Lk 24:33)
assembly= ekklēsia (2/0/0-23, 0)
to-assess= anakrinō (0/0/1-5, 0)
to-assist= sunantilambanomai (Lk 10:40)
as-soon-as= epan (1/0/2-0, 0)
to-astound= thambeō (0/3/0-0, 0)
at-a-distance= porrōthen (Lk 12:17)
at-all= holōs (Mt 5:34)
at-any-time= pōpote (0/0/1-0, 4)
at-night= ennuchos (Mk 1:35)
at-once= parachrēma (2/0/10-6, 0)
to-attack-with-questions= apostomatizō (Lk 11:53)
to-attain= tugchanō (0/0/1-5, 0)
attempt= epicheireō (0/0/1-2)
to-attend= parakoloutheō (0/1/1-0, 0)
attendant= hupēretēs (2/2/2-4, 9)
to-attire= amphiezō (Lk 12:28)
Augustus= Augoustos (Lk 2:1)
authority= exousia (10/10/16-7, 8)
automatically= automatos (0/1/0-1, 0)
to-awake= diegeirō (1/0/2-0, 0)
away-from-home= apodēmos (Mk 13:34)
awkward= dusbastaktos (1/0/1-0, 0)
axe= axinē (1/0/1-0, 0)
Azor= Azōr (2/0/0-0, 0)

B

to-babble= battalogeō (Mt 6:7)
baby= brephos (0/0/5-1, 0)
Babylon= Babulōn (3/1/0-1, 0)
bad= kakos (3/2/2-4, 2)
badly= kakōs (7/4/2-1, 1)
bailiff= praktōr (Lk 12:58)
to-bandage= katadeō (Lk 10:34)
bandit= lēstēs (4/3/4-0, 3)
to-banish= methistēmi (0/0/1-2, 0)
banker= trapezitēs (Mt 25:27)
banquet= deipnon (1/2/5-0, 4)
to-banquet-on= deipneō (0/0/2-0, 0)
baptism= baptisma (2/4/4-6, 0)
baptist= baptistēs (7/2/3-0, 0)
to-baptize= baptizō (7/13/10-21, 13)
Barabbas= Barabbas (5/3/1-0, 1)
Barachiah= Barachias (Mt 23:35)
Bar-Jonah= Bariōna (Mt 16:17)
barley= krithinos (0/0/0-0, 2)
Bartholomew= Bartholomaios (1/1/1-1, 0)
Bartimaeus= Bartimaios (Mk 10:46)
basket= kophinos (2/2/1-0, 1)
to-batter= proskoptō (2/0/1-0, 2)
battle= polemos (2/2/2-0, 0)
to-be= eimi (common)
to-be-able= dunamai (common)
to-be-accustomed= eiōthō (1/1/1-1, 0)
beach= aigialos (2/0/0-3, 1)
to-be-a-disciple= mathēteuō (3/0/0-1, 0)
to-be-advantageous= lusiteleō (Lk 17:2)
to-be-agitated= adēmoneō (1/1/0-0, 0)
to-be-alarmed= ptoeō (0/0/2-0, 0)
to-be-amazed= ekplēssō (4/5/3-1, 0)
to-be-angry= orgizō (3/0/2-0, 0)
to-bear= bastazō (3/1/5-4, 5)
to-bear-fruit= karpophoreō (1/2/1-0, 0)
to-bear-out= anaplēroō (Mt 13:14)

to-be-arrayed= periballō (5/2/2-1, 1)
to-be-ashamed= aischuomai (Lk 16:3)
to-be-ashamed-of= epaischunomai (0/2/2-0, 0)
to-be-a-slave= douleuō (2/0/3-2, 1)
to-be-a-soldier= strateuomai (Lk 3:14)
beast= thērion (0/1/0-3, 0)
beast-of-burden= hupozugion (Mt 5:21)
to-be-astonished= thaumazō (7/4/13-5, 6)
to-beat= derō (1/3/5-3, 1)
to-be-at-one's-disposal= huparchō (3/0/15-25, 0)
to-beat-on-the-head= kephalioō (Mk 4:12)
to-be-at-peace= eirēneuō (Mk 9:50)
because= heineka (Lk 4:18)
because-of= heneka (7/5/4-3, 0)
to-become-an-adulterer= moichaō (2/2/0-0, 0)
to-become-discouraged= egkakeō (Lk 18:1)
to-become-drowsy= nustazō (Mt 25:5)
to-become-less-important= elattoō (Jn 3:30)
to-become-old= palaioō (Lk 12:33)
to-become-tasteless= mōrainō (1/0/1-0, 0)
to-become-wrathful= thumoō (Mt 2:16)
to-be-completely-astonished= ekthaumazō (Mk 12:17)
to-be-concerned= skopeō (Lk 11:35)
to-be-confused= diaporeō (0/0/1-3, 0)
to-be-content = eudokeō (3/1/2-0, 0)
to-be-covered-with-sores= helkoō (Lk 16:20)
to-be-customary= ethizō (Lk 2:27)
bed= koitē (Lk 11:7)
to-be-deficient= hustereō (1/1/2-0, 1)
to-be-demon-possessed= daimonizomai (8/4/1-0, 1)
to-be-disloyal= apisteō (0/2/2-1, 0)
to-be-distracted= perispaomai (Lk 10:40)
to-be-drunk= methuō (1/0/0-1, 0)
bee= melissos (textual variant found at Lk 24:42)
to-be-early= orthrizō (Lk 21:38)
Beelzebul= Beelzeboul (3/1/3-0, 0)
to-be-endangered= kinduneuō (0/0/1-2, 0)
to-be-enough= arkeō (1/0/1-0, 2)
to-be-epileptic= selēniazomai (2/0/0-0, 0)
to-be-feverish= puressō (1/1/0-0, 0)
to-be-fiery= purrazō (2/0/0-0, 0)
to-be-fixed-on= atenizō (0/0/2-10, 0)
before= pro (5/1/7-7, 9)
before-the-Sabbath= prosabbaton (Mk 15:42)
to-be-founded= themelioō (Mt 7:25)
to-be-full= gemō (2/0/1-0, 0)
to-be-fully-armed= kathoplizō (Lk 11:21)
to-beg= erōtaō (4/3/15-7, 28)
to-beget= gennaō (45/1/4-7, 18)
to-begin= archō (13/27/31-10, 2)
beginning= archē (4/4/3-4, 8)
to-be-glad= agalliaō (1/0/2-2, 2)
to-be-greatly-surprised= ekthambeō (0/4/0-0, 0)
to-be-grieved-deeply= sullupeō (Mk 3:5)
to-behead= apokephalizō (1/2/1-0, 0)
to-be-healthy= hugiainō (0/0/3-0, 0)
behind= opisō (7/6/7-2, 7)
to-behold= emblepō (2/4/2-2, 2)
to-be-hostile= enechō (0/1/1-0, 0)
to-be-ignorant= agnoeō (0/1/1-2, 0)
to-be-ill= astheneō (3/1/1-3, 8)
to-be-imaginable= endechomai (Lk 13:33)
to-be-impossible= adunateō (1/0/1-0, 0)
to-be-in-debt= opheilō (6/0/5-1, 2)
to-be-indignant= aganakteō (3/3/1-0, 0)
to-be-insane= mainomai (0/0/0-3, 1)
to-be-inside= eneimi (Lk 11:41)
to-be-king= basileuō (1/0/3-0, 0)
beloved= agapētos (3/3/2-1, 0)
below= katō (2/2/1-2, 2)
to-be-loyal= pisteuō (common)
belt= zōnē (2/2/0-0, 0)
to-be-made-into-a-eunuch= eunouchizō (Mt 19:12)
to-be-merciful= eleeō (9/3/4-0, 0)
to-be-merry= euphrainō (0/0/6-2, 0)
to-bend= kuptō (0/1/0-0, 1)
to-bend-down= parakuptō (0/0/1-0, 2)
to-bend-over= sugkuptō (Lk 13:11)
to-be-nearly-smothered= tuphomai (Mt 12:20)
beneath= hupokatō (1/3/1-0, 1)
benefaction= charis (0/0/8-17, 4)
to-be-of-doubtful-mind= meteōrizomai (Lk 12:29)
to-be-of-right-mind= sōphroneō (0/1/1-0, 0)
to-be-quiet= sigaō (0/0/3-3, 0)
to-be-ready= proskartereō (0/1/0-6, 0)
to-be-ruler= hēgemoneuō (0/0/2-0, 0)
to-be-sad= stugnazō (1/1/0-0, 0)
to-be-sane= sōphroneō (0/1/1-0, 0)
to-be-seated= kathizō (8/8/7-9, 3)
to-be-seated-near= parakathezomai (Lk 10:39)
to-be-seated-together= sugkathizō (Lk 22:55)
to-beseech= diastellō (1/5/0-1, 0)
to-be-silent= siōpaō (2/5/2-1, 0)
to-besmirch= deigmatizō (Mt 1:19)
to-be-sorry= metamelomai (3/0/0-0, 0)
to-be-spellbound= ekkremanummi (Lk 21:48)
to-be-startled= throeō (1/1/0-0, 0)
to-be-stirred-up= thorubeō (1/1/0-2, 0)
to-bestow= dōreomai (Mk 15:45)
to-be-straightened-up= anorthoō (0/0/1-1, 0)
to-be-suitable= prepō (Mt 3:15)
to-be-superior= diapherō (3/1/2-2, 0)
to-be-surprised= existēmi (1/4/3-8, 0)
to-be-swamped= sumplēroō (0/0/2-1, 0)
to-be-taken-captive= aichmalōtizō (Lk 21:24)
to-be-tetrarch= tetrarcheō (0/0/3-0, 0)
Bethany= Bēthania (2/4/2-0, 4)
to-be-there= pareimi (1/0/1-5, 2)
to-be-thirsty= dipsaō (5/0/0-0, 6)
Bethlehem= Bēthleem (5/0/2-0, 1)
Bethphage= Bēthphagē (1/1/1-0, 0)
Bethsaida= Bēthsaida (1/2/2-0, 2)
Bethzatha= Bēthzatha (Jn 5:2)
between= metaxu (2/0/2-3, 1)
to-be-uncertain= aporeō (0/1/1-1, 1)
to-be-unoccupied= scholazō (Mt 12:44)
to-be-unresponsive= hēsuchazō (0/0/2-2, 0)
to-be-unrighteous= adikeō (1/0/1-5, 0)
to-be-wealthy= plouteō (0/0/2-0, 0)
to-be-with= suneimi (0/0/2-1, 0)
beyond= peran (7/7/1-0, 8)
to-bid-goodbye= apotassomai (0/1/2-2, 0)
bier= soros (Lk 7:14)
bill-of-divorce= apostasion (2/1/0-0, 0)
to-bind= desmeuō (1/0/1-1, 0)
to-bind-himself-by-a-curse= anathematizō (0/1/0-3, 0)
binding= desmos (0/1/2-5, 0)
bird= peteinon (4/2/4-2, 0)
birth= gennēsis (textual variant found at Mt 1:18)
birthday= genesia (1/1/0-0, 0)

birth-pain= ōdin (1/1/0-1, 0)
to-bisect= dichotomeō (1/0/1-0, 0)
bitter-gall= cholē (1/0/0-1, 0)
bitterly= pikrōs (1/0/1-0, 0)
black= melas (Mt 5:36)
to-blackmail= sukophanteō (0/0/2-0, 0)
blame= aitios (0/0/3-1, 0)
blameless= anaitios (2/0/0-0, 0)
to-blaspheme= blasphēmeō (3/4/3-4, 1)
blasphemy= blasphēmia (4/3/1-0, 1)
bleacher= gnapheus (Mk 9:3)
to-bless= eulogeō (5/5/13-1, 1)
blessed= eulogētos (0/1/1-0, 0)
to-bless-greatly= kateulogeō (Mk 10:16)
blind= tuphlos (17/5/8-1, 16)
to-blind= tuphloō (Jn 12:40)
blood= haima (11/3/8-11, 6)
blow= plēgē (0/0/2-2, 0)
Boanerges= Boanērgos (Mk 3:17)
Boas= Boos (Lk 3:32)
boat= ploion (13/18/8-19, 7)
Boaz= Bōes (2/0/0-0, 0)
bodily= sōmatikos (Lk 3:22)
body= sōma (14/4/13-1, 6)
body-part= melos (2/0/0-0, 0)
boldness= parrēsia (0/1/0-5, 9)
bone= osteon (1/0/1-0, 1)
book= biblos (1/1/2-3, 0)
booklet= biblion (1/1/3-0, 2)
born= gennētos (1/0/1-0, 0)
bosom= kolpos (0/0/3-1, 2)
both= amphoteroi (3/0/5-3, 0)
to-bother= skullō (1/1/2-0, 0)
bowl= chalkion (Mk 4:7)
bramble-bush= batos 1 (0/1/2-2, 0)
branch= klados (3/2/1-0, 0)
bravo= euge (Lk 19:17)
bread= artos (common)
to-break= klaō (3/3/2-4, 0)
to-break-apart= diaspaō (0/1/0-1, 0)
to-break-in= diorussō (3/0/1-0, 0)
breaking= klasis (0/0/1-1, 0)
to-break-to-pieces= sunthlaomai (1/0/1-0, 0)
to-break-up= kataklaō (0/1/1-0, 0)
breast= mastos (0/0/2-0, 0)
to-breast-feed= ektrephō (textual variant found at Lk 23:29)
to-breathe-upon= emphusaō (Jn 20:22)
to-bribe= diaseiō (Lk 3:14)
bride= numphē (1/0/2-0, 1)
bridegroom= numphios (6/3/2-0, 4)
briefly= suntomōs (textual variant found at Mk 8:16)
to-bring= eispherō (1/0/4-1, 0)
to-bring-around= peripherō (Mk 6:55)
to-bring-charges= diaballō (Lk 16:1)
to-bring-down= kathaireō (0/2/3-3, 0)
to-bring-in-for-marriage= eggamizō (textual variant found at Mt 24:38)
to-bring-into-sight= anaphainō (0/0/1-1, 0)
to-bring-out= ekpherō (0/1/1-4, 0)
to-bring-safely-through= diasōzō (1/0/1-5, 0)
to-bring-together= suzeugnumi (1/1/0-0, 0)
to-bring-up= anapherō (1/1/1-0, 0)
broiled= optos (Lk 24:42)
fragment= klasma (2/4/1-0, 2)
brood= nossia (Lk 13:34)
brother= adelphos (common)
brow= ophrus (Lk 4:29)
to-bruise= katakoptō (Mk 5:5)
to-bud= mēkunō (Mk 4:27)
to-build= oikodomeō (8/4/12-4, 1)
building= oikodomē (1/2/0-0, 0)
bull= tauros (1/0/0-1, 0)
bunch-of-grapes= staphulē (1/0/1-0, 0)
to-bundle= eneileō (Mk 15:46)
burden= phortion (2/0/2-1, 0)
to-burden= phortizō (1/0/1-0, 0)
burial= entaphiasmos (0/1/0-0, 1)
burial-place= taphē (Mt 7:27)
to-kindle= kaiō (1/0/2-0, 2)
to-burn-down= empimprēmi (Mt 22:7)
to-burn-incense= thumiaō (Lk 1:9)
burnt-offering= holokautōma (Mk 12:33)
to-burst-upon= prosrēgnumi (0/0/2-0, 0)
to-bury= thaptō (3/0/3-4, 0)
bushel= modios (1/1/1-0/0)
business= emporia (Mt 22:5)
but= alla (common)
to-buy= agorazō (7/5/5-0, 3)
by-all-means= pantōs (0/0/1-2, 0)
by-foot= pezē (1/1/0-0, 0)
by-no-means= oudamōs (Mt 2:6)

C

Caesar= Kaisar (4/4/7-10, 3)
Caesarea= Kaisareia (1/1/0-15, 0)
Caiaphas= Kaiaphas (2/0/1-1, 5)
Cainan= Kainam (0/0/2-0, 0)
calf= moschos (0/0/3-0, 0)
to-call= kaleō (26/4/43-18, 2)
called= klētos (Mt 22:14)
to-call-together= sugkaleō (1/0/4-3, 0)
to-call-upon= epikaleō (1/0/0-20, 0)
calm= galēnē (1/1/1-0, 0)
camel= kamēlos (3/2/1-0, 0)
to-camp-out= aulizomai (1/0/1-0, 0)
Cana= Kana (0/0/0-0, 4)
Canaanean= Kananaios (1/1/0-0, 0)
Canaanite= Chananaios (Matt 15:22)
Capharnaum= Kapharnaoum (4/3/4-0, 5)
captive= aichmalōtos (Lk 4:18)
to-capture= zōgreō (Lk 5:10)
to-care-for= episkeptomai (2/0/3-4, 0)
carefully= epimelōs (Lk 15:8)
carpenter= tektōn (1/1/0-0, 0)
to-carry= pherō (4/15/4-10, 16)
to-carry-away= apopherō (0/1/1-1, 0)
to-carry-from= parapherō (0/1/1-0, 0)
cash= kerma (Jn 2:15)
cash-changer= kermatistēs (Jn 2:14)
to-cast-out= ekballō (28/18/20-5, 6)
casting-net= amphiblēstron (Mt 4:18)
catch= agra (0/0/2-0, 0)
to-catch-fish= halieuō (Jn 21:3)
to-catch-sight-of= theōreō (2/7/7-14, 24)
to-cause-to-stumble= skandalizō (14/8/2-0, 2)
cave= spēlaios (1/1/1-0, 1)
to-cease= kopazō (1/2/0-0, 0)
cellar= kruptē (Lk 11:33)
to-censure= embrimaomai (1/2/0-0, 2)
centurion= kenturiōn (0/3/0-0, 0)
Cephas= Kēphas (Jn 1:42)
certainty= asphaleia (0/0/1-1, 0)
cervix= mētra (Lk 2:23)
chaff= achuron (1/0/1-0, 0)
chain= halusis (0/3/1-4, 0)
chance= sugkuria (Lk 10:31)
chaos= akatastasia (Lk 21:9)
charcoal-fire= anthrakia (0/0/0-0, 2)
to-charge= entellō (4/2/1-2, 4)
chasm= chasma (Lk 16:26)
cheek= siagōn (1/0/1-0, 0)
to-cheer-up= tharseō (3/2/0-1, 1)
chest= stēthos (0/0/2-0, 2)
to-chew= trōgō (1/0/0-0, 5)
child= pais (8/0/9-6, 1)
childhood= paidiothen (Mk 9:21)
to-choke= sumpnigō (1/2/2-0, 0)
to-choose= eklegomai (0/1/4-7, 5)
Chorazin= Chorazin (1/0/1-0, 0)
chosen= eklektos (4/3/2-0, 0)
Chuza= Chouzas (Lk 3:8)
to-circle= kukloō (0/0/1-1, 1)

to-circumcise= peritemnō (0/0/2-5, 1)
citizen= politēs (0/0/2-1, 0)
city= polis (27/8/39-42, 8)
clay-jar= keramion (0/1/1-0, 0)
clay-tile= keramos (Lk 5:19)
to-cleanse= diakathairō (Lk 3:17)
clearly= tēlaugōs (Mk 8:25)
Cleopas= Kleopas (Lk 24:18)
to-cling= kollaomai (1/0/2-5, 0)
to-cling-to= proskollaō (Mk 7:10)
to-cloak= perikaluptō (0/1/1-0, 0)
Clopas= Klōpas (Jn 19:27)
close-by= homou (0/0/0-1, 3)
to-close-in= episuntrechō (Mk 9:25)
cloth= soudarion (0/0/1-1, 2)
to-clothe= enduō (3/3/4-1, 0)
clothes= enduma (7/0/1-0, 0)
cloud= nephelē (4/4/5-1, 0)
club= xulon (2/2/2-4, 0)
coastal-region= paralios (Lk 6:17)
coat= himation (14/12/10-8, 6)
cohort= speira (1/1/0-3, 2)
coin= nomisma (Mt 22:19)
cold-water= psuchros (Mt 10:42)
to-collapse= sumpiptō (Lk 6:49)
to-collect= episunagō (3/2/3-0, 0)
colt= pōlos (3/4/4-0, 1)
to-come= erchomai (common)
to-come-through= dierchomai (2/2/10-21, 2)
to-come-about= sumbainō (0/1/1-3, 0)
to-come-back-through= epanerchomai (0/0/2-0, 0)
come-here= deuro (1/1/1-2, 1)
to-come-in-upon= epeiserchomai (Lk 21:35)
come-on!= deute (6/3/0-0, 2)
to-come-out= exerchomai (common)
to-come-together= sunerchomai (2/1/2-16, 2)
to-come-upon= eperchomai (0/0/3-4, 0)
coming-day= epiousios (1/0/1-0, 0)
commandment= entolē (6/6/4-1, 10)
to-commend= epaineō (Lk 16:8)
to-commission= anadeiknumi (0/0/1-1, 0)
to-commit-adultery= moicheuō (4/1/2-0, 1)
common= koinos (0/2/0-5, 0)
commotion= thorubos (2/2/0-3, 0)
companion= koinōnos (1/0/1-0, 0)
company= sunodia (Lk 2:44)
comparable-to= homoios (9/0/9-1, 2)
to-compare= homoioō (8/1/3-1, 0)
compassionate= oiktirmōn (Lk 6:36)
to-compel= anagkazō (1/1/1-2, 0)
to-compile= anatassomai (Lk 1:1)
to-complete= teleō (7/0/4-1, 2)
completely= pantelēs (Lk 13:11)
completion= apartismos (Lk 14:28)
to-comprehend= suniēmi (9/5/4-4, 0)
comprehension= sunesis (0/1/1-0, 0)
comrade= hetairos (3/0/0-0, 0)
to-conceal= sugkaluptō (Lk 12:2)
to-concede= eaō (1/0/2-7, 0)
to-conclude= sunteleō (0/1/2-1)
conclusion= sunteleia (5/0/0-0, 0)
to-condemn= katadikazō (2/0/2-0, 0)
to-confer= diatithēmi (0/0/1-1, 0)
to-confess= homologeō (4/0/2-3, 3)
to-confess-freely= anthomologeomai (Lk 2:38)
to-confirm= bebaioō (Mk 16:20)
to-confront= machomai (0/0/0-1, 1)
confusion= aporia (Lk 21:25)
to-congratulate= makarizō (Lk 1:48)
to-consent= sugkatatithēmi (Lk 23:51)
consequently= ara (7/2/7-6, 0)
to-consider= phroneō (1/1/0-1, 0)
to-consign= tassō (1/0/1-4, 0)
consolation= paraklēsis (0/0/2-4, 0)
constellation= astron (0/0/1-2, 0)
to-consume= katesthiō (1/2/3-0, 1)
container= aggos (Mt 13:48)
to-contaminate= miainō (Jn 18:28)
contentment= eudokia (1/0/2-0, 0)
to-control= sunechō (1/0/6-3, 0)
to-converse= homileō (0/0/2-2, 0)
to-convey-for-burial= ekkomizō (Lk 7:12)
to-convulse= sparassō (0/2/1-0, 0)
cooked-food= opsarion (0/0/0-0, 5)
to-cool= katapsuchō (Lk 16:24)
copper= chalkos (1/2/0-0, 0)
cor= koros (Aramaic) (Lk 16:7)
corner= gōnia (2/1/1-2, 0)
corpse= ptōma (2/2/0-0, 0)
correctly= orthōs (0/1/3-0, 0)
to-corrupt= diaphtheirō (Lk 12:33)
to-count= arithmeō (1/0/1-0, 0)
to-count-worthy= kataxioō (0/0/1-1, 0)
to-cover= kaluptō (2/0/1-0, 0)
to-create= ktizō (1/1/0-0, 0)
to-cross-over= diaperaō (2/2/1-1, 0)
to-crucify= stauroō (10/8/6-2, 11)
to-crucify-with= sustauroō (1/1/0-0, 1)
to-crush= likmaō (1/0/1-0, 0)
to-cry= krazō (12/11/3-11, 4)
to-cry-out= anakrazō (2/0/3-0, 0)
Cosam= Kōsam (Lk 3:28)
costly= polutelēs (Mk 3:14)
cot= klinidion (0/0/2-0, 0)
council= boulē (0/0/2-7, 0)
council-member= bouleutēs (0/1/1-0, 0)
council-of-elders= presbuterion (Lk 22:66)
courtyard= aulē (3/3/2-0, 3)
covenant= diathēkē (1/1/2-2, 0)
covetousness= pleonexia (0/1/1-0, 0)
craftiness= panourgia (Lk 20:23)
creation= ktisis (0/3/0-0, 0)
criminal= kakourgos (0/0/3-0, 0)
cripple= anapeiros (0/0/2-0, 0)
crooked= skolios (0/0/1-1, 0)
cross= stauros (5/4/3-0, 4)
crow= korax (Lk 12:24)
crowd= ochlos (common)
crown= stephanos (1/1/0-0, 2)
cubit= pēchus (1/0/1-0, 1)
to-cultivate= exanistēmi (0/1/1-1, 0)
cumin= kuminon (Mt 23:23)
cunning= dolos (1/2/0-1, 1)
cup= potērion (8/6/5-0, 1)
cure= iasis (0/0/1-2, 0)
to-cure= iaomai (4/1/11-4, 3)
to-curse= katathematizō (Mt 26:74)
curtain= katapetasma (1/1/1-0, 0)
cushion= proskephalaion (Mk 4:38)
custodia= koustōdia (3/0/0-0, 0)
custom= ethos (0/0/3-7, 1)
to-cut= koptō (3/1/2-0, 0)
to-cut-away= apokoptō (2/0/0-1, 2)
to-cut-off= ekkoptō (4/0/3-0, 0)
Cyrenian= Kurēnaios (1/1/1-3, 0)

D

daily= biōtikos (Lk 21:34)
Dalmanoutha= Dalmanoutha (Mk 8:10)
to-damn= kakologeō (1/2/0-1, 0)
to-dance= orcheomai (2/1/1-0, 0)
dancing= choros (Lk 15:25)
Daniel= Daniēl (Mt 24:15)
to-dare= tolmaō (1/2/1-2, 1)
dark= skotia (1/0/1-0, 8)
to-darken= skotizomai (1/1/0-0, 0)
darkness= skotos (7/1/4-3, 1)
darksome= skoteinos (1/0/2-0, 0)
daughter= thugatēr (8/5/9-3, 1)
David= Dauid (17/7/13-11, 1)
to-dawn= epiphōskō (1/0/1-0, 0)
day-of-unleavened-bread= azumos (1/2/2-2, 0)

day= hēmera (common)
dead= nekros (12/8/14-17, 8)
deadly-poison= thanasimos (Mk 16:18)
to-deal-mercifully-with= hilaskomai (Lk 18:13)
death= thanatos (7/6/7-8, 8)
debauchery= kraipalē (Lk 21:34)
debit= opheilē (Mt 18:32)
debt= opheilēma (Mt 6:12)
debtor= opheiletēs (2/0/1-0, 0)
Decapolis= Dekapolis (1/2/0-0, 0)
to-deceive= planaō (8/4/1-0, 2)
deceiver= planos (Mt 27:63)
to-deceive-thoroughly = apoplanaō (Mk 13:22)
deception= planē (Mt 27:64)
to-decide= horizō (0/0/1-5, 0)
to-decipher= diermēneuō (0/0/1-1, 0)
to-declare= exaggelē (textual variant found at Mk 16:8)
decline= ptōsis (1/0/1-0, 0)
decree= dogma (0/0/1-2, 0)
to-deduce= aisthanomai (Lk 9:45)
deed= praxis (1/0/1-1,0)
to-deem-worthy= axioō (0/0/1-2, 0)
deep= bathus (0/0/1-1, 1)
deep-part= pelagos (1/0/0-1, 0)
to-defeat= nikaō (0/0/1-0, 1)
to-defend= apologeomai (0/0/2-6, 0)
deficiency= husterēma (Lk 4:21)
deficit= husterēsis (Mk 12:44)
to-defile= koinoō (5/5/0-3, 0)
definitely= ontōs (0/1/2-0, 1)
to-defraud= apostereō (Mk 10:19)
to-delay= chronizō (2/0/2-0, 0)
to-deliberate-on= enthumeomai (2/0/0-0, 0)
deliberation= enthumēsis (2/0/0-1, 0)
to-deliver= paradidōmi (common)
deliverance= apolutrōsis (Lk 21:28)
demand= aitēma (Lk 23:24)
to-demand-back= apaiteō (0/0/2-0)
to-demolish= kataluō (5/3/3-3, 0)
demon= daimonion (11/13/23-1, 6)
denarius= dēnarion (6/3/3-0, 2)
to-denounce= oneidizō (3/2/1-0, 0)
to-deny= arneomai (4/2/4-4, 4)
to-depart= diachōrizō (Lk 9:33)
deportation= metoikesia (3/0/0-0, 0)
to-deposit= apotithēmi (1/0/0-1, 0)
depth= bathos (1/1/1-0, 0)
to-descend= katabainō (common)
descendant= teknon (14/9/14-5, 3)
descendantless= ateknos (0/0/2-0, 0)
to-describe= exēgeomai (0/0/1-4, 1)
deserted= erēmos (8/9/11-9, 5)
deserted-place= erēmia (1/1/0-0, 0)
to-designate= prostassō (2/1/1-3, 0)
desire= epithumia (0/1/1-0, 1)
to-desire= epithumeō (2/0/4-1, 0)
to-desist-from= dialeipō (Lk 7:45)
desolation= erēmōsis (1/1/1-0, 0)
to-despise= kataphroneō (2/0/1-0, 0)
destitute= penichros (Lk 2:21)
to-destroy= apollumi (common)
destruction= apōleia (2/1/0-1, 1)
to-detain= katechō (0/0/3-1, 0)
to-devastate= rhēgnumi (2/2/2-0, 0)
devastation= rhēgma (Lk 6:47)
devil= diabolos (6/0/6-2, 3)
to-devour= bibrōskō (Jn 6:13)
to-dialogue= dialegomai (0/1/0-10, 0)
didramcha= didrachmon (Mt 17:24)
to-die= thnēskō (1/1/2-2, 2)
to-dig= skaptō (0/0/3-0), 0
difficultly= bareōs (1/0/0/0-1, 0)
to-dig-a-hole= orussō (2/1/0-0, 0)
dill= anēthon (Mt 23:23)
to-dine= anakeimai (5/3/1-0, 4)
dinner= dochē (0/0/2-0, 0)
to-dip= embaptō (1/1/0-0, 0)
to-direct= suntassō (3/0/0-0, 0)
dirt= chous (Mk 6:11)
to-discharge= sunairō (3/0/0-0, 0)
disciple= mathētēs (common)
to-discipline= paideuō (0/0/2-2, 0)
to-disclose= mēnuō (0/0/1-1, 1)
to-discuss= suzēteō (0/6/2-2, 0)
disease= nosos (5/1/4-1, 0)
to-disfigure= aphanizō (3/0/0-1, 0)
disgrace= oneidos (Lk 1:25)
dish= trublion (1/1/0-0, 0)
dishonorable= atimos (1/1/0-0, 0)
disloyalty= apistia (1/3/0-0, 0)
disobedient= apeithēs (0/0/1-1, 0)
to-disown= aparneomai (4/4/3-0, 0)
to-disperse= skorpizō (1/0/1-0, 2)
to-display= hupodeiknumi (1/0/3-2, 0)
dispute= philoneikia (Lk 22:24)
to-disregard= akuroō (1/1/0-0, 0)
distant= makros (1/0/3-0, 0)
to-distort= diastrephō (1/0/2-3, 0)
to-distract= thorubazō (Lk 10:41)
distress= thlipsis (4/3/0-5, 2)
to-distribute= diadidōmi (0/0/2-1, 1)
to-disturb= tarassō (2/2/2-3, 6)
to-disturb-deeply= diatarassō (Lk 1:29)
disunity= diamerismos (Lk 12:51)
ditch= bothunos (2/0/1-0, 0)
to-divide= merizō (3/4/1-0, 0)
to-divide-up= diamerizō (1/1/6-2, 1)
to-divulge= ereugomai (Mt 13:35)
to-do= poieō (common)
dog= kuōn (1/0/1-0, 0)
to-do-good= agathopoieō (0/0/4-0, 0)
to-do-ill= kakopoieō (0/1/1-0, 0)
to-don= phoreō (1/0/0-0, 1)
donkey= onikos (1/1/0-0, 0)
door= thura (4/6/4-10, 7)
door-keeper= thurōros (0/1/0-0, 3)
double= diplous (Mt 23:15)
to-doubt= distazō (2/0/0-0, 0)
dove= peristera (3/2/2-0, 3)
drachma= drachmē (0/0/2-0, 0)
to-drag= katasurō (Lk 12:58)
to-drag-down= buthizō (Lk 5:7)
dragnet= sagēnē (Mt 13:47)
to-draw= spaō (0/1/0-1, 0)
to-draw-away= apospaō (1/0/1-2, 0)
to-draw-out= anaspaō (0/0/1-1, 0)
dream= onar (6/0/0-0, 0)
to-dress= amphiennumi (2/0/1-0, 0)
to-drink= pinō (common)
to-drink-down= katapinō (Mt 23:24)
to-drive= elaunō (0/1/1-0, 1)
drop= thrombos (Lk 22:44)
to-drown= pnigō (2/1/0-0, 0)
drunkenness= methē (Lk 21:34)
to-dry= ekmassō (0/0/2-0, 3)
dung= koprion (Lk 13:8)
dung-heap= kopria (Lk 14:35)
to-dunk= baptō (0/0/1-0, 1)
dusk= dusis (textual variant found at Mk 16:8)
dust= koniortos (1/0/2-2, 0)
to-dwell-nearby= perioikeō (Lk 1:65)

E

each= hekastos (4/1/5-11, 4)
eagle= aetos (1/0/1-0, 0)
ear= ous (7/4/7-5, 0)
early= prōi (3/6/0-1, 2)
early-in-the-day= orthrinos (Lk 22:24)
early-morning= orthros (0/0/1-1, 1)
ear-of-grain= stachus (1/3/1-0, 0)
earthquake= seismos (4/1/1-1, 0)
easier= eukopōteros (2/2/3-0, 0)
east= anatolē (5/1/2-0, 0)
to-eat= esthiō (common)
to-eat-with= sunesthiō (0/0/1-2, 0)
Eber= Eber (Lk 3:35)
ecstasy= ekstasis (0/2/1-4, 0)

edge= peras (1/0/1-0, 0)
edible= brōsimos (Lk 24:41)
to-educate= katēcheō (0/0/1-3, 0)
effort= ergasia (0/0/1-4, 0)
egg= ōon (Lk 11:12)
Egypt= Aigyptos (4/0/0-15, 0)
eight= oktō (0/0/3-2, 2)
eighteen= dekaoktō (0/0/2-0, 0)
eighth= ogdoos (0/0/1-1, 0)
eighty= ogdoēkonta (0/0/2-0, 0)
to-elapse= diaginomai (0/1/0-2, 0)
elder= presbuteros (12/7/5-18, 1)
elderly= presbutēs (Lk 1:18)
Eleazar= Eleazar (2/0/0-0, 0)
to-elect= suntithēmi (0/0/1-1, 1)
eleven= hendeka (1/1/2-2, 0)
eleventh= hendekatos (2/0/0-0, 0)
ēli= ēli (Aramaic) (2/0/0-0, 0)
Eliakim= Eliakim (2/0/1-0, 0)
Eliezer= Eliezer (Lk 3:29)
Elijah= Ēlias (9/9/7-0, 2)
Elioud= Eliud (2/0/0-0, 0)
Elisabet= Elizabeth (0/0/9-0, 0)
Elisaios= Elisha (Lk 4:27)
Elmadam= Elmadam (Lk 3:28)
elōi= elōi (Aramaic) (0/2/0-0, 0)
elsewhere= allachou (Mk 1:38)
to-embark= embainō (5/5/3-0, 3)
embassy-of-elders= presbeia (0/0/2-0, 0)
to-embrace= enagkalizomai (0/2/0-0, 0)
Emmanuel= Emmanouēl (Matt 1:23)
Emmaus= Emmaous (Lk 24:13)
emphatically= ekperissōs (Mk 14:31)
empty= kenos (0/1/3-1, 0)
to-encloak= diazōnnumi (0/0/0-0, 3)
to-enclose= sugkleiō (Lk 5:6)
encounter= apantēsis (1/0/0-1, 0)
to-encounter= apantaō (0/1/1-0, 0)
end= telos (6/3/4-0, 1)
enemy= echthros (7/1/8-2, 0)
to-energize= energeō (1/1/0-0, 0)
to-enflame= anaptō (Lk 12:49)
to-enjoin= paraggellō (2/3/4-11, 0)
to-enlarge= platunō (Mt 5:23)
to-enlist= aggareuō (2/1/0-0, 0)
enmity= echthra (Lk 23:12)
Enoch= Enoch (Lk 3:37)
Enos= Enōs (Lk 3:38)
enough= arketos (2/0/0-0, 0)
to-ensnare= agreuō (Mk 12:13)
to-enter= eiserchomai (common)
to-enter-with= suneiserchomai (0/0/0-0, 2)
to-entrap= pagideuō (Mt 15:22)
to-entreat= parabiazō (0/0/1-1, 0)
envy= phthonos (1/1/0-0, 0)
eon= aiōn (8/4/7-2, 13)
ephphatha= ephphatha (Aramaic) (Mk 7:34)
equal= isos (1/2/1-1, 1)
Er= Ēr (Lk 3:28)
ere= enantion (0/0/3-2, 0)
to-escape= ekchōreō (Lk 21:21)
escort= hodēgos (3/0/0-1, 0)
to-escort= hodēgeō (1/0/1-1, 1)
Esli= Hesli (Lk 3:25)
to-establish= kathistēmi (4/0/3-5, 0)
to-estimate= psēphizō (Lk 14:28)
eternal= aiōnios (6/4/4-2, 17)
eunuch= eunouchos (3/0/0-5, 0)
to-evaluate= diakrinō (2/1/0-4, 0)
even= te (3/0/8-100+, 3)
even-as= hōsper (10/0/2-3, 2)
even-if= kan (2/3/3-1, 4)
evening= opsia (7/5/0-0, 2)
even-still= akmēn (Mt 15:16)
event= pragma (1/0/1-1, 0)
ever= an (common)
everyone= hapas (3/4/11-12, 1)
everywhere= pantachou (0/2/1-3, 0)
evil= ponēros (26/2/13-8, 3)
evilness= ponēria (1/1/1-1, 0)
evil-spirit= daimōn (Mt 8:31)
to-exalt= hupsoō (3/0/6-3, 5)
to-examine= dokimazō (0/0/2-0, 0)
example= hupodeigma (Jn 13:15)
to-exceed= perisseuō (5/1/4-1, 2)
exceedingly= lian (4/4/1-0, 0)
except-for= parektos (1/0/0-1, 0)
excess= perisseuma (1/1/1-0, 0)
excessive= perissos (2/1/0-0, 1)
excessively= perissōs (1/2/0-1, 0)
exchange= antallagma (1/1/0-0, 0)
to-exclaim= anaphōneō (Lk 1:42)
to-exclude= aphorizō (2/0/1-2, 0)
to-excuse= aphiēmi (common)
executioner= spekoulatōr (Mk 6:27)
to-exhaust= hupōpiazō (Lk 5:18)
to-exhort= parakaleō (9/9/7-22, 0)
to-exist-previously= prouparchō (0/0/1-1, 0)
exodus= exodos (Lk 9:31)
to-expand= epathroizō (Lk 11:29)
to-expect= prosdokaō (2/0/6-5, 0)
to-expend= prosanaloō (Lk 8:43)
to-expire= teleutaō (4/2/1-2, 1)
to-explain= diasapheō (2/0/0-0, 0)
to-explicate= epiluō (0/1/0-1, 0)
to-expose= elegchō (1/0/1-0, 3)
expense= dapanē (Lk 14:28)
expiration= teleutē (Mt 2:15)
to-extend= ekphuō (1/1/0-0, 0)
to-extinguish= sbennumi (2/1/0-0, 0)
eye= ophthalmos (common)
eyeball= omma (1/1/0-0, 0)
eyelet= trupēma (Mt 19:24)
eyewitness= autoptēs (Lk 1:2)

F

face= prosōpon (10/3/12-12, 0)
to-face-death= apothnēskō (5/8/10-4, 28)
to-face-death-with= sunapothnēskō (Mk 14:31)
to-fail= ekleipō (0/0/3-0, 0)
to-faint= ekluō (1/1/0-0, 0)
to-fall= piptō (19/8/17-9, 3)
to-fall-asleep= aphupnoō (Lk 8:23)
to-fall-down= katapiptō (0/0/1-2, 0)
to-fall-in= empiptō (1/0/2-0, 0)
to-fall-out= ekpiptō (text variant found at Mk 13:25)
to-fall-to= prospiptō (1/3/3-1, 0)
falsely-anointed-one= pseudochristos (1/1/0-0, 0)
false-prophet= pseudoprophētēs (3/1/1-1, 0)
false-witness= pseudomartus (Mt 26:60)
false-witness-testimony= pseudomarturia (2/0/0-0, 0)
famine= limos (1/1/4-2, 0)
far= porrō (1/1/1-0, 0)
far-away= makran (1/1/2-3, 1)
farmer= geōrgos (6/5/5-0, 1)
far-off= makrothen (2/5/4-0, 0)
farther= porrōteros (Lk 24:28)
to-fast= nēsteuō (8/6/4-2, 0)
fasting= nēsteia (0/0/1-2, 0)
father= patēr (common)
father-in-law= pentheros (Jn 13:18)
to-fathom= epistamai (0/1/0-9, 0)
fattened= siteutos (0/0/3-3, 0)
fattened-calf= sitistos (Mt 22:4)
faultless= amemptos (Lk 1:6)
fear= phobos (3/1/7-5, 3)
to-fear= phobeomai (18/12/23-14, 5)
fearful-event= phobētron (Lk 11:21)
fearlessly= aphobōs (Lk 1:74)
feast= heortē (2/2/3-0, 17)
to-feed= chortazō (4/4/4-0, 1)
feeding-trough= phatnē (0/0/4-0, 0)
fellow-slave= sundoulos (5/0/0-0, 0)

female= thēlus (1/1/0-0, 0)
female-slave= doulē (0/0/2-1, 0)
fever= puretos (1/1/2-1, 1)
few= oligoi (6/2/3-2, 0)
field= agros (17/9/9-1, 0)
fierce= chalepos (Mt 8:28)
fifteenth= pentekaidekatos (Lk 1:3)
fifty= pentēkonta (0/1/3-1, 2)
fig= sukon (1/1/1-0, 0)
fig-tree= sukē (5/4/3-0, 2)
to-fill= pimplēmi (2/0/13-9, 0)
to-filter-out= diulizō (Mt 23:24)
to-find= heuriskō (common)
fine= kalos (21/11/9-0, 7)
finger= daktulos (1/1/3-0, 3)
to-finish= teleioō (0/0/2-1, 5)
to-finish-off= ekteleō (0/0/2-0, 0)
fire= pur (12/4/7-4, 1)
first= prōtos (17/10/10-12, 6)
first-born= prōtotokos (Lk 2:7)
fish= ichthus (5/4/7-0, 3)
fisher= halieus (2/2/1-0, 0)
fish-hook= agkistron (Mt 17:27)
fit= hikanos (3/3/9-17, 0)
five= pente (12/3/9-5, 5)
five-hundred= pentakosioi (Lk 7:41)
five-thousand= pentakischilioi (2/2/1-0, 1)
flame= phlox (0/0/1-1, 0)
to-flash= astraptō (0/0/2-0, 0)
to-flash-like-lightning= exastraptō (Lk 9:29)
flashing-light= astrapē (2/0/3-0, 0)
flask= aggeion (Mt 25:4)
to-flatten= edaphizō (Lk 19:44)
to-flavor= artuō (0/1/1-0, 0)
to-flavor-with-myrrh= smurnizō (Mk 15:23)
flax-linen= bussos (Lk 16:19)
to-flee= pheugō (7/5/3-2, 2)
to-flee-away= ekpheugō (0/0/1-2, 0)
flesh= sarx (5/4/2-3, 13)
flight= phugē (Mt 20:24)
to-flip= anatrepō (Jn 2:15)
flock= poimnē (1/0/1-0, 1)
flood= kataklusmos (2/0/1-0, 0)
flood-tide= plēmmura (Lk 6:48)
to-flourish= phuō (0/0/2-0, 0)
to-flourish-with= sumphuomai (Lk 8:7)
flow= pēgē (Mk 5:29)
flute-player= aulētēs (Mt 9:23)
fold= poimnion (0/0/1-2, 0)
to-follow= akoloutheō (common)
to-follow-after= katakoloutheō (0/0/1-1, 0)
following-day= hexēs (0/0/2-3, 0)
to-follow-upon= epakoloutheō (Mk 16:20)
folly= aphrosunē (Mk 7:22)
food= chortos (3/2/1-0, 1)
fool= rhaka (Mt 5:22)
foolish= anoētos (Lk 24:25)
foot= pous (10/6/19-19, 14)
foot-shackle= pedē (0/2/1-0, 0)
foot-soldier= stratopedon (Lk 21:20)
footstool= hupopodion (1/0/1-2, 0)
for= gar (common)
to-force= biazō (1/0/1-0, 0)
forceful-one= biastēs (Mt 11:12)
forecourt= proaulion (Mk 14:68)
foreign-born= allogenēs (Lk 17:18)
foreigner= allotrios (2/0/1-1, 1)
forelimb= agkalē (Lk 2:28)
to-forerun= proporeuomai (0/0/1-1, 0)
to-forfeit= zēmioō (1/1/1-0, 0)
form= eidos (0/0/2-0, 1)
fornication= porneia (3/1/0-3, 1)
fornicator= pornē (2/0/1-0, 0)
for-one= men (20/6/10-47, 8)
to-forsake= egkataleipō (1/1/0-2, 0)
for-show= prophasis (0/1/1-1, 1)
for-this-reason= dio (1/0/2-7, 0)
fortunate= makarios (13/0/15-0, 2)
forty= tesserakonta (1/1/1-8, 1)
for-what-reason= hinati (2/0/1-2, 0)
foundation= themilios (0/0/3-0, 0)
four= tessares (1/2/1-6, 2)
four-drachma= statēr (Mt 17:27)
four-fold= tetraplous (Lk 8:19)
four-month= tetramēnos (Jn 4:35)
fourteen= dekatessares (3/0/0-0, 0)
fourth= tetartos (1/1/0-1, 0)
four-thousand= tetrakischilioi (2/2/0-1, 0)
fox= alōpēx (1/0/2-0, 0)
fragrance= osmē (Jn 3:12)
fragrant-spice= arōma (0/1/2-0, 1)
frankincense= libanos (Mt 2:11)
free= eleutheros (1/0/0-0, 1)
freely= dōrean (1/0/0-0, 1)
frequently= puknos (0/0/1-1, 0)
fresh= neos (2/2/4-0, 0)
fresher= neoteros (0/0/3-1/1)
to-fret= odunaō (0/0/3-1, 0)
friend= philos (1/0/15-3, 6)
frightened= emphobos (0/0/2-2, 0)
from= apo (common)
from-behind= opisthen (2/1/2-0, 0)
from-everywhere= pantothen (0/1/1-0, 0)
from-here= enteuthen (0/0/2-0, 6)
from-outside= exōthen (3/2/2-0, 0)
from-there= ekeithen (12/5/3-4, 1)
from-the-start= anōthen (1/1/1-1, 5)
from-this-place= enthen (1/0/1-0, 0)
from-where= pothen (5/3/4-0, 13)
from-which= hothen (4/0/1-3, 0)
from-within= esōthen (4/2/3-0, 0)
froth= aphros (Lk 9:39)
to-froth= aphrizō (0/2/0-0, 0)
fruit= karpos (19/5/12-1, 10)
fruitless= akarpos (1/1/0-0, 0)
to-fulfill= plēroō (16/2/9-16, 15)
fulfillment= teleiōsis (Lk 1:45)
full= plērēs (2/2/2-8, 1)
fullness= plērōma (1/3/0-0, 1)
full-of-light= phōteinos (2/0/3-0, 0)
furlong= stadion (1/0/1/-0, 1)
furnace= klibanos (1/0/1-0, 0)

G

Gabriel= Gabriēl (0/0/2-0, 0)
Gadarene= Gadarēnos (Mt 8:28)
Galilean= Galilaios (1/1/5-3, 1)
Galilee= Galilaia (common)
to-gain= kerdainō (6/1/1-1, 0)
to-garb= perizōnnumi (0/0/3-0, 0)
garden= kēpos (0/0/1-0, 3)
gardener= kēpouros (Jn 15:20)
gate= pulē (4/0/1-4, 0)
gateway= pulōn (1/0/1-5, 0)
to-gather= sunagō (24/5/6-11, 7)
Gehenna= geenna (7/3/1-0, 0)
general= stratēgos (0/0/2-8, 0)
generation= genea (13/5/15-5, 0)
genesis= genesis (2/0/1-0, 0)
Gennesaret= Gennēsaret (1/1/1-0, 0)
gentile= ethnikos (3/0/0-0)
gentle= praus (3/0/0-0, 0)
genuine= alēthinos (0/0/1-0, 9)
Gerasene= Gerasēnos (0/1/2-0, 0)
to-germinate= blastanō (1/1/0-0, 0)
to-gesture= enneuō (Lk 1:62)
to-get-drunk= methuskō (Lk 12:45)
Gethsemane= Gethsēmani (1/1/0-0, 0)
to-get-near-to= suntugchanō (Lk 8:19)
to-get-out= apobainō (0/0/2-0, 1)
to-get-up= anistēmi (4/17/27-45, 8)
gift= dōron (9/1/2-0, 0)
girl= korasion (3/5/0-0, 0)
to-give= didōmi (common)

to-give-a-drink= potizō (5/2/1-0, 0)
to-give-as-a-benefaction= charizomai (0/0/3-4, 0)
to-give-away-in-wedlock= ekgamiskō (textual variant found at Mt 24:38)
to-give-birth-to= tiktō (4/0/5-0, 1)
to-give-in-marriage= gamizō (2/1/2-0, 0)
to-give-in-wedlock= gamiskō (Lk 20:34)
to-give-life= zōogoneō (0/0/1-1, 0)
to-give-light= epiphainō (0/0/1-1, 0)
to-give-notice= diaggellō (0/0/1-1, 0)
to-give-over= apodidōmi (18/1/8-4, 0)
to-give-relief= anapauō (2/2/1-0, 0)
to-give-strength= enischuō (0/0/1-1, 0)
to-give-thanks= eucharisteō (2/2/4-2, 3)
to-give-the-impression= prospoieomai (Lk 24:28)
to-give-to= epididōmi (2/0/5-2, 0)
gladly= hēdeōs (0/2/0-0, 0)
to-glean= trugaō (Lk 6:44)
to-glisten= stilbō (Mk 9:3)
gloomy= skuthrōpos (1/0/1-0, 0)
to-glorify= doxazō (4/1/9-5, 23)
glorious= endoxos (0/0/2-0, 0)
glory= doxa (7/3/13-4, 19)
gluttonous= phagos (1/0/1-0, 0)
gnat= kōnōps (Mt 23:24)
to-go= erchomai (common)
goat= eriphos (1/0/1-0, 0)
to-go-away= aperchomai (common)
god= theos (common)
to-go-deep= bathunō (Lk 6:48)
god-fearing= eulabēs (0/0/1-3, 0)
to-go-down= katerchomai (0/0/2-13, 0)
gold= chrusos (5/0/0-1, 0)
Golgotha= Golgotha (1/1/0-0, 1)
Gomorrah= Gomorra (Mt 10:15)
good= agathos (15/3/15-3, 3)
goods= chrēma (1/0/1-4, 0)
to-go-on-through= diodeuō (0/0/1-1, 0)
to-go-out= exerchomai (common)
to-go-over= diabainō (0/0/1-1, 0)
gossip= phēmē (1/0/1-0, 0)
to-go-through= dierchomai (2/2/10-21, 2)
to-go-up= anerchomai (Jn 6:3)
to-grab= sunarpazō (0/0/1-3, 0)
grainfield= sporimos (1/1/1-0, 0)
to-grasp= katalambanō (0/1/0-3, 4)
grave= mnēma (0/2/3-2, 0)
to-graze= boskō (2/2/3-0, 2)
great= megas (20/15/26-31, 5)
greater= meizōn (10/3/7-0, 14)
greek= hellēnikos (textual variant found at Lk 23:38)
green= chlōros (Mk 6:39)
to-greet= aspazomai (2/2/2-5, 0)
greeting= aspasmos (1/1/5-0, 0)
grief= lupē (0/0/1-0, 4)
to-grieve= lupeō (6/2/0-0, 2)
to-grind= trizō (Mk 9:18)
to-grind-grain= alēthō (1/0/1-0, 0)
grinding= brugmos (6/0/1-0, 0)
to-grip= sullambanō (1/1/7-4, 1)
to-groan= stenazō (Mk 7:34)
to-groan-loudly= anastenazō (Mk 8:12)
groundward= chamai (0/0/0-0, 2)
group= prasia (0/2/0-0, 0)
to-grow= auxanō (2/1/4-4, 1)
to-grow-cold= psuchō (Mt 12:24)
to-grow-together= sunauxanō (Mt 13:30)
to-grumble= gogguzō (1/0/1-0, 4)
to-grumble-loudly= diagogguzō (0/0/2-0, 0)
to-guard= phulassō (1/1/6-8, 3)
guest-room= kataluma (0/1/2-0, 0)
to-guide= kateuthunō (Lk 1:79)
guileless= akeraios (Mt 10:16)

H

ha= oua (Mk 15:29)
habit= sunētheia (Jn 18:39)
Hades= hadēs (2/0/2-2, 0)
to-hail= hupodechomai (0/0/2-1, 0)
hair= thrix (3/1/4-1, 2)
half= hēmisus (0/1/1-0, 0)
half-dead= hēmithanēs (Lk 10:30)
hand= cheir (common)
to-handle= psēlaphaō (0/0/1-1, 0)
to-hang= kremannumi (2/0/1-3, 0)
to-hang-oneself= apagchomai (Mt 27:5)
to-happen= ginomai (common)
to-happen-to-come-together= sumparaginomai (Lk 23:48)
to-harass= kolaphizō (1/1/0-0, 0)
harbor= limnē (0/0/5-0, 0)
hard= sklēros (1/0/0-1, 1)
to-harden= pōroō (0/2/0-0, 1)
hardly= molis (0/0/0-4, 0)
hardness-of-heart= sklērokardia (1/3/0-0, 0)
to-harm= blaptō (0/1/1-0, 0)
harsh= austēros (0/0/2-0, 0)
harvest= therismos (6/1/2-0, 2)
to-harvest= therizō (3/0/3-0, 4)
haste= spoudē (0/1/1-0, 0)
hastily= spoudaiōs (Lk 7:4)
to-hate= miseō (5/1/7-0, 12)
to-haul= helkuō (0/0/0-2, 5)
to-have= echō (common)
to-have-as-one's-lot= lagchanō (0/0/1-1, 1)
to-have-authority-over= exousiazō (Lk 22:25)
to-have-lunch= aristaō (0/0/1-0, 2)
to-have-on= endiduskō (0/1/1-0, 0)
to-have-pity= splagchnizomai (5/4/3-0, 0)
to-have-the-opportunity= eukaireō (0/1/0-1, 0)
to-have-the-strength= ischuō (4/4/8-6, 1)
he/she/it = autos (common)
head= kephalē (12/8/7-4, 5)
to-head-back= anakamptō (1/0/1-1, 0)
to-head-out= metabainō (5/0/1-1, 3)
to-heal= therapeuō (16/5/14-5, 1)
healing= therapeia (0/0/2-0, 0)
healthy= hugiēs (2/1/0-1, 6)
to-hear= akouō (common)
heart= kardia (16/11/23-20, 7)
to-heave= pneō (2/0/1-1, 2)
heaven= ouranos (common)
heavenly= ouranios (7/0/1-1, 0)
heavenly-host= stratia (0/0/1-1, 0)
hebraic= hebraikos (textual variant found at Lk 23:38)
hedge= phragmos (1/1/1-0, 0)
height= hupsos (0/0/2-0, 0)
Heli= Ēli (Lk 3:23)
Hellene= Hellēnis (0/1/0-1, 0)
to-help= boētheō (1/2/0-2, 0)
hen= ornis (1/0/1-0, 0)
her/its= autēs (common)
herd= agelē (3/2/2-0, 0)
here= hōde (18/10/15-2, 5)
Herod= Hērōdes (13/8/14-8, 0)
Herodians= Hērōdianoi (1/2/0-0, 0)
Herodias= Hērōdias (2/3/1-0, 0)
herself= heautē (4/3/4-1, 0)
to-hew= latomeō (1/1/0-0, 0)
Hezekiah= Hezekias (2/0/0-0, 0)
Hezron= Hesrōm (Lk 3:33)
hidden= kruptos (5/1/2-0, 3)
hidden-away= apokruphos (0/1/1-0, 0)
to-hide= kruptō (7/0/2-0, 3)
to-hide-away= apokruptō (Lk 10:21)
hiding= kruphaios (2/0/0-0, 0)
high= hupsēlos (2/1/2-1, 0)
high-priest= archiereus (common)

higher= anōteros (Lk 14:10)
hill= bounos (0/0/2-0, 0)
himself= heautos (8/6/31-11, 19)
to-hinder= kōluō (1/3/6-6, 0)
to-hire= misthoō (2/0/0-0, 0)
hired-laborer= misthōtos (0/1/0-0, 2)
his/its= autou (common)
to-hit= tuptō (2/1/4-5, 0)
to-hold-fast= antechō (1/0/1-0, 0)
hole= phōleos (1/0/1-0, 0)
holiness= hosiotēs (Lk 1:75)
holy= hagios (10/7/20-53, 5)
home= oikia (25/18/24-11, 4)
homeland= patris (2/2/2-0, 1)
honey= meli (1/1/0-0, 0)
honey-comb= kērion (textual variant found at Lk 24:42)
honor= timē (0/2/0-6, 1)
to-honor= timaō (6/3/1-1, 6)
honored= entimos (Lk 7:2)
to-hope= elpizō (1/0/3-2, 1)
to-hope-for= apelpizō (Lk 6:35)
horn= keras (Lk 1:69)
hosanna= hōsanna (3/2/1-0, 0)
hour= hōra (common)
house= oikos (10/12/33-25, 4)
house-dog= kunarion (2/2/0-0, 0)
household= oiketeia (Mt 24:45)
house-member= oikiakos (2/0/0-0, 0)
house-servant= oiketēs (0/0/1-1, 0)
housetop= dōma (2/1/3-1, 0)
how= pōs (common)
however= mentoi (0/0/0-0, 5)
how-great?= posos (8/6/6-1, 0)
how-often= posakis (2/0/1-0, 0)
humble= tapeinos (1/0/1-0, 0)
to-humble= tapeinoō (3/0/5-0, 0)
humiliation= tapeinōsis (0/0/1-1, 0)
hundred-fold= hekatontaplasiōn (1/1/1-0, 0)
to-hunger= peinaō (9/2/5-0, 1)
hungry= nēstis (1/1/0-0, 0)
to-hurry= speudō (0/0/3-2, 0)
hypocrisy= hupokrisis (1/1/1-0, 0)
hypocrite= hupokritēs (13/1/3-0, 0)
hyssop-branch= hussōpos (Jn 19:29)

I

I= egō (common) NB: as in English, the other forms of "I" (me, my, we, us, our) do not have separate dictionary entries.
idle= argos (3/0/0-0, 0)
Idumea= Idoumaia (Mk 3:8)
if= ei (common)
if-ever= ean (common)
to-ignite= periaptō (Lk 22:55)
to-ignore= parakouō (2/1/0-0, 0)
ill= asthenēs (3/1/2-3, 0)
illness= astheneia (1/0/4-1, 2)
to-illumine= phōtizō (0/0/1-0, 1)
image= eikōn (1/1/1-0, 0)
to-imagine= hupolambanō (0/0/2-2, 0)
immediately= euthus (5/41/1-1, 3)
imminent-judgment= prosdokia (0/0/1-1, 0)
imperishable= aphthartos (textual variant found at Mk 16:8)
to-implore= deomai (1/0/8-7, 0)
impossible= adunatos (1/1/1-1, 0)
improper= atopos (0/0/1-2, 0)
in= en (common)
in-as-much-as= epeidēper (Lk 1:1)
incense= thumiama (0/0/2-0, 0)
to-incinerate= katakaiō (3/0/1-1, 0)
to-incite= anaseiō (0/1/1-0, 0)
incredible= paradoxos (Lk 5:26)
indecency= aselgeia (Mk 7:22)
indeed= dē (1/0/1-2, 0)
indeed-not= ouchi (8/0/18-2, 5)
to-indicate= sēmainō (0/0/0-2, 3)
in-effect= ge (4/0/8-4, 0)
inevitable= anagkē (1/0/2-0, 0)
infant= nēpios (2/0/1-0, 0)
to-inform= apaggellō (8/5/11-15, 1)
in-front= emprosthen (18/2/10-2, 5)
in-Greek-letters= Hellēnisti (0/0/0-1, 1)
inhabited-earth= oikoumenē (1/0/3-5, 0)
in-Hebrew= Hebraisti (0/0/0-0, 5)
in-here= enthade (0/0/1-5, 2)
to-inherit= klēronomeō (3/1/2-0, 0)
inheritance= klēronomia (1/1/2-2, 0)
inheritor= klēronomos (1/1/1-0, 0)
inn= pandocheion (Lk 10:34)
inn-keeper= pandocheus (Lk 10:35)
innocent= athōos (2/0/0-0, 0)
in-order-that= hina (common)
in-place-of= anti (5/1/4-1, 1)
to-inquire= punthanomai (1/0/2-7, 2)
in-Roman-letters= Rhōmaisti (Jn 19:20)
to-inscribe= epigraphō (0/1/0-1, 0)
inscription= epigraphē (1/2/2-0, 0)
to-insert= egkruptō (1/0/1-0, 0)
inside= entos (1/0/1-0, 0)
insight= phronēsis (Lk 1:17)
insignificant= elaphros (Mt 11:30)
to-insist= diischurizomai (0/0/1-1, 0)
instantly= eutheōs (13/1/6-9, 3)
instruction= didachē (3/5/1-4, 1)
instructor= kathēgētēs (2/0/0-0, 0)
to-insult= hubrizō (1/0/2-1, 0)
insurrection= stasis (0/1/2-5, 0)
insurrectionist= stasiastēs (Mk 15:7)
intellect= nous (Lk 24:45)
intelligent= sunetos (1/0/1-1, 0)
intelligently= nounechōs (Mk 12:34)
to-intend= mellō (9/2/12-34, 12)
intense-sorrow= rhomphaia (Lk 2:35)
interest= tokos (1/0/1-0, 0)
to-interpret= phrazō (Mt 15:15)
interwoven= uphantos (Jn 19:23)
in-the-same-way= hōsautōs (3/2/3-0, 0)
in-the-sight= enōpion (0/0/22-13, 1)
into= eis (common)
in-unison-with= hama (2/0/0-2, 0)
to-invest= pragmateuomai (Lk 13:19)
invisible= aphantos (Lk 24:31)
to-invite-in-return= antikaleō (Lk 14:12)
iota= iōta (Mt 5:18)
Isaac= Isaak (4/1/3-4, 0)
Isaiah= Hēsaias (6/2/2-3, 4)
Iscariot= Iskariōtēs (2/2/2-0, 5)
Israel= Israēl (12/2/12-15, 4)
Israelite= Israēlitēs (0/0/0-5, 1)
issue= rhusis (0/1/2-0, 0)
it/he/she= autos (common)
it-is-necessary= dei (8/6/18-22, 10)
it-is-of-concern= melei (1/2/1-1, 1)
I-too= kagō (8/0/6-4, 30)
its/her= autēs (common)
its/his= autou (common)
Ituraea= Itouraios (Lk 3:1)

J

Jacob= Iakōb (6/1/4-8, 3)
jail= desmōtērion (1/0/0-3, 0)
Jairus= Iairos (0/1/1-0, 0)
James= Iakōbos (6/15/8-7, 0)
Jannai= Iannao (Lk 3:24)
Jared= Iaret (Lk 3:37)
Jechoniah= Iechonias (2/0/0-0, 0)
Jehosaphat= Iōsaphat (2/0/0-0, 0)
Jeremiah= Ieremias (3/0/0-0, 0)
Jericho= Ierichō (1/1/3-0, 0)
Jerusalem= Hierosalēm (common)
Jerusalemites= Hierosolumitēs (0/1/0-0, 1)
Jesse= Iessai (2/0/1-1, 0)
Jesus= Iēsous (common)
Joanan= Iōanan (Lk 3:27)
Joanna= Iōanna (0/0/2-0, 0)
Joda= Iōda (Lk 3:26)

John= Iōannēs (common)
Jonah= Iōnas (5/0/4-0, 0)
Jonam= Iōnam (Lk 3:30)
Joram= Iōram (2/0/0-0, 0)
Jordan= Iordanēs (6/4/2-0, 3)
Jorim= Iōrim (Lk 3:29)
Josech= Iōsēch (Lk 3:26)
Joseph= Iōsēph (11/2/8-7, 4)
Joses= Iōsēs (1/3/0-0, 0)
Joshua= Iēsou (Lk 3:29)
Josiah= Iōsiah (2/0/0-0, 0)
Jotham= Iōatham (2/0/0-0, 0)
journey= poreia (Lk 13:22)
joy= chara (6/1/8-4, 9)
jubilation= agalliasis (0/0/2-1, 0)
Judah= Ioudas (10/4/8-8, 9)
Judea= Ioudaia (8/3/10-12, 6)
Judean= Ioudaios (5/7/5-79, 71)
judge= kritēs (3/0/6-4, 0)
to-judge= krinō (6/0/6-21, 19)
to-judge-against= katakrinō (4/3/2-0, 2)
judgment= krisis (12/0/4-1, 11)
judicator= dikastēs (textual variant found at Lk 12:14)
judicial-bench= bēma (1/0/0-8, 0)
to-jump-up= anapēdaō (Mk 10:50)
just-as= kathōs (3/8/17-11, 31)
justifiably= dikaiōs (Lk 23:41)
to-justify= dikaioō (2/0/5-2, 0)
just-like= katha (Mt 27:10)

K

to-keep= tēreō (6/1/0-8, 18)
to-keep-in-seclusion= perikrubō (Lk 1:24)
key= kleis (1/0/1-0, 0)
Kidron= Kedrōn (Jn 18:1)
to-kill= apokteinō (common)
to-kill-by-stoning= katalithazō (Lk 20:6)
kin= suggenēs (0/1/4-1, 1)
kind= chrēstos (1/0/2-0, 0)
kindred= suggeneia (0/0/1-2, 0)
king= basileus (common)
kingdom= basileia (55/20/46-8, 5)
kinswoman= suggenis (Lk 1:36)
kiss= philēma (0/0/2-0, 0)
to-kiss= kataphileō (1/1/3-1, 0)
knee= gonu (0/1/2-4, 0)
to-kneel= gonupeteō (2/2/0-0, 0)
to-knock= krouō (2/0/4-2, 0)
to-know= ginōskō (common)
knowledge= gnōsis (0/0/2-0, 0)
korban= korban (Aramaic) (Mk 7:11)
koum= koum (Aramaic)

L

to-labor= kopiaō (2/0/2-1, 1)
to-lack= leipō (Lk 18:22)
lamb= amnos (0/0/0-1, 2)
lame= chōlos (5/1/3-3, 1)
Lamech= Lamech (Lk 3:36)
lamentation= odurmos (Mt 2:18)
lamp= lampas (5/0/0-1, 1)
lamp-stand= luchnia (1/1/2-0, 0)
land= gē (common)
laneway= rhumē (1/0/3-0, 0)
to-languish= pentheō (2/1/1-0, 0)
lantern= luchnos (2/1/6-0, 1)
large-basket= spuris (2/2/0-1, 0)
large-sea-creature= kētos (Mt 12:40)
last= eschatos (10/5/6-3, 7)
lastly= eschatōs (Mk 5:23)
late= opsios (Mk 11:11)
late-afternoon= hespera (0/0/1-2, 0)
late-in-the-day= opse (1/2/0-0, 0)
later= epeita (0/0/1-0, 1)
latin= rhōmaikos (textual variant found at Lk 23:38)
latrine= aphedrōn (1/1/0-0, 0)
to-laugh= gelaō (0/0/2-0, 0)
to-laugh-heartily= katagelaō (1/1/1-0, 0)
law= nomos (8/0/9-17, 15)
lawless= anomos (0/0/1-1, 0)
lawlessness= anomia (4/0/0-0, 0)
lawyer= nomikos (1/0/6-0, 0)
to-lay/lie= keimai (3/0/6-0, 7)
to-lay-around= perikeimai (1/0/1-1, 0)
to-lay-upon= epikeimai (0/0/2-1, 2)
Lazarus= Lazaros (0/0/4-0, 11)
lazy= oknēros (Mt 25:26)
to-lead= agō (4/3/13-26, 13)
to-lead-ahead= proagō (6/5/1-4, 0)
to-lead-around= periagō (3/1/0-1, 0)
to-lead-away= apagō (5/3/4-2, 0)
to-lead-down= katagō (0/0/1-7, 0)
to-lead-in= eisagō (0/0/3-6, 1)
to-lead-out= exagō (0/1/1-8, 1)
to-lead-to= prosagō (0/0/1-2, 0)
to-lead-up= anagō (1/0/3-17)
leaf= phullon (2/3/0-0, 0)
leafy-branch= stibas (Mk 11:8)
to-lean= anapiptō (1/1/4-0, 5)
to-leap= skirtaō (0/0/3-0, 0)
to-learn= manthanō (3/1/0-1, 2)
to-lease= ekdidōmi (2/1/1-0, 0)
least= elachistos (5/0/4-0, 0)
leather= dermatinos (1/1/0-0, 0)
to-leave= hupagō (19/15/5-0, 32)
to-leave-home= apodēmeō (3/1/2-0, 0)
leaven= zumē (4/1/2-0, 0)
to-leaven= zumoō (1/0/1-0, 0)
left= euōnumos (5/2/0-1, 0)
left-hand= aristeros (1/1/1-0, 0)
legion= legiōn (1/2/1-0, 0)
legion-leader= chiliarchos (0/1/0-17, 1)
lema= lema (Aramaic) (1/1/0-0, 0)
to-lend= kichrēmi (Lk 11:5)
to-lend-a-hand= prospsauō (Lk 11:46)
leprosy= lepra (1/1/2-0, 0)
leprous= lepros (4/2/3-0, 0)
lepton= leptos (copper coin worth ½ quadrans, or 1/128th denarius) (0/1/2-0, 0)
less= katōterō (Mt 2:16)
lesson= didaskalia (1/1/0-0, 0)
lest= mēpote (8/2/7-2, 1)
to-let-down= kathiēmi (0/0/1-3, 0)
letter= gramma (0/0/2-2, 2)
level= pedinos (Lk 6:17)
Levi= Leui (0/1/4-0, 0)
Levite= Leuitēs (0/0/1-1, 1)
to-lick= epiliechō (Lk 16:21)
to-lie= pseudomai (0/1/0-2, 0)
to-lie/lay= keimai (3/0/6-0, 7)
to-lie-down= katakeimai (0/4/3-2, 2)
life= zōē (7/4/5-8, 36)
to-lift-up= epairō (1/0/6-5, 4)
light= phōs (7/1/7-10, 23)
like= hōs (common)
to-like= phileō (5/1/2-0, 13)
likewise= homoiōs (9/0/9-1, 2)
lily= krinon (1/0/1-0, 0)
linen-sheet= sindōn (1/4/1-0, 0)
lip= cheilos (1/1/0-0, 0)
liquid= pistikos (0/1/0-0, 1)
liter= litra (0/0/0-0, 2)
little= oligos (0/2/3-8, 0)
little-bit= brachus (0/0/1-2, 1)
little-boy= paidarion (Jn 6:9)
little-daughter= thugatrion (0/2/0-0, 0)
little-ear= ōtarion (0/1/0-0, 1)
little-loyalty= oligopistos (4/0/1-0, 0)
littleness-of-loyalty= oligopistia (Matt 17:20)
little-sandal= sandalion (0/1/0-1, 0)
to-live= zaō (6/3/9-12, 17)
to-live-again= anazaō (0/0/2-0, 0)
livelihood= bios (0/2/5-0, 0)
to-live-outdoors= agrauleō (Lk 2:8)
loan= daneion (Mt 18:27)
loan-shark= danistēs (Lk 7:41)
to-loan= danizō (1/0/3-0, 0)
to-locate= aneuriskō (0/0/1-1, 0)

to-lock= kleiō (3/0/2-2, 2)
to-lock-up= apokleiō (Lk 13:25)
locust= akris (1/1/0-0, 0)
log= dokos (3/0/2-0, 0)
look!= idou (62/7/57-23, 4)
look= ide (4/9/0-0, 18)
to-look= blepō (common)
to-look-around= periblepō (0/6/1-0, 0)
to-look-up= anablepō (3/6/7-5, 4)
to-look-upon= epiblepō (0/0/2-0, 0)
to-loom= phthanō (1/0/1-0, 0)
to-loose= luō (6/5/7-6, 6)
lord= kurios (common)
to-lose-heart= apopsuchō (Lk 21:26)
to-lose-sight-of= pariēmi (Lk 11:42)
Lot= Lōt (0/0/3-0, 0)
love= agapē (1/0/1-0, 7)
to-love= agapaō (8/5/13-0, 37)
lovely= hōraios (1/0/0-2, 0)
to-lower= chalaō (0/1/2-3, 0)
loyal= pistos (5/0/6-4, 1)
loyalty= pistis (8/5/11-15, 0)
lure= apatē (1/1/0-0, 0)
lustre= pheggos (1/1/0-0, 0)
luxurious= truphē (Lk 7:25)
Lysanius= Lusaias (Lk 3:1)

M

Maath= Maath (Lk 3:26)
made-by-hand= cheiropoiētos (0/1/0-2, 0)
madness= anoia (Lk 6:11)
Magadan= Magadan (Mt 15:39)
Magdalene= Magdalēnē (3/4/2-0, 3)
magistrate= archōn (5/1/8-11, 7)
to-magnify= megalunō (1/0/2-3, 0)
Magus= magos (4/0/0-2, 0)
maimed= kullos (3/1/0-0, 0)
majesty= megaleiotēs (0/0/1-1, 0)
to-make-a-careful-search= exetazō (2/0/0-0, 1)
to-make-apologies= paraiteomai (0/1/3-1, 0)
to-make-apparent= emphanizō (1/0/0-5, 2)
to-make-desolate= erēmoō (1/0/1-0, 0)
to-make-dull= pachunomai (1/0/0-1, 0)
to-make-firm= stērizō (0/0/3-0, 0)
to-make-friends= eunoeō (Mt 5:25)
to-make-fun-of= ekmuktērizō (0/0/2-0, 0)
to-make-holy= hagiazō (3/0/1-2, 3)
to-make-known= gnōrizō (0/0/2-1, 2)
to-make-peace= diallassomai (Mt 5:24)
to-make-ready= hetoimazō (7/5/14-1, 2)
to-make-salty= halizō (1/1/0-0, 0)
to-make-secure= peripoieō (0/0/1-2, 0)
to-make-signs= dianeuō (Lk 1:22)
to-make-straight= euthunō (Jn 1:23)
to-make-strong= krataioō (0/0/2-0, 0)
to-make-visible= phaneroō (0/3/0-0, 9)
to-make-white= leukainō (Mk 9:3)
Malaleel= Maleleēl (Lk 3:37)
Malchus= Malchos (Jn 18:10)
male= arsēn (1/1/1-0, 0)
man= anēr (8/4/26-100, 8)
to-manage= oikonomeō (Lk 16:2)
management= oikonomia (0/0/3-0, 0)
manager= oikonomos (0/0/4-0, 0)
Manasseh= Manassēs (Mt 1:10)
manner= tropos (1/0/1-4, 0)
many= polus (common)
many-thousands= murias (0/0/1-2, 0)
many-times-more= pollaplasiōn (Lk 18:30)
market= agora (3/3/3-2, 0)
to-marry= gameō (6/4/6-0, 0)
to-marry-off= ekgamizō (textual variant found at Mt 22:30 and 24:38)
to-marshal= sustrephō (1/0/0-1, 0)
Martha= Martha (0/0/4-0, 9)
Mary= Maria (11/8/17-2, 5)
master= despotēs (0/0/1-1, 0)
master-of-the-house= oikodespotēs (7/1/4-0, 0)
Mattatha= Mattatha (Lk 3:31)
Mattathias= Mattathias (0/0/2-0, 0)
Matthan= Matthan (Mt 1:15)
Matthat= Maththat (0/0/2-0, 0)
Matthew= Maththaios (2/1/1-0, 0)
mattress= krabattos (0/5/0-2, 4)
meal= ariston (1/0/3-0, 0)
to-mean= hermēneuō (0/0/0-0, 2)
measure= metron (2/1/2-0, 1)
to-measure-in-return= antimetreō (Lk 6:38)
to-measure-out= metreō (2/2/1-0, 0)
to-meet= hupantaō (2/1/2-1, 4)
meeting= hupantēsis (2/0/0-0, 1)
to-meet-with= sunantaō (0/0/2-2, 0)
Melchi= Melchi (0/0/2-0, 0)
Melea= Melea (Lk 3:31)
memory= mnēmosunon (1/1/0-0, 0)
Menna= Menna (Lk 3:31)
merchandise= emporion (Jn 2:16)
merchant= emporos (Mt 13:45)
merciful= eleēmōn (Mt 5:7)
mercy= eleos (3/0/6-0, 0)
messiah= messias (0/0/0-0, 2)
to-metamorphize= metamorphoō (1/1/0-0, 0)
Methusala= Methousala (Lk 3:37)
middle= mesos (7/5/14-10, 6)
midnight= mesonuktion (0/1/1-2, 0)
might= ischus (0/2/1-0, 0)
mile= milion (Mt 5:41)
miller's-stone= mulikos (Lk 17:2)
mill-stone= mulos (2/1/0-0, 0)
mina= mna (0/0/9-0, 0)
mind= dianoia (1/1/2-0, 0)
ministry= leitourgia (Lk 1:23)
mint= hēduosmon (1/0/1-0, 0)
to-mistreat= epēreazō (Lk 6:28)
to-mix= meignumi (1/0/1-0, 0)
mixture= migma (Jn 19:39)
to-mock= empaizō (5/3/5-0, 0)
moisture= ikmas (Lk 8:6)
molding= katabolē (2/0/1-0, 1)
moment= stigmē (Lk 4:5)
money= mamōnas (1/0/3-0, 0)
moneybag= ballantion (0/0/4-0, 0)
money-box= glōssokomon (0/0/0-0, 2)
money-changer= kollubistēs (1/1/0-0, 1)
money-lover= philarguros (Lk 14:16)
to-monitor= epechō (0/0/1-2, 0)
month= mēn (0/0/5-5, 0)
moon= selēnē (1/1/1-1, 0)
to-moor= prosormizō (Mk 6:53)
more= pleion (7/1/9-18, 5)
more-excessive= perissoteros (1/3/4-0, 0)
more-honored= entimoteros (Lk 14:8)
more-nicely= kompsoteron (Jn 4:52)
moreover= eita (0/4/1-0, 3)
more-persistently= ektenōteros (textual variant found at Lk 22:44)
more-quickly= tachion (0/0/0-0, 2)
more-sensible= phronimōteros (Lk 8:16)
more-tolerable= anektoteros (3/0/2-0, 0)
more-weighty= baruteros (Mt 23:23)
morning= prōia (1/0/0-0, 1)
moronic= mōros (6/0/0-0, 0)
Moses= Mōusēs (7/8/10-19, 13)
most= pleistos (2/1/0-0, 0)
most-excellent= kratistos (0/0/1-3, 0)
most-high= hupsistos (1/2/7-2, 0)
moth= sēs (2/0/1-0, 0)
mother= mētēr (common)
mother-in-law= penthera (2/1/3-0, 0)
to-motion-toward= kataneuō (Lk 5:7)
to-mount= epibainō (1/0/0-5, 0)
mountain= oros (16/11/13-3, 5)

mountainous= oreinos (0/0/2-0, 0)
to-mourn= thrēneō (1/0/2-0, 1)
mouth= stoma (11/0/9-12, 1)
to-move= kineō (2/1/0-3, 0)
to-move-up= prosanabainō (Lk 10:14)
mulberry-tree= sukaminos (Lk 17:6)
to-mull-over= sumballō (0/0/2-4, 0)
to-multiply= plēthunō (1/0/0-5, 0)
multitude= plēthos (0/2/8-16, 2)
murder= phonos (1/2/2-1, 0)
to-murder= phoneuō (5/1/1-0, 0)
murderer= phoneus (1/0/0-3, 0)
music= sumphōnia (Lk 15:25)
mustard= sinapi (2/1/2-0, 0)
mute= kōphos (8/3/4-0, 0)
to-muzzle= phimoō (2/2/1-0, 0)
my-own= emos (4/2/3-0, 40)
myrrh= smurna (1/0/0-0, 1)
myself= hemautos (1/0/2-4, 16)
mystery= musterion (1/1/1-0, 0)

N

Naaman= Naiman (Lk 4:27)
Naggai= Naggai (Lk 3:25)
Nahor= Nachōr (Lk 3:34)
Nahshon= Naassōn (1/0/1-0, 0)
Nahum= Naoum (Lk 3:25)
Nain= Nain (Lk 7:11)
naked= gumnos (4/1/0-1, 1)
name= onoma (common)
to-name= onomazō (0/1/2-1, 0)
nard= nardos (0/1/0-0, 1)
to-narrate= diēgeomai (0/1/2-3, 0)
narrative= diēgēsis (Lk 1:1)
narrow= stenos (2/0/1-0, 0)
Natham= Natham (Lk 3:31)
Nathan= Nathan (textual variant found at Lk 3:31)
Nathanael= Nathanaēl (0/0/0-0, 6)
nation= ethnos (15/6/13-43, 5)
Nazara= Nazara (1/0/1-0, 0)
Nazarene= Nazarēnos (0/4/2-0, 0)
Nazaret= Nazaret (1/1/0-0, 2)
Nazareth= Nazareth (1/0/4-1, 0)
Nazarite= Nazōraios (2/0/1-7, 1)
near= eggus (3/2/3-3, 11)
to-near= eggizō (7/3/18-6, 0)
nearby-dweller= perioikos (Lk 1:58)
neck= trachēlos (1/1/2-2, 0)
need= chreia (6/4/7-5, 4)
to-need= chrēzō (1/0/2-0, 0)
needle= rhaphis (1/1/0-0, 0)
needy-debtor= chreopheiletēs (0/0/2-0, 0)
to-neglect= epilanthanomai (1/1/1-0, 0)
neighbor= plēsion (3/2/3-1, 1)
neither= oute (6/4/4-14, 8)
Nephthali= Nephthalim (2/0/0-0, 0)
Neri= Nēri (Lk 3:27)
net= diktuon (2/2/4-0, 4)
never= oudepote (5/2/2-3, 1)
never-decreasing= anekleiptos (Lk 12:33)
nevertheless= plēn (5/1/15-4, 0)
new= kainos (4/5/5-2, 2)
next-day= epaurion (1/1/0-10, 5)
next-door-neighbor= geitōn (0/0/3-0, 1)
next-generation= paliggenesia (Mt 19:28)
Nicodemus= Nikodēmos (0/0/0-0, 5)
night= nux (9/4/7-16, 6)
nine= ennea (2/0/3-0, 0)
ninety= enenēkonta (2/0/2-0, 0)
Ninevite= Nineuitēs (1/0/2-0, 0)
ninth= enatos (3/2/1-3, 0)
no= mē (common)
Noah= Nōe (2/0/3-0, 0)
noble= eugenēs (0/0/1-1, 0)
to-nod= neuō (0/0/0-1, 1)
noise= ēchos (0/0/1-1, 0)
no-longer= ouketi (2/7/3-3, 12)
nonsense= lēros (Lk 24:11)
no-one= oudeis (common)
nor= oude (common)
north= borras (Lk 13:29)
not= ou/ouk/ouch (common)
not-any-longer= mēketi (1/4/1-3, 2)
not-easily= duskolōs (1/1/1-0, 0)
not-easy= duskolos (Mk 10:24)
not-even= mēte (6/0/6-8, 0)
nothing= outheis (0/0/2-3, 0)
notice= titlos (0/0/0-0, 2)
to-notice= theaomai (4/2/2-3, 6)
not-made-by-hand= acheiropoiētos (Mk 14:58)
not-one= mēdeis (5/9/9-22, 0)
notorious= episēmos (Mt 27:16)
not-possible= anendektos (Lk 17:1)
not-quite-yet= oudepō (0/0/0-1, 3)
not-yet= oupō (2/5/1-0, 12)
to-nourish= trephō (2/0/3-1, 0)
nourishment= trophē (4/0/1-7, 1)
now= nun (4/3/14-25, 29)
number= arithmos (0/0/1-5, 1)
to-nurse= thēlazō (2/1/2-0, 0)

O

Obed= Iōbēd (2/0/1-0, 0)
to-obey= hupakouō (1/2/2-2, 0)
observable-signs= paratērēsis (Lk 17:20)
to-observe= katamanthanō (Mt 6:28)
obstinacy= pōrōsis (Mk 3:5)
to-obtain= komizō (1/0/1-0, 0)
obvious= dēlos (Mt 26:73)
to-offer= prospherō (15/3/4-3, 2)
officer= hekatontarchēs (4/0/3-13, 0)
offspring= gennēma (3/0/1, 0)
often= pollakis (2/2/0-1, 1)
oh= ō (common)
ointment= muron (3/3/4-0, 4)
old= palaios (3/3/5-0, 0)
old-days= palai (1/1/1-0, 0)
olive= elaia (3/3/4-1, 1)
olive-oil= elaion (3/1/3-0, 0)
omen= teras (1/1/0-9, 1)
on-account-that= kathoti (0/0/2-4, 0)
on-behalf= huper (5/2/5-7, 13)
one= heis (common)
one-another= allēlōn (3/5/11-8, 15)
one-eyed= monophthalmos (1/1/0-0, 0)
one-hundred= hekaton (4/3/3-1, 2)
one-must-throw= blēteos (Lk 5:38)
only= monon (7/2/1-8, 5)
only-born= monogenēs (0/0/3-0, 4)
on-the-contrary= menoun (Lk 11:28)
to-open= anoigō (11/1/6-16, 11)
opening= trumalia (Mk 10:25)
openly= phanerōs (0/1/0-1, 1)
to-open-up= dianoigō (0/1/4-3, 0)
opponent= antidikos (2/0/2-0, 0)
opportune= eukairos (Mk 6:21)
opportune-time= eukairia (1/0/1-0, 0)
opportunity= eukairōs (Mk 14:11)
to-oppose= antikeimai (0/0/2-0, 0)
opposite= antipera (Lk 8:26)
to-oppress= thrauō (Lk 4:18)
or= ē (common)
to-order= keleuō (7/0/1-17, 0)
other= heteros (10/1/32-17, 1)
our-own= hēmeteros (textual variant found at Lk 16:12)
out= ek (common)
outer= ektos (1/0/0-1, 0)
outer-ear= ōtion (1/0/1-0, 1)
outer-garment= ependutēs (Jn 21:7)
out-front-of= enanti (0/0/1-1, 0)
outmost= exōteros (3/0/0-0, 0)
outside= exō (9/10/10-10, 13)
oven= kaminos (2/0/0-0, 0)
to-overcome= periechō (Lk 5:9)
over-excessively= huperperissōs (Mk 7:37)
to-over-flow= huperekchunnō (Lk 6:38)

overflowing= mestos (1/0/0-0, 2)
to-over-power= katischuō (1/0/2-0, 0)
overseer= epistatēs (0/0/7-0, 0)
to-overshadow= episkiazō (1/1/2-1, 0)
to-overspend= prosdapanaō (Lk 10:35)
own= idios (10/8/6-16, 15)
ox= bous (0/0/3-0, 3)

P

pair= zeugos (0/0/2-0, 0)
palace= basileios (Lk 7:25)
palm-branch= baion (Jn 12:13)
palm-tree= phoinix (Jn 12:13)
to-panhandle= prosaiteō (textual variant found at Mk 10:46)
panhandler= prosaitēs (0/1/0-0, 1)
parable= parabolē (17/13/19-0, 0)
paradise= paradeisos (Lk 23:43)
paralytic= paralutikos (5/5/0-0, 0)
parent= goneus (1/1/6-0, 6)
parentage= patria (0/0/1-1, 0)
part= meros (4/1/4-7, 4)
partner= metochos (Lk 5:7)
party= sumposion (0/2/0-0, 0)
to-pass= diistēmi (0/0/2-1, 0)
passage= diexodos (Mt 22:9)
to-pass-away= parerchomai (9/5/9-2, 0)
to-pass-by= paragō (3/3/0-0, 1)
to-pass-by-on-the-other-side= antiparerchomai (0/0/2-0, 0)
passover= pascha (4/5/7-1, 10)
to-pass-sentence= epikrinō (Lk 23:24)
patch= epiblēma (1/1/2-0, 0)
path= tribos (1/1/1-0, 0)
patience= hupomonē (0/0/2-0, 0)
pay= opsōnion (Lk 3:14)
to-pay-attention-to= eisakouō (1/0/1-1, 0)
to-pay-close-attention= prosechō (6/0/4-6,0)
peace= eirēnē (3/1/14-7, 6)
peacemaker= eirēnopoios (Mt 5:9)
pearl= margaritēs (3/1/0-0, 0)
to-peddle= pipraskō (3/1/0-3, 1)
Peleg= Phalek (Lk 3:35)
people-of-high-status= megistan (Mk 6:21)
to-perceive= noeō (4/3/0-0, 1)
Peres= Phares (1/0/1-0, 0)
Perez= Phares (1/0/1-0, 0)
perfect= teleios (2/0/0-0, 0)
to-perform= epiteleō (textual variant found at Lk 13:32)
perhaps= isōs (Lk 20:13)
to-perish= koimaomai (2/0/1-3, 2)
persecution= diōgmos (1/2/0-2, 0)
to-persevere= stēkō (0/2/0-0, 0)
to-persist-in= epimenō (0/0/0-6, 1)
person= anthrōpos (common)
perspiration= hidrōs (textual variant found at Lk 22:44)
to-persuade= peithō (3/0/4-17, 0)
Peter= Petros (common)
petition= deēsis (0/0/3-0, 0)
Phanouel= Phanouēl (Lk 2:36)
Pharisee= Pharisaios (common)
Philip= Philippos (3/3/2-16, 12)
phylactery= phulaktērion (Mt 5:23)
physician= iatros (1/2/3-0, 0)
to-pick= sullegō (7/0/1-0, 0)
piece-of-cloth= rhakos (1/1/0-0, 0)
to-pierce= nussō (Jn 19:34; textual variant found at Mt 27:49)
pig= choiros (4/4/4-0, 0)
Pilate= Pilatos (9/10/12-3, 20)
pinnacle= pterugion (0/1/1-0, 0)
pit= phrear (0/0/1-0, 2)
pity= splagchnon (0/0/1-1, 0)
place= topos (common)
to-place= epitithēmi (7/8/5-14, 2)
to-place-before= paratithēmi (2/2/5-4, 0)
place-of-honor= prōtoklisia (1/1/3-0, 0)
plague= loimos (0/0/1-1, 0)
to-plan= bouleuō (0/0/1-1, 2)
plant= phuteia (Mt 13:15)
to-plant= phuteuō (2/1/4-0, 0)
plate= paropsis (2/0/0-0, 0)
platter= pinax (2/2/1-0, 0)
to-play-the-flute= auleō (1/0/1-0, 0)
pleasant= eudia (Mt 16:2)
to-please= areskō (1/1/0-1, 0)
pleasure= hēdonē (Lk 8:14)
plot= sumboulion (5/2/0-0, 1)
to-plot-against= enedreuō (0/0/1-1, 0)
plow= arotron (Lk 9:62)
to-plow= arotriaō (Lk 17:7)
to-pluck= tillō (1/1/1-0, 0)
to-plunder= harpazō (3/0/0-2, 4)
pod= keration (Lk 15:16)
to-point-out= epideiknumi (3/0/1-2, 0)
to-ponder= dialogizomai (3/7/6-0, 0)
Pontius= Pontios (0/0/1-1, 0)
pool= kolumbēthra (0/0/0-0, 3)
poor= ptōchos (5/5/10-0, 4)
portico= stoa (0/0/0-2, 2)
portion= meris (0/0/1-2, 0)
possessions= ktēma (1/2/0-2, 0)
possible= dunatos (3/5/4-6, 0)
pot= xestēs (Mk 7:4)
potion= posis (Jn 6:55)
potter= kerameus (2/0/0-0, 0)
pouch= pēra (1/1/4-0, 0)
to-pounce-on= thēreuō (Lk 11:54)
to-pour-on= epicheō (Lk 10:34)
to-pour-out= ekcheō (1/0/2-5, 1)
to-pour-over= katacheō (1/1/0-0, 0)
to-pour-perfume-on= murizō (Mk 14:8)
power= dunamis (12/10/15-10, 0)
to-practice= prassō (0/0/6-13, 2)
praetorium= praitōrion (1/1/0-1, 4)
praise= ainos (1/0/1-0, 0)
to-praise= aineō (0/0/3-3, 0)
to-pray= proseuchō (15/10/19-16, 0)
prayer= proseuchē (2/2/3-9, 0)
to-preach= kērussō (9/14/9-8, 0)
preaching= kērugma (1/1/1-0, 0)
to-precede= proerchomai (1/2/2-3, 0)
precept= entalma (1/1/0-0, 0)
precious= barutimos (Mt 26:7)
pregnant= egkuos (Lk 2:5)
preparation-day= paraskeuē (1/1/1-0, 3)
to-prepare-ahead-of-time= promeletaō (Lk 14:21)
to-prepare-for-burial= entaphiazō (1/0/0-0, 1)
presence= parousia (2/0/0-0, 0)
present= doma (1/0/1-0, 0)
to-present= parechō (1/1/4-5, 0)
presentation= prothesis (1/1/1-2, 0)
to-preserve= diatēreō (0/0/1-1, 0)
to-preside-over= epitassō (0/4/4-1, 0)
to-press-against= thlibō (1/1/0-0, 0)
to-press-down= piezō (Lk 6:38)
to-press-forward= hēkō (4/1/5-0, 4)
to-press-upon= sunthlibō (0/2/0-0, 0)
to-pretend= hupokrinomai (Lk 20:20)
to-prevent= diakōluō (Mt 3:14)
priest= hiereus (3/2/5-3, 1)
priestly-division= ephēmeria (0/0/2-0, 0)
priestly-office= hierateia (Lk 1:9)
prince= dunastēs (0/0/1-1, 0)
prior-to= prin (3/2/2-3, 3)
prison= phulakē (10/3/8-16, 1)
prisoner= desmios (2/1/0-6, 0)
private-room= tameion (2/0/2-0, 0)
to-proclaim= euaggelizō (1/0/10-15, 0)
proclamation= euaggelion (4/8/0-2, 0)
produce= genēma (1/1/1-0, 0)
to-produce= propherō (0/0/2-0, 0)
to-produce-good-crops= euphoreō (Lk 12:16)

to-produce-mature-fruit= telesphoreō (Lk 8:14)
to-profane= bebēloō (1/0/0-1, 0)
to-profit= diapragmateuomai (Lk 19:15)
to-progress= prokoptō (Lk 2:52)
promise= epaggelia (0/0/1-8, 0)
to-promise= epaggelomai (0/1/0-1, 0)
to-promise-in-marriage= mnēsteuō (1/0/2-0, 0)
to-prompt= probibazō (Mt 8:14)
promptly= exautēs (0/1/0-4, 0)
to-prophesy= prophēteuō (4/2/2-4, 1)
proper-time= kairos (10/5/13-9, 3)
property= ousia (0/0/2-0, 0)
prophecy= propheteia (Mt 13:14)
prophet= prophētēs (common)
prophetess= prophētis (Lk 2:36)
propitious= hileōs (Mt 16:22)
proselyte= prosēlutos (1/0/0-3, 0)
to-protect= suntēreō (1/1/1-0, 0)
psalm= psalmos (0/0/2-2, 0)
public-appearance= anadeixis (Lk 1:80)
to-pull-out= exaireō (2/0/0-5, 0)
to-pull-up= anabibazō (Mt 13:48)
to-pulverize= katagnumi (1/0/0-0, 3)
punishment= kolasis (Mt 25:46)
pure= katharos (3/0/1-2, 4)
to-purge= diakatharizō (Mt 3:12)
purification= katharismos (0/1/2-0, 2)
to-purify= katharizō (7/4/7-3, 3)
purple= porphurous (0/0/0-0, 2)
purple-cloth= porphura (0/2/1-0, 0)
to-pursue= diōkō (6/0/3-9, 2)
to-pursue-closely= katadiōkō (Mk 1:36)
to-put= tithēmi (5/11/16-23, 17)
to-put-a-coat-on= himatizō (0/1/1-0, 0)
to-put-around= peritithēmi (3/3/0-0, 1)
to-put-forward= proballō (0/0/1-1, 0)
to-put-in= katagtuō (0/0/1-7, 0)
to-put-out= epanagō (1/0/2-0, 0)
to-put-to-death= thanatoō (3/2/1-0, 0)
to-put-to-shame= kataischunō (Lk 13:17)
to-put-upon= epibibazō (0/0/2-1, 0)
to-put-up-with= anechomai (1/1/1-1, 0)

Q

quadrans= kodrantēs (1/1/0-0, 0)
to-quarrel= erizō (Mt 12:19)
queen= basilissa (1/0/1-1, 0)
to-question= eperōtaō (8/25/17-2, 2)
quickly= tachus (3/1/1-0, 1)
Quirinius= Kurēnios (Lk 2:2)
to-quit= kataleipō (4/4/4-5, 1)

R

rabbi= rabbi (4/3/0-0, 8)
Rabbouni= rabbouni (0/1/0-0, 1)
Rachel= Rachēl (Mt 2:18)
Rahab= Rachab (Mt 1:5)
to-raid= diarpazō (1/2/0-0, 0)
raiment= esthēs (0/0/2-3, 0)
rain= brochē (2/0/0-0, 0)
to-rain= brechō (1/0/3-0, 0)
to-raise/rise= egeirō (common)
Rama= Rama (Mt 2:18)
rampart= charax (Lk 19:43)
ransom= lutron (1/1/0-0, 0)
rather= mallon (9/5/5-7, 4)
ration= sitometrion (Lk 12:42)
to-ravel= ptussō (Lk 4:20)
ravenous= harpax (1/0/1-0, 0)
to-reach-out= ekteinō (6/3/3-3, 1)
to-read= anaginōskō (7/4/3-7, 1)
ready= hetoimos (4/1/3-2, 1)
ready-to-bear-fruit= hapalos (1/1/0-0, 0)
to-realize= plērophoreō (Lk 1:1)
reaper= theristēs (2/0/0-0, 0)
reason= aitia (3/1/1-8, 0)
to-rebuff= ameleō (Mt 22:5)
to-rebuke= epitimaō (7/9/12-0, 0)
to-recall= mnēmoneuō (1/1/1-2, 3)
to-receive= dechomai (10/6/16-8, 1)
to-receive-a-benefaction= charitoō (Lk 1:28)
to-receive-back= apolambanō (0/1/5-0, 0)
to-receive-in-full= apechō (5/2/4-2, 0)
recklessly= asōtōs (Lk 15:13)
to-recline= klinō (1/0/4-0, 1)
to-recline-at-table= kataklinō (0/0/6-0, 0)
to-recognize= oida (common)
redemption= lutrōsis (0/0/2-0, 0)
reed= kalamos (5/2/1-0, 0)
to-refuse= atheteō (0/2/5-0, 1)
to-refute= antilegō (0/0/3-4, 1)
region= chōra (3/4/9-8, 3)
to-register= apographō (0/0/3-0, 0)
registration= apographē (0/0/1-1, 0)
Rehoboam= Rhoboam (2/0/0-0, 0)
to-reject= apodokimazō (1/2/3-0, 0)
to-rejoice= chairō (7/2/12-7, 9)
to-rejoice-with= sugchairō (0/0/3-0, 0)
to-release= apoluō (19/12/14-15, 5)
relief= anapausis (2/0/1-0, 0)
to-remain= diamenō (0/0/2-0, 0)
to-remain-alert= agrupneō (0/1/1-0, 0)
remainder= loipos (4/3/6-6, 0)
to-remain-hidden= lanthanō (0/1/1-1, 0)
to-remember= mimnēskomai (3/0/6-2, 3)
remembrance= anamnēsis (Lk 22:19)
to-remind= anamimnēskō (0/2/0-0, 0)
to-remind-about= hupomimnēskō (0/0/1-0, 1)
remission= aphesis (1/2/5-5, 0)
to-remove= airō (common)
to-rend= diarrēgnumi (1/1/2-1, 0)
to-repay= antapodidōmi (0/0/2-0, 0)
repayment= antapodoma (Lk 14:12)
to-repent= metanoeō (5/2/9-5, 0)
repentance= metanoia (2/1/5-6, 0)
to-report-exactly= diagnōrizō (textual variant found at Lk 2:17)
to-reprimand= epiplēssō (textual variant found at Lk 23:43)
to-request= exaiteō (Lk 22:31)
requirements= dikaiōma (Lk 1:6)
to-rescue= rhuomai (2/0/1-0, 0)
to-resemble= paromoiazō (Mt 23:27)
to-resist= anthistēmi (1/0/1-2, 0)
to-resolve= apallassō (0/0/1-1, 0)
to-respect= entrepō (1/1/3-0, 0)
respectable= euschēmōn (0/1/0-2, 0)
to-rest= epanapauomai (Lk 10:6)
to-restore= apokathistēmi (2/3/1-1, 0)
restoration-of-sight= anablepsis (Lk 4:18)
to-restrain= deō (10/8/2-12, 4)
resurrection= egersis (Mt 27:53)
to-retire= analuō (Lk 12:36)
to-retreat= anachōreō (10/1/0-2, 1)
to-return= hupostrephō (0/0/21-11, 0)
Reu= Rhagau (Lk 3:35)
to-reveal= apokaluptō (4/0/5-0, 1)
revelation= apokalupsis (Lk 2:32)
to-revere= sebō (1/1/0-8, 0)
Rhesa= Rhēsa (Lk 3:27)
right= dexios (12/7/6-8, 2)
righteous= dikaios (17/2/11-6, 3)
righteousness= dikaiosunē (7/0/1-4, 2)
right-now= arti (7/0/0-0, 12)
ring= daktulios (Lk 15:22)
to-rinse= plunō (Lk 2:5)
rip= schisma (1/1/0-0, 3)
to-rip= schizō (2/2/3-2, 2)
to-rise/raise= egeirō (common)
rise= anastasis (4/2/6-11, 4)
ritual-washing= baptismos (Mk 7:4)
river= potamos (3/1/2-0, 1)
roadway= amphodon (Mk 11:4)
robe= stolē (0/2/2-0, 0)

rock= petra (5/1/3-0, 0)
rock-hewn= laxeutos (Lk 23:53)
rocky-ground= petrōdes (2/2/0-0, 0)
to-roll= proskuliō (1/1/0-0, 0)
to-roll-around= kuliō (Mk 9:20)
to-roll-away= apokuliō (1/2/1-0, 0)
Roman= rhōmaios (0/0/0-11, 1)
roof= stegē (1/1/1-0, 0)
roomy= euruchōros (Mt 7:13)
rooster= alektōr (3/4/3-0, 2)
rooster-sound= alektorophōnia (Mk 13:35)
root= rhiza (2/3/2-0, 0)
rope= schoinion (Jn 2:15)
rotten= sapros (5/0/1-0, 0)
rough= trachus (Lk 3:5)
rough-waves= kludōn (Lk 8:24)
royal-official= basilikos (0/0/0-2, 2)
to-rub= psōchō (Lk 1:6)
to-rule= hēgeomai (1/0/1-4, 0)
to-rule-over= katexousiazō (1/1/0-0, 0)
to-run= trechō (2/2/2-0, 2)
to-run-ahead= protrechō (0/0/1-0, 1)
to-run-around= peritrechō (Mk 6:55)
to-run-to= prostrechō (0/2/0-1, 0)
to-run-together= suntrechō (0/1/0-1, 0)
to-rush= hormaō (1/1/1-2, 0)
Rufus= Rhouphis (Mk 15:21)
rule= hēgemonia (Lk 3:1)
ruler= hēgemōn (10/2/1-6, 0)
rumination= dianoēma (Lk 11:17)
rumor= akoē (4/3/1-2, 0)
rust= brōsis (2/0/0-0, 4)
Ruth= Rhouth (Mt 1:5)

S

sabachthani= sabachthani (Aramaic) (1/1/0-0, 0)
Sabbath= sabbaton (common)
sack-cloth= sakkos (1/0/1-0, 0)
sacred= hieros (textual variant found at Mk 16:8)
sacrifice= thusia (2/1/2-2, 0)
sacrificial-altar= thusiastērion (6/0/2-0, 0)
sacrificial-lamb= arēn (Lk 10:3)
Sadducee= Saddoukaios (7/1/1-5, 0)
to-safeguard= diaphulassō (Lk 4:10)
to-sail= pleō (0/0/1-3, 0)
to-sail-along= katapleō (Lk 8:26)
sake= charin (Lk 7:47)
Sala= Sala (0/0/2-0, 0)
Salathiel= Salathiēl (2/0/1-0, 0)
Salmon= Salmōn (2/0/1-0, 0)
Salome= Salōmē (0/2/0-0, 0)
salt= halas (2/3/2-0, 0)
salvation= sōteria (0/1/4-6, 1)
Samaria= Samareia (0/0/1-7, 3)
Samaritan= Samaritēs (1/0/3-1, 4)
sanctuary= naos (9/3/4-2, 3)
sand= ammos (Mt 7:26)
sandal= hupodēma (2/1/4-2, 1)
Sanhedrin= sunedrion (3/3/1-14, 1)
to-satisfy= empimplēmi (0/0/2-1, 1)
saton= saton (1/0/1-0, 0)
to-save= sōzō (15/15/17-13, 6)
saving-power= sōterion (0/0/2-1, 0)
savior= sōtēr (0/0/2-2, 1)
to-say= legō (common)
scandal= skandalon (3/0/1-0, 0)
scarcely= mogis (Lk 9:39)
scarcely-able-to-talk= mogilalos (Mk 7:32)
scarlet= kokkinos (Mt 27:28)
to-scatter= diaskorpizō (3/1/3-1, 1)
scented-herb= pēganon (Lk 11:42)
to-scoop= exorussō (Mk 2:4)
to-scorch= kaumatizō (1/2/0-0, 0)
scorching-heat= kausōn (1/0/1-0, 0)
scorpion= skorpios (0/0/2-0, 0)
scourge= mastix (0/3/1-1, 0)
to-scourge= mastigoō (3/1/1-0, 1)
scrap-of-food= psichion (1/1/0-0, 0)
scream= kraugē (1/0/1-1, 0)
to-scream= kraugazō (1/0/1-1, 6)
scribe= grammateus (22/21/14-4, 1)
sea= thalassa (16/19/3-10, 9)
to-seal= sphragizō (1/0/0-0, 2)
seamless= araphos (Jn 19:23)
to-search= zēteō (common)
sea-side= parathalassios (Mt 4:13)
seat= kathedra (2/1/0-0, 0)
seat-of-honor= prōtokathedria (1/1/2-0, 0)
to-seat-oneself= kathezomai (1/0/1-2, 3)
second= deuteros (3/3/3-5, 2)
second-coming= eleusis (textual variant found at Lk 23:42) (0/0/0-1, 0)
secretly= lathra (2/0/0-1, 1)
section= klisia (Lk 9:14)
to-secure= asphalizō (3/0/0-1, 0)
securely= asphalōs (0/1/0-2, 0)
to-see= horaō (common)
to-see-clearly= diablepō (1/1/1-0, 0)
seed= sperma (7/5/2-4, 3)
seedling= sporos (0/2/2-0, 0)
to-seek= epizēteō (3/0/2-3, 0)
to-seek-out= ekzēteō (0/0/2-1, 0)
to-seize= krateō (12/15/2-4, 2)
to-select= hairetizō (Mt 12:18)
self-indulgence= akrasia (Mt 23:25)
to-sell= pōleō (6/3/6-3, 2)
Semein= Semein (Lk 3:26)
to-send= pempō (4/1/10-11, 32)
to-send-forth= exapostellō (0/1/3-7, 0)
to-send-off= apostellō (common)
to-send-up= anapempō (0/0/3-1, 0)
sensible= phronimos (7/0/1-0, 0)
sensibly= phronimōs (Lk 8:16)
to-separate= chōrizō (1/1/0-3, 0)
sepulcher= taphos (6/0/0-0, 0)
Serug= Serouch (Lk 3:35)
servant= diakonos (3/2/0-0, 3)
to-serve= diakoneō (6/5/7-2, 2)
service= diakonia (0/0/1-8, 0)
to-set= dunō (0/1/1-0, 0)
to-set-free= lutroō (Lk 24:21)
Seth= Sēth (Lk 3:38)
to-settle= katoikeō (4/0/2-20, 0)
seven= hepta (9/9/6-8, 0)
seventh= hebdomos (Jn 4:52)
seven-times= heptakis (2/0/2-0, 0)
seventy= hebdomēkonta (0/0/2-3, 0)
seventy-times= hebdomēkontakis (Mt 18:22)
to-sew-on= epiraptō (Mk 2:21)
sewing-needle= belonē (Lk 18:25)
shade= skia (1/1/1-1, 0)
to-shake= seiō (3/0/0-0, 0)
to-shake-off= apotinassō (0/0/1-1, 0)
to-shake-out= ektinassō (1/1/0-2, 0)
to-shake-up= saleuō (2/1/4-4, 0)
shame= aischunē (Lk 14:9)
shameless-persistence= anaideia (Lk 11:8)
shape= morphē (Mk 16:12)
to-share-with= metadidōmi (Lk 3:10)
to-shatter= suntribō (1/2/1-0, 1)
she/he/it = autos (common)
sheath= thēkē (Jn 18:11)
to-shed= ekchunnomai (2/1/1-1, 0)
sheep= probaton (11/2/2-1, 19)
sheep-gate= probatikos (Jn 2:5)
Shem= Sēm (Lk 3:36)
shepherd= poimēn (3/2/4-0, 6)
to-shepherd= poimainō (1/0/1-1, 1)
to-shine= lampō (3/0/1-1, 0)
to-shine-around= perilampō (0/0/1-1, 0)
to-shine-forth= eklampō (Mt 13:43)
to-shorten= koloboō (2/2/0-0, 0)
shoulder= ōmos (1/0/1-0, 0)
to-shout= boaō (1/2/4-3, 1)

to-shout-out= anaboaō (Mt 27:46)
to-show= deiknumi (3/2/5-2, 7)
shower= ombros (Lk 12:54)
to-shroud= parakaluptō (Lk 9:45)
shrub= lachanon (1/1/1-0, 0)
to-shut= kammuō (1/0/0-1, 0)
to-shut-up= katakleiō (0/0/1-1, 0)
sickle= drepanon (Mk 4:29)
sickness= malakia (3/0/0-0, 0)
side= pleura (0/0/0-1, 4) (textual variant found at Mt 27:49)
Sidon= Sidōn (3/2/3-1, 0)
Sidonite= Sidōnios (0/0/1-1, 0)
to-sift= siniazō (Lk 22:31)
sight= horama (1/0/0-11, 0)
sign= sēmeion (13/7/11-13, 17)
signal= sussēmon (Mk 14:44)
Siloam= Silōam (Lk 13:4)
silver= arguros (1/0/0-1, 0)
silver-coin= argurion (9/1/4-5, 0)
similar= paromoios (Mk 7:13)
Simon= Simōn (common)
simpleton= aphrōn (0/0/2-0, 0)
sin= hamartia (7/6/11-8, 17)
to-sin= hamartanō (3/0/4-1, 4)
since= epeidē (0/0/2-3, 0)
sinful= hamartōlos (5/6/18-0, 4)
sinfulness= hamartēma (0/2/0-0, 0)
to-sing-a-hymn= humneō (1/1/0-1, 0)
to-sink= katapontizō (2/0/0-0, 0)
sinless= anamartētos (Jn 8:7)
sister= adelphē (3/5/3-1, 6)
to-sit= kathēmai (19/11/13-6, 4)
to-sit-around= perikathizō (textual variant found at Lk 22:55)
to-sit-at-table= sunanakeimai (2/2/3-0, 0)
to-sit-together= sugkathēmai (0/1/0-1, 0)
to-sit-up= anakathizō (0/0/1-1, 0)
to-sit-upon= epikathizō (Mt 21:7)
six= hex (1/1/2-3, 3)
sixth= hektos (2/1/3-1, 2)
sixty= hexēkonta (2/2/1-0, 0)
skull= kranion (1/1/1-0, 1)
slap= rhapisma (0/1/0-0, 2)
to-slap= rhapizō (2/0/0-0, 0)
to-slaughter= thuō (1/1/4-4, 1)
slave= doulos (30/5/26-3, 11)
slave-girl= paidiskē (1/2/2-2, 1)
to-slay= katasphazō (Lk 19:27)
sleep= hupnos (1/0/1-1, 1)
to-sleep= katheudō (7/8/2-0, 0)
to-slice= dichazō (Mt 10:35)
slow= bradus (Lk 24:25)
small= mikros (6/4/3-2, 11)
small-bit-of-bread= psōmion (0/0/0-0, 3)
small-boat= ploiarion (0/1/0-0, 4)
smaller= mikroteros (2/1/2-0, 0)
small-fish= ichthudion (1/1/0-0, 0)
small-region= chōrion (1/1/0-7, 0)
small-town= kōmopolis (Mk 1:38)
to-smear= aleiphō (1/2/3-0, 2)
smooth= leios (Lk 3:5)
snake= ophis (3/1/2-0, 1)
snow= chiōn (Mt 3:28)
so= de (common)
so-and-so= deina (Mt 26:18)
Sodom= Sodoma (3/0/2-0, 0)
soft= malakos (2/0/1-0, 0)
soldier= stratiōtēs (3/1/2-13, 6)
soldier's-robe= chlamus (2/0/0-0, 0)
Solomon= Solomōn (5/0/3-3, 1)
so-many= tosoutos (3/0/2-2, 4)
some= tis without accent (common)
something-edible= episitismos (Lk 9:12)
something-to-eat= prosphagion (Jn 5:21)
sometime= pote (without accent) (Lk 22:32)
son= huios (common)
so-not= mēde (11/6/7-2, 2)
so-now= toinun (Lk 20:24)
sore= helkos (Lk 16:21)
so-that= hopōs (17/1/7-14, 1)
so-then= oukoun (Jn 18:37)
soul= psuchē (16/8/14-15, 10)
to-sound-a-trumpet= salpizō (Mt 6:2)
sour-wine= oxos (1/1/1-0, 3)
south= notos (1/0/3-2, 0)
to-sow= speirō (17/12/6-0, 2)
to-sow-in-addition= epispeirō (Mt 13:25)
sparrow= strouthion (2/0/2-0, 0)
to-speak= phēmi (16/6/8-25, 3)
to-speak-out= diaphēmizō (2/1/0-0, 0)
spear= logchē (Jn 19:34; textual variant found at Mt 27:49)
spectacle= theōria (Lk 23:48)
speech= rhēma (5/2/19-14, 12)
speechless= alalos (0/3/0-0,0)
speed= tachos (0/0/1-3, 0)
to-spend= dapanaō (0/1/1-1, 0)
to-spend-the-night= dianuktereuō (Lk 6:12)
to-spin= nēthō (1/0/1-0, 0)
spirit= pneuma (common)
to-spit= ptuō (0/2/0-0, 1)
to-spit-on= emptuō (2/3/1-0, 0)
splendidly= eu (2/1/0-1, 0)
splinter= karphos (3/0/3-0, 0)
to-split= diaireō (Lk 15:12)
spoil (from plunder)= skulon (Lk 11:22)
sponge= spoggos (1/1/0-0, 1)
to-spread-out= strōnnuō (2/2/1-1, 0)
to-spread-right-out= hupostrōnnuō (Lk 19:36)
to-sprout-up= exanatellō (1/1/0-0, 0)
spy= egkathetos (Lk 20:20)
squall= lailaps (1/0/1-0, 0)
to-squeeze= apothlibō (Lk 8:45)
staff= rhabdos (1/1/1-0, 0)
to-stand= histēmi (common)
to-stand-by= ephistēmi (0/0/7-11, 0)
to-stand-with= sunistēmi (Lk 9:32)
star= astēr (5/1/0-0, 0)
to-stay= menō (3/2/7-13, 40)
to-stay-awake= grēgoreō (6/6/1-1, 0)
to-stay-behind= hupomenō (2/1/1-1, 0)
to-stay-warm= thermainō (0/2/0-0, 3)
to-stay-with= prosmenō (1/1/0-3, 0)
to-steal= kleptō (5/1/1-0, 1)
steep-bank= krēmnos (1/1/1-0, 0)
sterile= steira (0/0/3-0, 0)
stern= prumna (1/0/0-2, 0)
steward= epitropos (1/0/1-0, 0)
stomach= gastēr (3/1/2-0, 0)
stone= lithos (11/8/14-2, 7)
to-stone= lithoboleō (2/0/1-3, 0)
to-stop= pauō (0/0/3-6, 0)
to-stop-breathing= ekpneō (0/2/1-0, 0)
storehouse= apothēkē (3/0/3-0, 0)
to-store-treasure= thēsaurizō (2/0/1-0, 0)
stormy= cheimōn (2/1/0-1, 1)
straight= eutheias (1/1/2-3, 0)
to-straighten-up= anakuptō (0/0/2-0, 2)
stranger= xenos (5/0/0-2, 0)
strap= himas (0/1/1-1, 1)
straw= klēros (1/1/1-5, 1)
strength= kratos (0/0/1-1, 0)
stretcher= klinē (2/3/3-0, 0)
to-stretch-out= anaklinō (2/1/3-0, 0)
to-strike= paiō (1/1/1-0, 1)
to-strike-down= patassō (2/1/2-3, 0)
to-strip= ekduō (2/1/1-0, 0)
stroke= keraia (1/0/1-0, 0)
strong= ischuros (2/2/3-0, 0)
strong-drink= sikera (Lk 1:15)
stronger= ischuroteros (1/1/2-0, 0)
to-struggle= agōnizomai (0/0/1-0, 1)

to-stuff= gemizō (0/2/1-0, 2)
to-submit= hupotassō (0/0/3-0, 0)
successively= kathexēs (0/0/2-3, 0)
such= hode (0/0/1-1, 0)
such-as= hoios (1/2/0-0, 0)
such-as-this= toioutos (3/6/2-4, 3)
suddenly= exaiphnēs (0/1/2-2, 0)
to-suffer= paschō (4/3/6-5, 0)
to-suffer-chronic-bleeding= haimorroeō (Mt 9:20)
suffering-from-dropsy= hudrōpikos (Lk 2:14)
to-suffocate= apopnigō (0/0/2-0, 0)
sulfur= theion (Lk 17:29)
summer= theros (1/1/1-0, 0)
to-summon= proskaleomai (6/9/4-9, 0)
sumptuous= lampros (0/0/1-1, 0)
sumptuously= lamprōs (Lk 16:19)
sun= hēlios (5/4/3-4, 0)
to-suppose= dokeō (10/2/10-8, 8)
surely-not= mēti (4/2/2-1, 3)
to-surround= perikukloō (Lk 19:43)
surrounding-region= perichōros (2/1/5-1, 0)
sustenance= brōma (1/1/2-0, 1)
Suzanna= Sousanna (Lk 8:3)
to-swap= antiballō (Lk 24:17)
to-swear= horkizō (0/1/0-1, 0)
to-swear-falsely= epiorkeō (Mt 5:33)
to-swear-under-oath= exorkizō (Mt 26:63)
to-sweep= saroō (1/0/2-0, 0)
swell= salos (Lk 21:25)
sword= machaira (7/3/5-2, 2)
sworn-oath= horkos (4/1/1-1, 0)
sycamore-tree= sukomorea (Lk 19:4)
Symeon= Sumeōn (0/0/3-2, 0)
synagogue= sunagōgē (9/8/15-21, 2)
synagogue-leader= archisunagōgos (0/4/2-3, 0)
Syria= Suria (1/0/1-5, 0)
Syrian= Suros (Lk 4:27)
Syrophoenician= Surophoinikissa (Mk 7:26)

T

table= trapeza (2/2/4-2, 1)
to-tag-along= sunakoloutheō (0/2/1-0, 0)
to-take= lambanō (common)
to-take-along= paralambanō (16/6/6-6, 3)
to-take-aside= proslambanō (1/1/0-5, 0)
to-take-away= aphaireō (1/1/4-0, 0)
to-take-before= prolambanō (Mk 8:14)
to-take-care= epimeleomai (0/0/2-0, 0)
to-take-hold-of= epilambanomai (1/1/5-7, 0)
to-take-into-account= logizomai (0/0/1-1, 1)
to-take-leave= metairō (2/0/0-0, 0)
to-take-notice-of= ephoraō (0/0/1-1, 0)
to-take-up= apairō (1/1/1-0, 0)
talant= talanton (14/0/0-0, 0)
talitha= talitha (Aramaic word) (Mk 5:41)
talk= lalia (1/0/0-0, 2)
to-talk= laleō (common)
to-talk-about= dialaleō (0/0/2-0, 0)
to-talk-with= sullaleō (1/1/3-1, 0)
Tamar= Thamar (Mt 1:3)
to-tame= damazō (Mk 5:4)
tassel= kraspedon (3/1/1-0, 0)
to-taste= geuomai (2/1/2-3, 2)
tax= kēnsos (3/1/0-0, 0)
tax-booth= telōnion (1/1/1-0, 0)
tax-chief= architelōnēs (Lk 19:2)
tax-collector= telōnēs (8/3/10-0, 0)
to-teach= didaskō (common)
teacher= didaskalos (12/12/17-1, 8)
teacher-of-the-law= nomodidaskalos (0/0/1-1, 0)
tear= dakruon (0/0/2-2, 0)
teeth= odous (8/1/1-0, 0)
to-tell-before= prolegō (1/1/0-1, 0)
temple= hieron (11/9/25-25, 11)
temple-treasury= korbanas (Mt 27:6)
temporary= proskairos (1/1/0-0, 0)
ten= deka (3/1/11-1, 0)
tent= skēnē (1/1/2-3, 0)
tenth= dekatos (Jn 1:39)
to-tenth= apodekateuō (textual variant found at Lk 18:12)
ten-thousand= murioi (Mt 18:24)
Terah= Thara (Lk 3:34)
terribly= deinōs (1/0/1-0, 0)
terrified= ekphobos (Mk 9:6)
territory= horion (6/5/0-1, 0)
test= peirasmos (2/1/6-1, 0)
to-test= peirazō (6/4/2-5, 2)
to-testify= martureō (1/0/1-11, 33)
to-testify-against= katamartureō (2/1/0-0, 0)
to-testify-falsely= pseudomartureō (1/3/1-0, 0)
testimony= marturion (3/3/3-2, 0)
tetrarch= tetraarchēs (1/0/2-1, 0)
Thadeus= Thaddaios (1/1/0-0, 0)
thankless= acharistos (Lk 6:35)
that= ekeinos (demonstrative pronoun) (common)
that= hoti (conjunction) (common)
the= ho (common)
to-the-point= mechri (2/1/1-2, 0)
theft= klopē (1/1/0-0, 0)
their/theirs= autōn (common)
themselves= heautous (19/15/20-8, 6)
then= tote (90/6/14-21, 10)
the-name-of-whom= tounoma (Mt 27:57)
Theophilos= Theophilos (0/0/1-1, 0)
there= ekei (common)
therefore= oun (56/6/33-61, 200)
they= autoi (common)
thief= kleptēs (3/0/2-0, 4)
to-think= nomizō (3/0/2-7, 0)
to-think-about= katanoeō (1/0/4-4, 0)
third= tritos (7/2/9-4, 1)
thirdly= triton (0/1/1-0, 1)
thirty= triakonta (5/2/1-0, 2)
this= houtos (common)
thistle= tribolos (Mt 7:16)
Thomas= Thōmas (1/1/1-1, 7)
thorny= akanthinos (0/1/0-0, 1)
thorny-plant= akantha (5/3/4-0, 1)
thought= dialogismos (1/1/6-0, 0)
thousand= chilias (0/0/1-1, 0)
to-thrash= susparassō (0/11/1-0, 0)
three= treis (12/7/10-13, 4)
three-hundred= triakosioi (0/1/0-0, 1)
three-times= tris (2/2/2-2, 1)
threshing-floor= halōn (1/0/1-0, 0)
throne= thronos (5/0/3-1, 0)
through= dia (common)
through-that= dioti (0/0/3-5, 0)
throw= bolē (Lk 22:41)
to-throw= ballō (common)
to-throw-a-net= amphiballō (Mk 1:16)
to-throw-in= emballō (Lk 12:5)
to-throw-off= apoballō (Mk 10:50)
to-throw-on= epiballō (2/4/5-4, 2)
to-throw-up= paremballō (Lk 19:43)
thunder= brontē (1/0/0-0, 1)
thus= houtōs (common)
Tiberias= Tiberias (0/0/0-0, 3)
Tiberius= Tiberios (Lk 1:3)
till= achri (1/1/4-15, 0)
Timaeus= Timaios (Mk 10:46)
time= chronos (3/2/7-17, 4)
time-of-marriage= parthenia (Lk 2:36)
tiny-seed= kokkos (2/1/2-0, 1)
tip= akron (2/2/1-0, 0)

to-tithe= apodekatoō (1/0/2-0, 0)
to= pros (common)
today= sēmeron (8/1/11-9, 0)
together-with= sun (4/6/22-51, 3)
tomb= mnēmeion (7/8/8-1, 16)
tomorrow= aurion (3/0/4-4, 0)
tongue= glōssa (0/3/2-6, 0)
torch= phanos (Jn 3:18)
torment= basanos (1/0/2-0, 0)
to-torment= basanizō (3/2/1-0, 0)
tormenter= basanistēs (Mt 18:34)
to-toss= rhiptō (3/0/2-2, 0)
to-toss-down= katabibazō (textual variant found at Mt 11:23)
to-toss-on= epiriptō (Lk 19:35)
to-toss-over= katakrēmnizō (Lk 4:29)
to-touch= haptō (9/11/13-1, 1)
towel= lention (0/0/0-0, 2)
tower= purgos (1/1/2-0, 0)
Trachonitis= Trachōnitis (Lk 1:3)
to-track-down= anazēteō (0/0/2-1, 0)
tradition= paradosis (2/5/0-0, 0)
traitor= prodotēs (0/0/1-1, 0)
to-transgress= parabainō (2/0/0-1, 0)
to-translate= methermēneuō (1/3/0-2, 2)
to-transport= analambanō (0/1/0-8, 0)
transportation= analēpsis (Lk 9:51)
trap= pagis (Lk 21:35)
to-travel= poreuomai (29/3/51-37, 16)
to-travel-in= eisporeuomai (1/8/5-4, 0)
to-travel-by= paraporeuomai (1/4/0-0, 0)
to-travel-out= ekporeuomai (5/11/3-3, 2)
to-travel-through= diaporeuomai (0/0/3-1, 0)
to-travel-to= epiporeuomai (Lk 8:4)
to-travel-together-with= sumporeuomai (0/1/3-0, 0)
to-travel-toward= prosporeuomai (Mk 10:35)
to-tread= pateō (0/0/2-0, 0)
to-tread-upon= katapateō (2/0/2-0, 0)
treasure-box= thēsauros (9/1/5-0, 0)
treasury= gazophulakion (0/3/1-0, 0)
to-treat-contemptously= exoudeneō (Mk 9:12)
to-treat-dishonorably= atimazō (0/1/1-1, 1)
tree= dendron (12/1/7-0, 0)
to-tremble= tremō (0/1/1-0, 0)
tremor= tromos (Mk 8:16)
tribe= phulē (2/0/2-1, 0)
tribute= phoros (0/0/2-0, 0)
troop= strateuma (1/0/1-3, 0)
trouble= kopos (1/1/2-0, 1)
true= alēthēs (1/1/0-1, 14)
truly= alēthōs (3/2/3-1, 7)
trumpet-blast= salpigx (Mt 24:31)
truthfulness= alētheia (1/3/3-3, 25)
to-try= ekpeirazō (1/0/2-0, 0)
to-tug= surō (0/0/0/3, 1)
tunic= chitōn (2/2/3-1, 2)
turn= taxis (Lk 1:8)
to-turn= strephō (6/0/7-3, 4)
to-turn-against= epanistamai (1/1/0-0, 0)
to-turn-away= apostrephō (2/0/1-1, 0)
to-turn-back= epistrephō (4/4/7-11, 1)
to-turn-up= anastrephō (textual variant found at Mt 17:22)
turtle-dove= trugōn (Lk 2:24)
twelve= dōdeka (13/15/12-4, 5)
twenty= eikosi (0/0/1-2, 1)
twice= dis (0/2/1-0, 0)
Twin= Didumos (0/0/0-0, 3)
two= duo (common)
two-hundred= diakosioi (0/1/0-2, 2)
two-thousand= dischilioi (Mk 5:13)
two-years-old= dietēs (Mt 2:16)
type= genos (1/2/0-9, 0)
Tyre= Turos (3/3/3-2, 0)

U

unclean= akathartos (2/11/6-5, 0)
uncleanliness= akatharsia (Mt 23:27)
under= hupo (28/12/31-41, 2)
to-understand= epiginōskō (6/4/7-13, 0)
unencumbered= haplous (1/0/1-0, 0)
unexpectedly= aiphnidios (Lk 21:34)
unfaithful= apistos (1/1/2-1, 1)
unintelligent= asunetos (1/1/0-0, 0)
unmarked= adēlos (Lk 11:44)
unmarried-girl= parthenos (4/0/2-1, 0)
unquenchable= asbestos (1/1/1-0, 0)
unrighteous= adikos (1/0/4-1, 0)
unrighteousness= adikia (0/0/4-2, 1)
to-unroll= anaptussō (Lk 4:17)
to-unroof= apostegazō (Mk 2:4)
unsalty= analos (Mk 9:50)
unshrunken= agnaphos (1/1/0-0, 0)
until= heōs (common)
unwashed= aniptos (1/1/0-0, 0)
unwell= arrōstos (1/3/0-0, 0)
up= ana (3/1/3-0, 1)
upon= epi (common)
to-uproot= ekrizoō (2/0/1-0, 0)
upstairs-room= anagaion (0/1/1-0, 0)
to-urge= epischuō (Lk 23:5)
Uriah= Ourias (Mt 1:6)
usable= euthetos (0/0/2-0, 0)
to-utter= epilegō (0/0/0-1, 1)
Uzziah= Ozias (2/0/0-0, 0)

V

vainly= matēn (1/1/0-0, 0)
valley= pharagx (Lk 3:5)
valuable= polutimos (1/0/0-0, 1)
various= poikilos (1/1/1-0, 0)
vat= batos (Lk 16:6)
to-venerate= latreuō (1/0/3-5, 0)
to-venture= hodeuō (Lk 10:33)
verdant= hugros (Lk 23:31)
verdict= krima (1/1/3-1, 1)
very= sphodra (7/1/1-1, 0)
very-grieved= perilupos (1/2/2-0, 0)
vessel= skeuos (1/2/2-5, 1)
victory= nikos (Matt 12:20)
to-view-with-disdain= exoutheneō (0/0/2-1, 0)
vigorously= eutonōs (0/0/1-1, 0)
village= kōmē (4/7/12-1, 3)
vine= ampelos (1/1/1-0, 3)
vine-dresser= ampelourgos (Lk 13:7)
vineyard= ampelōn (10/5/7-0, 0)
violent-greed= harpagē (1/0/1-0, 0)
viper= echidna (3/0/1-0, 0)
visible= phaneros (1/3/2-2, 0)
vision= optasia (0/0/2-1, 0)
to-visit= paroikeō (Lk 18:24)
visitation= episkopē (0/0/1-1, 0)
voice= phōnē (7/7/13-27, 15)
votive-gifts= anathēma (Lk 21:5)
to-vow= omnuō (13/2/1-1, 0)

W

wage-laborer= misthios (0/0/2-0, 0)
wages= misthos (10/1/3-1, 1)
to-wail-loudly= alalazō (Mk 5:38)
wailing= klauthmos (7/0/1-1, 0)
waist= osphus (1/1/1-1, 0)
wash-basin= niptēr (Jn 13:5)
to-wait-for= prosdechomai (0/1/5-2, 0)
to-wake-up= diagrēgoreō (Lk 9:32)
to-walk-around= peripateō (7/9/5-8, 17)
to-want= boulomai (2/1/2-14, 1)
to-warn= chrēmatizō (2/0/1-2, 0)
to-wash= niptō (2/1/0-0, 13)
to-wash-off= aponiptō (Mt 27:24)
to-watch-closely= paratēreō (0/1/3-1, 0)
water= hudōr (7/5/6-7, 21)
waterless= anudros (1/0/1-0, 0)

wave= kuma (2/1/0-1, 0)
way= hodos (22/16/20-20, 4)
wealth= ploutos (1/1/1-0, 0)
wealthy= plousios (3/2/11-0, 0)
weapon= hoplon (Jn 18:3)
to-wear= hupodeomai (0/1/0-1, 0)
to-weave= plekō (1/1/0-0, 1)
to-wed= epigambreuō (Mt 22:24)
wedding= gamos (9/0/2-0, 2)
wedding-hall= numphōn (1/1/1-0, 0)
weed= zizanion (8/0/0-0, 0)
to-weep= klaiō (2/4/11-2, 8)
to-weigh-down= bareō (1/0/2-0, 0)
weight= baros (1/0/0-1, 0)
weighty= barus (1/0/0-2, 0)
to-welcome= apodechomai (0/0/2-5, 0)
well= kalōs (2/6/4-3, 4)
west= dusmē (2/0/2-0, 0)
what= tis with accent (common)
what-kind-of= poios (7/4/8-4, 4)
whatsoever= hosos (common)
what-sort-of= potapos (1/2/2-0, 0)
wheat= sitos (4/1/4-1, 1)
wheat-flour= aleuron (1/0/1-0, 0)
when?= pote (with accent) (7/5/4-0, 2)
when= hote (common)
whenever= hotan (common)
where= hopou (13/15/5-2, 30)
wheresoever= pou (4/3/7-0, 19)
which/who/whom= hos (common)
whip= phragellion (Jn 2:15)
to-whip= phragelloō (1/1/0-0, 0)
white= leukos (3/2/1-1, 2)
to-white-wash= koniaō (1/0/0-1, 0)
who/whom/which= hos (common)
whoever/whichever= hostis (30/4/20-23, 3)
whole= holos (22/18/17-19, 7)
whole-people= laos (14/2/36-48, 3)
whom/who/which= hos (common)
wick= linon (Mt 12:20)
wickedness= kakia (1/0/0-1, 0)
wide= platus (Mt 7:13)
wide-street= plateia (2/0/3-1, 0)
widow= chēra (0/3/9-3, 0)
wild= agrios (1/1/0-0, 0)
will= thelēma (6/1/4-3, 11)
willing= prothumos (1/1/0-0, 0)
wind= anemos (9/7/4-4, 1)
wine= oinos (4/5/6-0, 6)
wine-drinking= oinopotēs (1/0/1-0, 0)
wine-press= lēnos (Mt 21:33)
wine-press-pit= hupolēnion (Mk 1:12)
wine-skin= askos (4/4/4-0, 0)
wing= pterux (1/0/1-0, 0)
winnowing-shovel= ptuon (1/0/1-0, 0)
winter-stream= cheimarros (Jn 1:18)
to-wipe-off= apomassō (Lk 10:11)
wisdom= sophia (3/1/6-4, 0)
wise= sophos (2/0/1-0, 0)
to-wish= thelō (common)
with= meta (common)
to-withdraw= hupochōreō (0/0/2-0, 0)
to-withdraw-back= apochōreō (1/0/1-1, 0)
to-wither= xērainō (3/6/1-0, 1)
withered= xēros (2/1/3-0, 1)
within= esō (1/2/0-1, 1)
without= chōris (3/1/1-0, 3)
without-delay= tacheōs (0/0/2-1, 3)
without-worry= amerimnos (Mt 28:14)
with-the-result-that= hōste (15/13/4-8, 1)
witness= martus (2/1/2-13, 0)
witness-testimony= marturia (0/3/1-1, 14)
woe= ouai (13/2/15-0, 0)
wolf= lukos (2/0/1-1, 1)
woman= gunē (common)
wonder= thambos (0/0/2-1, 0)
wonderful= thaumasios (Mt 21:15)
word= logos (common)
wordiness= polulogia (Mt 6:7)
work= ergon (6/2/2-10, 27)
to-work= ergazomai (4/1/1-3, 8)
to-work-with= sunergeō (Mk 16:20)
worker= ergatēs (6/0/4-1, 0)
worker-of-kindess= euergetēs (Lk 22:25)
world= kosmos (9/3/3-1, 77)
worm= skōlēx (Mk 9:48)
worry= merimna (1/1/2-0, 0)
to-worry= merimnaō (7/0/5-0, 0)
to-worry-ahead-of-time= promerimnaō (Mk 11:13)
worse= cheirōn (3/2/1-0, 1)
to-worship= proskuneō (13/2/3-4, 11)
worthless= achreios (1/0/1-0, 0)
worthy= axios (9/0/8-7, 1)
wound= trauma (Lk 10:34)
to-wound= traumatizō (0/0/1-1, 0)
to-wrap= entulissō (1/0/1-0, 1)
to-wrap-in-baby-clothes= sparganoō (0/0/2-0, 0)
to-wrap-up= apokeimai (Lk 19:20)
wrapping= othonion (0/0/1-0, 4)
wrath= thumos (0/0/1-1, 0)
wrist= pugmē (Mk 3:7)
to-write= graphō (common)
writing= graphē (4/3/4-7, 12)
writing-tablet= pinakidion (Lk 1:63)
wrongdoing= paraptōma (3/1/0-0, 0)

X

Y

y'all's-own= humeteros (0/0/2-1, 3)
year= etos (1/1/15-11, 3)
to-yell= phōneō (5/10/10-4, 13)
to-yell-out= epiphōneō (0/0/1-3, 0)
yes= nai (9/1/4-2, 3)
yesterday= echthes (0/0/0-1, 1)
yet= eti (7/5/14-1, 1)
to-yield= prosergazomai (Lk 16:19)
yoke= zugos (2/0/0-1, 0)
you= su (common) NB: as in English, the other forms of "you" (singular 'you' as object, plural 'you' as subject and object, your, etc.) do not have separate dictionary entries.
young= nossos (Lk 2:24)
young-bird= nossion (Mt 23:37)
young-child= paidion (18/12/13-0, 3)
young-donkey= onarion (Jn 12:14)
young-goat= eriphion (Mt 25:33)
young-man= neaniskos (2/2/1-4, 0)
your-own= sos (8/2/4-3, 7)
yourself= seautos (5/3/6-3, 9)
youth= neotēs (0/1/1-1, 0)

Z

Zacchaeus= Zakchaios (0/0/3-0, 0)
Zachariah= Zacharias (2/0/10-0, 0)
Zadok= Sadōk (Mt 1:14)
Zarepheth= Sarepta (Lk 4:26)
zeal= zēlos (0/0/0-2, 1)
zealot= zēlōtēs (0/0/1-3, 0)
Zebedee= Zebedaios (6/4/1-0, 1)
Zebulon= Zaboulōn (2/0/0-0, 0)
Zerah= Zara (Mt 1:3)
Zerubbabel= Zorobabel (2/0/1-0, 0)
Zion= Siōn (1/0/0-0, 1)